THE ACTS

OF

THE APOSTLES.

WITH NOTES, COMMENTS, MAPS, AND ILLUSTRATIONS.

BY

REV. LYMAN ABBOTT,

AUTHOR OF "DICTIONARY OF RELIGIOUS KNOWLEDGE," "JESUS OF NAZARETH," AND "COMMENTARY ON MATTHEW AND MARK."

A. S. BARNES & COMPANY,

NEW YORK, CHICAGO, AND NEW ORLEANS.

1876.

PUBLISHERS' NOTICE.

THE object of this Commentary, as defined by the author, is to aid those who desire to learn, or to promote in others a knowledge of the principles which Jesus Christ came to propound and establish. Vol. I. contains Matthew and Mark, and also an Introduction to the study of the New Testament, comprising a consideration of its origin and authority, the nature and evidences of its inspiration, the history of the canon, the text, and the English translation, and a brief summary of the principles of interpretation, together with a condensed Life of Christ and a tabular harmony of the Gospels. Vol. II. will contain Luke and John; its preparation is well advanced; but its publication was temporarily delayed, in compliance with numerous requests, to enable the publishers to issue the present volume in time for the use of Sabbath-schools in 1876. It is expected that the whole work will be completed in four volumes of about 500 pages each. The present volume constitutes Part I. of Vol. III. of the completed work.

PREFACE.*

THE object of this Commentary is to aid in their Christian work those who are endeavoring to promote the knowledge of the principles which Jesus Christ came to propound and establish—clergymen, Christian parents, Sunday-School teachers, Bible-women, lay-preachers. Intended for Christian workers, it aims to give the results rather than the processes of scholarship, the conclusions rather than the controversies of scholars; intended for laymen as well as for clergymen, it accompanies the English version of the New Testament, in all references to the original Greek gives the English equivalent, and translates all quotations from the French, German, Latin and Greek authors.

The introduction on pages 31–34, contains a statement of those principles of interpretation which appear to me to be essential to the correct understanding of the Word of God. This Commentary is the result of a conscientious endeavor to apply those principles to the elucidation of the New Testament.

It is founded on a careful examination of the latest and best text; such variations as are of practical or doctrinal importance are indicated in the notes. It is founded on the original Greek; wherever that is inadequately rendered in our English version, a new translation is afforded by the notes. The general purpose of the writer or speaker, and the general scope of the incident or teaching, is indicated in a Preliminary Note to the passage, or in an analysis, a paraphrase, or a general summary at the close. Special topics, such as The Baptism, The Temptation, The Trial, and The Crucifixion of Jesus are treated separately in preliminary or supplementary notes. This volume contains thirty such excursus. The results of recent researches in Biblical archæology have been embodied, so as to make the Commentary serve in part the purpose of a Bible Dictionary. A free use is made of illustrations, from antiques, photographs, original drawings, and other trustworthy sources. They are never employed for mere ornament, but always to aid in depicting the life of Palestine, which remains in many respects substantially unchanged by the lapse of time. Since the Commentary is prepared, not for devotional reading, but for practical workers, little space has been devoted to hortatory remarks or practical or spiritual reflections. But I have uniformly sought to interpret the letter by the spirit, and to suggest rather than to supply moral and spiritual reflections, a paragraph of hints is affixed to each section or topic, embodying what appears to me to be the essential religious lessons of the

* From Volume I—MATTHEW and MARK.

incident or the teaching; sometimes a note is appended elucidating them more fully. The best thoughts of the best thinkers, both exegetical and homiletical, are freely quoted, especially such as are not likely to be accessible to most American readers; in all such cases the thought is credited to the author. Parallel and contrasted passages of Scripture are brought together in the notes; in addition, full Scripture references are appended to the text. These are taken substantially from Bagster's large edition of the English version of the Polyglot Bible, but they have been carefully examined and verified in preparing for the press, and some modifications have been made. For the convenience of that large class of Christian workers who are limited in their means, I have endeavored to make this Commentary, as far as practicable, a complete apparatus for the study of the New Testament. When finished it will be fully furnished with maps;—there are four in this volume; a Gazetteer gives a condensed account of all the principal places in Palestine, mentioned in our Lord's life; and an introduction traces the history of the New Testament from the days of Christ to the present, giving some account of the evidence and nature of inspiration, the growth of the canon, the character and history of the manuscripts, the English version, the nature of the Gospels and their relation to each other, a brief life of Christ, and a complete tabular harmony of the four Gospels.

The want of all who use the Bible in Christian work is the same. The *wish* is often for a demonstration that the Scripture sustains the reader's peculiar theological tenets, but the *want* is always for a clearer and better knowledge of Scripture teaching, whether it sanctions or overturns previous opinions. I am not conscious that this work is written in the interest of any theological or ecclesiastical system. In those cases in which the best scholars are disagreed in their interpretation, the different views and the reasons which lead me to my own conclusions have been given, I trust, in no controversial spirit. For the sole object of this work is to ascertain and make clear the meaning of the Word of God, irrespective of systems, whether ecclesiastical or doctrinal.

No work is more delightful than that which throws us into fellowship with great minds; of all work the most delightful is that which brings us into association with the mind of God. This is the fellowship to which the student of the Bible aspires. I can have for those who use this work no higher hope than that they may find in its employment some of the happiness which I have found in its preparation, and that it may serve them as it has served me, as a guide to the Word of God, and through that Word to a better acquaintance with God himself.

CORNWALL-ON-HUDSON, *May*, 1875. LYMAN ABBOTT.

TABLE OF CONTENTS.

LIST OF ILLUSTRATIONS.

The illustrations accompanying this volume have been derived from a number of sources. Some of the smaller outline engravings of implements, utensils, etc., have been taken from *Rich's Dictionary;* several of the illustrations of ancient sites have been taken from *Lewin's Life and Epistles of St. Paul;* some from *Murray's Illustrated New Testament;* the maps have been taken from *Conybeare and Howson's Life and Epistles of St. Paul*, but have been carefully revised for this work. A large proportion of the engravings, however, especially those illustrating ancient manners and customs, have been drawn and engraved expressly for this volume, from sketches by Mr. A. L. Rawson.

MAPS AND PLANS.

THE ACTS

OF

THE APOSTLES,

WITH

NOTES AND COMMENTS.

THE ACTS OF THE APOSTLES.

INTRODUCTION.

By whom written. That the author of the Book of Acts is the same as that of the third Gospel is evident from several considerations: from the address to Theophilus, and the reference to a previous treatise similarly addressed (comp. Acts 1 : 1 with Luke 1 : 3); from the strong resemblance in the style of the two books; from parallelisms particularly noticeable in the description of the shipwreck in Acts and the storm on the Sea of Galilee in the Gospel; from intimations, slight, and yet noticeable, of the author's knowledge of disease and his use of medical terms (comp. Luke 4 : 38; 8 : 43, 44, with Acts 3 : 7; 12 : 23; 13 : 11; 28 : 8); and from the fact that Luke, who describes himself as the traveling companion of Paul even to Rome itself, is several times referred to by Paul as being with him in Rome (comp. Acts 28 with Col. 4 : 14; 2 Tim. 4 : 11; Phil. 24). That the author of both is Luke is the universal testimony of antiquity.

Several other hypotheses of authorship have been suggested; such as, that the book is the work of a later date, being compiled from various documents in the churches, descriptive of the apostolic labors; that it was edited by Luke, but contains narratives written by other authors; *e. g.*, that Timothy was Paul's traveling companion, and that where the narrative implies that it was written by one who was accompanying Paul on his journey (Acts 16 : 10; 20 : 13, etc.), the journal of Timothy has been bodily incorporated in the narrative; that Silas (ch. 15 : 13) was the author of parts of the book; or that Silas and Luke are different names for the same person. It would be foreign to my purpose to discuss at length these and kindred hypotheses. There is no just reason for questioning the universal testimony of tradition, which, from the earliest ages, has ascribed the book to Luke, and there is abundant reason in the structure of the book itself for rejecting the notion that it is the work of more than one author. Its style is the same throughout, except where it professes to report the speeches or writings of others; its narrative is continuous and harmonious; it gives no hint of incorporating foreign material; it fulfills (see below on Objects of the Book) a definite literary and religious design; in brief, it has all the marks of careful and individual authorship, none of a careless compilation. The curious student will find a discussion of these various theories in Alford's New Testament, Prolegomena, and in Davidson's Introduction to the N. T., Vol. II.

Luke. Very little is really *known* of Luke; traditions are untrustworthy; and hypotheses, whether formed by skeptics or Christians, are valueless. His name is only mentioned three times in the N. T. (Col. 4 : 14; 2 Tim. 4 : 11; Philemon 24, *Lucas*). He is thought not to have been of Jewish birth, since in Col. 4 : 11–14 Paul apparently distinguishes him from those who are of the circumcision. He was by profession a physician. This neither proves high birth nor remarkable attainments, since the medical art of that day was of the rudest description, and was sometimes practiced by slaves. Early tradition fixes his birthplace at Antioch; one less trustworthy describes him as a painter. The date of his conversion is unknown; he was not one of the twelve, nor, it would appear from Luke 1 : 2, an eye and ear witness of the works and words of our Lord. There is nothing inherently improbable in an early tradition which makes him one of the seventy whose appointment he alone describes (Luke 10 : 1). Assuming him to have been the author of the book of Acts, he joined Paul at Troas (Acts 16 : 10), and was thereafter Paul's traveling companion, though not continuously. (See below, Sources of Information.)

Authenticity. Whatever doubts may exist respecting the authorship of the Book of Acts, there is no room for reasonable doubt respecting its authenticity, *i. e.*, that it was written probably during the first century, certainly by a contemporary and companion of the apostles, who was an eye and ear witness of most of the scenes which he describes. The evidences of this are twofold:

(1.) The book abounds with references to the geography of Asia Minor and the manners and customs of the ancient Greeks and Romans. It contains allusions to more than one hundred towns and cities. It describes, in some cases with considerable detail, the journeys of Paul from place to place. It describes characteristically different experiences in different places—the scornful skepticism of Athens, the worldly indifference of Corinth, the witchcraft of Ephesus and the mob there incited by the makers of Diana's silver shrines. Both history and geography confirm the accuracy of these accounts. We are able to retrace the journeys of Paul; and the ruined cities remain to attest the perfect accuracy of the history. We know something of their ancient character, and that they correspond with the record which Luke has given. We know that Athens was a city of intelligence, philosophy, and of superabundant superstitions; that Corinth was a commercial metropolis, likely to be coldly indifferent to a

Gospel which proclaimed a crucified God; that Ephesus was the heart of a semi-Asiatic witchcraft, and famous for its temple to Diana and the silver shrines which its workmen sent throughout all Greece. We are able, by aid of comparatively recent exhumations, to test the accuracy of Luke's incidental references to the manners and customs of ancient Greece and Rome; no work of a later age could bear the test as his narrative does. These confirmations of his account are referred to throughout the notes; see especially on ch. 27.

(2.) Claiming to be contemporaneous with this Book of Acts are thirteen letters, purporting to be written by the apostle Paul, whose life and labors constitute the main portion of Luke's narrative. The authorship of some of these letters the most determined infidel does not question; others are questioned, but can hardly be called questionable. For while the authorship of some of the N. T. books, the Epistle to the Hebrews and 2 Peter, for example, is somewhat doubtful, that of Paul's epistles is as certain as the authorship of any books of equal antiquity. These letters of Paul abound with references to his own personal experience, and a careful comparison of these personal experiences with Luke's history shows a great number of what Dr. Paley has aptly called "undesigned coincidences." The more obscure of these parallelisms the stronger the argument derived from them. A subsequent writer, having Paul's letters before him, might incorporate a few references borrowed from them. But when we find that the life of Paul, as delineated by Luke, corresponds in even the minutest detail with the experience of Paul as described by himself, and that the coincidences are in many cases such that only a careful study makes them apparent, we may safely conclude that the life is authentic. For the argument from these undesigned coincidences the reader is referred to Dr. Paley's *Horæ Paulinæ;* to aid those who have not access to that book, and yet wish to get some idea of the nature of the argument, I append a list of some of the more important parallel passages, premising that, in some cases, the parallelism will manifest itself, not to the casual reader, but only to the careful student:

Acts.	Epistles.
8 : 3.	Gal. 1 : 13. 1 Tim. 1 : 12, 13.
9 : 23-25.	2 Cor. 11 : 32, 33.
13 : 50. 14 : 5. 19.	2 Tim. 3 : 10, 11.
16 : 1.	2 Tim. 1 : 4. 2 Tim. 3 : 15.
16 : 22.	Phil. 1 : 29, 30.
16 : 3. 21 : 23, 26.	1 Cor. 9 : 20.
18 : 1, 5.	2 Cor. 11 : 9. 2 Cor. 1 : 19.
18 : 2.	Rom. 16 : 3.
18 : 3.	1 Cor. 4 : 11, 12.
18 : 8.	1 Cor. 1 : 14.
18 : 6, 18.	Rom. 16 : 4.
18 : 24-28	1 Cor. 1 : 12. 1 Cor. 3 : 6.
18 : 27.	2 Cor. 3 : 1.
19 : 21.	Rom. 1 : 13.
19 : 21, 22.	1 Cor. 4 : 17-19.
19 : 28-34.	2 Cor. 1 : 8-10.
19 : 29.	Col. 4 : 10.
20 : 4.	Rom. 16 : 21-23.
20 : 22, 23	Rom. 15 : 30.
20 : 24.	2 Thess. 3 : 9.
22 : 3.	Gal. 1 : 14.
22 : 17, 18.	Gal. 1 : 18.

Date. The date of publication of the Book of Acts cannot be fixed with certainty. The absence of all reference to the destruction of Jerusalem, and the implication throughout that it is still standing, justifies the opinion, universal throughout the Christian Church, that it was published previous to that event, which occurred A. D. 70. The best opinion fixes the publication at about the time indicated by the close of the book, *i. e.*, during Paul's first imprisonment in Rome. This would bring it about A. D. 63. It may be said with certainty that it was published not before A. D. 61 or 62, and not later than A. D. 70.

Sources of information. The writer of the Book of Acts was with Paul at Troas (Acts 16 : 10-13), left him at Philippi (ch. 17 : 1), rejoined him there seven years later (ch. 20 : 5), and continued with him throughout his perilous voyage to Rome (ch. 27 : 1, 7, 39, etc.). A considerable portion of the narrative, therefore, is a journal of events which he himself witnessed, and in which he participated. But there is no external evidence, and nothing in the book itself, to indicate that he was an eye and ear witness of the events recorded in the first fourteen chapters. He does not mention himself in this portion of the narrative. It is probable, therefore, that he derived his information respecting the events there recorded from those who were eye-witnesses. This inherently reasonable opinion is confirmed by the fact that he derived the information for his Gospel from such eye-witnesses (Luke 1 : 2), and by the minute details in his narrative. Thus, for example, in the account of the deliverance of Peter from prison (ch. 12 : 1-17), the very name of the servant who opened the door is given; and in the account of Paul's conversion, the name of the street where Saul tarried in Damascus (ch. 9 : 11). A comparison of the three accounts of that conversion (ch. 9 : 1-9; 22 : 1-16; 26 : 12-18) indicates clearly that Luke derived his information respecting it from Paul; and it is scarcely less evident from the narrative itself that the writer's knowledge of the call of Cornelius, and the revelation to Peter that the Gospel was a gift to the Gentiles as well as to the Jews (ch. 10), was derived from Peter.

A more interesting and difficult question is, Whence did Luke derive his reports of the speeches which constitute so important a part of his narrative? These he publishes in full; and, at least in some instances, apparently *verbatim*. Of such speeches those of Peter at Pentecost (ch. 2 : 14-36) and in the Temple (ch. 3 : 12-26), of Stephen (ch. 7), and the various speeches of Paul (ch. 13 : 16-41 ; 17 : 22-31 ; 22 : 1-21 ; 24 : 10-21 ; ch. 26), are notable illustrations. There are three explanations as to the sources from which he derived or the method in which he made his reports of these addresses. (1.) It is supposed that they were disclosed to him by the Holy Spirit, being in fact a matter of divine revelation. But no such claim is made either by or for his narrative in the N. T. The same reverence which leads us to accept the inspiration claimed by the N. T. leads to caution in imputing to it an inspiration which it does not claim. While the divine inspiration quickens the human faculties it does not provide a substitute for their activity; and it is safe to say that God never reveals, supernaturally, truth which man can ascertain by natural means. (2.) It is suggested that Luke has not given verbatim reports of what was said, but has embodied in his own language the substance of the speaker's thoughts, as he was able to gather it from oral tradition, and that for greater dramatic effect he has put it in the form of a direct and verbatim report. This was a common method among ancient historians, and is indeed pursued by some very popular historians at the present day. But this hypothesis is open to a twofold objection: (*a*.) It deprives the account of much of its credibility. We are left at a loss to determine what is history and what the imagination of the narrator. It supposes a sacrifice of simple truth to dramatic effect. (*b*.) It does not accord with the language of the original Greek. In numerous instances, not patent to the English reader, there is a marked difference in style and language between that of Luke the historian and that of Peter or Paul the speaker; and this change is such as to indicate that in some instances, and to some considerable extent, the exact words of the speaker have been caught and preserved. (3.) It is supposed that these addresses were preserved in documentary form in the churches, and that these documentary reports constituted the material which Luke employed in his narrative. But this does not wholly solve the problem, for the question still remains, Whence these documentary reports? It is quite impossible to suppose that Peter wrote his Pentecostal sermon, or Paul his speech at Athens, either before delivering it, or after delivery, and a strictly verbatim report could not have been taken down by any method known to the ancients. (4.) I am compelled therefore to adopt an hypothesis composed of these three; *i. e.*, I suppose it probable that reports, more or less full, were taken at the time and preserved; that these written reports, or the memory of auditors, afforded Luke the material for his history; that composing his reports of speeches from this material he embodied it in the form of *verbatim* reports, according to the custom of his age, and in the manner still pursued by the skillful reporter of to-day, who often condenses into half a column the address of half an hour, and yet succeeds in preserving the style and even the very language of the orator; and that in this work Luke was so aided by the influence of the Holy Spirit that we have in all cases the substance, and, where it is important, the very words of the inspired speaker. It must be remembered that in an age of scant literature and much public speaking, hearers would naturally remember better than now, not only the substance but even the very words of memorable addresses; that they did so, is made evident by classical literature. That Luke has sometimes condensed a long address into a short report, and yet given it in the words, or substantially the words, of the speaker, is indicated by Acts 2 : 40. The student must, however, bear in mind that these are only hypotheses, and that the N. T. itself is silent as to the method in which Luke prepared his history, or the material which he employed in its preparation.

Object and nature of the book. This is indicated by what I believe to have been its original title, viz., The Acts; the words, *Of the Apostles*, are wanting in the Sinaitic manuscript, and omitted by Tischendorf; they were probably added by a copyist to explain the brief and somewhat enigmatical original title. That it was no part of the purpose of the author to narrate the acts of the apostles is evident from the contents of the book itself.

Of the original twelve after the list in ch. 1 : 13 it only mentions by name three, Peter, James and John. It does not describe in any detail the labors, nor does it mention the death, of either one of these three. The life of Paul is partially, but only partially given. Clearly the lives and labors of the apostles were not the chief theme of this writer. He is not a biographer. Nor can this book be correctly characterized as The Acts of the Holy Spirit. True, it does describe the initiation of the work of the Holy Spirit, as the four Gospels describe the earthly life and work of Jesus Christ. But the Acts of the Holy Spirit began long before the Pentecost (see ch. 2 : 4, note) and have continued with increasing demonstrations of power to the present day. It appears to me then, that, as the Gospels reveal the religion of Jesus Christ as embodied in his own life and teachings, and as the Epistles reveal it as embodied in more systematic and didactic forms, and as applied by the inspired apostles to the various experiences of individual and church life, this book reveals it as embodied in action. It teaches Christianity by recording the acts of Christ's disciples in labors for its promotion and extension. Thus we have in the Gospels the fundamental principles of Christianity, in the Epistles the doctrinal and practical teachings of Christianity, and in this book the Acts of Christianity or Christianity in action. The book, thus interpreted, is not fragmentary, nor is its ending abrupt. It begins with the descent of the Holy Spirit in Jerusalem, the capital of Judea. It carries on the record of the work of the church, until its leading mind has preached the Word in Rome, the capital of the Gentile world. Thus it records, not indeed the final and complete, but what I may call the prophetic, fulfillment of Christ's promise, "Ye shall be witnesses unto me, both in Jerusalem, and in all Judea, and in Samaria, and unto the uttermost parts of the earth," (ch. 1 : 8), and the methods in which, and the measures by which, the early church obtained the fulfillment of this promise.

The book may be regarded as divided into three sections, viz., (1) The founding of the Church at Jerusalem by the descent and work of the Holy Ghost and the preaching of the twelve, especially Peter (chaps. 1-5); (2) the growth, development, and organization of the church,—its growth in numbers, its development in doctrine and in spiritual life from a reformed Jewish sect into a Catholic church; its organization into a body with officers and somewhat defined methods of procedure,—all in preparation for its work of preaching the Gospel unto every creature, the Jew first, but also the Gentile (chaps. 6-12); (3) its missionary work, beginning with the departure of Paul and Barnabas from Antioch, and closing with the preaching of the Gospel in the city of Rome (chaps. 13-28).

Uses of the book. What is the use of the Book of Acts to *us;* what have *we* to learn from it? Largely it has been regarded by the church as a text-book in all matters of ecclesiastical organization, ceremonial, and discipline. The Congregationalist points to the election of Matthias (Acts 1 : 23) as an evidence that the authority of the early churches was vested in the whole body of believers; the Presbyterian, to the existence of elders (ch. 20 : 17) as an evidence that there was a body of officers entrusted with the administration of church affairs answering to the modern session; the Episcopalian, to the oversight exercised by the apostles over all the churches as an evidence of the apostolic origin of Episcopacy. This use of the Book of Acts assumes (1) That Christ founded a church with a definite organization and definite rules for its guidance, and that, therefore, the church of the first century is the inspired and authoritative model for the churches in all ages; (2) that the apostolic *example* as well as the apostolic teaching is inspired and authoritative, and that, therefore, if we can learn how the apostles organized and administered the churches, we shall be sure to organize and administer wisely in following their example; (3) that there was one method of organization and administration which was common to all the churches in the first century. There is small warrant in Scripture for either of these assumptions.

(1.) That Christ intended that his disciples should organize in Christian communities to carry on Christian work is certain; but he nowhere prescribes how those communities shall be organized and governed; neither do his disciples. There is not in the N. T. anything answering to the ecclesiastical canons of modern times. If he had intended to leave an authoritative rule for future ages, it is hardly conceivable that he would have left it to be deduced from casual and often ambiguous references scattered through a history of what one or two only of his apostles did, in organizing the first churches. (2.) That the apostles spoke by inspiration of God, and that as teachers they are trustworthy and authoritative guides in moral and spiritual truth, is, I believe, clear, from a variety of considerations. (See Vol. I, Introduction, p. 14.) But they nowhere claim to be inspired and authoritative examples, unless 1 Cor. 4 : 16; 11 : 1; Phil. 3 : 17; 1 Thess. 1 : 6; 2 Thess. 3 : 9, be thought to suggest such a claim. Christ is our example, not the apostles. Their lives, like those of the O. T. saints and patriarchs afford warning as well as guidance. Illustrations of their mistakes are afforded by the quarrel between Paul and Barnabas (ch. 15 : 38, 39), the refraction of Peter (Gal. 2 : 12-14), the failure of Paul's device in Jerusalem (ch. 21 : 20-30). If, therefore, we were able to ascertain the manner and form of organization of the apostolic churches, it would not follow that we must of necessity organize ourselves in this country in the same manner. (3.) There is very inadequate ground for the assumption that the apostolic churches were all formed on one pattern. It might safely be presumed that this would not be the case. Where a church of instructed Christians was formed it would assume naturally the charge of its own affairs (ch. 1 : 23-26; 2 : 44-47; 6 : 5); where a church was gathered out of a purely heathen community, unfitted by either religious or political education for self-government, its affairs would be administered for it by its appointed pastor, and its officers selected for it by the apostle who organized the church (Acts 14 : 23; Tit. 1 : 5); where the majority of the newly organized church were Jews, the form of ecclesiastical government with which they were most familiar, that of the Jewish synagogue, would be naturally adopted. In other words, the church would be Congregational, Episcopalian, or Presbyterian, according to the peculiar circumstances and conditions of the church and community. And this in fact appears to have been the case. There is nothing in the Book of Acts to indicate that the Apostles undertook to provide one form of ecclesiastical organization for all localities, even in their own time, much less for all places and all times. In short, there is but little to indicate what was the organization, if any, of the apostolic churches, and nothing to indicate that this organization, whatever it may have been, is the best for our own changed times and circumstances.

The true use of the Book of Acts for us is indicated by its object, as defined above. In it we study the church of God in action. We are to imbibe the spirit of the apostles, learn the principles which gave them their power, and imitate, though not blindly, nor without regard to the change of times and conditions, the methods which they employed. He who does this, studies the Book of Acts to far wiser purpose than he who endeavors to construct out of its imperfect and fragmentary hints, a complete system of church government and order. Thus, for example, the remarkable specimens of sacred oratory which this book contains, constitute models for the study of the Christian worker in all ages. In Peter's Pentecostal address we have the apostolic revival sermon; in Stephen's dying speech, the martyr's plea; in Paul's sermon at Antioch in Pisidia, the apostle's sermon to the Jews; in his speech to the people of Lycaonia, the apostolic missionaries' address to the heathen; in his speech at Athens, the apostle's argument with rationalism. So, again, while the government of the primitive churches is uncertain, even if they had one common form of government, which is doubtful, the spirit of prayer, of consecration, of rejoicing, of spiritual sympathy, and of practical helpfulness which inspired them, and which is indicated by such pictures as that of ch. 2 : 42–47 (see notes there), is not doubtful, nor is the force of its example weakened by change of time, place, or circumstances. In brief, the important theme for our study is not the external form, but the inward Spirit; not the mechanism, but the power which moved it; not the body, but the soul; not the anatomy, but the psychology of the apostolic churches.

The life of the Apostle Paul. Our only authentic information respecting the life and labors of the first and the greatest missionary of the Gospel is wholly derived from the Book of Acts. For the convenience of those who wish to study that life I embody here a brief outline, referring the reader, for a consideration of all doubtful questions in chronology, to the notes, and for a consideration of the date and composition of the epistles to the introductions which accompany them.

All that we know of the early life of Paul is derived from occasional passages in his letters and speeches; *e. g.*, Acts 21 : 39; 22 : 3; Phil. 3 : 4–6. He was born in Tarsus of Cilicia, and brought up to the occupation of a tent-maker. His father being a Roman citizen, Saul,[1] as he was then called, was free-born. By reason of intercourse with the Greek population of his native city, he acquired the Greek language; but his parents, being of the stricter sect of Pharisees, had therefore an abhorrence of Greek culture, and there is no reason to believe he received an education in the schools for which Tarsus was then famous. He was early sent to Jerusalem, where he was "brought up," *i. e.*, from early youth,[2] at the feet of Gamaliel, the most distinguished doctor of the Jewish law. He learned to regard the Jewish law as an object of almost idolatrous regard, and whatever seemed to weaken its authority he conceived to be a foe to God, to be resisted unto death. His intense zeal against the new religion made him a leader of persecution against the early Christians, and it is as such we first meet him.[3] When Stephen, the first martyr, was slain, Saul is described as consenting to his death, and holding the outer garments of the witnesses who cast the first stones. He persecuted the disciples from city to city, pursuing them even to death. Of his miraculous conversion while pursuing the disciples to Damascus, the three accounts (chaps. 9, 22, 26), though differing in some unimportant details, agree in the substantial facts.[4] They all come from Paul himself, and appear never to have been denied during his lifetime. From his conversion to the commencement of his first missionary journey his life is involved in some obscurity, our knowledge being derived almost entirely from incidental allusions. From a comparison of Acts 9 : 19–30; 11 : 25, 26, 30; 22 : 17–21, and Gal. 1 : 17–24, we learn that he immediately commenced preaching at Damascus, which so excited the enmity of the Jews that he escaped death only by being let down by the wall in a basket, probably from the house of some Christian disciple, which stood upon or constituted a part of the wall of the city. After three years

[1] For explanations of his double name see ch. 13 : 9, note.... [2] See chap. 22 : 3, note.... [3] See chap. 26 : 10, 11, note; comp. 1 Tim. 1 : 13.... [4] See note on Saul's conversion, chap. 9 : 1–9.

(part of this time being spent in Arabia, probably studying the O. T. Scriptures), he went to Jerusalem, which was still the centre of the Christian Church, where the disciples viewed him with suspicion, and it was not until Barnabas told the story of his conversion that he was received among them. His first desire being to preach the Gospel to his own nation, when the Lord appeared to him in a trance in the Temple, and bade him leave Jerusalem, he remonstrated, believing that as the Jews had known him as a persecutor, they would be more ready to receive his testimony to the power of the truth; but, when the command was repeated, he yielded and returned to Tarsus, where he remained until Barnabas went for and brought him to Antioch. From this time the Book of Acts is little else than the story of his life and missionary labors. It may be conveniently divided into four sections.

First missionary tour. As the result of a special occasion of fasting and prayer, Paul and Barnabas are ordained as the first missionaries, and set out, taking with them John Mark as an assistant. They embark at Seleucia, the port of Antioch, for the island of Cyprus. Here the Roman proconsul, Sergius Paulus, is converted, and Elymas, or Bar-jesus, is smitten with blindness. From this time the apostle adopts his new name, Paul, which is now first mentioned, and by which he is always subsequently called.

From Cyprus John Mark returns, probably deterred by the dangers of the journey, while Paul and Barnabas cross over to Perga, on the main coast, intending to penetrate the districts of Pisidia and Lycaonia. Their first stopping place was Antioch in Pisidia; driven thence by persecution, they visited in succession the cities of Iconium, Lystra, and Derbe. At Lystra a miracle performed upon a cripple brought together a crowd of ignorant people, who are subsequently incited by Jews from Antioch and Iconium, and stone Paul, leaving him for dead, though only stunned. But these persecutions do not prevent him from visiting all these cities on his return to Antioch in Syria, after an absence which is supposed to have lasted about a year. The broad command to "preach the Gospel to every creature" was evidently but very imperfectly understood by the Apostolic Church. Many disciples were not prepared to go further than to say that heathen might become Christians by submitting to circumcision, accepting the Jewish law, and so becoming Jews. Paul and Barnabas, on the contrary, maintained that Christ was free to every creature. To settle this dispute a council was called at Jerusalem, which resulted in the unanimous approval of the work of Paul and of his principles.

Second missionary journey. This occupied three or four years. The incidents are recorded in Acts 15 : 36–41 to 18 : 22. It is memorable for its extent, duration, and the introduction of Christianity into Europe. Paul proposing to Barnabas to revisit the churches they had established, Barnabas insisted on taking John Mark with them, to which Paul would not consent. A dispute arose, which resulted in their separation, and Paul departed, accompanied by Silas. Beginning at Antioch in Syria, he visited Cilicia, Lycaonia, Phrygia, Galatia, Mysia, and the Troad, and in Europe, Macedonia, Athens, and Corinth; thence he crossed the Ægean Sea to Ephesus, and thence, by Cæsarea, to Jerusalem, whence, after a hasty visit, he returned to Antioch in Syria. It was on this journey he organized the churches at Thessalonica and Philippi, and also first preached the Gospel at Athens. At Philippi the arrest and imprisonment of Paul and Silas, and the conversion of the jailor, occurred.

Third missionary tour. The account of this tour is contained in Acts 18 : 23 to 21 : 17. His course, as indicated in the accompanying map, is somewhat hypothetical. He passed through Galatia and Phrygia, "strengthening all the disciples" (Acts 8 : 23), and thence came into Ephesus. This city was to the Asia of the N. T. what Corinth was to Greece and Rome to Italy, and it may be regarded as the central object of this third apostolic journey. Here occurred his conflict with the witchcraft of which Ephesus was headquarters, and here he spent over two years in the ministry of the Gospel. His subsequent course may be traced with considerable accuracy in Acts, ch. 20. From Ephesus he went up the coast to Troas (2 Cor. 2 : 12), and thence into Macedonia, probably visiting the churches at Philippi, Thessalonica, Perea, etc., and spending three months in Greece, probably in Corinth. Thence he returned, partly by land and partly by water, along the coast of the Ægean Sea. At Potara he took ship direct to Tyre, and so came, via Cæsarea, to the end of his third missionary tour at Jerusalem.

Arrest, imprisonment, and shipwreck. Acts 21 : 18 to chap. 28. In consequence of a mob incited by the Jews against Paul, he is arrested by the Roman authorities, sent to Cæsarea, the Roman military headquarters of Judea, tried first before Felix, then before Festus and Agrippa, and finally, having appealed to Cæsar, which every Roman citizen had a right to do, is sent to Rome. The minute account of this voyage, its perils and shipwreck, afford a remarkable opportunity for the verification of N. T. history. See notes on chap. 27.

Subsequent history. The N. T. history of Paul ends with his first imprisonment in Rome. His subsequent history is not known with certainty. It appears probable, however, that at the end of two years his case was heard by Nero, who acquitted him (A. D. 63); that he then spent a period, which some reckon at five years, others at two or three, in journeys of uncertain extent, but which brought him again to Ephesus. Here he is supposed to have been again arrested and carried to Rome; but at all events it is tolerably certain that he was imprisoned there a second time, condemned by Nero, and put to death in the great persecution of the Christians by that emperor. According to the uniform tradition the apostle was beheaded, without scourging (as the privilege of his citizenship), outside the gate leading to the port of Ostea. The date of his death appears to have been about midsummer, A. D. 66 or 67.

Chronology. The chronology of the Book

MAP OF PAUL'S FIRST AND SECOND MISSIONARY JOURNEYS.

of Acts is involved in much obscurity, and has given rise to much discussion among scholars. It can probably never be settled with any degree of certainty. The following table, taken substantially from Conybeare and Howson, may help the student in tracing the course of its history, though he must not forget that the dates are largely hypothetical. A more complicated and elaborate table will be found in Alford's Greek Testament, with dates different in some respects; and in Davidson's Introduction to the N. T. (Vol. II) is one giving in a tabular form the various views of thirty-four different scholars.

CHRONOLOGICAL TABLE.

A. D.	New Testament History.	Contemporary Events.
30	The ascension (May 18).	
30 to 36	The events related in Acts, ch. 2 : 42 to 6 : 8. Martyrdom of Stephen; extension of church through persecution, chaps. 6 : 8 to 8 : 40.	Tiberius emperor of Rome.
36	St. Paul's conversion.	Death of Tiberius and accession of Caligula (March 16).
37	At Damascus.	
38	Flight from Damascus to Jerusalem, and thence to Tarsus.	
39	During three years St. Paul preaches in Syria and Cilicia, making Tarsus his head-	
40	quarters, and probably undergoes most of	Death of Caligula and accession of Claudius
41	the sufferings mentioned at 2 Cor. 11 : 24–27,	(Jan. 25), Judæa and Samaria given to
42	viz., two of the Roman and the five Jewish	Herod Agrippa I.
43	scourgings, and three shipwrecks.	Invasion of Britain by Aulus Plautius.
44	He is brought from Tarsus to Antioch (Acts 11 : 26), and stays there a year before the famine.	Death of Herod Agrippa I (Acts 12). Cuspius Fadus (as procurator) succeeds to the government of Judæa.
45	He visits Jerusalem with Barnabas, to relieve the famine.	
46	At Antioch.	Tiberius Alexander made procurator of Judæa (about this time).
47	At Antioch.	
48	His "First Missionary Journey," from Antioch to Cyprus, Antioch in Pisidia, Iconium, Lystra, Derbe,	Agrippa II (Acts 25 : 24) made king of Chalcis.
49	and back through the same places to Antioch.	Cumanus made procurator of Judæa (about this time).
50	St. Paul and Barnabas attend the "Council of Jerusalem."	Caractacus captured by the Romans in Britain. Cogidunus (father of Claudia (?), 2 Tim. 4 : 21), assists the Romans in Britain.
51	His "Second Missionary Journey," from Antioch to Cilicia, Lycaonia, Galatia,	
52	Troas, Philippi, Thessalonica, Berœa, Athens, and Corinth—Writes 1 Thess.	Claudius expels the Jews from Rome (Acts 18 : 2).
53	At Corinth—Writes 2 Thess.	The tetrarchy of Trachonitis given to Agrippa II; Felix made procurator of Judæa.
54	(Spring)—He leaves Corinth and reaches (Summer) Jerusalem at Pentecost, and thence goes to Antioch. (Autumn)—His "Third Missionary Journey." He goes to Ephesus.	Death of Claudius and accession of Nero (Oct. 13).
55	At Ephesus.	
56	At Ephesus.	
57	(Spring) He writes 1 Cor. (Summer) Leaves Ephesus for Macedonia, (Autumn) where he writes 2 Cor., and thence (Winter) to Corinth, where he writes Galatians.	
58	(Spring) He writes Romans, and leaves Corinth, going by Philippi and Miletus (Summer) to Jerusalem (Pentecost), where he is arrested, and sent to Cæsarea.	
59	At Cæsarea.	Nero murders Agrippina.
60	(Autumn)—Sent to Rome by Festus (about August). (Winter)—Shipwrecked at Malta.	Felix is recalled, and succeeded by Festus.
61	(Spring)—He arrives at Rome.	Embassy from Jerusalem to Rome to petition about the wall.
62	At Rome. (Spring)—Writes { Philemon, Colossians, Ephesians. (Autumn)—Writes Philippians.	Burrus dies; Albinus succeeds Festus as procurator; Nero marries Poppæa; Octavia executed; Pallas put to death.
63	(Spring)—He is acquitted and probably goes to Macedonia (Phil. 2 : 24) and Colosse (Philemon 22).	Poppæa's daughter Claudia born.

MAP OF COUNTRIES MENTIONED IN THE BOOK OF ACTS: PAUL'S THIRD AND FOURTH JOURNEYS.

GAZETTEER.

Achaia. In the N. T. it signifies a Roman province which included the whole of the Peloponnesus, and the greater part of Hellas proper, with the adjacent islands. This province, with that of Macedonia, comprehended the whole of Greece; hence Achaia and Macedonia are frequently mentioned together in the N. T. to indicate all Greece. Acts 18 : 12.

Accho. Now called Acre, or more usually by Europeans, St. Jean d'Acre, the most important seaport town on the Syrian coast, about thirty miles south of Tyre. The only notice of it in the N. T. is in connection with Paul's passage from Tyre to Cæsarea, where it is called by its Egyptian name, Ptolemais. Acts 21 : 7.

Adria. This term occurs but once in the Scriptures. As there used it includes not only the Venetian Gulf, but all that part of the Mediterranean between Crete and Sicily. Ptolemy bounds Italy on the south, Sicily on the east, Greece on the south and west, and Crete on the west by Adria, or the Adriatic sea. Its bounds are only important as fixing the site of Paul's shipwreck. Acts 27 : 27.

Adramytium. A city of Asia, by some commentators erroneously confounded with Adrametum in Africa. It was situated on the coast of Mysia (*q. v.*) at the head of an extensive bay, facing the island of Lesbos. It has no Biblical interest except that Paul's voyage from Cæsarea was made in a ship belonging to this place. Acts 27 : 2.

Alexandria. A celebrated city and seaport of Egypt on the Mediterranean, twelve miles from the mouth of the river Nile, named in honor of Alexander the Great, who founded it B. C. 332. Acts 18 : 24.

Amphipolis. A city of Macedonia on the river Strymon, thirty-three Roman miles from Philippi. Its site is now occupied by a village called Neokhorio. Acts 17 : 1.

Antioch. Two cities of this name are in Syria, and Antioch in Pisidia, both connected with the life and labors of Paul. Antioch in Syria was a city with more than 500,000 souls. It is now a village of but a few thousand inhabitants, and the only remnant of Christianity is in the name of the eastern gate, which is called after Paul. Acts 11 : 19–30; 13 : 1–3; 14 : 26–28; 15 : 30–35. Antioch in Pisidia, a town on the border of Phrygia, was at the time of Paul a Roman colony. It is now identified with the modern Yalobatch. Acts 13 : 14; 14 : 19–22; 18 : 22.

Antipatris. A town in Palestine built by Herod the Great, and named after his father, Antipater. It is situated between Jerusalem and Cæsarea, and is now a village called *Kefr Saba*. Acts 23 : 31.

Apollonia. A city of Macedonia about thirty Roman miles from Amphibolis. Acts 17 : 1.

Appi Forum. A well known station forty-three miles from Rome in the Appian Bay leading from Rome to the Bay of Naples. The "Three Taverns" was a wayside inn, and a customary resort of travelers, ten miles nearer Rome. Both are mentioned by Cicero. Acts 28 : 15.

Areopagus, or **Mars Hill.** A narrow naked ridge of limestone-rock at Athens, sloping upward from the north, and terminating in an abrupt precipice on the south, fifty or sixty feet above a valley which divides it from the west end of the Acropolis. The court of the Areopagus was simply an open space on the highest summit of the hill, the judges sitting in the open air, on rude seats of stone hewn out in the solid rock. This was the site of what we may call the Supreme Court of Athens. On the spot occupied by this court, a long series of awful causes, connected with crime and religion, had been decided, beginning with the legendary trial by the other gods of Mars the god of war, for murder, which gave to the place its name. Acts 17 : 19.

Ashdod. The Azotus of the Greeks and Romans, a city of the Philistines, on the seacoast about midway between Gaza and Joppa. Acts 8 : 40.

Asia. The origin of this name is obscure, but as a designation of one of the greater divisions of the known world, it came into use in the fifth century before Christ. In the O. T. it does not occur. In the N. T. it is used in a narrower sense for a Roman province which embraced the western part of Asia Minor and of which Ephesus was the capital. Acts 2 : 9; 6 : 9; 16 : 6; 19 : 10, 22, 26.

Assos. A seaport of Lesser Mysia in the Ægean Sea. Its site is now occupied by a village called Beiram. Acts 20 : 13.

Athens. A city of Greece distinguished for the military talent, learning, and eloquence of its inhabitants. Devastated by war, by time, and by repeated changes of masters, it is now a mass of ruins. For description of its condition at the time of Paul's visit to it, see notes on Acts 17 : 16–34.

Attalia. A maritime town at the mouth of the river Catambactes, in Pamphylia, now existing under the name of Adalia; population 8000. Acts 14 : 25.

Azotus. See Ashdod. Acts 8 : 40.

Babylon. The name given to the capital of the Babylonian monarchy, and also to the monarchy itself. Babylon, the capital, was probably the largest and most magnificent city of the ancient world. It was built in the form of a square upon both sides of the Euphrates, and enclosed within a vast system of double walls, measuring, according to the least estimate, forty miles, or ten each way. Acts 7 : 43.

Berea. A city of Macedonia, now existing under the name of Verria, with a population of 18,000 or 20,000 and placed in the second rank of the cities of European Turkey. Acts 17 : 10–14.

Bithynia. A province of Asia Minor, mentioned only in Acts 16 : 7, and in 1 Peter 1 : 1.

Cæsarea. A celebrated city of Palestine on the Mediterranean sea-coast, about seventy miles N. W. of Jerusalem. It was sometimes called Cæsarea Palestina to distinguish it from Cæsarea Philippi. The site is still called Kaisariyeh. Acts 8 : 40; 9 : 30; 11 : 11; 12 : 19; 18 : 22; 21 : 8, 16.

Cappadocia. The most easterly region of Asia Minor. Acts 2 : 9.

Cenchrea. The eastern harbor of Corinth, from which it was distant about nine miles. The modern village of *Kikries* now occupies the site of Cenchrea, and some remnants of the moles are still visible. Acts 18 : 18.

Chanaan, or **Canaan.** The name given to that portion of Palestine which lay to the west of the Jordan to distinguish it from Gilead, the name given to the high table-land east of the Jordan. The territory so called extended from the boundary of Syria on the north to Gaza on the south, and from the Jordan to the Mediterranean. Acts 7 : 11.

Charran. See Haran. Acts 7 : 2, 4.

Chios. A beautiful island in the Ægean Sea between Samos and Lesbos. It is now called Scio. Acts 20 : 15.

Cilicia. The most southeasterly province of Asia Minor, divided by Mount Amanus from Syria, with which it is sometimes coupled. Acts 6 : 9; 21 : 39; 22 : 3.

Clauda. An island off the southwest coast of Crete, under the lee of which the vessel in Paul's voyage to Italy had to run. Now called Gozzo. Acts 27 : 16.

Cnidus. A peninsula at the entrance of the Ægean Sea, between the islands of Coos and Rhodes. Acts 27 : 7.

Corinth. This city is alike remarkable for its distinctive geographical position, its eminence in Greek and Roman history, and its close connection with the spread of Christianity. It was the capital of a small district called *Isthmus*, "a bridge of the sea," which joins the ancient Peloponnesus, the modern Morea, to the northern portion of Greece. Its position made it a great commercial metropolis. The city has now shrunk to a wretched village on the old site, bearing the corrupted name of Gortho. Acts 18 : 1.

Coos. A small island near the coast of Caria, now called Stanco. Acts 21 : 1.

Crete. A large island in the Mediterranean, anciently celebrated for its one hundred cities. Acts 2 : 11; 27 : 12; 13 : 21.

Cyprus. A large island in the Mediterranean, about sixty miles from the coasts of Syria and Asia Minor; is very frequently mentioned in Scripture. The first missionary journey of Paul and Barnabas commenced with Cyprus. Acts 4 : 36; 11 : 19, 20; 13 : 4–12.

Cyrene. A Libyan city founded by a colony of Greeks from Thera, an island in the Ægean Sea, about B. C. 632. Simon, who was compelled to bear our Saviour's cross, was a Cyrenian, so were some of the first Christian teachers. Acts 2 : 10; 11 : 20; 13 : 1.

Damascus. A city of Western Asia, formerly the capital of the kingdom of Syria, is one of the most ancient cities of the world. The population with its suburbs is estimated at 150,000. The principal street, about a mile in length, running through the city from east to west, is regarded by the Christian population as "the street which is called Straight," mentioned in Acts 9 : 11.

Derbe. A small town in Lycaonia, probably near the pass called the Cilician gates. The exact site is uncertain. Acts 14 : 6, 20; 16 : 1.

Egypt. A region important from the earliest times and more closely identified with Bible incidents than any other, except the Holy Land itself. The common name of Egypt in the Bible is "Mizraim" (*q. v.*) or more fully "the land of Mizraim." It occupies the northeastern angle of Africa, and its boundaries appear to have been always very nearly the same. Acts 13 : 17.

Ephesus. A celebrated city, the metropolis of Ionia, and of Proconsular Asia under the Romans; located in a fertile plain south of the river Cayster, not far from the coast of the Icarian Sea. It is now an uninhabited ruin; the retiring sea has left its harbor a pestilential morass. Acts 18 : 19.

Fair Havens, the. A harbor or roadstead off the south coast of Crete; mentioned only in Acts 27 : 8. See note there.

Galatia. A province which may be roughly described as the central region of the peninsula of Asia Minor, with the provinces of Asia on the west, Cappadocia on the east, Pamphylia and Cilicia on the south, and Bithynia and Pontus on the north. The Galatians were Celts or Gauls, and possessed that enthusiasm and fickleness which have ever been the characteristics of the Gallic race. For full description of their character see Introduction to the Epistle to the Galatians. Acts 16 : 6.

Galilee. In the time of Christ, Galilee embraced the whole northern section of Palestine, including the ancient territories of Issachar, Zebulon, Asher, and Naphtali. Acts 1 : 11.

Gaza. One of the five princely cities of the Philistines which has withstood the desolations of many generations, and continues to the present time a comparatively thriving and well peopled city. It may be regarded as one of the oldest cities of the world, since it is mentioned in Gen. 10 : 19 as one of the border towns of the Canaanites. The present Arabic name of the city is Ghuzzeh, and its population is estimated at from 15,000 to 20,000, mainly Mohammedans. Acts 8 : 26.

Greece. A country lying in the southeast of Europe between 36° and 40° north latitude. It is sometimes described as containing the four provinces of Macedonia, Epirus, Achaia or Hellas, and Peloponnesus, but more commonly is understood to comprise the two latter. Acts 20 : 2.

Haran. The Charran of Acts 7 : 2, 4, was situated in Mesopotamia, or more exactly, in Padanaram. It still exists in the modern village of Harrân on the river Belik.

Iconium. A city of Lycaonia between Ephesus and the more easterly cities of Tarsus and Antioch and the Euphrates. It is now called Konizeh. Population 30,000. Acts 13 : 51; 14 : 19; 16 : 22.

Italy. As used in the N. T. denotes the same extent of country that it does in modern times; it comprehends the whole peninsula which reaches from the Alps to the Straits of Messina. It but rarely occurs in the N. T., and only as a general designation. Acts 27 : 1.

Jerusalem. The ancient capital of the Holy Land, situated in Judea, and directly west of the north end of the Dead Sea. It is 2500 feet above the level of the Mediterranean Sea and 3600 feet above the Judean Valley. For description, topography, and map, see Vol. I, page 278. Acts 1 : 4.

Joppa, or **Japho.** A seaport on the southern coast of Palestine, forty miles west-northwest of Jerusalem, and one of the oldest cities of the world. It is the Jaffa of modern history. Present population 15,000. Acts 9 : 36, 42, 43.

Judea. This name is now frequently applied to the whole of the Holy Land, more generally designated as Palestine. Properly speaking, however, it only signifies one of the three provinces into which Palestine west of the Jordan was divided at the time of Christ—Galilee, Samaria, and Judea. The province of Judea comprised the territories of Judah, Benjamin, Simeon, and parts of Dan, and it extended from the Jordan to the Mediterranean, from the wilderness on the south to Shiloh on the north, running up, however, on the sea-coast west of Samaria to a point north of Cæsarea. Acts 1 : 8.

Lasea. A town in Crete near the Fair Havens where Paul for a time was detained. The place is nowhere else mentioned, but it has been identified in comparatively recent times, and the name is still borne by a few ruins. Acts 27 : 8.

Libya. A country west of Egypt, of which Cyrene was the capital. Acts 2 : 10.

Lycaonia. One of the provinces of Asia Minor. Acts 14 : 6.

Lystra. A city of Lycaonia south of Iconium. The exact site is unknown. Acts 14 : 6, 8; 16 : 1, 2.

Macedonia. An important kingdom of ancient Greece, and subsequently a Roman province, bounded on the north by Mœsia and Illyricum, on the south by Thessaly and Epirus, and on the east and west, respectively, by Thrace and the Ægean Sea, and by Epirus and the Adriatic. Its soil is fertile and its climate healthy. The churches at Thessalonica and Philippi were among the results of Paul's labors in Macedonia. Acts 16 : 9.

Madian. See note on Acts 25 : 34. Acts 7 : 29.

Mars Hill. See Areopagus. Acts 17 : 22.

Mesopotamia. A country deriving its name from its position between the great rivers Euphrates and Tigris. It is about 700 miles in length and varies in breadth from 20 to 240 or 250 miles. It is the northwestern part which is supposed to be the Mesopotamia of Scripture,—the land where Abraham's kindred dwelt. Acts 7 : 2.

Miletus. A city of Asia Minor twenty or thirty miles south of Ephesus, where Paul, when hastening to Jerusalem, summoned the elders of Ephesus that he might give them a solemn charge. Acts 20 : 15–17.

Melita. The name given in Acts 28 : 1 to the island on which Paul was shipwrecked. While there has been some difference of opinion among scholars, by the general consent of most of those who have investigated the matter, Melita is identified with the modern Malta. Acts 28 : 1.

Mitylene. The capital of the ancient island of Lesbos in the Ægean Sea. Acts 20 : 14.

Mount Sina, or **Sinai.** The wild mountain region in Arabia Petrea where the law was given to Moses. Indeed the whole peninsula which lies between the horns of the Red Sea has received the name of Sinai from the magnitude and prominence of the Sinaitic group of mountains which lies nearly in its centre. Acts 7 : 30.

Myra. One of the chief towns of the province of Lycia. Acts 27 : 5.

Mysia. The northwestern province of Asia Minor, comprising one of its richest and most populous regions. Acts 16 : 7, 8.

Neapolis. A seaport on the coast of the Ægean Sea about ten miles from Philippi. The village of Kavalla is on the site of Neapolis and contains at present 5000 or 6000 inhabitants. Acts 16 : 11.

Olivet (Mount of). Directly east of Jerusalem is a long ridge with four distinct summits, one outlier starting off to the north and another to the south. This ridge is that known both in the O. T. and the N. T. as the Mount of Olives or of Olivet. It was the "Park" of Jerusalem. Its green slopes, as seen in the early spring, even now stand out in refreshing contrast to the dreary and withered ruins of the city at its foot. Acts 1 : 9–12.

Pamphylia. One of the southern provinces of Asia Minor. At the time of Paul it formed a province together with Lycia. Acts 13 : 13; 14 : 24.

Paphos. A town at the western end of Cyprus. Acts 13 : 6.

Patara. A seaport of Lycia in Asia Minor. Acts 21 : 1.

Perga. A city of Pamphylia on the river Castrus. Acts 13 : 13.

Phenice, or **Phœnicia.** A narrow tract of country on the Mediterranean north of Palestine. Phenice also occurs in Acts 27 : 12 as the name of a town in Crete where the officers of the vessel in which Paul was shipwrecked desired to harbor. It has been identified with the modern Lutro.

Philippi. A city of Macedonia, about ten miles from Neapolis, its port, where Paul landed. The ancient name is still applied to the locality, but there are no inhabitants. So far as the N. T. history directly informs us, Philippi was the first city in Europe which heard the gospel preached. Acts 16 : 12.

Phrygia. A district of Asia Minor twice mentioned in the N. T. Its limits, as the term was used in the apostolic age, were very indefinite. Acts 16 : 6; 18 : 23.

Pisidia. An interior district of Asia Minor lying principally on Mount Taurus. Acts 13 : 14.

Pontus. A considerable district in Asia Minor three times mentioned in the N. T. It signified a country of various extent at various times. Acts 2 : 9; 18 : 2.

Ptolemais. See Accho. Acts 21 : 7.

Puteoli. This was the principal port of southern Italy, and commerce brought many Jews to Puteoli. Hence when Paul landed here on his way to Rome he found brethren ready to receive and speed him on his journey. It is now called Puzzuoli. Acts 28 : 13, 14.

Red Sea. A body of water lying east of Egypt and Nubia and separating them from Arabia. It is 1400 miles long, and 200 miles wide in its widest part. In Bible history it is famous for the passage made by Israel (Exodus, chap. 14) which took place near the head-waters of what is now known as the Gulf of Suez. In the N. T. it is referred to only in connection with this event. Acts 7 : 36. Heb. 11 : 29.

Rhegium. A city of Italy situated at the southern extremity of the peninsula, now called Reggio, where Paul landed on his journey to Rome. It is at present one of the most flourishing towns of southern Italy, with a population of 9000. Acts 28 : 13.

Rhodes. An island off the coast of Asia Minor, over against Caria. Its present population is about 20,000. Acts 21 : 1.

Rome (City of). The capital of the Roman Empire, situated on the Tiber about fifteen miles from its mouth. The famous seven hills which formed the nucleus of the ancient city still stand on the left bank, and the remains of many of the buildings erected by the Roman Emperors still remain. To the N. T. student the city is chiefly of interest in connection with the visit of Paul and the epistle to the Romans. At the time of this visit the city must be imagined as a large and irregular mass of buildings, unprotected by an outer wall; the streets were narrow and winding, the houses lofty and densely crowded. The population was probably a little larger than the city of New York in 1875; one-half were slaves, of the remainder a large proportion were paupers; there was a small proportion of wealthy and profligate nobility, but apparently no middle industrial classes. Untrustworthy traditions connect various sites with Paul's stay in the city. Some of the ruins are of value because illustrating Scripture. This is especially true of the famous Arch of Titus, erected to celebrate his triumph, and which contains bas reliefs of some of the sacred vessels of the Jewish Temple. Acts 2 : 10.

Rome (Empire of). The boundaries of the Roman Empire at the commencement of the Christian era were, the Atlantic on the west; the Euphrates on the east; the Desert of Africa, the Cataracts of the Nile, and the Arabian Deserts on the south; the British Channel, the Rhine, the Danube, and the Black Sea on the north. The only independent powers of importance were the Parthians on the east and the Germans on the north. The population of the empire in the time of Augustus has been variously estimated at from 85,000,000 to 120,000,000. This includes the population of the provinces, *i. e.* the countries conquered by Rome and usually governed by Roman officials.

Salamis. A seaport town on the eastern coast of Cyprus. It was here that Paul and Barnabas landed, being the nearest point to Seleucia. Acts 13 : 4, 5.

Salmone. A promontory on the eastern extremity of the island of Crete. Acts 27 : 7.

Samaria. The province of Samaria once included all of Palestine north of Judea. That portion east of the Jordan which originally belonged to it was taken away by the kings of Assyria; then the northern portion shared the same fate; and Samaria was reduced to the dimensions which it possessed at the time of Christ. Acts 1 : 8.

Samos. An island on the coast of Asia Minor midway between the points occupied by Ephesus and Miletus. Acts 20 : 15.

Samothracia. A lofty and conspicuous island north of Lemnos, in the Ægean Sea, off the coast of Thrace, now called Samotraki. Acts 16 : 11.

Saron, or **Sharon.** A level tract between Mount Carmel and Joppa, in which Lydda stood. Acts 9 : 35.

Seleucia. There are various cities of this name in Syria and Asia Minor, but the only one noticed in Scripture is the one which stood at the mouth of the Orontes, and formed the seaport of Antioch. Acts 13 : 4.

Sidon, or **Zidon.** An ancient city of Phœnicia about twenty miles north of Tyre, and nearly forty miles south of Beirut. The modern name is *Saida.* Acts 12 : 20.

Sychem. A celebrated city of Palestine called also Shechem, Sichem, and Sychar, and of great antiquity, for it was in existence when Abraham entered Canaan. It is located in a valley between Mount Ebal and Gerizim, about seven miles south of Samaria. Acts 7 : 16.

Syracuse. An ancient city in the southeastern coast of Sicily. Acts 28 : 12.

Syria. The region from east to west between the Mediterranean and the Euphrates, and from north to south between the Lebanon and the borders of the desert. Acts 18 : 18.

Tarsus. The capital of the province of Cilicia, a large and populous city on the river Cydmus. It is now a town with about 20,000 inhabitants, and is described as being a den of poverty, filth, and ruins. Acts 9 : 11, 30; 11 : 25.

Thessalonica. A city of Macedonia, now the second city of European Turkey with 70,000 inhabitants, under the slightly corrupted name of Saloniké. Acts 17 : 1–9.

Thyatira. A town of Lydia situated on the river Lycus. It is still a considerable town with many ruins, called Akhissar. Acts 16 : 14; Rev. 1 : 2.

Troas. A seaport town near to the Hellespont, sometimes considered as belonging to the Lesser Mysia. Acts 16 : 8, 11; 20 : 5, 6.

Trogyllium. A small town at the foot of the promontory of Mycale, opposite to the island of Samos. Acts 20 : 15.

Tyre. A celebrated city of Phœnicia, situated on the eastern coast of the Mediterranean. Present population 3000 or 4000, half being Christians. Acts 12 : 20.

TRADITIONAL PORTRAITS OF PETER AND PAUL.

These portraits are copied, same size as the original, from the bottom of a gilded glass cup, found in the Catacombs of St. Sebastian at Rome. The earliest interments by the Christians in the Roman catacombs included, besides Christian symbols, some objects of pagan regard. This having been the case in the section in which the glass cup bearing the group of the Saviour, Paul, and Peter was discovered, it seems conclusive that the age was probably the fourth, if not the third century. The absence of the nimbus (glory or circle) about the heads of Peter and Paul, and its presence around the Saviour's, may indicate the third century or early in the fourth; for the nimbus was generally used around the heads of all saints and divine persons in the latter half of the fourth century. Tertullian speaks of glass cups as used in sacramental services, as also does Eusebius. In this picture the Saviour is represented as presenting a crown of life to the apostles; the inscription is a prayer of the friends of the dead, who was laid in the tomb in the faith of Christ, and may be paraphrased, "Friendship's blessing; may you live forever with thy (Saviour)."

THE ACTS

OF THE APOSTLES.

CHAPTER I.

THE former treatise [a] have I made, O Theophilus,
of all that Jesus began both to do and teach,
2 Until [b] the day in which he was taken up, after
that he through the Holy Ghost had given commandments [c] unto the apostles whom he had chosen:
3 To whom also he shewed himself alive after his
passion, by many [d] infallible proofs, being seen of them
forty days, and speaking of the things pertaining to
the kingdom of God;
4 And being assembled together with *them*, commanded [e] them that they should not depart from Jerusalem, but wait for the promise of the Father, which,
saith he, ye [f] have heard of me:
5 For John [g] truly baptized with water; but ye shall
be baptized with the Holy Ghost,[h] not many days
hence.

a Luke 1:1-4, etc....b verse 9; Luke 24:51; 1 Tim. 3:16....c Matt. 28:19; Mark 16:15-19....d Luke 24:15; John, ch. 20, 21....e Luke 24:49....f John, ch. 14 to 16....g Matt. 3:11....h chap. 2:4; 10:45; 11:15.

Ch. 1:1-14. PREFACE. THE ASCENSION. THE CONDITION OF CHRISTIAN ACTIVITY, THE FULFILLMENT OF THE PROMISE OF THE FATHER.—THE LIMITS OF HUMAN KNOWLEDGE AND THE FOLLY OF HUMAN FORETELLING.—THE SOURCE OF THE CHRISTIAN'S POWER.—THE EXTENT OF THE CHRISTIAN'S MINISTRY.—THE ASCENSION AND THE NATURE OF CHRIST'S SECOND COMING.

A.D. 30. May. After a preface to his whole book (vers. 1-3) Luke briefly describes the ascension of our Lord (vers. 4-12) as a preliminary to the account, which immediately follows, of the apostolic selection of a successor to Judas Iscariot. The whole of Chap. I may be regarded as prefatory and preliminary to the main history which begins with the descent of the Holy Spirit on the day of Pentecost and the resultant revival (ch. 2).

1. The former treatise. The Gospel of Luke. Comp. its introduction ch. 1:1-4.—**O Theophilus.** Of this person nothing whatever is known except the facts implied here and in the notes to Luke's Gospel. The various conjectures may be seen in Smith's *Bible Dictionary*, article Theophilus. That he was a Christian appears clear from Luke 1:4; the title applied to him, *Most excellent Theophilus*, indicates rank as well as character (see Acts 23:26; 24:3; 26:25); hence it is probable that he held some high position, but what, or where, is wholly unknown. The theory advanced by some that the name, which signifies "Lover of God," was a fictitious one, and that the Gospel and this book were simply addressed to all that loved God, *i. e.* to all the disciples, is untenable. Both the treatises were probably dedicated somewhat after the manner of a modern book to Theophilus, but intended for a general circulation, which his name, appended, might even increase.—**Began both to do and to teach.** The Gospel records only the beginning of Christ's teaching, *i. e.*, the ministry of his earthly life; it is the object of the Book of Acts to record the continuance of his teaching, the ministry of the ascended Lord ever present with his church in fulfillment of the promise of Matt. 28:20. Thus the Gospel of Luke and the Book of Acts are parts of one connected Life of our Lord—one his life in the body, the other his life in the church. See Intro., pp. 15, 16.

2, 3. The construction of the original is a little difficult and uncertain. The best interpretation is that given by our English version—the ministry and teaching of Christ continuing after his resurrection and until his ascension. The commandments here referred to are especially those given in his last conferences with the eleven. (Matt. 28:19, 20; Mark 16:14-18; Luke 24:46-49; John 20:21-23; 21:15-17). The statement that they were given through the Holy Ghost, *i. e.* by the power of the Spirit of God speaking in and through Jesus Christ, accords with Christ's constant reference of his deeds and words to the Father, as the Power that dwelt in him. (John 5:30; 14:10.)—**To whom also he showed himself,** etc. On the nature and number of the appearances of Jesus Christ after his resurrection, and the proofs of that resurrection, and the slowness of the disciples to believe, see note on Resurrection of our Lord, Vol. I, p. 330. The appearances were as follows: To Mary Magdalene (John 20:11-18); to Peter (1 Cor. 15:5); to two disciples on the road to Emmaus (Mark 16:12, 13; Luke 24:13-35); to ten disciples (Mark 16:14; Luke 24:36-49; John 20:19-23; 1 Cor. 15:5); to Thomas with the rest (John 20:24-29); to the disciples by the sea (John 21:1-24); among the mountains (Matt. 28:16, 17; 1 Cor. 15:5); at the last commission (Matt. 28:18, 19; Mark 16:15-18); at the ascension (Mark 16:19; Luke 24:50-53; Acts 1:3-12). Whether the appearance described here in vers. 4, 5, is to be identified with some one of these other appearances, is uncertain.

4, 5. And being assembled together. A conference in Galilee is probably here described; for the indication is that they were assembled *for the purpose of meeting Christ*, and but one such gathering is intimated by the Evangelist (Matt 28:16). The *coming together* of ver. 6 is

6 When they therefore were come together, they
asked of him, saying, Lord, wilt[i] thou at this time restore[j] again the kingdom to Israel?
7 And he said unto them, It[k] is not for you to know
the times or the seasons, which the Father hath put in
his own power.
8 But ye shall receive power, after that the Holy
Ghost is come upon you: and ye[l] shall be witnesses
unto me, both in Jerusalem, and in all Judæa, and in
Samaria, and unto the uttermost part of the earth.
9 And when he had spoken these things, while they
beheld, he was taken up; and a cloud received him out
of their sight.

i Matt. 24 : 3, 4 . . . . j Isa. 1 : 26; Dan. 7 : 27 . . . . k Matt. 24 : 36; 1 Thess. 5 : 1, 2 . . . . l Matt. 28 : 19; Luke 24 : 47–49.

on a subsequent occasion and on the Mount of Olives, perhaps also by appointment. —**That they should not depart from Jerusalem.** That is, until they had received the promise of the Father.—**Which ye have heard of me.** The promise of the gift of *another* Comforter contained in Christ's last conversation with the eleven (John 14 : 16–20, 26; 15 : 26, 27; 16 : 13, 14). This was the promise of the Father, made in the Old Testament (Isa. 44 : 3; Ezek. 36 : 27; Joel 2 : 28–32), recalled to the remembrance of the nation by John the Baptist (Matt. 3 : 11), and renewed by the Son.

6. When they therefore were come together. Subsequently and in the vicinity of Jerusalem. This, which is the view of Calvin, Olshausen, and Hackett, appears more consonant with the narrative, than to understand that Luke again mentions the same coming together already referred to in ver. 4, as do Meyer and Alford.—**Wilt thou at this time restore again the kingdom to Israel?** They had not altogether passed beyond the Jewish idea of a temporal king, a re-established theocracy. The sufferings, death and resurrection which Christ had declared must precede the kingdom, had already taken place; they were anxious to know if the kingdom promised to Israel was immediately to be established. At the same time it seemed to them a thing incredible that it should be restored *at that time*, *i. e.*, to an Israel which had proved its unworthiness by crucifying its Lord.

7, 8. It is not for you to know, etc. Compare Christ's answer here with Matt. 24 : 36, 42; and Mark 13 : 32, note; and observe that it is fatal to all attempts to foretell the time of Christ's second coming, or even the definite signs of that second coming. Bengel's suggestion that the time has since been made known to the church through the Book of Revelation is inconsistent with the structure of this verse, which declares not merely the temporary veiling of information from the eyes of the apostles, but the limit put by the Providence of God on human knowledge. But Christ does not merely declare their ignorance of the time of his own second coming. The *times* are the succession of ages, greater or less in length, over which the history of the church should extend, before the end comes; the *seasons* are the successive phases of development, through and by means of which it would grow to its development. It is not in man either to know the length of time, or to understand beforehand the *necessary processes of growth;* it is his simply to perform the duty allotted to him, *leaving* the great movement of which he is a part, and to which he contributes, to be unfolded by God. He cannot read the book till God has unrolled it. Observe, too, the march of events, though above human control, is not above all control. The Father hath it in his own power.—**But ye shall receive power.** Comp. Luke 24 : 49; Rom. 15 : 13, 19; 1 Cor. 2 : 4; 2 Cor. 12 : 9; Phil. 3 : 10; 1 Thess. 1 : 5. These references will give the student an idea of the meaning of Christ's promise. It includes (1) the power of working miracles; (2) personal, moral and spiritual power in the conflicts and temptations of life, and especially in bearing suffering and persecution for Christ's sake; (3) power in the ministry of the word beyond that which belongs to human eloquence and wisdom, or even to the mere natural adaption of the truth to human wants.—**And ye shall be witnesses unto me.** See on verses 21, 22.—**In Jerusalem, and in all Judæa, and in Samaria, and even to the uttermost of the earth.** Observe the widening circle. Compare Luke 24 : 47; Matt. 28 : 19, 20; and contrast with the earlier commission (Matt. 10 : 5). By *uttermost* both time and space are included; to the remotest corners of the earth, to the remotest period of time. Christ's answer thus plainly implies that he will not immediately restore the kingdom to Israel. The then existing generation measurably fulfilled this command. The apostles began at Jerusalem (ch. 2 : 46; 4 : 1; 5 : 42); the disciples scattered abroad throughout Palestine preached the Gospel wherever they went (ch. 8 : 4; 11 : 19); Philip preached in Samaria (ch. 8 : 5); Peter traveled as far east as Babylon (1 Pet. 5 : 13); and Paul is believed to have carried the Gospel as far west as Spain. But it was not until Christ had interpreted this command (chaps. 10, 11; 22 : 21) that the apostles fully comprehended its nature. At first they regarded themselves as sent only to the dispersed Jews among the Gentiles (ch. 11 : 1–3; 15 : 1).

9. A cloud received him out of their sight. Comp. Matt. 17 : 5; Luke 9 : 34. The cloud was, I believe, the Shechinah of the O. T., the symbol of the divine presence and glory. In this cloud Christ will appear when he comes to

10 And while they looked stedfastly toward heaven, as he went up, behold, two[m] men stood by them in white apparel;
11 Which also said, Ye men[n] of Galilee, why stand ye gazing up into heaven? This same Jesus, which is taken up from you into heaven, shall[o] so come in like manner as ye have seen him go into heaven.
12 Then[p] returned they unto Jerusalem from the mount called Olivet, which is from Jerusalem a sabbath day's journey.

m John 20 : 12 . . . . n ch. 2 : 7; 13 : 31 . . . . o John 14 : 3; 1 Thess. 4 : 16 . . . . p Luke 24 : 52.

judge the world. (Rev. 1 : 7; 14 : 14; Comp. Matt. 24 : 30; 26 : 64; see note on Matt. 17 : 5.)

Of the ascension of our Lord we have three accounts, viz., Mark 16 : 19; Luke 24 : 50, 51 and here. Matthew and John do not mention it, yet they being of the twelve must have witnessed it, while it is not certain that Mark and Luke were eye-witnesses. The brevity of the description and the paucity of the subsequent N. T. references to it are noteworthy. In support of its credibility, however, are the following considerations. (1.) It is intimated by the O. T. writers (Psalm 24 : 7-10; 110 : 1; 68 : 18; with Ephes. 4 : 7, 8; Lev. 16 : 15 with Heb. 9 : 7-12); (2) and by Christ (John 6 : 62; 7 : 33; 20 : 17); (3) it is referred to by the apostles as a fact well recognized in the Christian church (Ephes. 1 : 20; Heb. 10 : 12; 1 Pet. 3 : 22); (4) it is an almost necessary sequel of the resurrection, since after the resurrection Christ must either have ascended into heaven, or lived a hidden life, and subsequently died a natural death. In respect to the body with which he ascended, it is easy to conjecture and impossible to know with assurance; but it is reasonable to suppose that the change which Paul declared will be wrought in the bodies of his saints at the last day, before their ascension (1 Cor. 15 : 51-54), was wrought in Christ's earthly body, which I believe to have been, prior to the ascension, unchanged (Luke 24 : 39, 40; John 20 : 27). If it be asked how, with a natural body, could he have passed through a closed door (John 20 : 19), or vanished from the disciples' sight (Luke 24 : 31), I reply, by the same miraculous power by which, with a natural body, he walked on the sea (John 6 : 19).

10, 11. Two men in white apparel. Angels in the form of men. Comp. Luke's description of the angels at the sepulchre with Matthew's (Luke 24 : 4; Matt. 28 . 2, 5).—**Ye men of Galilee.** This address indicates that only the eleven were present, all of whom were Galileans. —**Why stand ye gazing up into heaven?** The Christian may often profitably address this question to himself. His business on the earth is not to gaze into heaven for a glimpse of his ascended Lord, but to follow his example by his daily life on the earth. He is much more likely to find his Lord, by faithful life on earth, than by intent gazing into heaven.—**In like manner as ye have seen him go.** Not merely, As surely as he has departed, so surely will he return, but, In the manner in which he has departed he will return. The second coming of Christ, then, will not be like his first coming, obscure, and, as it were, in concealment. He will come in power and glory, on the clouds, and with his holy angels with him. Matt. 24 : 30, 31; 26 : 64; Rev. 6 : 13-17.

12. From the Mount called Olivet.

OLIVET, FROM ROAD TO BETHANY.
Jerusalem in the distance.

Luke's Gospel (24 : 50) places the ascension at Bethany, which was fifteen stadia or nearly two miles from Jerusalem. The description is more definite and probably more accurate here. In the Gospel, "Bethany" probably stands for the district or region about the town proper; and Alford suggests that the exactness of description

13 And when they were come in, they went up into
an upper room, where abode both Peter,[q] and James,
and John, and Andrew, Philip, and Thomas, Bartholo-
mew, and Matthew, James *the son* of Alphæus, and
Simon Zelotes, and Judas *the brother* of James.
14 These all continued with one accord in prayer
and supplication, with the[r] women, and Mary the
mother of Jesus, and with his brethren.
15 And in those days Peter stood up in the midst
of the disciples, and said (the number of names together were about an hundred and twenty),

q Luke 6 : 13-16. . . . r Luke 23 : 49, 55; 24 : 10.

here was for the purpose of correcting a misapprehension growing out of the former statement which implies a breach of the Rabbinical rule, against Sabbath traveling. This assumes, however, what is probable but not certain, that the ascension took place on a Sabbath. By a gloss on Exod. 16 : 29 the Rabbins fixed the limits beyond which the pious Jew might not go on the Sabbath, at 2000 paces from the walls of the city, equivalent to about a mile. This regulation is supposed to have been derived from the space between the arks and the tents, which tradition, following Josh. 3 : 4, fixed upon as 2000 cubits. It being a Sabbath duty to go to the ark, this 2000 cubits was adjudged a legitimate Sabbath-day's journey. The exact site of the ascension is unknown; tradition has fixed on one, however, which is occupied by a Roman Catholic church.

These first twelve verses of the first chapter of Acts constitute an introduction to the whole book. It is not by mere accident that Luke begins by describing the ascension of the Lord. By so doing he connects with the former treatise, which describes what Jesus began to say and to do in his earthly life, the present treatise, which describes what Jesus *continued* to say and to do, in and through his church after his ascension. Thus his ascension is the proper introduction to this, as the nativity is the proper introduction to that history.

13. And when they were come in. That is, into the city.—**They went up into an upper room.** This was a room in the second story, or sometimes on, or connected with, the flat roof. It was the practice of the Jews to retire to this upper room for the purpose of deliberation or prayer. This may well have been the upper chamber where the last supper was taken; and where, subsequent to his resurrection, the Lord had twice met his disciples (John 20 : 19-26). Perhaps they hoped that he would return thither again. For illustration and description of upper chamber see Luke 22 : 12.—**Where abode both Peter,** etc. Not, as our English version might seem to imply, the disciples, *i. e.*, some other disciples, went from the ascension to this upper chamber where Peter and the rest were dwelling, but, Peter and the rest went from the ascension to this upper chamber which was their temporary sojourning place in Jerusalem. Peter had a house at Capernaum (Mark 1 : 29), which there is no reason to suppose

ORIENTAL PRAYER-MEETING.

his family had left; and it appears probable that John had a house of his own in Jerusalem (John 19 : 27). There are four lists of the apostles in the N. T., the other three being found in Matt. 10 : 2-4; Mark 3 : 16, and Luke 6 : 14. They are substantially the same. For consideration of differences, see Matt. 10 : 2, note; for the lives and characters of the twelve, see note on The Twelve Apostles, Vol. I, p. 147.

14. These all continued with one accord. The original conveys a meaning not contained in our English version. The word rendered *continued* (προσκαρτερέω) signifies to *persevere, to be steadfast in;* despite no immediate answer they were not discouraged but continued instant in prayer. For meaning see Acts 6 : 4; Rom. 12 : 12; Col. 4 : 2. The word rendered *with one accord* (ὁμοθυμαδόν) is composed of two Greek words signifying unity in fervor or zeal. For meaning see Acts 7 : 57; 12 : 20; 18 : 12; 19 : 29. See also Exod. 19 : 8; Jer. 46 : 21. Their unity was not their intellectual accord, but their spiritual earnestness of desire for the divine blessing. They illustrate the condition of successful prayer, perseverance (Luke 18 : 1-8), accord (Matt. 18 : 19), and earnestness or fervor (Matt. 7 : 7).—**With the women.** Probably those who ministered to Jesus in Galilee (Luke 8 : 3) and were with him at the cross (John 19 : 25) and at the sepulchre (Mark 16 : 1). The Greek has been rendered *with the wives, i. e.*, of the apostles; it is capable of that translation, but the other and

16 Men *and* brethren, this scripture must needs have been fulfilled, which[s] the Holy Ghost by the mouth of David spake before concerning Judas, which was guide[t] to them that took Jesus.
17 For he[u] was numbered with us, and had obtained part of this ministry.

18 Now[v] this man purchased a field with the reward[w] of iniquity; and falling headlong, he burst asunder in the midst, and all his bowels gushed out.
19 And it was known unto all the dwellers at Jerusalem; insomuch as that field is called in their proper tongue, Aceldama, that is to say, The field of blood.

s Ps. 41 : 9; John 13 : 18.... t Matt. 26 : 47; John 18 : 3.... u Luke 6 : 16.... v Matt. 27 : 5-10.... w 2 Pet. 2 : 15.

more common rendering is more probable.—**And Mary.** This is the last mention of her in the New Testament. The later traditions are quite untrustworthy. Observe that she prays *with* the disciples, they do not pray *to* her, nor wait on her intercession with her son. —**With his brethren.** It is clear from the language here that these were not among the twelve, for they are distinctly discriminated from them. That they were real brethren, and not cousins or other remote relatives, seems to me very clear from a comparison of the New Testament teaching respecting them. See note on Brethren of Our Lord, Vol. I, p. 187. They were not believers in Christ in his earlier ministry (John 7 : 5), and John 19 : 25, 26 indicates that they were not so at the time of his crucifixion. That the crucifixion and subsequent resurrection were the means of their conversion is a reasonable hypothesis. It can hardly be doubted that they were believers at this time.

Ch. 1 : 15–26. CHOICE OF A SUCCESSOR TO JUDAS ISCARIOT. THE REWARD OF INIQUITY.—THE NATURE OF THE APOSTLES' OFFICE.—THE WORK OF MAN AND THE WORK OF GOD IN THE ORDERING OF THE CHRISTIAN CHURCH.—THE VALUE AND THE LIMITATION OF THE APOSTLES' EXAMPLE.

15. In those days. The days between the ascension of Christ and the descent of the Holy Ghost, while the disciples were thus engaged in prayer for the promised gift. This covered a period of ten days (ver. 3, with 2 : 1, note).—**About a hundred and twenty.** There were at least five hundred believers in all (1 Cor. 15 : 6), but of them only the hundred and twenty had gathered in Jerusalem. The meeting seems to have begun with the eleven, the women, and the brethren of Jesus, and to have increased in size by the coming in of other disciples. Alexander thinks that the reference to *names* indicates a registration, and that presupposes some kind of organization. It is very probable that this was a secret meeting, and that for fear of the Jews (John 20 : 19) precautions were taken to exclude any whose names were not known. More than this, it seems to me, the account does not imply.

16, 17. Men and brethren. This is an address of an equal to equals, not of a vicar of Christ to his ecclesiastical subordinates.—**This scripture must needs have been fulfilled.** The Scripture prophecy of Judas's treachery. See Psalm 55 : 12–14 and ref. below. It was a part of the divine purpose that Christ should be betrayed by one of his disciples; but this necessary fulfillment of the prophecy did not lessen the betrayer's guilt (Matt. 26 : 24; Acts 2 : 23).—**Which was guide to them that took Jesus.** Matt. 26 : 47–50.—**Numbered with us,** etc. Judas was among the twelve who were chosen and ordained as apostles, at the time of the Sermon on the Mount (Luke 6 : 13-16), and subsequently commissioned to preach the Gospel and endowed with miraculous powers (Matt. 10 : 1-4); and he was made or made himself the treasurer of the band (John 12 : 6; 13 : 29). Observe, that in Peter's characterization, no epithets are employed—even Judas is left to be judged by his own master.

18, 19. Now this man procured for himself. Not, necessarily, personally purchased. For meaning of the original verb (κτάομαι) comp. Matt. 10 : 9, where it is rendered *provide;* Luke 18 : 12, *possess;* Acts 22 : 28, *obtained.* Peter's language is that of irony. He represents Judas Iscariot as procuring for himself the field which the priests purchased with the blood-money for a burial-ground, and in which the traitor met with his horrible and mysterious death. Peter is not an historian, but an orator, and refers, oratorically, to facts well known to his auditors. This consideration sufficiently explains the difference between his language and the more prosaic and literal account of Matthew.—**Burst asunder.** Matt. 27 : 3–10 represents Judas as committing suicide. The two accounts are not necessarily inconsistent, though the reconciliations proffered are only hypothetical. The most probable one is that he hung himself upon a tree overhanging the valley, that the rope broke, and that he fell and was dashed upon the rocks below. For a consideration of the enigmatical character and mysterious death of Judas, see notes on Matthew, Vol. I, pp. 306, 307.—**Aceldama.** The site is unknown; the traditional site is just outside the walls of Jerusalem to the south of Mount Zion. The meaning of the word Aceldama, which is Aramaic, is *field of blood.* The title was given because it was purchased with blood-money. It was originally a potter's field, *i. e.*, a field of clay, which had been used for some well known pottery (Matt. 27 : 7, 8).

20. For it is written. The references are to Psalms 69 : 25 and 109 : 8. Both of these psalms appear from the titles to have been writ-

20 For it is written in the book of Psalms, Let[x] his habitation be desolate, and let no man dwell therein: and,[y] his bishopric let another take.
21 Wherefore of these men[z] which have companied with us all the time that the Lord Jesus went in and out among us,
22 Beginning from the baptism of John, unto that same day that he was taken up from us, must one be ordained to be a witness with us of his resurrection.
23 And they appointed two, Joseph called Barsabas,[a] who was surnamed Justus, and Matthias.

x Ps. 69 : 25. . . . y Ps. 109 : 8. . . . z Luke 10 : 1, 2 ; John 15 : 27. . . . a ch. 15 : 22.

ten by David, and to be applied by himself to himself. They appear to me to apply to Christ, not (*a*) because they were uttered by David pro-

THE TRADITIONAL ACELDAMA.

phetically, for there is nothing in their structure or tone to warrant that conclusion, and Psalm 69 : 5 is certainly not prophetically applicable to Christ; (*b*) nor by a mere accommodation of language, never intended by the Holy Spirit to apply to Christ, but seized on and applied to him by Peter, a theory which seems to me to do violence to Scripture, and to be inconsistent with the inspiration if not with the honesty of Peter; but (*c*) because David was himself a prophecy of the Messiah, and thus in these psalms, as in many others (e. g., Psalms 16, 22, 55, etc.), while he truly and literally described his own experiences of suffering and strength, he unconsciously prophesies both the suffering and the triumph of the Messiah. See Matt. 2 : 15, note.—**His bishopric.** The original signifies literally an office of overseer (ἐπισκοπή). Nothing can be deduced from it respecting the question whether in the early church the government was administered by or through bishops. There is certainly no evidence that the apostles were such bishops.

21, 22. Of these men which have companied with us. An intimation that Christ had been attended throughout his ministry, more or less continuously, by other disciples as well as the twelve.—**Beginning from the baptism of John.** Not from the baptism of Jesus by John, for the disciples did not join him at that time, but from the termination of John's baptizing by his imprisonment, at which time the public ministry of Christ began (Matt. 4 : 12).—**Must one be ordained.** The term is not used in an ecclesiastical sense; the original is simply, "There must be one to be a witness," etc.—**To be a witness with us of his resurrection.** This grand fact, the resurrection of Jesus Christ from the dead, was the burden of the earlier apostolic ministry (chap. 2 : 29-33 : 3 : 15; 13 : 30-37; 17 : 31), and on this fact, witnessed to by the apostles from their personal knowledge, the truth of the Christian religion was based. Observe, then, that the apostles were chosen *as personal witnesses of Christ's life, ministry, death and resurrection* (comp. John 15 : 27), that when Judas died, one was selected *able to bear this personal testimony from personal knowledge*, that Paul claimed to be an apostle *because he had seen the risen Lord* (1 Cor. 9 : 1; 15 : 8), and that thus *in the very nature of the case the apostles could have no successors after the then generation had passed away.*

23. And they appointed two. Peter did not make the appointment as primate, nor the eleven as ecclesiastical superiors. "They appointed, viz., *the whole company to whom the words had been spoken;* not the eleven apostles."—(*Alford.*)—**Joseph called Barsabas,** *i. e.*, Son of Sabba or Saba.—**Surnamed Justus.** A Roman cognomen.—**Matthias.** The name is a common Hebrew name meaning Gift of Jehovah, and differing slightly in form, as Matthew, Matthias, Mattatha and Mattathias. Nothing more is known with certainty respecting these two, than the fact here implied, that they had been

24 And they prayed, and said, Thou, Lord, which[b]
knowest the hearts of all *men*, shew whether of these
two thou hast chosen,
25 That he may take part of this ministry and apostleship, from which Judas by transgression fell, that he
might go to his own place.
26 And they gave forth their lots; and the lot fell
upon Matthias; and he was numbered with the eleven
apostles.

b Jer. 17 : 10; Rev. 2 : 23.

companions of Jesus Christ and the eleven throughout Christ's life, and were witnesses of his resurrection. Both are supposed by Eusebius to have been among the seventy ordained by Christ in Perea (Luke 10 : 1), and this is inherently probable. Joseph Barsabas is not to be confounded with Joses Barnabas (chap. 4 : 36), or Judas Barsebas (chap. 15 : 22). There is nothing in the fact that Joseph is mentioned first and described more fully, to warrant the deduction which has been made that he was the first choice of the meeting. We are neither told how, nor why, the two were chosen from whom the one should be selected. It is probable, however, that they were designated by a vote, that being a common method among the Jews, and the conjecture of Alexander is reasonable that they were the only two who had been witnesses and companions of Christ throughout his ministry, and the only two, therefore, who fulfilled the necessary conditions.

24, 25. Thou, Lord, who knowest the hearts of all. Some question has been made whether this prayer was made to Christ or to the Father, but the prayer itself does not determine. On the one hand, the language *Lord* might be addressed to the Father (chap. 4 : 29); on the other, the language *who knowest the hearts of all* might well be addressed, especially by Peter, to Christ (John 21 : 17). It is noteworthy, however, that the meeting decided for itself respecting the external qualifications of the two possible successors to Judas, for these they could personally know; but referred the final choice to the Lord, who could alone know the heart. The external knowledge and education was not, therefore, the only qualification which they recognized.—**Declare whom thou hast chosen.** The word rendered "shew" in our English version, is one employed in the Greek to designate the official and public announcement of the result of an election. The prayer assumes that the Lord has chosen, and will by the lot make known his choice. —**That he may take a place in this ministry and apostleship.** The best MSS. have here *place*, not *part*. So Alford and Tischendorf. Thus the contrast is noted between the place *from* which Judas fell and that *to* which he has gone.—**From which Judas by transgression fell.** Literally, *transgressed, stepped aside* (παραβαίνω).—**That he might go to his own place.** Not "go to the field of blood," which he had purchased, though he did go to it as his burial-place by his suicide; nor "go home," for though Numb. 24 : 25 gives some color to this interpretation, it is a weak and meaningless ending of the sentence, making the clause read, "From which Judas by transgression fell that he might go home"; nor "go to the place of the dead," for that was not *his* place more than the place of all humanity. The natural and obvious meaning is the correct one. He fell from his temporary place as an apostle, to go to *his own place* among the lost spirits, the place to which his evil nature drew him. And observe that heaven and hell are respectively to the Christian and the unrepentant their own places (Rev. 22 : 11). The curious student will find different interpretations in Dr. Adam Clarke's Commentary. It was a Rabbinical proverb, "'Whosoever betrays an Israelite into the hands of the Gentiles hath no part in the world to come.' If so, then where must he have his place who betrayed the very Messiah of Israel?"—(*Lightfoot.*)

26. They gave forth their lots. The casting of the lots was regarded among the heathen (see my *Relig. Dict.*, art. Lot) and among the Jews (Prov. 16 : 33) as a direct appeal to the Deity. It was employed in selecting men for an invading force (Judges 20 : 9), in partitioning the land among the tribes (Numb. 26 : 55; Josh. 18 : 10), in determining the location of families on the return from captivity (Neh. 11 : 1), in allotting the spoils of war (Joel 3 : 3; Nah. 3 : 10), in the detection of crime (Josh. 7 : 14, 18; 1 Sam. 14 : 41), in designating officers appointed by God, whose choice was indicated by the lot (1 Sam. 10 : 20, 21; 1 Chron. 24 : 31; 25 : 8; Luke 1 : 9). The practice was continued according to Bingham's *Antiquities*, as late as the seventh century, though applied only in exceptional cases, and there is no other instance of the employment of the lot in the Acts. The particular method employed here is uncertain. Probably the names were written on a piece of paper and put in an urn, and the first drawn was chosen. Chrysostom supposes that the lot was resorted to here, because, as yet, the apostles had not received the gift of the Holy Spirit for their direct guide in such matters.—**He was numbered with the eleven.** That is, he was counted in with them to make up the twelve.

In respect to this action of the early church, it is observable, (*a*) That in this, the first ecclesiastical action of the Church, Peter appealed to

CHAPTER II.

AND when the day of Pentecost[c] was fully come,
they[d] were all with one accord in one place.
2 And suddenly there came a sound from heaven, as
of a rushing mighty wind, and it filled[e] all the house
where they were sitting.
3 And there appeared unto them cloven tongues,
like as of fire, and it sat upon each of them :

c Lev. 23 : 15. . . . d chap. 1 : 14. . . . e chap. 4 : 31.

the entire body of disciples, women as well as men, and that, apparently, all participated in it, either directly or indirectly; (*b*) that the method pursued in filling up the vacancy, occasioned by the death of Judas, certainly gives no sanction to the theory that either Peter, or the eleven, considered themselves vested with especial authority as legislators or rulers in the church; (*c*) that, if the *example* of the apostles were a rule for the church universal, the lot should be employed in the selection of its officers, but, by almost universal consent, this apostolic method is not now employed, and there is no evidence that it was ever again employed in the apostolic church; (*d*) the inference is, that while the apostolic *principles* of action are an authority, their *methods* were determined by their peculiar exigencies, and were adapted to their special needs, and are therefore no authority for the modern church.

Ch. 2 : 1-13. THE GIFT OF THE HOLY SPIRIT. THE GIFT: THE PROMISE OF THE FATHER (chap. 1 : 4).—ON WHOM BESTOWED: ALL WERE FILLED WITH THE HOLY GHOST (ver. 4).—THE CONDITION OF RECEIVING: PATIENT WAITING, EARNEST HOPING, UNITED PRAYING (chap. 1 : 4, 14; 2 : 1).—THE ATTENDANT SYMBOLS: WIND FROM HEAVEN (John 3 : 8), TONGUES OF FIRE (Isaiah 6 : 6, 7; Matt. 3 : 11), THE UNIVERSAL LANGUAGE OF HEAVEN (Rev. 5 : 9).—THE RESULT: POWER TO WITNESS FOR CHRIST (chap. 1 : 8; 2 : 41). See note on Descent of the Holy Ghost, ver. 41.

A. D. 30, May 28, Lord's Day. The writer gives an account of the manifest outpouring of the Spirit of God upon the early church, with the audible and visible signs which accompany it (1-13), and reports Peter's sermon to the people (14-36), and its results upon the people (37-41), and in the church (42-47).

1. And when the day of Pentecost was fully come. This was one of the three great Jewish national festivals when all the males were required to go up to Jerusalem (Deut. 16 : 16). It was called Pentecost (a word meaning *fiftieth*) because it was the fiftieth day from the sixteenth day of Nisan, the second day of the Passover; it was also called *the feast of weeks* (Deut. 16 : 10), because seven weeks from the Passover; *the feast of harvest* (Exod. 23 : 16), because it was a feast of thanksgiving for the harvest (Deut. 26 : 5-10), and *the feast of first-fruits* (Numb. 28 : 26), because on this day the Jews offered to God the first-fruits of the wheat harvest, in bread made of the new grain (Lev. 23 : 15-21). The feast was also regarded as commemorating the giving of the law, which was delivered from Mount Sinai on the fiftieth day after the departure from Egypt, *i. e.*, after the institution of the Passover. If, as I believe to have been the case, the 16th of Nisan came, in the year of Christ's crucifixion, on Saturday, the Jewish sabbath, the day of Pentecost, when the gift of the Holy Spirit was bestowed, would have occurred on a Sunday. Among the modern Jews the feast of Pentecost includes two days, and is celebrated with the same strictness as the Passover. The Christian counterpart of this festival is Whit-Sunday, or White Sunday, so called, probably, from the white garments worn in the ancient church by those who were baptized on this day, which was one of the special seasons of baptism.—**They were all with united zeal.** See chap. 1 : 14, note.—**In one place.** From Luke 24 : 53 some commentators have supposed that this place was the temple. But that the disciples could have secured from the authorities a room in the temple is highly improbable, and that they met from day to day in a private house is indicated by chap. 1 : 13, and ver. 2 here.

2, 3. And suddenly. Without any previous indication, and unexpectedly to the disciples. They were expecting the fulfillment of Christ's promise (chap. 1 : 4, 8), but in what manner it would be fulfilled they did not know.—**A sound from heaven as of a rushing, mighty wind.** The wind is both in the O. T. and in the N. T. a symbol of the Spirit of God (Sol. Song 4 : 16; Ezek. 37 : 9; John 3 : 8; 20 : 22). The very word *inspiration*, meaning in-breathing, embodies an analogous metaphor.—**It filled all the house where they were sitting.** I see no adequate reason for the statement of Neander that "an earthquake, attended by a whirlwind, suddenly shook the building in which they were assembled," nor for the supposition of Alford, Hackett, and others, based on ver. 6, that the wind was heard throughout Jerusalem. It is not said that there was any wind, but *a sound as of a wind.* To suppose that there was literally a whirlwind, and that it blew over the whole city, seems to me to reduce the phenomenon from a special supernatural accompaniment of the descent of the Holy Spirit to a natural event, having no necessary connection with the new disclosure of the Spirit of God.—**And there appeared unto them.** That is,

4 And they were all filled[f] with the Holy Ghost, and began[g] to speak with other tongues, as the Spirit gave them utterance.
5 And there were dwelling at Jerusalem, Jews, devout men, out of every nation under heaven.
6 Now when this was noised abroad, the multitude came together, and were confounded, because that every man heard them speak in his own language.

f ch. 1 : 5. . . . g ch. 10 : 46 ; Mark 16 : 17.

to the entire assembly.—**Tongues as of fire.** Observe, not tongues of fire, but tongues of a fiery, burning appearance, though without real heat.—**Distributed** (among them) **and one sat upon each of them.** There is some uncertainty as to the proper translation of the original, but this appears to accord better with the grammatical construction of the Greek than does the meaning embodied in our English version. This rendering is defended by Bengel, Olshausen, De Wette, Baumgarten, Hackett, Robinson, and Meyer; the older view is adopted by Alford. As rendered above, the meaning is that a fiery appearance suddenly presented itself, and then divided, so that a part rested on each one in the assembly. Observe that it visited not merely the twelve; there appears to have been no discrimination between the apostles and the others, nor between the men and the women. Dr. Hackett says that it was a common belief, both among the Jews and the heathen, that an appearance like fire often encircled the heads of distinguished teachers of the law, and he supposes that God chose this symbol accordingly, much as he directed the magi to Christ by a star. Apart from this, the tongue of fire was a symbol of prophetic power, which, accompanied and interpreted as it was by the gift of tongues, could hardly be misunderstood. It indicated, not only the fulfillment of Christ's promise, but also the nature of the duty which that fulfillment laid on the disciples: "Ye shall receive power after that the Holy Ghost is come upon you; *and ye shall be witnesses unto me*" (chap. 1 : 8).

4. And they were all filled with the Holy Ghost. I see no warrant in Scripture for the very common impression that the Holy Spirit was now first given to the church. The same language here employed is used respecting Elizabeth (Luke 1 : 41), Zacharias (Luke 1 : 67), and John the Baptist (Luke 1 : 15); and the O. T. repeatedly makes mention of the influence of the Holy Spirit upon the minds of the prophets and others (Numb. 11 : 25, 26 ; 24 : 2, 3 ; 1 Sam. 10 : 10 ; 19 : 20 ; 2 Sam. 23 : 2 ; 2 Chron. 20 : 14 ; Neh. 9 : 30 ; Isaiah 48 : 16 ; Ezek. 2 : 2 ; 3 : 24 ; 11 : 5 ; Zech. 7 : 12 ; Matt. 22 : 43). That which was peculiar in this event is that (1) now for the first time *all* were filled with the Holy Ghost, not merely the apostles, but the entire Christian assembly; and (2) the influence was not occasional and transient, but abiding; the influence of the Holy Spirit was before exerted on man, he was now *given to* man as his divine inheritance. That which distinguishes the N. T. from the O. T. dispensation is that under the O. T. dispensation the Holy Spirit guided a few prophets, who thus became the inspired leaders of the people, while under the N. T. dispensation he is *given* to all; thus the wish of Moses is fulfilled (Numb. 11 : 29), the Lord puts his Spirit upon all his people (Acts 4 : 31 ; 10 : 44 ; Rom. 8 : 14 ; 1 Cor. 3 : 16 ; 12 : 7–11 ; Gal. 5 : 16, 18 ; Ephes. 3 : 16–19).

And began to speak with other tongues. The phenomenon here described is mysterious; neither its nature nor its object is well understood. It is wholly unknown in modern times; for though there was something externally analogous to it in the so-called gift of tongues among the Irvingites, 1831–1833, how far that was a mere nervous affection is uncertain. The principal Scripture passages bearing on this subject are the following: Mark 16 : 17 ; Acts 10 : 46 ; 19 : 6 ; 1 Cor. 12 : 10, 28 ; 13 : 1 ; 14 : 1–19. For a consideration of the nature and object of the gift of tongues, as indicated by Paul, see notes on latter passage. Without entering here into the discussion respecting the subject, it must suffice to say that the following facts are clear: (1.) The original word rendered *tongues* (γλῶσσα) signifies a dialect rather than a language, and this interpretation is confirmed by the narrative which follows. What the disciples spoke were probably various dialects of the Greek language. The difference was analogous to, but much greater, than those which now exist in France and Germany. (2.) These dialects were not known to the speakers by any natural process of education; a miraculous gift of speech is described. (3.) These "other tongues" were not mere rhapsodical utterances, because the various pilgrims testify that they hear and understand the various dialects spoken; nor a mere surprising recall of language which the disciples had previously heard and partially known, because it is distinctly said that they spake *as the Spirit gave them utterance.* (4.) It is not clear that the speakers themselves understood what they were saying; it is entirely consistent with the account to suppose that they were moved to the utterance of sounds dictated by the Holy Spirit, which they did not themselves comprehend, and this opinion receives some apparent confirmation from the language of Paul in 1 Cor. 14 : 14, 19. (5.) There is no authority whatever for the opinion that this gift of tongues was bestowed to enable the primitive Christians to preach the Gospel in the various languages of

7 And they were all amazed, and marvelled, saying one to another, Behold, are not all these which speak Galilæans?[h]

8 And how hear we every man in our own tongue, wherein we were born?

h ch. 1 : 11.

the world, without learning them. Greek was then spoken throughout the civilized world, so that such a gift for such a purpose was little needed. The implication of Acts 10 : 46 (comp. 1 Cor. 14 : 14-16) is that this gift was used, not in teaching, but in giving thanks to God; it is clear from 1 Cor., ch. 14, that the tongues were not comprehended in the Christian assemblies unless interpreted; in the case here recorded, the only sermon or address, apparently, was delivered by Peter, and in the Greek language; and in no instance in the N. T. is the gift of tongues ever recorded to have been used for the purpose of preaching the Gospel to those ignorant of that language. (6.) It is not an unreasonable hypothesis that the gift was bestowed as a symbol of the universality of the Gospel and its adaptation to all people, and of the time when those of every kindred, and tongue, and people, and nation, would unite in praising God in the church of the first-born above (Rev. 5 ; 9). Various rationalistic explanations have been attempted of this phenomenon, such as that the multitude heard in various languages what the believers spoke in their native tongue, that the believers spoke in an inarticulate and rhapsodical language, that they were themselves of different nationalities and spoke each in his native dialect, that Luke's language is exaggerated—rhetorical rather than historical—or that he has misapprehended and so misreported the facts. All of these, and other kindred interpretations, are plainly inconsistent with the historical authenticity of the narrative, and do not need to be considered by those who believe that the history is trustworthy, and who seek to interpret the record, not to substitute something else which they imagine more probable.

5. And there were dwelling at Jerusalem. Both permanent residents and pilgrims who had come up to the feast are probably included. See on ver. 10.—**Devout men.** Literally, *circumspect*, *i. e.*, toward God. The original (ἐυλαβής) occurs only here, in ch. 8 : 2, and in Luke 2 : 25. The latter passage illustrates its meaning. They were probably those who, like Simeon, were sincerely devout and God-fearing men, and waiting for the appearing of the promised Messiah. The fact that Peter's sermon was followed by so many conversions indicate that a large proportion of his auditors was composed, not of resolute foes to the truth, but of sincere inquirers after the truth.—**Out of every nation under heaven.** The dispersion of the Jews, since so effectually accomplished, had already begun to take place. These devout men included both dispersed Jews, who had returned either temporarily or permanently to Jerusalem, and proselytes of different nationalities, who had accepted the Jewish Scriptures and the worship of the one true God (ver. 10). The language is not to be accepted literally, yet most of the surrounding nations appear to have been represented.

6. Now when this sound was made. There is some uncertainty as to the meaning of the original, the literal translation of which is as above. Three interpretations are possible: (1) When the sound referred to in ver. 2, as of a rushing, mighty wind, occurred; (2) when the speech in other tongues (ver. 4) occurred; (3) when the rumor of the whole complex phenomenon, the sound as of wind, the tongues as of fire, the speaking in other tongues, was noised abroad. The first agrees best with the original Greek; the last better accords with the context. It is not necessary to suppose, however, that there was a wind heard and felt throughout Jerusalem. There would have been nothing in such a whirlwind to call particular attention to the house where the disciples were assembled. It may well be that some of the Christians hastened out to tell others who were not present, that the promise of Christ was being fulfilled in the outpouring of the Spirit, and that so the rumor spread quickly throughout the city.—**And were confounded.** Either the individuals were perplexed, or, more probably, the whole assembly were thrown into confusion and excitement, discussing the meaning of the singular phenomenon. See ch. 19 : 32; 21 : 31, where the verb is the same.—**Because they heard them speaking, each one in his own dialect.** See on ver. 4. The meaning is, not that all the disciples spoke all the dialects, but that each one spoke in some one, so that all were heard. We may reasonably assume that the disciples had come out of the upper chamber, and that the multitude was assembled in the courtyard of the house, or in some open square in the vicinity.

7, 8. Are not all these which speak Galileans? It is not probable that they were literally *all* Galileans; but certainly the greater part were so, and all the apostles and leading persons, who would probably be the prominent speakers.—**In our own tongue wherein we were born.** This testimony is conclusive against the theory that the speaking in other tongues was in an unmeaning language and in a

9 Parthians, and Medes, and Elamites, and the dwellers in Mesopotamia, and in Judæa, and Cappadocia, in Pontus, and Asia,
10 Phrygia, and Pamphylia, in Egypt, and in the parts of Libya about Cyrene, and strangers of Rome, Jews and proselytes,
11 Cretes and Arabians, we do hear them speak in our tongues[1] the wonderful works of God.

1 Cor. 12 : 10, 28.

state of ecstasy. The language was intelligible to the various auditors.

9-11. In the enumeration of the countries which follows, the writer proceeds from the northeast to the west and south. For their geographical position see map and Gazetteer, p. 23. The persons described Parthians, Medes, etc., are not the original heathen, who would not have been in Jerusalem, but either the Jews dispersed throughout those countries, or proselytes to the Jewish faith from the heathen nations (ver. 10).—**Parthians.** Parthia was in the extreme East, between the Caspian Sea and the Persian Gulf. The Parthian empire was founded by Arsaces I about 256 B. C., ultimately included the provinces of the earlier Persian kingdom, and extended westward until it met the Roman power on the Euphrates. It was never conquered by Rome, and continued until the third century after Christ acting as a counterpoise and a check to Rome, and furnishing a not intolerable refuge to such as had occasion to flee from the power of the Cæsars. It is mentioned in the N. T. only here. For an elaborate account of this empire, its history and its semi-civilization, see George Rawlinson's *Sixth Great Oriental Monarchy*.—**Medes.** Media lay west of Parthia, south of the Caspian Sea, east of Armenia, north of Persia. It was, historically, one of the five great oriental monarchies; in the seventh century before Christ embraced an area of territory as large as Great Britain, France, Spain, and Portugal together, but lacked unity and therefore real strength; was a *congeries* of kingdoms, each ruled by its own native prince; was conquered by Cyrus and merged in the Persian empire. It was subsequently overrun by Alexander the Great, and eventually passed over to and became a part of the Parthian monarchy, of which it was a province or dependency at this time. It is now included in the dominions of the Shah of Persia. —**Elamites.** It is difficult to define the boundaries of Elam; in general terms it may be described as southeast of Assyria, and south of Media. It was originally peopled by the descendants of Shem (Gen. 10 : 22), and subsequently became a province of Babylon, in fulfillment of prophetic denunciation (Isaiah 22 : 6; Jer. 49 : 34-39; Ezek. 32 : 24, 25; Dan. 8 : 1, 2). Its chief city, Susa, became the Persian metropolis. Captive Israelites were located in Elam (Isaiah 11 : 11), from whom were perhaps descended the Elamites of our text.—**Dwellers in Mesopotamia.** The original word *Mesopotamia* means between rivers; it designates a district lying between the Euphrates and the Tigris, the land from which Abraham was called, and Balaam came (Gen. 24 : 10; Acts 7 : 2; Deut. 23 : 4). It seems never to have been an individual state, but to have belonged successively to the Assyrian, Babylonian, Greek, Syrian, Roman, and Parthian empires.—**Judea.** Some difficulty has been experienced from the insertion of Judea in this list, since the language or dialect of Judea would be that of the disciples. There appears, however, to have been a difference in dialect between the Galileans and the Judeans (Matt. 26 : 73), and it may have been a cause of astonishment, if among the Galileans were those who spoke in the dialect and with the peculiar accent of the Judeans. If the Galileans, whose dialect was the subject of ridicule in Judea, spoke now a pure Hebrew, this would have been as notable a linguistic peculiarity as any.—**Cappadocia.** The most easterly region of Asia Minor, south of the Black Sea, and immediately west of Armenia. It was at this time a province of Rome; its inhabitants are thought to have been of Syrian origin; its dialect was probably a corrupt form of the Greek, but this is not certain.—**Pontus.** A district bordering on and immediately south of the Black Sea. It was at this time a Roman province. The inhabitants spoke a dialect compounded of the Persian and the Greek. Its religion was also a composition of the Greek, Persian and Scythian. It apparently contained many Jewish residents (ch. 18 : 2; 1 Pet. 1 : 1).—**Asia.** Not, of course, the continent, nor even what is now known as Asia Minor, and which includes Cappadocia and Pontus, but a small section of it, lying above the Ægean Sea, and having Ephesus for its capital. It was a province of Rome. Its boundaries cannot be defined with precision, since they were constantly undergoing change.—**Phrygia.** The same geographical indefiniteness attaches to this term. It did not form a distinct province, but was included in Asia. Its inhabitants, however, were in origin and character distinct; they were an Indo-Germanic race, who emigrated westward from Armenia. That this region contained many Jews is evident from ch. 14 : 1, 19. They were introduced there first by Antiochus the Great (Josephus' Ant. 12 : 3, 4).—**Pamphylia.** A small Roman province lying between Pisidia and the Mediterranean.—**Egypt.** The enumeration already given embraces the principal provinces of Asia

12 And they were all amazed, and were in doubt,
saying one to another, What[j] meaneth this?
13 Others, mocking, said, These men are full of new
wine.
14 But Peter, standing up with the eleven, lifted up
his voice, and said unto them, Ye men of Judæa, and
all *ye* that dwell at Jerusalem, be this known unto you,
and hearken to my words:
15 For these are not drunken, as ye suppose, seeing[k] it is *but* the third hour of the day.
16 But this is that which was[l] spoken by the prophet
Joel:

j ch. 17 : 20.... k 1 Thess. 5 : 7.... l Joel 2 : 28–32.

Minor. Egypt contained many Jews; two-fifths of the population of Alexandria are said to have been Jews.—**In the parts of Libya about Cyrene.** The name Libya is applied by the Greek and Roman writers to the African continent, generally excluding Egypt. Language corresponding to that used here is employed by Dion Cassius and Josephus to designate that portion of Africa constituting the district of Cyrenaica, on the southern coast of the Mediterranean and west of Egypt. There were many Jews settled in this district, the capital of which, Cyrene, was a Greek city (Matt. 27 : 32; Acts 6 : 9; 11 : 20; 13 : 1).—**Roman sojourners.** That is, Roman Jews, or proselytes from the Roman to the Jewish faith, residing at Jerusalem, or come thither temporarily on account of the feast.—**Jews and proselytes.** This characterizes the entire class described, who were not the heathen inhabitants of the districts mentioned, but either dispersed Jews, or heathens converted to the Jewish faith.—**Cretes and Arabians.** These are introduced, after the general description of the entire body in the previous clause, as though the writer had forgotten to enumerate them in their order, and added them as an afterthought. Cretes are inhabitants of the island of Crete in the Mediterranean, south of the Ægean Sea. Arabians are such as were scattered throughout Arabia Petrea, south of Palestine.—**In our tongues.** See on vers. 4 and 6.—**The wonderful works of God.** It can hardly be doubted that the theme of the disciples was the wondrousness of divine mercy shown in the life, the death, and the resurrection of the Messiah.

12, 13. They were all amazed and in doubt. That is, as to the significance of this phenomenon.—**What meaneth this?** Literally, *What will this be?* or, as we should say, *What is going to come of this?*—**Others, mocking, said.** Not others of the God-fearing men already described, but others beside them. Among the crowd drawn together by the event, were some hostile critics, who reviled. Revivals of religion have ever since provoked criticism as captious, and explanations as peurile, as those offered here.—**Sweet wine.** Not *new wine.* The Pentecost was in June, the first vintage not until August. From grapes dried in the sun and soaked in old wine a *sweet* wine was manufactured, which is said to have been especially intoxicating (Jahn's *Archæology*, § 69). Hence, "to be sweetened" was a Rabbinical equivalent for "to be drunk," and here, "They are full of sweet wine" is equivalent to "They are very drunk." So says Lightfoot, who suggests that this explanation came from those who, "knowing no other language but their own mother tongue, and not understanding what the apostles said, while they were speaking in foreign languages, thought they said nothing but mere babble and gibberish."

Ch. 2 : 14–36. ADDRESS OF PETER. JESUS PROVED TO BE BOTH KING AND SAVIOUR (ver. 36) BY (1) HIS FULFILLMENT OF PROPHECY (vers. 17–21), (2) HIS MIRACLES (ver. 22), (3) HIS RESURRECTION (ver. 24). HIS RESURRECTION ITSELF PROVED BY PROPHECY (vers. 2–31), BY APOSTOLIC TESTIMONY (ver. 32), BY THE GIFT OF THE HOLY GHOST BESTOWED THROUGH HIM (ver. 33).

14. But Peter standing up with the eleven. *With*, not apart from, them; their spokesman, not their superior. They stood up with him to give sanction to his address, especially to his appeal to them as witnesses of Christ's resurrection (ver. 32).—**Lifted up his voice.** The implication is, that the speaking in other tongues had been in the Christian assembly, not to the multitude. Peter now raised his voice and addressed the throng; probably outside the house in which the disciples had originally assembled.—**And preached to them.** The original implies a solemn and weighty utterance.—**Men, Judeans and all ye sojourners at Jerusalem.** Not *men of Judea.* The language here is like that of Anthony, "Friends, Romans, countrymen." Compare verses 29, 37, and ch. 1 : 16, where it is not Fraternal men, but Men, brethren. The Judeans are those whose home is in Judea; the sojourners at Jerusalem are those who have come up as pilgrims to the feast. The whole address was made by Peter as a Jew to Jews, and appeals to their national faith.

15, 16. For these are not drunken as ye suppose. In the original *not* is emphatic, and the word rendered *suppose* (*υπυλαμβανω*) is literally *to take up*, and indicates here a notion suggested by others, and caught up by the mind of the multitude. The sentence might be paraphrased, *It is not true, this idea that you have taken up.*—**Seeing it is but the third hour of the day.** Nine A. M., and the hour of morning prayer (see note on ch. 3 : 1), "Before which time, especially on the Sabbath and other feast days, the Jews were not wont so much as to taste anything of meat or drink."—(*Lightfoot.*) Moreover, it was irrational

17 And it shall come to pass in the last days, saith
God, I will pour out[m] of my Spirit upon all flesh: and
your sons and your daughters shall prophesy, and
your young men shall see visions, and your old men
shall dream dreams:
18 And on my servants and on my handmaidens I
will pour out, in those days, of my Spirit; and[n] they
shall prophesy:
19 And I will shew wonders in heaven above, and
signs in the earth beneath; blood, and fire, and vapour of smoke:

m Isa. 44:3; Ezek. 36:27.... n ch. 21:4, 9, 10; 1 Cor. 12:10.

to suppose that an assembly would be given up to drunkenness at so early an hour of the day, and that a solemn feast day. Observe the quietness and meekness with which Peter repels, without resentment, the insult and derision of the hostile Jews, exemplifying his own subsequent instruction (1 Pet. 2:20, 23; 4:19).—**But this is that which was spoken by the prophet Joel;** *i. e.*, a fulfillment of that prophecy. The quotation is from the *Septuagint* or Greek version, with very slight and quite immaterial variations. The passage quoted is Joel 2:28–32, which formed a part of the scriptural reading in the synagogues in the Pentecostal service, and Joel in this passage unmistakably points to the dispensation of the Spirit and the second coming of Christ. Tischendorf, following the Sinaitic manuscript, omits verse 21; Alford retains it. It unquestionably is a part of the original prophecy, and internal evidence indicates that it formed a part of Peter's quotation here.

17, 18. In the last days. In the original prophecy the language is *afterward*. *The last days*, or *the last time*, is used in the N. T. to describe the final dispensation, in which God speaks to the world through his Son and by the bestowal of his Spirit, in contrast with the previous dispensation in which he revealed himself in fragmentary utterances through prophets, and was approached by priests. See especially Heb. 1:1, 2, and comp. 2 Tim. 3:1; 1 Pet. 1:5, 20; 2 Pet. 3:3; 1 John 2:18; Jude 18. This period is called the "last days," or the "last time," not because when the apostles wrote the end was nigh at hand, but because it constituted the last dispensation of divine mercy, and the consummation of the conflict between the kingdoms of light and of darkness, of truth and error, of righteousness and sin, of God and Satan. The length of this dispensation, and so the day and hour of the second coming of Christ, was not revealed to the apostles, nor known to the angels, nor even to Christ himself (Mark 13:32), who warned his followers to be constantly watching for it (Matt. 24:42, 44). Doubtless the early church fell into the error of believing that the period was shorter and the hour of Christ's final manifestation nearer than they were. Our liability is to fall into the reverse error, and to cease to watch because we cease to expect it. Paul warns against the first error (2 Thess. 2:2-5), Peter against the second (2 Pet. 3:3-8).—**Saith God.** This language is Peter's, not Joel's; compare, however, Joel 2:12, 32. It is based on the assumption that Joel spoke by inspiration of God.—**I will pour out from my Spirit upon all flesh.** Not *gifts from my Spirit*, but *my Spirit itself*. Indeed, this is the language of the original Hebrew in Joel. The metaphor is taken from the rain, in which the cloud pours itself down upon the parched earth. Comp. Deut. 32:2; Ps. 72:6; Hos. 6:3; Hos. 10:12. Observe the extent of the promise, *upon all flesh*. Not the giving of the Spirit, but the outpouring upon the whole human race, is the characteristic of the dispensation of the last days. See vers. 4, 38, and notes. *All flesh* is not to be limited to all who seek. Under the N. T. the Spirit of God is poured out like the rain and the sun on *all*, but may be grieved and driven away by unbelief and indifference (Ephes. 4:30; 1 Thess. 4:19).—**Your sons and your daughters shall prophesy.** Not, Shall foretell future events, which is not the radical meaning of the word prophesy (see Stanley's *Jewish Church*, Vol. I: Lecture XIX), nor merely, as Calvin, Shall possess a "rare and excellent gift of understanding," but, as Hackett, "Shall communicate religious truth in general under a divine inspiration." Observe, this is a divine appointment of women as religious teachers in the church; in the gifts of the Spirit, as in the gift of personal salvation, there is neither male nor female (Gal. 3:28). It does not, however, indicate the *method in which* woman shall fulfill the function of religious teaching, whether in the pulpit, on the platform, by the pen, or in the home circle. That is left to be determined, either by other teachings of God's word, or by the later guidance of the Spirit, the instincts of humanity, and the circumstances of the individual.—**Your young men shall see visions and your old men shall dream dreams.** Visions are mentioned in the apostolic times (Acts 9:10, 12; 10:3, 17; 11:5; 16:9; 18:9; 26:19; 2 Cor. 12:1), but not dreams, which are throughout the Bible treated as an inferior form of divine revelation and generally confined to those not possessing any other revelation of the divine will (see Matt. 27:19, note). The *vision* differs from the dream in that it involves a real appearance to the soul in a waking and conscious state. The language here implies that God will still employ visions and dreams; but it does not imply their use under circumstances in which he never employed them in the

20 The [o] sun shall be turned into darkness, and the
moon into blood, before that great and notable day of
the Lord come:
21 And it shall come to pass, *that* whosoever [p] shall
call on the name of the Lord, shall be saved.

22 Ye men of Israel, hear these words; Jesus of
Nazareth, a man approved of God among you by miracles [q] and wonders and signs, which God did, by him,
in the midst of you, as ye [r] yourselves also know:

o Mark 13 : 24; 2 Pet. 3 : 7, 10.... p Ps. 86 : 5; Rom. 10 : 13; 1 Cor. 1, 2; Heb. 4 : 16.... q John 14 : 10, 11; Heb. 2 : 4.... r John 15 : 24.

past, and therefore not among a people possessing the far clearer revelation of an open word.—**And upon my man servants and upon my maid servants.** Neither sex, nor age, nor condition in life shall constitute any bar to this blessing. In fact, some of the greatest preachers have been men of lowly birth and condition.

19, 20. For reasons stated more fully in my notes on Matt. 24, especially verses 29–31, I think it clear that this language describes not phenomena attendant upon the destruction of Jerusalem, but those which are to precede and accompany the second coming of Christ. These will mark the end of the last days which were inaugurated at Pentecost, and in which we are living. Peter quotes the entire prophetic description of this era, without knowing how long a time must elapse before its consummation. The language of the prophet here and of Christ in Matthew should be compared. See also 1 Thess. 4 : 15–17; 2 Thess. 1 : 7; 1 Cor. 15 : 52; Rev. 6 : 12–14.—**Portents in the heavens above.** The original (τερας) signifies something foreboding calamity.—**And signs.** Evidences of divine presence and power.—**Blood and fire.** This may be taken symbolically to mean devastating wars, in which case the language here is parallel to Matt. 24 : 7, or, as Alford, bloody and fiery appearances of a supernatural character.—**Vapour of smoke.** That is, columns of smoke.—**Great and notable day of the Lord.** Tischendorf omits, Alford retains, the term *notable.* It is, however, without question, in the original prophecy, and its position renders it emphatic. The term signifies not a horrible day, as the Vulgate in Joel renders it, nor a notable, *i. e.*, remarkable day, as our English version renders it, but a day *clearly manifest*, *i. e.*, one the nature of which is not and cannot be hid from any. It thus answers to Christ's description in Matt. 24 : 27; see note there. Coming in mercy, he is hid from them that are lost (2 Cor. 4 : 3, 4; comp. Matt. 13 : 14, 15); coming in judgment, he will be manifest to all (Rev. 6 : 15, 16).

21. Whosoever shall have called on the name of the Lord shall be saved. The call must precede the salvation, and is a condition precedent to it. (Aorist subj. with ἄν is equivalent to fut. perf. in Latin. Winer, 307. See ver. 39, note.) The promise here, which ends the quotation from Joel, is applicable throughout the whole period of the "last days," from the descent of the Holy Spirit at Pentecost to the second coming of Christ in judgment. If verses 19 and 20 are regarded as descriptive of the destruction of Jerusalem, then this verse is simply a promise to save the inhabitants from that destruction; and this appears to be Henderson's interpretation, which seems to me to belittle the whole passage, and impair the force and meaning of Peter's entire address. He speaks, not to the Jews only, but through them to the whole world, not of national deliverance from earthly peril, but of soul salvation from sin and doom. To *call on the name of the Lord* is here equivalent to Return unto the Lord in Isaiah 55 : 7, or Look unto me in Isaiah 45 : 22, and nearly the same as Repent and be baptized in the name of Jesus Christ in ver. 38, though there baptism, as the sign of public confession of Christ, is added. "The gates of God's mercy are thrown open in Christ to all people: no barrier is placed, no union with any external association or succession is required: the promise is to individuals as individuals."—(*Alford.*) Nor is there required any rite or ceremony, or any theological knowledge or creed, *as a condition of salvation;* simply a calling on the name of the Lord, *i. e.*, Jesus Christ (ver. 36). See, for illustration of this truth, Luke 23 : 42.

22. Men, Israelites. Not *Men of Israel.* See note on ver. 14.—**Jesus the Nazarene.** Not without significance does Peter here and elsewhere (ch. 3 : 6; 4 : 10) accept and employ this opprobrious epithet. Him whom Israel despised God approved.—**Hear these words.** Consider the meaning of this prophecy, which accordingly Peter proceeds to expound.—**A man made manifest unto you by God.** The word *approve* is here used in the sense of *sanction.*—**By mighty works, and wonders, and signs.** These words indicate the Scriptural definition of a miracle, which is a *mighty work*, *i. e.*, something evidently wrought by superhuman power, a *wonder*, *i. e.*, something out of the ordinary course of nature, thus attracting attention and compelling investigation, and a *sign*, *i. e.*, such a wonder and work as is irresistibly a sign of the *divine* presence and power. By these Christ's character and authority were attested to the people of Israel. Observe that in the language of the N. T. there is no sanction whatever for the common but false definition of a miracle as an event contrary to the laws of nature.—**Which God did by him.** Observe the works are attributed by Peter, as by Christ (John 14 : 10), to the power

23 Him, being[s] delivered by the determinate counsel and foreknowledge of God, ye[t] have taken, and[u]
by wicked hands have crucified and slain:
24 Whom[v] God hath raised up, having loosed the
pains of death: because it was not possible[w] that he
should be holden of it.
25 For David speaketh[x] concerning him, I foresaw
the Lord always before my face; for he is on my right
hand, that I should not be moved:
26 Therefore did my heart rejoice, and my tongue
was glad; moreover also my flesh shall rest in hope:
27 Because thou wilt not leave my soul in hell,
neither wilt thou suffer thine Holy One to see corruption.

s ch. 3 : 18; Luke 22 : 22; 24 : 44....t ch. 5 : 30....u Matt. 27 : 1....v ch. 13 : 30, 34; Luke 24 : 1-6; 1 Cor. 6 : 14; Ephes. 1 : 20; Col. 2 : 12; 1 Thess. 1 : 10; Heb. 13 : 20; 1 Pet. 1 : 21....w John 10 : 18....x Ps. 16 : 8-11.

of Israel's God. Jesus Christ is never preached by the apostles so as to detract love and allegiance from the one God and Father of all.

23. Him, by the determinate counsel and foreknowledge of God, being given forth, ye, taking, and with lawless hands nailing (to the cross), **have slain.** Not, Delivered up by Judas *in accordance with* the will of God, but, Given up to humanity *by the will of God.* The declaration is parallel to John 3 : 16; Gal. 4 : 4, 5. Being thus given over to the world, the world knew him not, but taking him, nailed him to the cross. God is represented as holding a counsel with himself respecting man's redemption, as in Gen. 1 : 26 respecting his creation; and the adjective *determinate* (from ὁρίζω, *to put limits to*) implies that in this counsel the manner of the redemption, viz., by death, was also determined on. With this accords Christ's own declaration (Luke 22 : 22), and it is here asserted to show that the crucifixion was not due to the powerlessness of Christ, but to the purpose of God. The phrase *lawless hands* recalls the circumstances of the crucifixion, the original trial before the Sanhedrim being conducted in flagrant violation of the Jewish rules of precedent (see Vol. I, p. 298), the sentence of Pilate being coerced by a mob. *Nailing* emphasizes the brutal and cruel character of the deed; and the whole is charged upon Israel, not, as Olshausen, because "all mankind were in fact guilty of the death of Jesus," in which case Peter must have said "we," not "ye," but because, but for the popular outcry of Crucify him, Pilate would not have given sentence of death (John 19 : 6).

24. Whom God hath raised up, having destroyed the pains of death. Not, *Having released him from the bands of death*, for the word rendered pains (ὠδῖς) does not mean *bands*, but *sorrows; literally, travail pains;* nor, Having released him from the pains of death, *i. e.*, the physical pains, for, in fact, he bore them all to the end; nor, Having loosed death's pains, as though "death itself in holding him had pangs and was sore bestead" (Chrysostom); but, as in 1 Cor. 15 : 54-57, *Having by him and in his person destroyed the pain of death*, viz., sin, not for him only, but in and through him for all the world. It was because Christ knew no sin, that death could not hold him, as it is because the redeemed of the Lord are by his atonement freed from sin, that death, the penalty of sin, cannot hold them (Rom. 5 : 12, 21; John 11 : 25, 26).

25-28. The quotation is from Psalm 16 : 8-11, and the original is *verbatim* from the *Septuagint.* The context there clearly indicates that David spoke primarily of himself. Ver. 31 here clearly indicates that he foresaw, more or less clearly, in this utterance, a prophecy of Christ's resurrection. This double reference will surely give no trouble to those who believe that Christ was perfect man, and that in his resurrection as in his life, he exemplifies in its perfection that experience which is imperfectly exemplified in all his saints, and this whether they preceded and believed in a Messiah to come, or follow and believe in a Messiah who has been revealed.—**I am accustomed to see the Lord always before my face.** The verb is in the imperfect tense, implying a habit of life, and is interpreted by Heb. 12 : 2, "Looking unto Jesus"; and by 2 Cor. 5 : 7, "We walk by faith."—**For he is at my right hand that I should not be disturbed.** That is, mentally perturbed. The conscious presence of God gives peace to the godly (John 16 : 33; Heb. 11 : 27). Of this experience of steadfast peace David himself affords a marvelous illustration in Psalm 3, written during his flight from Absalom. See especially ver. 5.—**Therefore did my heart rejoice and my tongue give praise.** The one expression refers to the inward experience of joy, the other to its outward expression in thanksgiving.—**Moreover, also, my flesh shall tabernacle in hope that thou wilt not abandon my soul to Hades.** The original verb (κατασκηνόω) means literally, to pitch tent or encamp. Here, the meaning appears to me to be, not, My flesh shall rest in the grave in hope, because of the future resurrection, for hope does not abide in the grave, and can hardly, even by poetic license, be represented as dwelling there; but, My flesh, *i. e.*, I, myself, in my earthly life and nature, shall sojourn here in this life, sustained throughout by the hope that thou wilt not abandon my soul to the place of the dead. This, which was only a *hope* with the O. T. saints, and an uncertain one (see Ps. 88 : 10-12; 115 : 17), is a certainty of the Christian since Christ's resurrection. Thus interpreted, this verse, as an utterance of Christian experience, is parallel to Rom. 8 : 23, 24. *Hell* is not here the abode of the lost, but the abode of the dead (ᾅδης

28 Thou hast made known to me the ways of life;
thou shalt make me full of joy with thy countenance.
29 Men *and* brethren, let me freely speak unto you
of the patriarch David, that he is both dead and buried,
and his sepulchre is with us unto this day.
30 Therefore being[y] a prophet, and knowing that
God had sworn[z] with an oath[a] to him, that of the fruit
of his loins, according to the flesh, he would raise up
Christ to sit on his throne;
31 He, seeing this before,[b] spake of the resurrection
of Christ, that his soul was not left in hell, neither his
flesh did see corruption.
32 This[c] Jesus hath God raised up, whereof[d] we all
are witnesses.

y 2 Sam. 23 : 2. . . . z 2 Sam. 7 : 12, 13; Ps. 132 : 11. . . . a Heb. 6 : 17. . . . b 1 Pet. 1 : 11, 12. . . . c verse 24. . . . d Luke 24 : 48.

not γέενα).—**Neither deliver over thy saint to experience annihilation.** Not, as in our English version, *Thy Holy One.* The word so rendered is an adjective (ὅσιος) meaning *holy*, but is never used in the N. T. to designate Jesus Christ as *the* Holy One. Here the reference is primarily to David, and expresses his hope in the future life of all the saints of God. Neither does the word rendered *corruption* (διαφθορά) necessarily imply putrescence; rather, utter destruction. The expression implies a hope, not so much of the preservation of the body from decay, as of the life from extinction. *See* is equivalent to *experience*, as in Luke 2 : 26.—**The ways of life.** The ways of spiritual life here that lead to eternal life hereafter. Spiritual death and life both begin in time, and are carried out and consummated in eternity.—**Thou wilt make me full of joy with thy countenance.** In the future life, as in the earthly experience of the Christian, the conscious presence of God is the inspiration of his joy (Psalm 17 : 15). This experience of the Christian, as David here outlines it, is emphatically true of Christ, who dwelt contin-

TOMBS OF THE KINGS.—DAVID'S SEPULCHRE.

ually in God, and God in him (John 14 : 10); whose joy was full (John 15 : 11); whose *life*, as well as tongue, proclaimed the praise of the Father (John 17 : 4); who endured his earthly life and passion, despising the shame for the joy that was set before him (Heb. 12 : 2), knowing that death had no dominion over him (John 10 : 17), and would not have even over his body.

29, 30. Men, brethren, I may speak with freedom to you of the patriarch David. He does not ask permission; he asserts his right so to do. "*With freedom;* without fear of being thought deficient in any just respect to his memory."—(*Hackett.*)—**His sepulchre is with us unto this day.** David was buried at Jerusalem and on Mount Zion (1 Kings 2 : 10; Neh. 3 : 16). Josephus (Antiq. 7 : 15, 3) gives an account of the tomb being opened and rifled successively by Hyrcanus and King Herod. According to Jerome, it was known as late as the fourth century. The supposed site on the southern brow of Mount Zion is probably in the neighborhood of the actual one.—**And knowing that God had sworn.** Psalm 16 is supposed to have been written on the delivery of this promise by Nathan to David (2 Sam. 7 : 12-16). **That of the fruit of his loins one should sit on his throne.** This is the reading of Tischendorf, Alford and Lachmann, and is undoubtedly the correct one. The words, *according to the flesh he would raise up Christ*, were added as an explanation by some copyist.

31. He, foreseeing this. David then recog-

33 Therefore,[e] being by the right hand of God exalted, and having[f] received of the Father the promise of the Holy Ghost, he hath shed forth this,[g] which ye now see and hear.
34 For David is not ascended into the heavens: but he saith himself, The LORD[h] said unto my Lord, Sit thou on my right hand,
35 Until I make thy foes thy footstool.
36 Therefore let all the house[i] of Israel know assuredly, that[j] God hath made that same Jesus, whom ye have crucified, both Lord[k] and Christ.[l]

e ch. 5 : 31; Phil. 2 : 9....f ch. 1 : 4; John 16 : 7, 13....g ch. 4 : 31; 10 : 45....h Ps. 110 : 1; Matt. 22 : 44....i Zech. 13 : 1....j ch. 5 : 31....k John 3 : 35....l Ps. 2 : 2, 6-8.

nized in this psalm a prophetic import, though he may not have fully comprehended the meaning of what he wrote.—**Spake of the resurrection of the Messiah; for his soul was not abandoned to Hades, neither did his flesh experience annihilation.** Not, as in our English version, *That his soul was not left*, etc. Peter does not again quote David's prophecy, but states, as a fact, that the Messiah was not left subject to death, as an evidence that the prophecy of David, not perfectly fulfilled in his own experience, was fulfilled now—in the experience of Jesus the Nazarene. Observe the difference in language here and in ver. 27. David says, Thou wilt not suffer thy *saint* to experience annihilation; here Peter declares that even the *flesh* of Christ has not been destroyed.

32, 33. Whereof. Or, *Of whom.* See 3 : 15, note.—**We all are witnesses.** *All;* primarily, the twelve apostles (see ver. 14, note), but also many, doubtless, among the multitude of the disciples (1 Cor. 15 : 6).—**Receiving the promise of the Holy Spirit from the Father, he hath poured this out which ye now see and hear.** Not, these physical signs—the sound as of wind, and the tongues as of fire—but *the whole phenomenon*, including both the physical and the spiritual. Observe that the Father gives the Son to the world (John 3 : 16), and gives the Spirit to and through the Son, so that all is in and through and from the Father, that he may be all and in all (Rom. 11 : 36; 1 Cor. 15 : 28). The climax of the address, which throughout refers all to the one only God, is also noteworthy. Jesus Christ is accredited *by* God, by works wrought among you *by* God, being delivered over to you *by* God, and finally raised up *by* God, and *by* God made both Lord and Christ (vers. 22, 23, 36). It seems to me better to take the language here as in our English version, *by the right hand of God* (as Alford, Meyer, Calvin), rather than *to the right hand of God* (as Hackett, Olshausen, Neander). Either rendition is, however, grammatically admissible.

34, 35. For David is not ascended unto the heavens. The Jews generally believed that the dead awaited in Hades the appointed time for their resurrection, and entered into their final state after this intermediate state, which was brought to an end by a general judgment (Job 3 : 17-19; 14 : 12; John 11 : 24). To this belief Peter appeals, and his language here certainly implies that he shared this popular conviction that the saints, at least the O. T. saints, did not enter at once upon death into the full fruition of their heavenly state.—**But he saith himself.** In Psalm 110 : 1, which is believed to have been written on the same occasion as Psalm 16.—**The Lord saith unto my Lord.** In the original Hebrew two different words are used, rendered in the Greek and the English by the same word. The sense would be better given by translating, *Jehovah said to my Lord.* As David had in his lifetime no earthly superior, the reference to the Messiah, as his sovereign, is unmistakable. See Matt. 22 : 44, note.—**The footstool of thy feet.** See 2 Sam. 22 : 41. In this reference to Psalm 110, Peter fortifies his argument for the resurrection of Jesus Christ, by the explicit declaration of David that the Messiah should be raised up to sit on the right hand of God, sharing his dominion with him.

36. This verse is the consummation and climax of the whole discourse, viz., (1) that by the resurrection God hath certified that he has made Jesus the Nazarene both Lord, *i. e.* sovereign or king, primarily of the Jewish nation, secondarily of the whole earth, and Messiah, *i. e.* the Anointed One or priest, by whom there is alone access to God (Vol. I : 57, note on The Names of Jesus); and (2) that this their King and Messiah, thus certified to by miracles while he lived, by his resurrection, and by his fulfillment of prophecy, they had crucified.

PETER'S PENTECOSTAL SERMON.—This sermon I believe to be a model of what the revival sermon should be; not necessarily in its form, but in its structure and spirit. In studying it, observe that, (1) It does not appeal to the imagination; contains no word-painting, no sensuous images, no brilliant rhetoric; it is not sensational. (2.) It contains little exhortation, and no appeal to the feelings; it is not passional. (3.) It contains no metaphysical or abstruse teachings. It embodies the essential doctrine of the Gospel, but no refined speculations respecting them. It declares the work of the Spirit, but does not discuss how the Spirit works in the hearts of men; declares the truth of the resurrection, but does not discuss the nature of the resurrection; declares the foreknowledge and decrees of God, but does not discuss their relations to the free-will of man; declares the Messiahship of Jesus, but does not discuss his nature, or the cause of his atoning sacrifice, or the philosophy of the plan of salvation. It is doctrinal, but neither

37 Now when they heard *this*, they were pricked[m] in their heart, and said unto Peter and to the rest of the apostles, Men *and* brethren, what[n] shall we do?

38 Then Peter said unto them,[o] Repent, and be baptized every one of you in the name of Jesus Christ, for the remission of sins, and ye shall receive the gift of the Holy Ghost.

m Ezek. 7 : 16 ; Zech. 12 : 10. . . . n ch. 9 : 6 ; 16 : 30. . . . o ch. 3 : 19 ; Luke 24 : 47.

dogmatical nor metaphysical. (4.) It is mainly a statement of *facts*, Christ's character, life and miracles, his death, his resurrection, his ascension. (5.) The whole argument rests on these considerations: (*a*) facts known to the hearers—the miracles performed by Jesus, his crucifixion in disregard of law, the death and burial of David, etc.; (*b*) facts testified to by the apostles from their personal knowledge, Christ's resurrection and ascension; (*c*) the Scripture. (6.) Its object and effect is to produce a personal sense of sin, and that the particular sin of rejecting the Messiah and Saviour of the nation and the world.

Ch. 2 : 37-47. EFFECT OF OUTPOURING OF THE SPIRIT.—ON THE MULTITUDE: AWE (ver. 43), CONVICTION OF SIN (ver. 37), CONVERSION (ver. 41).—ON THE APOSTLES: EARNEST AND PERSONAL WORK FOR THE CONVERSION OF SOULS (ver. 37, 38).—ON THE CHURCH: DOCILITY, SYMPATHY, DEVOUTNESS, CHARITY, GLADNESS, SIMPLICITY, PUBLIC FAVOR (42-47).

37. They were pricked in their heart. Comp. Heb. 4 : 12. It must be remembered that the effect produced was largely on the strangers and pilgrims (vers. 9-11) as well as on those who had directly participated in the crucifixion. Observe that it is the story of the cross, not the preaching of the law, which produced conviction of sin; the preaching of the law is not a necessary preparation to the preaching of the cross. Comp. Zech. 12 : 10. Observe, too, that they were not only pricked in their heart, but were also obedient to Peter's counsel. "There must be added unto this pricking in heart, readiness to obey. Cain and Judas were pricked in heart, but despair did keep them back from submitting themselves unto God" (Gen. 4 : 13 ; Matt. 27 : 3).—(*Calvin.*)—**To Peter and the rest of the apostles.** The meeting now evidently broke up into fragments, *personal conversation with inquirers following the public sermon.* An inquiry meeting is not truly a new method.—**What shall we do?** This question is not exactly equivalent to the jailer's question, *What must I do to be saved?* (ch. 16 : 30). Convinced that the nation had put its Messiah to death, the people were overwhelmed with both sorrow and perplexity. They could not undo the deed; what could they do?

38. Repent and be baptized each of you upon the name of Jesus Christ for the remission of sins. In getting the exact meaning of Peter's directions to these inquirers, observe, (1) *Repent* (μετανοέω) is literally *to perceive afterwards*, and hence to *change the mind*, including one's view of life and truth, and hence one's purpose. See Matt. 3 : 2, note. Here it includes an entire change of opinion respecting Jesus Christ, from regarding him as an impostor to reverencing him as both Lord and Christ; but it also includes all that change of interior life and purpose which is consequent thereon. The Roman Catholic translation, *Do penance*, making the direction merely the observance of certain legal rites, is equally inconsistent with the original Greek and with the spirit of the entire passage. (2.) *Be baptized* follows in order the direction to repent. Baptism is not a regenerating ordinance, but a sign and symbol of repentance and a public confession of Christ. On the meaning of the word, see on Matthew, pp. 73 and 328. (3.) *Each of you* shows that the repentance and baptism must be a personal act. The multitude could not have been baptized under this direction, as some of the converts under Xavier's preaching were baptized in India, by being sprinkled all together as a multitude. (4.) *Upon the name of Jesus Christ* is as Dr. Hackett, "Upon the name of Jesus Christ as the foundation of the baptism, *i. e.*, with an acknowledgment of him in that act, as being what his name imports, the sinner's only hope, his Redeemer, Justifier, Lord, final Judge." (5.) *For the remission of sins* is not merely, as Dr. Hackett, "in order to the forgiveness of sins," but, *for the putting away of sins*, the entire cleansing of the heart from actual sin, as well as the pardon of those that are past. See Matt. 6 : 12, note; see also Isaiah 1 : 18; Matt. 1 : 21; 1 John 1 : 9. What the Gospel promises is pardon for the past and deliverance from the dominion of sin in the future (Rom. 6 : 14), on condition of repentance, *i. e.*, a change of heart, life, and purpose, and baptism, *i. e.*, a public confession of Jesus Christ as both Jesus, *i. e.*, Saviour, and Christ, *i. e.*, Lord or Master, the one involving trust in him for pardon, the other obedience to him for the future.—**And ye shall receive the gift of the Holy Ghost.** That is, on the conditions already explained, they should receive that same gift of the indwelling and inspiring presence of the Spirit of God, the manifestation of which they beheld in the apostles and other disciples. Whoever thus repented and were baptized should also be inspired. See on ver. 4. This is still more emphatically declared in the succeeding verse.

39. For the promise. What promise? That on which Peter has already expatiated, the

39 For the promise[p] is unto you, and to your children, and[q] to all that are afar off, *even* as many as the Lord our God shall call.
40 And with many other words did he testify and exhort, saying, Save yourselves from this untoward generation.
41 Then they that gladly received his word were baptized: and the same day there were added *unto them* about three thousand souls.

p Joel 2 : 28. . . . q Ephes. 2 : 13, 17.

promise of the Spirit of God (verses 17, 18; comp. 1 : 4; Ephes. 1 : 13).—**Is unto you and to your children.** The original (τέκνον) may mean either *descendants*, as in ch. 13 : 33, Matt. 27 : 25, or *children*, as in ch. 21 : 5, Matt. 7 : 11. The promise is, however, conditional on repentance and baptism, and therefore does not, by its terms, include any except such as are capable of repentance. The former meaning, *descendants*, suits the context better, for thus it includes the latter, *children*, and makes the promise include the whole family of mankind.—**And to all that are afar off.** All Gentile nations. The *near* are Jews, the *afar off* Gentiles (Isaiah 57 : 19; Zech. 6 : 15; Ephes. 2 : 13, 17). Some have questioned this meaning here, because Peter was subsequently surprised at the call of the Gentiles (chap. 10 : 28; 11 : 16, 17; Gal. 2 : 12); and others, not questioning the meaning, have doubted the fact that Peter uttered it. The difficulty is, however, purely imaginary. Not only the apostles, but also every pious Jew, expected the conversion of the Gentiles in great numbers; what surprised Peter, and what he and the other early Jewish Christians were slow to believe, was that they were to be admitted to the Church of Christ without first becoming Jews (ch. 15 : 1). — **As many as the Lord our God shall have called.** Not *shall call.* The reference is not to the calling by the Spirit of God, acting on the individual heart, but to the invitations of the O. T., which embrace both Jew and Gentile (Isaiah 55 : 7; 56 : 6-8; 60 : 3, 5-8: Joel 2 : 32; Micah 4 : 1, 2). That this is the meaning is evident (1) from the tense of the verb, which is past, not future (nearly equal to Latin future perfect; see Winer, 307; ver. 21, note); (2) from the word used (προσκαλέομαι), which is never used in the N. T. of the effectual calling of the individual by the influence of the Spirit of God; the word rendered *calling* in Rom. 11 : 29; Ephes. 4 : 4; 2 Tim. 1 : 9; 2 Pet. 1 : 10 is a different one (κλῆσις); (3) from the context; the ordinary interpretation makes Peter declare that the promise of the Holy Spirit is to all those who actually receive and accept its influence, which not only limits the promise, but makes it unmeaning.

40. And with many other words. This language implies that only the substance of the personal direction of the apostle to the inquirers is here given.—**Did he testify and exhort.** *Testify* as a witness to the truth of the promise of God, and *exhort* as an ambassador from God (2 Cor. 5 : 20), to its immediate acceptance. Gospel preaching is a testimony and an invitation.—**Be ye saved.** Not, *Save yourselves.* The original (σώθητε) is in the passive tense. Our English version neither agrees with the original here, nor with the current teaching of Scripture elsewhere (Ezek. 33 : 12; Dan. 9 : 18; Rom. 3 : 20; Ephes. 2 : 8, 9, 2 Tim. 1 : 9; Tit. 3 : 5).—**From this crooked generation.** The meaning is, both from the *evil influence of* and also from the *condemnation pronounced against* the Jewish nation. For significance of the epithet *crooked* (σκολιός), here rendered *untoward*, see Deut. 32 : 5; Phil. 2 : 15; 1 Pet. 2 : 18, in the latter passage rendered *froward.*

41. They therefore that received his word. Accepted it as true; they testified to their acceptance by complying immediately with

BAPTIZING IN THE EAST.

the external and visible condition, baptism. *Gladly* is wanting in the best manuscripts, and is omitted by Tischendorf and Alford.—**Were baptized.** Immediately, though not necessarily on the same day. The 3000 accepted the truth at once, but time may have been taken, necessary for the rite of baptism. How it was performed is not indicated in the narrative. We certainly cannot safely say that there was not time to baptize all by immersion, for what time was taken for the baptism we are not told; nor that there could have been no opportunity for immersion, for there were abundant pools of water in and about Jerusalem, in some of which bathing was certainly allowed (John 5 : 4; 9 : 7), and whether they could have been made available by the disciples for this purpose we have no means of knowing. The implication of the narrative is certainly that only those persons were at this time baptized who were old enough to accept, understandingly, the word.—**There were added about 3000 souls.** *Unto them* is an addition by the translators. The language here is absolute, as though these souls first found their true life when they found it in Jesus Christ. Comp. ch. 5 : 14; 11 : 24. Observe (1) that these converts were received into the church at once, on their profession of repentance and their consent to receive baptism, without waiting for instruction in Christian doctrine, of which they must have been almost wholly ignorant; (2) that they were received on the basis of personal repentance and acceptance of the word, as converts to the religion of Jesus Christ. This is implied, not only by the course of the narrative, but by the phraseology of ver. 47, The Lord added such *as were being saved;* (3) it is not impossible that the apostles may have received some who were not savingly converted, for they were not infallible in their spiritual judgments of men (chap. 8 : 13, 18-23). The language of ver. 47 implies that they were added to the church only as true disciples, and on the ground of their personal salvation, but not that no mistakes were made. It is very probable that some of these new converts brought into the primitive church the seeds of that Judaizing doctrine which regarded Christianity as only a phase of Judaism, and required circumcision of all Christian converts, and which afterward proved so hostile to the purity and the power of the early church; (4) it is, however, clear from the next verse that the majority of these converts were humble and docile recipients of the new faith, as taught by the apostles, and were steadfast in it.

NOTE ON THE OUTPOURING OF THE HOLY SPIRIT AT THE PENTECOST. (1.) *The fact.* The physical phenomena which accompanied the gift of the Holy Ghost, the sound as of wind and the tongues as of fire, are testified to by only one witness; whether he was an eye-witness or not we do not know; his description of the phenomena is so brief that their nature is a matter of uncertainty, and it affords a theme for curious rather than profitable inquiry. But the gift of tongues is so distinctly described in 1 Cor., ch. 14, the Pauline authorship of which is undoubted, that the existence of such a phenomenon in the early church cannot be questioned, though its nature is not and cannot be clearly known. The great fact, however, is that the Spirit of God, whose influence had hitherto been chiefly manifested in and through special individuals, appointed to be the inspired leaders of Israel, was now for the first time bestowed upon all men, on the simple conditions of repentance and baptism in the name of Jesus Christ. This fact is abundantly confirmed by the following considerations: (*a.*) It fulfills the promises of the O. T. prophets (see ver. 39, note and refs.) and of Jesus Christ (John 14 : 16-26; 15 : 26; 16 : 13, etc.). (*b.*) It is repeatedly testified to by Luke in the Book of Acts (ch. 4 : 31; 6 : 3; 8 : 15; 10 : 45; 11 : 15, etc.), and is one of the central truths dwelt upon by the apostles in their letters to the early churches (see ver. 4, note). (*c.*) It is demonstrated in the remarkable change wrought in the apostles, especially in Peter. Contrast the story of his denial of Christ (Matt. 26 : 69-75) with his courage and willing suffering after the descent of the Holy Spirit (Acts 4 : 13, 19; 5 : 29, 41, etc.). (*d.*) It is paralleled by a continuous series of revivals, extending from the day of Pentecost to the present time, the spiritual phenomena of which, in the new and devout life of awakened souls, are as truly remarkable as those of Pentecost. (2.) *The conditions of the gift.* The disciples were expecting the gift of the Holy Ghost. They believed the promise of their Lord, and waited in faith for its fulfillment. They were united in zealous hope and in prayer. There is no hint at this time of the jealousies and strifes which at other times divided them (Matt. 20 : 24; Mark 9 : 33, 34; Luke 22 : 24). They obeyed unquestioning the command of Christ (ch. 1 : 4), and again abandoning their fishing, which they had resumed after Christ's death (John 21 : 3), continued to assemble for ten days in the upper chamber at Jerusalem, without any indication of the fulfillment of the promise made by their departed Lord. They were united in patient, persevering prayer for the blessing. For illustration of these conditions see ch. 1 : 4, 8, 12-14; 2 : 1; comp. John 14 : 21-23. (3.) *The results of the gift.* On Peter and the apostles, a power of utterance accompanied with the demonstration of the Spirit (1 Cor. 2 : 4; 1 Thess. 1 : 5); on the people, the conversion of souls in multitudes; on the church, steadfastness, mutual sympathy and charity, joy, devoutness of spirit (verses 42-47; Gal. 5 : 22, 23). (4.) *The apostolic methods:* First, a prayer meeting, attended by those only who believed in and hoped for the fulfillment of Christ's promise; next, a sermon, presenting to the multitude simply, but with direct personal appeal, a crucified, risen, and ascended Saviour (1 Cor. 2 : 2); then a meeting for personal converse with inquirers, then the immediate baptism and reception into the church of all who professed repentance and were willing to make public confession of their new faith by baptism; finally, definite religious instruction in the truths of Christianity to such as accepted Jesus Christ as their personal Saviour and Lord. These facts, of the gift, the conditions on which it was obtained, the results on the community and the

42 And[r] they continued stedfastly in the apostles'
doctrine and fellowship, and in breaking of bread, and
in prayers.
43 And fear came upon every soul: and many[s] wonders and signs were done by the apostles.

44 And all that believed were together, and[t] had all
things common;
45 And sold their possessions and goods, and[u] parted them to all *men*, as every man had need.

r 1 Cor. 11 : 2; Heb. 10 : 25 . . . . s Mark 16 : 17 . . . . t ch. 4 : 32, 34 . . . . u Isa. 58 : 7; 2 Cor. 9 : 1, 9; 1 John 3 : 17.

church, and the apostolic methods of co-working with the Spirit of God, are recorded as an example and instruction to the universal church of Christ.

42. The following verses, to the end of the chapter, describe in general terms the condition of the church in this first phase of its existence. The duration covered is not indicated, but could not have been very long, for persecution soon ensued, which scattered the disciples and put an end to the temporary community of goods, and to "favor with all people."—**They,** *i. e.*, the new converts, **continued steadfastly.** Their new life was not a mere transient excitement, but a steadfast purpose, the strength of which was demonstrated by their perseverance.—**In the apostles' teaching;** *i. e.*, in the acceptance and maintenance of their teaching; they were docile scholars in the new faith.—**And in fellowship.** The original (κοινωνία) signifies literally a sharing in common. Here it probably implies both fellowship in spiritual things, a participation with each other in Christian sympathy and experience, and also practical charity—the sharing of goods with the poor indicated by ver. 45.—**And in breaking of bread.** There is some doubt as to the meaning of this phrase. I think it tolerably clear that an observance of the Lord's Supper is indicated, because (1) in ver. 46 *the breaking of bread* appears to be distinguished from an ordinary meal; (2) the language accords closely with that employed in the description of the institution of the Lord's Supper (Matt. 26 : 26; Mark 14 : 22; Luke 22 : 19. Comp. 24 : 35; 1 Cor. 11 : 23, 24); (3) and with that elsewhere employed to describe what was probably the Lord's Supper (Acts 20 : 7, 11; 1 Cor. 10 : 16.).—**And in prayers.** Probably here social gatherings for prayer, not merely individual prayers, are intended.

43-45. And fear came upon every soul. Fear in the sense of commingled awe and reverence; a fear not inconsistent with joy (ver. 46).—**And many wonders and signs were done by the apostles.** This general description includes the miracles described more in detail in subsequent chapters (ch. 3 : 1-8; 5 : 12, 15, 16).—**All that believed were together.** Not literally were in one place. No ordinary room, obtainable in Jerusalem, would have contained the 3,000. But they constituted a social community by themselves, separated from the rest of the people, not by local and physical barriers, but by their own mutual sympathies.—**And had all things in common; and sold their possessions and goods.** The term *possessions* (κτήματα) signifies property acquired, the term *goods* (ὑπάρξεις) simply that which belongs to one. Their property, whether acquired or inherited, was held subject to the claims of Christian charity. I see no adequate ground for Alford's distinction, who interprets *possessions* as landed property, and *goods* as moveables. But lands and houses, as well as moveable goods, were sold (ch. 4 : 34).—**And parted them to all.** Not to all *men*, but to *all* in the church.—**As every man had need.** This surrender of property was not instantaneous or absolute; it was only as need appeared in the church that such sale and distribution took place.

OF COMMUNISM IN THE EARLY CHURCH.—In respect to the communism described in the early church here and in chaps. 4 : 32-34; 5 : 1-4, the following facts should be noted by the student: (1.) The disciples did not sell to give to a hierarchy, but to the poor, and as the poor had need. They employed the apostles only as almoners of their bounty, and the apostles early declined this office, and the disciples appointed others for the purpose (ch. 6 : 1-5). There is, therefore, in this primitive example no precedent for the Romish endeavor to secure from its adherents the gift of their property to the church, as an ecclesiastical organization. (2.) The sale and gift were purely voluntary. No disciple was required, as a condition of joining the church, to surrender his property to the community; even after sale, he was free to give little or much as he chose (ch. 5 : 4). There is, therefore, in the apostolic example no warrant for the modern American socialistic communities, in which every member is *required* to surrender, not only his property, but his earnings, to the common stock. For brief account of these communities, see Lyman Abbott's *Dictionary of Religious Knowledge*, art. Socialism. (3.) The community was bound together by sympathies, not by rules and regulations; it did not at any time prevent the disciples from continuing to live separately in individual households and in their own houses (ver. 46; ch. 12 : 12). It did not, therefore, disrupt or weaken the family. (4.) It was confined to Jerusalem and to the early period of the Christian church, at a time when it was largely composed of pilgrims temporarily sojourning at Jerusalem, and dependent, according to the custom then, and even now to some extent prevailing in the East, on

46 And they, continuing daily with one accord in the temple, and breaking bread from house to house, did eat their meat with gladness and singleness of heart,

47 Praising God, and having favour[v] with all the people. And[w] the Lord added to the church daily such as should be saved.

v Luke 2 : 52; Rom. 14 : 18.... w chap. 5 : 14; 11 : 24.

the hospitality of the residents there. The Christian enthusiasm simply enlarged this hospitality, providing for the poorer pilgrims out of the abundance of the richer disciples. "No trace of its existence is discoverable anywhere else; on the contrary, Paul speaks constantly of the rich and poor. See 1 Tim. 6 : 17; Gal. 2 : 10; 2 Cor. 8 : 13, 15; 9 : 6, 7; 1 Cor. 16 : 2; also, James 2 : 1-5; 4 : 13."—(*Alford.*) (5.) Its origin may probably be looked for in the organization of the apostolic band, which, during Christ's earthly life, lived in voluntary poverty, and had a common treasury (Matt. 19 : 21; Luke 5 : 11; John 12 : 6; 13 : 29). Naturally, the first converts attempted to adopt the same principle, until experience demonstrated that the community of goods, applicable to the small and itinerant apostolate, was inapplicable to the large and increasing Christian brotherhood. (6.) For, the attempt to organize the Christian church on this basis and to have all things in common, failed and was soon abandoned. It led to disputes (ch. 6 : 1), was never extended beyond Jerusalem, nor even permanently maintained there (see references above), and its temporary adoption there perhaps accounts for the poverty of that church (ch. 11 : 29, 30: 24 : 17; Rom. 15 : 25, 26; 1 Cor. 16 : 1-3; with 2 Cor., ch. 8, 9). (7.) There is not in the N. T. any warrant for the belief that such communism as was practised temporarily in the church at Jerusalem, was directed by God, or is recorded as an example for us. It is not said to have been counselled by the apostles; their writings nowhere commend it; and while the inspired teachings of the N. T. writers are authoritative, there is no warrant in Scripture for the doctrine that the *example* of the early church is an *authority* for later ages. Christ is our only example. (8.) The principle underlying Christian communism, viz., that all possessing goods and industries are to be consecrated to God in the service of humanity, is a fundamental Christian principle (Matt. 25 : 14-30; Luke 13 : 6-9), but neither experience nor Scripture indicates that selling all and dividing to the poor, is the method best calculated to serve humanity, or even the poor.

46, 47. And they, persevering daily with one accord. On the meaning of the word (ὁμοθυμαδὸν), rendered *one accord*, see ch. 1 : 14 and note.—**In the Temple.** Thither they went up to pray (ch. 3 : 1), and to teach, the latter in Solomon's porch (ch. 3 : 11; 5 : 21). On the structure of the Temple and its adaptation to the purposes of religious teaching, see John 2 : 13-17, notes.—**And breaking bread from house to house.** Or, *in the house, i. e.*, in private. The original is capable of either interpretation. The essential fact is, that while they continued at this time in the observance of the Jewish forms of worship, they added gatherings for Christian worship in private houses. By "breaking bread," the observance of the Lord's Supper is probably intended. See ver. 42, note.—**They did eat their meat with gladness.** A very simple meal may be joyous.—**And singleness of heart.** Their simplicity, in contrast with the pride and rivalries of the Pharisaic feasts (Luke 14 : 7; Matt. 23 : 6), and the self-indulgent luxury of the later feasts of the Christian church (1 Cor. 11 : 20, 21), was in part the secret of their joy. "Singleness of heart accompanied the gladness; and in point of fact, wanting that companion, the gladness itself would soon disappear."—(*Arnot.*) The hint is practically valuable in these days when irrational luxury and pride and rivalry destroy the true gladness of social life.—**Praising God and having favor with all the people.** The *people* are here in contrast with the Jewish ecclesiastics. See chap. 4 : 1-4. As yet, however, persecution had not arisen; the beauty of holiness was perceived and admired by the people; its severe requirements and condemnation of popular sins was not at first felt. The spark was allowed to grow into a flame before the blast of persecution; then the storm did but increase and extend the flame (ch. 8 : 4).—**And the Lord added.** Not, *to the church*, which words are wanting in the best MSS.; but, *to himself* (ch. 5 : 16; 11 : 24).—**Such as were being saved.** Not such as *had been saved*, which would require the past tense, nor such as *certainly would be saved*, which would require the future, but such as *were in the way of salvation.* It is not necessarily implied that all were saved, some self-deceived and apostates might be among them; but it is implied that only those were accepted in the church who themselves professed to accept salvation through Jesus Christ as their Saviour. Conversion was a condition of church membership. Observe that they did not add themselves, and were not added by the church or the apostles, but *by the Lord* (1 Cor. 3 : 5-7). While this brief description (vers. 41-47) of the first experience of the primitive church affords but little light on the methods of church organization, it indicates very clearly the elements of spiritual life which gave the early church its power. It received the gift of the Holy Spirit, labored directly for the conversion of souls, received converts on their profession of repentance and faith in Christ,

CHAPTER III.

NOW Peter and John went up together into the temple at[x] the hour of prayer, *being* the ninth *hour*.
2 And a certain man, lame from his mother's womb, was carried, whom they laid daily at the gate[y] of the temple which is called Beautiful, to ask alms of them that entered into the temple;
3 Who, seeing Peter and John about to go into the temple, asked an alms.
4 And Peter, fastening his eyes upon him, with John, said, Look on us.

x Ps. 55 : 17; Dan. 6 : 10. . . . y John 9 : 8.

who entered the church as learners, whose experience was characterized by mutual sympathy, generous charity, social life, great joyousness, and whose services were simple, informal, non-ritualistic, and genuinely devout, being held in private houses, and consisting of social meals, accompanied by the memorial supper of the Lord, of instruction afforded by the apostles, of prayer, of singing, and of mutual fellowship in Christian experience.

Ch. 3 : 1-11. THE FIRST APOSTOLIC MIRACLE.—THE VALUE OF A LOOK ILLUSTRATED.—TWO PHASES OF FAITH EXEMPLIFIED.—IN THE NAME OF JESUS CHRIST. —THE HEALING POWER OF CHRIST IS THE GLORY OF GOD.

Date A. D. 30. Nothing indicates the exact time. It must have been soon after the day of Pentecost, but probably not on that day. It is the first miracle definitely described as performed by an apostle, though that they had wrought miracles during Christ's life is implied by Matt. 10 : 8. Comp. Luke 10 : 17. On one occasion they attempted and failed (Mark 9 : 18), but for their failure were rebuked by Christ, who attributed it to their spiritual deficiency (Mark 9 : 19, 28, 29). The miracle here is recorded for the sake of results to which it leads—the address to the people founded on it (vers. 12-26), the arrest of the apostles, and their first trial before the Sanhedrim (ch. 4 : 1-22), and the effect in strengthening the faith and courage of the early church (4 : 23-31).

1-3. Peter and John went up together. The personal friendship of these two disciples is illustrated by many incidents (Luke 5 : 1-11; John 13 : 23, 24; 18 : 15, 16; 21 : 7).—**At the hour of prayer, the ninth hour.** That is, 3 P. M. There were two fixed hours for sacrifice and prayer—the morning hour 9 A. M., and the evening hour 3 P. M. (Exod. 29 : 41). These, with one at noon, were observed as hours of prayers by the devout Jews, even when absent from Jerusalem and the Temple (Ps. 55 : 17; Dan. 6 : 10). Similar hours of prayer are established by ecclesiastical laws among the Mohammedans and the Roman Catholic priesthood. The later Jews were exacting in the observance of these occasions of prayer, continuing them scrupulously during Pompey's siege of Jerusalem (Josephus' Ant. 14 : 4, 3). The apostles went up, not to teach (*Calvin*), nor as a matter of expediency (*Chrysostom*), nor to commemorate Christ's perfect sacrifice by observing the typical sacrifice of the Temple (*Hackett*), but because they were still Jews as well as Christians, and had not yet learned the full meaning of Christ's declaration that he had fulfilled the law, and that time and place are unimportant in worship (Matt. 5 : 17; John 4 : 21-24). The maintenance of special hours of prayer, borrowed from the Jews, was continued in the Christian church and increased to seven daily occasions; these are still observed, in theory, if not in practice, by the Romish clergy. The literal observance of the entire prescribed service would occupy nearly the entire twenty-four hours.—**Lame from his mother's womb.** And he was now over forty years of age (ch. 4 : 22). The nature of the lameness, a congenital weakness of the feet and ankles, is indicated by ver. 7. —**Was being carried.** That is, as Peter and John entered the Temple, the cripple was being carried by friends to his accustomed place.—**At the gate of the Temple which is called Beautiful.** What gate is here indicated is not known. Some have identified it with the famous one which gave admission from the outer court of the Gentiles into the court of the women. But from the fact, that after the healing, the people ran together to them in Solomon's porch (ver. 11), which was without the Temple proper, it appears more likely that one of the exterior gates, leading from the city without to the courts within, is intended. There were two gates on the south side of the court of the Gentiles leading from Jerusalem into the Stoa Basilica or Solomon's Porch.—**To ask an alms.** The giving of alms was a sacred duty insisted on strenuously in the law, and in connection with the religious offerings at the Temple (Deut. 14 : 28, 29; 15 : 7, 11; 26 : 12, 13).

4, 5. Said, Look on us. Not because he "wished to see his countenance, in order to judge whether he was deserving of kindness" (*Meyer*), but simply to fix his attention, and awaken, even though vaguely, that spirit of the expectation and the obedience of faith, without which the cure could not have been wrought. Comp. with this look of the lame man that of the poisoned Israelite, in Numb. 21 : 8; both illustrate Isaiah 45 : 22. Quarles interprets the two looks of Peter and the lame man: "When thou seest misery in thy brother's face, let him see mercy in thine eye."—**Expecting to receive something.** This expectation is generally a condi-

5 And he gave heed unto them, expecting to receive
something of them.
6 Then Peter said, Silver and gold have I none; but
such as I have give I thee: In[z] the name of Jesus
Christ of Nazareth, rise up and walk.
7 And he took him by the right hand, and lifted *him*
up: and immediately his feet and ancle bones received
strength.
8 And he, leaping[a] up, stood, and walked, and entered with them into the temple, walking, and leaping,
and praising God.
9 And all the people saw him walking and praising
God:
10 And they knew that it was he which sat for alms
at the Beautiful gate of the temple: and they were
filled with wonder and amazement at that which had
happened unto him.
11 And, as the lame man which was healed held Peter and John, all the people ran together unto them, in
the porch[b] that is called Solomon's, greatly wondering.

z ch. 4 : 10.... a Isa. 35 : 6.... b ch. 5 : 12; John 10 : 23.

tion of receiving (Matt. 7 : 7, 8), but the gift exceeds the expectation (Ephes. 3 : 20), as it did here. Observe the illustration of two phases of faith; in the apostle, a clear knowledge of the benefit to be conferred, and of the divine power of him by whom it would be conferred; in the lame man, only a confidence in the charity of the two unknown, and a vague hope of *something*, he knew not what. But there was faith in both, in each according to the measure of knowledge.

6. Silver and gold is not to me. Not, *I have none with me now*, nor *I have none to give to thee*, nor, literally, *I have none*, for though Peter had left all to follow Christ (Matt. 19 : 27), he was not a mendicant; but, *Silver and gold is not for me to give*, *i. e.*, it is not my means for doing good. He speaks not for himself only, but also for John. —**But what I have, that give I to thee.** In a sense every disciple can say this. The moneyless can show mercy; the poorest can yet give to the poor sympathy and consideration (Ps. 41 : 1; Prov. 29 : 7).—**In the name of Jesus Christ the Nazarene.** Speaking for him and by his authority. Contrast the miracles of Christ performed never in the name of another, but with an "I say unto thee" (Luke 5 : 24; 7 : 14; 8 : 54, etc.). Why does he add *the Nazarene?* He adopts joyfully the appellation given in derision (Matt. 2 : 23; John 1 : 46), that he may share the obloquy of his Master and honor even his dishonored title.

7, 8. And he took him by the right hand and lifted him up. Not so much to strengthen his limbs as his faith.—**And immediately his feet and ankle-bones received strength.** Luke, who is a physician, intimates the nature of the disease, as well as the suddenness and radicalness of the cure.—**He leaping up, stood, and walked.** He leaped or sprang up from his sitting posture, stood for a moment to realize his new power, then walked, another evidence of the miracle, for walking is an acquired art, and he had never learned.—**And entered with them into the Temple, walking, and leaping, and praising God.** This fact, coupled with ver. 11, which indicates what part of the Temple they entered together, implies that the Beautiful gate was one exterior to the whole structure. His walking and leaping was in the exuberance of his new-found powers; his praising God either indicates that he possessed a truly devout spirit, or else, merely the habit of the orientals, who, much more than the Anglo-Saxon, attribute all remarkable events to God.

9-11. All the people. The miracle was publicly performed, and publicly recognized and appreciated. "They who have seen our infirmities should attest our change."—**And they recognized.** Literally, *Knew perfectly* (ἐπιγνωσκω). He was a well-known mendicant. There was no opportunity to question his identity, as in the case of the blind beggar (John 9 : 9).—**And they were filled with wonder.** In feeling; surprise intermingled with awe.—**And amazement.** In the understanding. They were dazed by the event.—**At that which had happened unto him.** They saw him leaping and walking, knew him to be the lame man, but knew not the circumstance of his cure, and were amazed and awe-struck, wondering what had occurred.—**And as he held Peter and John.** This reading is better than that of the Received Text, though the meaning is the same. He held them, not for support, because he was ignorant how to walk, nor for fear, lest the cure was not permanent and he should suffer relapse if he lost them, but from joy and gratitude.—**In the porch that is called Solomon's.** This porch, 600 feet in length and 75 in width, overhung the south wall of Jerusalem; it was open toward the Temple, but closed by a wall toward the country. For illustration, see Vol. I, p. 257; for description, John 2 : 13-17, notes.

Ch. 3 : 12-26. PETER'S ADDRESS TO THE PEOPLE. THE POWER OF THE APOSTLES: THE POWER OF FAITH (12, 16).—THE SIN OF ISRAEL: THE REJECTION OF THE MESSIAH (13-15).—IGNORANCE A PALLIATION BUT NOT AN EXCUSE FOR SIN (ver. 17 with 2 : 23).—EVEN THE WICKED FULFILL THE DIVINE PURPOSES (ver. 18).—THE FRUITS OF REPENTANCE: NEW SPIRITUAL LIFE AND THE SPIRITUAL RECEPTION OF CHRIST (19, 20).—THE HOPE OF THE CHURCH: THE SECOND COMING OF CHRIST (21).—THE WORLD'S SIN: HEEDLESSNESS OF CHRIST (22, 23).—THE PUNISHMENT OF THAT SIN: SOUL DESTRUCTION (23).—THE MISSION OF CHRIST: TO TURN MEN FROM THE WAY OF SIN (26).

There are two radically different interpretations of this address. One regards Peter as speaking throughout of the present dispensation.

12 And when Peter saw *it*, he answered unto the
people, Ye men of Israel, why marvel ye at this? or
why look ye so earnestly on us, as though by our own
power[c] or holiness we had made this man to walk?
13 The God[d] of Abraham, and of Isaac, and of Jacob, the God of our fathers,[e] hath glorified[f] his Son Jesus; whom ye delivered up, and denied him[g] in the presence of Pilate, when he[h] was determined to let *him* go.
14 But ye denied the Holy One[i] and the Just,[j] and
desired a murderer to be granted unto you;
15 And killed the Prince of life, whom God hath
raised[k] from the dead; whereof we[l] are witnesses.

c 2 Cor. 3 : 5....d Matt. 22 : 32....e ch. 5 : 30, 31....f John 17 ; 1; Ephes. 1 : 20 22; Phil. 2 : 9 11; Heb. 2 : 9; Rev. 1 : 5, 18....g John 19 : 15.... h Matt. 27 : 17-25: Luke 23 : 16 23....i Ps. 16 : 10; Luke 1 : 35....j ch. 7 : 52; 22 : 14....k Matt. 28 : 2-6; Ephes. 1 : 20....l ch. 2 : 32.

According to this view, "times of refreshing" (ver. 19) are seasons of spiritual refreshment coming to the individual soul; the promise "he shall send Jesus" (ver. 20) is fulfilled in Christ's spiritual presence in the hearts of his people, or in his presence in the world, in his church, and his Gospel; "until the times of restitution of all things" (ver. 21) is equivalent to "until the restitution or restoration which the Gospel is bringing about has been accomplished." The other interpretation regards Peter in this address as a prophet, and as referring to the second coming of the Lord, in glory and power, to establish his kingdom upon the earth. The student will find the former view in Barnes's notes, the latter in Alford. For reasons stated in the notes, I believe that neither interpretation is wholly true; but that in part of his address Peter refers to the present dispensation, and in part to the future coming of Christ. There is a contrast between this and Peter's former speech (ch. 2 : 14-36). There he appealed to the conscience of the people, and to the crucifixion of their King, which is past; in the present address he appeals rather to the hopes of the people, and to the coronation of their King, which is in the future. That address, however, is completed; this one is abruptly broken off by the arrest of the speaker (ch. 4 : 1).

12. And Peter seeing (the concourse of the people described in the previous verse), **answered unto the people.** To their looks of inquiry and amazement. The word *answered* does not imply any previous questioning; it is commonly used in the N. T. in describing the commencement of an address (Matt. 11 : 25; 22 : 1; Luke 7 : 22).—**Why marvel ye at this?** That is, at the man who had been cured, and who was holding to the apostles to express his gratitude to them.—**Or why on us gaze so intently?** The *us*, by its position in the sentence, as well as by the context, is made emphatic. Peter endeavors to turn the curiosity and interest in himself manifested by the staring of the crowd, to good account to their spiritual benefit. Contrast Peter's course here, in turning attention from himself, with Christ's course in Luke 4 : 16–22, when all eyes were fixed upon him, in accepting and concentrating this attention upon himself. One was the herald, the other the King.—**As though by our own power or piety we had made this man to walk.** The apostle disowns both any peculiar prerogative of working miracles and any peculiar privilege of access to God, any efficacy of prayer above that of a faith which may be exercised by any disciple.

13. The God of Abraham * * * the God of our fathers. "See how assiduously he thrusts himself upon the fathers of old, lest he should appear to be introducing a new doctrine."—(*Chrysostom.*) See, too, how he ranks himself with his hearers as an Israelite, by the phrase "*our* fathers," here and in ver. 25.—**Hath glorified his servant Jesus.** Not Son; the word is the same rendered *servant* in chap. 4 : 25 (παῖς, not υἱός). It is used in reference to Christ by Isaiah (chap. 42 : 1, Septuagint), and is interpreted by Heb. 10 : 7. See note on Acts 4 : 27. God had glorified Jesus by the miracles wrought through him during his earthly life (2 : 22), by his resurrection and ascension, by the spiritual blessings already conferred through him (2 : 24, 33), and now by this miracle wrought in Christ's name. The latter is the immediate reference here. By this miracle, Peter says, God glorifies not us, but him in whose name it was wrought (ver. 6).—**Whom ye delivered up.** As a nation, through their constituted rulers, the Jewish people delivered Jesus over to Pilate, the Roman governor, to be sentenced.—**And denied him to the face of Pilate.** Or, as in our English version, *in the presence of Pilate*; either rendering is admissible. *Denied* is here, not merely, denied that he was their Messiah and their King, though this is true (John 19 : 15), and is included in the statement, but, rejected him wholly, his claim, his authority, his salvation, his lordship, invoking his blood on their own heads (Matt. 27 : 25).—**When he** (Pilate) **had adjudged to release him.** Not, as in our English version, *was determined*, which indicates only a mental purpose, but had adjudged him innocent and decreed officially his release. Pilate did so adjudge, and retracted his decision and permitted the crucifixion, only in obedience to the clamor of the mob and the threats of the priests (Luke 23 : 14, 16; John 19 : 4; Matt. 27 : 24; Mark 15 : 15).

14, 15. But ye rejected the pure and just. The former conveys the idea of moral purity *within*, the latter uprightness in external life. Jesus was in *heart-life* sinless, and he had committed no *overt act* which contravened the law of the land. He was both *unjustly* and *illegally* put to death.—**And desired a murderer to be**

16 And his name, through faith in his name, hath made this man strong, whom ye see and know; yea, the faith which is by him hath given him this perfect soundness in the presence of you all.
17 And now, brethren, I wot that through ignorance[m] ye did *it*, as *did* also your rulers.

18 But those things,[n] which God before had shewed by the mouth of all his prophets, that Christ should suffer, he hath so fulfilled.
19 Repent[o] ye therefore, and be converted,[p] that your sins may be blotted[q] out, when the times of refreshing[r] shall come from the presence of the Lord;

m Luke 23 : 34; John 16 : 3; 1 Cor. 2 : 8....n ch. 26 : 22, 23; Luke 24 : 44....o ch. 2 : 38. ..p Isa. 1 : 16-20; Joel 2 : 13....q Isa. 43 : 25.... r Jer. 31 : 23-25; Zeph. 3 : 14-20; Rev. 21 : 4.

granted unto you. Barabbas (Luke 23 : 16-19).—**And killed the originator of life.** The word *prince* (ἀρχηγός) is literally *leader*, then the *progenitor* of a race, then the *originator*, the one from whom anything, whether good or bad, proceeds. This appears to be its sense here and in Heb. 2 : 10, where it is rendered "*captain* of our salvation." Comp. Heb. 12 : 2, "author of faith." Christ is the *author* of life, as he is also the *leader* into life eternal, being the first-fruits of them that rose from the dead (1 Cor. 15 : 23).—**Of whom we are witnesses.** Not merely *whereof*, as in our English version. The apostles were witnesses to Christ, his character, his life, his passion, and his resurrection. The latter is included in, but does not include all of, the apostolic testimony. Alford notices the striking antithesis in this sentence; the *pure and just* in contrast with *a murderer*, and the *author of life* with *ye killed.*

16. And by the faith of his name, him whom ye see (healed) **and know** (to have been a cripple), **his** (Christ's) **name hath made strong.—Yea, the faith which is through him** (*i. e.* given through Christ by God) **hath given him this perfect soundness in the presence of you all.** The apostle begins the first sentence, breaks it off, leaving it incomplete, and begins again, thus emphasizing the potency of Christ's name. In the second sentence, he adds that this faith is itself the gift of God, by whose mercy and love, uncaused and unconditional, this cure has been wrought. It seems to me clear that he speaks both of the faith of the apostles who wrought the cure and of the faith in the man cured, who could not have been healed if he had not exercised sufficient faith to attempt obedience to the apostolic direction, "Rise up and walk."

17, 18. And now, brethren. The appellation *brethren* softens the address, and reminds the hearers that, in nationality and religious faith, he is one with them.—**I know that because of ignorance ye did it, as also your rulers.** Undoubtedly ignorance of different degrees in different persons; the ignorance of Caiaphas and of the Roman soldiery was not the same; but not even Caiaphas, though he knew that Jesus wrought miracles, realized his full character and mission. Of all that participated in the crucifixion of our Lord, Judas is perhaps the only one who cannot be said to have done so in ignorance of what he was doing. But observe, though that ignorance is a *palliation*, it is not an *excuse* for the crime. The hands that slew him were *wicked hands* (ch. 2 : 23); for the people knew enough of Christ's character to be under obligation to inquire further and learn more. The next verse, referring to the prophets, with which they were or ought to have been familiar, enforces this truth. Comp. 2 Cor. 3 : 14, 15; 1 Tim. 1 : 13.—**But God, what things he had before announced by the mouth of all his prophets, that the Messiah should suffer, hath thus fulfilled.** The declaration is exactly parallel to that of ch. 2 : 23; the wicked hands, in crucifying, did but fulfill, not only the counsel and foreknowledge of God, but his declared word. Comp. also Luke 24 : 26. *All his prophets* is not to be taken literally, for though all the prophets foretold the days of the Messiah, they did not *all* foretell his passion and death. Peter speaks of them all as *one* body and actuated by *one* spirit; and as a body, their testimony is concurrent and harmonious, in pointing to a Messiah suffering, and triumphing in and by suffering. See Numb. 21 : 9, with John 3 : 14, 15; Ps. 22 : 16; Isaiah, ch. 53; Dan. 9 : 26; Zech. 11 : 13.

19. Repent ye, therefore, and be converted. On the meaning of the word *repent*, see ch. 2 : 38, Matt. 3 : 2, notes; on the meaning of the words *be converted*, see Matt. 18 : 3, note. The former indicates a change of aim and purpose, the latter a consequent change of direction and course in life, and both, changes wrought *by*, not *on*, the individual.—**Unto the blotting out of your sins.** The first effect of repentance is that past sins are erased from the book of God's remembrance. Comp. Ps. 51 : 9; Isaiah 1 : 18; Jer. 31 : 34; Micah 7 : 19.—**So that there may come seasons of reviving from the presence of the Lord.** The second effect of repentance, and in order of time following the pardon of sin, and dependent upon it. The meaning of the promise I take to be primarily, seasons, to the individual, of spiritual revival, *i. e.*, the bestowal of new life, of which God is the author, and which are always accompanied by a peculiar consciousness of his presence; and secondarily, similar seasons of reviving to the church or the community, but always on the same conditions, viz., repentance and a change of life, and always preceded by a free forgiveness through Jesus Christ. Thus the exhortation of this verse is exactly parallel to ch. 2 : 38: "Repent and be bap-

20 And he[s] shall send Jesus Christ, which before
was preached unto you:
21 Whom the heaven must receive until the times[t]
of restitution of all things, which God hath spoken[u] by the mouth of all his holy prophets since the world began.

s ch. 1 : 11; Heb. 9 : 28. . . . t Matt. 17 : 11. . . . u Luke 1 : 70.

tized for the remission of sins, and ye shall receive the gift of the Holy Ghost." The other interpretation is that by *times of refreshing* is meant "the great season of joy and rest which it was understood the coming of the Messiah in his glory was to bring with it" (*Alford*), and hence that Peter's reference is here to the second coming of Christ. This interpretation, though admissible, is, I think, less probable, because (1) the word *times* (καιρός) is without the article and is in the plural; the language therefore indicates repeated and frequent occasions, not a single definite occasion, though in the singular it undoubtedly is used to designate the second coming of Christ (see 1 Pet. 1 : 5; Rev. 1 : 3); (2) the word *refreshing* (ἀνάψυξις), literally, *breathe again*, though used in the N. T. only here, accords with those metaphors elsewhere which represent the effect of the spirit to be the bestowal of new spiritual life (see references below); (3) if that is not contained in the promise here, then that result of repentance and conversion, which is almost uniformly coupled in the Bible with the promise of pardon for past sin (Ps. 51 : 9, 10; Ezek. 36 : 25, 26; John 3 : 16; Acts 2 : 38; Rom. 8 : 1, 2) is altogether ignored by Peter here, and this simply to anticipate a promise of Christ's second and glorious coming, which is made more distinctly and emphatically immediately afterward (ver. 21); (4) moreover, if the promise here is of Christ's second coming, that is, by the construction of the sentence, made dependent on the repentance and conversion of the Jews, whereas, in fact, they did not, as a nation, repent and turn to the Lord, and were consequently rejected by him, and his second coming will assuredly take place, and this irrespective of the repentance and conversion of either individual or community; for he will come to assert and enforce his right to reign over all opposition and in spite of all unbelief (1 Thess. 4 : 16; Rev. 6 : 15–17; 19 : 11–16). I understand this verse, then, to be a promise of free forgiveness and a new spiritual life, *i. e.*, pardon and regeneration, upon the simple condition of a change in the purpose and direction of the sinner. Does any one ask, Does this gift of new life precede or follow the act of repentance and turning to the Lord? I answer, It accompanies it, as the act of the impotent man accompanied and was essential to the efficacy of the miracle which healed him (vers. 6–8. Comp. Job 5 : 8, 9).

20. And that he may send. (ἀποστείλῃ, *aor. subj.*) This sending is, by the construction of the Greek, dependent on their repentance, as is the *times of reviving*. In this respect, our English version is defective.—**The Messiah before prepared for you, Jesus.** This is the literal translation of the best reading, which gives *prepared*, not *preached*, and places Christ before Jesus. The *before prepared* refers to the appointment of God from before the foundation of the world (1 Pet. 1 : 20; Rev. 13 : 8). Most critics understand this passage as referring to the return of Christ at the end of the world. It is noticeable, however, (1) that nowhere else in the N. T. is God represented as *sending the Messiah* into the world in his second coming, which is described as in his own power, while in his mediatorial character he is habitually represented as *sent* into the world by the Father (Luke 4 : 18; John 6 : 57; 17 : 3, 18, 21, 23; 20 : 21; 1 John 4 : 9, 10, 14); (2) this sending is here made dependent upon the repentance of the sinner, while the second coming is not so. I therefore understand Peter here to refer to that spiritual sending of the Son by the Father to the individual soul, on condition of its repentance and conversion, without which Christ is never truly brought home to the soul, nor the soul led to accept him as its Saviour. See John 6 : 37, 39, 44, 45.

21. Whom the heaven must receive. Not, as Bengel, *who must receive*, *i. e.*, take possession, *of the heavens*, a meaning which does violence to the original Greek, and is proposed only because the other and natural interpretation is thought to imply that "heaven is greater than Christ," and to be "inimical to the loftiness of Christ above all heavens." Peter explains, in a word, that, as the Messiah must be crucified, so he must ascend up into heaven, and there await the time appointed of God for the fulfillment of his mission and the establishment of his kingdom.—**Until the times of the restoration of all things.** The reference is clearly to the anticipated restoration and glory of the theocracy, promised by the prophets and expected by the people to be realized by the Messiah. This seems to me to be clear (1) from the language itself, which clearly points to a future time or times of restoration; (2) from the reference to the prophecies, which do in fact point to such a final restoration of that which was lost by the fall; (3) from Peter's teaching on the subject, in his epistle, concerning the day of God, for which the saints are to look, and to which they are to hasten, a day that ushers in the new heavens and the new earth wherein dwelleth righteousness (2 Pet. 3 : 12, 13); (4) from the fact that Peter here employs substantially the language embodied in

22 For Moses truly said unto the fathers, A prophet[v]
shall the Lord your God raise up unto you of your
brethren, like unto me: him shall ye hear in all things,
whatsoever he shall say unto you.
23 And it shall come to pass, *that* every soul, which
will not hear that prophet, shall be destroyed from
among the people.
24 Yea, and all the prophets from Samuel, and those
that follow after, as many as have spoken, have likewise foretold of these days.
25 Ye are[w] the children of the prophets, and of the
covenant which God made with our fathers, saying
unto Abraham, And in[x] thy seed shall all the kindreds
of the earth be blessed.
26 Unto you[y] first, God, having raised up his Son
Jesus, sent him to bless you, in turning away[z] every
one of you from his iniquities.

v Deut. 18 : 15-19....w Rom. 9 : 4; 15 : 8....x Gen. 22 : 18....y Matt. 10 : 5; Luke 24 : 47....z Isa. 59 : 20; Matt. 1 : 21; Tit. 2 : 11-14.

the question of the apostles to Christ respecting his second coming, and addressed to him at the time of his ascension (Acts 1 : 6); (5) from the consideration that the language of Peter here, interpreted as a prophecy of Christ's second coming, corresponds exactly with Christ's own teaching, both with and without parable, viz., that he must depart for a season, until the appointed time was fulfilled, when he would return again and take possession of and perfect his kingdom. See particularly Matt., ch. 25. The other interpretations are, *Until the times when all things shall have been restored*, *i. e.*, by the gradual progress of the Gospel, which, as a translation, does violence to the Greek, and, *Until the times of the fulfillment of all things which God hath spoken*, etc., which imputes to the Greek word rendered *restitution* (ἀποκατάστασις) a meaning which in the N. T. Greek is never attached to it or the verb from which it is taken. Matt. 12 : 13; 17 : 11; Mark 3 : 5; 8 : 25; 9 : 12; Luke 6 : 10; Acts 1 : 6; Heb. 13 : 19, are the only passages in which the verb occurs in the N. T.; the noun occurs only here. In all these passages the idea of *restitution* is implied.—**Of which** (seasons) **God hath spoken through the mouth of his holy prophets.** *All* is omitted by the best manuscripts.—**Throughout the ages.** For some of the prophetic passages here referred to, see Isaiah 2 : 2-5; 11 : 6-9; Dan. 2 : 35, 44; 7 : 14; Micah 4 : 3, 4; Hag. 2 : 7-9; Zech. ch. 14.

22-24. For truly Moses said. Not, *Moses said truly.* Peter, in an address to the Jews, does not need to affirm the truth of Moses. The reference is to Deut. 18 : 15-19, a part of which only Peter quotes, and that not verbatim. The variations are immaterial. "*The fathers*" is wanting in the best manuscripts.—**A prophet shall the Lord your God raise up unto you from your brethren, like unto me.** That Christ was a prophet, and the last in the long line of prophets, is clearly implied by himself, even where he marks the difference between himself as a Son and them as servants (Matt. 22 : 33-39). He was not ashamed to call those whom he redeemed brethren (Heb. 2 : 11). He was like Moses in that both were mediators between God and man, unlike in the covenants or dispensations of which they were the respective representatives, and in the authority and permanence of their position in the household of God (Heb. 8 : 5, 6; 3 : 1-6).—**Him shall ye hear.** The language is mandatory, not prophetic. *Hear* is equivalent to *heed.*—**Shall be utterly destroyed from among the people.** In the original passage (Deut. 18 : 19), the language is more general, *I will punish*, or, in our English version, *I will require it of him*, *i. e.*, call him to account therefor. The spiritual significance of the warning here is given by Christ in John 3 : 18; 8 : 24. This verse thus interpreted indicates the nature of sin, under the N. T. dispensation, viz., a refusal to hear and heed Christ and the nature of punishment, spiritual destruction.—**Of these days.** Not, *those days*, *i. e.*, those of the future coming of Christ and consequent restoration of all things, but *the present days*, the dispensation of the Gospel. The declaration here is explicit that, underlying all minor prophecies and interwoven in the whole body of prophecy, the constant theme of them all, is the promise of the Redeemer and his redemption; a strong confirmation of that system of interpretation which recognizes in the history and ceremonialism of the O. T. a foreshadowing of the revelations of the N. T., and in many prophecies of the O. T. a double meaning, a Christly significance, shining through their historical and partial fulfillment, which makes history itself a prophecy.

25, 26. Ye are the sons of the prophets. Descended from them; belonging to the same nationality; therefore, these promises are peculiarly to you, and these warnings also. Comp. Rom. 3 : 2.—**And of the covenant.** Embraced in that covenant which was to Abraham and *his seed.* Paul applies this to Christ as the seed of Abraham (Gal. 3 : 16); but he was so because, according to the flesh, a Jew; and the promise was primarily to the Jewish nation, and to all the kindreds or families of the earth, through the Jewish nation, because through Jesus.—**Unto you first, God, having raised up his servant.** Not, Son (παῖς not υἱός). The word Jesus is not in the best manuscripts. It is a gloss added by a later hand, but correctly interprets the meaning of the passage.—**Sent him.** Not, *shall send him.* Observe, in confirmation of the interpretation I have given above of ver. 20, that God is represented as still sending Jesus into the world, in the dispensation of his Gospel, although, personally, Jesus has ascended into

CHAPTER IV.

AND as they spake unto the people, the priests, and
the captain of the temple, and the Sadducees,[a]
came upon them,
2 Being grieved that they taught the people, and
preached through Jesus the resurrection from the dead.
3 And they laid hands on them, and put *them* in hold
unto the next day: for it was now eventide.
4 Howbeit many[b] of them which heard the word believed; and the number of the men was about five
thousand.
5 And it came to pass on the morrow, that their rulers, and elders, and scribes,

---

a ch. 23 : 8; Matt. 22 : 23.... b ch. 28 : 24.

---

and remains in the heavens. Observe, too, that the language here implies that Peter recognized that this Gospel was for the Gentiles as well as for the Jews, but that it must first be preached to the latter. Not until later, however, did he learn that the Gentiles might come into the kingdom of Christ without first becoming Jews by submitting to the rite of circumcision (Acts 10 : 45; 15 : 1; Gal. 2 : 12).—**To bless you in turning away every one of you from his iniquity.** Not merely, nor even chiefly, in providing a pardon for sins that are past, but in saving from sins that are future: the former being the condition of and preparatory for the latter. See Matt. 1 : 21; 1 John 1 : 9. Peter's address is not apparently finished, but broken off by his arrest by the Temple officers.

Ch. 4 : 1-22. FIRST THREATENING OF PERSECUTION.—THE TRIAL OF THE APOSTLES' FAITH,—THEIR POWER, AND THEIR VICTORY. See note at end of section.

The arrest of the apostles occurred on the evening of the same day as the miracle; the conference with the apostles on the day following.

1-3. The priests, and the captain of the Temple, and the Sadducees. The *captain of the Temple* is the chief of the Temple police, a Levitical force for the preservation of order, and referred to, not only in the Rabbinical writings (see Lightfoot here, and on Luke 22 : 4) and Josephus (Wars of Jews 6 : 5, 3), but also in both the O. T. and the N. T. (2 Kings 11 : 9; Jer. 20 : 1; Luke 22 : 4, 52; John 7 : 32; 18 : 3). *Captains* of the Temple are referred to in Luke; probably the Temple guard was divided into several corps, each having its captain, but all under one chief who is here referred to. The priests probably incited the arrest, because the preaching of Jesus Christ was directly inimical to the hierarchy (see Matt. 26 : 61; Acts 6 : 14); the captain of the Temple arrested them on the pretext that the running of the people together (ch. 3 : 11) was disorderly; and the Sadducees participated for the reason stated in the next verse, *i. e.*, because the apostles testified to the resurrection. The Sadducees were the materialists and infidels of the first century and denied both spiritual existence and the resurrection (Matt. 22 : 23; Acts 23 : 8). See Matt. 3 : 7, note, for their history and principles. Observe in this first persecution of the church a type of all that follow: A corrupt priesthood lead the way; the civil power is its instrument; the infidel world combines with and sustains the two.—**Being exercised because they taught the people, and preached in Jesus the resurrection of the dead.** There is some question whether this clause describes the Sadducees only, or also the priests and the captain. The word rendered *grieved* is literally, *exercised; i. e.*, mentally disturbed and troubled. Two things aroused them, one that the disciples, without any official authority, assumed to teach the people; the other, the doctrine which they taught, which was not the general resurrection of the dead, except by implication (see ch. 17 : 31), but the resurrection *in the case of Jesus*, attested by the healing of the cripple (ch. 3 : 15, 16). Observe that infidelity as well as religion has its bigots.—**Laid hands on them.** Arrested them; the language implies some actual violence in the arrest.—**Put them in hold.** In a guard or watch-house. Where this was, and what its nature, is not known. On the Jewish prison, see notes on ch. 5 : 18-23; 12 : 3-11.—**Now eventide.** The miracle was performed at 3 P. M. The arrest was on the evening of the same day.

4. And the number of the men. The original (ἀνήρ not ἄνθρωπος) implies *male converts*, though this is questioned by some scholars. But the language does not justify the deduction that as yet only men attached themselves to the church (*Olshausen*); rather, as in Matt. 14 : 21, it indicates the number of males besides women and children, *i. e.*, the number, presumptively, of heads of households. In Jewish estimates, the number of women converted would be less significant.—**Was about five thousand.** Tischendorf omits *about;* Alford questions it. It is uncertain whether this number represents the new converts on this occasion, or the whole number of the church; probably the latter.

5, 6. Their rulers; *i. e.*, the rulers of the Jews, not those of the disciples or apostles. Nevertheless, they were the rulers of the latter, to be obeyed in all things in which the divine command was not contravened (Matt. 23 : 3). **And elders and scribes * * * were gathered together.** A meeting of the Sanhedrim is described. See Matt. 2 : 4, note, and for its history, organization and methods of procedure, Vol. I, p. 298. The elders (see Matt. 16 : 21, note) were political leaders, whose office dates from

6 And Annas[c] the high priest, and Caiaphas, and
John, and Alexander, and as many as were of the kindred of the high priest, were gathered together at Jerusalem.
7 And when they had set them in the midst, they
asked, By what[d] power, or by what name, have ye
done this?
8 Then Peter, filled[e] with the Holy Ghost, said unto
them, Ye rulers of the people, and elders of Israel,
9 If we this day be examined of the good deed done
to the impotent man, by what means he is made whole;
10 Be it known unto you all, and to all the people
of Israel, that by[f] the name of Jesus Christ of Nazareth, whom ye crucified, whom God raised from the
dead, *even* by him doth this man stand here before you
whole.
11 This is the stone[g] which was set at nought of you
builders, which is become the head of the corner.

c John 18 : 13. . . . d Matt. 21 : 23. . . . e ch. 7 : 55. . . . f ch. 3 : 6, 16. . . . g Ps. 118 : 22; Isa. 28 : 16; Matt. 21 : 42.

the patriarchal age; the scribes were the Jewish rabbis and commentators on the law. The meeting now convened was packed with the special friends of the hierarchy, the kinsfolk of the high-priest. Annas was appointed high-priest A. D. 7, but was removed by the Roman procurator A. D. 23. He continued, however, to bear the title and really to wield the powers of the office. He is called high-priest here, probably

AN ORIENTAL COURT.

because he is recognized as such by the Jews, the authority of the Romans to appoint to this sacred office being denied by them. Originally, the high-priesthood was a life office. Nothing is known with certainty of the individuals designated as John and Alexander.

7. By what power, or by what name, have ye done this? *i. e.*, this miracle. The question was not asked for information; for the apostles had already publicly declared that it was done by the power and the name of Jesus of Nazareth (ch. 3 : 6, 16); and it was this their declaration, not the healing, which led to their arrest (ver. 2). But a distinct statute provided (Deut. 13 : 1-5) that every prophet who should attempt to turn away the allegiance of the people from Jehovah, should be put to death; under this law Jesus had himself been condemned by the Sanhedrim (Vol. I, p. 298); and the question was asked here, either to lay a foundation for a charge of blasphemy against the apostles in attempting to win the allegiance of the people to Jesus, or to frighten the apostles into a retraction or modification of their assertion. The leaders of the hierarchy must have known that all Christ's disciples forsook him and fled at the time of his arrest and trial; to frighten them would not, therefore, seem impracticable.

8-12. Peter's answer, by its commingled boldness and wisdom, frustrates their design. He declares that the miracle was wrought in the name of Jesus of Nazareth, whom, by a single word, he pronounces the Messiah: to the unuttered objection of the Sanhedrim that this Jesus had already been condemned as an impostor, he responds by referring them to the prophecy of Ps. 118 : 22; and he concludes by at once, impliedly, denying that he is guilty of attempting to impair the allegiance due to Jehovah, and making the cure an occasion and a text for preaching the Gospel, by declaring that this Jesus whom they have rejected is the Saviour appointed by Jehovah and foretold in the O. T. —**Then Peter, filled with the Holy Ghost.** He relies upon and receives the fulfillment of Christ's promise in Luke 12 : 11, 12, and exemplifies his own exhortation, Add to your faith, virtue; *i. e.*, courage (2 Pet. 1 : 5).—**Rulers of the people and elders of Israel.** He addresses them with the respect due their office, though he does not hesitate to charge upon them the death of the Messiah. Comp. Paul's language ch. 22 : 1; 23 : 1, and Peter's direction to his readers in 1 Pet. 2 : 17, Honor all men, etc.—**Concerning the good deed done to the impotent man.** The goodness of the deed was not questioned; the man was present to attest it by his restoration (ver. 14). Thus Peter's opening sentence shows the false position of the court; for the apostles are charged with having done, not *evil*, but *good*. —**By what he has been saved.** The original verb is the same translated *saved* in ver. 12. Thus Peter makes the salvation of the impotent from his impotency a text for proclaiming the Gospel salvation. In this he follows the example set him by his Master (John 9 : 39-41; 6 : 35). *By what* includes both the questions addressed to Peter, viz., by what *power* and in what *name.*—**Be it known unto you all.** He neither conceals,

12 Neither is there salvation in any other: for there[h]
is none other[i] name under heaven given among men,
whereby we must be saved.
13 Now when they saw the boldness of Peter and
John, and perceived that they were unlearned[j] and
ignorant men, they marvelled; and they took knowledge of them, that they had been with Jesus.
14 And beholding the man which was healed standing with them, they could say nothing[k] against it.
15 But when they had commanded them to go
aside out of the council, they conferred among themselves,
16 Saying, What[l] shall we do to these men? for that
indeed a notable miracle hath been done by them *is*
manifest to all them that dwell in Jerusalem; and we
cannot deny *it*.
17 But that it spread no further among the people,
let us straitly threaten them, that they[m] speak henceforth to no man in this name.
18 And they called them, and commanded them not
to speak at all nor teach in the name of Jesus.

h ch. 10 : 43; 1 Tim. 2 : 5, 6.... i Ps. 45 : 17.... j Matt. 11 : 25; 1 Cor. 1 : 27.... k ch. 19 : 36.... l John 11 : 47.... m ch. 5 : 40.

prevaricates, nor hesitates. He understands the issue, and meets it with boldness.—**In the name of Jesus, the Messiah, the Nazarene.** *Jesus* the Saviour, *Christ* the Messiah, *the Nazarene* the despised. See on ch. 3 : 6.—**Whom ye crucified.** The arraigned arraigns his accusers. He implies, I know that you have condemned this man as a blasphemer and an impostor. I reassert his Messiahship, attested by this miracle wrought by his power.—**This is the stone set at naught by you, the builders.** The reference is to Ps. 118 : 22. Christ applies the same prophecy to himself in Matt. 21 : 42. On its meaning and application, see note there. The "head of the corner" is not the coping of the wall, but the corner-stone. On Christ as the corner-stone, see 1 Cor. 3 : 11; Ephes. 2 : 20–22; 1 Pet. 2 : 6, 7. Peter's object in the quotation here, is to show that their condemnation of Christ, by the Sanhedrim, as an impostor, fulfills O. T. prophecy respecting the promised Messiah.—**And there is not in any other the salvation.** Observe the definite article before the noun, unfortunately not expressed in the English version. *The* salvation indicates a salvation definitely conceived and assumed as known to the hearers; the salvation promised to Israel through the Messiah. The alternatives which have been proposed, Neither is there salvation to this lame man, and Neither is there salvation to us, *i. e.*, protection in our present emergency, are quite inadmissible, and would never have been devised but to avoid the doctrine of salvation exclusively through Jesus Christ.—**Neither is there any other name under heaven.** Equivalent to In all the earth.—**Given.** Bestowed by God.—**Among men.** Not *to* men, nor *for* men, but *among* men, as the sphere in which the salvation is provided. Observe, *men*, not *Jews;* the apostle recognizes that it is a salvation for humanity.—**Whereby we must be saved.** The preacher classes himself with the crucifiers as a fellow-sinner, equally with them needing salvation. Observe in this brief address the combined spirit of respect for the office of the rulers, of humility, and of courage in condemning their sin and testifying to Jesus Christ. Observe, too, that while salvation is exclusive, afforded only through Jesus Christ (comp. John 3 : 18; 10 : 8; 2 Cor. 11 : 4; Gal. 1 : 8, 9), it is not necessarily confined to those who *know* the name or *understand* the truth respecting Jesus (Matt. 8 : 11, 12; 25 : 37–39, see note; Acts 10 : 35; Rom 2 : 6, 7). *The name* here is equivalent to Jesus Christ himself in all his offices and attributes (see Matt. 28 : 19, note), and the salvation which he brings is larger than our comprehension of it.

13. Now when they saw the boldness of Peter and John. Literally *plain-spokenness.* There was none of that hesitation in speech which comes of timidity, and which, in the case of men unskilled in the arts of speech, would be natural before such a tribunal.—**And perceived that they were unlearned and ignorant.** *Unlearned* (ἀγράμματος) is *unversed in literature*, here, untaught in the Jewish schools, the Rabbinical being the only literature which the Pharisaic teachers recognized as legitimate subjects of study; *ignorant* (ἰδιώτης) is more probably *common* people, in contrast with public and recognized teachers. The first refers to their education, the second also to their social position (comp. 1 Cor. 1 : 27).—**They marvelled; also they recognized them that they were with Jesus.** Not merely *had been*, as in our English version, but *were*, that is, were customarily his associates and followers while he was living. "Their wonder sharpened their recollection" (*Meyer*); and considering more narrowly, they now, apparently for the first time, recognized in the two accused, disciples of Jesus Christ. Observe, what identified them with Jesus was their *boldness* of utterance. Observe too, that the influence of Christ's presence may and should be attested by the spirit of his followers.

14. The man * * * standing with them. Either arrested with the apostles the night before, as being in part the means of provoking disturbance, or summoned as a witness, or coming voluntarily before the court to testify for the apostles, or possibly as a mere spectator. All these conjectures have been suggested.

15-18. They conferred among themselves. We have only the substance of their deliberations. The court was obliged to sit with open doors; the facts would therefore be known.

19 But Peter and John answered and said unto them,
Whether it be right in the sight of God to hearken[n]
unto you more than unto God, judge ye.
20 For we[o] cannot but speak the things which we[p]
have seen and heard.
21 So when they had further threatened them, they
let them go, finding nothing how they might punish
them, because[q] of the people: for all *men* glorified
God for that which was done.
22 For the man was above forty years old, on whom
this miracle of healing was shewed.
23 And being let go, they went[r] to their own com-

n ch. 5 : 29.... o Jer. 20 : 9.... p ch. 22 : 15; 1 John 1 : 1, 3.... q ch. 5 : 26; Matt. 21 : 26.... r ch. 2 : 42

—**What shall we do to these men?** Observe, their question is in form analogous to that of the people in ch. 2 : 37, but in spirit how different!—**For that a well-known miracle hath been done through them.** *Well-known*, not notable. What troubled the council was not the remarkable character of the miracle, but the fact that it was known to all the people, and could not be gainsaid. *By them* (διά αὐτῶν) is rather *Through their means*, and indicates the apostles as the instrument, not as the original cause of the cure.—**Let us straitly threaten them.** Literally, With threatening let us threaten them.—**Not to speak nor to teach in the name of Jesus.** Literally *upon* the name (ἐπὶ), *i. e.*, "so as to make that name the subject (basis) of their discoursing."—(*Alford.*) The prohibition was twofold: they were not to act as public teachers at all, and especially they were not to teach the people respecting Jesus. The ostensible reason for this prohibition was that they were not authorized as teachers, and their doctrine was false; the real reason appears in ch. 5 : 28.

19, 20. Peter and John. Not necessarily both of them; one may have acted as spokesman for the other. But the utterance represented the spirit and purpose of both.—**In the sight of God.** "The world accounts many things right which in the sight of God are not right; and conversely." — (*Bengel.*) Observe that here they violate the letter of Christ's command in Matt. 23 : 3, that they may fulfill the spirit of his command in Matt. 26 : 19, 20.—**To hearken unto you rather than to God.** To hearken is not exactly synonymous with To obey. They will not even *hearken* to those who command disobedience to God. Thus, superior to all civil and ecclesiastical authority, they proclaim the authority of the word of God as interpreted by the individual conscience (Dan. 3 : 18; 6 : 10). Baumgarten interprets well both their courage and the lesson it conveys. "What a shock to the mind, what perplexity, weakness, and want of faith, would in these days show themselves, if the highest authority in sacred things were to decide against the truth. How many are there not at all times who are disposed to maintain inviolate a respect for such an authority, which they say is indispensable for the general good, even though truth would in some degree suffer thereby? How few in such a case would maintain either internal certainty or external firmness. And what is any sacred authority among ourselves, compared with the Sanhedrim of Israel in the first days after the Pentecost?"—**Judge ye.** The apostles still employ the language of respect, and appeal to the consciences of their judges.—**For we cannot but speak what we have seen and heard.** The Christian assurance of conviction compels courage in utterance (Amos 3 : 8; 1 Cor. 9 : 16). The *seen* here is the personal character and example of Christ; the *heard* are his instructions.

21, 22. So when they had further threatened them. The only effect was to increase the faith and courage of the apostles (ver. 29).—**Finding nothing how they might punish them.** No specious pretext for punishment.—**Because of the people.** Who would be rendered indignant by punishment inflicted for so great and so merciful a cure. Comp. ch. 2 : 47. The opposition to Christ and the primitive church came from the rulers (Ps. 2 : 2), not, in the first instance, from the common people. "Often the people are more rational than their rulers."—(*Bengel.*)—**Above forty years old.** An indication of the inveterate and incurable nature of his infirmity, which he had suffered from birth (ch. 3 : 2).

In considering the conduct of the apostles on this occasion, observe, (1) *The trial of their faith.* Not merely was there naturally personal fear of persecution, but also the fear of unskilled men, lest their imperfect presentation of a great cause, at a critical juncture, should prejudice it. For this was the first investigation by the Sanhedrim into the claims of Christianity, after the resurrection of Jesus Christ; the importance, in a human point of view, of a decision in its favor, we can hardly overestimate. And the popular movement had assumed such proportions that there may well have been a hope of securing in its favor the acquiescence of the rulers. (2.) *The apostolic spirit.* The apostles are respectful to the court, because of its official position, outspoken in the avowal of their own convictions, abating nothing of the claims of Jesus to be the only Messiah and Saviour, pointed in their condemnation of the sin of their accusers in crucifying the Messiah, humble in recognizing their own need of a Saviour, resolute in their expressed determination to obey God rather than man. (3.) *The secret of their power.* Peter was naturally pany, and reported all that the chief priests and elders had said unto them.

24 And when they heard that, they lifted up their voice to God with one accord, and said, Lord, thou[s] *art* God, which hast made heaven, and earth, and the sea, and all that in them is:

25 Who by the mouth of thy servant David hast said, Why did[t] the heathen rage, and the people imagine vain things?

26 The kings of the earth stood up, and the rulers were gathered together against the Lord, and against his Christ.

s 2 Kings 19 : 15....t Ps. 2 : 1, 2.

weak and wavering; both were uneducated, self-distrustful, and naturally liable to be overawed by the Supreme Court of Israel. But they were strong because filled with the Holy Ghost (Ephes. 6 : 13, 19).

Ch. 4 : 23-31. RELEASE OF THE APOSTLES, AND PRAYER OF THE CHURCH. THE APOSTLES' REFUGE: GOD THE ALL-MIGHTY (ver. 24), THE ALL-WISE (ver. 25-27), THE ALL-CONTROLLING (ver 28).—THE APOSTOLIC PRAYER: NOT TO BE RESCUED FROM TRIAL, BUT TO BE MADE VICTORIOUS IN TRIAL.

This meeting takes place on the same day as the trial reported above. By one of those dramatic changes common in life, we are suddenly transported from the council-chamber of the Sanhedrim into the midst of the Christian brotherhood. The malice and perturbation of the one, the purity and peace of the other, stand out the more clearly from the contrast. Defeated in their plea before the Sanhedrim, and forbidden to continue their ministry to the people, the disciples seek refuge in God.

23, 24. And being let go, they went to their own. Not to their own homes, nor to the twelve, but to the body of believers, who were probably praying together for them, as in ch. 12 : 12. Probably all were not gathered, but a representative number. Both sinners and saints, when released from temporary influence or restraint, go back to their own (ch. 1 : 25, note; 2 Tim. 4 : 10). Observe the evidence of vital Christian sympathy and fellowship in the primitive church. It is a good sign when the Christian goes to his church as to "his own," for sympathetic help in time of trouble.—**With one accord they lifted up a voice to God.** A concert of hearts, not of voices, is implied. One may have uttered a prayer for all, and one in which all spirits united, or, as suggested by Baumgarten, all may have said or sung the second Psalm, and then one of the company may have applied it to their condition. The report is probably not *verbatim*.—**Lord.** The prayer is addressed to the Father; it is doubtful whether the word here rendered Lord (Δεσπότης, not κύριος) is ever applied to Christ in the N. T., though 2 Pet. 2 : 1 may be an instance. It signifies literally *Master*, and is sometimes so rendered (1 Tim. 6 : 1, 2; 1 Pet. 2 : 18). From it comes our English word *despot*.—**Thou God, which hast made heaven,** etc. Not, as in our English version, and as Alford, "Thou *art* the God." The word *art* is added by the translators. The language is that of fervid appeal to God as the Creator. For parallel usage in prayers see Neh. 9 : 6; Jer. 32 : 17. The latter passage indicates the spiritual significance of the language here: "There is nothing too hard for thee." The apostles strengthen their faith by recalling the all-mighty power of their Divine Master.

25, 26. There is some uncertainty both as to the reading and the verbal meaning of these verses. The best MSS. give verse 25 as follows: *Who by the mouth of our father, thy servant David, by the Holy Spirit hast said.* This is the reading adopted by Lachmann, Tischendorf and Alford. It does not differ in meaning from the simpler form of the Received Text. The word rendered *rage* (φρυάσσω) is literally, to fume, as high-spirited horses, against control. That intolerance of control, which is the effect of pride, is indicated. *To imagine a vain thing* (μελετάω), is to purpose vain things; here, to lay plans which were both innately empty and worthless, and also in vain, as all plans in opposition to God must ever be. *Stood up* is equivalent to the English phrase, "took their stand," and indicates a fixed and determined resistance. *The rulers were gathered together* answers to, *Took counsel together*, in Ps. 2 : 2. The verb is in the passive voice, and the language indicates not merely, nor mainly, that they gathered in one place, but that they were drawn together by one purpose; (ἐπι indicates not the place where, but the object for which they gathered). *Against the Lord* is against God the Father, *against his Christ* is against his Anointed One, *i. e.*, the Messiah. The quotation here is from Ps. 2 : 3; the reference of which to Christ, and the persecution against him and his church, could hardly be doubted, even were it not here expressly so applied. The fulfillment of this prophecy was not, however, exhausted in the first century; "it runs parallel with the history of the conflict and the triumph of the cause of truth."—(*Hackett.*) The apostles recognized in the course of the Sanhedrim, not a mere transient outbreak from a single though powerful faction, but a manifestation of that hostility against the kingdom of Christ, which ancient prophecy had foretold. But they also recognized a fulfillment of the divine plan and purpose, and therefore, were neither surprised nor terrified. Observe that the language assumes the inspiration of the

27 For of a truth, against thy holy child Jesus, whom thou hast anointed, both Herod,[u] and Pontius Pilate, with the Gentiles, and the people of Israel, were gathered together,

28 For[v] to do whatsoever thy hand and thy counsel determined[w] before to be done.

29 And now, Lord, behold their threatenings: and grant unto thy servants, that with all boldness[x] they may speak thy word,

u Luke 23 : 1, 8, etc. . . . v ch. 3 : 18 . . . . w Prov. 21 : 30; Isa. 46 : 10; 53 : 10 . . . . x vers. 13, 31; ch. 14 : 3; 28 : 31; Ephes. 6 : 19.

psalm: "Thou, God, * * * by the mouth of thy servant David hast said."

27. For there were gathered together. The wicked unite as well as the holy, but "unity without truth is conspiracy."—(*Augustine.*)—**In truth, in this city.** The words *In this city* are found in the best MSS., and are added by Tischendorf, Alford, Hackett, etc. Alford sees in them a reference to Ps. 2 : 6; I should recognize them as simply emphatic of the truth of the prophecy, as if they said, "There were gathered *in this very city.*—**Both Herod and Pontius Pilate.** The accompanying face of Herod is from an ancient coin. Their union against Christ is narrated by Luke 23 : 12.—**Against thy holy servant Jesus.** The word rendered *child* in our English version is the same (παῖς) rendered servant in verse 25, and should be so translated here; but it is not the same which Paul so frequently employs in characterizing himself as the servant of Jesus Christ (Rom. 1 : 1; Gal. 1 : 10; Col. 4 : 12; δοῦλος). It corresponds to the French term *garçon*, and its nearest equivalent the word *boy;* it is rendered sometimes *servant* (Matt. 8 : 6, 8, 13; 12 : 18; 14 : 2; Luke 1 : 54); sometimes *child* or *son* (Matt. 17 : 18; 21 : 15; Luke 2 : 43; 9 : 42; John 4 : 51; Acts 3 : 13). Christ is in this an example to the Christian that he is both son and servant, a son that serves (Heb. 10 : 7, 9).—**Whom thou hast anointed.** Comp. Heb. 1 : 9. Anointing was a symbol of consecration, both to God and by God. This consecration was visibly and outwardly symbolized in the case of Jesus at his baptism (Matt. 3 : 16, 17). Anointing in the case of Jesus signifies not his royalty (*Hackett*), but his priesthood. Kings were not always anointed, the high-priest was, and to the Jew was known as the Anointed One. See note on The Names of Jesus, Vol. I, p. 57.—**Both Herod and Pontius Pilate, with the Gentiles and the peoples of Israel.** *Peoples* plural, not *people* singular. The reference is either to the different tribes of Israel, or, less probably, to the fact that they were now scattered in, and came from, different lands, representing different nationalities. Bengel notes the exact parallel between the prophecy and its fulfillment; Herod answers to the *Kings*, Pilate to the *Rulers*, the Gentiles here to the *Gentiles* in the psalm, and the peoples of Israel here to the *people* there. The Herod mentioned is Herod Antipas. See Vol. I, p. 58, 59. This verse definitely applies the prophecy of David to these recent events. The ground of the disciples' encouragement was twofold: (1) These events, however surprising and saddening to them, were not unexpected to their Divine Master; and (2) in the resurrection of their crucified Lord, in the outpourings of the Holy Spirit, and in the conversions to Christ, greater in a single day than during his whole life, they had experienced the futility of the concurrent opposition of Jew and Gentile, king, ruler and people to their KING.

28. To do whatsoever thy hand and thy counsel determined before to be done. In respect to the meaning of this declaration, it is to be observed, (1) that there is no question whatever respecting the authenticity of the verse; (2) and no serious question respecting the translation. Dr. Adam Clark does indeed suggest that the second clause of the preceding verse should be read as in a parenthesis; thus the meaning of the declaration would be, Herod, Pontius Pilate, etc., were gathered together against thy holy servant Jesus, whom thou hast anointed, to do whatsoever thy hand and thy counsel determined before. But this neither accords with the course of thought, nor with the natural construction of the original. His argument that it is "both impious and absurd" to suppose that "their rage and vain counsel would be such as God himself had determined should take place," is one never safe in the interpretation of the Scripture; we are to accept what Scripture does teach, not to overrule, set aside, or interpret its teachings according to our conception of what is pious and rational. (3.) The meaning then is sufficiently clear, however mysterious may be the truth it enunciates. The *hand* of God is his power, the *counsel* of God is his wisdom; the declaration, as in ch. 2 : 23, is that the arrest, condemnation and crucifixion of Jesus Christ, though wrought by the rage and vain counsel of wicked men, fulfilled the divine purpose and was carried out under, and subject to, the divine control. It belongs to the theologian, not to the commentator, to consider the relation of this truth, the absolute sovereign control of God over all life, to the freedom and responsibility of the individual; in my judgment, both truths are taught by life and by Scripture, but their reconciliation transcends the limit of

30 By stretching forth thine hand to heal; and that signs[y] and wonders may be done by the name of thy holy child Jesus.
31 And when they had prayed,[z] the place was shaken where they were assembled together; and they were all filled with the Holy Ghost, and they[a] spake the word of God with boldness.

y ch. 2 : 43; 5 : 12....z ch. 2 : 2, 4; 16 : 26....a verse 29.

human thought. It ought perhaps to be observed that the declaration is not made here that God determined *who* should execute his purpose, but only that the deeds done were what he had determined should be done.

29, 30. And now, Lord. *Now* is not merely a conjunction, but an adverb of time. It might be rendered, *At this present time.*—**Behold their threatenings.** See Exod. 3 : 7, etc.; 2 Chron. 16 : 9; Isaiah 66 : 18; Eccles. 5 : 8; Hosea 7 : 2. —**And grant unto thy servants.** *Slaves* will represent more literally, though perhaps less accurately, the meaning (δοῦλος not παῖς).—**That with all boldness.** *Plain-spokenness*, as in ch. 4 : 13.—**They may speak thy word in stretching forth thy hand to heal, and that signs and wonders may come to pass.** That is, By stretching forth thy hand to heal, and by miracles wrought as an evident token of thy presence and blessing, impart this courage.—**In the name of thy holy servant Jesus.** To his glory, not to their own. Observe, in respect to this prayer, that they ask, not to be rescued from persecution, nor to be relieved from the obligation of speaking, nor to be avenged on their enemies or God's, nor even for greater intelligence, acumen and skill, but (1) that they may continue to speak, (2) with boldness, *i. e.*, freedom and courage of speech, (3) the word of God, implying a request for a continual revelation of that word (John 14 : 26; 15 : 26), attested by manifestations, not of divine justice, but of mercy, (4) to the glory of Christ's name.

31. The place was shaken. Perhaps by an earthquake, or by a phenomenon producing the same apparent results. Such a moving of the foundation of the visible world would be a natural and apt sign of the presence and power of Him who made heaven and earth, and to whom the world and all therein are subject. It is recognized by heathen writers as such a symbol. Thus Virgil's Eneid 3 : 89:

> Grant now,
> Father, some sign, and glide into our souls.
> Scarce had I spoke, when everything around
> Suddenly trembled, all the sacred doors
> And laurels of the god. The mountain heaved.
> —*Cranch's Transl.*

It is also referred to as a sign of the divine presence in the O. T. (Isaiah 2 : 19, 21; 13 : 13; 24 : 20; Ezek. 38 : 19; Joel 3 : 16; Hag. 2 : 6, 7; Hab. 3 : 6, 10). Comp. also Christ's employment of similar symbolisms in Matt. 24 : 29; Mark 24 : 25.—**They were all filled with the Holy Ghost, and they spake the word of God with boldness.** The physical sign was only an accompaniment of the spiritual blessing. They had prayed for the impartation of courage of speech to the apostles (ver. 20); it was bestowed on all. Thus was indicated that the preaching of the Gospel was not confined to the twelve, but all were to witness to Christ with apostolic faith and courage.

The experience of the apostles in this chapter illustrates the declaration of the Psalmist (Ps. 46 : 1), God is our refuge and strength. Comp. this psalm throughout, and with it Ps. 91; 121; 125. Appointed without previous training, to represent the kingdom of God, after the departure of their Lord, the apostles are surprised by a popular movement which adds thousands to the infant church. In the midst of this popular uprising, they are brought before the supreme court, plead Christ's cause, fail to win the court, and are forbidden to continue preaching to the people. The court has apparently ample power to compel obedience. In this exigency they seek refuge in God, and in their prayer, which is less a petition or ascription of praise, than a communion with God, they dwell upon the facts that he is (1) All-mighty—the creator of the universe, and so of the very men whose opposition threatens to put an end to their work for God; (2) All-wise—he knew and centuries past foretold the very exigency that has now befallen his church; it is a surprise and disappointment to them, but not to Him; (3) All-controlling—the very events which, humanly speaking, seem so disastrous, have been predetermined by Him; the very enemies, whose threatening seems so ominous, are, despite themselves, carrying out His will. The all-mighty, the all-wise, the all-sovereign God, is the Christian's refuge in time of trouble.

Ch. 4 : 32–37. FURTHER DESCRIPTION OF THE STATE OF THE CHURCH.—ITS CHARACTERISTICS: UNITY, CHARITY, GOSPEL POWER, DIVINE GRACE.

With this description comp. ch. 2 : 37–47 and notes; especially for consideration of primitive practice of community of goods. Here the description is repeated, partly as an evidence of the divine answer to prayer, and of the spiritual quickening produced by the threatening of the Sanhedrim, and partly as an introduction to and explanation of the story of Ananias and Sapphira in ch. 5.

32, 33. Of them that had believed. That is, of the new converts. They entered into and shared the life of the company which they joined,

32 And the multitude of them that believed were
of one heart[b] and of one soul: neither said any *of them*
that aught of the things which he possessed was his
own; but they[c] had all things common.
33 And with great power[d] gave the apostles witness[e] of the resurrection of the Lord Jesus: and great
grace[f] was upon them all.
34 Neither was there any among them that lacked:
for as many as were possessors of lands or houses,
sold them, and brought the prices of the things that
were sold,
35 And laid[g] *them* down at the apostles' feet: and
distribution[h] was made unto every man according as
he had need.
36 And Joses, who by the apostles was surnamed
Barnabas (which is, being interpreted, The son of
consolation), a Levite, *and* of the country of Cyprus,
37 Having land, sold *it*, and brought the money,
and laid *it* at the apostles' feet.

---

b Rom. 15 : 5, 6; 2 Cor. 13 : 11; Phil. 2 : 2; 1 Pet. 3 : 8....c ch. 2 : 44....d ch. 1 : 8....e ch. 1 : 22; Luke 11 : 48, 49....f John 1 : 16.... g ver. 37; ch. 5 : 2....h ch. 2 : 45; 6 : 1.

---

and which Luke has already described.—**Were in heart and in life one.** In *heart* is in affection; in *life* (ψυχή) is in their inward life, their experience. See Matt. 22 : 37, note. The true unity of the members of the church is not in outward circumstance, nor in intellectual ability, but in heart sympathy and in spiritual life. This unifying power of Christ in the heart, overcoming all obstacles of race, nation, language, sex and condition, is exemplified in John 11 : 52; Phil. 2 : 2, 3; Col. 3 : 11; Rev. 7 : 9.—**Neither said any of them that aught of the things which he possessed was his own.** Not "Did not regard it as his own" (*Barnes*); on the contrary, the language implies that the individual ownership was recognized in the company, but the owner did not claim its sole use. "This very expression assumes that *ownership* was not entirely abolished." — (*Bengel.*) — **And with great power gave the apostles witness of the resurrection of the Lord Jesus.** This was the special theme of their early ministry (ch. 2 : 28–32; 3 : 21; 4 : 2, 10; 10 : 39, 40; 13 : 30–37; 17 : 31, 32); the witness was given by the apostles because they were eye-witnesses of the fact (ver. 20; ch. 1 : 22); the *power* was that conferred on them and on their word by the special gift of the Holy Spirit (1 Thess. 1 : 5). Three evidences of this gift are here mentioned, and always accompany a true revival of religion in the church, viz.: (1) unity in Christian life, (2) practical charity, (3) power in preaching the Gospel.—**And great grace was upon them all.** The same word rendered *grace* (χάρις) here is rendered favor in ch. 2 : 47. It may mean here either *favor* with the people (*Olshausen*, *Grotius*), or *grace* from God (*Alford*, *Meyer*, *Hackett*). The latter is the more probable meaning. See John 1 : 16, note.

34, 35. For neither was there any among them that lived in want * * * * And there was distributed to every one according as each had need. *For*, not rendered in our English version, indicates in this verse the reason for the statement in the preceding; their practical charity made them the recipients of both divine grace and popular favor (Matt. 10 : 42; Luke 6 : 38). Observe the implication that the rich did not give everything away, for then they would themselves have lived in want; and that there was not a miscellaneous distribution, nor, in strictness of speech, a communism, but only a liberal distribution wherever there was need. If, however, there is danger of misinterpreting the apostolic example, there is greater danger of losing the apostolic spirit. Calvin's note is applicable to our times: "They sold in times past their possessions, there reigneth at this day an insatiable desire to buy. Love made that common to the poor and needy which was proper to every man; such is the unnaturalness of some men now, that they envy the poor the common dwelling on the earth, and the common use of water, air and sky." See 1 John 3 : 17, 18.—**Lands or houses.** The one implies estate in the country, the other, perhaps, in the city; the earlier cities being very compact, and the houses having little or no ground attached to them.—**And brought the prices.** But not necessarily the full price (ch. 5 : 4, 8).—**Laid them down at the apostles' feet.** Alford supposes that "the apostles, like the prætor, probably sat upon a raised seat, on the step of which, at their feet, the money was laid in token of reverence." This seems to me purely gratuitous, and not in accordance with the simplicity of the early church. Did the apostles carry the raised seat with them from house to house? More probably the expression is simply figurative, to signify that the disciples committed the offering wholly to the apostles' care; the figure is taken from the oriental custom of laying offerings before the footstool of kings.

36, 37. Joses, who by the apostles was surnamed Barnabas. He is first mentioned here; whether a personal disciple of Jesus Christ is not known; he brought Paul to the apostles (ch. 9 : 27), and was afterward a fellow-laborer with him (ch. 11 : 25–30; 12 : 25; 13; 14; 15; Gal. 2 : 1–9).—**A Levite.** Therefore, under the old Mosaic Law, not entitled to a share in the original distribution of the land (Numb. 18 : 20–24; Deut. 10 : 8, 9). But after the captivity the Levites began to possess land (Jer. 32 : 7), and probably did so generally at this time.—**Of the country of Cyprus.** For some account of this island, see ch. 11 : 19, note. The account of this sale and gift is given here as an introduction to, and in contrast with, the fraudulent gift of Ananias and Sapphira.

CHAPTER V.

BUT a certain man named Ananias, with Sapphira,
his wife, sold a possession,
2 And kept back *part* of the price, his wife also
being privy *to it*, and brought[i] a certain part, and laid
it at the apostles' feet.
3 But Peter said, Ananias, why hath Satan[j] filled
thine heart to lie to[k] the Holy Ghost, and to keep[l]
back *part* of the price of the land?
4 Whiles it remained, was it not thine own? and
after it was sold, was it not in thine own power? Why
hast thou conceived this thing in thine heart? thou
hast not lied unto men, but unto[m] God.

i ch. 4 : 34, 37 . . . . j Luke 22 : 3 . . . . k verse 9 . . . . l Numb. 30 : 2 ; Deut. 23 : 21 ; Eccles. 5 : 4 . . . . m Ps. 139 : 4.

Ch. 5 : 1-16. SIN AND PUNISHMENT OF ANANIAS AND SAPPHIRA, AND THE RESULT. "THE HYPOCRITES IN HEART HEAP UP WRATH" (Job 36 : 13).—EFFECT OF THE JUDGMENT: IT REPELS HYPOCRITES (13); ATTRACTS BELIEVERS (14); EXTENDS THE FAME OF THE GOSPEL (15, 16).

The time of this occurrence is unknown; probably somewhere between A. D. 32 and A. D. 34. The sin and punishment of Ananias and Sapphira adds to the power because to the purity of the church, and leads to the second attempted persecution of the apostles, who are imprisoned and scourged, but, owing to the counsel of Gamaliel, are then released.

1, 2. But a certain man. *But* marks the transition from Barnabas to Ananias. Such contrasts between the true and false occur, both in God's word and in his providence, to teach the truth more clearly; *e. g.*, Saul and David, the publican and the Pharisee, the prodigal son and the elder brother, the five wise and the five foolish virgins. There is no ground for the hypothesis that Ananias was a person of special prominence in the church; rather we may assume that, like Simon Magus (ch. 8 : 18, 19), he endeavored to purchase prominence with his money.—**Ananias with Sapphira his wife.** *Ananias* means Jehovah is gracious; *Sapphira* either sapphire or beautiful. "Their names were favorable and beautiful; their principles bad."—(*Bengel.*)—**His wife also being privy to it.** The falsehood of these two differs from that of Peter (Matt. 26 : 69-75) not only in the motive—covetousness in the one case, fear in the other—not only in the sin indicated—hypocrisy in the one case, heedless self-confidence in the other—but also in its very nature; the falsehood of Ananias and Sapphira was deliberate and preconcerted, that of Peter unpremeditated. "It argues an extreme hardness of heart when two persons, united by the tenderest bonds, plan a lie together, and engage to support each other in carrying it out."—(*Arnot.*) There is small ground for the hypothesis of Henry that they sold the land intending to devote all the proceeds to the poor, "but when the money was received their heart failed them, and they kept back part of the price." Rather the inference is that the whole transaction was a deliberate and concerted falsehood.—**And laid it at the apostles' feet.** The indications are that this was done at and as part of a religious service. It was in an assembly of the believers; at a gathering which lasted three hours (ver. 7); apparently at a recognized meeting of the church (ver. 11); the object of the two, credit in the church, could have been attained only by a *public* offering; and the lie is characterized as one told to God, not to man (ver. 4). "Before the face of the apostles, therefore, and in the midst of that solemn assembly, engaged in prayer, must this lie have been uttered, for otherwise the object of this husband and wife could not have been gained."—(*Baumgarten.*)

3, 4. Why hath Satan filled thy heart? Observe, the cause of the overt act is a heart *filled* with sin. For that is why Satan fills the heart. See Matt. 15 : 19, and Gal. 5 : 19-21.—**To lie to the Holy Ghost.** There is no intimation that Ananias had directly uttered a falsehood, as did his wife (ver. 8); a lie in action may be as criminal as a spoken lie. They lied to the Holy Ghost, not merely because they lied to the church, which was the body of Christ, the temple of God, and filled with the Holy Ghost, or to the apostles, who were inspired by the Holy Ghost, and whose divine power of insight they ignored, but because the offering was made, not to the apostles, nor to the church, but to God, and the act was thus a direct falsehood addressed to Him.—**While it remained was it not thine own?** Clearly the communism of the early church was purely voluntary. Ananias and Sapphira could have retained the land, or the price, or any part of it. The sin consisted in offering a part *as the whole.* How Peter knew that only a part was offered is not stated. It may have been by natural means, or by divine revelation.—**Why hast thou conceived this thing in thy heart?** Literally, *Why hast thou put in thy heart this thing?* For meaning, see Dan. 1 : 8; Mal. 2 : 2. We are not responsible for suggestions which Satan addresses to our heart; he addressed evil suggestions to Christ (Matt. 4 : 3, 6, 9). We are culpable if we put them in our heart, *i. e.*, give them admission and harbor them.—**Thou hast not lied unto men, but unto God.** That is, Not merely unto men. See Mark 9 : 37; John 12 : 44. It is clear from this sentence that the death punishment was not inflicted for a lie told to men, and the warning of this death is not merely, nor mainly, against

5 And Ananias, hearing these words,[n] fell down, and gave up the ghost: and great fear[o] came on all them that heard these things.
6 And the young men arose, wound[p] him up, and carried *him* out, and buried *him*.
7 And it was about the space of three hours after, when his wife, not knowing what was done, came in.
8 And Peter answered unto her, Tell me whether ye sold the land for so much? And she said, Yea, for so much.
9 Then Peter said unto her, How is it that ye have agreed[q] together to tempt the Spirit of the Lord? behold, the feet of them which have buried thy husband *are* at the door, and shall carry thee out.

n vers. 10, 11.... o Ps. 64 : 9.... p John 19 : 40.... q verse 2; Ps. 50 : 18.

falsehood. See below. The sin was the lie *to God*. "Hypocrisy makes a sober jest of God and religion."—(*Pope.*) In Peter's language here Bengel sees a confirmation of the doctrine of the Deity and Personality of the Holy Spirit; His Deity it certainly demonstrates, but how does it bear on the question of His distinct personality?

5, 6. And Ananias hearing these words, fell down and gave up the ghost. Those who criticise the severity of the punishment find fault with God. It appears unduly severe only if our consciences fail to judge aright the heinousness of the sin. Observe, (1) That no sentence is pronounced by Peter. There is nothing even to indicate that he anticipated the death of Ananias. The death of Sapphira he foretold (ver. 9), but he did not inflict. There is, therefore, nothing in this account to justify the church in inflicting temporal punishments. (2.) The death of Ananias, if it stood alone, might, perhaps, be attributed to the natural effect of shame and remorse at the public exposure of his hypocrisy. Coupled with the immediately succeeding death of his wife, it is impossible for an unprejudiced reader to doubt that it was the special and direct infliction of God. In this the punishment of Ananias and Sapphira differs from that of Achan (Josh., ch. 7), with whose sin theirs has been compared.—**And the young men.** Literally, *The younger men.* Not a class of officers, for there is no evidence of any such class in the primitive church, but simply the younger of the men in the assembly. The religious service, whatever it was, continued; a few of the younger men carried out and buried the corpse.—**Wound him up.** Enveloped him for burial. It was customary among the Jews to bury the body in the same garment used in life, or in one resembling it. The body of Ananias was probably wrapped in his own burnoose. That it was not taken to his home is indicated by his wife's ignorance of what had occurred. The accompanying cut represents a body thus prepared for burial and attended by hired mourners; it represents the Moslem oriental burial custom, which is probably an exact copy of the ancient custom.—**And buried him.** It was, and in the East still is, customary among the Jews to bury soon after death, ordinarily on the same day, partly because decomposition takes place rapidly in the warm climate of Palestine, partly because of the peculiar Jewish feeling respecting defilement

PREPARED FOR BURIAL.

from the dead (Numb. 19 : 11, etc.). Burial was probably hastened somewhat in this case, and the body interred without the honors—washing, anointing, etc.—ordinarily paid to the dead (John 19 : 39, 40). Interments were outside the city walls; to take the corpse to the burial-place and inter it would therefore probably occupy the three hours referred to in the next verse; and not more than that, as no grave would have to be dug, entombment being generally in caves.

7, 8. About the space of three hours * * * came in. The implication is that she came into the Christian assembly, which was still in session.—**Answered her.** Possibly, Answered her salutation; but the phrase is a common Hebraistic one, indicating simply the commencement of a speech or of conversation (Job 3 : 2, marginal reading; 6 : 1, etc.; Isaiah 21 : 9).—**Tell me,** etc. Thorough trial precedes judgment, and an opportunity is given for repentance.—**Yea, for so much.** The lie in action leads to a lie spoken. "A willful falsehood is a cripple and cannot stand alone. It is easy to tell one lie, hard to tell but one lie."—(*Fuller.*)

9-11. That ye have agreed together to tempt the Spirit of the Lord. That is, to make trial; to prove whether there is a divine Spirit, and what is his knowledge. Comp. Judges 6 : 39; Luke 11 : 16; 20 : 23. Their action involved a practical if not a theoretical disbelief in

10 Then fell[r] she down straightway at his feet, and
yielded up the ghost: and the young men came in, and
found her dead, and, carrying *her* forth, buried *her* by
her husband.
11 And great[s] fear came upon all the church, and
upon as many as heard these things.

12 And by the hands of the apostles were many[t]
signs and wonders wrought among the people (and
they were all with one accord in Solomon's porch.
13 And[u] of the rest durst no man join himself to
them: but[v] the people magnified them.

r verse 5....s ch. 2:43....t ch. 4:30; Rom. 15:19; Heb. 2:4....u John 12:42....v ch. 4:21.

the presence and omniscience of the Spirit of God, to whom they had offered a part, seeking credit for the whole.—**The feet of them * * * are at the door.** Not that Peter heard the tread of the young men returning; not even, necessarily, that they had just then returned; they may have been standing without some time. The *feet* is a common expression for the person of a messenger or carrier (Isaiah 52:7; Nah. 1:15; Rom. 10:15).—**Shall carry thee out.** This is not a sentence of death. Peter speaks as a prophet, not as a judge; he does not give sentence, he foretells.—**Buried her by her husband.** Perhaps both were laid in the family tomb. Being apparently a family of competence, they would probably have possessed such a tomb.—**And great fear came upon the church.** Fear of the Lord, which is the beginning of knowledge (Prov. 1:7).

THE SIN OF ANANIAS AND SAPPHIRA.—This was not *merely* falsehood, and the warning is not *primarily* to the liar (see on ver. 4); nor was it the same as that of Achan or Gehazi (Josh., ch. 7; 2 Kings 5:20-24), with both of which it has been compared; nor was it merely the sin of attempting to serve two masters (Matt. 6:24), though Augustine's comment is certainly pertinent, "Woe to the double mind that shares God's own; half to him, half to the devil." It was the first incursion of Pharisaism in the primitive church, the first manifestation of that spirit of hypocrisy, the essence of which is lying to God, which does its righteousness to be seen of men (Matt. 6:1), against which Christ had so earnestly warned his followers in the Sermon on the Mount (comp. Luke 12:1) and inveighed in his last words in the Temple (Matt., ch. 23). Of all sins, this is the worst; "the only sin that cannot be forgiven is hypocrisy" (*Hazlitt*); of all sins, it is, to the church, the most insidious and the most dangerous; "when religion is in request, it (hypocrisy) is the chief malady of the church and numbers die of it, though, because it is a subtle and inward evil, it be little perceived."—(*Bishop Hall.*) The punishment of Ananias and Sapphira contrasts but does not conflict with Luke 9:52–56; for there the disciples proposed to destroy a village which, ignorant of Christ's true character, refused him hospitality because he was a Jew; here God struck dead professed disciples who did their works to be seen of men. He has infinite patience with ignorance and prejudice, but not with deliberate hypocrisy and false pretence. It teaches the same lesson as the punishment inflicted in the cases of Achan (Josh., ch. 7), Nadab and Abihu (Lev. 10:1, 2), Korah and his company (Numb. 16:31-33), the man who violated the Sabbath (Numb. 15:32-36), Uzzah (2 Sam. 6:6-8), and others, all of them illustrating Rom. 11:22 and 1 Pet. 4:17. It is a solemn testimony to God's abhorrence of all false pretence in his service, and symbolically teaches that the end of hypocrisy is death.

12. In the following verses (12-14) Luke, for the third time, gives, in a brief summary, a description of the state of the church, adding here some account of the excitement in the community. Comp. ch. 2:41–47; 4:31–35.—**Many portents and signs.** The first word strictly implies something foreboding of the future, as the death of Ananias and Sapphira, warned of a future judgment against all hypocrisy in the church; the second word indicates any event constituting a sign of the divine presence. See 2:22, note.—**And they were all with one accord.** *Accord*, not only in being there, but in the purpose with which they were there, viz., to preach the gospel. See ch. 1:14, note. The "all" are here the apostles (so Alford, Olshausen, Hackett); clearly not the people, nor, as Bengel and Meyer, all believers, for the *believers* are not the subject of the sentence, nor is it reasonable to believe that all, to the number of several thousands, would have assembled in Solomon's porch, nor would there have been any advantage in their so doing; this would indeed have impeded the work of the ministry.—**In Solomon's porch.** For description of Temple and plan, see John 2:19, 20; for illustration, Matt., ch. 24. Solomon's porch, minutely described by Josephus (Ant. 15:11, § 5), consisted of a nave and two aisles, that toward the Temple being open, that toward the country closed by a wall. The breadth of the centre aisle was 45 feet; of the side aisles, 30 feet from centre to centre of the pillars; their height was 50 feet, that of the centre aisle 100 feet; the total length was 600 feet. The roof of cedar, elaborately carved, was supported by 162 columns, arranged in four rows, forty in each row, the two additional pillars standing apparently at the end of the bridge leading over the ravine which separated the site of the Temple from that of Herod's palace. The floor was a mosaic of many-colored stones. Josephus says that this porch was built by Solomon, hence its name. But this statement is very doubtful, there is no evidence to support it, and the better

14 And believers were the more added to the Lord, multitudes [w] both of men and women.)
15 Insomuch that they brought forth the sick into the streets, and laid *them* on beds and couches, that at the least the shadow of Peter passing by might overshadow some of them.

w ch. 2 : 47.

SOLOMON'S PORCH.

opinion is that it was built in the time and under the direction of Herod the Great, by whom the entire Temple was rebuilt. The accompanying illustration, from a sketch by Mr. A. L. Rawson, is designed to present rather an aid to the imagination of the reader than any absolute information as to the exact architectural style of the structure, of which, of course, there are no remains. The object of the apostles in going to this porch was to preach the Gospel. See ver. 25, and comp. ch. 3 : 12, etc., and Luke 19 : 47.

13, 14. And of the rest durst no one join himself to them. Alford's interpretation seems to me extraordinary, "Of the rest, whether believers or not, none dared to *join himself to*, as being one of or equal to them (the apostles); but, so far was this from being the case, that the very people (the multitude) magnified them." This seems to me to be inconsistent (1) with the context. The *rest* is in contrast with the *all* of the preceding verse; and they (the disciples) were all in Solomon's porch, and of the rest (not disciples) durst no one, etc. (2.) With the free spirit of the early church, in which there was great reverence for the Lord, but no such fear of man, against which the apostolic instructions especially guard. (3.) With the meaning of the Greek verb rendered *join to* (κολλάω), which does not carry with it any idea of official or even necessarily personal equality and companionship (Luke 15 : 15; Acts 8 : 29; 9 : 26; 1 Cor. 6 : 16, 17). (4.) With the express language of the next verse, which implies that this very fear increased the number of believers. I understand, then, *the rest* to refer, as in Rom. 11 : 7; Ephes. 2 : 3; 1 Thess. 4 : 13; 5 : 6, to those without the church and the covenant of God, and the meaning to be that, after the death of Ananias and Sapphira, none such dared to join themselves to the church under pretence of an experience of faith and consecration. Nor is this inconsistent with the further declaration that the people, even those who did not heartily accept and consecrate themselves to the Lord, still magnified the apostles and the church, both for their power and their grace. So Arnot, "Those who were not of them dared not pretend to be of

16 There came also a multitude *out* of the cities
round about unto Jerusalem, bringing sick [x] folks, and
them which were vexed with unclean spirits: and they [y]
were healed every one.
17 Then the high priest rose up, and all they that
were with him, (which is the sect of the Sadducees,[z])
and were filled with indignation,
18 And laid their hands on the apostles, and put them
in the common prison.[a]

x Mark 16 : 17, 18; John 14 : 12. . . . y 1 Cor. 12 : 9, 28. . . . z ch. 4 : 1, 2. . . . a ch. 12 : 5-7; 16 : 23-27.

them. The stroke of judgment scared the hypocrites; but believers came flowing in like a stream."—**But believers were the more added to the Lord.** The *more* because of this fear; it repelled hypocrites; it attracted believers.—**Multitudes of both men and women.** *Multitudes*, for then, as now, religious life flows and ebbs in currents; *men*, because the strong in their pride were bowed down; *women*, because the Gospel both owns, and elevates, and enfranchises woman.

15, 16. Insomuch that they brought forth the sick. Not that the believers did this. The verb is impersonal and the meaning is simply that the sick were brought forth.—**Into the streets.** Literally, the *broad* streets. The word (πλατείας) is used in contrast with lanes in Luke 14 : 21.—**Upon couches and beds.** The former (κλίνη) was, in strictness of speech, a high bedstead, resembling a modern, so-called French bedstead (see Smith's *Dict. of Ant.*, art. Lectus); the latter (κράββατος) was, in form, like our modern trundle-bed. See illustration in Mark (ch. 2 : 4). Here, however, the words are probably used only pictorially, to indicate to the imagination various kinds of beds, as various classes of people.—**That at least the shadow of Peter passing by might overshadow some of them.** I do not see the least evidence that any were thus healed by his shadow. Such healing does not consort with God's method of cure in other cases. I have endeavored to show that in the apparently analogous case of the woman with an issue of blood, she was healed, not by touching Christ's garment, but by his conscious forth-putting of power. See Mark 5 : 25-34, notes. In Acts 19 : 12, where the sick were healed by handkerchiefs brought from Paul, the implication is that they could not conveniently come to him, nor he to them, and that the cure was wrought by his conscious act. It is not to the purpose to say, as Alford, "Cannot the Creator Spirit work with any instruments, or with none, as pleases Him?" The question is not what he *can* do, but what the Scripture asserts that he *has* done, and there is no such assertion here. Nor is this implied by the connection, as Baumgarten argues. For we are not told it "in the midst of a passage which evidently is intended to convey a notion of the infinite miraculous operations of the Apostle," but in one intended to convey a suggestion of the effects of the apostolic miracles on the entire community; these repelled some, attracted others, awoke a superstitious trust in the magical efficacy of Peter's shadow in some, and a lively faith in the power of God in and through him, in others. The next verse, which asserts that he healed those who were brought to *him*, rather implies that those who trusted in his shadow were not healed.—**Out of the cities round about.** This indicates the extent to which the fame of the Gospel spread, and also that some time elapsed before the second arrest of the apostles described in the next verse.—**Unclean spirits.** On demoniacal possession, see note on Matt., ch. 8 : 28-34, Vol. I, p. 123.

Ch. 5 : 17-42. IMPRISONMENT, MIRACULOUS LIBERATION, TRIAL, DEFENCE, AND FINAL DELIVERANCE OF THE APOSTLES. THE TRIUMPHS OF CHRISTIANITY ENRAGE ITS DETERMINED FOES (vers. 17, 33).—THE POWER OF THE LORD TO SUCCOUR HIS OWN (vers. 19, 23, 34-40).—THE MISSION OF THE MINISTRY (20).—THE GOSPEL POPULAR WITH THE UNPREJUDICED (26).—THE INCONSISTENCY OF THE WICKED (28, with Matt. 27 : 25).—THE APOSTLES' CREED (29-32).—A CHRIST-LIKE GLORYING IN SHAME (41).

17. But the high-priest rising up. The effect of the apostolic miracles on the ecclesiastical dignitaries is stated in contrast with the popular enthusiasm. This "rising up" was not to speak before the council, for that was not yet assembled; the language is simply expressive of the high-priest's anger. Whether Caiaphas or Annas is meant is uncertain; ch. 4 : 6 indicates the latter. See note there and on Luke 3 : 2.—**And all they that were with him.** That is, who agreed with him in feeling and doctrine, as explained by the next clause.—**Who, being of the sect of the Sadducees, were filled with heat.** The word (ζῆλος) rendered *indignation*, is from a verb meaning *to boil*, and is used in the N. T. in both a good and a bad sense, being rendered by *zeal* (John 2 : 17; Rom. 10 : 2; Col. 4 : 13), *fervent mind* (2 Cor. 7 : 7), *envy* (Acts 13 : 45; Rom. 13 : 13, etc.) and *jealousy* (2 Cor. 11 : 2). The Sadducees denied both Spirit and resurrection (see Matt. 3 : 7, note); and that these were Sadducees is stated in explanation of their special heat against the apostles, the central truth of whose preaching was the resurrection of Jesus from the dead. It appears from Josephus (Antiq. 20 : 9, 1) that Sadducees were appointed to the office of high-priest; the son of Annas and nephew of Caiaphas, who was appointed shortly subsequent to these events, was a Sadducee; they were severe and vindictive in their judgments,

19 But the angel of the Lord by night opened the
prison doors, and brought them forth, and said,
20 Go, stand and speak in the temple to the people
all[b] the words[c] of this life.
21 And when they heard *that*, they entered into the
temple early in the morning, and taught. But[d] the
high priest came, and they that were with him, and
called the council together, and all the senate of the
children of Israel, and sent to the prison to have them
brought.
22 But when the officers came, and found them not
in the prison, they returned and told,
23 Saying, The prison truly found we shut with all
safety, and the keepers standing without before the
doors: but when we had opened, we found no man
within.

b Exod. 24 : 3....c John 6 : 63, 68; 17 : 8....d ch. 4 : 5, 6.

while the administration of the Pharisees was of a more conservative and humane character.

18. And laid their hands on the apostles. Not directly, but sending the Temple police to arrest them.—**And put them in a common prison.** Rather, *guard-house;* probably a room connected with the Temple. Imprisonment was not practiced among the Greeks as a punishment, and rarely among the Romans or the Jews. In this case the apostles were simply confined until the morning should give opportunity for convening the Sanhedrim for their trial. On the Roman prisons, see Acts 12 : 4 and 16 : 24.

19, 20. But an angel of the Lord by night. Some time during the night. Observe, not *the* angel of the Lord, a phrase used in the O. T., as I believe, of One only, viz., the Son of God himself, but *an* angel, *i. e.*, a messenger. A similar supernatural deliverance is described in much greater detail in ch. 12. It has been objected to as a needless interposition of God, since the divine protection did not prevent the immediate rearrest of the apostles (ver. 26). The same objection applies with equal force to the falling back to the ground of the soldiers who came to arrest Jesus (John 18 : 6), to the deliverance of Peter, who was subsequently crucified, and indeed to every divine deliverance from death, since death is finally the lot of all. In the present case the deliverance of the apostles gave them both opportunity and courage to plead for the truth before the Sanhedrim.—**And brought them forth and said.** "The angel opened the prison, and carried to the prisoners the Master's message that they should continue to preach the Gospel; but the angel himself does not preach. You never find an angel calling on sinners to repent."—(*Arnot.*)—**All the words of this life.** By *this life* is meant, not the earthly life, for this had not been the theme of the apostles' preaching; nor the future life merely, though in a sense both would be included; but the spiritual and therefore immortal life, the life which Jesus Christ came to bring to light (2 Tim. 1 : 10). The expression should not be rendered, as Bengel, *These words of life.* See Winer, § 346. Observe the theme of the apostles' ministry: instruction respecting immortal life, both here and hereafter, and respecting Jesus Christ as the One who both manifests it and renders it possible to those that believe in him.

21. They entered into the temple at early morn. "The people of the East commence the day much earlier than is customary with us. The arrangements of life there adjust themselves to the character of the climate. During a great part of the year in Palestine, the heat becomes oppressive soon after sunrise, and the inhabitants therefore assign their most important duties and labors to the early hours of the day. Nothing is more common at the present time than to see the villagers going forth to their employment in the fields while the night and the day are still struggling with each other. Worship is often performed in the synagogue at Jerusalem before the sun appears above Olivet." —(*Hackett.*)—**But the high-priest came.** To the Temple. This being a large collection of buildings and courts, covering many acres, the apostolic teaching might have been going on in Solomon's porch, and the high-priest and the Sanhedrim, assembling in one of the side buildings, have known nothing of it.—**And they that were with him.** This indicates, if not a packed meeting, at least a preconcerted movement on the part of the Sadducees to condemn and destroy the apostles.—**And called the council together.** The Sanhedrim. See, on its character and customs, Matt. 26 : 57–68, note, Vol. I, p. 298.—**And all the senate.** Literally, *Eldership.* These were the lay members of the council (see Matt. 16 : 21, note). The Greek word here rendered *senate* (*γερουσία*) occurs nowhere else in the N. T. Alford suggests that it may be borrowed from the form of words in which they were summoned.

22-24. The prison truly we found shut in all security. That is, We found it closed and securely locked.—**And the guards standing at the door.** Probably Temple police, left to keep watch.—**Now when the high-priest,** etc. There is some uncertainty as to the meaning. Tischendorf omits the word *high-priest;* Alford retains it. *The captain of the Temple* is the chief of the Temple police, present probably in his official capacity; perhaps he was called to explain the disappearance of the prisoners.—**Doubted of them.** That is, Were in perplexity concerning the report thus made to them.—**Whereunto this would grow.** That is, What would come of it. They were probably equally perplexed to understand how the apostles could

24 Now when the high priest and the [e] captain of the
temple and the chief priests heard these things, they
doubted of them whereunto this would grow.
25 Then came one and told them, saying, Behold,
the men whom ye put in prison are standing in the
temple, and teaching the people.
26 Then went the captain with the officers, and
brought them without violence: for they [f] feared the
people, lest they should have been stoned.

27 And when they had brought them, they set *them*
before the council: and the high priest asked them,
28 Saying, Did not we [g] straitly command you, that
ye should not teach in this name? and, behold, ye have
filled Jerusalem with your doctrine, and intend to bring
this man's blood [h] upon us.
29 Then Peter and the *other* apostles answered and
said, We [i] ought to obey God rather than men.

e ch. 4 : 1.... f Matt. 21 : 26.... g ch. 4 : 18.... h ch. 2 : 23, 36 ; 7 : 52 ; Matt. 27 : 25.... i ch. 4 : 19.

have made their escape, and to foresee what would be the result thereof. Observe how the circumstance as attested by this examination demonstrated the supernatural character of the deliverance; the prison doors securely fastened, the prison guards before the door, and yet the prisoners released.

25, 26. Then came one. Apparently unconscious of the perplexity of the council, but surprised to find the imprisoned apostles publicly teaching in the temple. This fact demonstrated that they were not endeavoring to escape, and yet that they had no intention of yielding to the prohibition of the council.—**The captain with the officers.** With the subordinate police.—**For they feared the people.** One of the many indications in the N. T. that Christ and his truth were attractive to the common people, and that the opposition was instigated and persecution inaugurated by interested rulers. Men are not by nature *wholly* averse to the truth; they are attracted by it, and are opposed to it only as it opposes their self-interest or their pride.

27, 28. We straitway commanded you. So Alford and Tischendorf read, instead of interrogating, as in our English version. The language is literally, *With proclamation we proclaimed to you, i. e.*, officially, as magistrates.—**In this name * * * this man's blood.** Observe that the priests do not speak the name of Jesus. Was this a superstitious dread, an unconscious feeling that it might be the Messiah whom they had put to death? or merely the reluctance of murderers to speak directly of their victim? or simply a sign of their contempt? Contrast Peter's glorying in the name of Jesus Christ (30, 31).—**Ye have filled Jerusalem with your teaching.** Not, *doctrine.* The Jerusalemites had not generally accepted the truth of Christianity; but all Jerusalem was full of the fame of the apostles' teaching. Not the *truth*, but the *report* of the truth, filled Jerusalem.—**And intend to bring this man's blood upon us.** Not, as Alford seems to imply, You intend to incite the people to vengeance; there had been absolutely nothing in the apostolic teaching to give color to such a charge or occasion for such a fear; nor, You intend to bring us into divine judgment and punishment; for apostolic preaching could not do this; but, You intend to hold us before the people, answerable for the blood of Jesus, the Messiah of Israel; for this was the effect of Peter's preaching (ch. 2 : 36; 3 : 14; 5 : 30; ver. 30). Publicly, before Pilate, these same priests had taken Christ's blood upon them (Matt. 27 : 25), agreeing to be answerable for it, both as before God and man. In a true sense the apostles would fain have brought this man's blood on the rulers for the cleansing of their sin (Rom. 3 : 25; Ephes. 1 : 7; Col. 1 : 14); but they would not accept it.

29. The address which follows is almost in the nature of a syllogism; its logic is unanswerable. (1) We ought to obey God rather than man; (2) Israel's God has raised and exalted Jesus, whom ye slew; (3) by direct commission and by the impartation of the Holy Ghost we are directed to bear witness of these truths.—**Peter.** As spokesman.—**And the apostles.** Standing with him, as in ch. 2 : 14, and by their countenance and acquiescence accepting him as their representative.—**We ought to obey God rather than men.** The verb is impersonal, and might be rendered, One ought to obey. The apostle declares a general principle, not a special obligation resting peculiarly upon them. It is one which the rulers could not gainsay without denying one of the fundamental principles of the Hebrew theocracy (Gen. 3 : 17; 1 Sam. 15 : 24; Dan. 3 : 17, 18; 6 : 10). Parallel is Socrates' declaration in his defence (Apology 29), "Men of Athens, I honor and love you, but I shall obey God rather than you;" and again, "If when, as I conclude and imagine, God orders me to fulfill the philosopher's mission of searching into myself and other men, I were to desert my post through fear of death, or any other fear, that would indeed be strange, and I might justly be arraigned in court for denying the existence of the gods, if I disobeyed the oracle because I was afraid of death."—(*Jowett's Translation*, I : 327.) Observe that while this precept recognizes a higher than human law, and gives to the individual conscience a right of *disobedience* to the human in obedience to what is recognized as divine, and while the N. T. bases the duty of obedience to human law on the higher duty of obedience to the divine (Rom. 13 : 1, 2), neither by precept nor practice did the apostles justify *resistance* to human law in the name of God. They fled from persecution

30 The God of our fathers raised up Jesus, whom ye
slew and hanged[j] on a tree.
31 Him hath God exalted[k] with his right hand *to be*
a Prince[l] and a Saviour,[m] for to give repentance to
Israel, and forgiveness of sins.
32 And we are his witnesses[n] of these things; and
so is also the Holy Ghost,[o] whom God hath given to
them that obey him.
33 When they heard *that*, they[p] were cut *to the*
heart, and took counsel to slay them.

j Gal. 3 : 13; 1 Pet. 2 : 24....k Phil. 2 : 9....l Isa. 9 : 6....m Matt. 1 : 21....n Luke 24 : 48....o ch. 2 : 4....p ch. 7 : 54.

(Matt. 10 : 23; 2 Cor. 11 : 32, 33), but never resisted it (1 Pet. 2 : 22, 23).

30, 31. The God of our fathers. Peter still, as always heretofore, speaks as a Jew, and to them as Jews, ranking himself with them, and treating Christianity as God's gift to Israel in fulfillment of his covenant with that nation (ver. 31). Not until later did the apostles grow into the faith that it was equally for Gentile and Jew (Rom. 3 : 22, 29).—**Whom ye slew, hanging upon a tree.** He brings clearly before them the double act, (1) murder, for they coerced the death sentence from Pilate; (2) the means employed, the disgraceful Gentile cross.—**Him, a Prince and a Saviour, God hath exalted by his right hand.** On the meaning of the word (ἀρχηγός) rendered *prince*, see ch. 3 : 15. For its use in the O. T. as a title of the Messiah, see Dan. 8 : 25; 9 : 25; Isaiah 9 : 6; Ezek. 34 : 24. Here the double office of Christ is recognized, as King or Leader, to be obeyed and followed, and as Saviour, bringing redemption by his blood. The language, *by his right hand*, refers the glory of Christ's exaltation and of his kingly and mediatorial character to the Father; it is by the God of Israel that Jesus is made prince and Saviour (Heb. 1 : 8, 9). Observe the difference between the translation above and that of our English version, which is incorrect. It is not *Exalted him to be a prince and Saviour*, but *Him, who is a prince and Saviour, God hath exalted.*—**To give repentance to Israel and the remission of sins.** The object of the exaltation. The death, resurrection, ascension, and ever-living intercession are all part of one atoning work, having all the one object, the redemption of men from sin.—*To give repentance* is not merely to give an opportunity to exercise it, *i. e.*, to afford pardon to the repentant, but to impart the disposition to repentance. Both repentance and faith are represented in the N. T. as *gifts* of God, that all may be from Him (John 1 : 16; 16 : 7, 8; Acts 3 : 16; Rom. 2 : 4; Ephes. 2 : 8). *The remission of sins* is not merely pardon, *i. e.*, relief from the punishment of sin, but the cleansing of the soul from sin itself. See ch. 2 : 38, note and references.

32. And we are his witnesses. Christ's witnesses, *i. e.*, witnesses appointed by Christ. For the appointment see Luke 24 : 47–50, and observe in the parallel between the language there and here, an incidental evidence of the authenticity of the two accounts, and an indication that Luke's Gospel and The Acts were by the same pen.—**Of these words.** Not *things*, a meaning sometimes, but I think incorrectly, given to the original (ῥῆμα). It is from a verb meaning to speak, and always signifies what is spoken. Here it may mean, either, as Alford, *words of history*, *i. e.*, We, the apostles, personally know and testify to the truth of these words which I, Peter, have just spoken; or *words of prophecy*, *i. e.*, We are appointed as witnesses to the fulfillment of that holy word which foretold the coming of such a prince and Saviour; perhaps it is better to include both meanings.—**As also the Holy Ghost, whom God hath given to them that obey him.** The Holy Ghost was a witness to the truth of redemption, both by the special gifts conferred upon the apostles and early disciples—gifts of tongues, miracles, etc. (ch. 2 : 1-7; 10 : 45; 19 : 6; Mark 16 : 20); and by the internal witness afforded to the believer in his own experience (Rom. 8 : 16; Gal. 4 : 6; 1 John 3 : 24). Both kinds of testimony are included here, and on the three kinds of evidence here referred to Christianity rests; (1) *historical and human*, the testimony of credible witnesses to the life, character, miracles, death, and resurrection of Jesus of Nazareth; (2) *divine and external*, the evidence afforded by moral and spiritual changes in individuals and the community accounted for only by the presence of God's Spirit; (3) *divine and internal*, the inward realization of the Spirit of God in the heart of the believer. Observe the extent of the promise here, agreeing with the language of ch. 2 : 39; 3 : 25, etc.

Peter's address here exemplifies the fulfillment of Christ's promise in Matt. 10 : 19. I have already spoken above of its logical structure. Observe (1) *its brevity:* three sentences; (2) *its compactness and completeness;* it declares the crucifixion, resurrection, and ascension of our Lord, his double character as King and Saviour, his mission to cleanse away sin, the condition of receiving the benefits he affords, repentance which is itself his gift, and the twofold evidence of these truths, the human and the divine. It may fairly be called the true apostles' creed; (3) *its Christian spirit:* Courage without bitterness; in it Peter refuses obedience to the prohibition of the rulers, and accuses them of slaying on the cross the Prince of Israel, but preaches to them the Gospel of Salvation, and offers to them the gift of the Holy Ghost, on the conditions of repentance and faith.

34 Then stood there up one in the council, a Pharisee, named Gamaliel,[q] a doctor of the law, had in reputation among all the people, and commanded to put the apostles forth a little space;
35 And said unto them, Ye men of Israel, take heed to yourselves what ye intend to do as touching these men.

36 For before these days rose up Theudas, boasting himself to be somebody; to whom a number of men, about four hundred, joined themselves: who was slain; and all, as many as obeyed him, were scattered, and brought to nought.
37 After this man, rose up Judas of Galilee, in the days of the taxing, and drew away much people after

q ch. 22 : 3.

33. They were cut. The words *to the heart* are supplied by the translator. The original is literally *were sawed asunder*. It occurs only here and in Acts 7 : 54, and indicates intense exasperation. Observe the effect of faithful Gospel preaching; it pierces to the heart, either to awaken repentance and lead to forgiveness (ch. 2 : 37), or to awaken remorse and anger, and lead to an aggravation of guilt. — **Were taking counsel to slay them.** That is, were counseling how they might do it. To slay the apostles was not a simple matter, for (1) there was no ground on which to base a capital conviction. They could not be accused of blasphemy, for in all their addresses they had directed the reverence and allegiance of Israel to the God of their fathers. At most they could only be charged with delusion; (2) the people could not be incited to a mob as in the case of Stephen, for as yet the popular current was with the apostles (ver. 26); (3) capital punishment could only be inflicted by the Roman governor, and there was no charge that could be preferred to the Roman governor against Peter and the eleven.

34, 35. A Pharisee named Gamaliel. There were two Jewish rabbis of this name, Gamaliel I and II. Conybeare and Howson have confounded them, and attributed to Gamaliel I some anecdotes related of Gamaliel II. The one here mentioned, Gamaliel I, was a grandson of Hillel; in theology, his disciple, in spirit akin to Shammai, he occupied a position midway between the rigid and the liberal parties into which Phariseeism was divided. See Matt. 3 : 7, note. He insisted on the rigorous observance of the Sabbath, but decreed that all persons called on that day to assist in repelling invasion, or at inundations, fires, etc., or even at childbirth, might walk two thousand paces in any direction; he decreed the right to glean to the heathen poor; he sanctioned extending the greeting "Peace be with you" to the heathen; he modified the divorce laws, and alleviated the condition of women; he was himself a student of Greek literature; and to his influence may be attributed Paul's knowledge of the Greek poets (Acts 17 : 28; 1 Cor. 15 : 33; Titus 1 : 12), for he was Paul's preceptor (Acts 22 : 3). He died about 50 A. D. For an excellent account of him, see Kitto's *Cyclopedia;* on the character of his counsel here, see below.—**Had in reputation among all the people.** He was the first to receive the title of Rabban, and it is a Rabbinical proverb, "With the death of Gamaliel, reverence for the law ceased, and purity and abstinence died away."—**Commanded to put the apostles forth.** The ready acquiescence of the council indicates the degree of authority which he possessed. Lightfoot supposes him to have been the president.—**Take heed to yourselves.** Observe that the counsel of Gamaliel is addressed to their fears, not to their consciences; it is the counsel of the conservative and timid nature.

36, 37. The skill of Gamaliel is shown in his address. He begins by ranking the apostles with Theudas and Judas, impostors; he ends by suggesting that their work *may* be of God. If he had reversed the order, the result of his address might have been different.—**Theudas.** Josephus mentions an outbreak under a person of this name who pretended to be a prophet, and carried forth a multitude of followers to the Jordan. He was unexpectedly attacked, taken, and put to death by the Romans. This, however, occurred A. D. 44, eleven or twelve years after Gamaliel's speech. Skeptics have drawn from this the conclusion that Luke was mistaken in his date, and hence that his whole narrative is unreliable. It is far more probable that Josephus misplaced his Theudas; for he is often chargeable with inaccuracy. It is still more probable, however, that the two historians refer to two persons of the same name. Such impostures were not infrequent at the time, and the name was a common one. The attempt to identify this Theudas with some of the other leaders of outbreaks mentioned by Josephus (see Hackett) are not successful. It is, at all events, hardly possible, considering the time and the circumstances of the writing of the Acts, and the evident supervision of them by Paul, the pupil of Gamaliel, that a gross historical mistake should have been here put into his mouth, even if the writer be not regarded as inspired.—**Judas of Galilee.** According to Josephus, who is our only source of information respecting him or the insurrection, this man was a native of Gamala in Gaulonitis. At the time when Quirinus, the Cyrenius of Scripture, undertook to enroll the people of Judea, preparatory to taxation (Luke 2 : 2), this Judas incited to an unsuccessful revolt. His insurrection was of a semi-religious character, his followers claiming that God was the only ruler and lord. What became of Judas himself we do not know;

him: he[r] also perished; and all, *even* as many as
obeyed him, were dispersed.
38 And now I say unto you, Refrain from these men,
and let them alone: [s] for if this counsel or this work be
of men, it will come to nought.
39 But if[t] it be of God, ye cannot overthrow it; lest
haply ye be found even to fight[u] against God.
40 And to him they agreed: and when they had
called the apostles, and beaten[v] *them*, they commanded[w] that they should not speak in the name of Jesus,
and let them go.
41 And they departed from the presence of the council, rejoicing[x] that they were counted worthy to suffer
shame for his name.
42 And daily[y] in the temple, and in every house,
they ceased not to teach and preach Jesus Christ.

r Luke 13 : 1, 2....s Prov. 21 : 30; Isa. 8 : 10; Matt. 15 : 13....t Job 34 : 29; 1 Cor. 1 : 25....u ch. 9 : 5; 23 : 9....v Matt. 10 : 17.... w ch. 4 : 18....x Matt. 5 : 12; 2 Cor. 12 : 10; Phil. 1 : 29; James 1 : 2; 1 Pet. 4 : 13-16....y 2 Tim. 4 : 2.

but though his immediate followers were *dispersed*, the sect remained, denying the right of taxation to the Roman government, and giving rise to the Zealots and to subsequent insurrection. Thus Luke's discrimination between the followers of Theudas, "who came to naught," and those of Judas, who were "only dispersed," is strictly and noticeably accurate, an incidental evidence of the trustworthiness of the record.

38, 39. And for the present I say unto you, refrain from these men. That is, refrain from punishing them. The Greek word rendered *now* (τἀνῦν) is not a conjunction; it indicates present time, You regard these men as impostors; imposture comes to naught; for the present my advice is to leave them alone; if they are what you think, the imposture will soon run its course. This, in effect, is Gamaliel's advice. —**And let them alone.** Rather, *Suffer them to go on.*—**For if this counsel or this work.** *Counsel* signifies the general plan and purpose which the apostles were carrying out; *work*, the particular operations involved in executing it. The *counsel* was not comprehended by the Sanhedrim and only imperfectly by the apostles themselves. It really included the extension of Christianity over the whole world; for the counsel was God's. The work was the preaching of that Gospel then and there in Jerusalem, and the accompanying miracles; the work was the apostles', albeit God was working in them.—**Overthrow it.** Alford and Tischendorf both read *overthrow them.* The meaning is, If their purpose, what they are carrying out, and their work, what they are doing in carrying it out, are from God, they cannot be successfully resisted. There is some difference among scholars as to the construction of the Greek of ver. 39, but none as to its substantial meaning, as expressed in our English version.

40-42. And to him they agreed. In part; they did not, however, refrain from punishing the men, and would not have suffered them to go on with their work, if they could have prevented it.—**And beaten them.** Probably not with the scourge used in the Roman scourging. See Matt. 27 : 26-31, note. The verb there and here is different. Beating was employed by the Jews as a punishment. It was not improbably borrowed from the Egyptians, who used then, as now, the cruel bastinado. The offender is thrown on the ground and beaten, either on the back or on the soles of the feet. Jewish law confined the stripes to forty (Lev. 19 : 20; Deut. 22 : 18; 25 : 2, 3; 2 Cor. 11 : 24).—**That they were counted worthy to suffer shame for the name.** Not *his* name, but *the* name. The definite article attached, indicates it as the only name, the one above every other name, as the Scriptures are *the* writings, and the Bible is *the* book. Observe the contrast, counted *worthy* to suffer *shame*. Comp. Luke 16 : 15. "This influence of the holy name, which could transmute shame and suffering endured for its sake, into honor and rejoicing, greatly transcends all that

BASTINADO.

the name of Jehovah (in the O. T.) had ever accomplished. Here, therefore, we have actual demonstration that the name of Jesus is *the* name."—(*Baumgarten.*)—**And daily in the Temple, and from house to house.** The Greek is the same in ch. 2 : 46. See note there. —**To teach and to preach the Messiah, Jesus.** This language is not tautological. To *preach* Jesus is to proclaim to unbelievers that Jesus is the promised Messiah; to *teach* Jesus is to teach the believers the truths respecting him and his Messianic kingdom. See Christ's command in Matt. 28 : 19, 20, and notes there.

GAMALIEL'S COUNSEL.—The effect of Gama-

CHAPTER VI.

AND in those days, when the number of the disciples was multiplied, there arose a murmuring of
the Grecians[z] against the Hebrews, because their
widows were neglected in[a] the daily ministration.
2 Then the twelve called the multitude of the disciples *unto them*, and said, It[b] is not reason that we
should leave the word of God, and serve tables.
3 Wherefore, brethren, look[c] ye out among you
seven men of[d] honest report, full of the Holy Ghost
and wisdom, whom we may appoint over this business.
4 But we will[e] give ourselves continually to prayer,
and to the ministry of the word.

z ch. 9 : 29 ; 11 : 20 . . . . a ch. 4 : 35 . . . . b Exod. 18 : 17-26 . . . . c Deut. 1 : 13 . . . . d ch. 16 : 2 ; 1 Tim. 3 : 7, 8, 10 . . . . e 1 Tim. 4 : 15.

liel's counsel was the deliverance of the apostles, and this has led to a curiously false estimate of the man and his advice. He is commended as "right-minded in his judgment" (*Chrysostom*), and his speech as "humane, sensible, candid, and enlightened" (*Adam Clarke*), an "honest and intelligent argument" (*Conybeare* and *Howson*), "an instance of great shrewdness and prudence" (*Barnes*). He has been regarded as an apostle of the philosophy of toleration, and even as a defender of Christianity, and an ancient legend represents him to have been a secret Christian and subsequently baptized. The legend is untrustworthy and the commendations bestowed on him and his counsel are ill-judged. His address was indeed shrewd, but it was neither courageous, honest, nor sound. It certainly was not a plea for Christianity, for he apparently classifies the apostles with impostors; nor a plea for the right of private judgment in religion, the Biblical and the only sound basis for religious toleration. His counsel may be "salutary in a doubtful matter" (*Bengel*), *i. e.*, there may be cases in which only the result can determine the character and value of a great popular movement. But it is false in principle, for those things that come to naught are sometimes of God, witness the Asiatic churches planted by the apostles; those things that survive are not always from Him, witness Mahommedanism. It is false in reasoning; that God can give victory to his own is no reason for not contending against error and for the truth. "He who cannot decide until Christ and his church are completely victorious, will remain in doubt until the day of judgment arrives."—(*Lange's Commentary.*) It is false in its application; the miracles wrought by Jesus of Nazareth, his death and resurrection, the descent of the Holy Ghost, the movement of the people, and, above all, the peculiar character of the apostles' teaching and of Him whom they preached, sufficiently attested the counsel and work to be of God. The truth appears to be that Gamaliel was an Erasmus in times that needed a Luther; that he was in philosophy a fatalist, and in spirit a temporizer; that the humane teachings of Christ attracted him, but that he had not the courage nor the spiritual faith essential to a disciple; that he was really in some doubt as to the meaning and the probable result of this movement; that by aiding the Sadducees to put men to death for preaching the doctrine of the resurrection, he would be aiding the enemies of his own party, in an assault on the fundamental article of their faith, and he was wise enough to see it; and that he adopted an argument false in its premises, its conclusion, and its application, and temporizing in its spirit, to promote peace, and settle by compromise an issue which could only be settled by conflict and victory. This is in substance the estimate formed by Alford, Arnot and Calvin, the latter being, I believe, the first to call in question the soundness of Gamaliel's reasoning. His comments are admirable, and, provided we remember that God does not fulfill his designs in a lifetime, his deductions just. "That which is of God must needs stand, though all the world say nay; therefore, faith must stand without all fear, against all the assaults of Satan and men, seeing that faith is underpropped and supported with the eternal truth of God." Again, "Although the wicked attack whatsoever they can, and seek all means to destroy the church, although they furiously strive against Christ and his church so much as they are able, yet they shall not prevail, because it is the property of God to bring the counsels of man to naught."

Ch. 6 : 1-8. THE APPOINTMENT OF DEACONS. THE METHOD OF CHURCH ORGANIZATION IN APOSTOLIC TIMES.—THE METHOD OF DEALING WITH AND PREVENTING A CHURCH QUARREL.—THE OFFICE OF THE CHRISTIAN MINISTRY: PRAYER AND PREACHING.

1. In those days. An indefinite note of time equivalent to, During that period of the history of the church. Assuming that the conversion of Paul took place A. D. 30, the descent of the Holy Spirit at Pentecost A. D. 29 (see Chronological Table in Introduction), the date of this event would be fixed in the first year of the existence of the church. The date is further indicated by the second clause of the sentence. —**When the number of the disciples was multiplied.** The number was now several thousands (ch. 2 : 41; 5 : 14).—**Of the Grecians against the Hebrews.** Both terms are used in a popular and somewhat indefinite sense; the Grecians includes those who dwelt in Greece and had come up to attend the feast at Jerusalem, whether native Greeks and adopting the Jewish religion, or native Hebrews, adopting Greece as their abode; Hebrews includes those who dwelt in Judea retaining the Hebrew language and using the Hebrew Scriptures. The race prejudice between Greek and Hebrew was great. It affected the Jewish church and threatened the primitive Christian church (Rom. 2 : 9, 10; 1 Cor. 1 : 22-24; Ephes. 2 : 14; Col. 3 : 11). The murmuring here described was the first indication of danger. The word rendered *murmuring* (γογγυσμός) indicates that it was a suppressed and whispered discontent. The apostles did not wait for a public outbreak, but acted on the first suggestion of difficulty. "It is a point of prudence and godly carefulness in that they prevented the evil which began to arise without deferring the remedy."—(*Calvin.*)—**Their widows were neglected in the daily ministration.** Under the Mosaic law no definite provision was made for the maintenance of widows, who were dependent upon relatives, especially the eldest son, though they were protected from oppression by

A GRECIAN WIDOW.

special laws (Deut. 28 : 17; Job 24 : 3), and they were commended to the care of the community (Exod. 22 : 22; Deut. 27 : 19; Isaiah 1 : 17; Jer. 7 : 6; 22 : 3; Zech. 7 : 10). In compliance with the spirit of these regulations the early Christian church appear to have made special provision for the widows (comp. 1 Tim. 5 : 9). What was the nature of the daily ministration here referred to is not clear. The "tables" (τράπεζα) of verse 2 may mean either tables for meals or a money-changer's tables (Matt. 15 : 27; 21 : 12; Luke 16 : 21; 22 : 21). In Luke 19 : 23 the same word is rendered *bank.* Either money, or food, or both, may have been distributed. The phrase, "serve tables," does not, however, necessarily imply that this ministration took place literally at a table. The language may be regarded as simply metaphorical. It is supposed by many commentators that the apostles had already intrusted this distribution to deputies, not having the time to attend to it personally. But this is a gratuitous assumption, and does not accord with the narrative. If they had already appointed deputies, why do they refer to themselves as leaving the word of God to serve tables? The suggestion of deputies is made to avoid the supposed implication that the apostles were neglectful. But there is nothing to indicate whether the complaints were well grounded, or the product of a sensitive jealousy.

2-4. Then the twelve. The matter was evidently made a subject of consultation between them, and their action was concurrent.—**Called the multitude of the disciples together.** It is no more necessary to suppose that the entire number, five or six thousand, attended than that all the citizens attend every town meeting. It was a public gathering of the church, to which all could come who were so inclined. The open court-yard of any of the large houses of Jerusalem would afford a convenient place of meeting. —**It does not please us to leave the word of God.** The meaning of the original seems to be, It is not our choice to distribute the charities of the church; do you provide some one else to do it.—**Look ye out.** The whole multitude were to make their own selection. The course here pursued is hardly consistent with the theory of an apostolic authority *over* the church, still less with that of a papal primacy in Peter as vicegerent of Christ.—**Seven men.** "Why they should be just seven let him that hath confidence enough pretend to assign a reason."—(*Lightfoot.*) There has been no lack of this confidence in the commentators; Bengel says one deacon for each 1,000 converts; Meyer, the Jewish sacred number; Alford, some present consideration of convenience; Wordsworth, with reference to the sevenfold gift of the Spirit (Isaiah 11 : 2). Chrysostom's deduction is just and reasonable: "If there were need of seven men for this, how great in proportion must have been the sums of money that flowed in."—**Of honest report.** Not merely honest men, but men possessing the confidence of the disciples. A good reputation is sometimes a very necessary qualification for a public office. Comp. 1 Tim. 3 : 10.—**Full of the Holy Ghost and wisdom.** Purity alone does not suffice for church work; it must be mated to intellectual capacity.—**Whom we may appoint over this business.** Of distribution. The apostles being intrusted with the accumulated funds of the church, reserved the right to confirm or reject the selection of the multitude.—**To prayer and to the ministry of the word.** The word rendered *ministry* here is the same as that rendered *serve* in ver. 2. The apostles will serve the word of God, and leave to others to serve the charities of the church. There is a hint here of the inexpediency of placing the secular properties of the

5 And the saying pleased the whole multitude: and
they chose Stephen, a man full[f] of faith and of the
Holy Ghost, and Philip,[g] and Prochorus, and Nicanor,
and Timon, and Parmenas, and[h] Nicolas a proselyte
of Antioch:
6 Whom they set before the apostles; and when[i]
they had prayed, they[j] laid *their* hands on them.

f ch. 11 : 24. . . . g ch. 8 : 5, 26 ; 21 : 8 . . . . h Rev. 2 : 6, 15 . . . . i ch. 1 : 24; 13 : 3 . . . . j 1 Tim. 4 : 14 ; 5 : 22 ; 2 Tim. 1 : 6.

church in the hands of its ecclesiastics. Certainly the church which does this is not apostolic. Observe that prayer in the apostles' minds precedes and prepares for preaching. They that exhort us to prayer give themselves to it (Rom. 1 : 10). "So Moses did indeed exhort us unto prayer, but he went before them as a ringleader" (Exod. 17 : 11).—(*Calvin.*) Observe, too, that prayer and the ministry of the word appear to comprise the whole of the apostolic function, in which case we are all successors of the apostles—or ought to be.

5, 6. And these chose Stephen, etc. They were chosen by the whole multitude, that is, by Greek and Hebrew; but the fact that all the names are Greek, indicate that all the chosen were, if not Greeks, at least not likely to disparage or overlook the Greek element. The church apparently put the work of distribution largely in the hands of the complainants. Of these appointees only Stephen and Philip are again mentioned in the N. T. (ch. 8 : 5, 26, 40 ; 21 : 8). Nicolas was claimed by the heretical sect of Nicolaitanes (Rev. 2 : 6) as their founder, but this claim, though allowed by Epiphanius, is generally discredited by modern scholars. The fact that he was a proselyte of Antioch has been taken by some as an indication that all were proselytes; by others that he was the only proselyte. It seems rather to be a personal designation, perhaps to distinguish him from others of the same name.—**Whom they set before the apostles.** For their approval.—**And when they had prayed.** For guidance in the final decision (ch. 1 : 24, 25), and for divine blessing on those that were chosen (ch. 13 : 2, 3).—**They laid their hands on them.** This is the first mention in the N. T. of what has grown into an ecclesiastical rite. Its origin is to be traced in the O. T., and its significance found there. It was employed to indicate the bestowal of generally a blessing (Gen. 48 : 14; Matt. 19 : 13; Mark 8 : 33; 10 : 16); sometimes a physical cure (2 Kings 5 : 11; Mark 16 : 18); but also, in one notable instance, a curse (Lev. 16 : 21). It was employed by Moses in the ordination of Joshua (Numb. 27 : 18; Deut. 34 : 9). The same form was used by the apostles with the same significance, but always in the impartation of a blessing, never to indicate a curse. The laying on of hands accompanied the gift of healing (Acts 9 : 17, 18; 28 : 8); the consecration of disciples to a particular work, as in this case (Acts 13 : 3); or the impartation of the special gift of the Holy Spirit, followed, at least in some cases, by visible signs of his presence and power (ch. 8 : 17; 19 : 6). The rite has since passed into the Christian church; in nearly all denominations it is employed in the ordination of ministers, and in those in which the rite of confirmation, supplemental to baptism, is employed it is made an important part of that rite.

OF THE ORIGIN AND OFFICE OF DEACONS. (1) The word rendered (ver. 2) to *serve* is diakonein (διακονειν); from it undoubtedly comes our word deacon; and from the appointment here narrated this office is reasonably thought to have sprung. Such an officer certainly existed in apostolic times. In Phil. 1 : 1, Paul refers to the deacons as an order then existing; and in 1 Tim. 3 : 8–13, he prescribes their necessary qualifications. Deaconesses also were early appointed, probably in the apostolic age (Rom. 16 : 1; 1 Tim. 5 : 9–16). The office has been permanently retained in the Christian church, but with different functions in different denominations. In the Roman Catholic church the deacon is an assistant of the bishop; in the Episcopal church a clergyman, without, however, full ordination, not being allowed to consecrate the elements at the communion; in the Methodist Episcopal church he assists in the administration of the communion and as a teacher of the Scriptures; in the Congregational church the deacons are nominally the dispensers of the charities of the church, really the pastor's spiritual advisers; in the Presbyterian church the office is rarely practically maintained, its duties generally devolving upon the elders. Each denomination carefully defines the office; each endeavors to conform it to the apostolic model. In fact there is no apostolic model. For (2) observe the nature of the original appointment. A special exigency required special work, and officers were appointed for the purpose. The tenure of their office was not fixed; nor its permanence in the church prescribed; nor its duties defined; nor was even a name given to it. Apparently the fact of the appointment is only mentioned to explain the preaching and martyrdom of Stephen, and the subsequent conversion of Paul. There is no reason whatever to suppose that it was intended for a precedent, still less for a law, to succeeding generations; and all endeavors to conform the model to the ancient office are in vain, since the ancient office had no definite duties. Stephen and Philip both became well-known preachers; Philip is known as the Evan-

7 And[k] the word of God increased; and the number
of the disciples multiplied in Jerusalem greatly; and a
great company of the priests[l] were obedient to the
faith.
8 And Stephen, full of faith and power, did great
wonders and miracles among the people.

9 Then there arose certain of the synagogue, which
is called *the synagogue* of the Libertines, and Cyrenians, and Alexandrians, and of them of Cilicia and of
Asia, disputing with Stephen.
10 And they were not able[m] to resist the wisdom
and the spirit by which he spake.

---

k ch. 12 : 24 ; 19 : 20 ; Isa. 55 : 11. . . . l Ps. 132 : 9, 16 ; John 12 : 42. . . . m Luke 21 : 15.

---

gelist, not as the deacon (ch. 21 : 8); he administered baptism (ch. 8 : 38), and there is no reason to suppose that he might not with equal propriety have administered the communion. In short, the modern church cannot be conformed to the apostolic, because the apostolic church had no definite form. The constitution of the church was not framed by its founders like that of the United States; it grew like that of Great Britain. (3.) This appointment affords a model for the prevention of church quarrels. The apostles do not chide the complainants; nor wait till the quarrel assumes serious proportions; nor answer the complainants with self-justification; nor endeavor to allay the jealousy by rebuking it, or heal the schism by being leaders of either Greek or Hebrew party. They throw the responsibility on the church; turn over the administration largely to the complainants; and give themselves with increased consecration to spiritual work.

7, 8. The word of God increased. In power, in the church, and hence in extent, by addition to the church. The nature of the increase is explained by the subsequent clauses of the verse, which define its effects. This was both an evidence that harmony was restored and an effect of that harmony. When the church is united the word increases in power. As to the accession of priests, doubtless in the priesthood there were some honest and sincere inquirers after truth, ready to welcome it in spite of foes; others were easily swayed by the rising enthusiasm which pervaded Jerusalem. The number of priests at the return from Babylon (Ezra 2 : 36-38) was 4,289, and it was now probably still greater. It does not necessarily follow that all the new adherents to the church were spiritual converts. Many of these, like some of Christ's earlier disciples, probably apostatized from the faith, when they learned all that it involved (John 6 : 66). Such apostasy was evidently not unknown in the apostolic church (Heb. 6 : 4-6). This verse describes the culmination of the period of external prosperity in the church. "As yet all seemed going on prosperously for the conversion of Israel. The multitude honored the apostles; the advice of Gamaliel had moderated the opposition of the Sanhedrim; the priests were gradually being won over. But God's designs were far different. At this period another and important element in the testimony of the church is brought out in the person of Stephen—*its protest against Pharisaism.* This arrays against it that powerful and jealous sect, and henceforward it finds neither favor nor tolerance with either of the parties among the Jews, but the increasing and bitter enmity of them both."—(*Alford.*)—**Stephen full of grace and power.** *Grace,* not faith, is the best reading. It is here divine grace, and includes faith as one of the chief graces or free gifts of God's Spirit. *Power* is the divine power promised by Jesus Christ to his disciples in ch. 1 : 8, as manifested by signs and miracles, and also in the boldness and effectiveness of Stephen's preaching.

Ch. 6 : 9 to ch. 7 : 60. THE ACCUSATION, DEFENCE, AND MARTYRDOM OF STEPHEN. THE UNITY OF THE BIBLE.—THE CATHOLICITY AND SPIRITUALITY OF ITS RELIGION.—THE SOLE CONDITION OF THE DIVINE BLESSING, FAITH: ILLUSTRATED BY THE FAITH AND BLESSING OF ABRAHAM, MOSES, DAVID; BY THE REPEATED DISOBEDIENCE AND PUNISHMENT OF ISRAEL. See below, Stephen's address: prel. note.

A. D. 35 or 36, Dec. This address of Stephen marks a new era in the history of the church. Up to this time the preaching had been by Hebrews and addressed to Hebrews. Stephen, a Greek, untrammeled by the prejudices from which none of the twelve, not even Peter (ch. 10 : 14, 15), were emancipated, saw more clearly, and proclaimed more fearlessly, the radical and revolutionary character of the new religion, and especially its fitness for and its free offer to all nations. This catholic character of his ministry is indicated in the charge preferred against him; it is demonstrated in the speech he delivered in his own defence; it explains the bitterness of the persecution by the Pharisees which followed; it led, in the providence of God, to the dispersion of the church hitherto centred at Jerusalem, and the ministry of the word throughout Palestine; it prepared the way for the conversion of Paul. The careful student will find in Stephen's plea the germs of the doctrines of universal sin and universal grace, of which Paul became the most distinguished exponent, and which, I believe, he learned from the martyred Stephen. Though this address only inculcates what Christ taught in his first sermon (Luke 4 : 21-27), by a similar historical argument, it marks the practical transition of Christianity from a reformation of Judaism to a world religion, and is thus almost the most important of the speeches reported in the Book of Acts.

11 Then they suborned[n] men, which said, We have heard him speak blasphemous words against Moses, and *against* God.

12 And they stirred up the people, and the elders, and the scribes, and came upon *him*, and caught him, and brought *him* to the council,

n 1 Kings 21 : 10, 13; Matt. 26 : 59, 60.

9, 10. Then arose certain of the synagogue called of the Libertines, etc. For account of Jewish synagogue, see note on Matt. 4 : 23. For illustration, see Vol. I, frontispiece, and Luke 5 : 21. According to the Rabbinical books there were upwards of four hundred and fifty synagogues in Jerusalem; Jews of different dialects and provinces naturally worshipped together, and the synagogues naturally took their names from the nationality of the congregations. Whether here five synagogues are intended, or one or two, which embraced the worshippers of the different districts, is uncertain. In the synagogue services it was generally permitted to the leaders of any new school to set forth their opinions (ch. 13 : 15). Hence Stephen's preaching in the synagogue, which aroused the opposition of the Pharisees. The *Libertines* were Jews, who, having been taken prisoners and reduced to slavery, had afterwards been emancipated, and had returned to their national land. They had been allowed by Augustus to settle in a part of Rome, and to follow their own religious customs, but were expelled by Tiberius A. D. 19. Four thousand were sent to Sardinia, in the hope that they would there perish from the malaria; the rest were required to leave Italy, or abjure their religion. It is a reasonable conjecture that of these exiles enough may have found their way to Jerusalem to organize a synagogue of their own; and, having suffered persecution for their own faith, would be foremost in opposition to the new doctrine, as one "against this holy place and the law." For other but now generally discarded interpretations of the word Libertines, see Smith's *Bible Dictionary*. The *Cyrenians* were emigrants from Cyrene on the north of Africa. See ch. 2 : 10, note. The *Alexandrians* were from Alexandria, on the Mediterranean, twelve miles from the mouth of the Nile, a famous philosophical and literary centre. A large number of Jews were planted there by its founder, Alexander the Great; they possessed equal rights with the Greek population, had a part of the city allotted to them, were governed by their own code of laws, and at the time of Christ constituted one-third of the population of the city. *Cilicia* and *Asia* were Roman provinces; the latter including Mysia, Lydia, Cana, and Phrygia. See Gazetteer and map, p. 21.—**Disputing with Stephen.** *With* does not necessarily imply that he entered into any public debate or discussion with them. It is equally consistent with the account to suppose that he preached the truth affirmatively, and that they opposed, but could not successfully resist him. Comp. ch. 13 : 45.—**The wisdom and the spirit with which he spoke.** *Wisdom* is not equivalent to prudence, nor to learning, nor to dialectic skill, nor to mere theoretical knowledge, but to knowledge of truth coupled with skill in teaching and applying it. "In respect to divine things, wisdom (σοφία), *i. e.*, knowledge, insight, deep understanding, is represented everywhere as a divine gift, and includes the idea of practical illustration and application, thus distinguished from theoretical knowledge" (*Rob. Lex.*, σοφία). *The spirit* might either mean the Holy Spirit or Stephen's spirit; in the former case, the influence of the Holy Ghost accompanying his words; in the latter, the spiritual power which proceeded from his own spirit aroused and infused into his speech. Either interpretation would accord with the N. T. use of the language elsewhere. Comp. ch. 2 : 4; 10 : 19; 11 : 12, with 19 : 21; Rom. 1 : 9; 7 : 6, etc.; but the latter meaning agrees best with the context. The language cannot mean simply that he spoke in a spirited manner, *i. e.*, with vivacity and ardor; this meaning is never attached to the Greek word (πνεῦμα), here rendered *spirit*.

11, 12. Then they suborned men. The natural resource of bigotry when convicted of error is always the same; silenced by argument, it silences by persecution. *Blasphemy* under the Jewish law was any endeavor to turn away the allegiance of the people from the one true God. This was not only irreligion, but treason, and was punishable with death. See Matt. 12 : 32, note, and 26 : 57–68, prel. note. Its nature is partially indicated here by ver. 14. To speak against Moses was equivalent to speaking against God, because God spake through Moses (John 9 : 29). *The council* was the Sanhedrim, the supreme court of the Jewish nation, which tried and condemned Christ. For description, see Vol. I, p. 298; for illustration of oriental court, see on ch. 4, p. 58. The *elders* were semi-political leaders, answering to the modern sheik; the *scribes* were Jewish rabbis. See Matt. 16 : 21, note. The chief priests were also members of the Sanhedrim; they are not mentioned here, perhaps because they were principally Sadducees, and this persecution was instigated by the Pharisees. Stephen's enemies stirred up the people by misrepresentations of Stephen's preaching, in order that they might counteract the popular feeling, which was in favor of the Christians and which had hitherto served to protect them from perse-

13 And set up false witnesses, which said, This man
ceaseth not to speak blasphemous words against this
holy place, and the law:
14 For[o] we have heard him say, that this Jesus of
Nazareth shall[p] destroy this place, and shall change
the customs which Moses delivered us.
15 And all that sat in the council, looking stedfastly
on him, saw his[q] face as it had been the face of an
angel.

o ch. 25 : 8. . . . p Dan. 9 : 26. . . . q Exod. 34 : 30, 35.

---

cution (ch. 2 : 47; 4 : 17; 5 : 26). Their success is seen in the mob which brought the trial to a sudden close. The Sanhedrim had no longer power of inflicting death, which was reserved by the Roman government to itself (John 18 : 31). In the case of Christ they appealed to Pilate for a ratification of their sentence; in this case, the mob executed it. The *holy place* is primarily the Temple, and secondarily Jerusalem, which was made holy to the Jew by the Temple. *The law* is the system given by Moses, including the whole ceremonial and theocratic dispensation, which was now to come to an end, having fulfilled its mission.

14. Jesus of Nazareth shall destroy this place. Jesus has destroyed Jerusalem and the Temple, and had previously foretold their destruction; he has also changed the *customs* which Moses delivered; and the character of Stephen's speech leads to the belief that he perceived the catholicity of the Christian religion and the transitoriness of Judaism better than the Hebrew disciples. It is not, therefore, improbable that the testimony of these witnesses was measurably true; false in spirit rather than in words. They told the truth, but not the whole truth; and half a truth is often a whole lie. The charge of attempting to turn away the allegiance of the people from Jehovah and the system given by him through Moses, is the gravamen of their accusation. Stephen's plea is devoted to meeting this charge; in it he shows that throughout the sacred history Gentile ground was holy ground, and Gentiles were called to be divine instruments and recipients of the divine grace, and that thus the Gospel which he preached was not adverse to, but the culmination of this gracious history.

15. Saw his face as it had been the face of an angel. Comp. Exod. 34 : 35; Luke 9 : 29. Whether here the shining was a supernatural brightness, a special and divine radiance, or a natural effect of his own divinely-inspired peace and joy, is not an important question. In either case it was the direct result of the indwelling of God with him, the fulfillment of the promise of Christ (John 14 : 23, 27). That the manifestation of this inward life was not without its effect on the council, is indicated by the mildness of the high-priest's question, in striking contrast with the high-priest's treatment of Christ (Matt. 27 : 62, 63, 65), and Paul (ch. 23 : 2); and by the fact that the council heard Stephen's defence until his outburst of indignation at the close. Contrast 22 : 22.

Ch. 7 : 1-52. STEPHEN'S ADDRESS: PRELIMINARY NOTE. The connection of this address with the accusation preferred against Stephen is not clear; different interpretations have been proposed; some rationalistic scholars have even denied that there is any connection. An understanding of the spirit of the address as a whole, and its relation to the accusation and the martyrdom, are essential to its study in detail. (1.) *Stephen's object.* This is not to defend himself, but to convict his hearers of sin in crucifying their Messiah, and to proclaim to them salvation through Christ's name. Like the apostles, he seizes the occasion to preach the Gospel. We are not, therefore, to look for a definite answer to the charges preferred against him. (2.) If he had indicated his purpose at the outset, the council would not have listened to him. He must conceal it in order to accomplish it. We may, therefore, look for some obscurity, especially in the earlier portion of his address. (3.) It is partly interpreted by the charge against him, viz., blasphemy, in speaking against Moses, prophesying the destruction of Jews and the Temple, and the overthrow of Judaism; and probably, also, predicting the extension of the Gospel to the proselytes from other lands, like himself, and to the heathen. This catholicity of Christianity always aroused the especial anger of the Pharisees (ch. 22 : 21, 22). (4.) So interpreting it, we find in his historical summary an incidental reply to these charges. In his selection of historical facts he illustrates and enforces the following truths: (*a.*) The favor and blessing of God had not been confined to Judea and its people. They were shown in the facts that God appeared to Abraham in Mesopotamia, a land of idolatry, gave him not even a foot-breadth of soil in Canaan (ver. 5), caused his seed to dwell as strangers in a strange land, Egypt (vers. 8-13), and Moses to be educated in heathen (Egyptian) philosophy, and called the latter out of Midian to become the deliverer of Israel (vers. 20-29). (*b.*) Jerusalem and the Temple were not *alone* holy ground, and to prophesy their destruction was not to speak against the allegiance due to God and his holy religion; for God had appeared to Abraham before the days of Tabernacle or Temple (ver. 2); to Joseph in his bondage in Egypt (9, 10); to Moses in the burning bush, making, by his appearance, Midian holy

CHAPTER VII.

THEN said the high priest, Are these things so?
2 And he said, Men,[r] brethren, and fathers,
hearken; The God of glory appeared unto our father
Abraham when he was in Mesopotamia, before he
dwelt in Charran,
3 And said[s] unto him, Get thee out of thy country,

r ch. 22 : 1.

ground (vers. 30–33); to Israel in the church in the wilderness (ver. 38); to David, who was a man after God's own heart, yet was not even permitted to construct a temple for his dwelling-place (ver. 46); and when at length the Temple was built God declared that it could not confine him within its walls (ver. 48). (*c.*) Stephen did not speak against Moses nor against the law in proclaiming the Messiah, for Moses had himself foretold the Messiah's advent (ver. 37). (*d.*) Throughout all their history the Jewish nation had resisted the dispensation of divine mercy. This fact is illustrated by the selling of Joseph into Egypt by his brethren (ver. 9); by the repudiation of Moses by the Israelites (ver. 27); by the defection and apostasy of Israel at Mount Sinai (vers. 39–41); their subsequent idolatries (vers. 42, 43); and their persecution of the prophets (vers. 51, 52); it was, therefore, no strange nor blasphemous doctrine which he preached, that they had now rejected the Messiah himself, and that God wonld consequently reject them as a nation. (5.) Stephen's speech is interrupted at ver. 51. The sudden transition there probably indicates not an actual and violent interruption by the council, which would have been reported, but an outburst of indignation on Stephen's part at the relentless enmity manifested in the faces of his judges. He breaks off his argument and closes his speech in an indignant invective. (6.) The speech is analogous in structure and aim to that of Christ in Luke 4 : 21–29; like that is historical; like that traces the history of the O. T. for the purpose of showing that with it agrees the universality and catholicity of the Gospel; like that secures attention at the outset, and is interrupted by a violent outbreak at the close. (7.) The source whence Luke derived his knowledge of this speech is unknown. It is a reasonable hypothesis that the report came from Paul, who was present and consenting to Stephen's death, and whose conversion may, I believe, be traced to the influence of Stephen's plea and martyrdom; but this is only an hypothesis. (8.) The indications are that the address was made in the Greek language. Stephen was a Greek, and his quotations from the O. T. generally agree with the Greek version. (9.) There are several respects in which his historical allusions differ from the O. T. history either by variation or addition. The following are the principal points of difference:

Ver. 2 puts the call of Abraham before the migration to Haran; Gen. 12 : 1, 4, 5, in Haran.

Ver. 14 enumerates 75 souls in Jacob's migration; Gen. 46 : 27 enumerates 70.

Ver. 16 mentions the burial of the twelve patriarchs at Shechem; Exodus does not.

Ver. 16 describes the purchase of the tomb differently from Gen. 23 : 15. See note below.

Ver. 20 characterizes the beauty of Moses in childhood in stronger language than Exod. 2 : 2.

Ver. 22 specifies his Egyptian education; Exodus does not.

Ver. 22 characterizes him as mighty in words and deeds; Exodus says nothing of his early Egyptian life.

Vers. 22, 30, 36 mention three periods of forty years; the last only is so defined in the Pentateuch.

Ver. 32 describes Moses's terror at the burning bush; Exod. 3 : 3–5 does not.

Vers. 42, 43 add from Amos 5 : 25, 26 to the Mosaic narrative.

Ver. 53 refers to angels in the giving of the law; Exodus does not.

For interpretation and explanation of these variations in detail, see the notes below. Here it may suffice to say that I see no objection to the belief that Stephen referred to traditional sources, assuming as true the well recognized facts in the Jewish history, whether recorded in the O. T. or not; and that thus his address enforces the principle that all history is sacred, in that it illustrates sacred truth, and that the value of the O. T. history lies in its substantial facts, not in its literal and minute accuracy. (10.) The general lesson derivable by us from Stephen's address is the unity of the religion of the O. T. and the N. T. (*a*) The O. T. as well as the N. T. represents the divine mercy as unlimited by considerations of race or nationality; (*b*) the O. T. is a preparation for the fuller revelation of mercy through Jesus Christ in the N. T.; (*c*) the O. T., like the N. T., subordinates the instrument (the temple) to the soul (faith, humility, and mercy) of religion. The spirit which substitutes the creed, the ceremony, the church, or the book for the living God is always an irreligious spirit.

1. Are these things so? The high-priest was *ex-officio* president of the council. The accused had, under Jewish rules of law, a right to be heard in his own defence. Pleaders were unknown in the Jewish courts; the accused presented his own cause.

2, 3. Men, brethren and fathers, hearken. *Men* are all present, including *brethren*, his

and from thy kindred, and come into the land which I shall shew thee.
4 Then[t] came he out of the land of the Chaldæans, and dwelt in Charran: and from thence, when his father was dead, he removed him into this land, wherein ye now dwell.
5 And he gave him none inheritance in it, no not *so much as* to set his foot on: yet he promised[u] that he would give it to him for a possession, and to his seed after him, when *as yet* he had no child.
6 And God spake on this wise, That[v] his seed should sojourn in a strange land; and that they should bring them into bondage, and entreat *them* evil four[w] hundred years.

s Gen. 12 : 1.... t Gen. 12 : 5.... u Gen. 13 : 15.... v Gen. 15 : 13, 16.... w Exod. 12 : 40, 41.

equals, especially the public, who were always admitted to the Jewish trial as spectators, and *fathers*, the members of the council, whom he addresses in terms of respect because of their official position. Comp. Acts 22 : 1; 1 Tim. 5 : 1. Observe the respectfulness and the dignity of Stephen's opening.—**The God of glory.** Not merely equivalent to the glorious God. He dwells ever in glorious light unapproachable (1 Tim. 6 : 16), and in the O. T. appeared in a cloud of glory, the Shechinah, to his people (Exod. 40 : 34; Lev. 9 : 6; Ezek. 1 : 28), this appearance being a peculiar privilege granted to Israel (Rom. 9 : 4). Stephen, who speaks of the appearance of God to Israel from the days of Abraham to those of Christ, characterizes him as the God of glory, *i. e.*, whose character has ever been a glorious manifestation of himself to his people, a preparation for this last and most glorious self-disclosure (Heb. 1 : 1, 2).—**Our father Abraham.** Stephen identifies himself with his audience as a son of Abraham.—**When he was in Mesopotamia, before he dwelt in Charran.** Mesopotamia derives its name, which means *between rivers*, from its position between the Euphrates and the Tigris; is now called by the Arabs Al-Jezirah, the island; is about 700 miles in length, and from 20 to 250 miles in width. The Mesopotamia of the Bible is the northwestern portion of modern Mesopotamia. It was the dwelling-place of Balaam; became in succession subject to the Assyrian, Babylonian, Persian, Grecian, Syrian, Roman, and Parthian rulers. Ur (Gen. 11 : 28, 31), and Haran, the Charran of our text, were cities in Mesopotamia. The site of both cities is somewhat uncertain; Ur is probably the modern Mugheir; Haran, probably the modern Harran; the former on the right bank of the southern Euphrates, the latter in northwestern Mesopotamia, on the banks of a small tributary of the Euphrates, the river Belik. But different localities have been assigned for the Haran, the Ur, and the Mesopotamia of Scripture. See Smith's *Bible Dict.*, arts. Haran and Ur, and Abbott's *Religious Dict.*, art. Mesopotamia.—**Before he dwelt in Charran.** According to Gen. 11 : 31, Abram and his father Terah, and his nephew Lot, went from Ur to Haran, where Terah died. Then ch. 12 begins a new account, "Now the Lord said unto Abram, Get thee out of thy country. * * * So Abram departed, as the Lord had spoken unto him." Thus Genesis mentions the departure from Ur to Haran, but no appearance of the Lord to Abram in Ur. Our translators have thrown back the appearance of the Lord to Abram in Haran by the rendering, The Lord *had said;* but this they apparently did to make the account there agree with Stephen's representation here. This was quite needless. There is nothing inconsistent in the two accounts; Stephen simply tells us, what we should not have known otherwise, that the first departure from Ur was in obedience to a divine call. This, however, is indicated by the language of Gen. 11 : 31, which states that Abram's purpose in the first movement was to go to Canaan, a purpose impeded but not abandoned, in the delay at Haran; and this is confirmed by the language of Gen. 15 : 7; Josh. 24 : 3; Neh. 9 : 7; and by Jewish tradition, preserved in Philo and Josephus.

4. When his father was dead he removed him into this land. This accords with the account in Genesis, but the account there presents some difficulty; for, apparently, Terah was seventy years of age at the birth of Abram (Gen. 11 : 26), and Abram was seventy-five years of age at the time of his emigration (Gen. 12 : 4), which would make Terah only one hundred and forty-five years old at that time, while, according to Gen. 11 : 32, he was two hundred and five years old at the time of his death. It is scarcely probable, however, that Abram, Nahor and Haran were born the same year, and there is no evidence that Abram was the oldest; Jewish tradition makes him the youngest. If, then, we understand the declaration of Gen. 11 : 26, "Terah lived seventy years and begat Abram, Nahor and Haran," to mean that he was seventy years old before the first of his sons was born, he may have been one hundred and thirty years old when Abram was born, and two hundred and five when Abram's migration took place. And this is the most probable explanation of a difficulty in chronology, which is of small consequence, except that it has been used to impugn the accuracy of the history.—**Wherein ye now dwell.** Stephen begins with Abram and his migration into Canaan to show his auditors that the call of the Gentiles in the Gospel, so far from being inconsistent with the sacred history, agrees with its first and fundamental fact, the call of Abraham from idolatry, and the bequest of this very land to him, on the simple condition of faith in and obedience to God's word.

7 And the nation to whom they shall be in bondage
will I judge, said God: and after that shall they come
forth, and serve [x] me in this place.
8 And [y] he gave him the covenant of circumcision:
and so [z] *Abraham* begat Isaac, and circumcised him
the eighth day; and Isaac [a] *begat* Jacob; and Jacob [b]
begat the twelve patriarchs.
9 And the patriarchs, moved with [c] envy, sold Joseph
into Egypt: but [d] God was with him,
10 And delivered him out of all his afflictions, and
gave him favour and wisdom in the sight of Pharaoh
king of Egypt; and he [e] made him governor over
Egypt and all his house.
11 Now [f] there came a dearth over all the land of

x Exod. 3 : 12....y Gen. 17 : 9-11....z Gen. 21 : 1-4....a Gen 25 : 26....b Gen. 29 : 32, etc....c Gen. 37 : 28; Ps. 105 : 17....d Gen. 39 : 2, 21.... e Gen. 41 : 40....f Gen. 41 : 54.

5-7. Not so much as to set his foot on. Literally, *not a foot-step.* Comp. Deut. 2 : 5. Abraham lived in Palestine an itinerant life, as a pilgrim and stranger (Heb. 11 : 9, 10), never owning any part of the soil, except the burial-place of Sarah, his wife, near Hebron (Gen., ch. 23).—**When as yet he had no child.** Abraham was a hundred years old at the time of Isaac's birth (Gen. 21 : 5) and had therefore sojourned in Palestine a quarter of a century before there was any indication of the fulfillment of the promise made to him.—**And God spake on this wise.** Stephen's language implies that he does not quote verbally. The quotation is from Gen. 15 : 13, 14.—**Four hundred years.** This agrees with the language of Gen. 15 : 13; in Exod. 12 : 40, and Gal. 3 : 17, the time is stated with greater accuracy at four hundred and thirty years. It is uncertain whether this four hundred and thirty years is the period of Israel's sojourn in Egypt, *i. e.*, the time between the coming of Jacob with his household into Egypt and the exodus of Israel under Moses, as implied in Exod. 12 : 40, or the period of Israel's sojourn in Egypt and Canaan, *i. e.*, the time between the promise to Abraham and the exodus of Israel from Egypt, as implied in Gal. 3 : 17, and in some ancient copies of the O. T., which, in Exod. 12 : 40, read, "who dwelt in Egypt and the land of Canaan." The former opinion best agrees with the remarkable increase of Israel from seventy-five souls (ver. 14) to a great nation; the latter best agrees with the Hebrew genealogies. It is not important for the interpretation of Stephen's address to determine this question, which is one of the most perplexing and difficult in Hebrew chronology. I am inclined to take Exod. 12 : 40 as literally true, to believe that the sojourn in Egypt covered a period of four hundred and thirty years, and to believe that there is some hiatus in the genealogy of Moses, as is often the case with the Hebrew genealogies. See Gal. 3 : 17, note.—**And serve me in this place.** These words are not in Genesis. Instead is the promise, *They shall come out with great substance.* Analogous to Stephen's language here is God's promise to Moses in the region of Mount Sinai (Exod. 3 : 12). "When thou hast brought forth the people out of Egypt, ye shall serve God upon this mountain." The promise that they shall serve God in Canaan is however implied by the whole course of God's dealings with the patriarchs and their descendants, the object of which was to bring into the land a chosen people, who should serve him, and him only. Stephen's object in this reference here is to enforce the truth that the worship of God is not dependent on place—as it began before Jerusalem existed, so it may continue after Jerusalem is destroyed; nor exclusive—as it was permitted to Abraham, a stranger in Palestine, and to Israel, a stranger in Egypt, so should it be to the Gentile, a stranger in Stephen's time, in the land of Israel.

8. The covenant of circumcision. The covenant is recorded in Gen. 17 : 4-8, and is interpreted spiritually by Paul in Gal. 3 : 15-18. It embraced God's promise to be the God of Abraham and of his seed. Stephen, like Paul, traces back the promise of grace, which made Israel the people of God, to a period long preceding the giving of the law, and thus indicates, what Paul more directly argues, that God's covenant is not dependent on the law. Hence in prophesying a change of the customs which Moses gave (ch. 6 : 14), Stephen has said nothing against the God or the religion of Israel. Thus his unexpressed conclusion is the same as that expressed by Paul: "If the inheritance be of the law it is no more of promise; but God gave it to Abraham by promise." It is called the *covenant of circumcision*, because its acceptance by Abraham and his seed was signified by the rite of circumcision (Gen. 17 : 9-14). On the rite itself see notes on ch. 15.—**And so he begat Isaac.** *So; i. e.*, in accordance with and fulfillment of the divine covenant to give to him, and his seed after him, the land of Canaan.

9, 10. The patriarchs, moved with envy, sold Joseph into Egypt. The story of Joseph is told in Genesis, chaps. 37-50. This statement is the first item in Stephen's indictment of the children of Israel, consummated in the indignant outburst of vers. 51-53. Joseph's brethren know not their appointed deliverer, endeavor to make away with him, are restrained from murder only by prudential considerations. Yet, as later by the crucifixion of Jesus Christ (ch. 2 : 23), Israel unconsciously executes the purposes of God. If the descendants of Abraham had remained in the free nomadic life of Palestine, they would have been dispersed. In their servitude in Egypt they became compacted into the germ of a great nation.—**Grace and wis-**

Egypt and Chanaan, and great affliction: and our fathers found no sustenance.
12 But[g] when Jacob heard that there was corn in Egypt, he sent out our fathers first.
13 And at the second *time* Joseph[h] was made known to his brethren; and Joseph's kindred was made known unto Pharaoh.
14 Then sent Joseph, and called his father Jacob to *him*, and all[i] his kindred, threescore and fifteen souls.
15 So Jacob went down into Egypt, and died, he, and our fathers,
16 And[j] were carried over into Sychem, and laid in the sepulchre that Abraham bought for a sum of money of the sons of Emmor *the father* of Sychem.
17 But when the time of the promise drew nigh, which God had sworn to Abraham, the people[k] grew and multiplied in Egypt,
18 Till another king arose, which knew not Joseph.

g Gen. 42 : 1, 2 .... h Gen. 45 : 4, 16 .... i Gen. 46 : 27; Deut. 10 : 22 .... j Josh. 24 : 32 .... k Exod. 1 : 7-9.

dom in the sight of Pharaoh. Not merely *grace and wisdom*, but these qualities so developed and manifested as to be apparent to the Egyptian king. *Grace* here may either mean gracefulness in manner, which was apparently a characteristic of Joseph (Gen. 39 : 6; 41 : 14), or favor, *i. e.* with Pharaoh, or divine grace. The latter seems to me to be the best interpretation here, in the light of Gen. 41 : 38.—**Governor over Egypt, and all his house.** The former phrase signifies Joseph's civil authority in the land, the second his position in the royal household. He was both prime minister and lord chamberlain; was second in dignity only to the king, and practically, as is often the case with the prime minister, especially in oriental countries, was the ruler of the land. This elevation of Joseph, attributed by Stephen, as by the O. T., to the divine favor, is another evidence that religion and God are not confined to the Temple, to Palestine, and to the scrupulous observers of the ceremonial law.

11-13. There came a dearth. Such experiences of famine as are described in Gen. 41 : 54–57 are unhappily still common in the East. The Persian famine is still fresh in the minds of American readers. For a terribly graphic description of a modern Egyptian famine see Stanley's Jewish Church, Lect. IV.

14. And all his kindred three score and fifteen souls. In the O. T. history it is three score and ten (Gen. 46 : 27; Exod. 1 : 5; Deut. 10 : 22). Apparently Jacob's household (66), Jacob himself, Joseph, and Joseph's two sons (4), make up the seventy. In the Greek version of the O. T. the number in both Genesis and Exodus is changed to 75, showing that Stephen's statement accords with the popular reading of the O. T. at that time. No other explanation of the variation is necessary for those who believe that Stephen, in such a minor matter of detail, would have quoted the current version of the O. T., as we would to-day the current version of the Bible, without going into a critical examination of the passage in the original. The point he has to make, that Israel went down into Egypt a household, and came out of Egypt a nation, does not depend on the question whether there were 70 or 75 in the family.

15, 16. And were carried over into Sychem, etc. In two respects Stephen's account here differs from that of the O. T. (1.) He represents the sons of Jacob as buried in Sychem; the O. T. does not intimate that their remains were removed from Egypt (Gen. 50 : 26; Exod. 1 : 6). The explanation of this variance is very simple. Joseph's remains were taken to Canaan at the time of the exodus, and buried in Sychem (Exod. 13 : 19; Josh. 24 : 32); and though nothing is said in the O. T. of the removal of the other brothers, it is stated by Josephus that they were buried in Hebron, *i. e.*, in Abraham's purchase, and by the Rabbinical traditions that they were buried in Sychem, which agrees with the statement here. There is absolutely no reason whatever for supposing that Stephen confined himself to the O. T. history in his address; and no reason why he should not have referred to other sources of ordinarily accepted history among the Jews. (2.) But he also represents the burial as taking place in a field bought by *Abraham* of Hamor's sons (Emmor being the same as Hamor); whereas, according to the O. T., this purchase of the field in Sychem was made by *Jacob* (Gen. 33 : 19), and the burial of Jacob was in the field of Macphelah, in another part of Palestine, bought by Abraham of Ephron the Hittite. In respect to this variance there is more difficulty. It is to be observed, however, that Stephen does not say that Jacob was buried in Sychem. If we put a period at the end of verse 15, his language will even imply the reverse. "So Jacob went down into Egypt, and died, he and our fathers. And they (*i. e.*, our fathers) were carried over into Sychem," etc. His language, though on its face ambiguous, would not be so to his auditors, to whom the facts were familiar, of the burial of Jacob near Hebron and of his sons at Sychem. The only real difficulty, then, consists in the fact that Stephen attributes the purchase at Sychem to *Abraham*, whereas it was made by Jacob. The hypothesis (Smith's *Bible Dict.*, Am. ed.) that the land was twice purchased, first by Abraham at the time when he built there an altar to God (Gen. 12 : 6, 7), and afterward—the land having been reoccupied by the Shechemites —was repurchased by Jacob, is possible, but it is at best only a surmise. I should prefer to suppose, with Hackett, that in Stephen's address the word *Abraham* has been substituted in some

19 The same dealt subtilly with our kindred, and
evil-entreated our fathers, so[l] that they cast out their
young children, to the end they might not live.
20 In which time Moses[m] was born, and was exceeding
fair, and nourished up in his father's house three
months:
21 And when he was cast out, Pharaoh's daughter
took him up, and[n] nourished him for her own son.
22 And Moses was learned in all the wisdom of
the Egyptians, and[o] was mighty in words and in
deeds.
23 And[p] when he was full forty years old, it came

l Exod. 1 : 22 . . . . m Exod. 2 : 2, etc. . . . n Exod. 2 : 10 . . . . o Luke 24 : 19 . . . . p Exod. 2 : 11, etc.

very early copies for *Jacob;* or that Luke, in writing, or Stephen, in speaking, substituted the one word for the other by a natural mistake. And I quite agree with Dean Alford that "the fact of the mistake occurring where it does will be far more instructive to the Christian student than the most ingenious solution of the difficulty could be, if it teaches him fearlessly and honestly to recognize the phenomena presented by the text of Scripture, instead of wresting them to suit a preconceived theory."

17-19. The time of the promise. That is, the time for its fulfillment, as indicated in the promise itself (Gen. 15 : 13).—**Which knew not Joseph.** Not literally, knew nothing about him, but was indifferent to him and the service he had rendered the nation. The name Pharaoh is a general title by which the national kings of Egypt are all known; but it represents different and even antagonistic dynasties. The Pharaoh of the oppression belonged to a different dynasty from that of the Pharaoh of Joseph; but scholars are not agreed in their identification of him with any king known in Egyptian history.—**Dealt subtilely with.** Rather, *cunningly against.* The account is given in Exodus (ch. 1); the king first endeavored to destroy the male children by corrupting the midwives; not until that failed did he openly command that they should be murdered.—**In order that they might cast out their young children.** The original does not necessarily, as our English version, imply that the Israelites slew their own children; only that it was the purpose of the Egyptian king to make them do so.

20, 21. Was exceeding fair. Literally, *fair for God, i. e.,* in his sight. The language is simply a strong expression of his beauty as a babe, and answers to the description in Exodus (2 : 2), "goodly child," and in Hebrews (11 : 23), "proper child." The tradition embodied by Josephus indicates the popular belief concerning his remarkable infantile beauty. "It happened frequently that those who met him as he was carried along the road were obliged to turn again upon seeing the child; that they left what they were about, and stood still a great while to look on him; for the beauty of the child was so remarkable and natural to him, on many accounts, that it detained the spectators and made them stay longer to look upon him."—**Pharaoh's daughter took him up.** See Exod. 2 : 1-10. His name, Moses, signifies *drawn out,* and was given to him because he was drawn out of the water. Of Pharaoh's daughter mentioned here and in Exodus, nothing else is known.

22. And Moses was instructed in all the wisdom of the Egyptians. *Instructed,* not *learned;* the original indicates his education, not his proficiency. This is not stated in the O. T., but it is implied by the fact that he was adopted by the princess and educated as her own son. The education itself was a fitting, if not necessary, preparation for the predestined leader of Israel, and the fruits of it appear in their subsequent history. Some of their laws and customs, and many of their arts, had an Egyptian origin. The Egyptians were students of astronomy and chemistry, excelled in geometry and mathematics, were proficient in medicine, surgery and practical anatomy, were workers in fine flax, possessed and worked looms, were acquainted with glass and glass manufacture, with manufacture of pottery, iron and bronze, with the forceps, the blow-pipe, the bellows, the syringe, and the siphon, were skilled in the art of architecture, and made both sculptures and paintings; from the former we derive most of our knowledge of their life, since in them their trades and habits are fully illustrated.—**Mighty in words and in deeds.** This statement is not derived from the O. T., which even implies that he was, in his early career, slow of speech (Exod. 4 : 10-16). But the Jewish traditions attribute to him remarkable military achievements during his life as an Egyptian prince. Stanley thus condenses into a paragraph the substance of these extra Scriptural legends concerning his youth: "He was educated at Heliopolis and grew up there as a priest under his Egyptian name of Osarsiph or Tisithen. He learned arithmetic, geometry, astronomy, medicine and music. He invented boats and engines for building, instruments of war and of hydraulics—hieroglyphics—division of lands. He taught Orpheus and was hence called by the Greeks Musæus, and by the Egyptians Hermes. He was sent on an expedition against the Ethiopians. He got rid of the serpents of the country to be traversed by letting loose baskets full of ibises upon them. The city of Hermopolis was believed to have been founded to commemorate his victory. He advanced to the capital of Ethiopia and gave it the name of Meroe, from his adopted mother, Merrhis, whom he buried

into his heart to visit his brethren the children of Israel.
24 And seeing one *of them* suffer wrong, he defended *him*, and avenged him that was oppressed, and
smote the Egyptian:
25 For he supposed his brethren would have understood how that God by his hand would deliver them:
but they understood not.
26 And the next day he shewed himself unto them as
they strove, and would have set them at one again,
saying, Sirs, ye are brethren; why do ye wrong one
to another?
27 But he that did his neighbour wrong thrust him
away, saying, Who made thee a ruler and a judge
over us?
28 Wilt thou kill me, as thou didst the Egyptian
yesterday?
29 Then fled Moses at this saying; and was a
stranger in the land of Madian, where he begat two
sons.
30 And[q] when forty years were expired, there appeared to him in the wilderness of Mount Sina an angel
of the Lord, in a flame of fire in a bush.

q Exod. 3 : 2, etc.

there. Tharbis, the daughter of the king of Ethiopia, fell in love with him, and he returned in triumph to Egypt with her as his wife." There is nothing in all this inconsistent with the Scripture, which, after narrating his birth, begins the story of his subsequent life with his defence of an Israelite against an Egyptian and his consequent flight into Midian. Livingstone argues the substantial truth of these traditions, and hoped to discover in Central Africa some evidences of this early career; this was indeed one of the objects of his last expedition (*Last Journals*, p. 238).

23-25. And when he was full forty years old. Nothing is said in the O. T. of his age at this time, but this statement agrees with Jewish legends. See *Lightfoot*.—**To visit his brethren.** Literally, *To look after his brethren.* The original involves the idea of carrying succor (Matt. 25 : 36; Luke 1 . 68; 7 : 16; James 1 : 27). Comparing the language here with that of Luke 1 : 68 and Heb. 2 : 6, we may see how Moses was a type of Christ, and how Christ was a prophet like unto Moses (ch. 3 : 22), like him leaving a royal court and going out to look after and to redeem those whom he was not ashamed to call brethren (Heb. 2 : 11).—**And smote the Egyptian.** The oppressor; and slew him (Exod. 2 : 12).—**For he supposed his brethren would have understood how that God, by his hand, gave to them salvation.** This is the literal rendering of the original, and though the salvation here referred to is unquestionably temporal deliverance from their bondage, yet the use of the language is significant. It connects Moses with Christ, and leads up to the consummation of Stephen's speech, that Israel has always been blind to and rejected the proffered salvation of God. It is not implied in the O. T. that Moses at this time understood that he was called to be the deliverer of Israel; his surprise and remonstrance when sent by God to Pharaoh (Exod. 4 : 1, 10, 13) has been thought by some to imply that prior to that time he did not comprehend the purpose for which God had raised him up. This, however, does not necessarily follow; from Stephen's interpretation of O. T. history, it would appear that Moses in his youth lacked the needful self-restraint and patience for his work; that he undertook the task of deliverance in self-confidence and self-reliance; that his failure discouraged him; that he abandoned his purpose and fled; and that after the forty years of education and maturing in the land of Midian, God recalled him to his purpose for the accomplishment of which his spirit of mingled self-distrust and courage then fitted him. In Exod. 2 : 12, Moses undertakes to deliver; in Exod. 3 : 8, God avows himself Israel's deliverer. Observe the significance of the present tense; not, *would give*, but *is giving*. God gave Israel salvation when he raised up Moses, as he gave the world salvation when he sent into it his only begotten Son. But in both cases much remained to be done before the perfect fruits of the salvation could be realized.—**But they understood not.** Comp. John 1 : 10, 11.

26-28. And urged them to peace, saying, Sirs, ye are brethren. So the Gospel is a Gospel of peace, and urges to peace on the ground that God hath made of one blood all the nations of the earth. And observe that Moses, like Christ, is rejected at first, not because he offers deliverance, but because he demands righteousness.—**Thrust him away.** Another item in Stephen's indictment, Ye do always resist the Holy Ghost (ver. 51). So, Israel thrust Moses away and sought to turn back to Egypt (ver. 39); and finally, thrust away Christ as their King and Saviour (ch. 13 : 46); and so many still thrust away faith, *i. e.*, trust in Jesus Christ as their Saviour, and a good conscience, *i. e.*, obedience to him as their King (1 Tim. 1 : 19).

29, 30. Then fled Moses at this saying. Meanwhile the facts came to Pharaoh's ears and he sought to slay Moses (Exod. 2 : 15).—**And was a stranger in the land of Madian.** The founders of Israel, Abraham in Palestine, the patriarchs in Egypt, Moses in Madian, were all strangers in a strange land—a ground of appeal to them to exercise consideration to the stranger in their own land (Exod. 22 : 21; Lev. 19 : 34; Deut. 10 : 19). *Madian* is the same as *Midian*. The land was named from one of the sons of Abraham by Keturah (Gen. 25 : 1, 2, 4), by whose descendants it was peopled. As they were a nomadic people, the boundaries of their land were never clearly defined. It certainly embraced the Sinaitic penin-

31 When Moses saw *it*, he wondered at the sight:
and as he drew near to behold *it*, the voice of the Lord
came unto him,
32 *Saying*, I *am* the God[r] of thy fathers, the God of
Abraham, and the God of Isaac, and the God of Jacob.
Then Moses trembled, and durst not behold.
33 Then said the Lord to him, Put[s] off thy shoes
from thy feet; for the place where thou standest is
holy ground.
34 I have seen, I have seen, the affliction of my people which is in Egypt, and I have heard their groaning, and am come down to deliver them. And now
come, I will send thee into Egypt.

r Matt. 22 : 32; Heb. 11 : 16 .... s Josh. 5 : 15; Eccles. 5 : 1.

sula, for here it was that the Lord appeared to Moses (ver. 30), and his sojourn in this peninsula was a part of his preparation for conducting Israel through this region in their forty years' wandering in the wilderness. But the entire territory answered, probably, very nearly to the modern Arabia Petra, and the Midianites to the modern Arabs. The Midianites are first mentioned in connection with Moses (Exod. 2 : 15; 3 : 1). They subsequently became dangerous enemies of Israel, seduced the people to idolatry and to flagrant vice (Numb., ch. 25), and were subsequently engaged in wars with them (Numb., ch. 31; Josh. 13 : 21; Judges, chaps. 6, 7, 8). The overthrow of the Midianites by Gideon was so complete that they appear no more in sacred history, though referred to incidentally by the prophets (Isaiah 60 : 6; Hab. 3 : 7).—**Where he begat two sons.** His wife was Zipporah, the daughter of Reuel (Exod. 2 : 18), or Jethro (Numb. 10 : 29), a priest of Midian. The two sons were Gershom and Eliezer (Exod. 18 : 3, 4). The fact is here stated as indicating how thoroughly Moses made Midian his home. The law-giver of Israel was by adoption an Egyptian, by his own choice a Midianite; the adopted son of an Egyptian princess, the son-in-law of a Midianitish prince. The argument against the Jewish enmity to the Gentile and to the Gospel, because glad tidings to the Gentile as well as the Jew, was the more effective for not being directly stated, but only indirectly implied.—**And when forty years were expired.** The length of his sojourn in Midian does not appear in the O. T. But Exod. 7 : 7 fixes Moses' age at the time of God's appearing to him as eighty; subtracting the forty years spent in Egypt (ver. 23), will leave forty years in the land of Midian. And this agrees with Jewish traditions, which divide Moses' life into three eras of forty years each, one in Egypt, one in Midian, and one with the children of Israel in the wilderness.—**An angel.** The words, *Of the Lord*, are omitted by Tischendorf and Alford. Evidently, however, the visitor was, not *an* angel, but *the angel of the Lord*, *i. e.*, Jesus Christ, who in the O. T. as in the N. T. is the manifestation of God to man. That this phrase always indicates, not a messenger of God, but a manifestation of God, is clear from many passages (see Gen. 16 : 7-13; 22 : 11, 12, 15, 16; 31 : 11, 13; 48 : 15, 16, etc). He is called also the angel of his presence (Isaiah 63 : 9), and the messenger of the covenant (Mal. 3 : 1), and is identified with Christ by Paul (1 Cor. 10 : 9; comp. Heb. 11 : 26).—**In a flame of fire in a bush;** which was not consumed. This fact drew Moses' attention to it (Exod. 3 : 2, 3). The original indicates some kind of a bramble-bush. Fire is a frequent symbol in the O. T. of the divine presence, especially when manifested for the purpose of judgment, of punishment, and of purification (Psalm 97 : 3; Isaiah 33 : 14; Heb. 12 : 29; Rev. 2 : 18). Thus God manifested himself when he came to destroy Baal and purify the land of idolatry (1 Kings 18 : 38); thus now when he came to destroy Pharaoh and to redeem his own people; thus at the last he will appear in flaming fire when he comes to judge the world (2 Thess. 1 : 8; Heb. 10 : 27; 2 Pet. 3 : 7).

31-34. Stephen's account differs in two particulars from that in Exodus. There the fear and trembling is not stated; here it is given as a consequence of God's disclosure of himself in the words, "I am the God of thy fathers," etc. Here the command to unloose the shoes is put before, there subsequent to this disclosure. The variance is immaterial, and is such as might be expected in an *extempore* address and a free recital of the facts from memory.—**I am the God of thy fathers.** From this declaration Christ deduces the doctrine of the immortality of the soul (Matt. 22 : 32). It indicates not only that the patriarchs were living, but also that they were recognized as living by Moses and his generation.—**Put off thy shoes.** Rather *sandals*. The Eastern nations remove these as a token of reverence, as we our hats. The priests performed all their ministrations barefoot, and the modern Arabs always leave their shoes at the door of the mosque on entering. See Josh. 5 : 15.—**The place where thou standest is holy ground.** This was five hundred years before the Temple was built. As God revealed himself, and by the revelation sanctified the place, centuries *before* the Temple was built, so he might reveal himself elsewhere *after* the Temple should be destroyed. To prophesy that destruction was not blasphemy against God or his truth, as charged by Stephen's accusers (ch. 6 : 14). In brief, God is not identical with his church, nor religion with its temple and ordinances; by identifying them the Jews dishonored both God and divine truth; Stephen appeals to the O. T. history to show how God's revelation of himself was not confined

35 This Moses, whom they refused, saying, Who
made thee a ruler and a judge? the same did God send
to be a ruler and a deliverer, by the hand of the[t] angel
which appeared to him in the bush.
36 He brought them out, after[u] that he had shewed
wonders and signs in the land of Egypt, and in the
Red Sea, and in the wilderness, forty[v] years.
37 This is that Moses which said[w] unto the children
of Israel, A prophet shall the Lord your God raise up
unto you of your brethren, like unto me; him[x] shall
ye hear.
38 This[y] is he, that was in the church in the wilderness, with the angel[z] which spake to him[a] in the
Mount Sina, and *with* our fathers; who[b] received[c]
the lively oracles to give unto us:
39 To whom our fathers would not obey, but thrust
him from them, and in their hearts turned back again
into Egypt,
40 Saying[d] unto Aaron, Make us gods to go before
us: for *as for* this Moses, which brought us out of the
land of Egypt, we wot not what is become of him.
41 And they made a calf[e] in those days, and offered
sacrifice unto the idol, and rejoiced in the works of
their own hands.

t Exod 14 : 19; Numb. 20 : 16....u Exod. 7, 11, 14....v Exod. 16 : 35....w ch. 3 : 22; Deut. 18 : 15, 18....x Matt. 17 : 5....y Heb. 2 : 2....z Isa. 63 : 9; Gal. 3 : 19....a Exod. 19 : 3, 17....b Deut. 5 : 27, 31; John 1 : 17....c Rom. 3 : 2....d Exod. 32 : 1... e Deut. 9 : 16; Ps. 106 : 19, 20.

to temples made with hands, and could not be, consistently with his character.—**I have seen—I have seen.** Literally, *Seeing, I have seen.* An emphatic expression equivalent to *I have surely seen*, in Exodus.—**The affliction of my people.** The divine silence does not indicate divine indifference. For four hundred years this affliction had continued, and this groaning had gone up to God; he had seen and heard, but not interfered, because the time for the fulfillment of his design had not arrived. He always sees and hears.—**To deliver them.** Literally, *To take them out.* The idea of deliverance is accompanied with another, viz., that God chooses them as his peculiar people. The promise was fulfilled only partially at the escape of Israel from Egypt; it was consummated by the covenant at Mount Sinai (Exod. 19 : 5, 6).

35, 36. As Stephen proceeds the object of his address appears more evident, in the parallel between Moses and Christ. Both were rejected by the Jews (comp. Luke 19 : 14; Matt. 21 : 42); both were chosen of God to fill the office denied them by man. Observe the contrast between the estimate of Moses by the Israelites and by God; by the one he is assumed to be a ruler and *judge;* by the other he is sent a ruler and *deliverer*, literally a *ransomer*. The Greek word (λυτρωτής) is the same in root with that rendered *redeem* in Luke 24 : 21; Titus 2 : 14; 1 Peter 1 : 18, and *redemption* in Luke 2 : 38 and Heb. 9 : 12. The deliverance by Moses is historically a prophecy and type of the redemption by Christ.—**After he had shown wonders and signs.** A further suggestion of the hardness of Israel's heart, who for unbelief were condemned to forty years' wandering in the wilderness, and whose unbelief required the continuous miracles of mercy, and justified the divine penalties recorded in the history of that period.

37, 38. A prophet shall the Lord your God raise up. See ch. 3 : 22, note. Stephen reminds them that Moses foretold the advent of a Messiah *like himself.* He thus suggests to them that, in rejecting the Messiah, they are rejecting Moses; they, not he (ch. 6 : 11), are false to the law and the law-giver.—**This is he that was in the assembly in the wilderness.** Not, The church; the original (ἐκκλησία) stands in the Septuagint for the Great Congregation, or House of Parliament, the popular legislative body of the Jewish Commonwealth, an organization between a mass meeting and a representative congress (Numb. 14 : 1-5, 10; 27 : 18-23; 1 Kings 8 : 1-5; 1 Chron. 13 : 1-8; Ps. 22 : 22). As Moses was the leader of this Great Congregation, so Christ, his anti-type, is the leader of the church, *i. e.*, the entire body of Christ's disciples.—**With the angel** (Jehovah) * * * **and with our fathers.** With both, and therefore a mediator between them; as Christ, the anti-type which was to be. The argument is the same as that of Paul in Gal. 3 : 19, 20; Stephen's preaching of Jesus Christ as a mediator between God and man is not, as charged, blasphemy against God or Moses; it accords with the divine dispensation from the beginning; and it does not weaken but strengthens allegiance to God.—**Who received the living oracles.** Oracles (λόγιον) are condensed, pregnant words. They are called *living*, not because they are *life-giving*, for that is not the meaning of the original (ζῶν is never equivalent to ζωοποιῶν), and the law given by Moses has no power to give life (Rom. 8 : 3; Gal. 3 : 21); but because they are *words of life*, *i. e.*, words that point to and give counsel respecting spiritual life, not mere civil and ecclesiastical regulations, and because they have a vitality which has made them endure with undiminished power after all contemporaneous literature has perished (Matt. 5 : 18).

39-41. To whom our fathers would not obey. A further illustration of the persistent rejection of God and his appointed means and messengers by the Jews.—**And in their hearts turned back.** Not, Wished to return to Egypt; this wish was not until later in their history (Numb. 14 : 4); but in their hearts abandoned God, and so established the idolatrous worship of Egypt. The Jews (Exod. 32 : 4; Neh. 9 : 18) worshipped the golden calf for having brought them out of Egypt, not as a means of enabling them to return thither.—**Saying unto Aaron.** The account is in Exod. 32 : 1-6.—**This Moses.** The language is that of contempt. He had disappeared, and his disappearance was taken as an evidence

42 Then God turned, and gave[f] them up to worship
the[g] host of heaven; as it is written[h] in the book of
the prophets, O ye house of Israel, have ye offered to
me slain beasts, and sacrifices, *by the space of* forty
years in the wilderness?

43 Yea, ye took up the tabernacle of Moloch, and
the star of your god Remphan, figures which ye made,
to worship them: and I will carry you away beyond
Babylon.
44 Our fathers had the tabernacle of witness in the

f Ps. 81 : 12.... g Deut. 4 : 19; 2 Kings 17 : 16; Jer. 19 : 13.... h Amos 5 : 25, 26.

that his God was unworthy of their confidence. **They made a calf in those days.** The apis, or sacred bull, was one of the chief deities of Egypt; was kept at Memphis; had in its honor an annual festival lasting seven days, which was observed with songs and dancing analogous to the festivals of the Israelites before their golden calf. The Israelites had participated in the Egyptian idolatrous worship before leaving Egypt (Josh. 24 : 14). The golden calf was doubtless made to imitate this apis, but whether as a substitute for Jehovah is not clear. Possibly it was not even clear to the Israelites themselves. Calf-worship was afterwards introduced by Jeroboam into the Holy Land, at the time of the disruption of the kingdom, to prevent the northern tribes from going up to Jerusalem on the great feast-days (1 Kings 12 : 26-29), and was probably brought by him thither from Egypt (1 Kings 11 : 40). The ox was a common form of idol in the East, on account of his utility in agriculture; and recent discoveries in Nineveh have brought to light well-preserved colossal bulls.—**And rejoiced in the works of their own hands.** All substitution of self for God is in the nature of idolatry; it was in Stephen's time the sin of Israel, who trusted in their own righteousness, not in divine grace and mercy (Luke 18 : 11, 12).

42, 43. Then God turned. From mercy to judgment. Observe that the immutability of God is not inconsistent with either inflections of feeling or changes in providential dealing.—**And gave them up to worship the host of heaven.** The implication is, that they were preserved from idolatry only by the preventing grace of God, and that when that was withdrawn, they naturally gravitated into idolatries; and this agrees with the teaching of Scripture elsewhere (see Rom. 1 : 24, 26, 28; Hos. 4 : 17). There is no mention in the Pentateuch of star-worship; but there are frequent traces of it in the subsequent history of the Jews (2 Kings 21 : 3, 5; 23 : 4, 5; Jer. 19 : 13; Zeph. 1 : 5); and they were warned against it by Moses (Deut. 4 : 19; 17 : 3). It was a common form of idolatry in the East from the earliest ages.—**In the book of the prophets.** The reference is to Amos 5 : 25, 26.—**Have ye offered to me slain beasts and sacrifices?** etc. There is considerable difficulty in both the reading and the interpretation of this passage. Stephen quotes from the Septuagint, which differs from the original Hebrew. The English reader will readily perceive the difficulty by comparing the language here with the following translation of the Hebrew, from *Lange's Commentary:*

Did ye offer me sacrifice and food offerings
In the wilderness forty years, O house of Israel?
(No) but ye bore the tent of your King (tabernacle of Moloch),
And the pedestal of your images (and Chiun, your images),
The star of your God,
Which ye made for yourselves,
Therefore, will I carry you away captive beyond Damascus,
Saith Jehovah whose name is God of hosts.

There is some uncertainty about the proper rendering of the Hebrew in Amos, but this appears to me to give the sense accurately. How it has happened that the Septuagint differs from the Hebrew is not known. Accepting the reading of the Septuagint and the N. T. here, there is difficulty in its interpretation. Some suppose that the prophet contrasts the worship of the true God by Israel in the wilderness, with the later idolatries under the kings, thus rendering the passage, *Did ye not offer to me slain beasts and sacrifices forty years in the wilderness, but (now) ye have taken up the tabernacle of Moloch*, etc. But this does not accord with the correct grammatical rendering of the original, which employs the same tense in speaking of the sacrifices in the wilderness and the worship of Moloch. Others have supposed that the Israelites did actually carry a small movable shrine and image of heathen idols, and thus mingle idolatry with the worship of the true God in the wilderness. But nothing of the sort is mentioned in the Pentateuch, and God, who disclosed and punished the sin of Achan, would hardly have passed by such a secret idolatry among his people. It seems to me that the language is that of bitter sarcasm, such as is not unfrequently employed by the prophets. The context both here and in Amos confirms this view, as does the analogous teachings in Isaiah 66 : 3. Comp. Isaiah 1 : 10–15. So interpreted, the prophet refers to and rebukes the complacent satisfaction of Israel in the history of the fathers; self-complacency makes all worship vain. The tabernacle in which they gloried was like that of Moloch, and the worship like that of Remphan. So Lange (see above) apparently understands the original passage. Moloch was a Phœnician deity. "His image was of brass with the head of an ox, and outstretched arms of a

wilderness, as he had appointed, speaking unto Moses, that[i] he should make it according to the fashion that he had seen.
45 Which[j] also our fathers that came after, brought in with Jesus into the possession of the Gentiles, whom[k] God drave out before the face of our fathers, unto the days of David;
46 Who found favour[l] before God, and desired[m] to find a tabernacle for the God of Jacob.
47 But Solomon[n] built him an house.

i Exod. 25 : 40; 26 : 30; Heb. 8 : 5....j Josh. 3 : 14....k Neh. 9 : 24; Ps. 44 : 2; 78 : 55....l 1 Sam. 16 : 1....m 1 Chron. 22 : 7....n 1 Kings 6 : 1, etc.; 8 : 20.

man, hollow; and human sacrifices (of children) were offered, by laying them in these arms and heating the image by a fire kindled within."—(*Alford.*) To this image the Hebrews, in violation of explicit commands (Lev. 18 : 21; 20 : 2-5), offered worship (2 Kings 16 : 3; 17 : 17; 23 : 10), sacrificing their children to it (Jer 7 : 31; Ps. 106 : 37, 38; Ezek. 16 : 20, 21; 23 : 37), though this was long subsequent to the wanderings in the wilderness. Who the god Remphan is was long a matter of dispute. A tablet recently discovered in Egypt throws light on the problem; it represents a group of gods, two bearing the name of Rempu (Remphan) and Ken (Chiun). The reference is probably to the worship of these deities, the Hebrew in Amos employing the name of Ken or Chiun, and the Septuagint, and therefore Stephen, for some unexplained reason, substituting the name of the other deity, Rempu or Remphan.—**Beyond Babylon.** Stephen substitutes Babylon for Damascus in the original prophecy; perhaps, as Alford and Hackett suggest, because the Babylonian captivity was the one most memorable in the Jewish annals.

44-47. That Stephen understands the language quoted from Amos to be that of sarcasm is indicated by these verses. He goes on to say, that the tabernacle which they had, and which the prophet thus describes as the tabernacle of Moloch, was made by Moses according to the divine pattern, was carried by Israel into the holy land at the time when they drove out the Canaanites, and was the predecessor and germ of the Temple by which they set so much store. If the prophet could stigmatize it as the tabernacle of Moloch, and Solomon could declare of the Temple that it was not the true dwelling-place of God, Stephen was guilty of no blasphemy in what he had said concerning it and its impending destruction. Such appears to me to be the connexion.—**The tabernacle of witness.** The language is the same in the Greek version, though different in our English Bible, in Numb. 16 : 18, 19. The tabernacle was called the tabernacle of the congregation, because the place where the congregation of Israel, or their representative Moses, were to meet God; and the tabernacle of witness, because it was a perpetual witness to the covenant between God and his people. It was a movable structure, with board sides and tent roof, 15 × 15 × 45 feet. It was divided by a curtain into two apartments, the holy place and the Holy of Holies. In the first, or ante-room, was the altar of incense, the table of shew-bread, and the golden candle-stick; in the Holy of Holies was the ark of the covenant, with the mercy-seat above the ark, and the two tables of stone containing the ten commandments within it. For further description of tabernacle, with illustration and plan, see Heb., ch. 9, notes.—**According to the figure that he had seen.** God showed Moses the pattern in the Mount (Exod. 25 : 9, 40). Observe the contrast with ver. 43. The figure which God had shown, the prophet stigmatizes as the figures which *ye made.* As the brazen serpent made at God's direction by Moses, when employed as an object of idolatrous worship by Israel, became Nehushtan, a mere "thing of brass," and was broken in pieces (2 Kings 18 : 4), so the tabernacle and the Temple, made by divine direction, became the tabernacle of Moloch, and the figure of men's hands, when the nation transferred its worship from God to the house.—**Which also our fathers having inherited.** Not, as in our English version, *which came after.* The fact stated is that the tabernacle of the days of Joshua was inherited by Israel from the Mosaic dispensation in the wilderness.—**Brought in with Jesus.** That is, with *Joshua.* The Greek equivalent to Joshua, which is a Hebrew name, is Jesus; but the rendering here and in Heb. 4 : 8 is misleading to the English reader. The tabernacle went before Joshua when he crossed the Jordan (Josh., ch. 4), and was set up by him at Shiloh (Josh. 18 : 1), where it remained throughout the whole period of the Judges. It was finally merged in the Temple erected by Solomon at Jerusalem, where David had meanwhile constructed a new tabernacle (2 Sam. 6 : 17; 1 Chron. 16 : 1). All this sacred history did not prevent the prophets calling it the tabernacle of Moloch, when it became an object of idolatrous reverence among the people.—**In their taking possession of the Gentiles.** That is, at the time of their conquest of the land of the Gentiles. So Alford and Alexander. The ark, which sanctified the tabernacle, when carried by the priests about the walls of Jericho, led to the overthrow of that city, which was the key to the whole land (Josh., ch. 6). It is to the participation of the tabernacle in the campaigns of Joshua that Stephen here refers. —**Unto the days of David.** Not until his reign were the enemies of Israel completely subdued; not until then was Jerusalem captured and made a Jewish city (2 Sam., ch. 5).—**Who besought** (permission) **to find a dwelling for the God**

48 Howbeit,[o] the Most High dwelleth not in temples
made with hands; as saith the prophet,
49 Heaven[p] *is* my throne, and earth *is* my footstool:
what house will ye build me? saith the Lord: or what
is the place of my rest?
50 Hath not my hand made all these things?
51 Ye stiffnecked,[q] and uncircumcised[r] in heart and
ears, ye do always resist the Holy Ghost: as your fathers *did*, so *do* ye.
52 Which[s] of the prophets have not your fathers
persecuted? and they have slain them which shewed
before of the coming of the Just[t] One; of whom ye
have been now the betrayers and murderers:
53 Who have received the law by[u] the disposition
of angels, and have not kept *it*.

o ch. 17 : 24; 1 Kings 8 : 27....p Isa. 66 : 1, 2....q Exod. 32 : 9; Isa. 48 : 4....r Lev. 26 : 41; Jer. 9 : 26; Rom. 2 : 28, 29....s 2 Chron. 36 : 16; 1 Thess. 2 : 15....t ch. 3 : 14....u Gal. 3 : 19.

of Jacob. See 2 Sam. 7 : 2; 1 Chron. 22 : 7: Ps. 132 : 3–5. The Greek word is not the same as that rendered *tabernacle* in the preceding verses. David did pitch a *tent* for God's dwelling; he desired permission to build a *permanent temple*, but this was denied him. Some manuscripts have here *for the house of Jacob*, and this reading is adopted by Tischendorf. But Meyer's conjecture that it was early adopted to avoid a seeming discrepancy with ver. 48, seems to me reasonable. There is good authority for the ordinary reading, and the context requires it.—**But Solomon built him an house.** The worship of God went on under Moses, Joshua, Samuel, and David, before the Temple was built; how could the destruction of the Temple be a destruction of true worship, or Stephen's prophecy of its destruction be accounted blasphemy against God?

48-50. The historical argument that God and his worship are not dependent on, nor identical with, the Temple and its service, is confirmed by a quotation from the O. T. Ver. 48 embodies the declarations of Solomon (1 Kings 8 : 27) and David (2 Chron. 6 : 18). The language of the Greek is significantly terse, *The Most High dwells not in* (what is) *hand made.* Ver. 49 is quoted from Isaiah 66 : 1, 2. Observe Paul's declaration of the same truth in his address to the Athenians (ch. 17 : 24).

51-53. Stephen breaks off in the midst of his argument with this closing invective. Whether interrupted by some act or gesture on the part of the council or some of its members, or by seeing in their faces the gathering signs of pride and anger and disdain, as the full meaning of his historical survey, at first unperceived, dawns upon them, or by the fervor of his own spirit, as the dark succession of apostasies, idolatries, and murders, terminating in the crucifixion of the Messiah, unrolls itself before him, must be a matter merely of surmise. There is no indication of an actual interruption; the mere overflow of fervid indignation seems to me hardly compatible with the character of Stephen as indicated by the course of his address; I should, therefore, incline to attribute the sudden change in its tone to hostility, if not actual menace, manifest in the countenances of the council.—**Stiff-necked and uncircumcised in heart and ears.** The appellation of *stiff-necked* is borrowed from the Pentateuch (Exod. 32 : 9; 33 : 3, 5; Deut. 9 : 6, 13). It refers to the pride and stubbornness of Israel. *Uncircumcised in heart and ear* are figures also borrowed from the O. T. (Lev. 26 : 41; Deut. 30 : 6; Jer. 6 : 10; 9 : 26). Circumcision was a sign of covenant relations with God. To be uncircumcised in heart is to be in heart estranged from God and excluded from the privileges of his people; to be uncircumcised in ear is to be bereft of his word, the possession of which was accounted rightly the peculiar and the high privilege of the Jews (Rom. 3 : 2). Though in formal possession of it, the Jews, by closing their ears to its instructions, commands, and warnings (Matt. 19 : 15), were as the Gentiles who had no access to it. Thus both in heart and in ear they were as heathen (Rom. 2 : 25–29).—**Ye do always resist the Holy Ghost.** Observe the incidental evidence of the personality of the Holy Ghost, and that he was not first revealed at Pentecost, but dealt with and was resisted by Israel throughout their whole history (see notes on ch. 2 : 4, 38, 39).—**As your fathers did, so do ye.** Very analogous language is used of the fathers in Isaiah 63 : 10; and in the Epistles Christians are warned not to resist the Holy Spirit (Ephes. 4 : 30; 1 Thess. 5 : 19).—**Which of the prophets have not your fathers persecuted,** etc.? This language is not to be taken literally; all the prophets were not slain; it is a rhetorical expression signifying the general spirit of disobedience and hostility to God, which had characterized the Jewish nation. Comp. 2 Chron. 36 : 16; Matt. 21 : 35–39, and especially Christ's parallel denunciation, Matt. 23 : 34, 35. Observe the change in Stephen's language; he speaks no longer of *our* fathers (vers. 12, 15, 19), but of *your* fathers. Their father was the devil (John 8 : 44), and they and their ancestry partook of his nature.—**Of the Just One.** The Messiah. The phrase is one common in Rabbinical literature as a designation of the Messiah, and is probably thence borrowed by the N. T. (see chaps. 3 : 14; 22 : 14; 1 Pet. 3 : 18; James 5 : 6). It is an appropriate designation of the only One who is absolutely just, being without sin (1 Pet. 2 : 22, with 1 John 1 : 8, and Rom. 3 : 23).—**Betrayers and murderers.** *Betrayers*, by accepting and employing the treachery of Judas; *murderers*, by unjustly condemning Jesus to death, falsely accusing him before Pilate, and

54 When they heard these things,[v] they were cut to
the heart, and they gnashed on him with *their* teeth.
55 But he, being [w] full of the Holy Ghost, looked up
stedfastly into heaven, and saw the glory of God, and
Jesus standing on the right hand of God,

56 And said, Behold, I see the [x] heavens opened,
and [y] the Son of man standing on the right hand of God.
57 Then they cried out with a loud voice, and stopped
their ears, and ran upon him with one accord,
58 And cast[z] *him* out of the city, and stoned *him:*

v ch. 5 : 33.... w ch. 6 : 5.... x Ezek. 1 : 1.... y Dan. 7 : 13.... z Luke 4 : 29; Heb. 13 : 12, 13.

inciting the mob to clamor for his crucifixion. It is a noticeable fact that both the bargain with Judas and the plans to wrest an unjust sentence from Pilate were made by the Sanhedrim before which Stephen was now speaking (Mark 8 : 31; Matt. 26 : 14, 15; 27 : 1, 2).—**By the disposition of angels.** That is, through the ministrations of angels. The ministry of angels is frequently referred to in the O. T., but not directly in connection with the giving of the law. It was, however, a Jewish belief that they were present and acted as ambassadors or interpreters between God and Moses; this belief is referred to by Herod in an address to the Jews: "We have learned from God the most excellent of our doctrines and the most holy part of our law, by angels or ambassadors" (Josephus' Ant. 15 : 5, 3). It is embodied in the Septuagint version of the O. T. in Deut. 33 : 2, where in lieu of the expression, "From his right hand went a fiery law," is substituted the expression, "On his right hand angels with him." Finally, this belief is apparently sanctioned not only here by Stephen, but also by Psalm 68 : 17; Gal. 3 : 19, and Heb. 2 : 2.—**And have not kept it.** The Jews gloried in the fact that they had a law; Stephen turns it to their shame, that having the law they did not keep it. The argument of Paul is the same in Rom. 1 : 17–23.

54-58. They were cut to the heart (see ch. 5 : 33, note).—**Gnashed on him with their teeth.** The same language is used by our Lord to describe the finally lost (Matt. 8 : 12; 13 : 42, etc.), whose suffering is that of an impotent rage, not of a mere remorse, still less of a true sorrow for sin. Observe that the passions of hell break forth in manifestations of rage and malice even on earth.—**But he, being full of the Holy Ghost.** The divine presence grew the clearer as the human enmity grew stronger and more furious.—**Attent upon the heaven.** No longer concerned by the council before which he stood. The implication is that the council was held in some place where the heavens were visible; perhaps in one of the open courts of the Temple, or the court-yard of the high-priest's palace.—**Saw the glory of God.** The light unapproachable in which God is represented as clothed (1 Tim. 6 : 16), manifested in O. T. times by the appearance of the Shechinah, the cloud of light, called both in O. T. and N. T. the *glory* of God (Exod. 16 : 10; 24 : 17; Luke 2 : 9; Matt. 16 : 27). See Matt. 17 : 5, note, and observe how this close of Stephen's speech brings him back to his starting-point, the whole address having related to the God of glory (ver. 2), *i. e.*, to his self-manifestation, which began with his appearance to Abraham, and is consummated in the earthly life, and, finally, in the heavenly glory of Jesus Christ.—**And Jesus standing on the right hand of God.** The language certainly implies a difference of *persons* in the Godhead, and is inconsistent with Sabellianism, which represents the Trinity as one of manifestation only; for here Stephen, full of the *Holy Ghost*, sees at the same time the Father and the Son. Christ is represented as *standing*, not, as Chrysostom, that he may show his attitude of help to the martyr, for he does not interfere for Stephen's deliverance; rather to receive him. May it not be regarded as a mark of special honor that the Lord receives the first martyr standing? On the whole vision Alford well remarks: "Stephen, under accusation of blaspheming the earthly temple, is granted a sight of the heavenly temple; being cited before the Sadducaic high-priest, who believed neither angel nor spirit, he is vouchsafed a vision of the heavenly High-Priest, standing and ministering at the throne, amidst the angels and just men made perfect."—**The Son of man standing.** The phrase, *Son of man*, is used by Daniel prophetically of the Messiah, and by Christ of himself, but never in the N. T. by the sacred writers in speaking of him, except here and in Rev. 1 : 13; 14 : 14. Why is it used here? Stephen, impelled by the Holy Spirit, employs the very same words in which Jesus himself had, before this same council, foretold his second coming in glory (Matt. 26 : 64), and thus he indicates to them that the glorification of the Just One, whom they had betrayed and murdered, had already begun. Moreover, he thus emphasizes the truth that it is Christ in his mediatorial capacity, Christ the Saviour, Christ with all his human sympathies and affections, Christ the *Son of man*, no less than the Son of God, who is ever at the right hand of God, and who there awaits the coming of his own unto him. Observe in this revelation a confirmation of the reality and the nearness of the spirit world. Comp. 2 Kings 6 : 17.

57, 58. It appears to me very clearly that this was the act of a mob, not the regular and formal execution of a judicial sentence, which could not be executed legally by the Jews without the sanction of the Roman procurator (John

and the witnesses[a] laid down their clothes at a young man's feet, whose name was[b] Saul.
59 And they stoned Stephen, calling upon *God*, and saying, Lord Jesus, receive[c] my spirit!
60 And he kneeled down, and cried with a loud voice, Lord, lay[d] not this sin to their charge. And when he had said this, he fell asleep.

a ch. 6 : 13. . . . b ch. 8 : 1, 3; 22 : 20. . . . c Ps. 31 : 5; Luke 23 : 46. . . . d Matt. 5 : 44; Luke 23 : 34.

18 : 31). There is no indication here of any formal vote, or any sentence. Possibly the high-priest, having experienced so great difficulty in wresting a death-sentence from Pilate in the case of Jesus Christ, thought it easier to incite a mob to execute it directly, without the forms of law. But though not formally pronounced, it is clear that the informal sentence of the council was death, expressed rather by their actions than by their words. Stoning was a common method of executing the death penalty among the Jews, and

DEATH OF STEPHEN.

was especially prescribed for blasphemy (Lev. 24 : 16). It was necessarily without the walls of the city (Lev. 24 : 14; Numb. 15 : 35; 1 Kings 21 : 13; Heb. 13 : 12). The two witnesses who were required under Jewish law in order to the condemnation of every accused person, were, on the infliction of the sentence, to cast the first stones; afterward the people generally were to join (Deut. 17 : 5-7). In order to be disencumbered, they first laid off the outer garment, the cloak or mantle (ἱμάτιον), leaving on only the under-garment or tunic (χιτών). These cloaks are put in Saul's charge for safe-keeping. Of his age, the phrase *young man* gives little idea. He could hardly have been over forty; if, as was apparently the case from his participation in the action of the council here, and from the commission given to him in ch. 9 : 1, 2, he was a member of the Sanhedrim, he must have been more than thirty. The accompanying illustration represents the traditional site of Stephen's death, at St. Stephen's gate, now called Damascus gate. Some portions of it are very ancient, showing the Hebrew style of building.

59, 60. Calling upon God and saying, Lord Jesus, receive my spirit. The word *God* is added by the translators, but correctly represents the sense of the original which is literally, *Invoking and saying.* Observe that the N. T. represents Jesus Christ as an object of worship, here of petition in the supreme moment of life (comp. Matt. 28 : 17; Luke 24 : 52; Heb. 1 : 6; Rev. 5 : 13, 14), and that nowhere in the N. T. is such petition presented by any disciple to saint, angel, or other created being. Observe, too, that this prayer to Christ was uttered, and this vision of him, standing on the right hand of God, was vouchsafed, when Stephen was *full of the Holy Ghost;* the one is therefore assuredly no error, and the other no illusion. In Stephen's twofold prayer, *receive my spirit* and *lay not this sin to their charge*, he follows the example set him by his Lord (Luke 23 : 34, 46). The former petition is re-echoed in Paul's utterance, "I am persuaded that he is able to keep that which I have committed unto him against that day" (2 Tim. 1 : 12); and the whole scene may well have been present in the apostle's mind when he wrote Phil. 1 : 23 and 2 Tim. 4 : 8. Stephen's prayer for forgiveness of his enemies is a sufficient answer to those critics who have wished to see in the outbreak of vers. 51-53, an indication of unseemly passion. The original is literally, *Weigh not against them this sin*, and is well interpreted by Wordsworth, "When thou, the Judge of all, weighest their actions in thy balance, do not place this sin in the scale against them." The conversion of Saul was an answer to this prayer, for it shows that the perpetrators of the crime were not thereby excluded from the divine mercy. See 1 Tim. 1 : 16. Stephen's calm committal of his spirit to his Lord, is so palpably inconsistent with the doctrine of a state of purgatory, or sleep, between death and the judgment, that Roman Catholic theology exempts all martyrs from purgatorial discipline.—**He fell**

CHAPTER VIII.

AND Saul[e] was consenting unto his death. And at that time there was a great persecution against the church which was at Jerusalem; and they were all scattered[f] abroad throughout the regions of Judæa and Samaria, except the apostles.

2 And devout men carried Stephen *to his burial*, and made great lamentation over him.
3 As for Saul, he[g] made havoc of the church, entering into every house, and haling men and women, committed *them* to prison.
4 Therefore they that were scattered abroad, went every where preaching the word.

e ch. 7 : 58....f ch. 11 : 19....g ch. 26 : 10, 11; Gal. 1 : 13.

asleep. A characteristic Christian expression for death, though found also in the Hebrew Rabbinical writers. Augustine traces a parallel between the death of Stephen and that of Jesus Christ, the charges the same, the condemnation the same, the prayers the same. But observe also the contrast: Christ crucified, a lingering death; Stephen stoned, an almost immediate death; Christ forsaken of his Father (Matt. 27 : 46), Stephen with the glory of God and of his Lord and Saviour, radiant before him.

Ch. 8 : 1–4. FIRST POPULAR OUTBREAK AGAINST THE CHURCH, AND THE RESULT. GOD'S PROVIDENCE EXPELS HIS CHURCH FROM ITS REST AND IMPELS IT TO ITS APPOINTED WORK (Deut. 32 : 11).

March A. D. 35 or 36. The death of Stephen marks a transition in the history of the church (see p. 80). Henceforth the sacred narrative describes the diffusion of the Gospel throughout the Gentile world. The initiation of this movement is due to the persecution inaugurated by the martyrdom of Stephen; it begins by the preaching of the Gospel in Samaria; it is carried on without the apostles, chiefly by the Greek converts; it receives a new impulse in the conversion of Saul; it is directly sanctioned by the divine vision vouchsafed to Peter, and the commission given to him (chaps. 10, 11); and it is finally adopted as the doctrine and policy of the Christian church, by the commission of Paul and Barnabas as missionaries to the Gentiles (ch. 13 : 1–3).

1, 2. And Saul was consenting unto his death. Literally, *was taking pleasure in;* the original (συνευδοκέω) is so rendered in Rom. 1 : 32; and 1 Cor. 7 : 12, 13. The similarity of the language here and in Acts 22 : 20 raises the presumption that Luke's authority for this statement was Paul's speech in Jerusalem. We are not necessarily to suppose a malignant pleasure in Stephen's suffering; rather the pleasure of a perverted conscience in the punishment of what Saul regarded as a heinous crime.—**At that time.** Literally, *In that day.* Matt. 13 : 1; John 14 : 20; 16 : 23, 26, indicates that day need not necessarily be taken literally, but it may be so taken here. It will then indicate that the mob, incited by the work of their own passions, went directly from Stephen's corpse to the customary places of Christian assembly to disperse them. Why this popular outbreak against Christianity, when, up to this time, the people had welcomed and even defended it (ch. 2 : 41, 47; 4 : 21; 5 : 12–16, 26)? Such transitions of popular feeling, which is always fickle, are common. The triumphal entry and the crucifixion of Jesus Christ is parallel (Luke 19 : 37, 38; 23 : 18, 21, etc.). So long as the apostles, who were Hebrews, preached the Gospel to the Hebrews, and the issue was between them and the Sadducees, who were powerful but unpopular, the feeling of the people was with the apostles. When the Gospel was preached by a Greek, and accompanied with the declaration that Jerusalem and the Temple would be destroyed, and the offer of mercy made to all nations, it became odious. Comp. Luke 4 : 22, 28; John 6 : 15, 66.—**They were all dispersed.** Literally true, so far as this, that all the Christian assemblages were broken up, the body, which had hitherto met daily (ch. 2 : 46), was scattered; but all the disciples were not driven out of Jerusalem—**Except the apostles.** The twelve apostles represented the twelve tribes of Israel, and were appointed primarily to witness the truth to the Hebrews, with whom they were in national sympathy, and whose religious prejudices, to some extent, they shared (ch. 9 : 14). When the era of preaching to the Gentiles was inaugurated, it was, by divine providence, entrusted to Greeks; and we have no account of any ministry to the Gentiles by any of the twelve, except Peter and John. Observe, too, (1) the indication that the apostles were not the *authoritative* leaders of the early church; for this radical change in its ministry was inaugurated without them; it was a spontaneous, not an ecclesiastical movement; (2) that God, who called fishermen to be apostles, called laymen to be missionaries, that thus he might show that the power is of God, not of men. Why the twelve remained at Jerusalem is not clear. Perhaps they hoped for the speady manifestation of the Messiah there, in his second coming. The fact that they could so remain, shows that the persecution was, as yet, fitful, the action of a mob rather than of the authorities, and that in Jerusalem it spent itself in breaking up the Christian assemblies, except as Saul (ver. 3) pushed his inquisition further. — **Devout men.** Whether Christians, or godly Jews not yet brought to the acceptance of Christianity, but sincerely desiring to know the truth, and impressed by the sincerity and earnestness of Stephen, is uncertain;

5 Then Philip[h] went down to the city of Samaria,
and preached Christ unto them.
6 And the people with one accord[i] gave heed unto
those things which Philip spake, hearing[j] and seeing
the miracles which he did.
7 For[k] unclean spirits, crying with loud voice, came

h ch. 6 : 5....i 2 Chron. 30 : 12....j John 4 : 41, 42....k Mark 16 : 17.

probably the latter, since the phrase *devout men* is never used in the N. T. to describe Christians. Acts 22 :12 is not an exception, for there Ananias is described, not as a Christian, but as "a devout man *according to the law*," *i. e.*, according to the Jewish standard.—**Devout men * * * made great lamentation over him.** Literally, *made a great beating*, the ordinary Jewish lamentation being accompanied with beating on the breast and the like. See, for description, Mark 5 : 38, note. This language implies that these devout men were still Jews in their feelings and customs, whether in heart Christians or no.

3, 4. But Saul made havoc of the church. The original verb (λυμαίνομαι) "is properly used of wild beasts, or of hostile armies devastating or ravaging."—(*Alford.*)—**Entering from house to house.** Not *every house.* This is not asserted, and could hardly be literally true. This action of Saul is stated as exceptional. The intense fervor of his spirit showed itself in the vigor with which he prosecuted the persecution; he was determined to stamp out the heresy in its inception. On his character and previous life, see note on Saul's Conversion, ch. 9 :1-9. —**Haling men and women.** Dragging them forcibly before the Jewish magistrates, or to prison. The fact that women were victims of this persecution is stated to show the vehemence of Saul's persecuting spirit.—**Committed them to prison.** For trial. Paul gives some additional particulars concerning this persecution, which apparently lasted for some months; perhaps throughout the summer. The Christians were scourged in the synagogues; were imprisoned; in some instances were put to death; the only apparent escape was by blaspheming the name of Christ, *i. e.*, openly renouncing allegiance to him, and adopting the Jewish verdict, that he was an impostor worthy of death (Acts 22 : 4, 19; 26 : 9-11; 1 Tim. 1 : 13. See also 1 Cor. 15 : 9; Gal. 1 : 13).—**Went everywhere.** This has since become literally true; but at this time the dispersion of the Christians could hardly have extended beyond the bounds of Palestine. The original implies no more; it is literally *passed through*, *i. e.*, the country.—**Preaching the word.** Observe that this word requires no defining. As the O. T.

CITY OF SAMARIA, FROM THE SOUTH-EAST. (The Mediterranean in the distance.)

was to the Jews the Scriptures, *i. e.*, *the* writings, and the O. T. and the N. T. are to us the Bible, *i. e.*, *the* book, so, to these early Christians, the *only* word was the word of life through Jesus Christ.

Ch. 8 : 5-24. FIRST MISSIONARY PREACHING OF THE GOSPEL IN SAMARIA. CASE OF SIMON MAGUS. TRUE CONVERSION ILLUSTRATED BY A CASE OF SPURIOUS CONVERSION. See note below, On the case of Simon Magus.

5-8. Then Philip went down to a city of Samaria. It was literally *up* from Jerusalem, the city of Samaria being about forty miles, in a straight line, north, on the road to Galilee. The original is ambiguous, and may be rendered *the* city of Samaria, *i. e.*, the city of that name, or *a* city of Samaria, *i. e.*, a city in that district; some suppose Sychar. Samaria was built by Omri, king of Israel, about 925 B. C., on a hill; derived its name, probably, from the original

out of many that were possessed *with them:* and many taken with palsies,[l] and that were lame,[m] were healed.
8 And there was great joy in that city.
9 But there was a certain man, called Simon, which beforetime in the same city used sorcery,[n] and bewitched the people of Samaria, giving out[o] that himself was some great one:
10 To whom[p] they all gave heed, from the least to

l ch. 9 : 33, 34; Mark 2 : 3-11....m Matt. 11 : 5....n ch. 13 : 6; Rev. 22 : 15....o ch. 5 : 36; 2 Tim. 3 : 2, 5....p 2 Cor. 11 : 19.

owner of the hill, Shemer; was the capital of the ten tribes until the time of the captivity; was a prominent centre of the idolatrous worship introduced by Ahab, and the site of a temple to Baal built by him and destroyed by Jehu; was rebuilt by Herod, and called by him Sebaste, the Greek equivalent of Augustus, his imperial patron. It is the modern Sebastieh, a village constructed out of the ruins of the ancient city (1 Kings 16 : 24, 32; 2 Kings 10 : 27). *Philip* is the deacon (Acts 6 : 5), not the apostle (Matt. 10 : 3), as is evident from vers. 1 and 14. The persecution being, apparently, especially directed against the Greeks, he would naturally be driven out of Jerusalem by it. Except the description of his work here, nothing is known of him but the fact that he became a well-known preacher, was called Philip the evangelist, probably to distinguish him from the apostle, and had four daughters who became inspired teachers (Acts 21 : 8, 9).—**And proclaimed the Messiah unto them.** The verb signifies literally *to make proclamation* as a public herald. The Samaritans believed in the advent of a promised Messiah (John 4 : 25, 29); Philip proclaimed that he had already come. On the character of the Samaritans, see notes on John, ch. 4. They were descended from a mongrel population, made by an intermixture of Jews and heathen at the time when Israel was carried into captivity by the Assyrian king (2 Kings 17 : 24-29). This is the first public preaching of the Gospel to any outside the Jewish nation. Christ had confined his ministry, while alive, to Judea, Galilee, and Perea. Though he went into the coasts of Tyre and Sidon, it was not to preach. He stayed in Sychar, a city of Samaria, two days, on his way from Jerusalem to Galilee (John 4 : 40), and the remembrance of that visit, six or seven years previous, may have prepared the way for the reception of the Gospel now; but there is no statement in John that he preached the Gospel publicly at that time. He expressly forbade his apostles from preaching, either in the way of the Gentiles or the cities of the Samaritans, during their first missionary tour. See Matt. 10 : 5, 6, and note there, for explanation of that prohibition.—**Hearing them and seeing the miracles.** Not *hearing and seeing the miracles*. Two reasons are assigned for the public reception of Philip; one, the message which he brought, which was welcome to the Samaritans; the other, the miracles which he wrought, which compelled attention, and also gave sanction to his word.—**Unclean spirits.** On the nature of demoniacal possession, see Vol. I, p. 123.—**There was great joy.** Not only had the way been prepared among the Samaritans by the previous ministry of Jesus Christ, but there was no prejudice against the catholicity of the Gospel; the doctrine, unbearable to the Jew, that God was no respecter of persons, was a welcome doctrine to the despised Samaritan and the Gentile.

9-11. But a certain man named Simon was beforetime in that city. The intimation is that it had been for some time his residence. He is a prominent character in ecclesiastical history, but so much of his life is legendary that only its barest outlines can be given with any certainty. Some doubt even has been entertained whether the Simon of tradition and the one here mentioned are the same; but their resemblance in character is too marked to leave much room for reasonable doubt. The Simon of tradition was a native of Cyprus; professed to believe the oriental philosophy of his day; claimed to be himself an *eon* or emanation from the deity; traveled about with a beautiful prostitute, whom he represented as another divine emanation; aided Felix in seducing Drusilla, the queen of Emesa (see on Acts 24 : 24); subsequently came to Rome, where he continued to practice his magic arts, probably until his death, the legendary account of which is intrinsically improbable. He was the founder of an heretical sect, called from his name Simonians, the author of some extinct heretical books, and is accused of forging and circulating other books in the name of Christ and his disciples.—**Using sorcery.** From the Greek word here employed (μαγεύω, *maguo*) comes our English word *magi*, and the appellation *magus*, by which this Simon is commonly, in literature, distinguished from others of the same name in the N. T. He was probably a degenerate descendant of the magi or wise men of the East; for a description of their character and office, see Vol. I, p. 59. These traveling impostors swarmed over Greece and Rome, pretending to magical powers derived from the spirit world; they were readers of the stars, interpreters of dreams, fortune-tellers, medicine men—in brief, they exercised the same arts as the modern fortune-teller, and by much the same methods; but they were as much more successful in those days than these, as the age was more ignorant and credulous. See Acts 13 : 6-10; 19 : 18-20.—**And astonishing the**

the greatest, saying, This man is the great power of God.
11 And to him they had regard, because that of long time he had bewitched[q] them with sorceries.
12 But when they believed[r] Philip preaching the things[s] concerning the kingdom of God, and the name of Jesus Christ, they were baptized, both men and women.
13 Then Simon himself believed also: and when he was baptized, he continued with Philip, and wondered, beholding the miracles and signs which were done.

q Gal. 3:1....r verse 37; ch. 2:41....s ch. 1:3.

people of Samaria. Not bewitching them. The verb is the same rendered *wondered* in ver. 13. Our English version implies the real exercise of a supernatural witchery over the people, which is not indicated by the original.—**Saying that he himself was some great one.** The oriental philosophy taught that the Infinite was manifested to and dwelt with the race through *eons* or emanations. See notes on the doctrine of the *Logos*, John, ch. 1, Vol. II. Simon claimed to be himself one of these *eons*. I am inclined to think, from the language here and in the next verse, that among the Samaritans, where the Messiah was expected, he claimed to be that Messiah; and this is indicated by some of the patristic literature against the Simonians. This claim would be the more readily acceded to from the general and widespread expectation of a Deliverer, which was by no means confined to the Jewish nation. See Vol. I, p. 60, § 3.—**He is the power of God, called the great.** This is the literal rendering of the best manuscripts. The meaning is that he is that power of God which is known as *the great one*. Observe that there is in his history that which is common to that of all great impostors; he preferred the most extravagant claims concerning himself, and the people took him at his own self-estimate. His very audacity carried weight.—**To whom they gave heed.** The verb is the same so rendered above in vers. 6 and 10. The contrast with ver. 6 is instructive; to Philip they gave heed because of his doctrine and his miracles of beneficent healing; to Simon because of their astonishment at his works of witchcraft. *Mere wonder-working is never a sound basis for a religious belief*, a truth which the modern spiritists would do well to bear in mind.—**Because for a long time they were astonished** (not *bewitched*, see above) **at his sorceries.** There is no reason whatever to believe that these sorceries were other than the frauds which are to-day practised in the same country by Mohammedan astrologers; none to suppose that Simon possessed any supernatural power, or any actual communion with the unseen world. Whether all the witchcraft and pretended miracles of the O. T. are to be explained as frauds may not be so clear.

12, 13. Concerning the kingdom of God. Inaugurated by the advent, the crucifixion, and the resurrection of Jesus Christ. It means here, as always in the N. T., the state of allegiance to God, whether in the individual heart, the community, or the future life.—**And the name of Jesus the Messiah;** that is, Philip proclaimed him as Jesus, *i. e.*, the Saviour (Matt. 1:21), and as Christ, *i. e.*, the priest or Anointed One. See note on Names of Jesus, Vol. I., p. 57.—**They were baptized.** In the name of Jesus (ver. 16), and as a sign that they accepted him as their Messiah. Observe that the affirmative preaching of the Gospel is the best antidote to error. There is no indication that Philip said anything directly about the superstition of the people and the magical arts of Simon.—**Then Simon also himself believed.** Not "*professed* to believe," as Hackett, and, substantially, Alexander and others; the historical statement is clear that he *did believe*, and the facts are narrated partly for the purpose of showing what are the conditions of salvation, by showing what supposed conditions are insufficient. Of these belief is one. See below, *Note on case of Simon Magus*. And the nature of the belief is also indicated by the course of the narrative. Neander's interpretation, "He was convinced that Philip was in league with some powerful spirit," is a pure and groundless surmise, and not complimentary to the simplicity, the clearness, and the directness of Philip's preaching. Simon believed the creed which Philip preached, viz., that the kingdom of God was at hand, and that Jesus was the Messiah, whose advent, death, and resurrection was its inauguration. Of the nature of this kingdom he doubtless had a crude and false conception, interpreting it by his own previous conception of what it was to be; and the result shows that he attached himself to it for his own aggrandizement. In this respect his case resembles that of Judas Iscariot (see Vol. I., p. 307), and his belief that of the vagabond Jewish exorcists mentioned in ch. 19:13.—**And being baptized he continued with Philip.** Attached himself personally to Philip, apparently in a subordinate position as his assistant. See ch. 10:7, where the same verb, rendered *waited on him continually*, is used to describe the relations of certain military attendants of Cornelius. Observe, then, that though Simon believed, was publicly baptized, and joined the discipleship, his heart was not right in the sight of God, and he still had no true part with God's people (ver. 21). The doctrine of baptismal regeneration,

14 Now when the apostles which were at Jerusalem heard that Samaria had received the word of God, they sent unto them Peter and John:
15 Who, when they were come down, prayed for them, that they might receive the Holy Ghost:
16 (For as yet[t] he was fallen upon none of them; only they were[u] baptized in the name of the Lord Jesus.)
17 Then laid[v] they *their* hands on them, and they received the Holy Ghost.

t ch. 19 : 2.... u ch. 2 : 38; 10 : 48; 19 : 5, 6; 1 Cor. 1 : 13.... v ch. 6 : 6; Heb. 6 : 2.

i. e., that the subject of baptism is regenerated by grace in the sacrament itself, and irrespective of his own faith, needs no other refutation than the history of Simon Magus. "Through baptism the church brought forth Simon Magus * * * Yet because love was wanting he was born in vain."—(*Augustine.*).—**Wondered.** The same word rendered bewitched in ver. 9.—**Beholding the powers and signs wrought.** It was wonder, not conscience, faith, or love, that brought Simon to join the disciples. He coveted their power, the reality of which he did not doubt; this is evident from his subsequent course.

14-16. Now the apostles, in Jerusalem. Not those apostles which remained in Jerusalem, which might be the meaning attached to our English version. Evidently the Philip here is not the apostle of that name, for he remained at Jerusalem.—**Hearing that Samaria had accepted the word of God.** Tischendorf reads, *Of Christ.* It was not the mere fact that the word had been preached in Samaria, but that Samaria had *accepted* it, which led to this apostolic commission.—**Peter and John.** Who are throughout the N. T. history fast friends; attached to each other by the very dissimilarity of their characters (Luke 5 : 1-11; John 13 : 23, 24; 18 : 15, 16; 21 : 7; Acts 3 : 1; 4 : 13). The going two by two, according to Christ's direction in their first commission (Mark 6 : 7), seems to have been practised customarily in the missionary work of the church (ch. 13 : 2; 15 : 39, 40). This is the last mention of John in the Acts; except in Revelation he is only mentioned again in the N. T. in Gal. 2 : 9. It is a significant fact that the apostle who desired to call down fire from heaven on a Samaritan village because it rejected Christ (Luke 9 : 54), is the one to carry to Samaria the baptism of the Holy Ghost, the true fire from heaven, not to consume but to make alive.—**That they might receive the Holy Ghost: for as yet he was fallen upon none of them.** A careful consideration of parallel passages in Scripture would have saved the commentators some difficulty experienced in the interpretation of this declaration. How could the Samaritans be converted and baptized without the regenerating influence of the Holy Spirit? The answer is that this phrase is never used in the N. T. of that gift of the Holy Ghost which is promised to *all* on condition of repentance and baptism in the name of Jesus Christ (ch. 2 : 38), and which is the indispensable condition of entering into the kingdom of God (John 3 : 3, 5). It always signifies the fulfillment, in a special manner, of Christ's promise to the twelve, Ye shall receive *power* after that the Holy Ghost is come upon you (ch. 1 : 8), and always an impartation of such a special presence of the Holy Ghost as is accompanied with supernatural gifts. Here the clear implication of ver. 18 is that the gift of the Holy Ghost described was accompanied by phenomena that were visible to a purely worldly and selfish nature like that of Simon; in ch. 10 : 44-46, the bestowal of the Holy Ghost was accompanied by speaking with tongues; in ch. 11 : 15, Peter characterizes it as a peculiar gift: "The Holy Ghost fell on them *as on us at the beginning*," *i. e.*, in the same manner and with the same results described in ch. 2 : 1-4; in ch. 19 : 2-6 the reception of the Holy Ghost is accompanied with the same supernatural and visible tokens. The declaration, then, is not that the Samaritans had not been spiritually quickened by the presence and power of the Spirit of God, but that no miraculous power had been imparted to them, manifested in visible signs. It was for this the apostles prayed; this was granted in answer to their prayer; and in consequence of witnessing the phenomena which ensued, whether of speaking in tongues, or healing, or what we know not, Simon desired to purchase the power of bestowing the same miraculous powers, as a means of augmenting his own influence and reputation as a wonder-worker.—**In the name of the Lord Jesus.** There is no case in the N. T. in which the apostles are reported to have baptized in the name of the Father, the Son, and the Holy Ghost, a conclusive indication that they did not understand that Christ, in Matt. 28 : 19, prescribed that as a necessary formula. See note there. The customary form was that here indicated.

17. Then laid they their hands on them and they received the Holy Ghost. On the signification of the laying on of hands, see ch. 6 : 6. The passage here and in ch. 19 : 5, 6, are the chief authorities for the rite of confirmation, whereby in the Episcopal and Roman Catholic churches the bishop (answering to the apostle here) lays his hands upon such as have been baptized, and do accept the Christian faith, confirming them in that faith, and receiving them into full membership with the church. Among the Romanists this rite is regarded as a solemn sacra-

18 And when Simon saw that through laying on of the apostles' hands the Holy Ghost was given, he offered them[w] money,

19 Saying, Give me also this power, that on whomsoever I lay hands, he may receive the Holy Ghost.
20 But Peter said unto him, Thy money perish with

w 1 Tim. 6 : 5.

ment, "bringing down the Holy Ghost in a more particular manner to dwell in them, and to fortify and confirm us in our faith, and enable us more effectually to resist all the enemies of our souls." The other principal Scripture references cited in support of this practice are Matt. 3 : 16; 19 : 15; Heb. 6 : 2; Ephes. 1 : 13, 14; 4 : 30; 2 Cor. 1 : 21; 2 Tim. 2 : 19. The apostles' course here is referred to in the Episcopal Prayer Book as the example, if not the authority, for the church in maintaining the rite. "We make our humble supplications," says the bishop in the service, "unto thee, for these thy servants, on whom, *after the example of thy holy apostles*, we have now laid our hands." I have stated elsewhere (Intro., p. 16) my reasons for not regarding the *example* but only the *teaching* of the apostles as authoritative. That this act of laying on of hands was not intended by them as the initiation of a permanent ecclesiastical rite, and still less as a sacrament, to be ranked with baptism and the Lord's Supper, seems to me clear, for the following reasons: (1.) There is no Scriptural basis for the idea that the apostles had authority to establish a sacrament for the universal church and for all time, and no indication that Christ established the rite of confirmation or directed its establishment. Matt. 19 : 15 furnishes no ground for such belief. (2.) There is nothing in the account here, or in ch. 19, to indicate the establishment of a permanent rite, as there is in Christ's directions to his twelve respecting the Lord's Supper and the rite of baptism (Luke 22 : 19; Matt. 28 : 19). (3.) There is no evidence that it was habitually maintained in the apostolic churches, as certainly baptism and the Lord's Supper were. On the contrary, both here and in ch. 19, the laying on of hands appears to have been done for the especial purpose of affording the infant discipleship some ocular evidence of the presence and power of the Spirit of God, and to have been accompanied with demonstrations which confessedly never attend the rite of confirmation now. I agree, therefore, with Alford in thinking that the apostolic preaching here and in ch. 19, affords no *authority* for the modern rite of confirmation, and no basis for the doctrine that it was instituted by the apostles. That rite must rest on the fitness of such a solemn confirmation, especially in the case of one baptized in infancy, on ecclesiastical usage, and on a certain remote analogy to the practice of the apostles in one or two exceptional cases. The question then remains, why did the apostles go down to Samaria and lay their hands on the Samaritan converts? The circumstances afford the answer to this question. They thus set the seal of their disapprobation on that excessive and unrelenting hatred which separated the Jew from the Samaritan (John 4 : 9); they gave the sanction of their names and presence to the doctrine that the Gospel was offered unto every one that believed, and to the practice of preaching it to the outcasts of Judaism; and they strengthened the faith of the Samaritans, a credulous people, and therefore easy to be led astray, God affording them, by the outpouring of the Spirit, and by accompanying supernatural signs, the same evidence which he had already afforded to the church at Jerusalem.

18, 19. The magicians were accustomed to sell the knowledge of their arts; Simon ranked the apostolic power with his own magical performances. He rightly estimated the Holy Spirit as a gift conferred; he showed a total lack of spiritual apprehension in supposing that the power to bestow it could be purchased. Whether he openly proposed to buy, or whether his act was a secret one, in the nature of an attempted bribery, the account does not indicate; the latter supposition is the more inherently probable. Whether the apostles had laid their hands on him or not does not appear; Alford thinks the course of the narrative indicates that they had not. The language clearly implies that sensible effects, such as the speaking of tongues, followed this laying on of hands, for Simon *saw* that the Holy Ghost was given. His desire was to be the equal in rank and power of the apostles; his act shows that his real motive in joining the Christian community was self aggrandizement. From his act here the name of simony has been given to the offence of buying or selling ecclesiastical offices in the church,—one which can only exist in an established church, where the spiritual office is a means of temporal profit, and is at the disposal of a lay patron or an ecclesiastical superior.

20-22. Thy money go with thee to destruction. This is not an anathema, a consignment of Simon to destruction, for in the next sentence Peter admonishes him to pray for forgiveness. The apostle declares that Simon is for destruction, if he does not escape by repentance, and repels the proffered money by an expression which is weakened by attempting to give to the language a literal construction. The underlying truth is that gold is perishable, as all things earthly (comp. 1 Pet. 1 : 7, 18; 1 Cor. 6 : 13), and that he who expects to buy the gift of God, proves his

thee, because[x] thou hast thought that the gift[y] of God
may be purchased with money.
21 Thou hast neither part[z] nor lot in this matter:
for[a] thy heart is not right in the sight of God.
22 Repent therefore of this thy wickedness; and
pray God, if[b] perhaps the thought of thine heart may
be forgiven thee:

23 For I perceive that thou art in the gall of bitterness,[c] and *in* the bond[d] of iniquity.
24 Then answered Simon, and said, Pray[e] ye to the
Lord for me, that none of these things which ye have
spoken come upon me.
25 And they, when they had testified and preached

x 2 Kings 5 : 15, 16; Matt. 10 : 8....y ch. 10 : 45; 11 : 17....z Josh. 22 : 25....a Ps. 78 : 36, 37; Ezek. 14 : 3....b Dan. 4 : 27; 2 Tim. 2 : 25....c Jer. 4 : 18; Heb. 12 : 15....d Ps. 116 : 16; Prov. 5 : 22; Isa. 28 : 22....e Exod. 8 : 8; Numb. 21 : 7; 1 Kings 13 : 6; Job 42 : 8; James 5 : 16.

corrupt, earthly, and therefore perishable nature. It is "as if he should have said, Thou art worthy to perish with thy money, when thou dost so blaspheme the Spirit of God."—(*Calvin.*) —**Because thou hast thought.** Observe, not because he had offered money, but because he had *thought* money could purchase the divine gift. It is the *thought*, not the deed, which Peter characterizes as damnable. The grace of God is a free gift; the thought that it can be purchased is insulting to God.—**Thou hast neither part nor lot.** If there is any difference in these words, the first indicates a portion already assigned; the second, one yet to be assigned. The first would then indicate that Simon had no present portion in Christian gifts; the second, no share in the future inheritance of the saints. And this appears to me to be the meaning. By most commentators, however, the terms are taken as synonymous, and the double expression as simply emphatic.—**In this word.** (λογος.) Not this *matter* or *business;* it is doubtful whether the original is ever used with that signification in the N. T.; but *in this word of the Gospel*, *i. e.*, the glad tidings of present salvation, including pardon and divine life here, and the promise of glory hereafter.—**For thy heart is not right.** "Not in earnest in its seeking after the Gospel, but seeks it with unworthy ends in view."—(*Alford.*) The word here rendered *right* is rendered *straight* in Luke 3 : 5; Simon's was a crooked heart that must be made straight before it could receive the indwelling of the Lord.—**Repent, therefore, of this thy wickedness.** Not in offering the money, but in so thinking of the divine grace as to desire to make it a means of self-aggrandizement.—**And pray God.** The better reading is, *the Lord*, *i. e.*, Jesus Christ.—**If, perhaps, the thought of thy heart may be forgiven thee.** Observe again, it is the *thought* that needs forgiveness, and the thought, not of the *mind*, but of the heart; the thought is wholly wrong, because the affections are earthly and sensual. Observe, too, the doubt of forgiveness implied by *If perhaps.* The apostle does not attempt to determine what sins may and what may not be forgiven (Matt. 12 : 31; 1 John 5 : 16), still less to receive the confession and pronounce the absolution.

23, 24. Unto the gall of bitterness (equivalent to bitter gall) **and the bond of iniquity I see thou art.** The order of the words gives emphasis to those which characterize Simon's condition. The exact meaning is not quite clear. Gall was regarded by the ancients as the seat of the venom of poisonous reptiles; and is in the N. T. a symbol of sin, as the serpent is of Satan (see Job 20 : 14; Rom. 3 : 13). The preposition *in* (εἰς) is literally *unto.* It indicates aim or end toward which any thing tends. The meaning then may be, I see that thou hast fallen into the poison and the bond of sin, or, I see that thou art tending to it, or, it may be regarded as a prophecy, I see that thou art about to become gall of bitterness, *i. e.*, a deadly poison to others, and a bond of iniquity, an organizer of sin and error. This last interpretation accords with the actual history of Simon subsequent to events here narrated. See above on ver. 9.—**Pray ye the Lord.** There is no true penitence in this prayer; no sense of sin; no seeking for forgiveness. It is the language of fear, not of repentance, and resembles that of Saul to Samuel (1 Sam. 15 : 30), who desired not divine forgiveness, but escape from public censure and reprobation before the people.

THE CASE OF SIMON MAGUS. The N. T. contains many cases illustrative of true conversion; this narrative illustrates a spurious conversion. Simon really believes, intellectually, the Gospel preached by Philip; he accepts the creed of the church; he publicly renounces his errors; he is baptized and received into Christian fellowship; he engages in church work (ver. 13, note). But he is drawn to this by wonder, not by an awakened conscience; he does not repent of nor confess his sin; nor does he consecrate himself to the service of God (ch. 22 : 10). His real purpose is self-aggrandizement; the thought of his heart, in his adhesion to the new cause, is manifested by his application to Peter; the language of the apostle shows that he never had any real participation in the Gospel; and his language, even after this rebuke, indicates no spiritual sense of his sin, no sorrow for it, no conscious need of the Saviour. Comparing his case with those of the penitent thief (Luke 23 : 41) and Zaccheus (Luke 19 : 8), there is a notable absence of confession or attempted reparation for the wrong already done; comparing it with that of Paul (ch. 22 : 10), there is a notable absence of any consecration of heart

the word of the Lord, returned to Jerusalem, and preached the gospel in many villages of the Samaritans.
26 And the angel of the Lord spake unto Philip, saying, Arise, and go toward the south, unto the way that goeth down from Jerusalem unto Gaza,[f] which is desert.
27 And he arose and went: and, behold, a man of Ethiopia,[g] an[h] eunuch of great authority under Candace queen of the Ethiopians, who had the charge of all her treasure, and had come[i] to Jerusalem for to worship,
28 Was returning; and, sitting in his chariot, read Esaias the prophet.

f Josh. 15 : 47.... g Zeph. 3 : 10.... h Isa. 56 : 3-5.... i 2 Chron. 6 : 32, 33.

and life to Christ. Simon accepts Christianity to use it for his own profit; Paul offers himself to Christ to be used. The lessons of the incident are (1) against the substitution of the externals of religion—the creed, the ceremonial, the active service, for the essence of religion, a heart straight in the sight of God; (2) against all simony, all purchase or procurement of place or position in the church for worldly advantage; (3) all worldliness and self-seeking.

Ch. 8 : 25-40. CONVERSION AND BAPTISM OF THE ETHIOPIAN. THE SEEKER SOUGHT.—THE RESULTS OF OBEYING THE DIVINE IMPULSE: A SOUL BROUGHT TO THE LIGHT.—THE PROGRESS OF A SOUL FROM DARKNESS TO LIGHT AND JOY, ILLUSTRATED: FROM HEATHENISM TO WORSHIP; FROM WORSHIP TO STUDY OF THE WORD; FROM STUDY TO PERSONAL INQUIRY; FROM INQUIRY TO ACCEPTANCE.—THE CONDITION OF OBTAINING LIGHT: FIDELITY IN SEEKING.—Matt. 7 : 8 illustrated.

This narrative affords a further illustration of the progress of the Gospel in its extension beyond the bounds of Judaism. From preaching to the Samaritans, whose religion was Jewish, but corrupted, Philip is directed to preach it to a heathen, but one who has already, at least partially, accepted the Jewish faith. The eunuch, converted, carries the Gospel with him into his own country; Philip continues his ministry throughout the border cities of the Holy Land, which are largely Gentile.

25. They, testifying and preaching the word of the Lord, returned to Jerusalem. Not, *When they had testified*, as in our English version. Their journey home was a missionary tour.—**And preached the Gospel in many villages of the Samaritans.** In this tour John called down fire from heaven on these villages; but in a sense and for a purpose how different from that with which he had once proposed to call down fire to destroy a Samaritan village! (Luke 9 : 54.)

26. And an angel of the Lord. Not *the* angel, which signifies generally, if not always, the same person, viz., Jesus Christ himself. Observe, the first communication to Philip is by an angel, and presumptively by one appearing in vision or dream; the second communication is by the Spirit of God himself (ver. 28), and presumptively without appearance or audible voice. Obedience to the first direction leads to a higher and more direct communication. The case illustrates the ministration of angels, taught by Heb. 1 : 7; Psalm 104 : 4. For other illustrations in the Book of Acts see chaps. 5 : 19; 10 : 3; 12 : 7; 27 : 23.—**To the way that goeth down from Jerusalem unto Gaza.** Alford gives, in a condensed form, the history of this city. "The southernmost city of Canaan (Gen. 10 : 19); in the part of Judah (Josh. 15 : 47), but soon taken from that tribe by the Philistines, and always spoken of as a Philistian city (1 Sam. 6 : 17; 2 Kings 18 : 8; Amos 1 : 6-8; Zeph. 2 : 4; Zech. 9 : 5). In Jer. 47 : 1 we have 'before Pharaoh (Necho ?) smote Gaza'—implying that at one time it was under Egypt. Alexander the Great took it after a siege of five months, but did not destroy it, for we find it a strong place in the subsequent Syrian wars. It was destroyed by the Jewish king Alexander Jannæus (96 B. C), after a siege of a year, but rebuilt again by the Roman general Gabinius—afterward given by Augustus to Herod, and finally, after his death, attached to the province of Syria. Mela, in the time of Claudius, calls it 'a vast city and strongly fortified,' with which agree Eusebius and Jerome. At present it is a large town by the same name, with from 15,000 to 16,000 inhabitants. The above chronological notices show that it can not have been *desert* at this time."—**Which is desert.** It is the *way*, not the city, which is thus described, and the description is added by the angel to distinguish which road Philip should take. There are several; the most direct is now the desert road, without towns or villages. This desert way gave opportunity for the eunuch to read the Scripture, and to Philip to baptize him without attracting observation. Such a retired place is always the most appropriate for private personal religious conversation. So Christ talked with Nicodemus alone at night, and with the woman of Samaria alone at the well.

27, 28. A man of Ethiopia. In its largest sense the term Ethiopia was applied to all the African bands south of Egypt; more definitely, it included the modern Nubia, Senaar, Kordofan, and part of Abyssinia. Its inhabitants were black in color and large in stature. Their land appears to have been one of wealth, and to have maintained some commercial relations with Palestine. The Hebrew equivalent for Ethiopia is Cush, and by this name it is designated in Gen-

GAZA.

esis. Some have supposed that this Ethiopian was a Jew who lived in Ethiopia; more probably he was a heathen converted to Judaism. That he was Jewish in his religious faith is evident from the fact that he came to Jerusalem to worship.—**An eunuch.** The Greek signifies literally a *bed-keeper*, and the term designates those persons who had charge of the bed-chambers in palaces and larger houses. But as the jealous and dissolute temperament of the East required this charge to be in the hands of persons who had been deprived of their virility, the word eunuch, in common usage, denoted generally persons of that condition. It was not, however, unusual for eunuchs to rise to high consideration and influence about the court, and to become confidential advisers of their royal masters or mistresses; hence the word appears to have been occasionally employed to denote persons in such a position, without indicating anything of their proper manhood. Thus Potiphar is designated "a eunuch (translated *officer* in our version) of Pharaoh's captain of the guard" (Gen. 37 : 36). But the fact that this man was minister to a female sovereign makes it probable that he was a eunuch in the narrower sense of the term. Such persons were by Deut. 23 : 1 forbidden to enter the congregation of the Lord, the law of Moses rigidly forbidding all self-mutilation; but the prophets recognized the truth that grace and mercy were not excluded from the eunuch (Isaiah 56 : 3-5 ; Jer. 38 : 7-13 ; 39 : 16-18); and one object of this incident was, apparently, to teach that none of those external considerations, whether of race or of physical condition, which excluded from the congregation of the Lord under the law, were to exclude under the Gospel. — **A chief officer of Candace, queen of the Ethiopians.** Candace was the name of a dynasty, like Pharaoh in Egypt or Cæsar among the Romans. From secular history (Strabo and Dio) it is known that there was a queen bearing this title, who fought against the Romans in the twenty-second or twenty-third year of Augustus. Pliny refers to another queen with the same title, during the reign of Vespasian.—**Of all her treasure.** Treasure-houses were common in the East, where not only money but also important documents were kept (Ezra 5 : 17 ; Esther 4 : 7). Of these treasure-houses this eunuch was the custodian.—**For to worship.** He must then have been a believer in the God of Israel, and presumptively a proselyte, who had publicly accepted the Hebrew religion. His journey, his study of Scripture, and his readiness to receive the Gospel, all indicate a man of genuine religious spirit and purpose.—**Read Isaiah the prophet.** Probably aloud (ver. 30). It is still the

29 Then [j] the Spirit said unto Philip, Go near, and join thyself to this chariot.
30 And Philip ran thither to *him*, and heard him read the prophet Esaias, and said, Understandest [k] thou what thou readest?
31 And he said, How [l] can I, except some man should guide [m] me? And he desired Philip that he would come up and sit with him.
32 The place of the scripture which he read was this,[n] He was led as a sheep to the slaughter; and like a lamb dumb before his shearer, so opened he not his mouth:

j Isa. 65 : 24; Hosea 6 : 3.... k Matt. 13 : 23, 51; Ephes. 5 : 17.... l Rom. 10 : 14.... m Ps. 25 : 9.... n Isa. 53 : 7, 8.

custom of the Orientals to read audibly, though reading to themselves. "Painfully feeling his departure from the Temple of Jehovah, on the holy hill, and from his solemn worship, he clings

CANDACE, QUEEN OF ETHIOPIA.
(From the Egyptian monuments.)

to another sanctuary, which he carries with him, in order that at home, in his distant land and solitude, he might have a compensation for the richer blessings of the house of God—namely, to the writings of Moses and the prophets."—(*Baumgarten.*) Observe, too, that he reads not in the law or the history, but in the prophets, and of the prophets, in Isaiah, the evangelist of the O. T., and in Isaiah, the chapter which contains the clearest revelation of the incarnation.

29-31. Then said the Spirit. The Holy Spirit of God. It was a distinct divine impulse, but how coming we have no means of judging. I see no reason for believing that such impulses as are described here and elsewhere in the Bible (comp. ch. 13 : 2; 16 : 6, 7) were in any wise different from those calls to duty, common in Christian experience, which consist in special inward impulses, springing up within us, without any apparent cause.—**And Philip ran.** Observe the alacrity of his obedience to the divine monitor.—**And said, Understandest thou what thou readest?** "A strange address to an unknown and great man. In holy conversation we should come at once to the truth itself. Philip did not begin, as is common, with the weather, the news, etc."—(*Bengel.*) But in this case the way was opened to him by the eunuch's evident desire to learn. Christ began conversation with the Samaritan woman with a very simple request (John 4 : 7). A comparison of Christ's method of religious conversation there, and Philip's here, is instructive.—**How can I, except some man should guide me?** Observe the evidence of the eunuch's earnestness: he comes from Ethiopia to Jerusalem to worship, a long journey; his court duties do not detain him; returning, he studies the Word of God on his journey; though he does not understand, he reads and ponders; when explanation is offered he is quick to welcome it. Calvin's practical comment is good, that in reading the Scripture we must accept readily whatever is plain, and whatever things are hid from us, we must pass them over and wait for light. To which I add, God will send light to the diligent and desirous student.

32, 33. The quotation is from Isaiah 53 : 7, 8, and is from the Septuagint or Greek version. Probably it was from this version the eunuch was reading. The original prophecy was uttered seven centuries before the event, and was in direct opposition to the popular belief respecting the Messiah. It is so unmistakable that Bolingbroke asserted that Christ brought about his own crucifixion, in order to enable his disciples to appeal to the prophecy which he had thus fulfilled.—**He was led as a sheep to the slaughter.** The essential truth taught here by the figures of the sheep and lamb is the quiet non-resistance with which Christ submitted to all the indignity put upon him. The prophecy is fulfilled by his refusal to resist or allow resistance of the officers who came to arrest him (Matt. 26 : 52, 53), by his patience under the indignity inflicted on him by the servants of the high-priest (Matt. 26 : 67, 68) and the soldiers of Pilate (Matt. 27 : 27-31), and by his silence before Pilate (Matt. 27 : 12-14) and before Herod (Luke 23 : 9). But the context in Isaiah clearly indicates that there is also implied the truth that the Messiah should fulfill by his own death the type afforded by the slaying of sheep as sacrifices under the O. T. dispensation. The chapter from which it is taken contains no less than eleven distinct references to the vicarious character of Christ's sufferings.—**In his humiliation his judgment was taken away.** This follows

33 In his humiliation his judgment was taken away: and who shall declare his generation? for his life is taken from the earth.
34 And the eunuch answered Philip, and said, I pray thee, of whom speaketh the prophet this? of himself, or of some other man?
35 Then Philip opened his mouth, and began[o] at the same scripture, and[p] preached unto him Jesus.
36 And as they went on *their* way, they came unto a certain water: and the eunuch said, See, *here is* water; what doth[q] hinder me to be baptized?

o Luke 24 : 27. . . . p ch. 18 : 28. . . . q ch. 10 : 47.

the Greek version, which differs slightly from the Hebrew. Of the original passage, which is confessedly difficult, various interpretations are offered: thus, Through oppression and judgment he was taken away, *i. e.*, by violence which cloaked itself under the formalities of a legal process (*Lowth, Alford, R. Payne Smith*); Through oppression without judgment (Pilate not adjudging him guilty, but simply delivering him to the Jews, Luke 23 : 24, 25) was he taken away (*Henderson*); From oppression and from judgment he was taken away, *i. e.*, by death (*so Luther's version and the Vulgate*). None of these seem to me to satisfy the meaning of the Greek version here, or the spirit of the passage in Isaiah, which surely embodies a deeper declaration than merely the violent death of the Messiah. I understand, then, the meaning of the passage to be this: He who knew no sin was made sin for us (2 Cor. 5 : 21), and in him, thus made in the likeness of sinful flesh, God condemned sin (Rom. 8 : 3); laying on *him* the transgressions of us all (Isaiah 53 : 4, 5). He, by his voluntary humiliation, as described in Phil. 2 : 7, 8, took away this judgment against himself, as the representative of man, whose nature he bore (John 1 : 29), so that to those that are in Christ Jesus there is henceforth no condemnation (Rom. 8 : 1). We may, then, paraphrase the declaration thus: *In his humiliation the condemnation pronounced against him as the sinner's substitute is taken away.* Observe that it is the condemnation of him, as the sinner's substitute, that is taken away, and hence it is only those that are *in* him from whom condemnation is lifted by his atonement. Observe, too, that it is in his humiliation, not by his example and teaching, that he takes sin and condemnation away from his followers.—**Who shall declare his generation?** Meyer, De Wette, Robinson, Alford, and Henderson understand this as equivalent to, Who can describe the wickedness of the men of his time? but, though this is a legitimate rendering, it does not agree with the spirit of the passage, which is concerned with the humiliation of the Messiah, not with the character of the times in which he lived; Hengstenberg interprets it, Who shall declare his posterity? *i. e.*, his spiritual children, born of the travail of his soul; but this is doubtful as a translation, interjects in the middle of a passage descriptive of the Messiah's humiliation a suggestion of his triumphal future, and is inconsistent with the sentence which follows, "For he is taken from the earth." R. Payne Smith renders it, "Who will care to bestow thought on a career so prematurely cut short?" This agrees better with the spirit of the passage than either of the other interpretations, and though the Greek word rendered *generation* (γενεά) has nowhere else in the N. T. the sense of a single life, given to it by this translation, its Hebrew equivalent in the original prophecy has that meaning. Calvin's interpretation of the entire passage is ingenious and even beautiful, if I understand him aright; but I doubt if it be sound. It may be expressed tersely in a paraphrase: In his humiliation his righteousness was exalted (made manifest; comp. Phil. 2 : 9; Heb. 1 : 9), and who shall declare his (eternal) life (or perhaps his *generation*, which would then include all his saints, who share with him eternal life); for his life is taken from the earth. According to this interpretation, ver. 32 describes the Messiah's humiliation, ver. 33 his exaltation in consequence thereof.

34-36. Of whom speaketh the prophet this? The earlier Jewish authorities all understood ch. 53 of Isaiah to refer to the coming Messiah; the later Jewish writers treat it either as a composition of Jeremiah or Josiah, and as referring to the writer himself, or as fulfilled in and by the sufferings inflicted upon the Jewish nation as a nation. These interpretations need no other refutation than that contained in the chapter itself. The nation, as a nation, was not cut off from the land of the living, nor had its grave with the wicked, nor saw its seed and prolonged its days; nor can it be said of the nation that its suffering was for others; it was a just punishment for its own sins (Isaiah 1 : 4, 5; Jer. 17 : 1-4). "All attempts to find any solution other than the historical one supplied in the Gospels are but instances of the blindness over which the prophet lamented (in ch. 53 : 1), 'Who hath believed our report?'"—(*R. Payne Smith.*)—**Preached unto him Jesus.** Literally, *Announced to him the glad tidings, Jesus.* The name (Matt. 1 : 21) indicates the nature of the glad tidings announced, viz., that Jesus, by his fulfillment of this prophecy, had provided a way of salvation for all who accept him. The next verse indicates that the preaching included some explanation concerning the rite of baptism and its significance. Philip could hardly have expounded

37 And Philip said, If[r] thou believest with all thine
heart, thou mayest. And he answered and said, I[s] believe that Jesus Christ is the Son of God.
38 And he commanded the chariot to stand still: and
they went down both into the water, both Philip and
the eunuch; and he baptized him.
39 And when they were come up out of the water,
the Spirit of the Lord[t] caught away Philip, that the
eunuch saw him no more: and he went on his way
rejoicing.[u]
40 But Philip was found at Azotus: and passing
through, he preached in all the cities, till he came to
Cæsarea.

r ver. 12; Mark 16:16.... s John 11:27; 1 Cor. 12:3; 1 John 4:15.... t 1 Kings 18:12; Ezek. 3:12, 14.... u Ps. 119:14, 111.

the passage in question in Isaiah *to a heathen*, and not have himself obtained a broader conception of the universality of the Gospel than he ever had before. The case is one of the teacher taught.—**They came unto a certain water.** The site is absolutely unknown, and the attempts to identify it with any existing spring or wady are almost necessarily fruitless, since not even the road, much less the location on it, is known with any degree of certainty. The accompany-

PHILIP'S FOUNTAIN.

ing illustration shows one of the traditional sites, which derives its name from the incident here recorded. It is about five miles south-west of Jerusalem, near one of the roads to Gaza, and one less traveled than the others, a circumstance slightly confirmatory of the tradition which connects it with the eunuch's baptism, and which dates from about the time of the crusades. This spring is a favorite resort of the women, both for drawing water and for washing clothes.—**What doth hinder me to be baptized?** "Faith *within* and water *without* were ready."—(*Bengel.*)

37. This verse is wanting in the best manuscripts. It is omitted by Alford and Tischendorf. Dr. Hackett declares against it. It is thought to have been inserted from a primitive baptismal liturgy. Though probably not genuine, it unquestionably embodies the spirit of the rite, which, whether infants were baptized or not, was certainly never administered to adults except upon the condition of faith in Jesus Christ as a divine Saviour.

38-40. Into the water * * * out of the water. The original unquestionably implies a going, not *to*, but *into*, the water; but it does not necessarily imply immersion, still less complete submersion. The two may have stood in the water, while baptism was performed, either by sprinkling, pouring, or immersion. See Vol. I, p. 73, for note on Form of Baptism.—**He baptized him.** Without waiting further to instruct him, or delaying for a public ceremonial. There is nothing in the account to indicate that any were present, except Philip and the eunuch. —**The Spirit of the Lord caught away Philip.** The original is correctly rendered by the English version and seems to me to imply a sudden and supernatural removal of Philip. The expression in 1 Kings 18:12, and 2 Kings 2:16, and the disappearance of Christ in Luke 24:31, interpret the statement here. So Alford, Bengel, Baumgarten. Meyer, Olshausen, and Hackett understand that nothing is implied, but that Philip left the eunuch suddenly and under a divine impulse, as he joined him; but the Greek verb (ἁρπάζω, *caught away*) always indicates a forcible removal by some power from without, never a voluntary act under a mere internal impulse. See, for examples, Matt. 13:19; John 6:15; Acts 23:10; 2 Cor. 12:2, 4; Rev. 12:5. —**He went on his way rejoicing.** "He no more saw, nor cared to see Philip, by reason of joy. He who has obtained the Scripture and Christ, can now dispense with a human guide." —(*Bengel.*)—**Philip was found at Azotus.** Or Ashdod, a city of the Philistines, near the Mediterranean and about midway between Gaza and Joppa. It was never thoroughly subjugated by the Jews; was captured by Tartan the Assyrian general (Isaiah 20:1), and again by Psammetichus (Jer. 25 : 20). In the restoration, the daughters of Ashdod became a snare to Israel (Neh. 13 : 23, 24). In the N. T. it is mentioned only here; but in early ecclesiastical history, it became the seat of a Christian church. Its site is now called Esdud, and its ruins contain remains of pottery and other evidences of a former city of considerable size.—**In all the cities.** These would include Ekron, Jamnia, Joppa, Apollonia, and perhaps Lydda.

Cæsarea. There were two towns of this name in Palestine, both named from the Cæsars, one Cæsarea Philippi on the northern borders of the Holy Land, the other the Cæsarea mentioned here and sometimes called Cæsarea Palestinæ. It was on the Mediterranean coast, about seventy

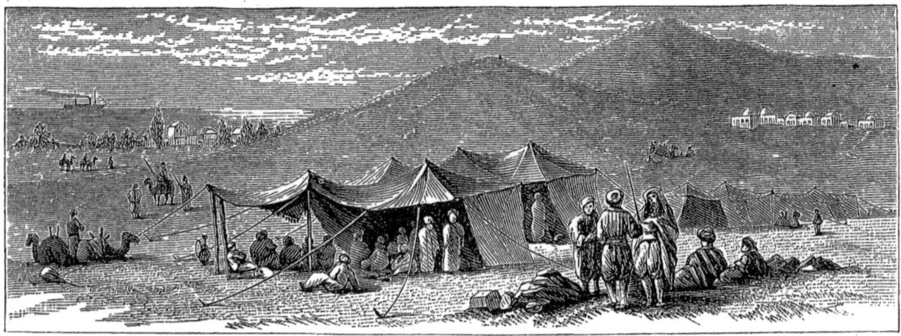

AZOTUS.—ASHDOD.

miles northwest of Jerusalem; was built by Herod the Great, who constructed a theatre and amphitheatre, some of the walls of which may still be traced. It is described as a magnificent city by Josephus, who speaks of an artificial harbor formed by a breakwater. However exaggerated his description may be, there is no doubt that the city was large, populous and prosperous. It was the residence of the Herodian family; the military headquarters of Rome; and conspicuous from the sea by reason of its fine public buildings. In N. T. history it is notable as the scene of Peter's visit to Cornelius (chaps. 10, 11), of Herod Agrippa's fatal stroke (ch. 12 : 19-23), and of Paul's imprisonment and trial (ch. 23 : 23, etc.). In ecclesiastical history, it is notable as the scene of Ori-

CÆSAREA PALESTINA. (From the north, showing the ruins of the harbor.)

gen's retirement, when excommunicated, and of the later and riper literary labors of his life. It is now utterly desolate; its ruins a quarry, out of which other towns are constructed; but its name still survives in the Arabic Kaisariyeh. It was at the time of Philip's visit, chiefly a Gentile city, and his preaching there was a continuance and an enlargement of the new dispensation, now opening before the church, in which the Gospel was to be preached to every creature, and prove itself the power of God unto salvation to Gentile as well as Jew.

Ch. 9 : 1-9. THE CONVERSION OF SAUL. THE NEW BIRTH ILLUSTRATED.

Of Saul's conversion there are three accounts

CHAPTER IX.

AND Saul, yet[v] breathing out threatenings and
slaughter against the disciples of the Lord, went
unto the high priest,
2 And desired of him letters to Damascus to the
synagogues, that, if he found any of this way, whether
they were men or women, he might bring them bound
unto Jerusalem.
3 And[w] as he journeyed, he came near Damascus:
and suddenly there shined round about him a light
from heaven:

v ch. 8 : 3; Gal. 1 : 13.... w 1 Cor. 15 : 8.

in the N. T., the one here by Luke, and two by Paul; one in his address to the mob at Jerusalem (ch. 22 : 1-11), the other in his address before Agrippa (ch. 26 : 8-18). The account here is presumptively derived from Paul, so that the three accounts come from one source. The date is involved in uncertainty; there is nothing to determine it. Opinions vary between A. D. 30 and A. D. 40. On the variations in the accounts and their reconciliation, the previous life of Paul, the authenticity and significance of the events here recorded, etc., see note on Conversion of Saul below.

1. But Saul. *But* (δέ) marks the contrast between the missionary zeal of Philip and the persecuting zeal of Saul. Both are zealous; but the conscience of the one is inflamed by hate, that of the other is inspired by love.—**Breathing out threatenings and slaughter.** A pregnant expression, signifying that his whole nature was full of an impassioned hate of the disciples of Christ. Paul expresses the same thing by describing himself as "exceeding mad against them" (ch. 26 : 11).—**Went unto the high-priest.** As president of the Sanhedrim. The whole council considered and acted on the application, the elders (ch. 22 : 5) and the chief-priests (ch. 26 : 12) uniting with the high-priest in conferring the commission.

A TURKISH FIRMAN.

2. And desired of him letters. It is customary in the East to issue letters of authority or protection, answering somewhat to the passport, always nominally, often practically, required in European countries. These sometimes carry with them some special commission or authority. Thus Nehemiah (ch. 2 : 7, 8) received letters from the king to the governors of Palestine; so at the present day the traveller in Turkey has to provide himself with letters (a firman) from the Porte or a pasha, commending him to the protection of the subordinate authorities. This firman must be authenticated by the Sultan's cipher, containing the interlaced letters of his name. Without this firman the traveller is always liable to arrest as a suspicious character. The letters granted to Paul probably partook of this character, and were necessary, both as a passport and as an authorization to the synagogue officers in Damascus.

Damascus. Probably the oldest existing city in the world. Its origin is lost in antiquity. According to Jewish tradition it was built by Uz, great-grandson of Noah. It was existing in Abraham's time (Gen. 14 : 15; 15 : 2), after which we hear no more of it until David subdued it (2 Sam. 8 : 6). In Solomon's time and under Rezon, it became the seat of the Syrian kingdom (1 Kings 11 : 23-25), and one of the most formidable rivals of Israel. The two Benhadads waged long and bloody wars with the contemporaneous kings of Israel (1 Kings 15 : 20); and when Hazael seized the throne of Damascus, the kingdom of Israel fared still worse. At length the rising monarchy of Assyria got possession of Damascus (2 Kings 16 : 9; Isaiah 10 : 9), and during the contests for empire that ensued for many centuries, while Damascus often changed its masters, it never became properly the capital of a kingdom. In N. T. history it is chiefly celebrated for being Paul's residence immediately after his conversion and the scene of his first Christian labors. In later history it became the seat of a Christian bishop, but in process of time the Christian influence in the city was overshadowed by the Mohammedan. It fell, A. D. 635, into the hands of the caliph Omar. Subsequently it shared in the manifold vicissitudes which passed over the provinces of Western Asia, till it fell, in 1516, into the power of Sultan Selim I. Since then it has remained under the sway of Turkey, the most populous and flourishing city which belongs to Asiatic Turkey. It occupies perhaps the most beautiful site in all Western Asia, at the eastern base of Anti-Libanus, in the centre of a large plain of great fertility, watered by the rivers Barada and

DAMASCUS, FROM THE JERUSALEM ROADS.
The foreground represents the traditional site of Saul's conversion.

Awaj, the ancient Abana and Pharpar of Scripture. Its trees and surrounding gardens impart to it a peculiarly picturesque appearance from a distance. Its beauty is illustrated by the legend that Mohammed once, on approaching the city, turned resolutely away after gazing upon it, saying: "Man can have but one paradise, and my paradise is fixed above." The more noticeable public buildings are the eastern gate, which exhibits some remains of Roman architecture, the castle, which in its foundation dates from the Roman period, and the great mosque of the Omniades. There are upward of eighty smaller mosques scattered through the city. The principal street, a long, wide thoroughfare leading from one of the gates to the castle or palace of the pasha, is regarded by the Christian population as "the street which is called Straight" (ver. 11), and tradition designates that part of the city wall by which the apostle made his escape from his first persecutors (ver. 25). It has a present population of upward of 150,000, composed of Jews, Moslems, and Christians; Alford's estimate of 250,000 is almost certainly quite too large. Its manufactures are still of some importance, though the famous Damascus blades exist no more, and its famed *damasks* have lost their ancient renown.

To the synagogues. This term, like our own word church, is ambiguous; it may mean either the building or the ecclesiastical organization. Here it designates the latter. For history and description of Jewish synagogues see Matt. 4:23, note. In the Jewish economy, in which church and state were one, the synagogue was both ecclesiastical and civil; it possessed judicial powers. It exercised these, however, in subjection to the Sanhedrim at Jerusalem, to which appeals were taken, and from which commands were received. Julius Cæsar, by imperial edict, B. C. 47, decreed that "Hyrcanus and his children do retain all the rights of high-priest, whether established by law or accorded by courtesy; and if hereafter any question arise touching the Jewish polity, I desire that the determination thereof be referred to him." This decree was subsequently confirmed by Augustus, and under these decrees, and the general policy which they embodied, the Sanhedrim at Jerusalem continued to exercise its judicial powers over the Jews wherever found, and were supported in this by the acquiescence, if not by the active co-operation, of the Roman authorities. Thus Paul's letters to the synagogues at Damascus were adequate for dealing with all Jewish Christians, and as yet the Christian religion had not considerably extended beyond the bounds of the Jewish church. The Jewish population at Damascus was 50,000; there would, therefore, have been a number of synagogues. Presumptively there were a number of Christians, perhaps converts returning after Pentecost from Jerusalem, or fugitives from the persecution in that city. Observe that Paul *applied* for the letters. He instigated the persecution.—**Of this way.** The way of salvation in Jesus Christ. The phrase is elsewhere used in the N. T. with the same significance, showing that it had become a common one among the Christians (ch. 19:9, 23; 24:22).—**Both men and women.** Comp. 8:3; 22:4. Religious persecution spares neither age nor sex.—**Unto Jerusalem.** For trial before the Sanhedrim, which alone had, under Jewish law, the power of pronouncing the death-sentence.

3. And as he journeyed. There are several roads from Jerusalem to Damascus; there is nothing whatever to indicate which he took. The distance is variously estimated from 120 to 150 miles, and would have taken five or six days. This gave Saul an opportunity for calm reflec-

4 And he fell to the earth, and heard a voice saying
unto him, Saul, Saul, why persecutest thou me? [x]
5 And he said, Who art thou, Lord? And the Lord
said, I am Jesus, whom thou persecutest: *it is* hard
for thee to kick [y] against the pricks.
6 And he trembling and astonished, said, Lord,

x Matt. 25 : 40, 45. . . . y ch. 5 : 39.

tion, compelled him to reconsider the Gospel which he had heard from the lips of Stephen, and made his heart accessible to the influence of the divine Spirit.—**He came near Damascus.** Dr. Barrows notes significance in the fact that Saul was not arrested until near the consummation of his journey: "God beholdeth violent men setting out in their unjust attempts. He letteth them proceed on in a full career, until they reach the edge of their design; then instantly he checketh, he stoppeth, he tumbleth them down or turneth them backward." Thus with Haman (Esther, ch. 3), Pharaoh (Exod., ch. 14), Abimelech (Judges 9 : 53), Absalom (2 Sam. 18 : 9), and Sennacherib (2 Kings 19 : 23).—**A light from heaven.** *From heaven*, but *about him.* It was not in the distant horizon, nor in the heavens above. It was midday; the sun was shining; this light shone above the brightness of the sun; it was seen by Paul's companions as well as himself (ch. 22 : 6, 9; 26 : 13). All attempts to explain this light as an electric phenomenon substitute the imagination of the commentator for the narrative of the historian. It was a great light, of what nature or how produced there is no hint. But we may naturally connect it with the fact that both the O. T. and the N. T. manifestation of God was often in or accompanied with a luminous cloud, very generally entitled the glory of the Lord (Exod. 3 : 2; 13 : 21, 22; 19 : 9, 18; 24 : 16; 40 : 34, 35; Deut. 31 : 15; 1 Kings 8 : 10; Luke 2 : 9; Acts 1 : 9, note; Rev. 1 : 7; 14 : 14). See Matt. 17 : 5, note. Observe that this phenomenon occurred at midday, and when Saul was journeying, surrounded by companions; the circumstances were not such as would tend to produce an imaginary vision.

4. He fell to the earth. Not necessarily in the greatness of his terror, which Bengel imputes to him. There is no intimation of terror here or in either of his own accounts; and his language of questioning, Who art thou? and What wilt thou have me to do? indicates that he did not lose his presence of mind. See below. —**Saul, Saul, why persecutest thou me?** The name is repeated for emphasis. So Martha, Martha (Luke 10 : 41); Simon, Simon (Luke 22 : 31); Jerusalem, Jerusalem (Matt. 23 : 37). There might be a question whether this was an audible voice, or whether it spoke only within Saul's soul, but for two circumstances: in his speech before Agrippa Paul says that it spake *in the Hebrew tongue*, and here, in ver. 7, it is said that *the men heard the voice.* It is, therefore, evident that there was an audible voice, not merely a spiritual impression produced on the mind of Saul. Observe the form of the question, Why persecutest thou *me?* not my disciples, nor my church. "Paul strikes in Damascus; Christ suffers in heaven."—(*Hall.*) Henry's comments on this question are very suggestive. It is personal, Why persecutest *thou* me (comp. 2 Sam. 12 : 7), shows the sin as one against the Son of God, Persecutest *me* (Matt. 25 : 45), and demands of his conscience a reason for his animosity, *Why* persecutest (Isaiah 1 : 18).

5, 6. And he said, Who art thou, Lord? It is reasonably evident, from several considerations, that Saul not only heard the voice, but saw Him who spake. This is implied by the declaration of ver. 8, that the men who were with him saw no man; by the language of Ananias, "Jesus that *appeared* unto thee in the way" (ver. 17, comp. 22 : 14); by the declaration of Barnabas, "how he (Paul) had *seen* the Lord in the way" (ver. 27); and from Paul's subsequent distinct declaration concerning himself that he had seen the Lord (1 Cor. 9 : 1; 15 : 8), where he unquestionably refers to this experience, for there is no indication that he ever saw the Lord prior to the crucifixion; indeed the language of 1 Cor. 15 : 8 implies the reverse. Observe that Saul does not yield allegiance to the unknown speaker until he has questioned him, and, by the disclosure of Saul's secret uneasiness (see next verse), the speaker has given evidence of divine omniscience. They entirely misread Saul's character and the narrative here, who attribute the change in him to the effect of mere terror.—**But he, I am Jesus, whom thou persecutest.** This is the literal rendering of the best manuscripts. Observe how the whole effect of this interview is to press home upon Paul's conscience his guilt as a persecutor *of the Lord*, and note its effect in his subsequent experience of humility and of thankfulness for divine grace (1 Cor. 15 : 9, 10; 1 Tim. 1 : 12-17). Observe, too, that the Lord calls himself here not Christ, the Messiah, the name of dignity, but Jesus, Saviour, the name of his earthly humiliation.—**It is hard for thee to kick against the goads. And he trembling and astonished said, Lord, what wilt thou have me to do? And the Lord said unto him.** These words are wanting in the best manuscripts. They are omitted by Alford, Tischendorf, Alexander, Hackett. For the statement that Saul trembled and was astonished there is, therefore, no authority, for this is not stated by him in either of the other accounts.

what[z] wilt thou have me to do? And the Lord *said* unto him, Arise, and go into the city, and it shall be told thee what thou must do.
7 And the men which journeyed with him stood speechless, hearing a voice, but[a] seeing no man.

8 And Saul arose from the earth; and when his eyes were opened, he saw no man: but they led him by the hand, and brought *him* into Damascus.
9 And he was three days without sight, and neither did eat nor drink.

z ch. 16 : 30.... a Dan. 10 : 7.

The rest of the narrative here is unquestionably accurate, having been transferred, partly from Paul's address before Agrippa (ch. 26 : 14, 15), partly from his address to the mob at Jerusalem (ch. 22 : 10). *It is hard for thee to kick against the goads* (*pricks*) is a proverbial expression, found both in Roman and Greek literature. It is derived from the use of the ox-goad. This in Palestine was a strong pole, eight or ten feet long, with a pointed prick at one end with which to urge on

ANCIENT OX-GOAD.

the oxen, and a kind of chisel at the other with which to clear the plowshare of earth and weeds. The size of the Jewish ox-goad is indicated by Judges 3 : 21. The ox, being driven from behind, not, as with us, from the side, would strike against the goad if it resisted by kicking. The figure is partially interpreted by Eccles. 12 : 11: "The words of the wise are as goads," because they direct into the right path and stimulate to energy. Paul's conscience, if he had followed it, would have similarly guided him out of the path into which the pride of a perverted intellect was leading him. Though he thought he was doing God service in opposing the Christian church (ch. 22 : 3; 26 : 9), he was all the time ill at ease. His soul was not at peace; his life was one of real resistance to the guidance and the goading of his own conscience, and it was *hard* for him. This single sentence, which revealed to Saul Christ's knowledge of his inmost soul, gives us a glimpse of it, and answers in the negative the oft-repeated question whether Saul was doing right in persecuting the church under the impulse of a genuine religious zeal (see ch. 26 : 10, 11, notes). *What wilt thou have me to do, Lord?* is incorporated in the narrative here from ch. 22 : 10. The question is that of one overpowered and bewildered, who does not understand; knows and feels that something must be done, but knows not what to do. It thus represents the natural inquiry of the awakened soul in its first surprise, when the claim of Christ as Master is really brought home to the consciousness. But the appellation Lord, indicates in Paul's mind a recognition of a Lord and Master in the Jesus whom he had before been persecuting, and the very form of the question implies a readiness to do what the Lord bids him, *whatever that may be;* and this implication is confirmed by his obedience to the divine directions. —**Arise and go into the city.** A severe test of his allegiance. He expected to enter the city with prestige, armed with letters from the high-priest, to be received and honored by the chief men of his own nation; he was commanded to enter it in humiliation, as a disciple of the Jesus whom he had publicly persecuted, and receive his instructions from one of the before-despised and outcast Christians.

7, 8. The men * * * stood. According to ch. 26 : 14, the men as well as Saul fell to the ground at the appearance of the light. On the reconciliation of these two accounts, see note below.—**Hearing a voice.** Literally, *Of the voice, i. e.*, the sound of a voice (on the significance of genitive after ἀκούω, see Winer, § 30, *c*); but they did not understand what was said; hence, in his speech to the mob in Jerusalem, Paul says, They heard not the voice of him that spake; *i. e.*, they did not hear it as an intelligible voice, so that they could comprehend its meaning.—**When his eyes were opened, he saw no one.** The reason is given in ch. 22 : 11, "When I could not see for the glory of that light." Its effect had been to blind him; and apparently (see below) he never fully recovered from the effects. *Saw no one*, signifies not merely that he no longer saw the divine Person with whom he had been speaking, but he was no longer able to see at all. This is indicated by the next clause of the verse.—**They led him by the hand.** This appearance of Christ does not appear from the narrative to have converted Saul's Jewish companions. So Christ's call to James and John was heard but apparently not heeded by their father (Matt. 4 : 21, 22). It is not for lack of evidence, but for lack of willingness, that souls remain out of Christ.

9. Neither did eat nor drink. It is hardly doubtful that this was a voluntary fast, undergone by Paul, in accordance with his Pharisaic education, in connection with prayer for pardon and guidance. This would have been in accord with his Pharisaic education, and would have naturally accompanied the highly wrought condition of his mind. The other explanations, that it was a medicinal abstinence for the restoration of his eyesight, or the mere natural effect of mental excitement, are improbable, the first highly so. His mental conflict is left undescribed; it must have been heightened by his loneliness.

"He could have no communion with the Christians, for they had been terrified by the news of his approach. And the unconverted Jews could have no true sympathy with his present state of mind."—(*Conybeare and Howson.*)

NOTE ON THE CONVERSION OF SAUL. I. *The fact.* There are three accounts of Saul's conversion, all contained in the same history, one by Luke, the other two in reported addresses by Paul. There are some differences in these accounts, which will appear clearly by a comparison of the following tabular analysis:

Acts 9 : 1–9. LUKE'S HISTORY.	Acts 22 : 3–11. PAUL'S SPEECH BEFORE THE MOB.	Acts 26 : 9–18. PAUL'S SPEECH BEFORE AGRIPPA.
	Saul describes his birth and education.	Saul thought he ought to oppose Christ.
Saul persecutes the Christian Church.	Persecutes the Christian Church.	Persecutes the Church.—*Details.*
Desires letters from the high-priest to the synagogues.	Receives letters from the high-priest *and elders unto the brethren.*	Receives commission from *the chief priests.*
To bring Christians, *both men and women*, to Jerusalem.	To bring Christians to Jerusalem *to be punished.*	
Near Damascus, a light suddenly shines about him.	*About noon*, near Damascus, a light suddenly shines about him.	At midday, near Damascus, a light suddenly shines about him, *above the brightness of the sun.*
He falls to the ground.	*He* falls to the ground.	*All* fall to the ground.
A voice addresses him: Saul, Saul, why persecutest thou me?	A voice addresses him: Saul, Saul, why persecutest thou me?	A voice addresses him *in the Hebrew tongue:* Saul, Saul, etc. It adds: *It is hard for thee to kick against the pricks.*
He responds: Who art thou Lord?	He responds: Who art thou Lord?	He responds: Who art thou Lord?
The Lord replies: I am Jesus whom thou persecutest.	The Lord replies: I am Jesus of Nazareth whom thou persecutest.	The Lord replies: I am Jesus of Nazareth whom thou persecutest;
His companions *stand* speechless, *hearing a voice*, but seeing no one. (See note on verses 5 and 6.)	His companions see the light but hear *not* the voice.	
	Saul asks: What shall I do?	
Saul is *directed to go to Damascus for instructions.*	And is *directed to go to Damascus for instructions.*	*And proceeds to give him his commission as a missionary to the Gentiles.*
He is blinded.	He is blinded *by the light.*	
And led into Damascus by the hand.	And led into Damascus by the hand.	Preaches first at Damascus, in obedience to the heavenly vision.

The variations in these accounts are indicated by the italics in the different columns. Of these only four are in the nature of discrepancies, and these present no serious difficulties, except to those who desire to find contradictions in the Scripture, or who needlessly multiply them by a theory of verbal inspiration, such as the Scriptures nowhere claim. (*a.*) In ch. 9 : 1, 2, Saul receives his commission from the high-priest, in ch. 22 : 5, from the high-priest and elders, in ch. 26 : 12, from the chief-priests. If granted by the Sanhedrim, this commission would be voted on by the body, comprising both elders and chief-priests, and would be issued in their name by the president of the Sanhedrim, the high-priest. Thus the same fact is in the three accounts described in different language. (*b.*) In ch. 26 : 14, *all* fell to the earth; in ch. 9 : 4, 7, Saul fell to the earth, while his companions *stood* speechless. The word rendered *stood* is here used in a general way, to signify, not their *posture*, but the effect of their astonishment in depriving them for the moment of power to move. They were both speechless and motionless. The difficulty is created in this case by a literalism which would not be applied to the interpretation of any other book than the Bible. (*c.*) In ch. 9 : 7, Saul's companions *hear a voice;* in ch. 22 : 9, they *hear not the voice* of him that spake to Saul. The most probable explanation of this discrepancy is that they heard a sound, but did not distinguish any words; and this view is confirmed by the language of the original. See note above. So in John 12 : 28, Christ, and perhaps his disciples, distinguished the words, but the unbelievers heard only an inarticulate and unmeaning sound. (*d.*) In ch. 9 : 6,

9, and 22 : 10, 11, Saul is represented as going into Damascus and there receiving his commission from Ananias; in ch. 26 : 16–18, this commission is represented as given directly and immediately by Christ, and nothing is said of Saul's going to Damascus. To me it appears clear that, in his speech before Agrippa, where details were needless, Paul summarizes the revelation of the divine will made to him by Ananias and subsequently at Jerusalem, his object being to present succinctly the cause of the Jewish enmity against himself; while, in his address to the mob at Jerusalem, he explains in detail how this commission to the Gentiles came to him first from Ananias, "a devout man according to the law," and afterward in a direct revelation from God, while he was praying in the Temple (ch. 22 : 13-18). So Alford on ch. 26 : 16–18. "There can be no question that Paul here condenses into one, various sayings of our Lord to him at different times, in visions, and by Ananias. Nor can this, on the strictest view, be considered any deviation from the truth. It is what all must more or less do who are abridging a narrative, or giving the general sense of things said at various times."

II. The essential fact in this narrative is the spiritual change wrought in the character of Saul, and this change there is no possible room to doubt. His unquestionably authentic letters indicate both the original nature and the subsequent Christian experience and character of the man. He was by birth a Hebrew, was educated at Jerusalem at the feet of Gamaliel, belonged to the strictest of the two parties into which the Pharisees were divided, was a believer in its ascetic philosophy, and zealous in its ascetic practices (ch. 22 : 2; 26 : 5; Phil. 3 : 5, 6). Thus he was taught that hate of the Gentile was a religious duty, that righteousness consisted in obedience to a rigorous ceremonial; that he must pray three times every day, fast twice a week, give tithes of all he possessed, wash ceremonially with scrupulous care before every meal. See for illustrations of Pharisaism, Luke 18 : 11, 12; Mark 8 : 3. He held these tenets and practices of his religion with so unyielding a faith, that no cruelty of punishment seemed to him too great for the new sect of Nazarenes who denied them (ch. 26 : 9, 10). He became after his conversion the exponent of all that was broad and catholic and progressive in the primitive church, preached that Jew as truly as Gentile is under the wrath of God (Rom. 3 : 9), that righteousness consists not in obedience to law, but in love for God and trust in him (Gal. 3 : 10-13), that days and weeks and ceremonies, even the most sacred ceremonial of Judaism, circumcision, are insignificant (Rom. 2 : 28, 29; Gal. 4 : 9–11), and gave his life to the propagation of those principles which before he had hated, and which to this day the Christian church is hardly able to comprehend or to accept in their fullness. That this change took place, and by the direct intervention and interposition of the Spirit of God, is the essential fact in the conversion of Paul. What were the external circumstances is a matter of secondary importance.

III. That a supernatural light shone, that an audible voice spoke, and that a real sight of the glorified Saviour was vouchsafed to Saul, is however unquestionably indicated by the N. T. history. And though, of the three accounts which we possess, two are certainly, and the third probably, derived from Saul, his narrative is confirmed by the following considerations: (*a.*) It is difficult, if not impossible, to account for a change so marvelous, so sudden, and so radical, except by means of a direct and supernatural appearance. (*b.*) Saul, in his subsequent ministry, frequently referred to the event (Rom. 1 : 1; 1 Cor. 1 : 1; 9 : 1; 15 : 8), and twice narrated it in detail. His companions on the journey were still living, knew whether the tale was true or false, and yet throughout his life, bitterly as he was opposed, both without and within the church, his account of his call and conversion never appears to have been questioned. (*c.*) He refers in somewhat enigmatical terms to the marks of the Lord Jesus Christ which he bore in his body, as an evidence of his apostleship (Gal. 6 : 17). What marks these were is not indeed known, but it is a reasonable surmise that they are the "thorn in the flesh" (2 Cor. 12 : 7), and the "infirmity of the flesh" (Gal. 4 : 13), and made his bodily presence "weak and contemptible" (2 Cor. 10 : 10); and his reference to the zeal of the Galatians, who "would have plucked out your own eyes and given them to me" (Gal. 4 : 15), coupled with the temporary blindness here described, gives color to the hypothesis that in all these passages he refers to a weakened eyesight which, to his death, confirmed his narrative of his miraculous conversion, at once a thorn in the flesh and a manifestation "of the power of Christ" upon him.

IV. The essential features of Saul's conversion, as an inward experience, afford a profitable theme for the devout student. Observe in respect to them: (1.) The divine preparation: (*a.*) Stephen's speech and heavenly vision; the former contains the germs of all Paul's subsequent theology; the latter is a forerunner of his own sight of the glorified Jesus of Nazareth. See ch. 7 and notes. (*b.*) Paul's own earnestness; honest zeal in a bad cause is a better preparation for the Gospel than indifference. (*c.*) His enforced quiet and time of thought during his week's journey to Damascus. (2.) The suddenness of the change. There is no long struggle, no bitter remorse, nor deep despair, no waiting for light, or for time to reform, or repair the past. Saul falls to the earth a persecutor, he rises a disciple. (3.) The nature

10 And there was a certain disciple at Damascus,
named Ananias;[b] and to him said the Lord in a vision,
Ananias. And he said, Behold, I *am here*, Lord.
11 And the Lord *said* unto him, Arise, and go into
the street which is called Straight, and inquire in the
house of Judas for *one* called Saul, of Tarsus; for, behold, he prayeth,
12 And hath seen in a vision a man named Ananias
coming in, and putting *his* hand on him, that he might receive his sight.
13 Then Ananias answered, Lord, I have heard by
many of this man,[c] how much evil he hath done to thy saints at Jerusalem:
14 And here he[d] hath authority from the chief priests
to bind all that call[e] on thy name.

b ch. 22 : 12. . . . c 1 Tim. 1 : 13. . . . d verse 21. . . . e 1 Cor. 1 : 2; 2 Tim. 2 : 22.

of the change. He has heretofore done according to *his own* will (ch. 26 : 9); he now avows a supreme allegiance to Christ's will (ch. 22 : 10). (4.) The test of that allegiance: obedience. He goes to Damascus, receives his instructions from a Christian disciple, preaches in the city where he came to persecute, accepts the service, of all most repellent to a Pharisee, the mission to the Gentiles, and after one remonstrance at Jerusalem (ch. 22 : 18-21), devotes himself unreservedly to it. Observe further, that this conversion involved in Saul a change of *creed:* from believing that he ought to do things against the name of Jesus of Nazareth (ch. 26 : 9), he became a worshipper (ver. 11) and a believer in and preacher of his divinity (vers. 20, 22); a change of *moral purpose:* from being a persecutor of Christ, he became a missionary of the cross; a change of *allegiance:* from doing what he thought in himself he ought to do, he became a devoted servant of Christ (ch. 26 : 9, note; Rom. 1 : 1, etc.), praying without ceasing, Lord, what wilt thou have me to do? a change of *spirit:* from being exceeding mad against the disciples of Jesus Christ (ch. 26 : 11), he became the chief exponent and apostle of love, patience and long-suffering. See epistles throughout. On his character before his conversion, see ch. 26 : 10, 11, note. Its key-note then was *pride*, henceforth it is *love*. See 1 Cor., ch. 13.

10, 11. Named Ananias. He was a Jew, "a devout man according to the law, having a good reputation of all the Jews which dwelt there" (ch. 22 : 12). Nothing is known of his history, except what is mentioned here and there, except the tradition that he was subsequently bishop of Damascus.—**In a vision.** By *vision* in the Bible is generally meant an experience in which the person retains his consciousness, in which respect it differs from a trance, and the object shown to him possesses a real existence, in which respect it differs from a dream. Thus the Transfiguration is spoken of as a vision (Matt. 17 : 9); so the appearance to Zacharias in the Temple (Luke 1 : 22), of the angel to Cornelius (ch 10 : 3), and to Peter (ch. 10 : 17), though in the latter case Peter was in a trance (ver. 10). For other illustrations of Biblical visions, see 1 Sam. 3 : 15; Dan. 2 : 19; 7 : 2; 8 : 1; Acts 16 : 9; 18 : 9; 26 : 19.—**The street that is called Straight.** This was the main thoroughfare of Damascus, being in a direct line from the eastern to the western gate. In the apostolic age it was a hundred feet wide, and divided by Corinthian colonnades into three avenues—the central and broadest for carriages and equestrians, and the two side pavements for foot passengers. At each end of the street were the city gates divided into three compartments corresponding to the roadways, while midway between them was a Roman triumphal arch. Remains of the gates and the colonnades are still to be seen. At present the street, now known as Sultany or Queen street, has been contracted by successive encroachments to one narrow passage—a mere by-lane. Near the west gate is shown the traditional house of Judas, and near the eastern gate that of Ananias, both of them in grottos.—**Of one Judas.** Nothing more is known of him; it is hardly probable that he was a Christian. The surmise of Dr. Wolcott, that he kept a public-house, in which case he must probably be known at least by reputation to Ananias, is reasonable.—**Of Tarsus.** See note on ver. 30.—**Behold, he is praying.** As a Pharisee, "touching the righteousness which is in the law blameless" (Phil. 3 : 6), he must have been accustomed to pray before (Matt. 6 : 5; 23 : 14), but the implication of the language here certainly is, that he now for the first time humbly solicited divine grace and guidance. "He prayeth" is always an indication, if not a demonstration, of the genuineness of conversion.

12-14. In a vision. Tischendorf and Alford omit these words, which were probably added by a copyist to explain the meaning of the original; the explanation is probably correct.—**A man named Ananias.** That is, in his vision, Saul had both seen the man and known his name.—**And putting his hand on him.** See ch. 8 : 17, note. Here the laying on of hands was to be accompanied by a miraculous evidence of the gift of the Holy Ghost in the restoration of Saul's sight (ch. 6 : 6, note).—**Ananias answered.** If we suppose that the Lord visibly appeared to Ananias, it is difficult to reconcile this answer with the spirit of reverence and allegiance to Christ. The impulse may have been so communicated as to leave Ananias in some doubt at first respecting its divine origin and authority.—**To thy saints.** This is the first time in the N. T. that this title is applied to the disciples of Christ; but it is the appellation commonly used by Paul in designating them. It

15 But the Lord said unto him, Go thy way: for[f] he
is a chosen vessel unto me, to bear my name before[g]
the Gentiles, and kings,[h] and the[i] children of Israel:
16 For I will shew him how great things he must
suffer[j] for my name's sake.
17 And Ananias went his way, and entered into the
house; and putting[k] his hands on him, said, Brother
Saul, the Lord, *even* Jesus, that appeared unto thee in
the way as thou camest, hath sent me, that thou mightest
receive thy sight, and[l] be filled with the Holy
Ghost.
18 And immediately there fell from his eyes as it had
been scales; and he received sight forthwith, and arose,
and was baptized.

f ch. 13 : 2; Rom. 1 : 1; 1 Cor. 15 : 10; Gal. 1 : 15; Ephes. 3 : 7, 8....g Rom. 11 : 13; Gal. 2 : 7, 8....h ch. 25 : 23, etc....i ch. 28 : 17, etc.... j ch. 20 : 23; 2 Cor. 11 : 23-27; 2 Tim. 1 : 11, 12....k ch. 8 : 17....k ch. 2 : 4.

is literally *holy ones*, and is applied to things or persons consecrated to the service of God; hence to disciples of Christ who are set apart as priests to his service (Rom. 1 : 7; 1 Cor. 1 : 2; Ephes. 1 : 4).—**All that call on thy name.** This language clearly implies that the speaker was Jesus Christ, and as clearly that it was the custom of Christians in the apostolic church to pray to Christ (see ch. 2 : 21; 7 : 59; 9 : 21; 22 : 16; 1 Cor. 1 : 2; 2 Tim. 2 : 22). That the fame of Saul's mission was noised abroad is evident from vers. 21, 26, ch. 22 : 19.

15, 16. But the Lord said unto him, Go. The words, *thy way*, are added by the translators, and weaken the force of the original. —**For he is a chosen vessel unto me.** Not, as Adam Clark, a choice or excellent instrument, the original does not bear that signification, but a *selected* instrument, *i. e.*, selected by God, and for the purpose indicated in the remainder of the sentence. Whether the reader considers that Saul was selected because of his character, education, and natural attainments, or that these were conferred upon him because God had chosen him for the work, will depend upon the reader's conception of the divine government. To the call or choice here indicated Paul often refers (Rom. 1 : 1; 1 Cor. 1 : 1; Gal. 1 : 1, etc.). The term rendered *vessel* is a general one, signifying any kind of implement.—**To bear my name.** This defines the object for which Saul was chosen, and the verse, taken as a whole, indicates rather that every Christian's work is allotted to him by God, than that he is chosen by God to be a special subject of redeeming grace. *To bear my name* is here to carry it as on a banner.—**Before the Gentiles, and kings, and the children of Israel.** This commission was repeated subsequently in Jerusalem (ch. 22 : 21), and fulfilled, as regards the Gentiles and Israelites, by Paul's whole missionary life, and as regards kings by his appearance before Agrippa (ch. 26), and probably before Nero.—**And I will shew him how great things he must suffer.** In fulfillment of this, see ch. 20 : 23, 25; 21 : 11. As illustrating the sufferings endured by Paul for Christ, see 1 Cor. 4 : 9-13; 2 Cor. 11 : 23-28.

17, 18. Putting his hands on him. On the laying on of hands, see ch. 8 : 17, note. Here evidently not an ordination to the ministry, but a symbol, in connection with which the Holy Spirit was conferred and the sight restored. That this was the object of the laying on of hands is clearly stated in ver. 12.—**Brother Saul.** The term *brother* seems to have been commonly used among the Jews in address, the kinship of nationality and religion binding all members of the race together as in one family (ch. 2 : 29, 37; 3 : 17). It was thence transferred to the Christian church, and became a common appellation of Christians in their conversation with each other. Its use here shows how fully and heartily Ananias had accepted the revelation and commission from God.—**And be filled with the Holy Ghost.** This is not in the commission given to Ananias *as reported* (vers. 12, 15, 16). It illustrates the truth, which the student of Scripture should ever bear in mind, that the Bible reports are rarely if ever *verbatim*. It is impossible to suppose that Ananias added this himself to the commission given him. Comp. with the language here that of ch. 26 : 16-18, which probably embodied the message of Ananias here together with the commission later given to Saul in Jerusalem, and observe the verbal differences.—**There fell from his eyes as it had been scales.** Not actual scales, but something resembling them. Dr. Buck, of New York, in a private letter in answer to a request for information, says that "The ophthalmia, so common in the East, and which occasions blindness by producing opacity of the cornea, presents a grayish white spot, occupying the centre and spreading toward the circumference, thus shutting out the entrance of light through the pupil into the interior of the eye. This opaque spot might readily suggest to the popular observer the idea of the presence of a scale in the eye, and give rise to the idea that the restoration of sight was effected by the falling of something resembling a scale."—**Arose and was baptized.** Observe that apparently here, and certainly in the case of the eunuch (ch. 8 : 38), this ordinance was administered privately, and not in connection with any church, nor as a rite of admission to any specific ecclesiastical organization. Observe, too, that it *was administered*, an indication that it had already been accepted by the church as the divinely-appointed symbol of conversion and a new life. Clearly in this case the Holy Ghost was imparted before baptism, and was the ground on which baptism was administered, as in the case of Cornelius and his

19 And when he had received meat, he was strengthened. Then was Saul certain days with the disciples
which were at Damascus.[m]
20 And straightway he preached Christ in the synagogues, that he is the Son of God.
21 But all that heard *him*[n] were amazed, and said,
Is not this he[o] that destroyed them which called on
this name in Jerusalem, and came hither for that intent, that he might bring them bound unto the chief
priests?
22 But Saul increased the more in strength,[p] and confounded the[q] Jews which dwelt at Damascus, proving
that this is very Christ.
23 And after that many days were fulfilled, the Jews
took counsel[r] to kill him.
24 But their laying await was known of Saul. And
they watched[s] the gates day and night, to kill him.
25 Then the disciples took him by night, and let[t] *him*
down by the wall in a basket.
26 And when Saul was come[u] to Jerusalem, he assayed to join himself to the disciples: but they were all
afraid of him, and believed not that he was a disciple.

m ch. 26 : 20; Gal. 1 : 17....n Gal. 1 : 13, 23....o ch. 8 : 3....p Ps. 84 : 7....q ch. 18 : 28... r ch. 23 : 12; 25 : 3....s 2 Cor. 11 : 26, etc.; Ps. 21 : 11; 37 : 32, 33....t Josh. 2 : 15....u Gal. 1 : 18.

companions (ch. 10 : 47). The question has been raised, Where was Saul converted—on the road, or at the visit of Ananias? It cannot be answered. Even in Saul's case the day and hour of the radical change cannot be fixed. But beware of assuming that he had not been subject to the influence of the Holy Ghost prior to the visit of Ananias, or even prior to the appearance of the Lord to him on the road. The gift of the Holy Ghost, which Ananias came to bring, was such a bestowal as would be accompanied with an external and miraculous sign, here the restoration of Saul's sight. See ch. 8 : 17, note.

19, 20. And when he had received meat, he was strengthened. The implication is that the fasting mentioned in ver. 9 had been so severe as to weaken him bodily.—**Certain days.** Not many. See next verse.—**And straightway.** *Immediately.* This word seems to me quite inconsistent with the theory of those who place the visit to Arabia, mentioned in Gal. 1 : 17, between Saul's conversion and his public preaching; and, what is more important, it is irreconcilable with Wordsworth's practical deduction: "Perhaps this retirement of Paul (into Arabia) after his conversion was designed to be exemplary and instructive, as intimating that new converts ought not to be admitted to exercise the functions of the ministerial office, without some probationary term of silence, after their conversion." On the contrary, the "*immediately*" here implies, so far as Saul's career is an example to be followed, that when the convert has had, as Paul, previous education that fits him for the work of the ministry, he should begin at once to proclaim to others the Gospel which he has found himself (comp. John 1 : 41, 45; Mark 5 : 19).—**Jesus in the synagogues.** Being educated as a Jewish Rabbi, he had no difficulty in securing an audience in the synagogues. On their form of service, see Matt. 4 : 23. The best manuscripts have here *Jesus* instead of *Christ.* And the difference is not merely verbal. What Saul preached was, not the doctrine that the Jewish Messiah was the Son of God, but the fact that Jesus of Nazareth was the Son of God, and the long-promised Messiah, "the very Christ" (ver. 22).

22. But Saul increased the more in strength. In all the elements of moral and spiritual strength—the ardor of his convictions, the resolution of his purpose, the clearness of his apprehension of the new interpretation of the O. T., and the peculiar and indefinable strength that comes from singleness of purpose and communion with God. For his own interpretation of this phrase, see Ephes. 3 : 16–19.—**Confounded the Jews.** Threw them into confusion and perplexity. There is nothing to indicate that this his first preaching was successful, except in compelling the Jews to consider the claims of Jesus, to which before they had probably paid little, if any, heed.—**Many days were fulfilled.** There is nothing to indicate how many. —**Took counsel to kill him.** Not after trial; for the synagogue courts of Damascus had no right, under Jewish law, to inflict the death sentence. That could only be done by the Sanhedrim at Jerusalem. A conspiracy to assassinate is indicated.

24, 25. Let him down by the wall in a basket. Paul's more accurate description in 2 Cor. 11 : 33, indicates the kind of basket (σαργάνη), viz., one made of rope woven together. He also tells us that he was let down *through a window.* These lattice-windows of the East are built like a modern bay-window, overlooking the street, and in some instances, where the house is built directly in the city wall, they extend beyond and over the wall, as in the annexed illustration, and look out upon the country beyond. Through one of these windows Saul made his escape, while the Jews were watching the gates which were customarily closed at night, and through which no one could pass without liability to scrutiny from the guard. The implication here, and still more in Corinthians, is, that the guard were directed to seize him if he attempted to make his escape.

Two somewhat difficult questions in chronology are connected with this account. I. In Gal. 1 : 17, Paul, giving an account of his personal experiences at this time, says, "Neither went I up to Jerusalem to them which were apostles before me: but I went into Arabia, and returned again unto Damascus. Then after three years I went up to Jerusalem." Luke says nothing of this visit to Arabia. When did it occur? Some commentators place it immediately after the restoration of Saul's sight, and before he commenced preaching, which seems to me inconsistent with the language of ver. 20, "*Straightway* he preached Jesus in the synagogues;" others place it during the period when he "increased in strength" (ver. 22); others again during the "many days" mentioned in ver. 23; and still others in the interval between vers. 25 and 26, *i. e.*, after the attempted assassination. The truth appears to be that we have no adequate data from which to determine the question. Luke does not mention

WINDOWS ON THE WALL—DAMASCUS.

the visit to Arabia, either because he did not know of it, or because it did not come within his scope, his object being not to write a biography of Paul, but to narrate his conversion and entrance into the ministry. Arabia is a very general term, indicating then, as now, a large area of country, and there is nothing to fix the time or place of his sojourn, and little to determine its object, though the context in Galatians indicates retirement for prayer and the study of God's word, rather than for the active preaching of the Gospel. See notes on Gal. 1:16–18. II. In 2 Cor. 11:32, 33, Paul, in referring to his escape from Damascus, says, "The governor under Aretas the king kept the city of the Damascenes." Aretas was king of Petra; Damascus was a Roman city. How, then, should the governor *under Aretas* have control of affairs in Damascus? There are no adequate materials to answer this question, except hypothetically; but certain well-known facts in history indicate the probable answer. War broke out about A. D. 32 between Herod Antipas and this King Aretas (see for explanation of this war, Matt. 14:1–12, notes), in which Herod was signally defeated. On this, Vitellius, Roman governor of Syria, was dispatched by Tiberius, the Roman emperor, to march against Aretas; but while he was on his way, Tiberius died and was succeeded by Caligula. The new emperor, who was a personal foe to Herod, soon after banished him to Lyons, made a new distribution of the provinces of the East, giving Herod's kingdom to Agrippa. That, in these changes, Damascus passed under the authority of King Aretas, is a reasonable surmise, and it is confirmed by the fact that while coins of Damascus are found with the heads of Augustus, Tiberius, and Nero, none are found with those of Caligula and Claudius, an indication that during their reigns, Damascus was not under Roman law. Aretas probably continued the Roman edicts, already referred to, so that the Jewish population were allowed not only the free exercise of their religion, but also to govern themselves, and punish offenders against their own laws. The governor referred to in Corinthians was probably the Jewish governor, *i. e.*, the chosen head of the Jewish population.

26, 27. And when Saul was come to Jerusalem. His object was to visit Peter; why him more than any of the other disciples can only be surmised. Perhaps he had heard of Peter's mission to the Gentiles, recounted in the next chapter, and so was drawn to him for conference and counsel. He also wanted to preach the Gospel in Jerusalem, believing that his previous course there, and the Jewish acquaintance with him, as a persecutor of the Christian church, would ensure him a hearing (ch. 22:19, 20). In this he was disappointed (ver. 29). Three years had elapsed since his conversion, spent in Damascus and Arabia (Gal. 1:18), but not necessarily three whole years. The expression in Galatians would be satisfied, according to Jewish reckoning, by one year and parts of two others. Saul, during this visit to Jerusalem, abode with Peter; it lasted fifteen days (Gal. 1:18); then, partly owing to direct instructions from the Lord in a vision (ch. 22:18, 21), and partly owing to the danger to his life (ver. 29), he retired to Tarsus, his native city. —**They were all afraid of him.** Believing the story of his conversion, which may have reached them, to be false, and that he was hypocritically endeavoring to unite himself to them, for the purpose of more effectually spying out and bringing to punishment their chief men.—

TARSUS, THE BIRTHPLACE OF ST. PAUL. (The spectator is looking north, and Mount Taurus is seen in the background.) *From Laborde.*

27 But Barnabas[v] took him, and brought *him* to the apostles, and declared unto them how he had seen the Lord in the way, and that he had spoken to him, and how he had preached boldly[w] at Damascus in the name of Jesus.
28 And he was with them coming in and going out at Jerusalem.
29 And he spake boldly in the name of the Lord Jesus, and disputed against the Grecians: but[x] they went about to slay him.
30 *Which* when the brethren knew, they brought him down to Cæsarea, and sent him forth to Tarsus.
31 Then[y] had the churches rest[z] throughout all Judæa and Galilee and Samaria, and were edified;[a] and walking[b] in the fear of the Lord, and in the comfort[c] of the Holy Ghost, were multiplied.[d]

v ch. 4 : 36....w vers. 20–22....x verse 23....y ch. 8 : 1; Zech. 9 : 1....z Ps. 94 : 13....a Rom. 14 : 19....b Ps. 86 : 11; Col. 1 : 10.... c John 14 : 16, 17....d Zech. 8 : 20–22.

But Barnabas took him. Barnabas was a native of Cyprus (ch. 4 : 36), itself only a few hours sail from Cilicia, and the schools for which Tarsus (see below) was famous may well have furnished Barnabas with a part of his education. It is therefore not improbable that Barnabas and Saul may have known each other in youth.—**How he hath seen the Lord.** Observe, not merely heard him. Comp. ver. 5, note and refs. —**And how in Damascus he had been outspoken in the name of Jesus.** Including his preaching, but not that alone. The emphasis of the original (παῤῥησιάζομαι) is not on the public preaching, but on the open and public avowal of his faith.

28-30. And he was with them. Of the apostles he saw at this time only Peter and James, the Lord's brother (Gal. 1 : 18, 19). Perhaps the others were absent from the city. On his second visit he saw John (Gal. 2 : 9). There is no evidence that he saw any others of the twelve.—**Coming in and going out.** A phrase significant of the closeness of his intimacy with them. See ch. 1 : 21.—**And disputed against the Grecians.** That is, in the synagogues of the Grecians in Jerusalem. It had been in these synagogues that Stephen had preached the Gospel; here he had argued, presumptively with Saul among others; and to these synagogues where Saul had reviled the name of Jesus, he now returned to honor it.—**They took it in hand** (ἐπιχειρέω) **to slay him.** Either by secret assassination, as in ch. 23 : 12, or by mob violence, as in ch. 21 : 31.—**Which, when the brethren knew.** There is no inconsistency between this account and that in ch. 22 : 17–21, which attributes Paul's departure from Jerusalem to a direct commission from God bidding him depart and preach the Gospel to the Gentiles. The providence and the word of God always agree; Luke speaks of the providence, Paul of the revealed word.—**Cæsarea.** Cæsarea Palestina on the Mediterranean coast. See ch. 8 : 40.

Sent him forth to Tarsus. Probably by ship. Paul's language in Gal. 1 : 21 is: "Afterward I came into the regions of Syria and Cilicia." This corresponds with the account in Acts. From Tarsus, the capital of Cilicia, Saul, at the solicitation of Barnabas, went to Antioch and preached there (ch. 12 : 25, 26). Tarsus (the word means *wing*), in Cilicia, chief town of the province, is principally illustrious as having been the birthplace of Paul, although it "was no mean city." It must have been of great extent, since the river Cydnus, a remarkably cold and swift stream, which then flowed directly through the city, dividing it in two wings, thus accounting for its name, is now more than a mile away, and recently-discovered ruins show that it is the city which has shrunken and not the river which has changed its course. It was a free city, *i. e.*, though under Roman rule, it made its own laws and chose its magistrates. This freedom did not confer the right of citizenship; and though Tarsus subsequently became a colony, and so was entitled to that right, it was not until after the time of Paul. In matters of education and learning it was the rival of Athens and Alexandria, and many famous men were educated there. It was also important commercially. The broad mouth of the river was artificially widened and docks constructed. After having been called by several different names, the place is now called Tersors, and contains some 30,000 inhabitants. It is no longer a place of wealth and learning, but a den of poverty, filth, and ruins. There is some reason to believe that Saul preached the Gospel effectually at the time of this visit, and that it was during this ministry that there were gathered into the Christian church some of those Christian kinsmen whom he mentions in Rom. 16 : 7, 11, 21.

31. Then had the churches rest. The best manuscripts have here *the church* in the singular; the difference is important only in its bearing on the question whether the Christian churches were united at this early period of their history in one ecclesiastical organization, or were independent of each other. Two causes combined in producing this rest: the conversion of Saul, who had chiefly instigated the persecution against the Christians (ch. 8 : 3, 4), and the fact that Caligula demanded that his statue should be set up in the temple, and be received, as elsewhere in the Roman empire, as a god. The excitement produced by the opposition to this demand distracted the attention of the Jews from the Christians (Josephus' Ant., 18 : 8, 2–9).—**Throughout all Judea and Galilee and Samaria.** This is the only distinct reference in the N. T. to

32 And it came to pass, as Peter passed throughout all *quarters*, he came down also to the saints which dwelt at Lydda.
33 And there he found a certain man named Æneas, which had kept his bed eight years, and was sick of the palsy.
34 And Peter said unto him, Æneas, Jesus Christ maketh[e] thee whole; arise, and make thy bed. And he arose immediately.
35 And all that dwelt at Lydda and[f] Saron saw him, and turned[g] to the Lord.

e ch. 3 : 6, 16; 4 : 10.... f 1 Chron. 5 : 16. ..g ch. 11 : 21; 2 Cor. 3 : 16.

Christian churches in Galilee.—**Being built up and walking in the fear of the Lord.** There should be no stop after edified, which in the original is a participle. Both the upbuilding and the walking were in the fear of the Lord; the former expression refers not to increase in numbers, but in spiritual life. Comp. 1 Cor. 8 : 1; 14 : 4; 1 Thess. 5 : 11, etc.—**The fear of the Lord;** that godly fear which leads to obedience of his commandments (Deut. 5 : 29; 6 : 2; Josh. 24 : 14), and accompanies trust and praise (2 Kings 17 : 36, 39; Psalm 22 : 33: 96 : 4; 115 : 11; Prov. 14 : 26); it is nearly equivalent to reverence and allegiance.—**And in the comfort of the Holy Ghost.** Rather in his *helpful presence*. No one English word is adequate to render the Greek (παράκλησις), which is derived from a verb meaning to call to one's help.—**Were multiplied.** This may mean either that the numbers of the churches or of the converts were multiplied, probably both.

Ch. 9 : 32-43. HEALING OF ENEAS AND RAISING OF DORCAS BY PETER. THE POWER OF THE GOSPEL AND THE POWER OF PRAYER ILLUSTRATED.—CHRISTIAN CHARITY EXEMPLIFIED.

The date of these events is uncertain. Peter was at Jerusalem at the time of Saul's visit (Gal. 1 : 18). This tour of Peter's must, therefore, have taken place prior or subsequent to that visit; more probably prior. Luke, having given the account of Paul's persecution of the church, his conversion, and his reception by the church at Jerusalem, goes back to recount the other important providences of God which opened the

LYDDA, WITH THE RUINS OF THE CHURCH OF ST. GEORGE.
(The tall minaret belongs to a mosque.)

door to the Gentiles. This account, including Peter's visit to and interview with Cornelius, being brought to an end at ch. 11 : 18, Luke there resumes his interrupted narrative, showing how the persecution under Saul led to the founding of the church at Antioch, and Paul's ministry there preliminary to his first missionary tour (ch. 11 : 19-30). If this view be correct, we can understand why Saul, having heard of Peter's mission to the Gentiles, should have been drawn to go up to Jerusalem to confer especially with him.

32. Peter passed throughout all. Not all *quarters*, as in our English version, but among all the churches referred to in the previous verse. This was not a missionary tour.—**To the saints.** Literally the *holy ones*, see ver. 13, note.—**At Lydda.** The Benjamitish town Lod of the O. T. (1 Chron. 8 : 12; Ezra 2 : 33; Neh. 11 : 35), although apart from the rest of the territory of the tribe. It was about nine miles from Joppa, on the road to Jerusalem. It is mentioned in the Apocrypha, and Josephus speaks of it as a village not inferior in size to a city. The miracle wrought by Peter quickened the interest in Christianity here, a church of some importance sprang up, and it became the seat of a bishopric frequently mentioned in ecclesiastical annals. It was probably the birthplace, and certainly the place of sepulchre, of the renowned St. George. At present Lydda, or Ludd, is only a considerable village, remarkable for nothing but the ruins of a magnificent church erected to the honor of St. George, and some fine surrounding gardens

36 Now there was at Joppa a certain disciple named Tabitha, which by interpretation is called Dorcas: this woman was full[h] of good works and almsdeeds which she did.

37 And it came to pass in those days, that she was sick, and died: whom, when they had washed, they laid *her* in an upper chamber.
38 And forasmuch as Lydda was nigh to Joppa, and

h 1 Tim. 2 : 10; Titus 2 : 7, 14.

and orchards. There is no further mention of it in the N. T.

33-35. A certain man named Eneas. Nothing is known of him except the mention here; his name indicates that he was a Greek or a Grecian Jew, and the connection that he was one of the *saints*, *i. e.*, a Christian disciple.—**Sick of palsy.** For description of palsy, see Mark 2 : 3, note.—**Jesus the Messiah healeth thee.** Observe that Peter makes this healing itself a proclamation that Jesus is the Messiah, and heals in the Messiah's name, not in his own. Comparing the N. T. with the O. T., observe that it is Jesus the Messiah "who forgiveth all thine iniquities, who healeth all thy diseases" (Psalm 103 : 3).—**And make thy bed.** Literally, *Spread for thyself;* the word bed is not in the original. This, which others had before done for him, he was now to do for himself, as an evidence of the thoroughness of his cure; arising showed strength in his lower limbs; spreading the bed showed command of his arms and hands. —**All that dwelt in Lydda and Saron saw him.** Not saw the cure, but saw him after he was cured, as in ch. 3 : 9, 10, and John 9 : 8. Saron was the district in which Lydda stood. It was a plain extending about thirty miles along the coast from Joppa to Cæsarea. It has been conjectured that there was a village of that name, but no trace of it has been found. Luke's meaning is that the inhabitants not only of Lydda, but of the plain generally, heard and believed. —**And turned to the Lord,** *i. e.*, to Jesus Christ. It is not meant that literally all the

VIEW OF JOPPA, FROM THE NORTHEAST.

inhabitants were spiritually converted to Christ, but that there was a general and popular recognition of Jesus founded on this miracle.

36. There was at Joppa. Joppa was an ancient Philistine city on the borders of Dan. Its name signifies *to be beautiful*, *to shine*, and was probably given because of the effect of the sunshine reflected from its houses which rose, as now, tier on tier, upon the hill sloping upward from the sea. It had a celebrated but not a very safe harbor, and has been since the days of Solomon the port of Jerusalem. Here were brought the fir trees and the cedar trees in the times of Hiram and Zerubbabel. Here Jonah took ship to flee from the Lord. It was a prominent fortification in the war of the Maccabees and in the later conflicts of the Crusades, when, for half a century, it was alternately built and destroyed. Judas Maccabeus, Antiochus, Herod, Cestius, Vespasian, Omar, Saladin, Richard, Godfrey, Napoleon, have all in turn laid siege to it, and it has at least once been entirely effaced. It is now called Jaffa, and has a population of 15,000, a large proportion of whom are Christians. Besides the beauty of the exterior of the city itself, are beautiful environs, with fragrant and shady groves of orange, lemon, olive, citron, mulberry, fig and palm trees. Commerce seems now to be returning to Jaffa with wonderful vigor, and a railroad, proposed between it and Jerusalem, is likely to greatly increase its importance. — **Named Tabitha.** This word is Aramaic; Dorcas is Greek. She is not again mentioned in the N. T. The name means gazelle, which was in the East a favorite type of beauty. See Solomon's Song 2 : 9, 17; 4 : 5; 7 : 3.—**Full of**

the disciples had heard that Peter was there, they sent unto him two men, desiring *him* that he would not delay to come to them.
39 Then Peter arose, and went with them. When he was come, they brought him into the upper chamber: and all the widows stood by him weeping, and shewing the coats and garments which Dorcas made, while[i] she was with them.
40 But Peter put[j] them all forth, and kneeled down, and prayed; and turning *him* to the body, said, Tabitha,[k] arise. And she opened her eyes: and when she saw Peter, she sat up.
41 And he gave her *his* hand, and lifted her up, and when he had called the saints and widows,[l] presented her alive.
42 And it was known throughout all Joppa: and[m] many believed in the Lord.
43 And it came to pass, that he tarried many days in Joppa, with one Simon a tanner.

i Eccles. 9 : 10....j Matt. 9 : 25....k Mark 5 : 41, 42; John 11 : 43....l 1 Kings 17 : 23....m John 12 : 11.

THE FOUNTAIN OF TABITHA, NEAR JOPPA.

good works and almsdeeds. Literally, *mercies.* The first phrase is general, the second specific, and is interpreted by ver. 39.—**She made.** With her own hands. She was not merely the almoner of others' charities.

37-39. Whom, when they had washed. For account of the preparation, according to Jewish customs, of the body for burial, see Mark 16 : 1, note; John 19 : 39, 40, note; Acts 5 : 6, note.—**In an upper chamber.** The houses of the poorer classes in the East have but one story. In the best houses, the best rooms are often on the second floor. See Luke 22 : 12, note. Here may be intended such a second-story room, but more probably a large, airy hall, not unfrequently constructed upon the roof of a house and forming a sort of third story. Here the Hebrews received company, gave feasts, and sometimes held religious services. Dr. Robinson (*Researches* 3 : 26) describes his reception in such an upper chamber. A similar apartment is common in Egypt and is called the "Kaah."—**Nigh to Joppa.** About nine miles (ver. 36, note).—**They sent unto him two men.** They desired his sympathy and ministry, and possibly having heard of the miracle at Lydda, had some vague hope of help.—**That thou wilt not delay to come to us.** This is the best reading and is adopted by Tischendorf and Alford. The variation is important only as the form is a slight indication that Luke was perhaps an eye and ear witness of what followed.—**Stood by him weeping.** Apparently there were no professional mourners and none of that ostentation of grief which Christ rebukes in Mark 5 : 39. That was a Jewish household; this is a Christian company.—**Coats and garments.** The former is the tunic, a loose shirt extending to the knees, the latter a large, loose cloak worn by day and used as a covering by night (Matt. 5 : 40; 24 : 18, notes).

40. Peter put them all forth. In imitation of his Lord's example (Mark 5 : 40). Perhaps as in 2 Kings 4 : 33, for privacy in prayer.—**And kneeled down.** This was a common attitude of prayer among the Jews (Ps. 95 : 6; Dan. 6 : 10; Luke 22 : 41; Acts 21 : 5).—**Tabitha, arise.** In one respect this miracle is peculiar, in that Peter performs it without any reference to Christ, and as if in his own name; but if his prayer were reported, we should probably find this otherwise singular omission supplied. The narrative implies that he prayed for the restoration of Dorcas as Elijah for the widow's son (1 Kings 17 : 20; comp. 2 Kings 4 : 33) and that he received such assurance of answer to his prayer as justified his authoritative tone.

AN ARAB WIDOW.

—**And she opened her eyes,** etc. "Observe how he, as it were, awakes her out of sleep; first she opened her eyes; then, upon seeing Peter, she sat up; then, from his hands she received strength."—(*Chrysostom.*)—**The saints and**

widows. *The saints* are her companions in Christian faith and works; the *widows*, those to whom she had ministered. The distribution of Christian charity inaugurated at Jerusalem (ch. 6 : 1) had been maintained in Joppa largely through the instrumentality of Dorcas. The accompanying illustration shows the Arab widow of modern times in her mourning. She is required by custom to wear garments dyed purple or dark brown. Some have an entire suit of purple, with heavy crimson fringe in wool. The head-vail is of wool, two yards by one, with fringe across each end, and half a yard along one side. When folded over the forehead, the extra fringe falls on the neck behind, as here indicated.

42, 43. Many believed in the Lord. Evidently, then, the miracle was performed in the name of the Lord, and was so understood throughout the community.—**Simon the tanner.** Only mentioned here and in the following chapter. His house was by the seaside (ch. 10 : 6), and one is now pointed out which Stanley thinks may occupy the original site. It is close to the sea-shore; the waves beat against the low wall. In the court-yard is a spring of fresh water, such as must always have been needed for the purposes of tanning. This occupation was in ill-repute among all ancient nations, especially the Jews. The latter considered entering into it after marriage ground for divorce, and forbade any tanner to become high-priest or king. Peter's selection of this abode indicates both the slight esteem in which the Christians were held by the Jews at Lydda, and the diminished hold which Judaism had upon the mind of Peter.

TRADITIONAL HOUSE OF SIMON THE TANNER.

Ch. 10 : 1–48. THE CALL AND BAPTISM OF CORNELIUS. THE CATHOLICITY OF THE GOSPEL: THE BLOOD OF JESUS CHRIST IS ABLE TO CLEANSE ALL SINNERS AND FROM ALL SIN.—THE CHARACTER ACCEPTABLE TO GOD: PIETY, CHARITY, JUSTICE.—WALKING ACCORDING TO PRESENT LIGHT THE WAY TO GREATER LIGHT.—THE TEACHER TAUGHT.—THE GOSPEL IN BRIEF (43).—BAPTISM THE SYMBOL, AND BAPTISM THE FACT (47).—See on verses 34, 35.

The date of this incident is uncertain. It was, perhaps, before Saul's conversion; more probably just subsequent; almost certainly, before Saul's visit to Jerusalem, recorded in the preceding chapter. See chap. 9 : 28, note. Nearly simultaneously the Lord commanded Saul to preach the Gospel to the Gentiles, and by a divine revelation taught Peter, and through him the church at Jerusalem, that the Gospel is for Gentile as well as Jew.

CHAPTER X.

THERE was a certain man in Cæsarea, called Cornelius, a centurion of the band called the Italian *band*,
2 *A* devout *man*,[n] and one that feared[o] God with
all[p] his house, which gave much alms to[q] the people,
and prayed[r] to God alway.
3 He saw in a vision evidently, about the ninth hour
of the day, an angel[s] of God coming in to him, and
saying unto him Cornelius.
4 And when he looked on him, he was afraid, and
said, What is it, Lord? And he said unto him, Thy
prayers and thine alms are come up for a memorial[t]
before God.
5 And now send men to Joppa, and call for *one* Simon, whose surname is Peter:

n ch. 8 : 2; 22 : 12....o Eccles. 7 : 18....p ch. 18 : 8; Gen. 18 : 19; Ps. 101 : 2-7....q Ps. 41 : 1....r Ps. 119 : 2; Prov. 2 : 3-5....s Heb. 1 : 14....t Isa. 45 : 19.

1, 2. In Cæsarea. For description and illustration, see ch. 8 : 40, note.—**A centurion of the cohort called the Italian.** The Roman army was divided into legions, each of which was subdivided into ten cohorts, each cohort into three maniples, and each maniple into two centuries, containing from fifty to one hundred men, under the command of a centurion, who thus answered to the captain of the modern army organization. The cohort to which Cornelius belonged was called the Italian, because composed of men levied in Italy, not in Syria. Cæsarea was the military headquarters of the Roman government in Palestine.—**A devout man and one that feared God.** The proselytes are divided in the Rabbinical books into two classes, "Proselytes of the gate," who accepted Jehovah as the true God, but were not circumcised, and "proselytes of righteousness," who formally united themselves to the Jewish church and accepted its whole ceremonial observance. See Matt. 23 : 15, note. Cornelius belonged to the first class. That he was not a proselyte of righteousness is clear from ver. 28. That he worshipped the true God is clear from the language of this verse. He knew something of the life of Jesus (ver. 37), but had no clear apprehension of Christ's character or work. Whether he was a true regenerate child of God before Peter came to him has been questioned, but chiefly because the supposition that he was so is inconsistent with our often too narrow theology. The very object of the narrative is to teach Peter, and through him the primitive church, the lesson which in all ages the church has been slow to learn, that God accepts every man, whatever his nationality or his religious ignorance, who reverences God, seeks further light from him, and does this in the way of practical righteousness (Rom. 2 : 6, 7; Matt. 8 : 10, 11, note). See further on ver. 35 and on ch. 11 : 14.—**Prayed to God always.** That is, his habitual devotions were offered to Jehovah; he had no sympathy with that spirit of Roman skepticism, repeated in our own day, which counted all religions as equally commendable.

3. He saw in a vision evidently. He was praying at the time. For what? Alford, following Neander, supposes that the subject of his prayers was that he might be guided into truth, and if so, hardly without reference to that faith which was now spreading so widely over Judea. He adds: "Further than this we cannot infer with certainty; but if *the particular difficulty present in his mind* be sought, we can hardly avoid the conclusion that it was connected with the apparent necessity of embracing Judaism and circumcision in order to become a believer in Christ." I should rather conclude, from ch. 11 : 14, that the burden of his prayer was the yearning desire for some clear revelation of redemption from sin, and some clear light in respect to human duty and the problem of the future, such as we elsewhere meet with, both in the writings of the best heathen philosophers and in the accounts of missionaries. For Scriptural illustrations, see Job 7 : 21; 9 : 33; 23 : 3; 31 : 5; Acts 17 : 27. On the nature of visions, see on ch. 2 : 17; 9 : 10. *Evidently* here indicates that there were some external and visible appearances; these are more fully described in ver. 30.—**About the ninth hour.** 3 P. M. This was a regular Jewish hour of prayer (ch. 3 : 1, note), and the language indicates that Cornelius observed, at least in part, the Jewish ritual.—**An angel of God.** The Jews believed that a guardian angel is assigned by God to each individual believer for his especial protection and spiritual help. See Matt. 18 : 10, note; Acts 12 : 15, note; 27 : 23; Heb. 1 : 14.

4. What is it, Lord? Rather *sire*. The language is that of reverence, but not necessarily of worship (see in Matt. 8 : 2).—**For a memorial before God.** Tischendorf omits the words *for a memorial*, but Alford retains them. The meaning is, God has heard and remembered them. See ver. 31, and comp. Rev. 5 : 8. The fact that the prayers of Cornelius were heard and answered, is of itself conclusive that, before hearing the Gospel from Peter, he was accepted as a child of God. See Ps. 66 : 18; Prov. 28 : 9; John 9 : 31.

5-8. With one Simon the tanner. See on ch. 9 : 43. *He shall tell thee what thou oughtest to do* is omitted by Tischendorf and Alford, but correctly interprets the object of the mission to Peter. *The household servants* were domestics belonging to the household; *the soldier*, probably a sentry belonging to the cohort. Joppa was about thirty miles south of Cæsarea. Observe in

6 He lodgeth with one Simon[u] a tanner, whose
house is by the sea side: he shall tell thee[v] what thou
oughtest to do.
7 And when the angel which spake unto Cornelius
was departed, he called two of his household servants,
and a devout soldier of them that waited on him continually;
8 And when he had declared all *these* things unto
them, he sent them to Joppa.
9 On the morrow, as they went on their journey, and
drew nigh unto the city, Peter went[w] up upon the
housetop to pray, about the sixth hour:
10 And he became very hungry, and would have
eaten: but while they made ready, he fell into a trance,
11 And saw[x] heaven opened, and a certain vessel
descending unto him, as it had been a great sheet, knit
at the four corners, and let down to the earth;
12 Wherein were all manner of four-footed beasts of
the earth, and wild beasts, and creeping things, and
fowls of the air.
13 And there came a voice to him, Rise, Peter; kill,
and eat.
14 But Peter said, Not so, Lord; for I have never
eaten any thing that is[y] common or unclean.

u ch. 9 : 43.... v ch. 11 : 14.... w ch. 11 : 5, etc.... x ch. 7 : 56; Rev. 19 : 11.... y Lev. 11 : 2, etc.; 20 : 25; Deut. 14 : 3, etc.; Ezek. 4 : 14.

the act of Cornelius the evidence of his faith. He sends a great distance, to one apparently unknown to him, for instruction, declaring to the messengers his object, thus confessing to them his faith and his hope. Contrast his humility with Naaman's pride (2 Kings 5 : 12). He received the kingdom of God as a little child.

A ROMAN SOLDIER.

9, 10. Peter went up upon the housetop. The housetop was flat, and was used commonly as a resort for conversation (1 Sam. 9 : 26), for sleeping (2 Sam. 16 : 22), for exercise (2 Sam. 11 : 2), for observation (Judges 16 : 27; Isa. 22 : 1), for idolatrous worship (2 Kings 23 : 12; Zeph. 1 : 5), for public mourning (Isa. 15 : 3; Jer. 48 : 38), for festival celebrations (Neh. 8 : 16), and for a variety of domestic purposes.—**About the sixth hour.** 12 M.—**Would have eaten.** Desired to eat.—**Fell into a trance.** His hunger was a preparation not for the trance, but for the vision which ensued. But for his hunger, the direction, Kill and eat, would have had less force. The trance is mentioned in the Bible only here, in ch. 22 : 17, and in Numb. 24 : 4, 16. Among scientific men it is a recognized mental condition, in which the mind loses the consciousness of outer objects, and is borne away, so to speak, into another world of thought. It differs from the dream in that it is unconnected with any natural sleep; and from the vision, because in the latter, the person retains his consciousness, and the objects shown to him possess a real existence.

11, 12. And saw heaven opened, etc. In interpreting this language we are to remember that it describes what was seen in a trance, and, like the ordinary descriptions of a dream, is incapable of exact interpretation. The vessel was not a great sheet, but something like a great sheet, let down by the four corners to the earth. It contained, not *all manner of four-footed beasts*, etc., a modification of the original unnecessarily made by the translators, but *all four-footed beasts*, etc.—*i. e.*, the impression on Peter's mind was that of the whole animal creation presented to him. To the Jew's mind the clean would have been polluted by contact with the unclean, so that all would have been alike prohibited. Neander suggests that in the four corners there is an intimation that men from the North, and the South, and the East, and the West, would appear as clean before God, and be called to a participation in his kingdom.

13, 14. There came a voice to him. Ch. 11 : 7 indicates an external and audible voice.—**Kill and eat.** This direction shows the dream-like character of the occurrence. He could not have eaten the animal food without cooking, for which there was no provision.—**By no means, Lord.** The negative is emphatic.—**Common and unclean.** This is the best reading; the conjunction *or* has been substituted for *and* to conform to ch. 11 : 8. The distinction between clean and unclean dates from as early as the flood (Gen. 7 : 2). It is incorporated in the Mosaic law; the fullest and most important account of its provisions on this subject are contained in Lev., chaps. 11–15. The most essential features of these provisions were the following: (*a.*) *All living animals* were clean, *all dead bodies* unclean, and this because death is the punishment of sin, and the corpse a symbol of moral putrefaction. (*b.*) It was necessary to make provision for human food; wherefore certain animals were allowed to be slaughtered for that purpose. The law pre-

15 And the voice *spake* unto him again the second time, What God hath cleansed,[z] *that* call not thou common.
16 This was done thrice: and the vessel was received up again into heaven.
17 Now while Peter doubted in himself what this vision which he had seen should mean, behold, the men which were sent from Cornelius had made inquiry[a] for Simon's house, and stood before the gate,
18 And called, and asked whether Simon, which was surnamed Peter, were lodged there.
19 While Peter thought on the vision, the Spirit[b] said unto him, Behold, three men seek thee.
20 Arise[c] therefore, and get thee down, and go with them, doubting nothing: for I have sent them.
21 Then Peter went down to the men which were sent unto him from Cornelius; and said, Behold, I am he whom ye seek: what *is* the cause wherefore ye are come?
22 And they said, Cornelius[d] the centurion, a just man, and one that feareth God, and of good report[e] among all the nation of the Jews, was warned from God by an holy angel, to send for thee into his house, and to hear words of thee.
23 Then called he them in, and lodged *them*. And on the morrow Peter went away with them, and certain[f] brethren from Joppa accompanied him.

z verse 28; Matt. 15 : 11; Rom. 14 : 14, etc.; 1 Cor. 10 : 25; 1 Tim. 4 : 4....a ch. 9 : 43....b ch. 11 : 12....c ch. 15 : 7....d verse 1, etc.... e ch. 22 : 12; Heb. 11 : 2....f verse 45.

scribed the animals and the method of slaughter. (*c.*) Its discrimination between clean and unclean animals, *i. e.*, between those permitted and those prohibited as food, accords with, though not necessarily founded on, those sanitary principles which experience indicates as of nearly universal application. The ancient heathen laws agreed substantially in their discrimination on this subject with the laws of Moses. (*d.*) There was one important exception, the Gentile laws applied only to the priestly classes, the Jewish law to all the people. The revelation to Peter here shows clearly that the distinction was not merely sanitary, but symbolical and spiritual. For while sanitary laws remain unchanged, the death of Christ has taken away the sting and shame of death (1 Cor. 15 : 55-57), and purified all things. See on next verse.

15, 16. What God hath cleansed call not thou common. The Lord, by his direction to Peter, declares the O. T. distinction between clean and unclean meats abolished, and this because Christ, by his death, has cleansed all things, for those who accept them in faith and with prayer and thanksgiving (Rom. 14 : 14-17; 1 Cor. 10 : 25, 26; 1 Tim. 4 : 4, 5), his redemption including in its scope and power the whole physical universe (Ephes. 1 : 10; Col. 1 : 20). But this is only the symbol; the especial truth symbolized is that Christ hath cleansed humanity, having taken away the sin of the world (John 1 : 29), so that henceforth there is no form of humanity, so debased in ignorance and vice, as to be common and unclean to him who sees in every human being a soul for which Christ has poured out his cleansing blood.—**Done thrice.** To render the communication more emphatic (Gen. 41 : 32).—**The vessel was received up again into heaven.** Perhaps the descent from heaven and the return to heaven may be taken to indicate that from both the clean (the Jew), and the unclean (the Gentile), is composed the host who have made their robes white in the blood of the Lamb (Rev. 7 : 14).

17, 18. Stood before the gate. Which closed the arched entrance to the courtyard around which the Jewish house was usually built. For plan and illustration, see Matt. 26 : 69, note.—**And called.** To the porter whose business it was to tend the door. There is no ground whatever for Neander's assertion that the voices of these messengers attracted Peter's attention; on the contrary, the implication of ver. 19 is that he knew nothing of their coming till the Spirit bade him go down.

19, 20. While Peter was revolving in his mind concerning the vision. Dreams and visions were universally regarded in those days as revelations of the divine will; Peter was still turning this vision over in mind to deduce from it the lesson intended, perhaps praying to God to interpret it to him, when, in answer to his prayer, came the message of the Spirit to him to go down and go with the men inquiring for him. Observe in his case, as in that of Cornelius, Peter was required *to do something* to show his obedience and faith, and this while the vision was still an unsolved mystery.—**Doubting nothing.** That is, without scruple or hesitation. When the invitation to preach the Gospel to a heathen was delivered to him by the messengers, he would, but for this revelation, have scrupled to comply. See ver. 28.—**I have sent them.** Because Cornelius, in sending them, acted under the guidance of the Holy Spirit.

21-23. Which were sent unto him from Cornelius. These words are wanting in the best MSS.—**A just man and one that feareth God.** Coupling this with the declaration of verse 2, that he *gave much alms to the people*, we have in Cornelius a character which corresponds to the divine requirement as interpreted by Micah 6 : 8, "What doth the Lord require of thee but to do justly, and to love mercy, and to walk humbly with thy God?" He was just in his military administration; he was charitable to the needy; he was a worshipper of Jehovah; and he had such respect to the Jewish religion as to be favorably regarded by the Jews.—**All the nation of the Jews.** That is, all of that nationality in Cæsarea, or its vicinity.—**And lodged them.** It was too late to return to Cæsarea the same day. The men had started

24 And the morrow after they entered into Cæsarea.
And Cornelius waited for them, and had called together his kinsmen and near friends.
25 And as Peter was coming in, Cornelius met him,
and fell down at his feet, and worshipped *him*.
26 But Peter took him up, saying, Stand[g] up: I myself also am a man.
27 And as he talked with him, he went in, and found
many that were come together.
28 And he said unto them, Ye know how that it is
an unlawful thing[h] for a man that is a Jew to keep
company, or come unto one of another nation; but
God hath shewed me[i] that I should not call any man
common or unclean.
29 Therefore came I *unto you* without gainsaying, as
soon as I was sent for: I ask, therefore, for what intent
ye have sent for me?
30 And Cornelius said, Four days ago I was fasting
until this hour: and at the ninth hour I prayed in my
house; and, behold, a man stood before me[j] in bright
clothing,
31 And said, Cornelius, thy[k] prayer is heard, and
thine alms are had in remembrance in the sight of
God.
32 Send therefore to Joppa, and call hither Simon,
whose surname is Peter: he is lodged in the house of
one Simon a tanner, by the sea side; who, when he
cometh, shall speak unto thee.
33 Immediately therefore I sent to thee: and thou
hast well done that thou art come. Now[l] therefore

g ch. 14:14, 15; Rev. 19:10; 22:9....h John 4:9....i ch. 15:8, 9; Ephes. 3:6....j ch. 1:10; Matt. 28:3 .. k verse 4, etc.; Dan. 10:12; Heb. 6:10....l Deut. 5:27.

after 3 P. M. of the preceding day (vers. 3, 7); they had thirty miles to travel, and could not, therefore, have reached Joppa till well on in the second day; it was noon when Peter went up on to the housetop to pray; and since then the trance had taken place. It was now, therefore, after noon, perhaps well on toward early evening.—**Certain brethren from Joppa accompanied him.** In the investigation which ensued, they confirmed Peter's account (ch. 11:12, note).

24-27. And the morrow after. That is, the day after starting. Thirty miles is more than a day's journey; the accuracy of statement in detail indicates that Luke's informant was an eye-witness of the events.—**Near friends.** Intimate friends. Observe the indication of the strength of his faith. He had sent a distance of thirty miles, after a stranger, yet such was his assurance of a favorable response that he had gathered his kinsfolk and friends before Peter's arrival.—**Fell down at his feet and reverenced him.** Not literally *worshipped him* (Matt. 8:2, note). The homage of an inferior to a superior is indicated here; Cornelius recognized in Peter a divine messenger, a prophet of the Lord. That a Roman centurion should have prostrated himself at the feet of a Jewish fisherman, is an evidence of his earnestness and his appreciation of divine things.—**I myself also am a man.** Comp. ch. 14:15; Rev. 22:8, 9. It would be well if Peter's successors had succeeded to Peter's feeling. Jesus never refused similar homage (Matt. 8:2; 9:18; 14:33, etc.). Was he less zealous for the worship of God than his disciples?—**He went in.** Cornelius, expecting him, had gone out and met Peter, perhaps at the gate, possibly on the road to Joppa.

28, 29. How that it is an unlawful thing for a man that is a Jew to keep company with, or come unto one of another nation. The O. T. law forbade intermarriage with the heathen, and discouraged intimacy of relationship with them (Deut. 7:1, 2, 16, 23-26; 12:27-32); but neither the O. T. nor the Rabbinical rules forbade all commerce between Jews and Gentiles. In that case the Jews could not have lived scattered throughout heathen lands. Social fellowship with Gentiles was, however, accounted unlawful. "Those foreigners who come to us, without submitting to our laws, Moses permitted not to have any intimate connection with us."—(*Jos.*, *Contra Apion*, 2:28.) So Juvenal says that the Jews "would not show the way, except to their fellow-religionists; nor guide any but a circumcised person to a fountain of which he was in search;" and Tacitus, that "they cherished against all mankind the hatred of enemies; they were separate in board and bed." So to-day, in India, the Hindoo deals with the English in business affairs, but rarely admits him to his house, or to any social fellowship. The language of ch. 11:3 indicates that on Peter's first entering, food was set before him, as, after a long journey, would naturally have been done, in accordance with almost universal Eastern custom. It was this social fellowship with Gentiles to which he here refers, and for which he was subsequently criticised.—**But God hath shewed me.** He now understood the vision. Cornelius preached the Gospel to Peter no less than Peter to Cornelius, each teaching the other its universality.—**Without gainsaying.** Contrast Peter's promptness with the hesitation of Moses (Exod. 4:10, 13) and of Jeremiah (Jer. 1:6), and his gladness with the moroseness of Jonah (Jonah 4:1).

30-33. Four days ago I was fasting. There is some difficulty about the proper rendering of this verse; but that afforded by our English version accords with the original, and is the most probable. The other view regards the fast of Cornelius as lasting for four days, *i. e.*, from the morning of the fourth preceding day to the time of this interview with Peter. But this is not a necessary translation, and why should he continue to fast after receiving an answer to his prayer (vers. 4-6)?—**A man stood before me in bright clothing.** He is here described according to his appearance, in verse 3 and in ch. 11:13 according to the reality; here as a *man*, there as

are we all here present before God, to hear all things
that are commanded thee of God.
34 Then Peter opened *his* mouth, and said, Of a
truth I perceive that God [m] is no respecter of persons:
35 But in [n] every nation he that feareth him, and
worketh righteousness, is accepted with him.
36 The word which *God* sent unto the children of Israel,
preaching peace [o] by Jesus Christ: (he is [p] Lord
of all:)
37 That word, *I say*, ye know, which was published
throughout all Judæa, and began from Galilee, after
the baptism which John preached;

m Deut. 10: 17; 2 Chron. 19: 7; Job 34: 19; Rom. 2: 11; Gal. 2: 6; 1 Pet. 1: 17....n Rom. 2: 13, 27; 3: 22, 29; 10: 12, 13; Ephes. 2: 13-18. ....o Isa. 57: 19; Col. 1: 20....p Ps. 24: 7-10; Matt. 28: 18; Rom. 14: 9; 1 Col. 15: 27; Ephes. 1: 20-22; 1 Pet. 3: 22; Rev. 17: 14.

an *angel.* Comp. Matt. 28 : 5 with Mark 16 : 5.—**Thy prayers are heard.** See on verse 4.—**Present before God * * * Commanded thee of God.** Observe that Cornelius is attentive, not to Peter the man, but to Peter as the commissioned messenger of God. The presence of God and the word of God are pre-eminent, the presence and word of Peter are subordinate.

34, 35. These two verses embody the lesson which this narrative is intended to teach. It contains a negative and an affirmative declaration. The negative, that God is no respecter of *persons*, literally of *faces*, is equivalent to, God does not judge men by their external circumstances and conditions. It is interpreted by James 2 : 1, 9, where the verb is the same; accords with the declaration of the O. T. (Deut. 10 : 17; Lev. 19 : 15; 1 Sam. 16 : 7), and is reiterated and confirmed by other passages in the N. T. (Rom. 2 : 11; Ephes. 6 : 9; Col. 3 : 25). The affirmative, In every nation he that feareth God and worketh righteousness is accepted with him, indicates that race and nationality are among the external circumstances which do not affect the divine judgment. Two fundamental traits of character secure his approval, viz., (1) a genuine reverence for and allegiance to the divine Being; (2) a sincere endeavor to show forth that allegiance and reverence by practical right-doing in daily life. With this accords the teaching of Rom. 2 : 6-11. How, then, as to the heathen? Taking the whole incident as a whole, noting the fact that in answer to the prayers of Cornelius Peter was sent to him, and the message with which he was charged was that of the Gospel, it clearly teaches, (1) that every man, whatever his race, education, or creed, who reverences God and shows forth his allegiance by right-doing according to his light, is accepted by God; (2) that this is no reason why the Gospel should not be preached to the heathen, both as a means for producing such reverence and righteousness of life, and also as an answer to the craving of soul of those in whom this spirit of piety is created; (3) that such are received not for their righteousness, but in God's mercy, on the ground of repentance, *i. e.*, abandonment of sin, and faith, which in their case is manifested, not by an acceptance of Christ before he has been preached to them, but by a yearning for Christ, that is quick to receive him when he is made known. The essential conditions of life eternal as here indicated are not different from, but identical with, those indicated elsewhere in the Scripture, as offered to those to whom the clear light of the Gospel is unknown. See Isaiah 55 : 7. The truth that this reverence for God and this working of righteousness are among the fruits of the Spirit, heard in the heart but not comprehended by it, is not in issue here, any more than the truth that God's grace seeks as well as saves the sinner is at issue in the parable of the prodigal son. Every part of the Bible does not teach *all* the Gospel. See further ch. 11 : 14, note.

36, 37. The construction of these verses is difficult. Some scholars take "*the word which God sent*" to be an interpretation of what precedes, thus reading the entire passage, "*I perceive that God is no respecter of persons, etc., according to the word which God sent.*" So substantially Bengel, De Wette, Alford. I think it better to understand it as in our English version, which makes *the word* (ver. 36) the object of the verb *know* (ver. 37). It is no objection to this view to say that Cornelius and his friends did not know the word preached, for how much they knew we have no means of ascertaining except from this narrative. Thus rendering the passage, the declaration of Peter is that his auditors knew that Jesus Christ ministered throughout Galilee, working miracles and preaching unto the children of Israel. It is now made known both to him and them that this Jesus is Lord of all, Gentile as well as Jew.—**Preaching peace through Jesus Christ.** Not, Preaching by Jesus Christ about peace, but, Proclaiming a peace afforded through the life and death of Jesus Christ. Here it is peace with God, soul-rest by his atonement and his indwelling (Matt. 11 : 29; Luke 1 : 79; 2 : 14; John 14 : 27).—**He is Lord of all.** That is, of all men. The larger truth that he is the Lord of all things, physical as well as spiritual (Col. 1 : 16, 18), is not referred to here.—**That word ye know.** That is, they knew that such a word had been preached to the children of Israel. That the fame of Christ's ministry extended beyond the bounds of Judea, even during his life, we know from the Gospels (Matt. 4 : 24, 25; Mark 7 : 24). Philip had subsequently preached the Gospel in Cæsarea (ch. 8 : 40). It is very probable, too, that some of the soldiers present at Jerusalem at the Passover had returned to Cæsarea, the Roman military headquarters, and had brought back reports of the

38 How God anointed[q] Jesus of Nazareth with the Holy Ghost and with power; who[r] went about doing good, and healing all that were oppressed[s] of the devil: for[t] God was with him.
39 And we[u] are witnesses of all things which he did, both in the land of the Jews, and in Jerusalem; whom they slew and hanged on a tree:
40 Him God raised up[v] the third day, and shewed him openly;
41 Not[w] to all the people, but unto witnesses chosen before[x] of God, *even* to us, who did eat and drink with him after he rose from the dead.
42 And he commanded us[y] to preach unto the people, and to testify that[z] it is he which was ordained of God *to be* the Judge of quick and dead.

q Luke 4 : 18; Heb. 1 : 9....r Matt. 12 : 15 ...s 1 John 3 : 8....t John 3 : 2....u ch. 2 : 32; Luke 24 : 48....v Matt. 28 : 1, 2....w John 14 : 22; 20 : 20....x John 15 : 16....y Matt. 28 : 19, 20....z ch. 17 : 31; John 5 : 22, 27; 2 Cor. 5 : 10; 1 Pet. 4 : 5.

ministry, the miracles, and the death of Jesus Christ; and it has even been suggested that Cornelius may have been the centurion who was present at Christ's crucifixion (Matt. 27 : 54; Mark 15 : 39).—**And began from Galilee.** It was from Galilee first that the fame of Jesus went abroad (Luke 4 : 14, 37, 44; 7 : 17; 9 : 6).—**After the baptism which John preached.** Christ's public ministry did not commence until John was cast into prison (Matt. 4 : 12), though some previous events in our Lord's life, including the conference with Nicodemus and the Samaritan woman, are recorded.

38. With the Holy Ghost and with power. The Holy Ghost descended upon Jesus immediately after his baptism. *Power* is not merely, as Dr. Hackett, the power to perform miracles, but the whole moral and spiritual might manifested by Christ's life of doing good and healing.—**Who went about doing good.** A suggestive characterization of what Christ's life was, and what the Christian's life should be. —**Healing all that were oppressed of the devil.** The reference is to the casting out of evil spirits from those possessed. See note on demoniacal possession, Vol. I., p. 123. This is singled out by Peter, as by Christ himself (Matt. 12 : 27, 28), as a conclusive demonstration of his divine power.—**For God was with him.** The secret of Christ's power, as of the power of his disciples, was God in him (John 14 : 10).

39-41. And we are witnesses. Having preached Christ, Peter declares to Cornelius his own mission and character. What his Gentile auditors knew only as a rumor, he has come to bear witness to as a fact.—**Whom they slew and hanged on a tree.** Alford notices the difference between the spirit of his address here to the Gentiles concerning the Jews, and his addresses to the Jews themselves (ch. 2 : 23; 3 : 14; 4 : 10; 5 : 30), when he was working conviction in the minds of those who had participated in the crucifixion. There he barely states the fact; there he characterizes and condemns the guilt of the people in the crucifixion.—**Him God raised up the third day.** On the resurrection of Jesus Christ, see Vol. I., p. 330.—**Not to all the people.** In fact, no appearance of Christ after the resurrection is recorded except to his own personal friends. This was perhaps for the same reason that he would not work miracles at the demand of the Pharisees, because he would not have the faith of the people rest upon signs and wonders (Matt. 12 : 38, 39; Luke 16 : 31). —**Unto witnesses chosen before of God.** They are represented in the Gospels both as chosen by Christ (Luke 6 : 13; John 15 : 16), and chosen by God and given to Christ (John 17 : 6).—**Who did eat and drink with him after he rose from the dead.** Luke 24 : 30, 41-43; John 21 : 12, 13, are instances of such meal-taking after the resurrection; the object of which appears to have been to afford tangible evidence of its reality.

42. And he commanded us to herald unto the people. Not as Alford, the *Jewish people.* It is true that the apostles at first so limited the commission, but at the time of Christ's birth his advent was announced as glad tidings to *all the people* (Luke 2 : 10); after his resurrection, in the great commission, he directed the apostles to preach the Gospel to every creature, teaching all nations (Matt. 28 : 19; Mark 16 : 15); and just before his ascension he promised them that they should be witnesses unto the uttermost part of the earth (ch. 1 : 8). Peter is beginning to understand the full meaning of the Lord's command, and his use of the term *the people,* without adding the qualifying phrase *of Israel* (ch. 4 : 10; 13 : 17, 24), indicates the change at work, under the influence of the Spirit of God, in his mind. This change is consummated when he sees the Holy Ghost evidently bestowed upon the Gentiles.—**And to testify.** This word suggests the solemn and weighty import and the certain truth of the words of the apostles, sworn, as it were, to speak the truth, the whole truth, and nothing but the truth. Observe the double office of the minister: he is a herald to announce news, and a witness to confirm it, by his own testimony and that (see next verse) of the word of God.—**Ordained by God, Judge of the living and the dead.** Not *to be* judge. The words *to be* are added needlessly by the translators. Christ *is now* the judge; his life and character are the standard by which every man is to judge himself; he shows what is the ideal of humanity, and so, how far we have fallen from it. He is also to be the judge, by announcing the divine judgments on the sons of men at the last day. See marg. ref. The *living and*

43 To him[a] give all the prophets witness, that through his name whosoever[b] believeth in him shall receive remission of sins.
44 While Peter yet spake these words, the Holy Ghost[c] fell on all them which heard the word.
45 And they[d] of the circumcision which believed were astonished, as many as came with Peter, because that on the Gentiles also was poured out the gift of the Holy Ghost:
46 For they heard them speak[e] with tongues, and magnify God. Then answered Peter,
47 Can[f] any man forbid water, that these should not be baptized, which have received the Holy Ghost as well as we.
48 And he commanded them to be baptized in the name of the Lord. Then prayed they him to tarry certain days.

a Luke 24 : 27, 44; John 5 : 39.... b John 3 : 14-17; Rom. 10 : 11.... c ch. 4 : 31.... d verse 23.... e ch. 2 : 4.... f ch. 8 : 12.

the dead are here to be taken, primarily, literally of all men, past, present, and to come; so taken, there is no objection to add, secondarily, a spiritual meaning, and understand it to indicate both saints and sinners. Observe how both here and in ch. 17 : 31, the judicial office of Christ is brought into prominence; a phase of his character and work rarely mentioned in modern preaching. He is Judge, as well as Saviour.

43. To him give all the prophets witness. Not necessarily to be taken literally. But it certainly implies the unquestionable truth that Jesus Christ was the central theme of the body of O. T. prophecy, both spoken and symbolical. See on ch. 3 : 21, 24.—**That through his name whosoever believeth in him shall receive remission of sins.** Another of Luther's "little Gospels," for which the apostles' speeches are very noteworthy. See ch. 2 : 38, 39; 3 : 19; 4 : 12; 5 : 31. Here is embodied (1) the only means of salvation, viz., the name of Jesus, which signifies Saviour from sin (Matt. 1 : 21, note; Acts 4 : 12); (2) the universality of the offer of salvation, *Whosoever* believeth; (3) the condition of salvation, *believeth in him*—not believing any doctrine *about* him, nor merely believing *what he says*, but believing, trusting, relying *upon him*, as the one supreme object of confidence (see Matt. 18 : 6, note); (4) the nature of salvation, *the remission of sins;* not merely the forgiveness, *i. e.*, the remission of the future penalty, but the remission of the sin itself, the cleansing from all unrighteousness. See ch. 2 : 38, note, and 1 John 1 : 9. It is very true that Peter's hearers probably did not, and even Peter possibly did not, fully comprehend the full significance of the language. The case is one in which the Holy Spirit conveys more than the immediate hearers could understand, and possibly more than the speaker himself understood.

44-46. While Peter was yet speaking. He was going on to say more, when interrupted by the manifestation of the gift of the Spirit (ch. 11 : 15).—**The Holy Ghost fell on them that heard the word.** Not merely moved on their hearts and minds; this he had done before, in awakening in them a desire for a knowledge of the truth (see on ver. 20); but, manifested his presence by an external revelation of his power, here by conferring on the Gentiles the power of speaking with tongues. See ch. 8 : 16, note.—**They of the circumcision,** etc. The Jewish Christians who had come with Peter (ch. 11 : 12).—**Speak with tongues.** See ch. 2 : 4, note. The gift of the Holy Ghost was bestowed on all that *heard*, and this declaration, coupled with the baptism which followed, implies that all accepted the word.

47, 48. Can any forbid the water that these should not be baptized? Alford's deduction from the form of expression here, *the* water, that "the practice was to bring the water to the candidates, not the candidates to the water," appears to me far-fetched. It is not by such inferences that we can learn the apostolic practice as regards baptism, if indeed, which I doubt, the form and method used by them is, or is meant to be, discoverable by us. But his comment on the fact that the bestowal of the Holy Ghost preceded baptism is both true and important. "The fire of the Lord fell, approving the sacrifice of the Gentiles (see Rom. 15 : 16), conferring on them the substance before the symbol, the baptism with the Holy Ghost before the baptism with water: and teaching us that as the Holy Spirit dispensed once and for all with the necessity of circumcision in the flesh, so can he also, when it pleases him, with the necessity of water baptism; and warning the Christian church not to put baptism itself in the place which circumcision once held."

He commanded them to be baptized. "By others; he devolved the service on his attendants."—(*Hackett.*) The facts that our Lord never baptized (John 4 : 2), and the apostles apparently rarely (1 Cor. 1 : 14), is significant, indicating that they held the rite to be quite subordinate to the preaching of the word, to which they chiefly gave themselves. It is also indicated that no ministerial ordination was required to perform the rite; there is nothing to indicate that any of Peter's companions held any official position in the Christian church.—**Certain days.** There is nothing to indicate how long Peter remained.

Ch. 11 : 1-30. RESULT OF THE REVELATION TO PETER. FURTHER OPENING OF THE DOOR TO THE GENTILES. THE TEACHING OF GOD'S SPIRIT ACCEPTED BY THE CHURCH.—THE GIFT OF GOD'S GRACE IS ALWAYS A SUFFICIENT TOKEN OF GOD'S APPROBATION.—THE

CHAPTER XI.

AND the apostles and brethren that were in Judæa
heard that the Gentiles had also received the
word of God.
2 And when Peter was come up to Jerusalem, they[g]
that were of the circumcision contended with him,
3 Saying, Thou wentest in to men uncircumcised,
and didst eat with them.
4 But Peter rehearsed *the matter* from the beginning,
and expounded *it* by order unto them, saying,
5 I was in the city of[h] Joppa, praying: and in a
trance I saw a vision, A certain vessel descend, as it
had been a great sheet, let down from heaven by four
corners; and it came even to me:
6 Upon the which when I had fastened mine eyes, I
considered, and saw four-footed beasts of the earth,
and wild beasts, and creeping things, and fowls of the
air.
7 And I heard a voice saying unto me, Arise, Peter;
slay, and eat.
8 But I said, Not so, Lord: for nothing common or
unclean hath at any time entered into my mouth.
9 But the voice answered me again from heaven,
What God hath cleansed, *that* call not thou common.
10 And this was done three times: and all were
drawn up again into heaven.
11 And, behold, immediately there were three men
already come unto the house where I was, sent from
Cæsarea unto me.

g ch. 10 : 23, 28; Gal. 2 : 12. . . . h ch. 10 : 9, etc.

SYMBOL UNIMPORTANT; THE SPIRIT ESSENTIAL.—THE CONFIRMATION OF PETER'S VISION IN THE CONVERSION OF THE GENTILES.—BARNABAS ILLUSTRATES THE TEACHABLE DISPOSITION OF THE TRUE DISCIPLE.—CHRISTIAN BENEVOLENCE SHOULD BE INDIVIDUAL, UNIVERSAL, VOLUNTARY, RELATIVE TO PECUNIARY ABILITY.—BENEVOLENCE AT HOME HELPS TO PREPARE THE CHURCH AT ANTIOCH FOR FOREIGN MISSIONARY WORK.

This chapter traces still further the development in the mind of the church of the truth that the Gospel is the power of God to every one that believeth, both Jew and Gentile. Peter's course in consorting with Gentiles is criticised; he submits himself to the investigation of the brethren at Jerusalem; on his account of the facts, they accept, with him, the manifest will of God; that will is further manifested by the influence of the Spirit of God, accompanying the preaching of the Gospel to the Greeks, especially in Antioch. This narrative leads to an account of the establishment of the Christian church there, the origin of the name Christian, the preparation for the subsequent missionary work of Paul and Barnabas, and in this connection Paul's second visit to the apostles at Jerusalem. The account is not chronological; at ver. 19 it goes back and recounts the effects of the persecution which Saul had instigated (ch. 8 : 2-4), and which, continuing after his conversion, paved the way for his subsequent Christian missionary work. Thus Luke brings together in this chapter the separate threads of his narrative, the whole of which is devoted to an account of the extension of the Gospel beyond the borders of Judaism, but by three concurrent instrumentalities: (1) by the dispersion of the Jewish Christians through the persecution inaugurated by Saul, narrated in ch. 8 : 2-4, and here in verses 19-21; (2) by the missionary labors of Philip (ch. 8 : 5-40), and Peter (9 : 32 to ch. 10 : 48), the preaching to and baptism of the Gentiles by the latter being confirmed by the church at Jerusalem (ver. 18); (3) by the labors of Saul, whose biography, broken off at ch. 9 : 30, is resumed here at ver. 25, to be broken off again, and again resumed in ch. 12 : 25, and made thereafter the centre of the history, as he was the great apostle to the Gentiles, and therefore the great instrument in spreading the Gospel among the heathen. The dates covered by the events in this chapter extend from A. D. 36 to A. D. 44 or 45. See chronological table in Introduction.

1-3. And the brethren that were throughout Judea. That is, belonging to the different churches in the province of Judea. With the exception of sojourners in Jerusalem, these would nearly all be Hebrews by birth and education.—**Had also accepted the word of God.** Not merely received the word, but acknowledged its truth and professed allegiance to it; their reception into the church is implied. *The word of God* is equivalent to the Gospel. Comp. ch. 4 : 31; 6 : 2; 8 : 14.—**They that were of the circumcision.** That is, the Hebrew Christians; probably such proselytes as were in Judea were not prominent in this complaint. Later, there grew up in the Christian church a considerable party who maintained that circumcision was a prerequisite to Christian discipleship; in other words, that the Gospel was offered only to those who were by birth, or by their own choice, Jews. Ch. 15 : 1; Gal. 5 : 1-6, 12; 6 : 12.—**And didst eat with them.** This social fellowship with the Gentiles was the gravamen of the charge against Peter. See ch. 10 : 28, note.

4. But Peter beginning set before them in order, saying. That is, he began at the beginning, and gave a consecutive narrative of his experience: his vision at Joppa, the message to him from Cornelius, the report by Cornelius of his own vision, the consequent preaching of the Gospel to him and his friends, and the result. Observe that Peter is called to an account not only by the apostles, but also by the laity (the brethren), that he recognizes their right, and answers their inquiries. He claims no apostolic—certainly no papal—authority.

5-10. See ch. 10 : 9-16, notes. One or two points in the narrative here are noticeable. *It came even to me*, indicates that the vision was not dim, distant, nor indistinct; *upon the which when I had fastened mine eyes I considered*, literally, *upon*

12 And the Spirit[i] bade me go with them, nothing
doubting. Moreover, these six brethren accompanied
me; and we entered into the man's house:
13 And he shewed us how he had seen an angel in
his house, which stood and said unto him, Send men
to Joppa, and call for Simon, whose surname is
Peter;
14 Who shall tell thee words,[j] whereby thou and all
thy house shall be saved.
15 And as I began to speak, the Holy Ghost fell on
them, as[k] on us at the beginning.
16 Then remembered I the word of the Lord, how
that he said, John[l] indeed baptized with water; but[m]
ye shall be baptized with the Holy Ghost.
17 Forasmuch then as God gave[n] them the like gift
as *he did* unto us, who believed on the Lord Jesus
Christ, what[o] was I, that I could withstand God?
18 When they heard these things, they held their
peace, and glorified God, saying, Then hath God also
to the Gentiles[p] granted repentance unto life.
19 Now they[q] which were scattered abroad upon the
persecution that arose about Stephen, travelled as far
as Phenice, and Cyprus, and Antioch, preaching the
word to none but[r] unto the Jews only.

i John 16 : 13....j Ps. 19 : 7-11; John 6 : 63, 68....k ch. 2 : 4....l ch. 1 : 5; Matt. 3 : 11; John 1 : 26, 33....m Isa. 44 : 3; Joel 2 : 28.... n ch. 15 : 8, 9....o Rom. 9 : 21-26....p Rom. 10 : 12, 13; 15 : 9, 16... q ch. 8 : 1....r Matt. 10 : 6.

which, intent, I considered, indicates that the voice did not speak to him until he not only observed but pondered the meaning; *I heard a voice*, indicates an audible voice.

11-14. See ch. 10 : 17-33, notes. Only from Peter's account here do we learn the number who accompanied him, *six brethren.* The language implies that they were present with him at this investigation to verify his account. *An angel*, should be rendered *the angel.* The use of the definite article implies that Peter's auditors had previously heard of the angelic appearance to Cornelius. *In his house* is inserted, it appears to me, not, as Alexander, to indicate that Cornelius was not liable to be deceived, since it appeared to him in his own house, but as an authority for Peter's course; if an angel of God could enter the house of a Gentile to bring a message of grace, surely Peter need not hesitate to do so.—**Who shall tell thee words whereby thou and all thy house shall be saved.** Comp. ch. 10 : 6, 33. The language here specifies more accurately than there the nature of the information which Cornelius was expecting. It does not, however, necessarily imply that he and his house were not already in the way of salvation, and ch. 10 : 2, 4, 31, 35 clearly indicates that before Peter came to him he was accepted by God. The language here, however, justifies the conclusion that he had no assurance of salvation, and that in his case it was the mission of the Gospel to bring peace by Jesus Christ (ch. 10 : 36) to a heart already saved by divine grace, but lacking that restful assurance of salvation which only the Gospel can impart. The promise to his house does not necessarily imply the salvation of the children on the faith of the father, for, in ch. 10 : 2, it is said that all his house feared God.

15-18. As I began to speak. Evidently the sermon (ch. 10 : 34-43) was broken off by the manifest descent of the Holy Ghost.—**As also upon us in the beginning.** That is, in the same manner as upon us, and so with evident manifestation of power (ch. 10 : 46).—**The word of the Lord.** See ch. 1 : 5. This outpouring of the Spirit recalled and gave new significance to Christ's promise.—**What was I, that I could restrain God?** The argument in the apostle's mind was this: Christ had promised the outpouring of his Spirit, that baptism of the Holy Ghost which John the Baptist had foretold (Matt. 3 : 11); of this, water-baptism was only the symbol; since this baptism of the Holy Ghost had been conferred by God upon the Gentiles, how could Peter refuse to confer the symbol? The argument is one of various application. Whenever we refuse to accept the work of God manifested in the hearts and lives of men, because it is not wrought according to our chosen ecclesiastical methods, or with the instruments which we have been accustomed to approve, we endeavor to restrain or limit God.—**They held their peace and glorified God.** Their objections were silenced; but praise was inspired. —**Surely then to the Gentiles also God has given repentance unto life.** Not *an opportunity to repent.* The Jews never doubted that the Gentiles might repent, be circumcised, and by thus becoming Jews become also heirs of eternal life. The language is to be taken literally; to the Gentiles, while still Gentiles, God had granted repentance, a change of heart and life. The church accepts Peter's argument and his conclusion; the divine result in gracious fruit is the conclusive demonstration of divine approval, however strange the method by which it is reached. Observe that repentance elsewhere commanded (Matt. 4 : 17; Acts 2 : 38) is here, as in ch. 5 : 31, treated as a divine gift, the disposition to repent being itself awakened by the Spirit of God. It makes no real difference in the spiritual meaning of the passage whether we connect *unto life*, as does Dr. Hackett, with repentance, understanding the meaning to be, *Repentance unto life* (2 Cor. 7 : 10), or, as Alford, with the verb *granted*, understanding the meaning to be, he has bestowed this gift of repentance that they may attain unto life. From this hour dates the division in the Christian church; one party, the Judaizing faction, putting the rite of circumcision above the spiritual significance of the rite, the other accepting the teaching of God's Spirit, and conferring baptism upon and extending Christian fellowship to the uncircumcised. In different forms the contest has reappeared in the Christian church whenever the external forms have been put above the inward spirit of religion. It is a noteworthy fact that, notwithstanding Peter was the first to extend Christian fellowship to the Gentiles, he subsequently drew back (Gal. 2 : 11-14).

19. Now they which were scattered abroad upon the persecution which arose about Stephen. As described in ch. 8 : 2-4. The historian goes back to the dispersion, there narrated, of the Jewish Christians, produced by the persecutions instigated by Saul, and traces its results down to the time subsequent to Saul's conversion and first visit to Jerusalem, and subsequent to the revelation to Peter, and his visit to Cornelius.—**Traveled as far as Phenice.** A small but important commercial country, from one to twenty miles wide, and from 150 to 180 miles long, lying between the crest of Lebanon and the sea. Itself a fruitful country, its fleets carried not only its own products, but those of Assyria, Babylon, and Egypt, to the Greeks and other inhabitants of Europe and of Northern and Western Africa. It was peopled by the descendants of Ham, and its principal cities, which were ordinarily independent, uniting only under the most powerful in time of danger, were Sidon, Tyre, Berytus, Byblus, Tripolis, and Aradus. Greece claims to have borrowed letters from the Phenicians, and their characters are unquestionably older than the Hebrew, of which they were perhaps the origin. They worshipped, in cruel rites, the sun, moon, and planets by the appellations of Baal and Ashtoreth, and had a most pernicious effect upon the Israelites. The land is frequently referred to in the O. T. by the title of its chief cities, Tyre and Sidon. Recent explorations bring to light much interesting proof of the proficiency of the Phenicians in many of the arts.

And Cyprus. A large island in the Mediterranean, about 60 miles from the coast of Palestine. It is fertile, though not extensively cultivated, and produces cotton, wine, and fruits. It has also some mineral products. After belonging to Egypt, Persia, and Greece, it became a Roman possession A. D. 58, and was added to Cilicia. It is frequently mentioned in Scripture, and is especially notable as being the birthplace of Barnabas, as early sending out Christian preachers, and as being the first point reached by Paul and Barnabas in their first missionary journey. Salamis, at one end of the island, and Paphos, at the other, were the principal cities. This island is now an object of great interest, since, in the recent explorations of Di Cesnola, a vast amount of treasure has been added to the antiquities which reveal so much respecting the ancients; while to the devout student of the Bible they are especially valuable, because in so many points they testify to its truth.

And Antioch. That is, Antioch in Syria. See map. This city, the capital of the Greco-Syrian

ANTIOCH IN SYRIA.

kings, was situated nearly in the angle formed by the coasts of Syria and Asia Minor, and in the valley where the river Orontes passes between the ranges of Lebanon and Tau. Its situation and circumstances were such as to make it a place of concourse for all classes and kinds of people. It possessed peculiar inland and maritime privileges. The trade of the Mediterranean and that of the caravans from Mesopotamia and Arabia met here. For the first two centuries of the Christian era it was the "Gate of the East," and only gradually did Constantinople win from it this honor. It was, in the time of Augustus, a tetrapolis, a union of four cities built by the first and second Seleucus and the third and fourth Antiochus. Prosperous as it was under the Greek kings of Syria, it became still more so under the Roman rule, when it was declared a

20 And some of them were men of Cyprus and Cyrene, which, when they were come to Antioch, spake
unto the Grecians,[s] preaching the Lord Jesus.

21 And the[t] hand of the Lord was with them: and
a great number believed, and turned[u] unto the Lord.
22 Then tidings of these things came unto the ears

s ch. 6 : 1; 9 : 29....t Luke 1 : 66....u ch. 15 : 19; 1 Thess. 1 : 9.

free city. Antioch was one to two miles wide, and between four and five miles long, from east to west. It was encompassed by walls 50 feet high and 15 feet thick, which were carried at a prodigious expense over ravines and the ridge of the mountain on the south, and whose remains even now, after all the ravages of time and the havoc of war, astonish the traveler. Within these walls the city was divided into four wards, each surrounded with its own wall. The streets, symmetrical and regular, were flanked by colonnades and decorated with statuary; and the main street, or *Corso*, built by Herod the Great, more than a league in length, and ornamented with four ranges of columns, formed two covered galleries, with a wide avenue in the midst. There were immense public buildings and wonderfully beautiful statues—the noblest specimens of Grecian art. Having, too, a most delightful climate, it is not strange that it gathered from every quarter a population reckoned at over 500,000, among whom the languages spoken and the costumes worn were singularly diverse. Foremost in refinement and culture, false though they were, Antioch was also foremost in luxury and vice. It is probable that no populations were ever more abandoned than those of oriental Grecian cities under the Roman empire, and of these cities Antioch was one of the greatest and worst. Frivolous amusements were daily occupations, and vice the business of life. Though the terrible degradation did not sink into mere ugly vulgarity, it was none the less terrible because surrounded by beauty of art and the infinite charm of nature. It was a city of races, games, dances, processions, fêtes, debaucheries, the fanaticism of the orgy, the most unhealthy superstitions, and the most unbridled luxury. Its famous suburb was an epitome of the city—the lovely Daphne, where the heathen gods Diana and Apollo were enshrined in a temple, embosomed in groves of cypresses and myrtles ten miles in circumference—with fountains and buildings, crowds of licentious votaries, and processions of pleasure-seekers intoxicated with sensuality—where "all that was beautiful in nature and in art had created a sanctuary for a perpetual festival of vice." To this city, with its outreaching radii, Divine wisdom directed the missionary disciples; upon this "heathen queen" they made their earliest attack, and their victory in the power of the Lord was here made memorable, though unwittingly, by those proud scorners who gave us the name of "Christians." Nothing but ruins remains of this one of the great cities of the world, and the changing of the river's course and the earthquake have almost obliterated these.

But unto the Jews only. This phrase shows that it is the ministry of the dispersed Jewish Christians immediately after Stephen's death that is here referred to, three years previous to Paul's visit to Jerusalem and conference with Peter (ch. 9 : 27, 28; Gal. 1 : 18), and probably some time previous to Peter's visit to Cornelius. Their preaching to the Jews only, accorded with Christ's commission to the twelve while he was still living (Matt. 10 : 5), and with their practice for the first few years after his resurrection and ascension. The first preaching, except to the Jews, was that of Philip in Samaria (ch. 8 : 5); the first public preaching to heathen, that mentioned in the next verse.

20, 21. Men of Cyprus and Cyrene. That is, natives; but probably Jewish proselytes who had become Christians. Less blinded by Jewish prejudice, these proselytes were more ready than the Jewish Christians to accept the doctrine that the Gospel was for Gentile as well as Jew. *Cyrene* was a city of Libya, on the north coast of Africa. For description, see Matt. 27 : 32, note. These exiles and missionaries traveled both north to Phenice and south and west to Africa. See map.—**Spake also unto the Grecians.** Rather the Greeks (ἕλληνας, not ἑλληνιστάς, is the best reading; see Hackett and Alford). Grecian Jews cannot be meant, for the Gospel had been already preached to them, and they were a recognized and even important part of the Christian church at Jerusalem (ch. 6 : 1); but the uncircumcised Greeks, the Gentiles, in opposition to the "*Jews only*" of the preceding verse, which would include proselytes as well as Jews by birth. Whether this preaching to the Gentiles took place prior or subsequent to Peter's visit to Cornelius we have no means of determining. Apparently the two events, the outpouring of the Holy Spirit there, and the conversion of the Gentiles here, with the report of Barnabas respecting it, were concurrent and nearly contemporaneous events, by which God's providence taught the church the full meaning of Christ's commission in Matt. 28 : 19 and Acts 1 : 8.—**Preaching the Lord Jesus.** That is, proclaiming him as both Lord of all, as in ch. 10 : 36, and Jesus, *i. e.*, Saviour (Matt. 1 : 21) for all; else there would have been no significance in the fact stated that they proclaimed him to the Greeks.—**The hand of**

of the church which was in Jerusalem: and they sent
forth Barnabas,[v] that he should go as far as Antioch.
23 Who, when he came, and had seen the grace of
God, was glad,[w] and exhorted[x] them all, that with
purpose[y] of[z] heart they would cleave unto the Lord.
24 For he was a good man, and full[a] of the Holy
Ghost and of faith: and[b] much people was added unto
the Lord.
25 Then[c] departed Barnabas to Tarsus, for to seek
Saul:

v ch. 9 : 27....w 3 John 4....x ch. 13 : 43; 14 : 22....y Ps. 17 : 3; 2 Cor. 1 : 17....z Prov. 23 : 26....a ch. 6 : 5....b verse 21....c ch. 9 : 27, 30.

the Lord. Comp. Luke 1 : 66. The hand is a symbol of power; here probably, as in ch. 4 : 30, it was stretched forth to heal, thus affording a manifest sign of Divine approval on this extension of the evangelistic work to the Gentiles.—**Turned to the Lord.** That is, turned from their heathen faith and practices, and accepted the new faith, and Christ as their Lord. This, no less than the miracles, afforded a sign of Divine approval; for though success is not always a proof of God's approbation, spiritual success in spiritual work always is.

22. They sent forth Barnabas. It is hardly doubtful what the object of this commission was. The Christians at Jerusalem criticised Peter for eating with uncircumcised heathen (ver. 3); and subsequently Christians from Jerusalem insisted on circumcision as a condition of admission to the church (ch. 15 : 1); we may assume, therefore, that these Jewish Christians would think the reception of Gentiles as Christian converts an offence. The object of this mission, then, was probably to inquire into the supposed irregularity, and to correct it. Yet it is a noticeable fact that they sent for this purpose not a Judean, but a native of Cyprus, and one therefore who would be in sympathy with those whose errors they thought required correction. This view of the mission of Barnabas is confirmed by the verses which follow. It is observable that not an apostle, but an unofficial member of the church, was sent on this mission, being selected from *personal*, not *official*, considerations. On the life and character of Barnabas, see ch. 4 : 36, note.—**To go through** (the churches) **even to Antioch.** He was to make a pastoral visitation of the churches between Jerusalem and Antioch, inquiring into their condition, and probably reporting results to the church at Jerusalem.

23, 24. Who when he came and had seen the grace of God. In the conversion of the Gentiles.—**Was glad.** An intimation that he had doubted whether he should find their conversion genuine.—**And exhorted them all.** Gentiles as well as Jews.—**That with purpose of heart.** Rather consecration of heart. The Greek word rendered *purpose* (πρόθεσις) means literally *setting forth*, and is used to designate the shew-bread (Matt. 12 : 4; Mark 2 : 26; Luke 6 : 4) which was set before and consecrated to the Lord. Here the "*purpose of heart*" is a heart similarly set before God by being wholly consecrated to his service.—**They would cleave unto the Lord.** Continue with him; abide in him (John 15 : 4). For meaning of the Greek word (προσμένω) rendered *cleave*, see Matt. 15 : 32; 1 Tim. 1 : 3; 5 : 5.—**For he was a good man,** etc. This explains the reason, not why he was sent on this mission, but why, in its execution, he recognized the work of God in calling and converting the uncircumcised. He was kind in disposition; the inspiration of his service was not ecclesiastical pride or ambition, but love and good-will (for this use of ἀγαθός, see Rom. 5 : 7; Titus 2 : 5); full of and ready to be guided by the Spirit of God; and of faith or spiritual insight, the power which sees the things that are unseen (Heb. 11 : 1), and hence was able to appreciate the spiritual. For these reasons he accepted the grace of God, literally *the grace which was of God* (*Alford*), manifested by the spiritual changes wrought in the character of the uncircumcised Greeks, as an evidence of the Divine approval which far outweighed his preconceived opinions as to the ecclesiastical regularity of the proceedings. The lesson for us is that spiritual results are always to be accepted with thanksgiving, whatever the seeming ecclesiastical irregularity of the method, and that they will be thus accepted by those whose religion is one characteristically of faith in God and good-will toward man.

25, 26. To Tarsus for to seek Saul. Convinced by what he had witnessed that the door was opened by the providence and Spirit of God to *preach the Gospel to the Gentiles*, and recalling Saul's commission to *preach it to the Gentiles* (ch. 9 : 15; 22 : 21), Barnabas, who had brought Saul to the apostles after his conversion (ch. 9 : 27), and perhaps had known him before, goes now to bring him to Antioch, to carry on the work assigned him by God. The date is uncertain; it was of course some time subsequent to Saul's departure from Jerusalem to Tarsus (ch. 9 : 30), and therefore more than three years subsequent to his conversion (Gal. 1 : 18). Meanwhile he had perhaps been preaching in Cilicia (Gal. 1 21), perhaps living in retirement, and devoting his time to the study of the Word. It would appear from ch. 22 : 19, as well as from his course immediately after his conversion (ch. 9 : 20, 29), that he at first desired to carry on a mission among his own people, the Jews; that his natural sympathies

26 And when he had found him, he brought him unto Antioch. And it came to pass, that a whole year they assembled themselves with the church, and taught[d] much people. And the disciples were called Christians first in Antioch.

27 And in these days came[e] prophets from Jerusalem unto Antioch.

28 And there stood up one of them, named Agabus,[f] and signified by the Spirit that there should be great dearth throughout all the world: which came to pass in the days of Claudius Cæsar.

d Matt. 28 : 19.... e ch. 2 : 17; 13 : 1; Ephes. 4 : 11.... f ch. 21 : 10.

were always strong is clear from Phil. 3 : 5 and Rom. 9 : 1-5; 10 : 1, and that he entered on his mission to the Gentiles only when the word and providence of God excluded him from Israel and opened the door to the Gentile. On Tarsus, see ch. 9 : 30, note.—**The disciples were called Christians first in Antioch.** The word *Christian* occurs in the N. T. only three times; here; in Agrippa's sarcastic response to Paul, "Almost thou persuadest me to be a Christian" (ch. 26 : 28); and in 1 Pet. 4 : 16, "If any man suffer as a Christian." The use of the term in the two latter passages, and the fact that it is never used by the disciples in speaking of themselves, indicates that it was first employed as a term of opprobium. It could not have been given by the Jews, for the term Christian (anointed one) was one of honor among the Jews, by whom the disciples were known as the "sect of the Nazarenes" (ch. 24 : 5; comp. Matt. 2 : 23); and Julian the Apostate later forbade their use of the name Christian, and decreed that they should be called Galileans. The inhabitants of Antioch are said to have been notorious for employing names of derision; and the probability is that this name was invented by the heathen of that city, in derision of the central doctrine of the new sect, the redemption offered through Christ Jesus, but was accepted and made an honored name by the disciples. So the words Methodist and Puritan were both originated as terms of derision, but became terms of honor. Throughout the N. T. Christians are called "believers," "the faithful," "saints," "brethren," or "disciples."

27. In those days. Comparing vers. 26 and 30, it was evidently during the year which Saul spent at Antioch that the prophecy of Agabus was uttered.—**Came prophets from Jerusalem.** The prophet was not necessarily a foreteller. The Hebrew word is derived from a root signifying to boil or bubble over, and simply conveys the idea of the bursting forth, as of a fountain, of truth with which God has inspired the soul. The early English kept tolerably near this original idea. Thus Jeremy Taylor, in the reign of Elizabeth, wrote a treatise on the *Liberty of Prophesying, i. e.*, of preaching. In the classics the Greek word (προφήτης) is used to describe those who interpreted the unintelligible oracles, and, metaphorically, the poets as interpreters of the gods or muses. In both the O. T. and the N. T. the prominent idea in prophecy and prophesying is not prediction, but inspiration; not telling before what is to happen, but delivering messages of warning, instruction, comfort, helpfulness, such as are commissioned by or given under the inspiration of the divine Spirit. This characteristic of prophecy appears very clearly from the titles given to the prophets in the Scriptures. He is called "the interpreter," "the messenger of Jehovah," "the man of Spirit," "the man of God;" and it is declared that the "Spirit of Jehovah" enters into him, or "clothes him," or, as here, that he speaks "by the Spirit" (Judges 2 : 1; 6 : 34, margin; 1 Sam. 2 : 27; 9 : 6; 1 Kings 12 : 22; 13 : 1, 2; 1 Chron. 12 : 18; 2 Chron. 24 : 20; Ezek. 2 : 2; Hos. 9 : 7; Hag. 1 : 13; Mal. 1 : 1). In the N. T. Paul gives some detailed description of prophesying, which is distinguished from what we should call preaching, only in that the presence and power of God is perhaps more prominent (see references below). Barnabas, literally Son of prophecy, is rendered rightly "Son of consolation" (Acts 4 : 36). The prophet might be of either sex (2 Kings 22 : 14; Acts 21 : 9). The other principal references in the N. T. to prophets and prophesying are the following: ch. 13 : 1; 15 : 32; 19 : 6; 21 : 9, 10; Rom. 12 : 6; 1 Cor. 12 : 10, 28, 29; 13 : 2, 8; 14 : 6, 29-37; Ephes. 2 : 20; 3 : 5; 4 : 11; 1 Thess. 5 : 20. The coming of prophets, *i. e.*, recognized inspired teachers from Jerusalem, is an indication that the church there was satisfied with and approved the ministry of Barnabas and Saul to the uncircumcised.

28, 29. Named Agabus. He is mentioned only here and in Acts 21 : 10. Nothing more is known of him.—**That there should be great dearth throughout the world.** Not throughout Palestine merely, but throughout the then known world (οἰκουμένη), including certainly the Greek and Roman, as well as the Jewish territory. See Matt. 24 : 14, note. Josephus, Dio Cassius, and Tacitus, all testify to the fulfillment of this prophecy, in several famines during the reign of Claudius Cæsar, extending not only throughout Judea, but also throughout Greece and Rome. Queen Helena of Actiabene, a Jewish proselyte, sent subsidies to the Jews, on the occasion of one of these, which Josephus designates as "the great famine." Many of the inhabitants were swept away by it. These famines were not contemporaneous, nor does this prophecy necessarily imply that they would be so. One affected chiefly Judea; another, Greece; two others,

29 Then the disciples, every man according to his ability, determined to send[g] relief unto the brethren which dwelt in Judæa:
30 Which also they did, and[h] sent it to the elders by the hands of Barnabas and Saul.

CHAPTER XII.

NOW about that time, Herod the king stretched forth *his* hands, to vex certain of the church.
2 And he killed James[i] the brother of John with the sword.

g Rom. 15 : 26; 1 Cor. 16 : 1; 2 Cor. 9 : 1, 2.... h ch. 12 : 25.... i Matt. 4 : 21; 20 : 23.

Rome.—**In the days of Claudius Cæsar.** See chronological table in Introduction. Claudius was emperor at the time of this prophecy, and the famines probably succeeded it very closely. This is indeed implied by the fact that provisions were, apparently immediately, sent to the brethren at Jerusalem. The date appears to have been about A. D. 45.—**Every one according to his ability.** Not every *man.* Observe the two elements which enter into Christian charity: every one shares; but each one grades his contribution according to his own pecuniary ability. Comp. 1 Cor. 16 : 2. It is indicated also that it was a purely voluntary contribution; each contributor determining for himself his own share; there was no ecclesiastical or priestly assessment.—**Unto the brethren which dwell in Judea.** This may imply that the famine for which they were providing was that which especially affected Judea. Antioch was, however, a wealthy commercial city; in Jerusalem the wealth was probably confined to the Pharisaic and *priestly party*, from which few or no converts had come into the Christian church.

30. To the elders. The affairs of each Jewish synagogue were managed by a college of elders (Matt. 4 : 23, note) resembling the modern session or classis; and the language here implies that the Christian church at Jerusalem was organized in a similar manner. The same form of organization appears to have been adopted elsewhere (ch. 20 : 17; Titus 1 : 5; 1 Peter 5 : 1, 2); but whether there was any distinction between governing and preaching elders, such as is now maintained in the Presbyterian church, is a disputed point. It is evident from a comparison of ch. 6 : 5 with ch. 6 : 10, and 8 : 5, that if this distinction was recognized, it was not rigorously maintained, and that officers in the church, appointed especially for the administration of its charities, assumed without hesitation and without rebuke the office of preachers and teachers.—**By the hands of Barnabas and Saul.** The Christian church at Antioch, the regularity of whose organization and procedure had been questioned, took the best way to approve to the church at Jerusalem the genuineness of their Christian character, viz., a practical manifestation of their Christian sympathy and love.

Ch. 12 : 1-25. PERSECUTION BY AND DEATH OF HEROD AGRIPPA. THE TWOFOLD OFFICE AND WORK OF ANGELS ILLUSTRATED: "THE ANGEL OF THE LORD ENCAMPETH ROUND ABOUT THEM THAT FEAR HIM" (Ps. 34 : 7). "LET THE ANGEL OF THE LORD PERSECUTE THEM" (Ps. 35 : 6).—THE POWER OF PRAYER AND THE WEAKNESS OF FAITH ILLUSTRATED.—THE DIVINE CONDEMNATION OF VANITY AND SELF-CONCEIT.—THE FOLLY OF FIGHTING AGAINST GOD ILLUSTRATED IN THE DELIVERANCE OF PETER AND THE DEATH OF HEROD.

From a description of the growth of the church, Luke turns aside to indicate the resistance which it encountered, exemplified in the death of James and the imprisonment and threatened death of Peter. This was, as is indicated by ver. 1, contemporaneous with the events recorded in the preceding chapter, or nearly so; the time of the year is definitely fixed by the language of vers. 3 and 4 as the spring; Josephus fixes the date of Herod's death as A. D. 44 (see *Conybeare and Howson*, Vol. II, p. 544, note A); the date of the events recorded in this chapter is therefore March or April A. D. 44. The indications are that the imprisonment of Peter and the subsequent death of Herod Agrippa occurred during the visit of Paul and Barnabas to Jerusalem (ch. 11 : 30) and prior to their return to Antioch (ch. 12 : 25). The minute details in the narrative,—the number and arrangement of the watch (ver. 4), Peter's adjustment of his dress (ver. 8), his exit and his own personal feeling (verses 9, 11), and the name of the damsel that came to the door (verses 12, 13), indicate that Luke derived his information from Peter himself. On the twofold office of angels, as indicated in this account, the reader will do well to examine the following passages. On angels as messengers to and guardians of God's people, Gen. 19 : 1, etc.; 1 Kings 19 : 5, 7; 2 Kings 6 : 17; Ps. 91 : 11, 12; Dan. 3 : 25, 28; 6 : 22; Matt. 18 : 10, note; Acts 5 : 19, 20; 10 : 3; 27 : 23. On angels as ministers of God's judgments, Gen. 3 : 24; 2 Sam. 24 : 16; 2 Kings 19 : 35; Ps. 78 : 49; Rev., chaps. 7, 8, 9, 15.

1, 2. About that time. That is, about the same time as the visit of Paul and Barnabas referred to in the closing verses of the preceding chapter.—**Herod the king.** Herod Agrippa. He was a grandson of Herod the Great, and father of the Agrippa mentioned in chaps. 25 and 26; was brought up at the court of the Emperor Tiberius; received from the Emperor Caligula the tetrarchies of Philip and Lysanias; won the title of king; subsequently the tetrarchy of Antipas was added to his dominions; and finally by Claudius

3 And because he saw it pleased[j] the Jews, he proceeded further to take Peter[k] also. (Then were the days[l] of unleavened bread.)
4 And when he had apprehended him, he put *him* in prison, and delivered *him* to four quaternions of soldiers, to keep him; intending after Easter to bring him forth to the people.
5 Peter therefore was kept in prison: but prayer

j ch. 24 : 27.... k John 21 : 18.... l Exod. 12 : 14, 15.

he was set over the whole territory that had formerly been subject to the rule of Herod the Great. He assiduously cultivated the good-will of the Jews. He was an Idumean by birth, and a Roman by education, and excessively luxurious in his personal tastes, so that he introduced into Jerusalem theatres, and amphitheatres, and games, and gladiatorial spectacles; but he was also, both from policy and from a certain sentiment of superstitious reverence, ardently attached to the Jewish ceremonial, and regular in his offering of sacrifices in the Temple. Thus his twofold character accords with his course here; he would be naturally hostile to a faith which was subversive of Judaism, ready to conciliate Jewish favor by persecuting its adherents, and quick to accept the deification proffered him by the multitude. For some account of the Herodian family, see Vol. I, pp. 58, 59; for a condensed life of Herod Agrippa, see Lewin's *St. Paul*, ch. 7.—**To maltreat.** *Vex*, in its ordinary signification, is not adequate as a translation of the original Greek, which is interpreted by the account which follows, of his slaying of James and imprisonment of Peter.—**James the brother of John.** He was probably own cousin to our Lord; is not to be confounded with James the Lord's brother, the probable author of the Epistle of James. On the life and character of this apostle, of whom very little is known, see Vol. I, p. 148.—**With the sword.** That is, by beheading. This was accounted a specially disgraceful mode of punishment among the Jews. It is a noticeable fact that this James asked for a first place in Christ's kingdom, and declared in response to Christ's questioning, that he was able to drink of Christ's cup and be baptized with Christ's baptism (Mark 10 : 35-39); and that he was the first apostle to suffer a martyr's death, and the only apostle of whose death the N. T. gives us any account. It is also noteworthy that Luke, who gives a full account of the circumstances of Stephen's death, sums up that of James, the apostle, in a single sentence. We may safely assume that if his death had been

ORIENTAL PRISON.

accompanied by any such ministry of the word, or any such gracious revelation of the Master in heaven waiting to receive his apostle, it would have been recorded, and, with Baumgarten, that "James, the very reverse of Stephen, met his bloody end quite like an ordinary being, without any special or singular signs accompanying it." It is not the manner of our death, but the spirit of our life which affords the true test of our discipleship.

3, 4. And seeing that it pleased the Jews. The implication is that the slaying of James was instigated rather by state policy than by any personal religious participation in their zeal against the new faith.—**Then were the days of unleavened bread.** The passover. It was not lawful, under Jewish rules, to put to death during this feast. Peter, therefore, was kept in custody until the festival should have passed, when he was to be brought forth for public execution.—**In prison.** The accompanying illustration gives the reader a good idea of the modern Oriental prison, which, probably, in its general character, resembles that of ancient times. It is usually connected with the governor's house; the prisoners are allowed the freedom of the yard by day; the guards *sit* about armed, and often conversing with their prison-

was made without ceasing of the church unto God for
him.
6 And when Herod would have brought him forth,
the same night Peter was sleeping between two soldiers, bound with two chains; and the keepers before
the door kept the prison.
7 And, behold, the angel[m] of the Lord came upon
him, and a light shined in the prison; and he smote
Peter on the side, and raised him up, saying, Arise up
quickly. And[n] his chains fell off from *his* hands.
8 And the angel said unto him, Gird thyself, and
bind on thy sandals: and so he did. And he saith unto
him, Cast thy garment about thee, and follow me.
9 And he went out, and followed him; and wist not[o]
that it was true which was done by the angel; but
thought he saw a vision.[p]

m ch. 5:19; Ps. 37:32, 33....n ch. 16:26....o Ps. 126:1....p ch. 10:3, 17.

ers. People come and go, bringing provisions. Prisoners of state are sometimes chained to their guards.—**Four quaternions of soldiers.** A quaternion is a guard of four soldiers; two kept watch within the prison-yard, two before the gate leading out into the street. These are the first and second ward referred to in ver. 10. The night was divided into four watches (Mark 13:35) and each quaternion took one watch.—**After Easter.** After the Passover, *i. e.*, the last day of the Passover. Easter celebrates the resurrection of our Lord, which took place during the Passover week, which lasted from 14th to 21st Nisan; the phrase has been improperly used here by our translators, in order to designate to the English reader the real time of the occurrence. The word so rendered is everywhere else in the N. T. translated Passover.

5. But earnest prayer was made. Not *without ceasing*, a meaning which the Greek will not bear. For significance, see Luke 22:44, where the original is the same. The object of their prayer is generally assumed to have been the deliverance of Peter; the Lord had before delivered him out of prison (ch. 5:18-20), and this fact may well have awakened the hopes of the disciples. But as help delayed to come, hope grew less; that they did not really expect his deliverance is evident from their surprise at his appearance (ver. 15). Probably anticipating the death of Peter to follow that of James, their prayer was that he might be rescued if it was the Lord's will, otherwise that he might be strengthened to suffer and die for him. Remembering how before he had denied his Lord, the disciples may well have been intense in their prayer for divine grace to sustain him now. The trial of his faith in this imprisonment and waiting was especially severe to a man of Peter's impetuous disposition, who could *dare* much, but by nature *endure* but little.

6. And when Herod was about to bring him forth, that same night. That is, the night before he was expecting to bring him forth for execution.—**Peter was sleeping.** An indication, when coupled with his subsequent history, of his trust in God, and of his steadfast purpose. If he had been divided in mind between the purpose of fidelity and the desire of personal safety, he would not have slept. Comp. Psalm 127:2: "He giveth his beloved sleep;" and, in illustration of this promise, Psalms 3:5; 4:8. Comp., too, the experience of Paul and Silas in prison at Philippi (ch. 16:25).—**Bound with two chains.** Probably to the two soldiers. It was the custom to chain the prisoner to his guard (see ch. 28:16, 20; Josephus' Ant. 18:6-8); the chains resembled our own except in the handcuff. The accompanying illustration represents some links of an ancient chain, now preserved as a sacred relic in the church of *S. Pietro in Vinculis* (St. Peter

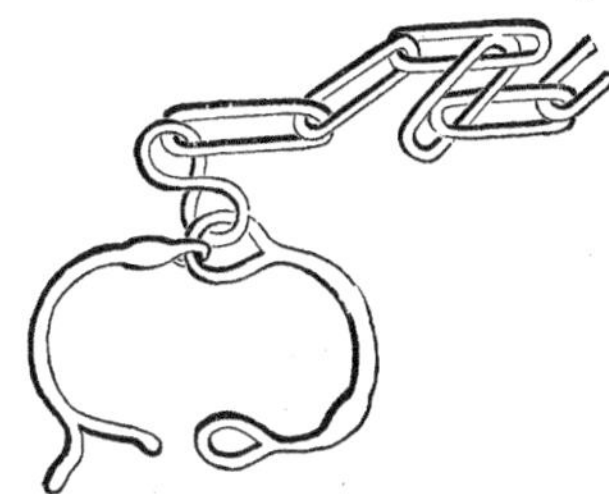

LINKS OF AN ANCIENT CHAIN.

in chains) at Rome; it is said to be the identical one with which Peter was chained in Rome. It is not necessary to credit this legend in order to recognize in the chain a valuable *antique*, indicating the kind used in ancient times.—**The keepers before the door kept the prison.** The other two soldiers. The door here is probably the gate leading out into the street from the inner court-yard, around which the prison was built.

7-9. An angel of the Lord. Not *the* angel, which always designates one and the same person, viz., Jesus Christ himself, the angel of the covenant (Numb. 22:23; Judges 6:12; 1 Chron. 21:15-30). For illustration of angels as messengers of the Lord—in the O. T. sometimes messengers of wrath, but in the N. T., except in Revelation, always harbingers of mercy—see Matt. 1:20; 2:13; Luke 1:11, 26; 2:9; Acts 5:19; 10:3; 27:23.—**Stood by.** Peter did not see him coming; but, roused out of his sleep, beheld him present.—**In the prison.** Rather *in the chamber;* not throughout the whole prison, but in the room where Peter was sleeping. The word here is not the same as that rendered *prison* above.—**He smote Peter on the side.** This, and the direction to gird him-

10 When they were past the first and the second ward, they came unto the iron gate that leadeth unto the city, which opened to them of his own accord; and they went out, and passed on through one street; and forthwith the angel departed from him.
11 And when Peter was come to himself, he said, Now I know of a surety, that the Lord hath sent[q] his angel, and hath[r] delivered me out of the hand of Herod, and *from* all the expectation of the people of the Jews.
12 And when he had considered *the thing*, he came to the house of Mary the mother of John, whose surname was Mark; where many[s] were gathered together, praying.

q 2 Chron. 16:9; Ps. 34:7; Dan. 3:28; 6:22; Heb. 1:14....r Ps. 33:18, 19; 97:10; 2 Cor. 1:10; 2 Pet. 2:9....s verse 5.

self, etc., in the next verse, was to arouse Peter, to convince him that it was not a dream, and to leave in his recollection a testimony of the reality of the angelic appearance. So Christ bade the disciples *touch* him, to satisfy themselves that he was really in bodily presence with them (Luke 24:39; John 20:20, 27).—**Raised him.** Assisted him to rise, partly as a further means of arousing him and bringing him to himself.—**Gird thyself.** The girdle had been loosed for sleeping; he was now to put on the girdle as a preparation for going forth.—**And bind on thy sandals.** For illustration of sandals, see Vol. I., p. 362. The sandal, which did not cover the foot, but was simply a sole of wood or leather underneath the foot, was bound on to it by straps or thongs of leather in a manner analogous to that of a skate in modern times.—**Cast thy cloak about thee.** This cloak (ἱμάτιον) was an outer garment, a sort of shawl or blanket used as a cloak by day and a covering by night. For illustration and description, see Vol. I., p. 261. This had been Peter's covering; he was to wrap it about him as a protection in going out into the night air. These directions all indicate a certain degree of leisure, and also the completeness of his deliverance. He not only escapes himself, he leaves no article of his attire behind him.—**Thought he saw a vision.** Its reality seemed incredible; he was in a maze; it appeared as a dream, or a divine revelation of something yet to come, like that vouchsafed to him when praying on the housetop at Joppa (ch. 10:10-17). Evidently this report of his own *thoughts* must have come from himself.

10. And passing through the first guard and the second. That is, passing between the two soldiers who lay sleeping at his side, and between the other two who guarded the outer gate, but were within it. This seems to me the most natural meaning. Alford concludes that the "first guard" cannot be the one to which he was chained, because in the preceding verse it says he "went out." But it does not necessarily follow that the passing of the guard here mentioned was subsequent to that going out. This verse simply adds details descriptive of the going out.—**The iron gate that leadeth unto the city.** It is probable that the prison was within the city, and the gate here referred to was the one leading from the prison court-yard out into the street. "The gates are large, massive, and two-leaved, built of heavy timber, plated with iron. A strong iron bar, hooked at one end, hangs from a heavy ring of the same metal, made fast in a strong post, built into the wall behind each fold of the gate. When the gate is closed, the hooks are set into other iron rings, on the back of its folds, enabling the gate to resist a very heavy pressure from without. The lock is massive and of wrought iron, and the long-handled, ponderous key is carried by the keeper of the gate in his belt, or hung from a nail in his little room close by." This description of the gate of an Eastern city, from Van Lennep's *Bible Lands*, represents the probable structure of this outer prison gate.—**Opened to them of his own accord.** That is, without the action of either the angel or Peter; it was opened by an invisible power. In ch. 5:19-23, the prison doors were closed afterward and fastened securely. Whether that was the case here is uncertain.—**Through one street.** The angel still guiding him, partly, perhaps, to give him assurance and enable him to come to a full sense of the deliverance which had been wrought.—**And immediately the angel departed from him.** Having no further service to render Peter, and without waiting for his thanks.

11, 12. And when Peter was come to himself. Fully come to a consciousness of what had occurred and where he was. "He was before in the half consciousness of one who is dreaming, and knows that it is a dream; except that, in his case, the dream was *the truth*, and his supposition the unreality." —(*Alford.*)—**And hath delivered me.** This deliverance may be rightfully regarded as a symbol of divine redemption in that it is by one whom the Lord hath sent, is afforded to those in captivity and without hope, and ransoms from the king and kingdom of evil and from death.—**And when he had considered.** Either, what had already occurred (*Alford*, *Hackett*), or, what he would next do, or both.—**He came to the house of Mary the mother of John, whose surname was Mark.** She is mentioned only here; but we learn from Col. 4:10, that she was *aunt* (not *sister*) to Barnabas (see note there). It is surmised that when Barnabas sold his land for the benefit of the church, she opened her house to be used as one of its chief places of meeting. Tradition

13 And as Peter knocked at the door of the gate, a
damsel came to hearken, named Rhoda.
14 And when she knew Peter's voice, she opened
not the gate for gladness, but ran in, and told how Peter stood before the gate.
15 And they said unto her, Thou art mad. But she
constantly affirmed that it was even so. Then said
they, It is his[t] angel.
16 But Peter continued knocking: and when they
had opened *the door*, and saw him, they were astonished.
17 But he, beckoning[u] unto them with the hand, to
hold their peace, declared[v] unto them how the Lord
had brought him out of the prison. And he said, Go,
shew these things unto James, and to the brethren.
And he departed, and went into another place.

t Gen. 48 : 16 ; Matt. 18 : 10.... u chaps. 13 : 16 ; 19 : 33 ; 21 : 40.... v Ps. 66 : 16.

fixed the site as on the upper slope of Zion, and affirmed that the building, saved from the general destruction at the capture of Jerusalem by Titus, was still used as a church in the fourth century. She is here designated as the mother of John, not only to distinguish her from other Marys, but because it was a common practice among the Hebrews, as it still is among the Arabs, to entitle parents by their children, and women by the father or husband (Gen. 11 : 29; 1 Sam. 18 : 20; 25 : 44; 2 Sam. 17 : 25; John 2 : 1). John is Hebrew, Mark (*Marcus*) is Latin. The person is doubtless the author of the Gospel of Mark ; he was converted through the instrumentality of Peter (1 Pet. 5 : 13). On his life, see Introduction to Mark, Vol. I, p. 337.—**Gathered together praying.** For Peter, but not necessarily for his release. See ver. 5, note.

13-16. At the door of the gate. For plan of Jewish house, see Vol. I, p. 303. It was built around an open court-yard ; the entrance into this court-yard was closed by a heavy gate, in which was a small wicket for single persons. The porter, answering to the French *concierge*, was often a maid-servant (comp. John 18 : 17). The language here all indicates that the house of Mary was one of some size, and she a woman in at least comfortable, if not affluent circumstances. The verb rendered *to hearken* is one used in the classics to signify an answer to a knock or call at the door. —**And knowing Peter's voice.** An indication that Peter had before been a frequent visitor at the house. Her gladness indicates that she shared the anxiety of the disciples for him, and perhaps his kindness and consideration for one who occupied the inferior station of a portress. His epistle indicates sympathy with servants and an appreciation of their peculiar trials (1 Pet. 2 : 18-20). The minuteness of the narrative here indicates that Luke's informant was an eye and ear witness ; I believe him to have been Peter himself. See above on verses 9-11. Rhoda is not again mentioned in the N. T. —**It is his angel.** Not, *A messenger from him ;* for though the Greek word (ἄγγελος) has sometimes the signification of a human messenger (Mark 1 : 2; Luke 7 : 27; 9 : 52; James 2 : 25), it is rarely used in this sense, and the construction of the sentence in the original would have been different if so used here ; it would have been, not *his messenger* (ἄγγελος αὐτοῦ), but, a *messenger from him* (ἄγγελος ἀπό αὐτοῦ). Nor can we render the words *his ghost or spirit*, for the word translated *angel* never has this meaning in the N. T., for which a different Greek word (πνεῦμα or φάντασμα) is used. The Jews believed, not only in the doctrine of angelic communications with men, which is plainly confirmed by Scripture, but also that each individual had his own special guardian angel, who sometimes assumed the appearance and the voice of the person himself. See Lightfoot on this passage. Matt. 18 : 10 (see note there) lends some confirmation to the doctrine of special guardian angels ; but it cannot be deduced from the language here, since we do not know who were the speakers, nor whether their expression implies anything more than their own acceptance of a common, but possibly false, belief ; and while the doctrine of guardian angels is clearly implied by our Lord's language in Matthew, and by angelic appearances in both the O. T. and the N. T., it cannot with safety be concluded from any Scriptural teaching, that each individual has a special angel assigned to him.—**But having opened** (the door), **they saw him and were astonished.** The implication is that the party, or at least several of them, went to and opened the door. If their prayer was for Peter's liberation, their astonishment indicates how small was their expectation of an answer. How often are we astonished at an affirmative reply to even our most earnest and hopeful prayers!

17. But he motioned unto them with his hand to keep silence. The tumult of their joy, and the confusion of their congratulation and questioning, was such that he could not at first make himself heard. This, rather than a fear of being overheard, and so attracting the attention of his enemies and theirs, was the reason for desiring their silence.—**Go shew these things unto James, and to the brethren.** The James here mentioned is not the apostle of that name, who had already been put to death (ver. 2), but the one known as the Lord's brother (Gal. 1 : 19), who appears to have occupied a position of prominence in the church at Jerusalem (ch. 15 : 13; 21 : 18; Gal. 2 : 9, 12), and whom I believe to be one of the brethren of the Lord mentioned in Matt. 13 : 55; John 7 : 5; Acts 1 : 14; 1 Cor. 9 : 5. Whether he was a real brother or a cousin of our Lord, is one of the disputed questions in

18 Now as soon as it was day, there was no small
stir among the soldiers, what was become of Peter.
19 And when Herod had sought for him, and found
him not, he examined the keepers, and commanded
that *they* should be put to death. And he went down
from Judæa to Cæsarea, and *there* abode.
20 And Herod was highly displeased with them of
Tyre and Sidon: but they came with one accord to
him, and, having made Blastus the king's chamberlain, their friend, desired peace; because their[w] country was nourished by the king's *country*.
21 And upon a set day, Herod, arrayed in royal
apparel, sat upon his throne, and made an oration unto
them.
22 And the people gave a shout, *saying*, *It is*[x] the
voice of a god, and not of a man.

w 1 Kings 5 : 9, 11; Ezek. 27 : 17 .... x Jude 16.

Biblical criticism; I believe the former opinion to be clearly the only one consonant with Scripture. See note on Brethren of the Lord, Vol. I, p. 187. The disciples were to report the facts to James, probably as pastor of the church at Jerusalem and a recognized leader in the churches of Judea. Peter's enforced exile would debar him from exercising the same influence within the kingdom of Herod Agrippa which he had done theretofore.—**And he departed and went into another place.** The place is not mentioned, partly, perhaps, because there may have been reasons, even at the time of the first publication of Luke's account, for keeping concealed the names of those who harbored Peter and aided his escape, and partly because it was no part of Luke's purpose to trace further Peter's personal history. He subsequently returned to Jerusalem at the time of the council (ch. 15 : 7), probably afterward went to Antioch (Gal. 2 : 11-14). He preached the Gospel in the East, going as far as Babylon (1 Peter 5 : 13), and from 1 Cor. 1 : 2 is thought to have preached it also in Greece, as far west as Corinth, in confirmation of which are early and apparently trustworthy traditions. If he ever visited Rome, which is uncertain, it may be considered as settled that his visit followed that of Paul, and did not take place till near the end of his own life.

18, 19. Now as soon as it was day, there was no small stir. As the guard was changed four times in the night (ver. 4, note), the presumption is that Peter's escape was in the morning watch; otherwise it would have been discovered before the break of day, at the change of guards following the escape. And this indicates the earnestness of the disciples, who continued all night in prayer.—**They should be put to death.** Not, probably, all the guards, but the two who were especially in charge of Peter, and to whom he had been chained (ver. 6). The guards under Roman law were held to a strict accountability for the safekeeping of their prisoners; hence the jailer at Philippi would have killed himself when he thought his prisoners had escaped (ch. 16 : 27). Here the implication is that the guards were sleeping, and therefore really culpable, though they could not, if awake, have prevented the escape of their prisoner.—**From Judea to Cæsarea, and abode there.** Cæsarea Palestinæ, on the Mediterranean coast; for illustration and description, see ch. 8 : 40, note. It was the military headquarters of the Roman governors. Herod's usual residence was in Jerusalem; he went to Cæsarea to preside at the public games in honor of the emperor Claudius (Jos. Ant. 18 : 8, 2). *Abode* (διατρίβω) signifies not that he made it his permanent residence, but that he went there to spend some time.

20. Herod was highly displeased with them of Tyre and Sidon. Not engaged in open war with them; for, though the original Greek (θυμομαχῶν) is capable of this meaning, Tyre and Sidon were in the Roman Empire, and an open war between two Roman provinces would not have been allowed. They were commercial cities of importance and renown; not improbably the quarrel arose out of commercial rivalry between them and Cæsarea, also a harbor of importance, but a comparatively modern city. On their history, see Matt. 11 : 21, note. Of the quarrel here referred to, secular history makes no mention; nothing more is known of it.—**Blastus the king's chamberlain.** Mentioned only here. His office is indicated by the original, which describes him as *over the king's chamber* (ἐπὶ τοῦ κοιτῶνος τοῦ βασιλέως). He was a servant who had the charge of his master's sleeping apartment, and, to some extent, of his person; was charged with the duty of introducing visitors to him; usually remained for this purpose in an ante-room during the hours when the king received guests; was often a person of high rank, and always maintained a peculiarly confidential relation to the king or chief person whom he served.—**Because their country was nourished by the king's.** Tyre and Sidon depended chiefly on Palestine for their bread-stuffs. See 1 Kings 5 : 11; Ezek. 27 : 17.

21-23. Arrayed in royal apparel. See below for description.—**Sat upon his throne** (ἐπὶ τοῦ βήματος). This was a platform used by governors, generals, and others from which to deliver public addresses or to administer justice. It was sometimes of stone and stationary, sometimes of wood and movable. For illustration, see John 19 : 13, note.—**The voice of God and not of man.** It was customary for the Greeks and Romans to deify their dead, many of their gods being ancient heroes. From this sprung up the practice, in these degenerate days of

23 And immediately the angel of the Lord smote him, because he gave not God the glory: and he was eaten of worms, and gave up the ghost.
24 But the word of God grew [y] and multiplied.

25 And Barnabas and Saul returned from Jerusalem, when they had fulfilled *their* ministry, and took with them John, whose surname was Mark.

y Isaiah 55 : 11 ; chaps. 6 : 7 ; 19 : 20 ; Col. 1 : 6.

MODERN SHEIK ON HIS THRONE.

Rome, of deifying the living. The attempt of Caligula to set up his image in the Temple at Jerusalem had already outraged the Jewish people, and had been abandoned at the petition of Herod Agrippa (Josephus' Ant., 18 : 8, 2-9).—**An angel of the Lord.** Not *the* angel. There is no reason whatever to suppose that any angel appeared, or that a physical and literal smiting is intended. The language is simply that of one who recognizes in the sudden and mortal illness which ensued what we should still call, in analogous language, "a stroke of Providence." Eusebius, misquoting Josephus' account of this event, substitutes, for the owl which he mentions, an angel, and this perhaps has led some to imagine, from the account here, the visible appearance of an angel. But this is not probable, and is not indicated by the account.—**And he was eaten of worms and expired.** Alford quotes several instances from ancient history, in which a similar disease is reported and attributed to Divine judgment. What is known in modern times as Trichiniasis answers to the description here. In this disease minute worms, called *trichinæ*, scarcely visible to the naked eye, introduced by the eating of meat, insufficiently cooked, containing their germs, pierce the mucous coats or walls of the intestines, enter the capillaries, and are transported by the blood throughout the whole muscular system. Their multiplication is enormous, reaching thousands and even millions in a single case. The disease is exceedingly painful and generally fatal.

Of Herod's death Josephus (Ant. 19 : 8, 2) gives a fuller account, but one which in all its essential particulars agrees with the account here. For the convenience of those who have not access to his history I transcribe, partly condensing, his account: "Now, when Agrippa had reigned three years over all Judea, he came to the city Cæsarea, which was formerly called Strabo's Tower; and there he exhibited shows in honor of Cæsar. On the second day of which shows he put on a garment made wholly of silver, and of a contexture truly wonderful, and came into the theatre early in the morning; at which time the silver of his garment being illuminated by the fresh reflection of the sun's rays upon it, shone out after a surprising manner, and was so resplendent as to spread a horror over those that looked intently upon him; and presently his flatterers cried out, one from one place and another from another (though not for his good), that he was a god; and they added, 'Be thou merciful to us; for although we have hitherto reverenced thee only as a man, yet shall we henceforth own thee as superior to mortal nature.' Upon this the king did neither rebuke them nor reject their impious flattery. But, as he presently afterwards looked up, he saw an owl sitting on a certain rope over his head, and immediately understood that this bird was the messenger of ill tidings, as it had once been the messenger of good tidings to him; and fell into the deepest sorrow. A severe pain also arose in his belly, and began in a most violent manner. He therefore looked upon his friends and said: 'I, whom you call a god, am commanded presently to depart this life; while Providence thus reproves the lying words you just now said to me; and I, who was by you called immortal, am immediately to be hurried away by death. But I am bound to accept of what Providence allots, as it pleases God; for we have by no means lived ill, but in a splendid and happy manner.'" He died, according to Josephus, after five days' illness, in the 54th year of his age and the seventh of his reign.

24, 25. Luke, in these verses, resumes his narrative where it was broken off by the introduction of the account of the death of James and the imprisonment of Peter (ch. 12 : 1).—**The word of God grew and was multiplied.** *Grew* in its actual power in the church, by rea-

CHAPTER XIII.

NOW there were in the church that was at Antioch, certain prophets and teachers; as Barnabas, and Simeon that was called Niger, and Lucius of Cyrene, and Manaen, which had been brought up with Herod the tetrarch, and Saul.
2 As they ministered to the Lord, and fasted, the

son of increasing faith in and allegiance to it; *was multiplied*, in the community, by the additions made to the church. *The word of God* is here, as generally in the N. T., not the *abstract truth*, but the truth as *practically held by men*. So our term *creed* means, properly, not a system of truth, but a belief. So in Matt. 13 : 19 the seed sown and the product of conviction in the hearer are treated as identical, though the identity is obscured by the mistranslation of the passage. See note there.—**When they had fulfilled their ministry.** The particular service for which they went up to Jerusalem, viz., to carry succor to the brethren (ch. 11 : 29, 30).—**John.** See above on ver. 12. The implication appears to me to be that the visit of Saul and Barnabas took place at or about the same time with the events recorded in this chapter. These verses introduce the account of the first missionary tour by Paul, Barnabas, and Mark, contained in the following chapter.

Ch. 13 : 1-12. THE FIRST MISSIONARY TOUR TO THE GENTILES BEGUN. THE HOLY GHOST THE ORIGINATOR OF FOREIGN MISSIONS.—THE FIRST MISSIONARY CONTRIBUTION: THE PRIMITIVE CHURCH GIVES ITS MINISTERS.—THE PREPARATION FOR SPECIAL RELIGIOUS UNDERTAKINGS IS PRAYER AND FASTING.—THE SIN AND PUNISHMENT OF ELYMAS: HE WHO WOULD KEEP OTHERS IN DARKNESS IS HIMSELF BLINDED.—ANGER AS WELL AS LOVE IS INSPIRED BY THE HOLY GHOST.

A. D. 47-48. See Chronological Table, Intro., p. 20. Luke here begins the third part of his history (Intro., p. 16). Having described (1) the founding of the church at Jerusalem (chaps. 1-5), and its growth and development by the initiatory teachings of the Holy Spirit and of divine Providence, necessary to prepare it for its missionary work (chaps. 6-12), he begins in this chapter a narrative of that work, beginning with the first missionary journey of Barnabas and Paul, and ending with the preaching of the Gospel by Paul in Rome. Henceforth his narrative follows substantially the course of Paul's missionary labors, and affords really a biography of the great apostle to the Gentiles, though not in a strictly biographical form. For map tracing the course of this journey, see Intro., p. 19. Starting from Seleucia, the port of Antioch in Syria, crossing over to Salamis, the eastern port of the island of Cyprus, he traverses that island, comes to Paphos on its western coast, where Elymas is struck with blindness, thence, following the natural course of commerce, crosses the Mediterranean to the mainland at Perga, and, journeying inland, visits in succession the following cities in Asia Minor: Antioch of Pisidia, Iconium, Lystra, Derbe, whence he returns by the same course to the sea-coast, embarking at Attalia, near Perga, direct for Antioch in Syria. The entire journey lasts probably about a year.

The general character of the provinces of Asia Minor visited by Paul at this time are well described by Renan. A more minute description is given by Conybeare and Howson. The external difficulties which Paul had to encounter were not few. The region is wild, rugged, mountainous; an almost Alpine country, with numerous lakes and rivers, which, with the melting of the spring snows, become suddenly dangerous torrents; the roads were bad and were infested with robbers; brigandage was common; in Lycaonia the scenery changes, but the difficulties increase; the land is unwatered by streams; Strabo mentions one place where water was even sold for money. To no part of Paul's life would the description better apply which he affords of his life: "In perils of waters, in perils of robbers, * * * in perils in the wilderness, * * * in hunger and thirst often" (2 Cor. 11 : 26). On the other hand, the character of the people was favorable to the apostle's mission. They were a wild rather than a corrupt race. Their speech was rude (ch. 14 : 11), their ignorance and superstition great; but they were not rendered skeptical by the cynical culture which at once developed and degraded the great commercial and philosophical centres of the Roman world. They were simple-hearted, and not encased in either the prejudices of a fossilized conservatism or in the indifference of a scoffing skepticism. There were many Jews scattered through this region. Far removed from Jerusalem and the influence of the hierarchy, they were less embittered in their hostility to the Gentiles than those of Judea. Jew and Gentile met in the synagogue; intermarriages were not uncommon (ch. 13 : 44; 16 : 1). Why Paul chose this region as the field of his first missionary tour is a matter only of surmise. It is however a fact, possibly of significance, that the whole district was one with which his residence in Tarsus must have made him familiar.

1. Now there were in the church. That is, the Christian church which had grown out of the ministry described in ch. 11 : 19-26.—**At Antioch.** In Syria, near the Mediterranean coast. For illustration and description, see ch. 11 : 19, note.—**Certain prophets and teachers.** It is not possible to ascertain with accuracy and certainty the nature of the distinctions

Holy Ghost said, Separate[z] me Barnabas and Saul for the work[a] whereunto I have called them.

3 And when they had fasted and prayed, and laid *their* hands on them, they sent *them* away.

z Rom. 1 : 1; Numb. 8 : 14; Gal. 1 : 15.... a Matt. 9 : 38; Rom. 10 : 15; 1 Tim. 2 : 7.

in the offices of the early church. Paul mentions, in Ephes. 4 : 11, four classes—apostles, prophets, evangelists, and pastors and teachers. The language there implies that pastors and teachers are different terms for the same office. By *prophets* here are meant teachers possessing in a special manner the inspiration of the Spirit of God, indicated in some peculiar supernatural gift, as that of healing or of foretelling (see ch. 11 : 27, note); by *teachers* are meant stated and permanent teachers, answering somewhat to the pastor of a modern church. The former may have included some of the prophets who came from Jerusalem (ch. 11 : 27).

Barnabas. See ch. 4 : 36, note.—**Simeon that was called Niger.** To distinguish him from Simon Peter, Simon and Simeon being the same name. Niger means *black;* and it is not an unreasonable surmise that he was an African convert.—**Lucius of Cyrene.** A person of the same name is described by Paul as one of his kinsmen (Rom. 16 : 21), and is said by tradition to have been ordained bishop of the church of Cenchreæ, and their identity is not improbable. He is not Luke, the author of the Gospel and of the Book of Acts and the Lucas of Phil. 24, who is in two other places mentioned by Paul in his epistles (Col. 4 : 14; 2 Tim. 4 : 11), but never as a kinsman; moreover, the names, though similar, are not the same. *Cyrene* was a province of Northern Africa (see ch. 2 : 10, note), and this Lucius was very probably a proselyte from that district, who heard the Gospel in his native dialect on the day of Pentecost, and also one of the "men of Cyrene" who subsequently were scattered abroad with others preaching the word as far as Antioch (ch. 11 : 19, 20).—**Manaen which had been brought up with Herod the tetrarch.** Herod Antipas, son of Herod the Great, appointed by his father tetrarch of Galilee and Perea, subsequently banished and dying in exile. See Vol. I., pp. 58, 59, 189. *Brought up with* indicates that Manaen was nurtured from infancy with this Herod, as his foster-brother. One of the same name, Manahem, an Essene, when Herod the Great was a boy, patted him on the back, saying: "Mark, boy! you will live to be king." When Herod became king he remembered the prophecy, and held Manahem and the Essenes generally in the highest honor (Jos. Ant. 15 : 10, 5). This Manaen was probably his grandson, though Alford supposes that he may have been no relation, but simply have received his name in honor of Manahem.—**And Saul.** Of Tarsus. From the mention of his name here it is evident that he was either recognized as a prophet, or, more probably, was looked up to by the church at Antioch as one of its official teachers.

2, 3. As they ministered to the Lord. Not, *as they preached* (*Chrysostom*); nor, *as they offered mass*, which is the interpretation of the Romanist expositors; nor can any conclusion be justly deduced from the fact that from the original Greek word (λειτουργέις) is derived our word *liturgy.* The word is used in classic Greek to designate certain public services connected more or less remotely with religious rites, which were provided by the wealthier citizens of Athens under the Grecian laws, such as vocal and instrumental choruses for the Greek festivals, gymnastic performances, races, and religious embassies to the oracles, often conducted with great magnificence. It is used in the N. T. both of ministrations of charity (Rom. 15 : 27; 2 Cor. 9 : 13; Phil. 2 : 25) and of the public services of the Jewish Temple (Luke 1 : 23; Heb. 10 : 11). It was while the church was engaged in its Christian services, whatever those were, probably substantially as described in ch. 2 : 42, 46, and including prayer, praise, and teaching, that the commission to the first missionary work was given by the Spirit of God.—**And fasting.** Fasting in the N. T. appears to have always accompanied some special service, and been indicative of some special desire for divine guidance or assistance (ch. 10 : 30; 14 : 23). It is therefore reasonable to suppose that this service was special in its character; not improbably the disciples were seeking for guidance on the question of their duty toward the great outlying heathen population. As the truth dawned on the church, that the door of the Gospel was opened alike to Gentile and Jew, the full significance of Christ's commission to preach the Gospel to all nations, would be impressed upon them (ch. 11 : 15-18), while how to fulfill it, they would not know.—**Separate now for me.** That is, *Set apart unto me*, for this special service. Comp. Rom. 1 : 1, where Paul apparently refers to this consecration to the special work of preaching the Gospel in heathen lands; and Gal. 1 : 15, where he refers to the grace of God consecrating him to himself from infancy. *Now* (δή), not in our English version, gives emphasis and precision to the command, as one to be immediately obeyed. They were not to wait for any other door of opportunity, any providential opening of the way to the Gentiles. Observe that they are set apart to this work by the direction of the Holy Ghost, and derive their mission

4 So they, being sent forth by the Holy Ghost, departed unto Seleucia; and from thence they sailed to Cyprus.

5 And when they were at Salamis, they preached the word of God in the synagogues of the Jews: and they had also John to *their* minister.

and authority, not from men, not from the church, but from God, a fact on which Paul, in Gal. 1:1 lays emphasis. But observe also that not till this call of God, although it had been before privately given, is accepted and interpreted by the church in a regular and orderly manner, does Paul commence his mission to the Gentiles.—**Whereunto I have called them.** Paul had previously been called directly by the Lord to this work of apostleship to the Gentiles (chaps. 9:15; 22:21); Barnabas had been called to an analogous work by the providence of God, which, through the action of the church at Jerusalem, had sent him down to Antioch, where, by the Spirit of God, he had been led to confirm the faith of the Gentile converts (ch. 11:23).—**And when they had fasted and prayed.** As a special preparation for the ordination of Barnabas and Saul. In the Roman Catholic and Anglican churches, certain special seasons of fasting—in the latter the Wednesday, Friday, and Saturday after the first Sunday in Lent, after Whit Sunday, after the 14th of September, and after the 13th of December—are set apart for special prayer and fasting for God's blessing on the ordination of the clergy. These weeks are called Ember weeks; the practice has been maintained since the fifth century, prior to which time there were no stated seasons for ordination in the church (Bingham's Antiq., B. 6, ch. 6:56). There are none in most of the Protestant churches, and ordination is not ordinarily preceded by any church fast, though often by special devotional exercises.—**And laid their hands on them.** On the laying on of hands, see ch. 8:17, note.—**They sent them away.** Observe that this little church gives, not money out of its treasury, but ministers, to the missionary cause; and that it surrenders to this purpose its two most prominent pastors. Missionary work requires the best men the church possesses.

4. They being sent forth by the Holy Ghost. In the manner already described. It is a striking illustration of the amazing blindness of the church that, notwithstanding this direct divine endorsement of the work of Christian missions, the modern missionary movement should have been vehemently opposed, and its expediency should be still doubted, in the church of Christ.—**Departed unto Seleucia.** The sea-

SELEUCIA AND MT. PIERIA.

port of Antioch in Syria, and on the Mediterranean sea, near the mouth of the Orontes river. It was founded by Seleucus Nicator, who died B. C. 280. The ruins of both the upper and lower towns are extensive. The walls of the port are still visible on the sea, and are so strong that Ali Pasha once intended to repair them and clear out the sand, so as to fit the port for use. The mountain near the village is Pieria, a part of Lebanon.—**And from thence they sailed unto Cyprus.** The lofty outline of this island is distinctly visible from Seleucia, between 60 and 70 miles distant. For description, see ch. 11:19, note.

5. And when they were at Salamis. The nearest port to Seleucia, on the eastern side of the island. It possessed a good harbor. It was ruined by an earthquake under Constantine the Great, but was rebuilt and called Constantia. Its remains are yet to be seen near the modern Famagosta.—**In the synagogue of the Jews.** It was the custom of the apostles first to

6 And when they had gone through the isle unto Paphos, they found a certain sorcerer, a false prophet, a Jew, whose name *was* Bar-jesus:

7 Which was with the deputy of the country, Sergius Paulus, a prudent man; who called for Barnabas and Saul, and desired to hear the word of God.

ANCIENT SALAMIS (MODERN FAMAGOSTA).
Ruins of St. Sophia Christian Church.

preach the Gospel to the Jews, and after their rejection of it to proclaim it to the Gentiles (chaps. 13 : 46; 17 : 2; 18 : 4; Rom. 1 : 16); and this, not because of any divine partiality for the Jewish nation, but because it was permitted to them to receive and become the heralds to others of the grace of God, if they had chosen so to do.—**John to their minister.** As their assistant. The Greek word (ὑπηρέτης) signifies literally an *under-rower*, then, in a wider sense, an assistant of another. In classic Greek it signifies the heralds, messengers, or assistants of public officers; in Luke (4 : 20), a subordinate officer in a Jewish synagogue; elsewhere in the Gospels, the subordinate officials of the high-priest (Matt. 26 : 58; Mark 14 : 54, 65; John 7 : 32, etc.); and three times in the N. T., in a spiritual sense, it is used for ministers or servants of Christ (Luke 1 : 2; Acts 26 : 16; 1 Cor. 4 : 1). The meaning here appears to be that Mark went in the capacity of an agent or assistant of the apostles, to make provision for their entertainment and their journeys, and also, perhaps, to act as the amanuensis of Paul. It has been suggested that he may have administered the rite of baptism, which Paul himself rarely did (1 Cor. 1 : 14-17). The value of his services Paul recognized in his letter to Timothy twenty years later (2 Tim. 4 : 11).

6. And when they had gone through the whole island unto Paphos. This city was at the western end of Cyprus, and, by a road which certainly existed A. D. 230, and very probably earlier, 100 miles from Salamis. New Paphos is intended, about eight miles north of the Paphos celebrated in classic poets for the temple and worship of Venus. — **A certain sorcerer.** Rather, magician. On the magi, their origin, history, and practices, see Matt. 2 : 1, note; Acts 8 : 9, note. The magicians did not merely pretend to foretell the future, but also to influence it, by the control which they claimed to exercise over the inferior gods or demons; it was called white or black art, according as the gods were good or evil. While the Jewish laws rigorously forbade all practice of witchcraft and magic, punishing it with death (Exod. 22 : 18; Deut. 18 : 9-22; Lev. 19 : 31), the Jewish nation at this time, in common with other Eastern nations, contributed necromancers, soothsayers, and wonder-workers, who played upon and profited by the superstitions of the people, and who brought under their influence not only the lower classes, but also the aristocracy, the governors, and even the emperors of Rome. Marius, Pompey, Crassus, Cæsar, and Tiberius all consulted them. It was not, therefore, strange that Sergius Paulus should have had such a magician as an adviser. For some account of their arts and influence, see Conybeare and Howson, ch. 5.—**A false prophet.** Not merely *a false teacher*, but one falsely professing to be an ambassador from and inspired by God. The language here and in verse 10 implies that he was a deliberate and conscious impostor.—**Bar-jesus.** A Hebrew word meaning Son of Joshua; the name below, *Elymas*, is of Arabic origin, signifying *the wise man*, and appears to be a title which he had assumed, the equivalent of which is the *magian*, mistranslated *the sorcerer*.

7, 8. Which was with the deputy of the country. Literally, the *proconsul*. The Roman provinces were of two kinds, imperial and senatorial; the former, those most requiring the presence of military force and military law, were

8 But Elymas the sorcerer (for so is his name by interpretation) withstood[b] them, seeking to turn away the deputy from the faith.

9 Then Saul, (who also *is called* Paul,) filled with the Holy Ghost, set his eyes on him,
10 And said, O full of all subtilty and all mischief,

b 2 Tim. 3 : 8.

governed by prefects called proprætors, who were appointed by the emperor, and were responsible to him; the latter, of a more peaceful character, were governed by officers, called proconsuls, appointed by the senate. Sergius Paulus was such a proconsul. The emperor Augustus at first reserved Cyprus to himself, and it was accordingly governed by proprætors, and, this fact appearing in Strabo, it was for a time supposed that Luke had erred in giving the title *proconsul* to Sergius Paulus. But a passage has since been discovered in Dio Cassius which stated that Augustus subsequently relinquished Cyprus to the senate, and that it was henceforth governed by proconsuls; and coins struck in the reign of Claudius, *i. e.*, about the time of Paul's visit, have been found, on one of which this very title proconsul is applied to a governor of Cyprus. Such minute historical confirmations show clearly that the Book of Acts was written at or about the time of the events narrated, and its accuracy.

Sergius Paulus, a prudent man. That is, *an intelligent* or *thoughtful man.* With this agrees Pliny, who cites him as an authority on questions of natural philosophy, and Galen, who refers in flattering terms to the philosophical ability of a son or grandson of the same name. Because Bar-jesus was his counsellor, it does not follow that he accepted unquestioningly the impostor's teachings; indeed, the reverse is implied by the course of the narrative.—**Desired to hear the Word of God.** He sent to the apostles to come to his court for this purpose; similar experiences are recorded by modern missionaries in foreign lands. The report of the preaching at the synagogue had probably reached him, and aroused his curiosity, if not his spiritual interest.—**The Word of God.** The Gospel; that is, the means of salvation through Jesus Christ.—**But Elymas.** See above, on ver. 6.—**From the faith,** *i. e.*, from accepting it; because with its acceptance the influence of Elymas would be at an end.

9. Then Saul, who is also called Paul. Up to this time he is designated in Luke's narrative only by the Hebrew name Saul; henceforth, in the narrative, only by the Latin name Paul, except in his own account of his conversion (ch. 22 : 7, 13; 26 : 14). Why this change of name? And why does it take place at this time? The N. T. does not answer these questions. Several hypothetical reasons have been assigned: (1.) That he takes the name of Sergius Paulus to commemorate the first remarkable victory in his missionary work; so Jerome, and, apparently, Augustine; but this is quite inconsistent with the spirit of one who always refused to glory, save in Jesus Christ his Lord (2 Cor. 12 : 5-9; Gal. 6 : 14); or, (2) he adopts Sergius Paulus as his patron, assuming his name in token of his dependence; so Renan; but this is equally inconsistent with Paul's notable independence of character; (3) that he abandoned the name Saul, because, though acceptable to the Hebrews, it carried with it a degrading idea in Greece, the word meaning *conceited;* but this suggestion is also at variance with the character of the apostle; (4) that he adopted the word Paul, meaning *little*, as a title of humility, and to indicate that he regarded himself as the least of the apostles on account of his previous persecutions of the church (1 Cor. 15 : 9), this is a possible, but not probable explanation; it savors too much of the ostentation of humility, and suggests no reason for the change *at this time;* (5) that both names were borne by him from childhood, Saul being his Hebrew, and Paul his Roman name, and that he from this time adopted the latter, partly to obtain the more readily the advantages which were afforded by his Roman citizenship, partly because it would better give him access to the Gentile world. The use of two names were common among the Jews, and may be traced through all the periods of Hebrew history. Thus Joseph took the name Zapherathpaaneah (Gen. 41 : 45), Daniel was entitled Belteshazzar (Dan. 1 : 7), Esther received the name Hadassah (Esther 2 : 7). So in the N. T. we have the Greek names Philip and Alexander, and the Roman names Crispus, Justus, Niger, given to Jews, and this practice of taking Gentile names has been continued among the Jews to the present day. This explanation seems to me the most reasonable, and it partly explains why the change is introduced in the narrative, at the time of, and in connection with, the apostles' first missionary journey.

Filled with the Holy Ghost. Paul's invective was not then inspired by any personal irritation of spirit, but by a holy wrath against imposture and the impostor who was attempting to prevent the work of God's grace and truth.—**Set eyes on him.** So Peter fastened his eyes upon the lame man in the Temple (ch. 3 : 4), and Paul on the impotent man at Lystra (ch. 14 : 9), and again upon the council before which he was summoned for trial (ch. 23 : 1). The language is that of an eye-witness, who was impressed by the intensity and power of Paul's gaze. Alford's *thou* child of the devil, *thou* enemy of all righteousness, wilt thou not cease to pervert the right ways of the Lord?

11 And now, behold, the hand of the Lord *is* upon thee, and thou shalt be blind, not seeing the sun for a season. And immediately there fell on him a mist and a darkness; and he went about seeking some to lead him by the hand.

12 Then the deputy, when he saw what was done, believed, being astonished at the doctrine of the Lord.

---

conjecture that it refers to some imperfection in his sight, as though he looked intently in order clearly to perceive Elymas, seems to me far less probable than that there was in his look a peculiar moral power, a piercing through the outer shell, which attracted the attention of the original narrator of this incident.

10. O full of all subtilty and mischief. *Deceit and recklessness.* The Greek word rendered *subtilty* (δόλος) primarily means a bait for fish; then, any deception; then, a desire or disposition to deceive; the word rendered *mischief* (ῥᾳδιουργία) signifies what is done lightly, recklessly, and hence an unscrupulousness in doing evil. I see no ground for Dr. Hackett's distinction that "*deceit* refers to his occupation, *wickedness* to his character;" rather both refer to his character—one to its falsity, the other to its utter unscrupulousness.—**Son of the devil.** Because a liar, and so a child of the father of lies (John 8 : 44). Meyer supposes an indignant allusion to his name Bar-jesus, Son of Joshua or Son of Jesus.—**Enemy of all righteousness.** He was not merely an opposer of Christianity, which one may be honestly and sincerely, as Saul himself, through the perversion of pride (ch. 26 : 9), but an enemy of *all righteousness*, and therefore opposed to Christianity, because it conducted men to righteousness; and this secret hostility to truth, purity, and love, is the general cause of open opposition to the religion of Jesus Christ.—**Wilt thou not cease to pervert the straight ways of the Lord?** Not, as Dr. Hackett, *to misrepresent and malign the ways which the Lord requires men to follow*, for there is no evidence that Elymas had misrepresented the doctrine of the Gospel, which indeed he had but little opportunity to do, with Paul present to correct the misrepresentation, and *to pervert* (διαστρέφω) has not properly the meaning of *malign;* nor, as Alexander, is the language equivalent to *turn away from the right ways of the Lord*, for it was not Sergius Paulus, but the *right ways of the Lord*, which Elymas was turning aside. These *right ways* are the same as the "path of the Lord," which John the Baptist urged his hearers to make *straight*, that He might come to Israel (Matt. 3 : 3; Mark 1 : 3), the way from God unto the hearts of men. The doctrine that the Holy Spirit holds communion with men, and that angels are the ministering spirits of the Most High to man, and that evil spirits are among man's spiritual foes (John 14 : 17; Ephes. 6 : 12; Heb. 1 : 14), Elymas, in common with all sorcerers of his day and ours, perverted into a doctrine of spiritism, and a practice of pretended communication with spirits. Thus he *perverted, turned aside, from a high and holy use, the truth*, making it a means of evil, and out of it a degrading error. The most dangerous errors are always those which are perversions of the straight ways of the Lord.

11. The hand of the Lord (is) **upon thee.** A frequent Biblical expression for the manifestation of the power of God, either in punishment (Exod. 9 : 3; 1 Sam. 5 : 11), or in mercy (Acts 4 : 30; 11 : 21; Ezra 7 : 9; Neh. 2 : 8).—**Not seeing the sun for a season.** This phrase indicates total blindness. In case of partial blindness, the eye cannot discern *objects*, but is able to recognize the *light;* when the sun cannot be discerned, the blindness is absolute. It is common for oculists to test the character of the difficulty by directing the eyes of the patient toward a strong light, and inquiring if anything of it can be recognized. That the blindness was temporary is indicated clearly by the language here; but how long it lasted, or when or how it was cured, we have no means of knowing. Nothing is known of Elymas except what is recorded here.—**A mist and darkness.** This indicates that the blindness came on in successive stages, as the cure was wrought on the man at Bethsaida (Mark 8 : 22-26). This description affords no hint of the nature of the blindness, whether an opacity on the eye, or a sudden failure in the optic nerve. In both classes of cases the blindness comes on, as here, in successive stages, first a mist, then a darkness, and in neither is it ever so suddenly produced as in this case.

12. Then the deputy * * * believed. That he was spiritually converted is not certain, for precisely the same language is used of Simon Magus (ch. 8 : 13). He was convinced by this miracle of the power of the Lord Jesus, whose ambassadors Paul and Barnabas were; that he gave his personal allegiance to Christ does not necessarily follow; it is not stated that he was baptized; and the implication that astonishment was the basis of his belief, does not favor the hypothesis that he became a true child of God. —**At the doctrine of the Lord.** That is, at the manner of the teaching, not at the truths taught. Comp. Mark 1 : 27. He was astonished at teaching accompanied by signs and wonders so much surpassing any that Elymas had produced by his arts.

In considering the practical and spiritual significance of this miracle, observe, (1) its parallel to

13 Now when Paul and his company loosed from Paphos, they came to Perga in Pamphylia; and John departing [c] from them, returned to Jerusalem.

14 But when they departed from Perga, they came to Antioch in Pisidia, and went into the synagogue [d] on the sabbath day, and sat down.

c ch. 15 : 38 .... d chaps. 16 : 13; 17 : 2; 18 : 4.

the conflict between Moses and the magicians of Egypt (Exod., chaps. 7, 8). In both, the powers of light and darkness are seen in conflict; in both, the hand of the Lord is heavy in punishment upon the workers of deceit and wickedness. (2.) The symbolic character of the punishment. He who was endeavoring to lead others into darkness, is himself blinded; so ever the framers and maintainers of superstition and ignorance are by it brought into blindness of mind and of soul. (3.) The admonition to all, who, in our own time, seek to turn inquirers away from the faith, or to pervert into error, for their own purposes, the truths of God's word. (4.) Its direct and divine sanction of indignation against the deliberate and purposed opposers of the truth, who resist it because they are enemies of all righteousness.

Ch. 13 : 13–52. PAUL'S SERMON AT ANTIOCH. THE GOSPEL REJECTED BY THE JEWS. THE APOSTOLIC MISSIONARY TO THE JEWISH PEOPLE.—THE DOCTRINE OF JUSTIFICATION BY FAITH UNFOLDED.

With this address of Paul should be carefully compared the parallel address of Peter in ch. 2, and the partially parallel one of Stephen in ch. 7. Observe, however, that Paul brings out far more distinctly and sharply the doctrine of justification by faith in contrast with justification by law, than either of the others.

13, 14. Paul and his companions. From this time Paul is not only the chief speaker (ch. 14 : 12), but the leader; Barnabas occupies a secondary, if not a subordinate position.—**They came to Perga.** An ancient and important city of Pamphylia, situated on the river Cestrus, at a distance of eight or ten miles from its mouth,

PERGA IN PAMPHYLIA.

and celebrated in antiquity for the worship of Artemis (Diana), whose temple stood on a hill outside the town. The goddess and the temple are represented in the coins of Perga. The Cestrus was formerly navigable to Perga. The modern traveler finds here only the encampments of shepherds, who pasture their cattle amidst walls and towers, columns and cornices, a theatre, a broken aqueduct encrusted with the calcareous deposit of the Pamphylian streams, and tombs scattered on both sides of the town. Nothing else remains of Perga but the beauty of its natural situation, between and upon the sides of two hills, with an extensive valley in front, watered by the river Cestrus, and backed by the mountains of the Taurus.—**In Pamphylia.** One of the southern provinces of Asia Minor. As in the case of most other provinces of Lesser Asia, the boundaries of Pamphylia were frequently changed, but it may be roughly said to have been separated from Pisidia by the Taurian range. The valleys are rich and fertile, but toward the sea unhealthy. At the time of Paul it formed a province together with Lycia. It was then a flourishing commercial province; the rivers, now rendered useless for ships by the formation of bars across their mouths, were then navigable to a considerable extent. The inhabitants were

15 And after the reading[e] of the law and the prophets, the rulers of the synagogue sent unto them, saying, *Ye* men *and* brethren, if ye have any word[f] of exhortation for the people, say on.

16 Then Paul stood up, and beckoning with *his* hand, said, Men of Israel, and ye that fear God, give audience.

e verse 27....f Heb. 13 : 22.

mild and courteous in manners, and largely engaged in commerce, to which, indeed, they were led by the peculiarly favorable situation of the country.

And John departing from them returned to Jerusalem. John Mark, the author of the Gospel of Mark; on his life and character, see Vol. I, p. 337. No reason is assigned for this departure; that it seemed unreasonable to Paul, and an evidence of weakness, irresolution, or lack of faith, is evident from the apostle's refusal to take him as a traveling companion on the second missionary tour (ch. 15 : 37, 38). Various explanations have been proposed; as that he feared the dangers of the hazardous journey; that he hesitated to commit himself to the work of preaching the Gospel to the Gentiles; that he was offended because Barnabas, who was a relative of Mark's, no longer held the foremost place, which was henceforth occupied by Paul; that his mother dwelt at Jerusalem (ch. 12 : 12), and that fear and filial love combined to call him back. However this may be, if he was, as ver. 5 implies (see note there), the agent and servant of Paul and Barnabas, having charge of all arrangements for their entertainment, etc., and answering to the modern courier, his departure would have necessarily involved great personal inconvenience to them, and a serious embarrassment in their work, quite adequate to account for Paul's subsequent unwillingness to take him again in the same capacity.—**They came to Antioch in Pisidia.** So entitled to distinguish it from the more important Antioch in Syria. It was built

ANTIOCH IN PISIDIA.

on a hill between two plains, one of which was in Pisidia and the other in Pamphylia. The site is near the modern village of Yalobatch. There are remains of three temples, a theatre, several churches, and an aqueduct, all of stone and well built.—**And went into the synagogue.** For illustration of Jewish synagogue, see Vol. I, frontispiece; for a description of synagogue and its services, Matt. 4 : 23, note.

15. After the reading of the law and the prophets. The reading of the Scripture formed an important part of the synagogue services (ver. 27). They were arranged in lessons, somewhat as in the Episcopal church of to-day, one selection being taken from the law the first five books, the other from the prophets, which included the books of Joshua, Judges, Samuel, and Kings. The lessons on this day were probably Deut., ch. 1, and Isaiah, ch. 1. See Bengel on verses 17–19, quoted below.—**The men of the synagogue.** The synagogue was governed by a board of elders; the term *ruler* is usually applied to the

17 The God of this people of Israel chose[g] our fathers, and exalted the people when they dwelt[h] as strangers in the land of Egypt, and with an high[i] arm brought he them out of it.

18 And about the time of forty[j] years suffered he their manners in the wilderness.

19 And when he had destroyed[k] seven nations in the land of Chanaan, he[l] divided their land to them by lot.

g Deut. 7 : 6, 7....h Ps. 105 : 23....i Exod. 13 : 14, 16....j Exod. 16 : 35....k Deut. 7 : 1....l Josh. 14 : 1, etc.

president of this board, but here, and in Mark 5 : 22, it appears to be equivalent to elders. Perhaps the president or ruler invited Paul to speak, after consulting with the other elders.—**Sent to them.** They were sitting with the congregation. Possibly something in the dress of Paul and Barnabas indicated that they were rabbis; Paul had received a regular theological education at Jerusalem from Gamaliel, and thus occupied in Jewish eyes the position of an ordained minister in our own times. Or, perhaps, they had already taught in private in Antioch, and the elders desired to give them an opportunity to explain their views publicly. It was customary to allow in the synagogue service any rabbi to expound the Scripture, and to make it the occasion for explaining the tenets of any new sect or school of Judaism. Comp. with the account here Luke 4 : 16–20.

16. And Paul stood up. The Jews appear to have given their instructions ordinarily, as the Orientals still do in their schools, sitting, and Jesus did so (Matt. 5 : 1; Luke 4 : 20). But the apostles appear to have spoken standing (Acts 1 : 15; 11 : 28; 15 : 7).—**And beckoning with his hand.** As a means of silencing the assembly and securing their attention. There is no reason for regarding this gesture as a peculiarity of Paul. See ch. 12 : 17; 19 : 33. The indication is of a murmur of curiosity to hear the new and strange doctrine, some rumors of which had probably already gone abroad, and a stir in the assembly, when Paul came forward to speak, and this he hushed with an uplifted hand, as a preparation for speaking.—**Men of Israel, and ye that fear God.** Two distinct classes are included by the apostle, *Men of Israel*, are the Hebrews by birth; *ye that fear God*, are Jewish proselytes, converted from heathenism to the worship of Jehovah, and attending the synagogue service. This phrase certainly does not include any Gentiles who did not accept and worship Jehovah.—**Give audience.** He speaks as one who has an important message to deliver, as a herald summoning attention to his proclamation.

17-19. "The beginning of this discourse, verses 17, 18, 19, has three Greek words which are both rare and altogether peculiar to the Scripture (ὕψωσεν, *exalted;* ἐτροποφόρησεν, *suffered their manners;* and κατεκληρονόμησεν, *divided by lot*); of which the first occurs in Isaiah 1 : 2 (*brought up*), the second and third in Deut. 1 : 31, 38. And moreover, these two chapters, Deut. 1 and Isaiah 1, are to this day read on the one Sabbath; whence it is sufficiently certain that both were read on that very Sabbath, and in Greek, and that Paul referred especially to that reading of Moses and the prophets mentioned in ver. 15. For even the mention of the Judges (ver. 20) agrees with the lesson Isaiah 1 : 26, and the Jews are wont to take their discourses, or their beginnings, from the Sabbath lesson in the synagogue."—(*Bengel.*)—**Chose our fathers.** The choice was first manifested in the call of Abraham (Gen. 12 : 1-3), who is the father, not only of the Jews, but of all believers (Matt. 3 : 9; Gal. 3 : 14). This doctrine, that the religion of the Bible, of the O. T. as well as of the N. T., is one which embraces in its promises all peoples, more fully declared by Paul in his epistles, especially to the Romans and the Galatians, is intimated by his language here, *our fathers*, which is addressed to Greek proselytes as well as to the Jews.—**And exalted the people.** Not *brought them up* (*Alford*), a meaning never given in the N. T. to the original (ὑψόω); Isaiah 1 : 2, which he quotes, does not sustain this translation; the original would there be better rendered *exalted*. Nor is the reference here to Joseph's exaltation (*Grotius*), for Paul says that God exalted the *people;* nor to their miraculous deliverance (*Calvin*, *Meyer*), for he says God exalted the people *when they dwelt* (literally, *during their sojourning*) *in the land of Egypt*. Their humiliation was their exaltation. They went thither 75 souls, of separate families; they were compacted by their servility into a united nation, made strong by suffering (ch 7 : 14, 17). So, by the American Revolution, God exalted the American colonists into a great nation.—**And about the time of forty years he nursed them in the wilderness.** This is the best MS. reading (τροφοφορέω, not τροποφορέω). The original is compounded of two Greek verbs, one signifying *a nurse*, the other *to carry;* God is represented as carrying the Israelites in his arms, as a nurse carries the child. See Numb. 11 : 12; Deut. 1 : 31; comp. 1 Thess. 2 : 7. Analogous is the imagery of Isaiah 40 : 11.—**Seven nations.** Deut. 7 : 1; Josh. 3 : 10; 24 : 11, give the names of these seven nations: The Hittites, the Girgashites, the Amorites, the Canaanites, the Perizzites, the Hivites and the Jebusites. They were the descendants of Canaan, and most of them take their names from his children (Gen. 10 : 15-19). They were not utterly destroyed; fragments remained down to and through Solomon's time (1 Kings 9 : 20).

20 And after that, he gave *unto them* judges,[m] about
the space of four hundred and fifty years, until Samuel
the prophet.
21 And afterward they[n] desired a king: and God
gave unto them Saul[o] the son of Cis, a man of the
tribe of Benjamin, by the space of forty years.
22 And when he[p] had removed him, he raised up
unto them David[q] to be their king; to whom also he
gave testimony, and said, I have found David the *son*
of Jesse, a man[r] after mine own heart, which shall ful-
fil all my will.

m Judith 2 : 16.... n 1 Sam. 8 : 5.... o 1 Sam. 10 : 1.... p 1 Sam. 31 : 6.... q 2 Sam. 5 : 3.... r 1 Sam. 13 : 14.

The fact that God ordered their destruction has given rise to much perplexity. Concerning this, it must suffice here to say: (1.) That the divine command to destroy these nations is not more perplexing than the divine providence which has uniformly destroyed or driven out savage tribes to make room for a people possessing a higher civilization. The extermination of the aborigines of Palestine is not a stranger fact, to one who believes in God's controlling providence, than the extermination of the aborigines of North America. (2.) That God deals with nations as well as individuals, and when a nation becomes hopelessly corrupt he destroys it; that in his Word he repeatedly declares this principle of his government in the most solemn manner (Isaiah 5 : 1-6; Jer. 4 : 27-31; Ezek., chaps. 15, 25, 26, etc.); and that Israel was the executioner appointed to inflict his judgment upon an idolatrous, cruel, lascivious, and hopelessly corrupt people. On their character, see Lyman Abbott's *Religious Dict.*, art. Canaanites. —**By Lot.** The division of the land among the twelve tribes was effected by lot, by Joshua (Josh. ch. 13, etc.).

20. And after that he gave judges. The history of the Jewish people may be divided politically into four eras: (1) the formative period under Moses and Joshua; (2) that under the judges, from the death of Joshua to the days of Samuel; (3) that under the kings, from the accession of Saul to the captivity; (4) that in which the remnant of the nation were tributary to and dependent on other nations, from the days of Nehemiah to the destruction of Jerusalem. The judges here mentioned were the executive head of the nation during the period between the occupancy of Palestine under Joshua and the accession of Saul. They were specially raised up and appointed by God for the deliverance and government of the nation; were generally military leaders; were sometimes contemporaries, two governing at the same time in different portions of the country. Their history is all contained in the book of Judges. There were fifteen in all, viz.: Othniel, Ehud, Shamgar, Deborah and Barak, Gideon, Abimelech, Tola, Jair, Jepthah, Ibzan, Elon, Abdon, Samson, Eli and Samuel.—**About the space of four hundred and fifty years.** This agrees with the chronology of Josephus, who allows for the entire period from the Exodus to the building of the temple, 592 years (Ant. 8 : 2-11), that is, in the wilderness 40 years, under Joshua 25 years (Ant. 5 : 1, 29), under judges 443 years, under Saul 40 years, under David 40 years, under Solomon prior to the beginning of the Temple 4 years (1 Kings 6 : 1), total 592. It agrees also with the chronology of the book of Judges, the spaces of time in which book, added together, equal 450 years. It does not agree with 1 Kings 6 : 1, which states that Solomon began the construction of the Temple in the 480th year after the children of Israel were come out of the land of Egypt. Allowing as before 40 years for the wilderness, 25 under Joshua, 80 under Saul and David, and 4 under Solomon, total 149, but 331 years would be left for the period of the Judges. There is, however, good reason to doubt the authenticity of the date given in 1 Kings 6 : 1. It is the only passage in the O. T. which contains the idea of dating from an era. The verse is quoted by Origen without the date, and it is believed by good critics to be an interpolation of the third century. (See *Bible Commentary* on 1 Kings 6 : 1.) Here, at all events, Paul follows the chronology generally received among the Jews, as is evident both from Josephus and from the book of Judges. For other explanations of the seeming discrepancy see *Alford's Greek Testament.*—**Until Samuel the prophet.** So designated, not because the first of the prophets, for Melchizedek, Moses, and others were prophets before him, but because the first of the line of prophetic teachers, which continued without a break from his time down to and through the captivity, and because he organized the school of the prophets, and gave to this form of religious teaching an impulse which was never lost so long as the nation preserved its individuality.

21. And afterward they desired a king. 1 Sam., ch. 8. So little Biblical authority is there for the doctrine of the divine right of kings, that the inauguration of kingly authority in Israel was in the nature of an apostasy. It was demanded by the people, who were dissatisfied with the government which God had appointed, and who desired a king in order to be like the other heathen nations.—**By the space of forty years.** The length of Saul's reign is not mentioned in the O. T.; the statement here agrees with Josephus (Ant. 6 : 14, 9).

22. And when he had removed him. The decree of the removal and the immediate

23 Of this man's seed hath God, according to *his*
promise, raised[s] unto Israel[t] a Saviour, Jesus:
24 When John[u] had first preached, before his coming, the baptism of repentance to all the people of Israel.
25 And as John fulfilled his course, he said, Whom
think ye that I am? I am not *he*. But, behold, there
cometh one after me, whose shoes of *his* feet I am not
worthy to loose.
26 Men *and* brethren, children of the stock of Abraham, and whosoever among you feareth God, to you[v]
is the word of this salvation sent.
27 For they that dwell at Jerusalem, and their rulers, because they knew him not, nor yet the voices of
the prophets which are read every sabbath day, they[w]
have fulfilled *them* in condemning *him*.
28 And though they found no cause of death *in him*,
yet desired they Pilate that he should be slain.
29 And when they had fulfilled all that was written
of him, they took *him* down from the tree, and laid
him in a sepulchre.
30 But God raised him from the dead:
31 And he was seen[x] many days of them which
came up with him from Galilee to Jerusalem, who are
his witnesses unto the people.

s Ps. 132 : 11.... t Matt. 1 : 21.... u Matt. 3 : 1-11.... v Matt. 10 : 6.... w Luke 24 : 20, 44.... x ch. 1 : 3.

cause of it is reported in 1 Sam., ch. 15; David was almost immediately after anointed, privately (1 Sam., ch. 16); but Saul was not finally removed till twenty-five or thirty years later, when slain on the field of battle, and not till then was David publicly recognized as king.—**To whom also he gave testimony.** No passage in the O. T. exactly corresponds to the language here. The reference is probably to 1 Sam. 15 : 14; comp. Psalm 89 : 20, 21. The latter clause of the sentence here interprets the first clause; David was a man after God's own heart, because the dominant purpose of his life was to do God's will, not his own, and to exalt God, not himself. In this respect he was a type of the Messiah. (Psalm 40 : 7; Heb. 10 : 7). If Deut. ch. 1 was the Scripture lesson for the day (see vers. 17, 18, note), we have a key to the structure of Paul's discourse. He begins there, with Exodus, and leads on, by a rapid historical *résumé*, to the time of David, through whom the Messiah was promised to Israel.

23. According to his promise. See Psalm 89 : 35-37; 132 : 11; Isaiah 11 : 1-10; Jer. 23 : 5, 6; 33 : 15, 16. These promises were so explicit that it was the uniform belief of the Pharisees that the Messiah would be of the seed of David. See Matt. 22 : 42.—**Raised unto Israel.** Rather, *Brought unto Israel.* (The best reading is ἤγαγεν not ἤγειρεν.) The original does not imply that the Messiah was raised up *for* Israel, to the exclusion of others, but brought *unto* Israel, whether for them only, or for others through them, is not indicated.—**When John had first preached.** *Heralded*, going before, as a courier before the king. See Luke 3 : 1-18. Christ did not begin his public ministry till John's was closed by his imprisonment (Matt. 4 : 12). As the clearest prophecies of the Messiah's coming were made to and through David, so the last were made by John, whose preaching had aroused the whole nation; the rumors of it doubtless had extended among all the dispersed Jews (Matt. 3 : 5; John 1 : 35, 44; Acts 19 : 3).—**To all the people of Israel.** Not that he had preached to all Israel, for his ministry was local, confined not only to Palestine, but apparently to one locality in Palestine; but he preached the necessity of repentance to all, Pharisee and Sadducee as well as publican (Matt. 3 : 7, 8).—**As John fulfilled his course.** His appointed mission. He filled it to the full and departed; Christ's mission is not fulfilled and will not be till the end come, and he see of the travail of his soul and is satisfied.—**He said.** *Was accustomed to say.* The imperfect tense carries with it the idea of habitual action. For illustration of such saying see John 1 : 19-23. For explanation of metaphor of shoe-latchet, see Matt. 3 : 11, note.

26-28. Children of the stock of Abraham, and whoever among you feareth God. This includes both Jews and those Gentiles who accepted Jehovah as their God, and this whether they had been circumcised or no. See on verse 16.—**To you.** Some MSS. have *to us;* Tischendorf adopts that reading; Alford retains the reading of the text.—**The word of this salvation.** The news that such a Saviour has come into the world. Observe that, impliedly, faith in and allegiance to one Supreme God is a condition precedent to the acceptance of Christianity; the Gospel is offered only to those *that fear God.* On the nature of the fear here indicated, see ch. 9 : 31, note. —**Because they knew him not.** The rulers then did not recognize in Jesus the Messiah of prophecy. With this agrees ch. 3 : 17; and it interprets Christ's prayer (Luke 23 : 34), showing it applicable to all who partook in the crucifixion.—**Nor yet the voices of the prophets.** See 2 Cor. 3 : 14. For explanation of this ignorance see Matt. 13 : 14, 15. The same ignorance exists to-day, not only among the Jews, but in all who either read the Bible with indifference and unconcern, or interpret it through their prejudices and prepossessions. Observe that ignorance is not always an excuse for sin.—**Have fulfilled them in condemning him.** See ch. 2 : 23, note.—**Though they found no cause of death in him, yet desired they Pilate that he should be slain.** This is literally true. Even in the trial before the Sanhedrim, no ground for Christ's condemnation could be made out by even suborned witnesses (Matt. 26 : 60), and he was at last condemned to die on his own declaration of his

32 And we declare unto you glad tidings, how that
the promise[y] which was made unto the fathers,
33 God hath fulfilled the same unto us their children,
in that he hath raised up Jesus again; as it is also
written in the second psalm, Thou[z] art my Son, this
day have I begotten thee.
34 And as concerning that he raised him up from
the dead, *now* no more to return to corruption, he
said on this wise, I will give you the sure mercies of
David.
35 Wherefore he saith also in[a] another *psalm*, Thou
shalt not suffer thine Holy One to see corruption.
36 For David, after he had served his own generation by the will of God, fell[b] on sleep, and was laid
unto his fathers, and saw corruption:
37 But he, whom God[c] raised again, saw no corruption.

y Rom. 4 : 13....z Ps. 2 : 7....a Ps. 16 : 10....b 1 Kings 2 : 10....c ch. 2 : 24.

mission, demanded of him by the high-priest. When brought before Pilate the priesthood were equally unable to assign a cause for the sentence which they required (Luke 23 : 22, 23).

29-31. They took him down from the tree. The body of Jesus was taken down and entombed by friends, Joseph of Arimathea and Nicodemus (John 19 : 38-42), but it was done by permission of Pilate, and the tomb was afterward sealed and a watch set by the Pharisees and by Pilate's direction (Matt. 27 : 62-66). Thus, here, Paul, who enters into no detail, treats the entombing as part of the endeavor of Christ's foes to insure his utter destruction, and as increasing, as it did, the triumph of his resurrection.—**But God raised him from the dead.** He passes by the crucifixion in a word, to dwell on the resurrection as the great and indisputable evidence of Christ's mission and authority. So also Peter in chaps. 2 and 3, and Paul in 1 Cor., ch. 15.—**Who are his witnesses unto the people.** Of the evidence of the resurrection of Jesus, see Vol. I, p. 330.

32-37. The apostle now comes to the conclusion of his sermon, to which he has gradually led the way by this historical summary, viz., the glad tidings that the promised Messiah has come to Israel, this fact being certified by the resurrection of Jesus from the dead.—**The promise which was made unto the fathers.** The apostle treats the O. T., with all its types and prophecies, as one promise of a Messiah, who should be both a Prince and a Deliverer.—**In that he hath raised up Jesus.** Not *again*, which does not represent any equivalent expression in the original. Some scholars understand that Paul here refers to the fact that God raised up Jesus by sending him into the world to fulfill the special mission of salvation. For analogous use of the same phraseology, see Exod. 9 : 16; Judges 2 : 16; Luke 1 : 69; Acts 3 : 22. It is so interpreted here by Calvin, Bengel, Olshausen, and Alexander. In support of this view is the fact that Psalm 2 : 7, Thou art my Son, this day have I begotten thee, refers not to the resurrection, but to the incarnation of Jesus Christ. Others understand that Paul here refers to the resurrection of Jesus from the dead. So Luther, Meyer, Alford, Hackett. This seems to me clearly the correct view. (1) It agrees with the context; for Paul is speaking here not of the incarnation, but of the resurrection; (2) it best agrees with the original, the verb rendered *raised up* (ανίστημι) when used by Paul of Christ being always employed to designate the resurrection; (3) it does not disagree with the Psalm; for though Christ was not begotten as the Son of God on the day of his resurrection, that resurrection is the chief external evidence that he is in a peculiar sense the Son of God.—**Second Psalm.** Some MSS. have *first* Psalm, what we now regard as the first Psalm having been regarded in ancient times by some as an introduction to the whole collection. The reference is to Psalm 2 : 7.—**Now no more to return to corruption.** Comp. Rom. 6 : 9, and observe in the analogy of the language one of the numerous parallels between Paul's speeches in the Book of Acts and his epistles.—**I will give you the sure mercies of David.** That is, the assured mercies promised to David—*sure*, because promised by Him whose word cannot be broken; *mercies*, because not deserved, and not bestowed on the ground of desert, but out of God's free, unbought love. Chief among these mercies was the promise to raise up of David's seed a Messiah unto Israel. See verse 23, note and ref. See also Psalm 89.—**After he had served his own generation.** Or, as in the margin, *served in his own generation.* Either translation is admissible; the former is preferable, in that it brings out more clearly the truth that he served *men* in obeying the will of God. Observe that only thus can we serve God, by obeying his will in serving our fellow-men (Matt. 25 : 31-46).—**Fell on sleep.** An old English expression, equivalent to *fell asleep.* It indicates a peaceful death, in the inner experience, not necessarily in the outer circumstances, for it is used of the martyr Stephen (ch. 7 : 60). It is employed in the O. T. in describing David's death (1 Kings 2 : 10). The argument of Paul here is precisely the same in spirit with, though different in form from, that of Peter in ch. 2 : 25-31. See notes there. David speaks primarily of himself; his hope of immortality for himself and all the saints of God was realized in the undying life of the soul; but the body was made subject to decay, and saw corruption;

38 Be it known unto you therefore, men *and* brethren, that through[d] this man is preached unto you the forgiveness of sins:
39 And by him,[e] all that believe are justified from all things, from which ye could not be justified by the law of Moses.
40 Beware, therefore, lest that come upon you, which is spoken of in[f] the prophets;
41 Behold, ye despisers, and wonder, and perish: for I work a work in your days, a work which ye shall in no wise believe, though a man declare it unto you.
42 And when the Jews were gone out of the syna-

d Dan. 9 : 24; Luke 24 : 47; 1 John 2 : 12.... e Isa. 53 : 11; Hab. 2 : 4; Rom. 3 : 28; 8 : 1.... f Isa. 29 : 14: Hab. 1 : 5.

Christ saw *no* corruption; his body knew not the dissolution of death; and in him, not in David, was the hope of the Psalmist fully realized.

38, 39. Be it known therefore to you, men, brethren, that through this one to you is proclaimed the remission of sins; and from all from which you could not, in the law of Moses, be justified, in him every one having faith is justified. Comp. carefully with the English verse this, which is as nearly as possible a literal translation of the original. The passage itself is one of special importance, because it is the *first clear enunciation by Paul of the doctrine of justification by faith alone, which forms the central truth of Pauline theology.* For his fuller statement of this doctrine, see Rom., chaps. 1–3, and notes there. Observe here, (1) that Paul does not say, as in our English version, through *this man;* there is not in the original the verbal infelicity involved in representing the remission of sins by or through *man,* or even through Jesus Christ as the Son of man; (2) that which is proclaimed is not merely the *forgiveness,* but the *remission, i. e.,* the putting away of sins, as explained by Psalm 51 : 1, 9; Isaiah 1 : 18; Micah 7 : 19 (comp. Matt. 1 : 21, note); (3) that the doctrine of the absolute remission of sins was proclaimed in the O. T. in these and many kindred passages, and by abundant symbols (see John 1 : 29, note), but that it was reserved for the N. T. to reveal clearly the One through whom this remission of sins is afforded, by whose voluntary sacrifice God can be both just and the justifier of them that believe; (4) that the latter clause (ver. 39) is not additional to, but explanatory of, the preceding clause (ver. 38); there are not two things proclaimed, the remission of sins *and* justification, but remission of sins, which is explained *to include* justification from all things from which the law could not justify; (5) that in ver. 39, Paul does not intimate that the law justifies from some things and Christ completes the work, justifying from those things from which the law cannot, for the law is wholly without power to justify (Rom. 3 : 20; 8 : 3; Gal. 3 : 11); the language here is equivalent to *From all* (*sins*) *every one having faith is justified in him, from* (*none of*) *which sins could ye be justified in the law;* (6) *in the law* is not equivalent to *by the law;* the declaration is much broader than our English translation renders it; not only we cannot be justified *by* the law, but we cannot while remaining in (*under*) it, and endeavoring to secure divine favor by works of merit of our own; see Gal. 5 : 4; Phil. 3 : 9; (7) *in him* is to be construed not with believe, but with justified; *i. e.,* Paul does not say every one *believing in him* is justified, but every one having faith is *justified in him;* Cornelius was justified *in* Christ, having faith in the divine grace and goodness before the news of Christ's sacrifice for sin had been proclaimed to him (ch. 10); (8) beware of taking the phrase which I have rendered *having faith* (πιστεύων) as equivalent to *believing,* in the intellectual sense; the original rarely, if ever, has that signification in the N. T., certainly not here; to have faith is to trust in the mercy of God simply, in contrast with the spirit which seeks to stand in the divine presence on the ground, in whole or in part, of personal merit, or righteousness, or works wrought; (9) on the meaning of the term *justified,* see Rom. 3 : 20–31, notes; here it must suffice to say that to be *justified* is not, in Paul's use of the term, if ever in the N. T., to be *made* just or righteous, but to be put in the place of one against whom no sentence of condemnation has been pronounced; it is interpreted by such passages as Rom. 8 : 1. Some of my statements in this note involve disputed points in criticism and theology. To enter into these discussions would far transcend the limits of this work. Incidentally, the different points are elsewhere discussed in this Commentary, as indicated by the references given.

40, 41. Paul closes his address by a warning against rejecting the Gospel, possibly incited thereto by signs of that opposition which the declaration that its offer of mercy was to *every one having faith* always provoked among the Jews, and which broke out in violent and blasphemous opposition here (ver. 45). The quotation is from Habakkuk 1 : 5, and follows the Septuagint; for variations between that and the Hebrew, comp. the language here with that in Habakkuk. The prediction there refers to judgments to be inflicted by the Chaldean armies on the Jewish nation. Observe that Paul does not here say that this prophecy was about to be fulfilled. He simply uses the language of the prophet to enforce his own warning, "as if he had said, 'Be upon your guard, lest, by rejecting the salvation which I have now offered in the name of your Messiah, you should call down judgments on yourselves as fearful and incredi-

gogue, the Gentiles besought that these words might
be preached to them he next sabbath.
43 Now when the congregation was broken up,
many of the Jews and religious proselytes followed
Paul and Barnabas: who, speaking to them, persuaded them to continue[g] in the grace of God.
44 And the next sabbath day came almost the whole
city together, to hear the word of God.
45 But when the Jews saw the multitudes, they were
filled with envy, and spake against those things which
were spoken by Paul, contradicting[h] and blaspheming.
46 Then Paul and Barnabas waxed bold, and said,
It was necessary that the word of God should first[i]
have been spoken to you: but seeing ye put it from
you, and judge yourselves unworthy of everlasting life,
lo, we[j] turn to the Gentiles.
47 For so hath the Lord commanded us, *saying*, I[k]
have set thee to be a light of the Gentiles, that thou
shouldest be for salvation unto the ends of the earth.

---

g ch. 14 : 22; Heb. 6 : 11, 12; 12 : 15....h ch. 18 : 6....i Matt. 10 : 6; Luke 24 : 47; Rom. 1 : 16....j Deut. 32 : 21; Matt. 21 : 43; Rom. 10 : 19.... k Isa. 49 : 6.

---

ble as those predicted by Habakkuk and inflicted by the hands of the Chaldeans on our unbelieving fathers.' "—(*Alexander.*)

42, 43. But as they were going out of the synagogue they besought that these words might be preached to them. This is the best reading, and is adopted by both Alford and Tischendorf. It has been changed to the form in our English version, probably because it was considered necessary to show that this request was preferred by the Gentiles, otherwise it would be inconsistent with the hostility of the Jews indicated in verse 45. In fact, however, the change in popular sentiment is just such as often occurs where convictions are not deeply settled; moreover it is neither necessary to suppose that all the Jews united in this request, or in that persecution.—**The next Sabbath.** Or, *The Sabbath between.* The original is capable of either translation, but that of our English version is adopted by the best critics (Meyer, Alford, Alexander and Hackett); if the other be adopted the meaning will be, on one of the week-day meetings of the synagogue. These were held on Monday and Thursday, and are said to have been arranged by Ezra.—**Now when the congregation was broken up.** Dismissed; set free. —**Many of the Jews and religious proselytes.** Literally, *The worshipping strangers;* here, the Greeks who accepted Jehovah as their God, and worshipped with the Jews. On the proselytes, and their division into two classes, see Matt. 23 : 15, note.—**To remain in the grace of God.** Or, *Of the Lord*, *i. e.*, Christ; there is good authority for either reading. The burden of the apostolic preaching was that they should accept salvation as a free gift, and rest on the free grace of God, not on their own obedience to the law. Comp. Phil. 3 : 9.

44, 45. Came almost the whole city together. To the synagogue. The throng embraced both Jew and Gentile; not merely the proselytes, but also those who had not theretofore accepted Judaism. It was this thronging of their synagogue by the Gentiles which aroused the opposition of the Jews. "They could not endure the notion of others being freely admitted to the same religious privileges with themselves. This was always the sin of the Jewish people. Instead of realizing their position in the world as the prophetic nation, for the good of the whole earth, they indulged the self-exalting opinion that God's highest blessings were only for themselves." — (*Conybeare and Howson.*) The same feeling still underlies race and national pride and prejudice. — **Filled with envy.** Rather, *With zeal.* On the meaning of the word (ζῆλος) see ch. 5 : 17, note. It is literally *heat* or *boiling.*—**Contradicting and blaspheming.** Not only opposing by argument, but also by sneers, and denunciation, and evil speaking. To *blaspheme* is here, not to take God's name in vain, but to speak evil and slanderous words. In the first centuries various forms of licentiousness and unnatural crime were charged upon the Christians, for the purpose of bringing them and their doctrines into disrepute.

46, 47. Then Paul and Barnabas speaking, boldly said. They had before implied (see ver. 26), rather than openly and freely asserted, the universality of the offer of salvation.—**It was necessary that the word of God should first have been spoken to you.** Not, *It was proper*, nor, *It was our duty*, but, *It was necessary;* because it was the divine purpose, that the Jews should have the opportunity to accept and become themselves the bearers to others of the message of salvation. See ch. 3 : 26; Rom. 1 : 16.—**Since ye thrust it away.** As Christ rejected the human (John 6 : 15) so these the divine crown. Comp. for meaning of the word and illustration of their Spirit ch. 7 : 27, 39; 1 Tim. 1 : 19. See also Luke 19 : 14.—**And judge yourselves not worthy of eternal life.** Observe that as every soul by its memory keeps the record of its own life (Luke 16 : 25), so every soul utters its own condemnation. We are daily judging ourselves unworthy of divine grace in every act of refusal to accept and rely upon it.—**We turn to the Gentiles.** Hitherto their preaching had been to the Jews; the Gentiles had been only incidentally included in their meaning. So Wesley and Whitfield went to the fields to preach when the pulpits were closed against them.—**So hath the Lord commanded.** The quotation is from Isaiah 49 : 6.

48 And when the Gentiles heard this, they were
glad, and glorified the word of the Lord: and as many[l]
as were ordained to eternal life, believed.
49 And the word of the Lord was published throughout all the region.
50 But the Jews stirred up the devout and honourable
women, and the chief men of the city, and raised[m]
persecution against Paul and Barnabas, and expelled
them out of their coasts.
51 But they shook[n] off the dust of their feet against
them, and came unto Iconium.
52 And the disciples were filled with joy,[o] and with
the Holy Ghost.

l ch. 2 : 47; Rom. 8 : 30.... m 2 Tim. 3 : 11.... n ch. 18 : 6; Mark 6 : 11; Luke 9 : 5.... o Matt. 5 : 12; 1 Thess. 1 : 6.

The command there is clearly given to Christ, and to his ministers only through him. Comp. with it Matt. 4 : 16; 8 : 11.

48. They were glad. Not all the Gentiles; but as it was characteristic of the Jews that they contradicted and blasphemed the Gospel, so it was characteristic of the Gentiles that they rejoiced in and honored it.—**As many as were ordained to eternal life believed.** This verse is a battle-ground. By Calvin and by Calvinistic commentators generally it is regarded as a proof-text of the doctrine of predestination. "This ordaining can be referred only to the eternal decree of God. It is a ridiculous cavil to refer it to the mind of those who believed, as if they received the Gospel who were properly disposed in their minds."—(*Calvin.*) The Arminian commentators understand the word rendered *ordained* as indicating not the will of God, but the disposition of the believers. So, apparently, Adam Clarke: "The verb (τάττω or τάσσω) signifies to place, set, order, appoint, dispose; hence it has been considered here as implying the disposition or readiness of mind of several persons in the congregation, such as the religious proselytes mentioned (ver. 43), who possessed the reverse of the disposition of those Jews who spake against those things, contradicting and blaspheming." An intermediate view is taken by some commentators; thus Alford: "The Jews had judged themselves unworthy of eternal life: the Gentiles, as many as were disposed to eternal life, believed. By whom so disposed is not here declared; nor need the word be in this place further particularized. We know that it is God who worketh in us the will to believe, and that the preparation of the heart is of Him: but to find in this text pre-ordination to life asserted, is to force both the word and the context to a meaning which they do not contain." That the word here rendered *ordained* signifies not merely a disposition of mind in the actor, but a determination or decision affecting him by some one else, and here by God, is, I think, clear from the following considerations: (1) the form of the verb which is the passive participle; they *were disposed by* some power or influence acting upon them; (2) from the verb itself (τάσσω) which signifies not a mere mental disposition or choice, but a determination or decree. For its use by Luke, see Luke 7 : 8; Acts 15 : 2; 22 : 10; 28 : 23; (3) from other parallel teachings of the N. T., which represent faith as the result of divine grace, working in the heart of the believer. For Luke's recognition of this truth, see Luke 7 : 8; Acts 2 : 47; 5 : 14; 22 : 10. Comp. 1 Cor. 3 : 6; Phil. 2 : 13; Rom. 8 : 29, 30.

ICONIUM—KONIYEH.

CHAPTER XIV.

AND it came to pass in Iconium, that they went both together into the synagogue of the Jews, and so spake, that a great multitude, both of the Jews and also of the Greeks, believed.
2 But the unbelieving Jews stirred up the Gentiles, and made their minds evil affected against the brethren.
3 Long time therefore abode they speaking boldly in the Lord, which gave[p] testimony unto the word of his grace, and granted signs and wonders to be done by their hands.
4 But the multitude of the city was divided: and part[q] held with the Jews, and part with the apostles.
5 And when there was an assault made, both of the Gentiles and also of the Jews, with their rulers, to use *them* despitefully, and to stone them,
6 They were ware of *it*, and fled[r] unto Lystra and Derbe, cities of Lycaonia, and unto the region that lieth round about:

p Mark 16 : 20; Heb. 2 : 4. . . . q ch. 28 : 24. . . . r Matt. 10 : 23.

But there is certainly nothing in this passage to indicate that the divine disposing of the Gentiles to believe was an eternal or an irresistible decree; nothing more is indicated than an effectual work of grace, accepted by the Gentiles and for that reason effectual.

49-52. Was published throughout all the region. Not by the Apostles, for the history goes on with the record of their personal labors, but by the private ministry of the new disciples, as in ch. 8 : 14; 11 : 19.—**But the Jews stirred up the devout and honorable women.** That is, Jewish proselytes of social influence. *Honorable* refers to social position, not to personal character. Women exerted a strong influence both for and against Christianity. It was probably by them that the opposition of the chief men of the city was incited. To the persecution here mentioned Paul refers in 1 Tim. 3 : 11.—**They shook off the dust off their feet.** As Christ directed in the first commission of the twelve. See Matt. 10 : 14 and note there for explanation of this symbolic act.

Iconium. A considerable city of Asia Minor, generally considered as belonging to Lycaonia. It lay in a fertile plain at the foot of Taurus, on the great line of communication between Ephesus and the more eastern cities of Tarsus and Antioch, and the Euphrates. From Pliny's description it would appear to have been a populous and important city at the time of Paul's visit. Under the Byzantine emperors it was the metropolis of Lycaonia, was subsequently captured by the Turks and made the capital of an empire whose sovereigns took the title of Sultans of Iconium. During this period of its history it acquired its greatest celebrity. It is now called Koniyeh, has a population variously estimated from twenty to thirty thousand. The houses are mostly of stone or sun-dried brick, and are poorly built, except the mosques and palaces. The place contains some remains and inscriptions, mostly of the Byzantine period. —**And the disciples were filled with joy.** A practical commentary on Matt. 5 : 11, 12. Comp. Acts 5 : 41. The *disciples* are not merely Paul and Barnabas, but also the new converts.

Ch. 14 : 1-28. THE MISSIONARY TOUR OF THE APOSTLES CONTINUED. THE GOSPEL A SWORD (Matt. 10 : 34)—CREDULITY IS AS ANTAGONISTIC TO THE GOSPEL AS SKEPTICISM.—THE APOSTLES BUT SERVANTS; CHRIST THE ONLY DIVINE MASTER.—THE APOSTLES' MISSIONARY ARGUMENT TO PAGANS.

For some account of the general region through which the apostles passed in this chapter see Prel. Note, p. 144.

1-3. The length of this ministry in Iconium is not known; in so rapid a missionary journey a few months would answer to the description here, *a long time*. The *Greeks* who believed were probably Jewish proselytes, since they attended the synagogue service; the public ministry of the apostles in Iconium appears to have been confined to the synagogues. How the unbelieving Jews evil affected the minds of the Gentiles is not indicated; not impossibly by exciting political prejudice against them as preachers of another kingdom and another king than Cæsar (ch. 16 : 20, 21); or it may be that their ministry against idolatry was made an occasion for provoking a Gentile persecution (ch. 19 : 26); or there may be some historical basis for the Roman Catholic legend of St. Thecla. According to this story she was converted by the apostle's preaching, and refused to marry her betrothed; the refusal resulted in Paul's imprisonment and banishment. See Conybeare and Howson, Vol. I, ch. 6, or Mrs. Jameson's *Sacred and Legendary Art*, Vol. II, p. 556. The language here, *evil affected against the brethren*, which term is a customary N. T. designation of Christian disciples (ch. 15 : 1, 3, 22, 23, etc.) indicates, however, not a mere personal opposition to Paul, but an enmity aroused against all the Christain converts.

4-7. The populace of the city was divided. The division of sentiment affected not merely the worshippers in the synagogue, but the people throughout the city. Such public contentions were not uncommon in the heterogeneous populations of these Grecian cities.—**And when there was a purpose * * * to use them despitefully.** Not, *an assault made.* Of course they would have been aware of that.—**And fled.** As Christ had directed (Matt. 10 : 23). Prudence is the twin of true courage.—**Lystra and Derbe.** The site of both towns is uncertain. *Lystra* was undoubtedly in the eastern part of the great plain of Lycaonia; and there

7 And there they preached the gospel.
8 And there sat a certain man at Lystra, impotent in
his feet, being a cripple[s] from his mother's womb, who
never had walked:
9 The same heard Paul speak: who stedfastly beholding him, and perceiving that he had faith[t] to be
healed,
10 Said with a loud voice, Stand upright on thy feet.
And he leaped[u] and walked.
11 And when the people saw what Paul had done,
they lifted up their voices, saying in the speech of Lycaonia, The gods[v] are come down to us in the likeness
of men.
12 And they called Barnabas, Jupiter; and Paul,
Mercurius, because he was the chief speaker.

s ch. 3 : 2. . . . t Matt. 9 : 28, 29. . . . u Isa. 35 : 6. . . . v ch. 28 : 6.

are very strong reasons for identifying its site with the ruins called Bin-bir-Kilisseh, at the base of a conical mountain of volcanic structure, named the Karadagh. Here are the remains of a great number of churches; and it should be noticed that Lystra has its post-apostolic Christian history, the names of its bishops appearing in the records of early councils. *Derbe* was in the eastern part of the great upland plain of Lycaonia, somewhere near the place where the pass called the Cilician Gates opened a way from the low plain of Cilicia to the table-land of the interior; and probably it was a stage upon the great road which passed this way. Lystra was the home of Timothy, and as he knew of the persecutions suffered by Paul in this tour (2 Tim. 3 : 10, 11), and was already a disciple at the time of Paul's second visit to Lystra (Acts 16 : 1), it is reasonably surmised that his conversion to Christianity took place at this time; that he was converted under Paul's ministry, is indicated by 1 Cor. 4 : 15, 17. It is a notable evidence of the accuracy of Luke's narrative that no persecution in Derbe is indicated in this chapter, and none in Paul's reference in 2 Tim. 3 : 10, 11, to the persecutions suffered during this journey. — **Lycaonia.** One of the provinces of Asia Minor, formerly within the limits of Phrygia, but made a separate province by Augustus. It is a bare and dreary region, unwatered by streams, though in parts liable to occasional inundations. The Lycaonians seem to have had a language, or rather a dialect, of their own, but we have no traces of it remaining. The best authorities speak of it merely as a corrupt Greek. The people were a fierce and warlike race, never fully subdued by the Persians, and conquered rather than amalgamated by the Greeks.—**They were preaching the Gospel.** The imperfect tense indicates a ministry extending over some period of time.

8-10. There sat a certain man. No mention is made of any synagogue in Lystra; it is therefore probable that Paul was preaching in the market-place (see ch. 17 : 17) or in some broad thoroughfare of the city. In a similar manner the missionaries of to-day avail themselves of the squares and public streets as preaching places. The lame man was sitting near by, perhaps brought hither to beg, as the one mentioned in ch. 3 : 2.—**Who never had walked.** An indication of the hopeless nature of his disease.—**The same was hearing.** (ἤκουεν, imperfect tense.) Not merely *heard*, but *was listening* to Paul.—**Who * * * perceived that he had faith to be saved** (σωθῆναι). This is the literal meaning of the original and I believe its meaning here; if so, what Paul perceived in the cripple was not an expectation of a miraculous cure, but a spiritual acceptance of the Gospel of Christ. This made the remedy possible. This faith Paul perceived in the expression of the countenance. There is no implication of any supernatural knowledge; rather the reverse; it was in *stedfastly beholding him* that Paul perceived his faith. —**With a loud voice.** Raising his voice to attract the cripple's attention.—**Stand upright on thy feet.** It is noteworthy that Paul, in performing this miracle, makes no reference to Christ or to God. This remarkable omission may be due to the brevity of Luke's narrative; or it may be that the theme of Paul's preaching was the life and ministry of Christ and especially his miracles, and rendered the usual reference to the Lord as the source of his own authority unnecessary; or may we consider that the misapprehension of the people, as indicated by their endeavor to offer sacrifices to Paul and Barnabas, was possibly partly due to the unintentional failure of the apostle to make unmistakably apparent the divine source of his authority?—**He leaped and walked.** An indication that the cure was instantaneous and complete.

11, 12. In the speech of Lycaonia. The nature of this speech, probably a corrupted dialect of the Greek, is not known with any certainty. The fact is here stated to explain why the apostles did not earlier interfere. The people generally would have understood the Greek language in which Paul spoke, but he would not have understood the native dialect of the people, especially in the babble and confusion of voices which ensued.—**The gods are come down to us in the likeness of men.** The Greek and Roman gods were deified men; it was not therefore strange that the people should believe, as they did, that these gods would on occasion visit the earth in human likeness. — **Jupiter * * * Mercurius.** *Jupiter*, "the heavenly father," was the highest and most powerful among the gods, had control over all changes in

13 Then the priest of Jupiter, which was before their
city, brought oxen and garlands unto the gates, and
would[w] have done sacrifice with the people.
14 *Which* when the apostles, Barnabas and Paul,
heard *of*, they[x] rent their clothes, and ran in among
the people, crying out,
15 And saying, Sirs, why do ye these things? We[y]
also are men of like passions with you, and preach
unto you, that ye should turn from these vanities[z]
unto[a] the living God, which made heaven,[b] and earth,
and the sea, and all things that are therein:
16 Who[c] in times past suffered all nations to walk in
their own ways.
17 Nevertheless,[d] he left not himself without witness, in that he did good, and gave us rain[e] from heaven, and fruitful seasons, filling our hearts with food
and gladness.

w Dan. 2 : 46....x Matt. 26 : 65....y ch. 10 : 26; James 5 : 17; Rev. 19 : 10....z 1 Sam. 12 : 21; 1 Kings 16 : 13; Jer. 14 : 22; Jonah 2 : 8; 1 Cor. 8 : 4....a 1 Thess. 1 : 9....b Gen. 1 : 1; Ps. 33 : 6; 146 : 6; Rev. 14 : 7....c ch. 17 : 30; Ps. 81 : 12....d Rom. 1 : 20....e Job 5 : 10; Ps. 147 : 8; Matt. 5 : 45.

the heavens, determined the course of all earthly affairs, was the guardian of the law, and was invoked at the beginning of every undertaking, and publicly worshipped at the return from every successful campaign. *Mercurius* was the messenger of the gods, hence the god of eloquence and prudence, qualities combined in the classical representations of him with cunning, fraud, perjury, and even theft. He was also a customary companion of other deities and attended Jupiter in his expeditions. Each of the Grecian cities was supposed to be under the especial protection of some deity; Jupiter appears to have been the tutelary deity of Lystra, and his temple, or possibly his statue, stood just outside the walls of the city (ver. 13). It was a common belief among the ancients that the gods occasionally visited the earth in the form of men, and Ovid (Met., B. 1, v. 211) has preserved a special tradition of such a visit by Jupiter and Mercury to the house of Lycaon, the supposed founder of one of the principal cities of Lycaonia. Thus the account here given of the reception accorded to the apostles agrees singularly with what we know of the character of the people and their traditions. Observe that it is Barnabas and not Paul who is regarded as Jupiter, and compare this with the statement of his enemies that his bodily presence is weak (2 Cor. 10 : 10); hence we may reasonably surmise that he was of small stature. Of his power as a speaker, the Book of Acts affords many illustrations.

13, 14. But the priest of the Jupiter which was before their city. There is better authority for reading *city* than *gates*, but the meaning in either case is substantially the same; his temple or statue stood probably at or near the chief entrance to the city.—**Brought oxen and garlands.** The former to sacrifice, the latter either to decorate the animals or to crown the apostles, or decorate their house. The annexed illustration of an ancient sacrifice and altar, which represents the essential features of this scene, is from an antique medal.—**Unto the doors.** Not the *gates* of the city, but the door or gate leading into the court-yard of the house where the apostles were. Paul had finished his sermon and gone into the house, and knew nothing of what was going on, until the priest and the multitude appeared in the street. This is implied both here and in the language of the next verse.—**But the apostles, Barnabas and Paul, hearing.** Not *hearing of* the popular impulse by the reports of others, but *hearing the tumult* before their doors.—**Rending their clothes.** To the Jew a natural symbol of grief or horror.—**Rushed forth among the people.** That is, from the house. The language implies intense vehemence of action. They were horror-stricken at the idea that the result of their ministry, the object of which had been to lead these heathens to Jesus Christ as their Saviour, had, in fact, brought them to offer an idolatrous worship to his apostles.

ANCIENT SACRIFICE AND ALTAR.

15. We are also of like passions with yourselves, men. Emphasis is placed on the phrase *of like passions*.—**And herald unto you as glad tidings.** This message is *glad tidings* because it is not merely a command to abandon idolatry, but also a revelation of the true God. —**That ye should turn from these vanities.** That is, from these vain and profitless gods. Comp. Ps. 115 : 4-8; Isaiah 40 : 18-20; 42 : 17, 18. In contrast with these inanities is the *living God.* God is frequently thus described in the Bible, especially by Paul. See Rom. 9 : 26; 2 Cor. 3 : 3; 6 : 16; 1 Thess. 1 : 9; 1 Tim. 3 : 15; 4 : 10. In a peculiar sense the preaching of Jesus Christ as the incarnation of the Deity was a preaching of a living God, *i. e.*, of a personal being entering into sympathetic relations with man. See Matt. 16 : 16, note. —**Which made heaven and earth,** etc. The Greeks generally did not regard the gods as the creators of material things; matter was eternal; the gods

18 And with these sayings scarce restrained they the people, that they had not done sacrifice unto them.
19 And there came thither *certain* Jews from Antioch and Iconium, who persuaded the people, and, having stoned[f] Paul, drew *him* out of the city, supposing he had been dead.
20 Howbeit, as the disciples stood round about him, he rose up, and came into the city: and the next day he departed with Barnabas to Derbe.
21 And when they had preached the gospel to that city, and had taught many, they returned again to Lystra, and *to* Iconium, and Antioch,

f 2 Cor. 11 : 25.

themselves were created in time; thus Zeus was the son of Chronos and Rhea, and Mercury was the son of Zeus, or Jupiter; and in their mythology the various domains of nature had each its own deity.

16, 17. Who, in bygone generations, suffered all the Gentiles to walk in their own ways. The word (ἔθνος) rendered *nation* is capable of either that rendering or the one I have given. The latter meaning seems best to suit both the context and the actual facts. The law was given only to the *Jews;* the *Gentiles* were left without any other law than that afforded by nature and conscience. — **Nevertheless, he left not himself without witness,** etc. Observe that the essential element in the argument from nature, as the apostle presents it, is the *beneficence* of God—the adaptation of nature to provide for the wants of man, both those of the body and of the heart: he did good, gave us rain, filled our hearts. The reference to rain was specially significant in a province where water was so scarce that it is said to have been sometimes sold for money. The authorship of this speech is confirmed by some striking coincidences between the phraseology employed here and elsewhere by the same speaker. See Acts 17 : 30; Rom. 3 : 25; 1 Thess. 1 : 9. Especially should the student examine Rom., chaps. 1, 2, where Paul elaborates the argument. He there explains why God left the nations to their own ways, viz., because they first left him, describes what those ways were, and draws clearly the contrast between the Jews who know the law, and the Gentiles who are without it.

18, 19. The revulsion in public sentiment indicated in these verses is not without parallels in both sacred and secular history; and the Lycaonians were a notoriously fickle people. Mr. Howson suggests that the Jews who came from Antioch and Iconium attributed the miracle of healing to diabolical agency, as did the Pharisees in the case of Christ and his miracles (Matt. 12 : 24). The popular interpretation of what they had witnessed having been disavowed by the apostles, the people would readily adopt a new interpretation, suggested by those who appeared to be well acquainted with the strangers, and who had followed them from distant cities. Paul refers to the stoning here mentioned in 2 Cor. 11 : 25, "Once I was stoned." From a comparison of the account here and in ver. 5, with Paul's reference in 2 Corinthians, Dr. Paley draws a forcible argument for the authenticity of Luke's account. "Had the assault (in Iconium) been completed, had the history related that a stone was thrown, as it relates that preparations were made both by Jews and Gentiles to stone Paul and his companions, or even had the account of this transaction stopped, without going on to inform us that Paul and his companions were 'aware of the danger and fled,' a contradiction between the history and the epistles would have ensued. Truth is necessarily consistent; but it is scarcely possible that independent accounts, not having truth to guide them, should thus advance to the very brink of contradiction without falling into it." Two other incidental coincidences confirm the narrative: (1) the persecution which was instigated by the Jews, was carried out by stoning, a Jewish mode of punishment; (2) this attempted infliction of death, in Palestine, would not have been permitted within the city (ch. 7 : 58); in this heathen city no scruple prevented it.

20, 21. As the disciples stood round about him. Not in order to bury him, but contemplating mournfully his insensible form. Timothy was not improbably one of this group; he resided at Lystra (ch. 16 : 1), and knew of, if he did not witness, this persecution (2 Tim. 3 : 11).—**He rose up and came into the city.** Alford and Meyer regard this as a supernatural recovery; Hackett the reverse; Alexander is doubtful. I see no reason to regard it as anything more than a recovery after being stunned; there is nothing in the fact that he came into the city to indicate "his immediate restoration to his usual activity and vigor"; the disciples were there to assist or even to carry him, if helpless, and his departure on the following day to Derbe was a natural means of safety. The suggestion, referred to by Alexander, that Paul's swoon at Lystra is to be identified with the trance described in 2 Cor. 12 : 1-4 is more ingenious than sound. A swoon is a state of unconsciousness, a trance is a state of exalted spiritual consciousness; there is nothing akin in them.—**Derbe.** For description, see ver. 6.—**Had taught many.** Rather, had made many disciples; the success of their ministry is indicated.—**They returned again to Lystra.** "Advancing still eastward from this point, they would soon have reached the well-known 'Cilician Gates,' through which they

22 Confirming the souls of the disciples, *and* exhorting them to continue[g] in the faith, and that we[h] must through much tribulation enter into the kingdom of God.
23 And when they had ordained them elders in every church, and had prayed with fasting, they commended them to the Lord, on whom they believed.
24 And after they had passed throughout Pisidia, they came to Pamphylia.
25 And when they had preached the word in Perga, they went down into Attalia:
26 And thence sailed to Antioch, from[i] whence they had been recommended to the grace[j] of God for the work which they fulfilled.
27 And when they were come, and had gathered the church together, they rehearsed[k] all that God had done with them, and how he had opened[l] the door of faith unto the Gentiles.
28 And there they abode long time with the disciples.

g ch. 13 : 43....h Rom. 8 : 17; 2 Tim. 3 : 12....i ch. 13 : 1, 3....j ch. 15 : 40....k ch. 15 : 4....l 1 Cor. 16 : 9; 2 Cor. 2 : 12; Rev. 3 : 8.

could have descended easily to Cilicia, and then have embarked from Tarsus for Antioch. They had the choice, therefore, of a nearer way to Syria; but their solicitude for the welfare of the newly-founded churches constrains them to turn back, and revisit the places where they had preached."—(*Hackett.*)

22, 23. Exhorting them to remain in the faith. Not merely in the belief that Jesus is the Messiah, though this belief might be shaken by his failure to protect them from persecution, but, *in the life of faith*, that is, in that life whose present strength and future hope is derived from a personal trust in a personal Saviour. Comp. 1 Cor. 16 : 13; 2 Cor. 13 : 5; Gal. 3 : 24-26; Col. 1 : 23.—**And that we must through much tribulation enter into the kingdom of God.** For the reason why tribulation is necessary, see Rom. 5 : 3-5; Heb. 12 : 11. Comp. Luke 14 : 25-33. It was by this exhortation, not by any special rite, that the apostles confirmed the souls of the disciples. There is some question among the critics as to the significance of the pronoun *we* in this sense; some regard it as indicating a general law applicable to all Christians; the meaning then would be, We as Christians enter the kingdom through tribulation. Others regard it as an indication that the words of the apostle are in part quoted; they refer to the persecutions which they have themselves suffered, as an evidence that all must enter the kingdom of God in the same way. Alford regards it as an indication that Luke has rejoined the apostles, having remained at Antioch during the journey to Iconium and back; but there is nothing in ch. 13 to indicate that Luke was with the apostles during any part of this missionary tour.—**And when they had ordained them elders in every church.** The word here rendered *ordained* (χειροτονέω) is etymologically and in classic Greek, to choose by a show of hands, a customary method of election in the Grecian public assemblies. In the N. T. the word occurs only here and in 2 Cor. 8 : 19, but in composition with the preposition *before* (πρό) it occurs in Acts 10 : 41, where it describes a choice exercised by God. In later ecclesiastical Greek the word is used to designate the ordination of a church officer by his ecclesiastical superior. On this state of facts three interpretations are afforded of this verse. The first imputes to the word *ordained* its later ecclesiastical meaning, and understands, as our English translators seem to have done, that the apostles appointed the elders over the churches by their own ecclesiastical authority. The second view imputes to it the etymological and classical meaning of an election by a show of hands, and understands that the elders were thus elected by vote of the church members, as were the deacons in ch. 6 : 5, and their choice was then ratified by the action of the apostles, who solemnly set apart the elders to their office, as Paul and Barnabas had been set apart by special religious services for their missionary work (ch. 13 : 3). This apparently is Alford's view: "The apostles ordained the presbyters whom the churches elected." The third view, which seems to me the correct one, takes the word (χειροτονέω), rendered *ordain*, in its secondary meaning as equivalent to *select* or *appoint*, and understands the declaration to be that the apostles appointed elders, without any indication whether the selection was made by themselves, or first by the lay members of the church and ratified by the apostles, or by the concurrent action of the two. In these Gentile cities, where the converts were largely without previous religious instruction in either the truths or the forms of religion, it seems very probable that the apostles would have exercised a controlling influence in the selection of church officers. There is nothing to indicate what was the authority of these elders except the facts that the name is applied in the O. T. to officers exercising certain undefined political functions, analogous to those of the modern shiek (Matt. 16 : 2, note), and also to designate officers who administered the affairs of the Jewish synagogue (Matt. 4 : 23, note). That their authority was confined to the local church is implied by the expression *elders in every church.* While no very clear and definite lesson respecting church action is conveyed by this passage, one practical lesson is plain and important: the apostles did not *merely* preach the Gospel, they also gathered the Christian converts into definitely organized churches, with officers duly appointed, and, presumptively, with the ordinances duly administered. They brought them into the visible, as well as into the invisible kingdom of God.—**Commended them to the Lord.** Rather, *Set them before the Lord;* a formal religious service participated in by the apostles is certainly implied. Comp. 1 Tim. 5 : 22 ; 2 Tim. 1 : 6; Tit. 1 : 5.

24, 25. Pisidia. A province in Asia Minor. See ch. 13 : 14, note.—**Pamphylia.** Another province. See ch. 13 : 13, note.—**Perga.** The first point which they had reached on the main road after leaving Cyprus. See ch. 13 : 13, note. —**Attalia.** A coast town of Pamphylia, in the immediate vicinity of Perga; it was founded by Attalus Philadelphus, and is still an important place, with a population of 8,000; it is now known as Cittalia, at least this is the better opinion, though there is some uncertainty respecting its identification. The apostles apparently went to Attalia not for the purpose of preaching, but as a convenient point from which to take ship for Antioch.

26-28. They had gathered the church together. A special meeting was held to hear their report. It is not improbable that there were several churches in Antioch whose members were convened on this occasion.—**They rehearsed all that God had done with them.** Perhaps this rehearsal furnished Luke with the material for his narrative. Observe how Paul here recognizes the truth afterwards insisted on in 1 Cor. 3 : 6-9. This was a true "praise meeting."—**Opened the door of faith unto the Gentiles.** That is, had by his grace given admission into the kingdom of faith unto the uncircumcised heathen. The metaphor is a favorite one with Paul (1 Cor. 16 : 9; 2 Cor. 2 : 12; Col. 4 : 3).—**Long time.** One or two years. Probably A.D. 48, 49. See Chronological Table, p. 20.

Ch. 15 : 1-35. THE SO-CALLED COUNCIL AT JERUSALEM. THE RELATION OF RITES TO THE RELIGION OF JESUS CHRIST.—THE TEACHINGS OF DIVINE PROVIDENCE AN AUTHORITY IN RELIGION.—HOW TO PREVENT CHURCH QUARRELS.—PRINCIPLE PERMANENT, POLICY TEMPORARY.

PRELIMINARY NOTE.—This chapter divides the Book of Acts into two nearly equal portions. The first fourteen chapters describe chiefly the operations of divine providence which brought the church to the decision here finally announced, that the Gospel is for the Gentile as well as the Jew, that Christianity is for humanity, not for a single nation; the second fourteen chapters recount the methods pursued by the church, under the guidance of God, in carrying the Gospel to the Gentiles. In studying this chapter consider the following facts: (1.) Circumcision was ordained by God in the days of Abraham. It was the sign of the covenant between himself and his people. It was a public profession of faith in and consecration to him. It opened the door of and gave admission to his kingdom. To be uncircumcised was to be a heathen, a stranger from the commonwealth of Israel, without a part in the divine inheritance (Gen. 17 : 14; Ezek 28 : 10, etc). To deny circumcision therefore, seemed to a Jewish conscience equivalent to denying God's covenant and kingdom. It was not an unmeaning ceremony. It was as important a part of religion as any ceremony ever is or ever can be; to deny that it was essential to salvation was equivalent to denying that any ceremonial is essential to religion. (2.) Jesus Christ had not repealed, set aside, or said aught to weaken the obligation of circumcision. He was himself circumcised (Luke 2 : 21). Accused by his enemies of relaxing the laws of Moses he had denied the imputation (Matt. 5 : 17, note). He had chosen all his apostles from among the circumcised. In his first commission he had bid them go not to any heathen province or Samaritan village (Matt. 10 : 5). The full meaning of his subsequent commissions (Matt. 28 : 19, 20; Acts 2 : 8) the apostles themselves did not at first comprehend. They had no direct *external* authority for abandoning a test of character which God had ordained, and which had been maintained for over 1,800 years. (3.) The apostles themselves had issued no decree on the subject. Christ had appointed them to sit as judges of Israel. He had conferred upon them an authority, vague certainly, but not insignificant, and they had been silent. The first preaching to the Greeks was by Philip, a Greek (ch. 8 : 5, 40). The second was by Peter, but the case was exceptional; he had been called to account for it; no permanent ministry to the heathen had resulted (chaps. 10, 11). Neither of them had organized the uncircumcised into Christian churches, or assumed to place Jew and Gentile on the same footing before God and the church. The action of Paul and Barnabas and the church at Antioch was therefore wholly without external or ecclesiastical authority. They not only appeared to disregard the traditions of the church, to reject the ordinance established by God, to abandon a ceremonial hallowed by immemorial usage, but to do this without authority from Christ or his apostles. Pride and conscience reenforced each other in the complaint preferred against them for this seemingly flagrant irregularity. (4.) This conference, usually called a council, was not one, in the modern sense of that term. The churches of Palestine were not represented; nor even the churches of Judea. It was simply a meeting of the church at Jerusalem. It was not called to settle authoritatively the question. In the mind of Paul there was no question. The complaints of the Pharisees awakened no hesitation in his mind (Gal. 2 : 5). He would not have yielded his convictions, no, not

CHAPTER XV.

AND[m] certain men which came down from Judæa taught the brethren, *and said*, Except[n] ye be circumcised after[o] the manner of Moses, ye cannot be saved.

2 When therefore Paul and Barnabas had no small dissension and disputation with them, they determined

m Gal. 2 : 12....n John 7 : 22....o Lev. 12 : 3.

to an angel from heaven (Gal. 1 : 7, 8). He did not even go up to Jerusalem till directed by a special divine revelation (Gal. 2 : 2). When he went he emphasized his own convictions by taking an uncircumcised Greek with him (Gal. 2 : 3). The church at Antioch was as little in doubt as himself. It accompanied Paul, Barnabas and Titus out of the city, giving him a public ovation (Acts 15 : 3). As the three journeyed to Jerusalem, they visited the churches on their route, narrating with thanksgiving the labors, for the irregularity of which they were called to account. Paul refused to recognize in the apostles any authority over him and superior to his own (Gal. 1 : 1, 11, 12, 17-22), and arriving at Jerusalem, entered into no debate or defence; he simply gave an account of what he had done. If we could imagine the Judaizing party securing the decision of the church in their favor, we could not imagine Paul's yielding to it. The genesis of this conference was simply this: Pharisaic believers came from Jerusalem to Antioch, claimed to speak by authority, and demanded the circumcision of the Gentile converts. The Christians at Antioch sent Paul and Barnabas to Jerusalem to learn whether this self-constituted delegation possessed the authority it claimed; whether the church had authorized or would ratify their action. (5.) The constitution and forms of proceedings of the so-called council are uncertain. I believe, however, that the matter was first discussed in private between the apostles and elders, that a result was reached, that it was then laid before the entire church and ratified by them, and that the addresses of Peter and the narrative of Paul and Barnabas, as well as the final utterance of James, are part of this report, prepared, as it was, in committee. See ver. 6, note. (6.) The result included both a principle and a policy. The *principle* is embodied by Peter's declaration that God recognizes no difference between Jew and Gentile, purifying all hearts by faith (ver. 9). Faith is not only the ground of salvation, it is the *only* ground. Nothing else is necessary. No ceremonial is of the essence of Christianity. No ceremonial could be more sacred, either from its origin, its usage, or its import, than circumcision. The *policy* is embodied in the counsel of James (vers. 20, 21, note), that the Gentiles abstain from certain practices out of regard to the consciences of their Jewish brethren. The principle is eternal. It is the same to-day as in the first century. The policy was perhaps never fully carried out. It certainly did not outlast the time of Paul. He openly declares the right of a Christian to eat meat offered to idols, though he advises, in the spirit of this conference, that the right be yielded for the sake of others (Rom. ch. 14 ; 1 Cor. ch. 8). (7.) This result was not obtained by an appeal to *church authority*:—neither to the O. T., though James quotes a passage from the prophets to show that the O. T. does not contravene their conclusion; nor to Jesus Christ, who is not quoted at all; nor to the Church, for only the opinion of a local church was asked, except as the apostles may be regarded as representatives of the church universal:—but by an appeal to *divine providence*. The ways of God are as authoritative as his word; and the teachings of the one, if not as plain, are as decisive as the teachings of the other. For the discontinuance of a ceremonial as old as the nation, the primitive church required no other authority than the evident blessing of God bestowed upon those who had not accepted and performed it (vers. 8-10). (8.) If I have read aright this narrative, it throws small light on methods of ecclesiastical procedure in N. T. times; it gives no *authority* for church councils, as a divinely appointed method of settling questions in church government or administration; but it attests the truth, which even the church of Christ has not yet learned, that religion consists *wholly* in heart-life and its issues, not at all in any rite or ceremony, however sacred in origin or hallowed by usage; it points out the method of preventing ecclesiastical contentions and quarrels, and it indicates the difference between principle and policy—the former to be held with inflexible tenacity, the latter to be readily yielded in accommodation to even unreasonable prejudices (comp. vers. 20, 21 with Gal. 2 : 5).

1. And certain men which came down from Judea. They were evidently members of the Christian church in Jerusalem. See ver. 5. In Galatians Paul characterizes them as "false brethren unawares brought in." They believed that Jesus was the Messiah, but regarded Christianity only as a reformation of Judaism.—**Except ye be circumcised.** Circumcision was first ordained by God in his covenant with Abraham (Gen. 17 : 10-14). It probably fell into disuse, for it was renewed in the person of the son of Moses, a little before the exodus (Exod. 4 : 24-26). It had been practised by other nations than the Jews—the Egyptians, Ethiopians, Tro-

that[p] Paul and Barnabas, and certain other of them,
should go up to Jerusalem, unto the apostles and elders,
about this question.
3 And being[q] brought on their way by the church,
they passed through Phenice and Samaria, declaring
the conversion[r] of the Gentiles: and they caused
great joy[s] unto all the brethren.
4 And when they were come to Jerusalem, they
were received of the church, and *of* the apostles and
elders, and they[t] declared all things that God had
done with them.
5 But there rose up certain of the sect of the Pharisees
which believed, saying,[u] That it was needful to
circumcise them, and to command *them* to keep the
law of Moses.
6 And the apostles and elders came together,[v] for to
consider of this matter.

p Gal. 2 : 1 . . . q Rom. 15 : 24; 1 Cor. 16 : 6, 11; 3 John 6 . . . r ch. 14 : 27 . . . s Luke 15 : 7, 10 . . . . t ch. 21 : 19 . . . u ver. 1 . v Matt. 18 : 20.

glodytes, Caffres of South Africa, and Islanders of the Pacific Ocean, and is still practised both by Mussulmans and modern Jews. It was performed on all males on the eighth day after birth (Lev. 12 : 3), and accompanied the naming of the child (Luke 1 : 59; 2 : 21). It was a painful ceremony, and was especially odious to the Gentiles, because in the public baths to which they resorted, the circumcised were subjected to cruel insults. So far was this carried that the Jews sometimes endeavored to efface the evidences of circumcision by a surgical operation. See 1 Cor. 7 : 18.—**Ye cannot be saved.** The point of the teaching was not therefore that it was expedient to be circumcised as a concession to the prejudices of others, but that *circumcision was essential to salvation.* It was this substitution of an external rite for the spiritual life of faith in a personal Saviour which rendered their teaching subversive of the soul. See ver. 24, note.

2. No small dissension and disputation with them. The former word (στάσις) elsewhere rendered *insurrection*, *sedition* and *uproar* (Mark 15 : 7; Luke 23 : 19, 25; Acts 19 : 40) implies a vigorous and determined resistance to the Judaizers by Paul and Barnabas; the latter word (ζήτησις) literally *questioning* (1 Tim. 1 : 4; 6 : 4) implies debate; the doctrine and the authority of these Judaizers were probably both questioned. In fact they had no authority to speak for the church at Jerusalem (ver. 24, note).—**They determined.** That is, the church at Antioch determined. It appears also from Gal. 2 : 2 that Paul received a direct revelation from heaven. There is nothing inconsistent in the two accounts. The revelation may have been afforded him by the voice of prophets in the church (ch. 13 : 2, note), or it may be that a private revelation to Paul and the action of the church combined in sending this delegation. So Paul was sent from Jerusalem both by the word and the Providence of God (ch. 9 : 29, 30 with ch. 22 : 18, 21).—**Certain other of them.** Titus was one (Gal. 2 : 1, 3), and the fact that he accompanied Paul, being an uncircumcised Greek, as well as the statement in the next verse, indicates that the mind of the church was with Paul and Barnabas, not with the Judaizers.—**About this question.** There is nothing to indicate an appeal to the church at Jerusalem as having *authority* to settle the question. The language of Gal. 2 : 5 implies the reverse; there was no question in Paul's mind, and we may reasonably doubt whether he would have gone on this mission but for the direct revelation made to him. The false teachers came from Judea claiming to speak for the church there; the brethren of Antioch sent to Jerusalem to learn the truth of their representations.

3. Being brought on their way by the church. Officially escorted by delegates from the church.—**Passed through Phenice and Samaria.** "As Galilee is not mentioned, they traveled probably along the coast as far south as Ptolemais (ch. 21 : 7), and then crossed the plain of Esdraelon into Samaria."—(*Hackett.*)—**Declaring the conversion of the Gentiles.** In the missionary tour from which they had just returned. That they were not going to Jerusalem to learn from the church there whether Gentiles could be converted without circumcision is very evident. Their account was given to the Christian churches which had previously been established along the line of their route (ch. 8 : 5, 40; 9 : 32; 11 : 19).—**Caused great joy unto all the brethren.** The Judaic faction had small influence in these churches.

4, 5. They were received of the church. That is, *cordially received.* Apparently prior to any public meeting, Paul privately communicated with the leaders in the church (Gal. 2 : 2). In the public meeting observe that he takes no part in the discussion, except to give a simple narrative of the work which had been done through him and Barnabas, and of God's blessing upon it, both in the conversion of the Gentiles, and in the wonders and miracles wrought among them.—**There rose up certain of the sect of the Pharisees.** For description of the Pharisees, see Matt. 3 : 7, note. We are not to understand that this is a part of Paul's report, an account of the opposition encountered at Antioch; these Pharisees rose up at this time in the assembly, and demanded that these Gentile converts should be circumcised and required to keep the whole law; in other words, that they must become Jews before they could become Christians. Humanly speaking, the future of the church depended on the decision of this question. If the Pharisaic party had triumphed, the Christian church would have been buried in the grave of Judaism.

7 And when there had been much disputing, Peter
rose up, and said unto them, Men *and* brethren, ye
know[w] how that a good while ago God made choice
among us that the Gentiles by my mouth should hear
the word of the gospel, and believe.
8 And God, which[x] knoweth the hearts, bare them
witness, giving them the Holy Ghost, even as *he did*
unto us;
9 And put no difference between us and them, purifying[y] their hearts by faith.
10 Now therefore why tempt ye God, to put a yoke[z]
upon the neck of the disciples, which neither our fathers nor we were able to bear?
11 But we believe that through[a] the grace of the
Lord Jesus Christ we shall be saved, even as they.
12 Then all the multitude kept silence, and gave au-

w ch. 10 : 20; Matt. 16 : 18, 19....x ch. 1 : 24....y Heb. 9 : 13, 14; 1 Pet. 1 : 22....z Gal. 5 : 1....a Rom. 3 : 24; Ephes. 2 : 8; Tit. 3 : 4, 5.

6. It is not easy to determine what was the constitution of this so-called council; the language of this verse implies that the matter was brought before the apostles and elders for *their* deliberation; the language of ver. 12, "*all the multitude*," implies that the laity of the church generally were present; and the language of ver. 22, "then pleased it the apostles and elders, *with the whole church*," implies that they participated in the final action; while the language of ver. 19 seems to imply that James, as president of the council, formally announced the decision. I suggest, as a reasonable surmise, harmonizing the various expressions in the narrative, that after Paul's account given to the church, and the criticisms on his course consequent thereon, the apostles and elders met as a committee, and after much discussion, settled upon their report; that to prepare the way for it, Peter first presented his account of the teachings of divine Providence several years before; that Paul and Barnabas followed with their account of their missionary work and God's approval of it by miracles and wonders; that James then announced the decision which the officers recommended; and that, finally, this report being ratified by the whole church, was embodied in the official document contained in vers. 23–29. It must not, however, be forgotten that this was not a representative council of the churches of Christendom, nor even of Palestine, but only the officers and laity of the church at Jerusalem, together with the apostles; the latter, as the immediate life companions of our Lord, would have had great influence, irrespective of any ecclesiastical authority which they may have possessed.

7-9. When there had been much disputing. A promiscuous debate, but whether among the apostles, or among the multitude, is uncertain; if the surmise above is correct, only the apostles and elders took part in this discussion.—**How that a good while ago.** The conversion of Cornelius was not far from fourteen years previous to this time, assuming that Paul's expression in Gal. 2 : 1, "fourteen years after," dates from his conversion. Peter refers to the lapse of time to show that the question has long since been settled by the revealed will of God. See chaps. 10, 11.—**And the heart-knowing God.** The value of circumcision consisted in its evidence of consecration to God. To the Judeans a refusal to be circumcised was an evidence of imperfect repentance and consecration, as with us a refusal to be baptized, or to make a public profession of faith. To this unexpressed feeling, Peter replies, The heart-knowing God (Jer. 17 : 10) has borne witness to the genuineness of their godly character by giving to them the Holy Ghost.—**Even as he did unto us.** That is, with the same miraculous gifts (ch. 11 : 15, note).—**Put no difference.** Rather recognized no difference; did not discriminate between them and us, having broken down by Christ the middle wall of partition between Jew and Gentile. See Ephes. 2 : 14.—**Purifying their hearts by the faith.** Even the O. T. recognized the truth that circumcision, unaccompanied by purification of heart, was valueless (Jer. 9 : 26). Comp. Col. 2 : 11. This circumcision of the heart had been granted to the Gentiles, who thus were received into the covenant of God. The faith by which their hearts were purified is not merely, as Dr. Hackett, a "belief in the truth," but, as explained by Peter himself, in 1 Pet. 1 : 22, that faith which obeys the truth through the spirit unto unfeigned love. The essential truth underlying Peter's argument, and equally applicable to modern times, is that he whose heart has been purified by the Spirit of God, and who gives evidence thereof by the fruits of the Spirit, as portrayed in Gal. 5 : 22, 23, is a child of God, however he may fall short of the ecclesiastical requirements of the church.

10, 11. Now, therefore, why tempt ye God? By requiring any other evidence of the universality of his grace.—**To put a yoke upon the neck of the disciples.** That is, by attempting to put such yoke upon them.—**Which neither we nor our fathers were able to bear.** This yoke is not the external observance of the ceremonial law, for that the Jews did bear, but the burden to the conscience of one who accounts obedience to such law essential to salvation. It cannot be borne because it is not the object of the law to give salvation, but to afford a knowledge of sin. See Rom. 3 : 19, 20; 7 : 9–24. In the latter passage Paul illustrates the burdensomeness of this yoke. Contrast Christ's yoke (Matt. 11 : 29, 30).—**But through the grace of the Lord Jesus we trust to be saved, in which way they**

dience to Barnabas and Paul, declaring what miracles
and wonders God had wrought[b] among the Gentiles
by them.
13 And after they had held their peace, James answered, saying, Men *and* brethren, hearken unto
me:
14 Simeon hath declared[c] how God at the first did
visit the Gentiles, to take out of them a people for his
name.
15 And to this agree the words of the prophets; as
it is written,[d]
16 After this I will return, and will build again the
tabernacle of David, which is fallen down; and I will
build again the ruins thereof, and I will set it up:
17 That the residue of men might seek after the Lord,
and all the Gentiles, upon whom my name is called,
saith the Lord, who doeth all these things.
18 Known[e] unto God are all his works, from the beginning of the world.
19 Wherefore my sentence is, that we trouble not
them, which from among the Gentiles are turned[f] to
God:

b ch. 14 : 27.... c Luke 2 : 31, 32.... d Amos 9 : 11, 12.... e Isa. 46 : 10.... f 1 Thess. 1 : 9.

also. This is the literal rendering of ver. 11, which consummates the apostle's argument; the Jewish Christians are saved, not through circumcision, but through the grace of Jesus Christ, and that which does not bring salvation to the Jew, cannot to the Gentile.

12. From the effect upon the multitude, it is evident that Peter's address was delivered to the church as a whole, not merely to the apostles and elders. Paul and Barnabas then rehearsed the miracles and wonders wrought by them among the Gentiles (ch. 13 : 11; 14 : 3, 8-10) as an evidence of the divine approval of their work in preaching the Gospel to the uncircumcised.

13. James answered. Called in Gal. 1 : 19 the Lord's brother, and, as I believe, the literal brother of Jesus, not a cousin or other relative. See note on Brethren of the Lord, Vol. I, p. 87. He was not one of the twelve, though designated by Paul as an apostle. He is probably the author of the Epistle General of St. James. In ecclesiastical history he is designated James the Just, and is reported by tradition to have been appointed bishop of Jerusalem by the Lord himself. That he occupied a prominent and influential position in the primitive church is evident. Comp. ch. 12 : 17; 21 : 18; Gal. 2 : 9. Tradition attributes to him an austere and ascetic character, whose sympathies would naturally be with the Hebraistic party in the church, and whose decision would therefore have special weight with the Hebrew Christians. Of all the books of the N. T., his epistle probably most strongly emphasizes the necessity of works of righteousness, and says least of the inward experience of faith. It accords with this aspect of his character that he refers to Peter by his Hebrew name, and to the O. T. Scriptures in support of the admission of uncircumcised Gentiles to the Christian church.

14-18. Simeon. The Greek form of the Hebrew name; used once by Peter of himself (2 Pet. 1 : 1), but in connection with his Christian name. The name Peter was given to Simon by Christ (John 1 : 42; Matt. 16 : 18).—**God at the first.** So Peter (ver. 7) says *a good while ago.* James recalls the fact that God's visiting the uncircumcised Gentiles is not new in the experience of the Christian church.—**To take out of them a people for his name.** Comp. 1 Pet. 2 : 9; Matt. 21 : 43, note.—**The words of the prophets.** The quotation which follows is from Amos 9 : 11, 12; it does not agree verbally with either the Septuagint or the Hebrew version. The original passage is thus translated by Schmoller (*Lange's Com.*):

In that day will I raise up
The fallen hut of David,
And wall up its breaches,
And raise up its ruins,
And build it as in the days of old;
That they may possess the remnant of Edom
and all the nations
Upon whom my name is called,
Saith Jehovah who doeth this.

Edom is specified in the original prophecy because while they were related to Israel they were especially hostile; to receive possession of Edom was therefore symbolical of Israel's greatest glory. The fulfillment of this prophecy began with the coming of Christ the Son of David, and will be perfected when he is fully recognized King of all the nations of the earth. The *tabernacle of David* is not the divine tabernacle, the precursor of the Temple; the kingdom is described not as the *palace* nor as the *house*, but as the *booth* or *hut* of David, to indicate its fallen condition. The *residue of men*, literally the *forsaken*, is a designation of the Gentiles. So in Ephes. 2 : 3; 1 Thess. 4 : 13; 5 : 6, *the others* are the heathen (there οἱ λοιπός, here κατάλοιπος). *Upon whom my name is called* is equivalent to, Who are surnamed by my name, that is, Who are called Christians. The quotation from Amos ends with ver. 17; ver. 18 is added by James. The best reading is, *Known from the beginning of the world*, the words *unto God are all his works* being added; so Meyer, Tischendorf, Alford. The variation is not immaterial; adopting the better reading, the meaning of James appears to be that this call of the Gentiles is not a new revelation, but something made known from the beginning by the prophets. The passage in Amos, then, as interpreted by James, declares that after the desolation of Israel foretold in the preceding verses God will return in mercy and

20 But that we write unto them, that they abstain
from pollutions of[g] idols, and *from* fornication,[h] and
from things strangled, and *from* blood.[i]
21 For Moses of old time hath in every city them
that preach him, being[j] read in the synagogues every
sabbath day.

22 Then pleased it the apostles and elders, with the
whole church, to send chosen men of their own company to Antioch, with Paul and Barnabas; *namely*,
Judas surnamed Barsabas,[k] and Silas, chief men among
the brethren:
23 And they wrote *letters* by them after this man-

g Exod. 20 : 4, 5; 1 Cor. 8 : 1, etc.; 10 : 28; Rev. 2 : 14, 20; 9 : 20....h 1 Cor. 6 : 9, 18; Col. 3 : 5; 1 Thess. 4 : 3....i Lev. 17 : 14; Deut. 12 : 16, 23....j ch. 13 : 15, 27....k ch. 1 : 23.

rebuild the kingdom of David in such a way that the Gentiles, accepting the name of Christ, may themselves enter and share in the kingdom of God.

19, 20. Wherefore my sentence is. Literally, Wherefore I judge. The original (κρίνω) signifies not merely an opinion, but a positive decision. See Matt. 7 : 5, note. But it does not indicate that the speaker's authority was greater than that of the others. The phrase was a common formula in the Greek assemblies, by which individual members gave expression to their verdict or decision after discussion. "The whole proceeding is analogous to that which continually takes place in our own church-courts, when the roll is called to give the members present an opportunity of stating their judgment upon some important question."—(*Alexander*.)—**That we trouble not them.** By laying upon them burdensome ceremonial regulations. Comp. Gal. 5 : 12. That circumcision was peculiarly burdensome to the Gentiles, see ver. 1, note.—**Are turned to God.** Rather *are turning*. The judgment of James was against imposing any burdens upon and hindrances to those Gentiles who, under the influence of the Gospel, were turning to the Lord.—**From pollutions of idols.** The animals sacrificed to the gods were not wholly consumed in burnt offerings; certain portions were destroyed, and the remainder were eaten by men in a festive meal, or sometimes sold in the markets. These meats were accounted an abomination among the Jews, and to partake of them knowingly was a heinous offence (Ps. 106 : 28). To guard against the possibility of unwittingly partaking of such meat, some confined themselves to herbs (Rom. 14 : 2). Paul subsequently declares that these are needless scruples, and that there is nothing unclean in such meats (Rom. 14 : 3, 14; 1 Cor. 8 : 4-8), with which agrees Christ's instructions in Mark 7 : 14-23; at the same time he recommends the Gentile Christians to abstain from eating them if partaking will be a temptation or an offence to others (Rom. 14 : 15-21; 1 Cor. 8 : 9-13); and that appears to be the principle upon which the recommendation to abstinence is given here by James.—**And from fornication.** It has been a perplexity to the commentators that this positive sin should be included with other matters in themselves indifferent. The explanation is, not that the word fornication is used in any other than its natural sense, but that this vice, when practised by men, was not regarded as blameworthy in Greek society; public opinion in the ancient Greek cities upon this subject is illustrated by, but was far worse than, that which still exists in some European capitals. "The young men of Athens, previous to their marriage, spent a great part of their time in the company of mistresses, without its being thought blameable in any respect whatever. Marriage, indeed, produced on the whole a change in this mode of living of young men, but in innumerable instances even married men continued their intercourse with mistresses, without drawing upon themselves the censure of public opinion."—(*Smith's Dict. of Ant.*) The Jews, on the other hand, are and always have been a characteristically chaste people. In specifying, therefore, those peculiarities which distinguished the Jews from the Gentiles, and which Christian converts were to maintain, it was necessary to include personal chastity.—**From things strangled and from blood.** The Jewish law forbade the partaking of blood in any shape (Gen. 9 : 4; Lev. 17 : 13, 14; Deut. 12 : 23, 24), and this therefore involved a prohibition of eating animals killed by strangling, because they would contain the blood. To the present day the Jews maintain separate butchers' establishments, and kill their meat in a peculiar manner, on account of these prohibitions.

21. This verse assigns the reason for the admonitions given to the Gentile converts. The primitive Christian churches were composed of three classes: heathen, proselytes, Jews—the two latter, attendants upon the synagogue, would hear the prohibitions of the ceremonial law constantly read; if their fellow-Christians disregarded them, controversies, and perhaps schisms, would then ensue. It was for the sake of peace that the Gentile Christians were to submit to a temporary limitation of their Christian liberty.

22. With the whole church. Observe that this commission was sent, not by the apostles alone, nor by a council of churches, but by the church at Jerusalem.—**Of their own.** The word *company* has no equivalent in the original. The meaning is, members of their own church.—**Judas.** Nothing further is known of him except that he was a prophet (ver. 32, note). The fact that this Judas was surnamed Barsabas, while Judas the apostle (ch. 1 : 13) was surnamed Lebbæus or Thaddæus (Matt. 10 : 3; Mark 3 : 18), indicates that this one is not the apostle.—**Silas.** Always so

ner; The apostles, and elders, and brethren, *send*
greeting unto the brethren which are of the Gentiles in
Antioch, and Syria, and Cilicia:
24 Forasmuch as we have heard, that certain[l] which
went out from us have troubled[m] you with words,[n]
subverting your souls, saying, *Ye must* be circumcised, and keep the law: to whom[o] we gave no *such*
commandment:
25 It seemed good unto us, being assembled with one
accord, to send chosen men unto you, with our beloved
Barnabas and Paul,
26 Men that have hazarded[p] their lives for the name
of our Lord Jesus Christ.

l verse 1....m Gal. 5:12....n Gal. 5:4....o Gal. 2:4....p ch. 13:50; 14:19.

named in the Acts, always Silvanus in the Epistles; the former was probably his Jewish, the latter his Gentile name. He is believed to have been a Grecian Jew; Acts 16:37 indicates that he was a Roman citizen. He accompanied Paul on his second missionary journey through Asia Minor to Macedonia (ver. 40; ch. 17:4), remained behind in Berea (17:10, 14), and joined Paul again in Corinth (18:5; 1 Thess. 1:1; 2 Thess. 1:1), where he preached with Paul and Timotheus (2 Cor. 1:19). Whether he was the Silvanus who conveyed Peter's first Epistle to Asia Minor (1 Pet. 5:12) is doubtful, though the probabilities are in favor of the identity.—**Leading men among the brethren.** Personal influence rather than official position is probably indicated.

23. And they wrote by them. The indication is that an exact transcript of the original letter is given. The words *after this manner* are wanting in the best manuscripts.—**The apostles and elders, brethren.** The word *and* is wanting in the ancient manuscripts; the apostles and elders are not masters but themselves brethren (Matt. 23:8; 1 Tim. 5:1; 1 Pet. 5:3).—**Throughout Antioch and Syria and Cilicia.** An indication both that Christian churches had been organized throughout those regions, and also that the Judaizers had demanded elsewhere than in Antioch the circumcision of Gentile converts.—**Cilicia** was the most south-easterly province of Asia Minor, divided by Mount Amanus from Syria. When Cicero was proconsul of Cilicia, B. C. 51–50, it included Pamphylia, Pisidia, Lycaonia and the island of Cyprus, and although subsequently reduced under Augustus to much narrower dimensions, the term is probably here used in the larger sense, for it is almost certain that the letter would be sent to the churches which Paul had organized in his missionary tour throughout Pamphylia, Pisidia, Phrygia, and Lycaonia, as well as to those which presumptively grew out of his previous ministry in Tarsus, the capital of Cilicia proper (ch. 9:30). *Syria*, an abbreviation or modification of Assyria, like all the ancient provinces, had indeterminate because variable boundaries, differing at different periods of its history. In general terms they may be described as the Mediterranean on the west, the Euphrates on the east, the range of Amanus and Taurus on the north, and the great desert of Arabia on the south; these include the provinces of Judea, Samaria and Galilee, and the country of Phœnicia, known in the N. T. from its principal cities, as the coasts of Tyre and Sidon. Possibly the letter was sent to the churches throughout all these provinces, including those converted through the ministries described in ch. 8:25, 26, 40; 9:22, 32–43; 11:19, 20.

24–26. Have troubled you. Here in the sense of throwing into agitation and perplexity.—**Subverting your souls.** Because reliance upon rites and ceremonies always leads the soul away from reliance upon Christ (Gal. 5:2–4).—**Saying, Ye must be circumcised and keep the law.** These words are omitted by Alford and Tischendorf; they were probably added by some scribe as an explanation, but it is a needless one. "The persons to whom the epistle was addressed would very well know what it was that had disturbed their minds, and the omission of formal mention of it would be natural, to avoid prominent cause of offence to the Jewish converts, by an apparent depreciation of circumcision and the observance of the law."—(*Alford.*)—**To whom we gave no commandment.** The word *such* is added by the translators; the declaration of the letter is that this self-constituted delegation was not authorized to speak for the church at Jerusalem. That they had pretended to do so is implied here, and is perhaps confirmed by Paul's characterization of them in Gal. 2:4, as "false brethren."—**Being assembled with one accord.** Or, *agreed with one consent.* Neander and Alford give the former, Bengel, Meyer, Hackett and Alexander the latter, which seems to me better to agree both with the meaning of the original and with the context. The Greek (ὁμοθυμαδὸν) signifies heartiness of accord (see ch. 1:14, note); and while there is no special significance in stating that the church had assembled together, there is evident reason why they should state that the decision was unanimous and after discussion.—**Our beloved Barnabas and Paul.** An incidental but strong indorsement of them whose character and authority had been impugned by the Judaizers (Gal. 2:4–6).—**Men that have hazarded their lives for the name of our Lord Jesus Christ.** This is the meaning given by all the commentators. , Literally rendered, however, the verse would read, *Men who have given their lives for the name of our Lord*

27 We have sent therefore Judas and Silas, who shall
also tell *you* the same things by mouth.
28 For it seemed good to the Holy Ghost, and to us,
to lay upon you no greater burden [q] than these necessary things:
29 That ye abstain [r] from meats offered to idols, and
from blood, and from things strangled, and from fornication: from which if ye keep [s] yourselves, ye shall do
well. Fare ye well.
30 So when they were dismissed, they came to Antioch: and when they had gathered the multitude together, they delivered the epistle:
31 *Which* when they had read, they rejoiced for the
consolation.
32 And Judas and Silas, being prophets also themselves, exhorted the brethren with many words, and
confirmed [t] *them*.
33 And after they had tarried *there* a space, they were
let go [u] in peace from the brethren unto the apostles.
34 Notwithstanding, it pleased Silas to abide there still.
35 Paul also and Barnabas continued in Antioch,
teaching and preaching the word of the Lord, with
many others also.
36 And some days after, Paul said unto Barnabas,
Let us go again and visit our brethren in [v] every city
where we have preached the word of the Lord, *and see*
how they do.
37 And Barnabas determined to take with them
John,[w] whose surname was Mark.
38 But Paul thought not good to take him with them,
who departed [x] from them from Pamphylia, and went
not with them to the work.
39 And the contention was so sharp between them,
that they departed asunder one from the other: and so
Barnabas took Mark, and sailed unto Cyprus:
40 And Paul chose Silas, and departed, being recommended [y] by the brethren unto the grace of God.
41 And he went through Syria and Cilicia, confirming [z] the churches.

q Rev. 2 : 24....r verse 20....s 2 Cor. 11 : 9; James 1 : 27; 1 John 5 : 21; Jude 20, 21....t ch. 14 : 22....u 1 Cor. 16 11; 2 John 10.... v ch. 13 : 4, etc....w ch. 12 : 12, 25; Col. 4 : 10....x ch. 13 : 13....y. chaps. 14 : 26 : 20 : 32....z ch: 16 : 5.

Jesus Christ, and this appears to me to be its true significance. It is not the risks they have run which makes them beloved, but the fact that they have wholly consecrated their lives to honoring Christ's name. The verse is interpreted by Paul's account of his own experience in Phil. 3 : 8. He employs the same verb (*παραδίδωμι*) in describing Christ's love, in Gal. 2 : 20, "who loved me and *gave himself* for me."

27-29. Who shall tell you the same things by mouth. Not the same things that Paul and Barnabas had preached, but the same things contained in this letter; they would certify to its authenticity, and answer any questions respecting the decision of the church at Jerusalem.—**To the Holy Ghost and to us.** The claim implied to speak authoritatively for the Spirit of God indicates unmistakably their belief in their own divine inspiration. It accords with the promise made by Christ to the apostles in Matt. 28 : 20 and John 14 : 26.—**These necessary things.** *Necessary*, because Christian charity required the Gentile converts to avoid needlessly offending their Jewish brethren. Observe the radicalism of this letter; circumcision, ablutions, the observance of days, the discrimination between clean and unclean things, together with the whole Jewish ritual, was swept away. Take note also that the observance of the Jewish Sabbath is not among the necessary things laid upon the Gentile Christians.—**That ye abstain,** etc. See on ver. 20.—**Fare ye well.** The customary conclusion of epistles. Comp. 23 : 30. The literal meaning is *Be ye strong*. Together with this official letter, were instructions to Paul and Barnabas to remember the poor (Gal. 2 : 10), *i. e.*, the poor at Jerusalem, and it is not improbable that Judas and Silas, when they returned from their mission (ver. 33), carried back with them from Antioch the contributions of the brethren there.

30-35. They came to Antioch. Whence, probably, copies of the letter were sent to the other churches.—**For the consolation.** In the assurance that the question was peacefully settled, and that there was no danger of schism.—**Being prophets.** *Inspired teachers.* See ch. 13 : 1, note. Their exhortations, therefore, possessed a special and recognized authority.—**Had tarried a space.** There is nothing to indicate the length of time.—**Let go in peace.** *With peace, i. e.*, with the customary Jewish salutation, Peace be with you; here, with something of the significance imparted to it by Christ (John 14 : 27).—Ver. 34 is wanting in the best manuscripts, and has probably been inserted to harmonize the statement in ver. 23, implying that Silas returned to Jerusalem, with that in ver. 40, that he shortly after accompanied Paul in his second missionary journey.—**Teaching and preaching.** Teaching the Christian disciples; preaching, as heralds, the Gospel to those that knew it not. This is the twofold function of the ministry.

Ch. 15 : 36 to ch. 16 : 13. PAUL RESUMES HIS MISSIONARY LABORS. HE ILLUSTRATES THE SPIRIT OF THE COUNSEL OF THE CHURCH AT JERUSALEM, THOUGH HE GOES BEYOND ITS LETTER (ver. 3).—GREAT WORK, FEW WORDS (ver. 6).—EVEN PAUL GOES TO THE GENTILES ONLY WHEN COMPELLED BY THE SPIRIT OF GOD (vers. 7-10).—THE FIRST PUBLIC PREACHING OF THE GOSPEL IN EUROPE (ver. 13).

The account of Paul's second missionary journey, in which Silas is his companion, instead of Barnabas, occupies up to ch. 18 : 22. It lasted three or four years, A. D. 51–54. During this journey he revisits the churches in Syria and Cilicia, thence passing rapidly through Asia Minor, crosses into Europe, preaches the Gospel at Philippi, Thessalonica and Berea in Macedonia, at Athens and Corinth in Greece, and thence returns by ship to Cæsarea, stopping at Ephesus on the way, and reaches Antioch probably in the summer or fall of A. D. 54. During this time he is thought to have written the two

CHAPTER XVI.

THEN came he to Derbe[a] and Lystra: and, behold, a certain disciple was there, named Timotheus,[b] the son of a[c] certain woman, which was a Jewess, and believed; but his father *was* a Greek:
2 Which was well[d] reported of by the brethren that were at Lystra and Iconium.

a ch. 14 : 6.... b ch. 19 : 22; Rom. 16 : 21; 1 Cor. 4 : 17.... c 2 Tim. 1 : 5.... d ch. 6 : 3; 1 Tim. 5 : 10.

epistles to the Thessalonians. See Chron. Table, p. 20.

36-41. Some days after. A comparatively short period is probably indicated.—**How they do.** "In faith, love and hope" (*Bengel*). Paul was not content to measure his work by the number of conversions, but sought to strengthen converts in the faith, and assure himself of their well-being. This was that "care of the churches" which came on him daily (2 Cor. 11 : 28). See ch. 18 : 23; 1 Thess. 3 : 5; 2 Cor. 11 : 2, 3.—**And Barnabas purposed to take with them John.** Who was a relative (Col. 4 : 10, note).—**But Paul thought proper, as to one who had fallen off from them from Pamphylia, and had not gone with them to the work, not to take with them that man.** This, which is Alford's translation, represents more accurately than our English version the rugged force of the original.—**And the contention was so sharp.** The original (*παροξυσμός, contention*) indicates bitterness in the controversy, and implies blame on both sides. The event illustrates Paul's declaration in ch. 14 : 15. Paul's subsequent reference both to Barnabas (1 Cor. 9 : 6) and to Mark (2 Tim. 4 : 11) indicate that the separation was not permanent.—**So Barnabas took Mark and sailed unto Cyprus.** His native country (ch. 4 : 36). Christianity subsequently became established in this island, a fact presumptively due, at least in part, to his labors. But he is not again mentioned in Acts, nor is anything of his subsequent history known. The fact that a spurious letter of Barnabas existed as early as the second century indicates that he occupied a prominent place in the Christian church, otherwise his name would not be forged to such a document.—**And Paul chose Silas.** Who had perhaps not gone back to Jerusalem with Judas (ver. 34, note), or possibly had returned again to Antioch; perhaps at the request of Paul to be his companion on this journey.—**Being recommended by the brethren.** It is not without significance that Barnabas is represented as setting out upon his journey with his nephew without any special sympathy or approval, while Paul is commended to the grace of God by the assembled church. We may hence fairly conclude that in this controversy the judgment of the brethren went, in the main, with Paul.—**Syria and Cilicia.** See on ver. 23. The churches visited in Syria would possibly include those in and about Damascus. In the sketch of his journey which follows we have no other indications to guide us than the mountain passes and some remains of ancient Roman roads. From these indications we judge that he crossed Mt. Amanus, the natural boundary between Syria and Cilicia, by the gorge anciently called the Syrian Gate, now known as the Beilan Pass. In Cilicia, whatever other churches he visited, he probably did not omit that which had been almost certainly established by his labors in his native city of Tarsus. Thence he must have crossed Mt. Taurus into the province of Lycaonia, probably through the great fissure known in ancient days as the Cilician Gates, a gorge extending, from north to south, a distance of some 80 miles.

Ch. 16 : 1, 2. Derbe and Lystra. Paul's course, as above described, would bring him first to Derbe, then to Lystra. For description of these cities, see ch. 14, note; in the latter city he had been stoned and left for dead.—**A certain disciple was there.** That is, at Lystra. The language of ch. 20 : 4 does not imply that Timothy came from Derbe, rather the reverse. He had probably been converted at Paul's previous visit to Lystra. See ch. 14, note. His mother's name was Eunice, his grandmother's name Lois (2 Tim. 1 : 5); they were both Christians, probably having been converted at Paul's previous visit. From childhood he had been instructed in the Jewish Scriptures (2 Tim. 3 : 15) at home, for there is no indication of any synagogue at Lystra; the father's name is unknown, he was a Greek, possibly, though that is entirely uncertain, a proselyte. Marriages with the heathen were forbidden by the O. T. (Deut. 7 : 3, 4), but this law was often disregarded by Jews residing in foreign lands (Ruth 1 : 4). Timothy, being both of Jewish and Greek extraction, would be thus peculiarly fitted to be Paul's coadjutor in his missionary work. The two epistles written by Paul to him contain indications of his character; he was not robust (1 Tim. 5 : 23), naturally shrank from opposition and responsibility (1 Tim. 4 : 12-16; 5 : 20; 6 : 11-14; 2 Tim. 2 : 1-7), was tender and sensitive (2 Tim. 1 : 4), and devout and earnestly consecrated to the service of God—this last being indicated by his abandonment of his home to accompany the apostle, and by his submission to the rite of circumcision.—**A Jewess and believed.** A Jewess by birth and education; a Christian believer by personal conviction.—**Which was well reported of by the brethren.** This is stated of Timothy, not of

3 Him would Paul have to go forth with him; and took and circumcised him,[e] because of the Jews[f] which were in those quarters: for they knew all that his father was a Greek.
4 And as they went through the cities, they delivered them the decrees for to keep, that were ordained[g] of the apostles and elders which were at Jerusalem.
5 And so were the churches[h] established in the faith, and increased in number daily.
6 Now when they had gone throughout Phrygia and

e Gal. 2 : 3-8; 5 : 1-3.... f 1 Cor. 9 : 20.... g ch. 15 : 28, 29.... h ch. 15 : 41.

his father; it has been surmised that the father was dead. Observe the indication that Paul made careful inquiries before taking Timothy as a companion; he acts upon the counsel which he subsequently gave to him, Lay hands suddenly on no man (1 Tim. 5 : 22).

3. And took and circumcised him. This action seems to some critics inconsistent with Paul's refusal to circumcise Titus (Gal. 2 : 3), his condemnation of Peter for refusing fellowship with the Gentiles (Gal. 2 : 12-14), and his subsequent condemnation of those who demanded circumcision of the Galatian Christians (Gal. 5 : 2). These critics, however, fail to notice the fact that Timothy was by his mother's side a Jew; that Paul was going, not to visit Christian churches, but to preach the Gospel in new regions; that it was always his custom to preach first to the Jews, and in the synagogue when there was one in the place, and that to have taken with him an *uncircumcised Jew* would not have helped but must only have hindered him. He acted here upon the principle enunciated to the Corinthians in 1 Cor. 9 : 20, 21. That neither he nor Timothy nor the Christian churches in that region perceived any inconsistency between the circumcision of Timothy and the resolution of the church at Jerusalem, is indicated by the next verse. After Timothy's circumcision he was specially ordained to the Gospel ministry by the laying on of hands (see chaps. 6 : 6; 8 : 17, notes) by Paul and the elders (1 Tim. 4 : 14; 2 Tim. 1 : 6), with which possibly was combined the good profession before many witnesses referred to in 1 Tim. 6 : 12.

4, 5. As they went through the cities. Not merely of Cilicia, the whole revisitation of the Christian churches established by Paul and Barnabas (ver. 36) is referred to.—**They delivered them the resolutions for to keep, that were determined by the apostles and elders in Jerusalem.** The language of this verse in our English version indicates an authoritative decree by the meeting at Jerusalem binding on all the churches; but it is at least doubtful whether this meaning is sustained by the original. The word rendered *decrees* (δόγμα) in classical Greek signifies, first an opinion, then a public resolution, finally an authoritative governmental decree, in which sense it is ordinarily used in the N. T. (Luke 2 : 1; Acts 17 : 7). Nothing more, however, is necessarily indicated here than that Paul and Silas reported to the Christian churches the judgment or opinion of the church at Jerusalem as embodied in their public resolution, to which, confirmed as it was by the unanimous agreement of the life-companions of their Lord, Gentile Christians would naturally yield a ready compliance. That it was not regarded by Paul as a law of permanent obligation is evident from his language subsequently to the Corinthians (1 Cor. ch. 8. Comp. Rom. 14 : 14).—**Therefore were the churches established in the faith.** *Therefore*, both because peace was secured between the Jewish and Gentile converts, and also because both were taught to rest their hope, not upon rites and ceremonies, the righteousness that is of the law, but upon the mercy of God through Jesus Christ. **And increased in number daily.** Not the number of churches, but the number of Christians in the churches increased.

6-8. For the course of Paul's journey so briefly indicated in these verses, see map, p. 19. The route there marked is wholly hypothetical in its details; we only know that he preached the Gospel in the provinces of Phrygia and Galatia, then passing through the provinces of Asia and Mysia on the Ægean Sea, crossed over into Europe, landing at Neapolis, the seaport of Philippi, in Macedonia. Apparently Paul would have confined his ministry mainly to the Jews and Jewish proselytes; but he was compelled by the Spirit of God to leave Asia Minor and carry the Gospel over into Greece proper, the heart of the heathen world; even here he does not straightway preach the Gospel to the heathen; at Philippi he is driven from his comparative retirement with the few Jewish women at the riverside, by the providence of God; in Thessalonica and Berea he preaches only to the Jews (ch. 17 : 1-10); in Athens chiefly to the Jews and proselytes, until invited by the Gentiles to Areopagus (ch. 17 : 17-19); and in Corinth he remains a considerable time in "weakness, and in fear, and in much trembling" (1 Cor. 2 : 3) before he turns from the Jews to preach to the Greeks (ch. 18 : 6).

Phrygia. This was one of the most important provinces of Asia Minor. The Phrygians are believed to be descendants from the Armenians; their legends contain an account of the flood. The Trojans, Mysians, and other populations of ancient Greece seem to be branches of this race. They were of a peaceful disposition; agriculture was their chief occupation; their country was rich in various products, especially

the region of[i] Galatia, and were forbidden of[j] the
Holy Ghost to preach the word in[k] Asia,
7 After they were come to Mysia, they assayed to go
into Bithynia: but the Spirit suffered them not.
8 And they passing by Mysia, came down to[l] Troas.
9 And a vision appeared to Paul in the night; There
stood a man[m] of Macedonia, and prayed him, saying,
Come over into Macedonia, and help us.

i Gal. 1:2; 1 Pet. 1:1....j Amos 8:11, 12; 1 Cor. 12:11....k Rev. 1:4, 11....l 2 Cor. 2:12; 2 Tim. 4:13....m ch. 10:30.

metals, marble, wine and sheep; their religion, a modified form of the Greek mythology, appears to have combined, in the worship, with the Greek rites, some of the peculiarly impure ceremonies of the Syro-Phœnician tribes. At the time of Paul's visit Phrygia was not a distinct Roman province. The term as used here indicates rather a race of people than a geographical or political division of country. We cannot therefore define its boundaries more accurately than by saying that with Galatia it occupied the great central space of Asia Minor.—**The region of Galatia.** This region was inhabited by the descendants of the Gauls, who invaded Greece and Asia in the third century B. C., and finally settled and became mixed with the Greek population. The Galatians were a brave, freedom-loving, enthusiastic, but fickle people, the Frenchmen of Asia Minor. On the history of this province and the character of its people, see Intro. to and notes on Epistle to the Galatians. During this visit Christian churches were established both in Phrygia and Galatia (ch. 18:23). Some details of Paul's experience in Galatia, particularly the enthusiastic reception accorded to him, are indicated in Gal. 4:13–15.—**Were forbidden of the Holy Ghost to preach the word in Asia.** How forbidden, whether by some special providence, or by the direct communication of the Spirit, is not indicated. *Asia* is of course not the continent of that name, nor Asia Minor, but a Roman senatorial province bordering the Ægean Sea. In the N. T. the phrase is always thus used to designate this particular province. Why Paul was forbidden to preach the Gospel in Asia and subsequently in Mysia and Bithynia can be only matter of surmise. I believe it was because God willed that he should carry the Gospel into the heart of heathendom. See note on vers. 6–8.

Mysia. A province, sometimes regarded as included in Asia. Like Phrygia, the term is

TROAS FROM TENEDOS.

used to designate a people rather than a political division.—**They essayed to go into Bithynia.** That is, prevented from preaching in Asia and Mysia, they attempted to go northward into the province of Bithynia. This province borders on the Euxine or Black Sea, embracing the northernmost portion of Asia Minor, and extending from the Black Sea on the East to the Bosphorus on the West. Bithynia and Mysia are mentioned in the N. T. only here.—**They passing by Mysia came down to Troas.** That is, as Alford, passing it by as regards the work of their preaching. They must have passed through Mysia to reach Troas, where they embarked for Macedonia. Troas is the ancient Troy, rendered famous by Homer, though the

10 And after he had seen the vision, immediately we
endeavoured to go[n] into Macedonia, assuredly gathering that the Lord had called us for to preach the gospel unto them.

11 Therefore loosing from Troas, we came with a
straight course to Samothracia, and the next *day* to
Neapolis;
12 And from thence to Philippi,[o] which is the chief

n 2 Cor. 2 : 13. . . . o Phil. 1 : 1.

exact site of the ancient city is probably several miles inland. The Troas here intended is either a seaport town, Alexandria Troas, named in honor of Alexander, or the district in its immediate vicinity. The town was a free city (see ver. 12, note) and was not reckoned as belonging to either Asia or Bithynia; the district was an undulating plain extending about eight geographical miles inland. The accompanying illustration represents the plain of Troy as seen from the neighboring island of Tenedos, with Mt. Ida in the distance.

9. A vision appeared to Paul. On the nature of visions, see ch. 9 : 10, 11. The apostle having been led by the spirit of God to the seashore, and prohibited from further missionary labors in Asia Minor, the Spirit now directly indicates to him the will of God, that he shall pass over from Asia Minor into Europe.—**A man of Macedonia.** Something in the attire or appearance of the visitant, or possibly his language, Come over into Macedonia, indicated the appeal as coming from that district. This vision has been rightly recognized by the church as interpreting the unuttered cry of heathendom for help. The annexed illustrations, showing the difference in dress and appearance between the Arab and the Greek, will indicate better than a description will do, that this Macedonian might have been recognized by his appearance; the dialect also was peculiar.

ARAB.

GREEK.

Into Macedonia. This was an important kingdom of ancient Greece, and subsequently a Roman province. At the accession of Alexander the Great, the kingdom was bounded on the north by Mœsia and Illyricum, on the south by Thessaly and Epirus, and on the east and west respectively, by Thrace and the Ægean Sea, and by Epirus and the Adriatic. The country may be described as an undulating plain, into which run the spurs of several ridges of mountains, and surrounded on three sides by the mountains themselves. Among the most distinguished of these are Athos and Olympus. Its ancient capital was Pella, the birth-place of Alexander; other important cities were Philippi, Thessalonica, Amphipolis, Apollonia, and Berea. The soil is fertile, and the climate healthy and temperate, though considered more severe than that of the more southerly parts of Greece. The ancient Macedonians were a hardy and warlike people, and their military system was considered very perfect. The civilization of Athens reached them but slowly, and they never, even under Alexander, attained to an equality with the more favored parts of Greece. To the Biblical student Macedonia is interesting chiefly as the site of Paul's successful labors. The churches at Thessalonica and Philippi were among the results of his missionary labors there; and, from Paul's references to them in subsequent epistles, we are assured that the Gospel found a readier entrance and a warmer welcome among the hardy Macedonians than among the more cultured Athenians, and was more generously supported and carried out in subsequent contributions than among the wealthier Corinthians. Comp. Acts 17 : 10–12 with 16, 32; 1 Thess. 1 : 5 with 1 Cor. 3 : 1; and Rom. 15 : 26; Phil. 4 : 10, 15, with 1 Cor. 9 : 7–14; 16 : 1; 2 Cor., ch. 9.

10. After he had seen the vision, we endeavored to go. By seeking for a ship in which to cross the Ægean Sea. It is notable that now, for the first time in his account, Luke employs the first person: *we* endeavored to go. Whether Luke was with Paul prior to this time is uncertain; it is reasonably certain that he was Paul's traveling companion in most of the events hereinafter narrated. See Intro., p. 14. It has been conjectured, and the surmise is not unreasonable, that he joined the apostle at Troas as a physician, on account of Paul's broken health.

11. We came with a straight course. That is, with a fair wind. The journey took but two days. When subsequently going in the opposite direction, the voyage occupied five days (ch. 20 : 6). It is only a strong southerly breeze which will overcome the current which runs from the Dardanelles by Tenedos, and this, combined with the short passage, is one of the many

city of that part of Macedonia, *and* a colony: and we
were in that city abiding certain days.
13 And on the sabbath we went out of the city by a
river side, where prayer[p] was wont to be made; and we sat down, and spake unto the women which resorted *thither*.

p ch. 21 : 5.

marks of the veracity of our narrative.—**To Samothracia.** An island in the Ægean Sea, 38 miles from the coast of Thrace, and about midway between Troas and Neapolis. It is of an oval shape, 8 miles long, 6 broad, and remarkable for its extreme elevation, rising 5,240 feet above the elevation of the sea. It is without good harbors, but affords safe anchorage. If, as was apparently the case, the wind was from the south, there would have been smooth water anywhere along the north shore. The implication is that the ship spent the night at anchor, proceeding the next day on its course.—**Neapolis.** The name is the same as Naples, and means New City; this was the seaport of Philippi, from which it was 10 miles distant. Immediately back of the town the land rises to a considerable height, on the other side of which is the plain of Philippi. Traces of paved military roads are still found, as well as the remains of a great aqueduct on two tiers of arches with Latin inscriptions. Over one of these roads Paul must have passed to his destination, led by the voice of the mysterious vision to he knew not what dangers and perils.

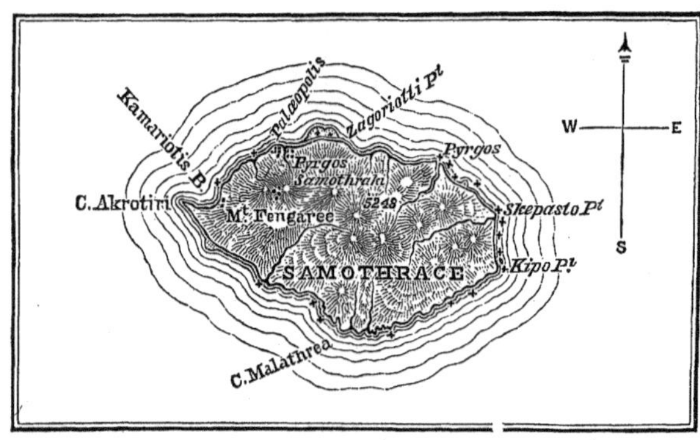

MAP OF SAMOTHRACIA. (From Lewin, Vol. I, p. 200.)

12. To Philippi. A city of Macedonia which took its name from its founder, Philip, the father of Alexander. The new city, built by the Romans, appears not to have been on the site of the old, but in its immediate proximity. The ancient name is still applied to the locality, but there are no inhabitants. The line of the walls may be traced, and there are two lofty gateways amidst the fragments that are left. There are also the remains of an amphitheatre on the sides of the overhanging hill, the seats of which are quite perfect. So far as the N. T. history directly informs us, Philippi was the first city in Europe which heard the Gospel message. How minute the seed, a conversational service with a few women outside the gates of Philippi! how great the tree, European Christendom! Comp. Matt. 13 : 31, 32. On the character and subsequent history of the church founded at this time by Paul, see Epistle to the Philippians, Notes and Intro.—**The chief city of that part of Macedonia.** Either *one of the principal cities of the province*, a statement which would be true of Philippi; or *the first city of Macedonia, i. e.*, the first one to which Paul came after landing. Either interpretation is admissible; Paul's visit to Neapolis is not inconsistent with the latter rendering, both because Neapolis, strictly speaking, belonged to Thrace, and also because it was only the seaport of Philippi and in the nature of a suburb.—**And a colony.** This word occurs only here in the N. T. With this characterization of the city, agrees Luke's reference to the *magistrates* (στρατηγός, vers. 20, 22, 35, 36, 38) and *sergeants* (ῥαβδοῦχος, vers. 35, 38). The fact that Philippi was a colony is mentioned here in explanation of the events which followed. The phrase is a technical one, applied in Roman literature to certain communities possessed of peculiar privileges. No colony was established without special authority from the parent government at Rome, and no Roman could be sent out as a colonist without his free consent. When the place of destination had been selected, the law passed and the volunteers organized, they were sent to their destination in the form of an army; the limits of the city, which was always an essential part of a Roman colony, were marked out by a plow; religious ceremonies accompanied; and the anniversary was ever afterward sacredly observed. The city thus founded was a miniature of Rome; its members had all the rights of Roman citizens; the Latin language was spoken and the Roman law administered; the coinage had Latin inscriptions. The government of the city was administered by magistrates, Duumviri, who frequently took the name of *prætors*

14 And a certain woman named Lydia, a seller of
purple, of the city of Thyatira, which worshipped God,
heard *us*: whose heart[q] the Lord opened, that she attended unto the things which were spoken of Paul.
15 And when she was baptized, and her household,
she besought[r] *us*, saying, If ye have judged me to be
faithful to the Lord, come into my house, and abide
there. And she constrained us.
16 And it came to pass, as we went to prayer, a certain damsel possessed[s] with a spirit of divination met
us, which brought her masters much gain[t] by soothsaying:

q Luke 24 : 45 .... r Heb. 13 : 2 .... s 1 Sam. 28 : 7 .... t ch. 19 : 24.

(στρατηγός), and who exercised functions in the colony analogous to that of the consul at Rome in the days of the republic. Attendant upon them were the lictors, the *sergeants* of vers. 35, 38, who were charged with inflicting punishment upon those who were condemned by the magistrates or Duumviri. Philippi, though originally founded by the Greeks, was subsequently made a colony by Augustus. The evidences that Philippi was such a colony appear in Latin inscriptions still found among the ruins.—**Abiding certain days.** Perhaps some days previous to the Sabbath mentioned in the next verse.

13. On the Sabbath we went out of the gates by a river side. "After about twenty minutes' ride from the Khan, over ground thickly strewed with fragments of marble columns and slabs that have been employed in building, a river-bed 66 feet wide is crossed, through which the stream rushes with great force, and immediately on the other side the walls of the ancient Philippi may be traced. Their direction is adjusted to the course of the stream; and at only 350 feet from its margin there appears a gap in their circuit indicating the former existence of a gate. This is, no doubt, the gate out of which the apostle and his companion passed to the 'prayer-meeting' on the banks of a river, where they made the acquaintance of Lydia, the Thyatiran seller of purple. The locality, just outside the walls, and with a plentiful supply of water for their animals, is exactly the one which would be appropriated as a market for itinerant traders."—(*Smith's Bib. Dict.*) It would also be an appropriate place for the religious meetings of the Jews, who were accustomed, when practicable, to hold their religious services near the water, probably on account of the frequent ablutions customary among them, the obligation of which would be especially urgent upon those living among the heathen. The river was the Gangites or Gangas. The best readings give here as I have, out of the *gates*, not out of the *city*, as in our English version.—**Where prayer was wont to be made.** There appears to have been no synagogue at Philippi (comp. ch. 17 : 1); perhaps here was one of those buildings called *proseuchæ*, which were distinguished from the synagogues by being slighter in structure, and sometimes simple enclosures open to the sky; or it may be, as our English version would indicate, that a mere spot by the river bank had been selected for open-air meetings, which appear to have been attended only or chiefly by women.

Ch. 16 : 14-40. PAUL AT PHILIPPI. THE TRUE AND THE FICTITIOUS SAVIOUR IN CONFLICT.—THE SPIRIT OF COVETOUSNESS THE SECRET OF MUCH OF RELIGIOUS PERSECUTION.—GRACE TO THE OPPRESSED IS TROUBLE TO THE OPPRESSOR.—SONGS IN THE NIGHT.—CONVERSION ILLUSTRATED.—THE DIGNITY OF THE TRUE CHRISTIAN.—THE SEED OF SORROW BRINGS FORTH THE FRUITS OF LOVE AND JOY. See Epis. to Phil.

14. A certain woman named Lydia. That she was a Jewish proselyte is indicated by the language, *which worshipped God;* ver. 15 indicates that she had her residence in or near Philippi; she is not mentioned again in the N. T., but may well have been one of those women which labored with Paul in the Gospel, and referred to in Phil. 4 : 3.—**A seller of purple.** Either the dye stuff, or robes dyed with purple; these were not only worn by kings and other officials, but also by the wealthy and luxurious (Jer. 10 : 9; Ez. 27 : 7; Luke 16 : 19; Rev. 17 : 4; 18 : 16). Dyeing is still a customary trade in the East; the dyer's shop, a room not more than 10 or 12 feet square,

THE DYER'S SHOP.

is usually placed directly on the street among others of the same trade; the cloths, after dipping in the vats, are hung outside to dry, the passers in the street avoiding them if they can.

It is not improbable that Lydia was carrying on the dyeing trade and had her shop just outside the city gates.—**Of the city of Thyatira.** A considerable city of the province of Asia where Paul had been prevented from preaching the Gospel; "thus, although forbidden to preach the Gospel in Asia, their first convert at Philippi is an Asiatic."—(*Alford.*) Here a Christian church was subsequently established (Rev. 1:11). It is called by Strabo a Macedonian colony, and although it seems clear that it existed prior to the Macedonian empire, it may have been greatly increased by colonists from Macedonia. In the middle ages the Turks changed the name to Akhissar, which it still bears. Among the guilds which existed in this city dyers are especially mentioned in the ancient inscriptions, and dyeing seems to have flourished here from a very early period. Thus Homer (Book 4:141):

"As when some Carian or Mæonian dame
Tinges with purple the white ivory,
To form a trapping for the cheeks of steeds."

The fact that Lydia is described as *of the city of Thyatira* does not indicate that Philippi was not at this time her permanent residence. Similarly Paul speaks of himself as a Jew of Tarsus in ch. 21:39; 22:3.—**Whose heart the Lord opened.** Observe the incidental recognition here of the truth that the word of God is efficacious only as it is blessed by the Spirit of God (1 Cor. 7:6; 2 Cor. 4:6. Comp. Matt. 13:16). "The heart is of itself closed; but it is for God to open it."—(*Bengel.*)

15. And when she was baptized and her house. This text is often quoted in support of the doctrine of infant baptism; thus Mr. Barnes: "No mention is made of their having believed, and the case is one that affords a strong presumptive proof that this was an instance of household or infant baptism." Similarly Bengel: "Who can believe that in so many families there was no infant? And that the Jews, who were wont to circumcise, and the Gentiles, who purified them by washings, did not also present them for baptism." To me it appears very clear that there is no *authority* for the practice of *infant* baptism in such incidental historical references such as this; for (1) *infant* and *household* baptism are not the same; there is nothing to indicate that there were any infant children in this household, or that Lydia was a married woman. On the other hand, it is hardly credible that there should have been no *adults*, and it will hardly be argued, that because their faith is not stated, they were baptized upon the faith of Lydia; (2) assuming that there were infants in the household in this and analogous cases mentioned in the N. T., it does not follow that they were baptized. If it was not the usage in the primitive church to baptize infants, but only adults, and upon a personal confession of faith, the historian would assume, and the reader would understand, that only those capable of making an intelligent confession of faith were included in the baptism. Thus, if a modern writer were to use the phraseology, "Mr. A. and his family have been baptized and joined the Baptist church," it would be assumed by both writer and reader that only those capable of making an intelligent confession of faith were included. The whole question of infant baptism must be determined, not by doubtful deductions from incidental references to the baptism of households, but by the view which the Bible student takes of the nature of the church of Christ, whether an organization of households or of individuals, and by his view of the covenant of God with his people, whether that covenant is entered into for each soul alone, or with Christian parents for their children. What may fairly be deduced from the language of this verse is this: that by reason of Lydia's faith her household were brought unto Christ and his church. The first field for the ministry of the young convert is his home.

If ye have judged me to be faithful unto the Lord. Not merely an earnest, but also a modest petition. She asks as a favor the privilege of conferring her hospitality. Comp. the story of the woman of Shunem, 2 Kings 4:8–10. See also Heb. 13:2.—**She constrained us.** By much entreaty. So in Luke 24:29, the disciples constrained Christ to accept their hospitality.

16. As we went to prayer. Rather to the *place of prayer* referred to in ver. 13. See note there.—**Possessed with a spirit of divination.** Literally, *of Python.* This was originally the name of a mythological dragon who guarded the Delphic oracle; Apollo having slain the monster, took possession of the oracle, hence to him was sometimes given the name of Python. He was the god of prophecy, punished and destroyed the wicked, and had the power of warding off evil, or at least of suggesting by his oracles the means by which it could be averted. According to Müller, the essential feature in the character of Apollo is that of the averter of evil; and the title of *Saviour* is one given to him by Greek writers. Thus, this damsel was, as it were, an apostle of the heathen Saviour, a fact which gives especial significance to her testimony to Paul and his companions, as those who show the "way of salvation."—**Brought her masters much gain by soothsaying.** It was a customary belief among the ancients that certain persons were possessed by the spirits of the gods; Apollo was generally the source from which the heathen diviners and seers professed to obtain their knowledge of the future. These heathen prophets were not only tolerated, but

17 The same followed Paul and us, and cried, saying, These men are the servants of the most high[u] God,
which shew unto us the way of[v] salvation.
18 And this did she many days. But Paul, being
grieved, turned and said[w] to the spirit, I command thee
in the name of Jesus Christ, to come out of her. And[x]
he came out the same hour.
19 And when her masters saw that the hope of their
gains[y] was gone, they caught Paul and Silas, and drew
them into the marketplace, unto[z] the rulers,

u Gen. 14 : 18-22 .... v ch. 18 : 26; Heb. 10 : 20 .... w Mark 1 : 25, 34 .... x Mark 16 : 17 .... y ch. 19 : 24-27 .... z Matt. 10 : 18.

protected and honored by the government, were consulted by leading men, and were honored counsellors in the public assemblies. Besides these more respectable prophets, there were numbers of diviners of an inferior order, who professed to explain signs and tell fortunes, and were popular with the lower classes of society; they were not infrequently slaves, as in the case of this woman, who was owned apparently by two or three masters in common. Whether shê was literally possessed by an evil spirit, or was simply a lunatic, whose maniacal utterances were turned to profitable account by her unscrupulous masters, who professed to interpret them as prophecies, is a question difficult to determine. Alford, Alexander, and Conybeare and Howson, hold the former view; Lewin, Meyer, and, apparently, Hackett, hold the latter view. That there is no demon or evil spirit corresponding to Apollo or Python is clear from 1 Cor. 8 : 4; that demoniacal possession is a real phenomenon, see note on Demoniacal Possession, Vol. I, p. 123. It seems to me both from Paul's language and from Luke's, in ver. 18, that this was a case of such possession, and that the act of Paul did not merely expose a fraud, nor calm the perturbed mind of a lunatic, but really delivered this unfortunate from the evil spirit which possessed her.

17, 18. The same followed Paul and us and cried saying, etc. This may have been a supernatural recognition of the power of God in the apostles; see the analogous cases in Matt. 8 : 29; Mark 3 : 11; Luke 4 : 41; 8 : 28; and this is the view of most commentators; or it may have been a cry of sarcasm and derision, the

RUINS IN THE MARKET-PLACE OF PHILIPPI.

possessed following Paul with this outcry, somewhat as a crowd of boys might do; and this I am inclined to think more probable, since otherwise her masters would have interfered to prevent her testimony.—**The way of salvation.** Or, *the way of safety;* in this more general sense the words would be understood by the heathen population.—**But Paul being grieved.** Rather being indignant, literally *exercised.* See ch. 4 : 2, note, where the Greek word is the same. "Not

20 And brought them to the magistrates, saying,
These men, being Jews, do exceedingly trouble[a] our
city,
21 And teach customs, which are not lawful for us to
receive, neither to observe, being Romans.

22 And the multitude rose up together against them:
and the magistrates rent off their clothes, and commanded to beat *them*.
23 And when they had laid many[b] stripes upon
them, they cast *them* into prison, charging the jailer to
keep them safely:

a ch. 17 : 6 ; 1 Kings 18 : 17 .... b 2 Cor. 6 : 5 ; 11 : 23, 25 ; 1 Thess. 2 : 2.

mere annoyance is expressed by this word, but rather holy indignation and sorrow at what he saw and heard; the Christian soldier was goaded to the attack, but the mere satisfaction of anger was not the object, any more than the result, of the stroke."—(*Alford.*) Why Paul allowed the evil spirit to go on unrebuked for many days it is difficult to say, unless it be an indication of hesitation, if not timidity, of which other indications are afforded by his course, in preaching only to the proselytes at Philippi (ver. 13), to the Jews only at Thessalonica and Berea (ch. 17 : 2, 10), and his first ministry at Corinth (ch. 18 : 1-5 ; 1 Cor. 2 : 3). From prudential motives he perhaps hesitated to provoke a controversy with heathenism by a direct attack on one of its most cherished and potent superstitions.—**In the name of Jesus Christ.** As a herald in the name and with the authority of his King, Paul speaks.—**He came out the same hour.** See Mark 1 : 27. In this miracle Christ fulfils the promise of Mark 16 : 17; Luke 9 : 1. Comp. Luke 10 : 17.

19. The hope of their gains was gone. The first heathen persecution, like that subsequently at Ephesus (ch. 19 : 25-27), was set on foot by covetousness. Comp. 1 Tim. 6 : 9, 10. Like the Gergesenes (Matt. 8 : 28-34) they cared nothing that a soul had been saved in comparison with the loss of their gains.—**They caught Paul and Silas.** The idea of violence is conveyed in the original. Luke and Timothy seem not to have been seized, either because they were not present, or because they were less prominent, or because, not being Jews, they were less obnoxious to the Greek population.—**Drew them into the market-place.** Or *Agora;* a public square, used not merely for purposes of market, but for assemblages and other public business. For description and illustration see 17 : 17, note. The accompanying illustration from Lewin gives the present aspect of the ruins of the Agora at Philippi, which indicates the solid character of the structure enclosing it.—**Unto the rulers.** (ἄρχων.) This term is here a general one, equivalent to the more specific one of *magistrates* in the next verse.

20. To the magistrates (στρατηγός). The duumviri or prætors; the former was their proper name, the latter, as one of greater honor, was frequently used by them. See note on ver. 12.—**Being Jews.** An appeal to the natural prejudice against the Jewish nation who were held in peculiar contempt amongst the Romans.—**Do exceedingly trouble our city.** By curing this poor lunatic. To cast out ungodliness is a trouble to those that get gain by it.—**And teach customs which are not lawful for us to receive, being Romans.** Observe the contrast: they, *Jews*, trouble us, *Romans*. While the Roman government allowed in the provinces the original religion of the inhabitants, they forbade the introduction of innovations in religion, especially into Roman cities like that of Philippi, as calculated to unsettle the minds of the people and create political disturbance. "How often in the ages of our fathers was it given in charge to the magistrates, to prohibit the performance of any foreign religious rites; to banish strolling sacrificers and soothsayers from the forum, the circus, and the city; to search for, and burn, books of divination; and to abolish every mode of sacrificing that was not conformable to the Roman practice."—(*Livy*, B. 39, ch. 16.) Thus, though the apostles had acted with all possible prudence, there was color for the charge brought against them. Moreover, every city had its own special protecting deities; to bring into it a new worship was an invasion which the people were as ready to resent as the magistrates to punish. Observe that in the superstitious city of Philippi these prejudices were easily aroused, but not in the philosophical and skeptical city of Athens, nor in the commercial city of Corinth (chaps. 17, 18).

22-24. The multitude rose up together. * * * **the magistrates rent off their clothes.** The clothes of Paul and Silas. The mob and the magistrates acted together; but the implication is that the magistrates acted under the impulse of and to please the mob, as did Pilate in the case of Christ. No attempt at inquiry was made, no opportunity was given to the accused for defence or to plead their Roman citizenship. Parallel to the course of the mob here is that in ch. 19 : 28, 34; 21 : 30.—**Commanded to beat them.** The command was given to the lictors, the sergeants of ver. 35, and the beating was inflicted with the lictor's rod or *fasces*. These consisted of a number of rods cut from the elm or birch tree and bound together with thongs; they were carried by the lictors before certain of the

24 Who, having received such a charge, thrust them
into the inner prison, and made their feet fast in the
stocks.
25 And at midnight Paul and Silas prayed,[c] and
sang [d] praises unto God: and the prisoners heard them.

26 And suddenly there was a great earthquake, so [e]
that the foundations of the prison were shaken: and
immediately [f] all the doors were opened, and every
one's bands were loosed.
27 And the keeper of the prison awaking out of

c James 5 : 13.... d Ps. 34 : 1.... e ch. 4 : 31.... f chaps. 5 : 19; 12 : 7, 10; Isa. 42 : 7.

magistrates, and were used to inflict scourging. During the reign of the kings, and under the first years of the republic, an axe was likewise inserted amongst the rods, but after the consulate of Publicola, no magistrate, except a dictator, was permitted to use the fasces with an axe in the city of Rome; the employment of both together being restricted to the consuls at the head of their armies and to the quæstors in their provinces. The illustration affords an example of the *fasces* as they appeared with the axe inserted, from a bas-relief of the Mattei palace at Rome. That the beating in this instance was inflicted by the lictor with the fasces is indicated in the original by the verb (ῥαβδίζειν) which signifies literally to beat with a rod. Paul refers to this in 2 Cor. 11 : 25, "thrice was I beaten with rods;" the other two instances history has not recorded. That he keenly felt the degradation is evident from 1 Thess. 2 : 2. The beating was upon the bare back, the apostles' garments having been violently torn off by order of the magistrates, not probably by them personally; they are said to have done what they ordered to be done.—**The jailer.** On the character of Roman jailers, who are also executioners, see below.—**In the inner prison** * * * *

FASCES.

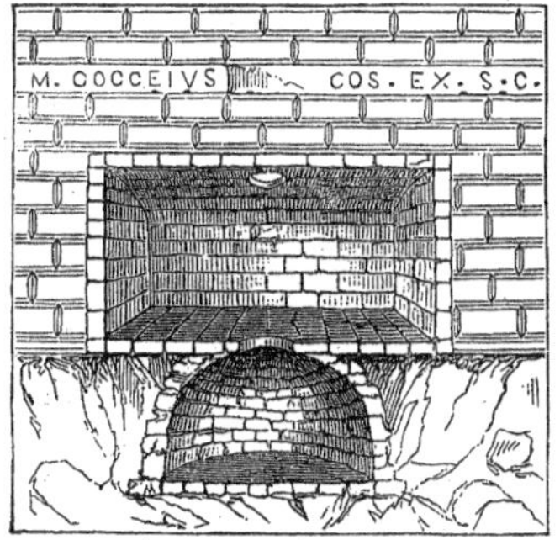

INNER PRISON—SECTIONAL VIEW.

fast in the stocks. The Roman prisons were customarily divided into three stories, one above the other, appropriated to different purposes. The lowermost was a dark underground dungeon entered through the floor of the cell above, and used only for execution when the criminal was condemned to death; the middle one, on a level with the ground, but like the other approached only through the roof, served as a place of confinement for the more dangerous prisoners. Filth, vermin, lack of air and light, and the often superadded chains of stocks, made this a veritable abode of torture. This was probably the *inner prison* into which Paul and Silas were thrust. The stocks were constructed like

IN THE STOCKS.

those of more modern times; they are still used, though now rarely, in the East, the criminal being ordinarily publicly exposed in the market-place, where he is an object of derision, and is sometimes pelted by the populace. Comp. with the treatment of Paul and Silas here that of Jeremiah in Jer. 20 : 2; 38 : 6.

25. And at midnight Paul and Silas in their prayers were singing praises unto God, and the prisoners were listening to them. This renders nearly literally the original; while they were singing, and while the prisoners were listening, the earthquake came. Their experience beautifully illustrates the reference of Job to God, "who giveth songs in the night," and emphasizes Paul's exhortation to the Philippian Christians, "Rejoice in the Lord alway" (Phil. 4 : 4). It is a significant fact that the most joyous of Paul's epistles is that written to the church at Philippi, born out of his experience

his sleep, and seeing the prison doors open, drew out
his sword, and would have killed himself, supposing
that the prisoners had been fled.
28 But[g] Paul cried with a loud voice, saying, Do
thyself[h] no harm; for we are all here.
29 Then he called for a light, and sprang in, and
came trembling,[i] and fell down before Paul and Silas,
30 And brought them out, and said, Sirs, what[j] must
I do to be saved?
31 And they said, Believe[k] on the Lord Jesus Christ,
and thou shalt be saved, and thy[l] house.
32 And they spake unto him the word of the Lord,
and to all[m] that were in his house.
33 And he took them the same hour of the night, and

g Prov. 24 : 11, 12; 1 Thess. 5 : 15....h Eccles. 7 : 15-17....i Jer. 5 : 22....j chaps. 2 : 37; 9 : 6....k ch. 13 : 39; Hab. 2 : 4; John 3 : 16, 36; 6 : 47....l ch. 2 : 39....m Rom. 1 : 14, 16.

of suffering. The Psalms afforded appropriate stanzas for their use. See Ps. 40 : 1–4; 79 : 12; 102 : 19, 20; 116 : 14; 142 : 8, 9; 146 : 6–8. Observe that the Christian's inward experience of joy is superior to outward experience of trouble: "Their legs in the stocks pained them not, whose souls were in heaven."—(*Tertullian.*) Also that the Christian's prayer, even in his direst extremity, should ever be with praise (Phil. 4 : 6; Col. 4 : 2; 1 Thess. 5 : 18).

26, 27. And suddenly there was a great earthquake. A remarkable illustration of answer to prayer; and observe that this answer involves a divine interference with nature, though not a violation of natural law. We must know a great deal more about earthquakes and their causes than we do now, to assert that it is irrational to believe that such an earthquake should be sent in answer to prayer.—**All the doors were opened and every one's bands were loosed.** Either by the action of the earthquake, or by the same supernatural power which produced the earthquake.—**The keeper of the prison.** The jailer of ver. 23; the Greek word is the same.—**Would have killed himself, supposing that the prisoners had been fled.** Under the Roman law the jailer was liable to undergo the punishment which the malefactors, who escaped by his negligence, were to have suffered. See ch. 12 : 19. Hence the pains which the soldiers took to make sure of the death of Christ (John 19 : 34). The jailer would have avoided death and disgrace by suicide. Notwithstanding some dissuasives from suicide by a few of the best ancient moralists, it was generally approved by the Romans. Among the defenders of the right of self-destruction are Seneca, Epicurus, Lucretius, Pliny; among those whose example sanctioned it are Cato, Cassius, Diodorus and Brutus.

28. Paul cried with a loud voice. The jailer's purpose must have been supernaturally communicated to him, for the prisoners were yet in darkness, and the jailer was not in nor probably very near to the inner prison.—**Do thyself no harm.** This is the message of the Gospel to man in despair. Contrast with it the counsel of Seneca, "If life pleases you, live; if not, you have a right to return whence you came."—**For we are all here.** Paul does not argue the sinfulness of suicide. He first removes the jailer's fears; he afterwards affords him religious instruction.

29, 30. Then he called for lights. Plural, not singular; sufficient to light the whole prison.—**And sprang in.** An indication of his excitement and eagerness.—**And came trembling.** The language of an eye-witness.—**And brought them out.** From the inner prison; perhaps into the court-yard, where may have occurred the speaking of the word by the apostles (ver. 32).—**Sirs, what must I do to be saved.** Not from the earthquake, for the danger from that was passed; nor from punishment, for his prisoners had not escaped; moreover Paul's answer is not responsive to the inquiry if this were its significance; faith in the Lord Jesus Christ would not secure him from the danger of punishment. These interpretations are curiously shallow, and ignore the ordinary effect of great events, and especially great dangers, upon the mind. Such an event as this earthquake brings the eternal world near, and gives to the dullest soul some sense of his spiritual needs; the same motive which leads the soldier in battle, and the sailor in storm, to pray, though he has never prayed before, led the jailer to ask one who had proved himself an unexpected friend, what he should do for personal salvation. Comp. the effect of Christ's miracle on Peter's mind in Luke 5 : 8.

31–33. And they said, Put thy trust on the Sire, Jesus Christ. There is a contrast between the jailer's question and the apostle's reply not preserved in the English version. The Greek for *Sirs* in ver. 30, and *Lord* in ver. 31, is the same. He addresses them as *Sires* or *Lords;* they reply, Trust in the one and only *Sire* or *Lord,* Jesus Christ. To believe here is, not to believe in any doctrine respecting the Lord Jesus Christ, for the jailer was a heathen who, so far as we know, knew nothing respecting him. Trust may and often does precede knowledge.—**And thy house.** The promise includes his as well as him. Not that they should be saved without faith, but that their faith should be awakened through his.—**And they spake unto him the word of the Lord.** Apparently either in the large room of the prison, or in the court-yard; certainly the members of his household, and possibly the other prisoners, were auditors with him.—**Washed their stripes and was baptized.** "He washed their stripes, was washed

washed *their* stripes; and was baptized, he and all his,
straightway.
34 And when he had brought them into his house,
he set meat[n] before them, and rejoiced,[o] believing in
God with all his house.
35 And when it was day, the magistrates sent the
serjeants, saying, Let those men go.
36 And the keeper of the prison told this saying to
Paul, The magistrates have sent to let you go: now
therefore depart, and go in peace.
37 But Paul said unto them, They have beaten us
openly uncondemned,[p] being Romans, and have cast
us into prison; and now do they thrust us out privily?
nay, verily; but let them come themselves,[q] and fetch
us out.

n Luke 5 : 29....o Rom. 5 : 11....p ch. 22 : 25....q Dan. 6 : 18, 19; Matt. 10 : 16.

from sin; he fed them and was fed."—(*Chrysostom.*)—**He and all his.** The *all* here, who were baptized, are the *all* to whom the word was preached (ver. 32), and the *all* who believed (ver. 34). It does not therefore seem to me that any were here baptized, probably except those who personally heard and accepted the word of God; but it would also seem not natural to suppose that the rite which was performed, if not before daybreak, certainly before the business of the day began (ver. 35), was by immersion. The authorities cited by Dr. Hackett, however, are sufficient to show that immersion was not impossible: "'The rite may have been performed,' says De Wette, 'in the same fountain or tank in which the jailer had washed them.' 'Perhaps the water,' says Meyer, 'was in the court of the house; and the baptism was that of immersion, which formed an essential part of the symbolism of the act.' (See Rom. 6 : 3, seq.) Ancient houses, as usually built, enclosed a rectangular reservoir or basin (the *impluvium*, so-called) for receiving the rain, which flowed from the slightly inclined roof. Some suggest that they may have used a κολυμβήθρα, or swimming bath, found within the walls of the prison. Such a bath was a common appurtenance of houses and public edifices among the Greeks and Romans."

34. He set meat before them. Literally, he *set a table.* The night which began in woe ended in rejoicing.—**And rejoiced believing in God.** Either, Rejoiced, having believed in God, or Rejoiced that he had been led to believe in God. Comp. ver. 31. Observe, Paul bids him believe on the *Lord Jesus Christ;* he believes in *God.* So in John 14 : 1, Ye believe in God, believe also in me.

ON THE CONVERSION OF THE JAILER.—Observe (1) The character of the man: a heathen, with no previous knowledge of the Gospel, and no faith in, probably no knowledge even of the one true God. That he was not a proselyte is certain from ver. 34; that he had no previous sympathy with the apostles is equally certain, from his treatment of them (ver. 24). Not only a heathen, but a man of probably brutal nature. The jailers were also torturers and executioners, were taken from the lower classes of society, and were brutalized by their vocation. No more hopeless case for conversion can be readily conceived. (2.) The condition of salvation: not any creed, nor any ceremony, nor any education or gradual process of reformation, but a simple trust in, and reliance upon, Jesus as his Lord, *i. e.*, his Sovereign and Master. (3.) The evidence he gave of the reality of his conversion: by listening to the word of the Lord, spoken by his prisoners; by accepting baptism at their hands; by releasing them from prison and the stocks, and making them his guests; all of which was done at the hazard of his office, if not of his life (see on verses 21, 27). (4.) The suddenness of his conversion. It is instant; it is instantly recognized by Paul and Silas; the same hour he is baptized and received into the visible church; there is no probation for a period of religious instruction and moral improvement. The church is for the weak and ignorant, as well as for the strong and wise. Neither did he require time to consider whether he would accept Christ, nor did Paul to consider whether he should be accepted. The apostles in officially accepting new members *act* the doctrine which they *preach,* viz., that faith in Jesus Christ is the only condition of salvation. Contrast with this simple and sublime declaration of Paul here, Put thy faith in the Lord Jesus Christ and thou shalt be saved, the declaration of a later dogmatism as embodied in the Athanasian creed, with its declaration, "He that will be saved must thus think of the Trinity."

35, 36. When it was day. All had occurred between midnight (ver. 25) and morning.—**Sent the sergeants.** Probably *the lictors* (ῥαβδοῦχος). The lictor was a public officer attached to the service of certain Roman magistrates, whom he preceded whenever he went abroad. He carried the *fasces* elevated on his left shoulder, and a rod in the right hand, with which he removed any persons obstructing the way, and knocked at the doors of those whom the magistrate visited. Six lictors attended the prætor. They also executed punishment on the condemned. See notes on vers. 12, 22.—**Let those men go.** The language implies contempt. Conybeare and Howson translate it, *Let those fellows go.* The action of the magistrates results, "either from reflecting that they had acted more harshly than the case had warranted, or from hearing a more accurate statement of facts, or through alarm caused by the earthquake, or through that vague

38 And the serjeants told these words unto the magistrates: and they feared, when they heard that they were Romans.
39 And they came and besought[r] them, and brought *them* out, and desired[s] *them* to depart out of the city.
40 And they went out of the prison, and entered into *the house of* Lydia:[t] and when they had seen the brethren, they comforted them, and departed.

CHAPTER XVII.

NOW when they had passed through Amphipolis and Apollonia, they came to Thessalonica, where was a synagogue of the Jews:
2 And Paul, as his manner was,[u] went in unto them, and three sabbath days reasoned with them out of the scriptures,

r Exod. 11 : 8; Rev. 3 : 9.... s Matt. 8 : 34.... t verse 14.... u chaps. 9 : 20; 13 : 5, 14; Luke 4 : 16.

THE LICTOR.

misgiving which sometimes, as in the case of Pilate and his wife, haunts the minds of those who have no distinct religious convictions."—(*Conybeare and Howson.*)—**Go in peace.** A common, here a Christian, salutation. The jailer accepts the message with joy, and anticipates its acceptance by Paul. To him it seems a great victory that Paul should be released; the manner of the release he does not consider.

37-40. Paul said unto them. Through the jailer. "Almost every word in this reply contains a distinct allegation. It would be difficult to find or frame a sentence superior to it in energetic brevity."—(*Hackett.*) They have been beaten *openly*, they will not be thrust out privily; they have been punished *uncondemned*, they will not be released unacquitted; they have been cast into prison before all the people, they will not go out of the prison as though they were fugitives. The demand of the apostle was not without reason; not only personal dignity justified him; it was also necessary for the protection of the infant church at Philippi. The scourging had been notorious; if they had departed secretly, the church would have been likely to suffer from the imputation that its founders were fugitives from justice.—**They feared when they heard that they were Romans.** The Roman law cared little for human rights, but a great deal for the rights of a Roman citizen. On the nature of those rights, and the nature of Paul's acquisition of them, see ch. 22 : 27, 28, note. The Valerian law exempted the Roman citizen from stripes and tortures until an appeal to the people was decided; the Porcian law absolutely forbade the infliction of stripes upon a Roman. The violation of these laws rendered the magistrate liable to indictment for treason, the penalty being death and the confiscation of his property.—**They came and besought them.** The word so rendered is the same one translated *comforted* in the next verse. They used fair words to atone for a foul deed; they were now as obsequious as they had been tyrannical.—**They comforted them and departed.** Rather *exhorted* or *encouraged* them. The apostles are not in haste to depart; but for the present the door is closed against their ministry; they do not remain.

This is the origin of the church at Philippi. Attached to Paul by peculiar sympathy in its origin, it is of all the churches the one most forward to manifest its love to him in all his subsequent afflictions (Phil. 4 : 10, 15); to it he seems to have been peculiarly attached (Phil. 1 : 3-5); originating with a few women, proselytes (ver. 13), women appear to have been among its most active members in its subsequent history (Phil. 4 : 2, 3). From the language of the verse here, which is in the third person, *they* comforted them and departed, with that of ver. 12, which is in the first person, *we* were in that city, it has been reasonably surmised that Luke, and perhaps Timothy (Phil. 2 : 19), remained for a time at Philippi after the departure of Paul and Silas.

CH. 17 : 1-15. PAUL CONTINUES HIS MISSIONARY TOUR; THESSALONICA; BEREA. THE UNSCRUPULOUSNESS OF RELIGIOUS ANIMOSITY.—THE WATER-MARKS OF AUTHENTICITY IN THE BOOK OF ACTS (vers. 5, 6, 8, notes).—TRUE NOBILITY; IT IS WILLING TO RECEIVE THE TRUTH; IT RECEIVES NOTHING AS TRUTH WITHOUT INVESTIGATION.

Paul apparently still desires to preach the Gospel first to his own nation, and is driven by the providence of God from the Jew to the Gentile. Thus he passes through Amphipolis and Apollonia, where, we may presume, there was no Jewish synagogue, preaches at Thessalonica to the Jews, driven thence by the mob, preaches in the synagogue at Berea, and not till he is driven from that city comes to Athens, the centre of Grecian philosophy and idolatry.

1. When they had passed through Amphipolis. A city of Macedonia, about 33 miles, or a day's journey, distant from Philippi. Standing in a pass traversing the mountains bordering the Strymonic gulf, thus commanding the only easy communication from the coast of that gulf to the great Macedonian plains, it was one of the most important strategic points in Greece, and it was, in consequence, an object of contention among the leading states. The ancient name of the place was "Nine Ways," from the great number of Thracian and Macedonian roads which here met. Situated on a tongue of land, formed by the bend of the River Strymon, it needed an artificial protection only on one side, across the isthmus, and the name Amphipolis, or Round-About Town, was given because of its being thus river-girt on three sides. It was his failure in an expedition against Amphipolis that caused the exile of Thucydides—a fortunate exile, since to it we owe his History of the Peloponnesian War. Amphipolis has no importance in the Scripture narrative, being only mentioned here. It is now only a mere village, called by the Greeks *Neokhorio*, by the Turks *Jeni-Keni*, or New Town.—**And Apollonia.** A city of Macedonia, in the district of Mygdonia, whose site is now only an object of conjecture. It has no other importance than as affording a possible lodging-place for Paul on his journey, and is believed to have been about midway between Amphipolis and Thessalonica, which were about two days' journey apart. The distance from Philippi to Amphipolis is 33 miles: Amphipolis to Apollonia, about 30 miles; Apollonia to Thessalonica, 37 miles. Thus the journey from Philippi to Thessalonica need not have occupied more than three days. Paul apparently did not preach in either Amphipolis or Apollonia, probably because there was no synagogue in either city.

Thessalonica. This city is situated on a declivity at the northeast corner of the bay of Thermæ. It was originally an inconsiderable town, known successively as Emathia, Halia,

THESSALONICA.

and Thermæ, was enlarged by Cassandra, one of Alexander's generals, and renamed Thessalonica in honor of his wife. At the time of Paul's visit it was the most important city of Macedonia, and its metropolis. Its commercial position, and its consequent communication with all parts of the world, made it a centre from which the Gospel was rapidly and widely disseminated (1 Thess. 1:8). It had been made by the Roman government a free city, that is, it had the right of self-government, the provincial governor did not interfere in its municipal affairs, the local magistrates, probably elected by the people, had the power of life and death, no Roman garrison was quartered within the city, a senate or an assembly, representing the people, made its municipal regulations, in short, it had many of the privileges and all the insignia of a free community; its allegiance to the central government at Rome was insured, for the possession of its privileges was dependent upon its good behavior. In such a city the charge of inciting treason (ver. 7) would be one peculiarly obnoxious both to magistrates and people. In ecclesiastical history, Thessalonica is an important object; it became the bulwark of Oriental Christendom, received the designation of the "orthodox city," and was one of the most important sees in the early church. Its commercial character has always given to it a large Jewish population, and it is said to embrace at the present day between 10,000 and 20,000 Jews. Its modern name is Salonica.

2-4. Paul, as his manner was. See ch. 13:14; 16:13; 17:10; 18:4.—**Three Sabbath days.** That is, three successive Sabbath days; this indicates, probably, only the duration of his ministry in the synagogue. The facts that the Philippians sent twice to him while at Thessalonica (Phil. 4:16), that heathen were converted and added to the church (1 Thess. 1:9), and that a Christian church was successfully organized (see

3 Opening and alledging, that Christ must[v] needs
have suffered, and risen again from the dead; and that
this Jesus, whom I preach unto you, is Christ.
4 And some[w] of them believed, and[x] consorted with
Paul and Silas; and of the devout Greeks a great multitude, and of the chief women not a few.
5 But the Jews which believed not, moved with
envy, took unto them certain lewd fellows of the baser
sort, and gathered a company, and set all the city on
an uproar, and assaulted the house of Jason,[y] and
sought to bring them out to the people.
6 And when they found them not, they drew Jason
and certain brethren unto the rulers of the city, crying, These[z] that have turned the world upside down
are come hither also;
7 Whom Jason hath received: and these all do contrary[a] to the decrees of Cæsar, saying that there is
another king, *one* Jesus.

v ch. 18 : 28; Luke 24 : 26, 46; Gal. 3 : 1....w ch. 28 : 24... x 2 Cor. 8 : 5; 1 Thess. 1 : 5, 6....y Rom. 16 : 21....z ch. 16 : 20; Luke 23 : 5.... a Luke 23 : 2; John 19 : 12.

on ver. 4) indicates a longer ministry; Lewin supposes that Paul remained in the city for two or three months.—**Opening and alleging.** That is, opening to them the O. T. Scriptures by interpreting aright their prophecies. Comp. Luke 24 : 32.—**That the Messiah must needs have suffered and risen from the dead.** Comp. Luke 24 : 26. The character of his preaching here is illustrated by his sermon at Antioch in Pisidia (ch. 13. Comp. ch. 9 : 22). His preaching comprised two parts: first, that the Messiah, in order to fulfill O. T. prophecy, must be a suffering, a crucified, and a risen Messiah; and second, that the life, death, and resurrection of Jesus of Nazareth, accorded with O. T. prophecy in these respects.—**And some of them believed.** Some, that is, of the synagogue worshippers; mainly the proselytes, not the Hebrews by birth. —**And consorted with Paul and Silas.** Cast in their lot with Paul and Silas; not only accepted theoretically their interpretation of prophecy, but practically adopted the Christian life with all the dangers which such a course entailed. This interpretation is much more natural than that preferred by Alford, "were added as if by lot, *i. e.* by God, "to the great family of which Paul and Silas were members." —**Devout Greeks.** Greek proselytes to the Jewish religion.—**Chief women.** From the earliest ages women have been among the first converts to Christianity (vers. 12, 34; ch. 16 : 13). The epistles to the Thessalonians give us some additional information in respect to Paul's course during this ministry and its results. He labored by night that he might not be a charge upon the infant church (1 Thess. 2 : 9); set them an example of purity and industry (1 Thess. 2 : 10-12); suffered not his boldness to be checked by the persecutions endured at Philippi (1 Thess. 2 : 2); made no endeavor to gain converts by flattery or by relaxing the obligations of the moral law (1 Thess. 2 : 4-6). His ministry was accompanied with the power and produced the fruits of the Spirit (1 Thess. 1 : 3-5), and while he presented a suffering Saviour, he also pointed the Thessalonians forward to the second coming of the Lord (ver. 7, note). Apparently at this time a Christian church was fully organized, comprising both Jewish and heathen converts, some of whom subsequently became Paul's traveling companions (ch. 20 : 4). It had regularly ordained pastors (1 Thess. 5 : 12, 13), with some provisions for discipline (2 Thess. 3 : 6, 14, 15), and it is reasonably surmised, from a comparison of 1 Thess. 5 : 1, 2, with Matt. 24 : 36, 42, 43, possessed a copy of the Gospel of Matthew.

5. But the Jews taking unto them of the market-men, certain wicked fellows, and raising a mob, produced an uproar in the city; and assaulting the house of Jason, sought to bring them out to their fellows. Comp. this translation, which follows very closely the original Greek, with the English version. In the Agora, or market-place, see ver. 17, note, of the ancient city gathered the market-men from the country about. These were often a rude and semi-barbaric people; sometimes, as to-day in some of the towns of North Africa, they were not even allowed to enter within the city walls, but were allotted a market-place without the gates; the market-women were as notorious for their foul language as those of the Billingsgate market of London. It is these market-men, who are not inaptly described in our English version as *fellows of the baser sort.* The *people* are not the inhabitants of the city, but the ruder country-folk who had come in, either to sell or to buy, and were easily incited to a riot. Their tumultuous proceedings excited the apprehensions of the people of the city (ver. 8). The Greek word rendered *people* in this verse is *demos* (δῆμος), and signifies, as in the earlier Greek poets, the outlying country population, not, as Conybeare and Howson apparently understand it, the municipal legislature of the city. In the N. T. it always has this sense of *people*, and generally in a tumultuous condition (ch. 12 : 22; 19 : 30, 33). The Greek word in ver. 8 is *oklos* (ὄχλος), a general term, ordinarily rendered in the N. T. *multitude*, and signifies here the whole population of the city. The riotous proceedings of the country-folk excited the apprehensions of the whole population. Of *Jason* nothing is known, except that he was a kinsman of Paul (Rom. 16 : 21).

6, 7. They drew Jason unto the rulers of the city. The *præfectus urbi.* This officer was ordinarily appointed by the emperor, though in a free city like that of Thessalonica, was generally chosen by the people. He had control of the police, and general jurisdiction over all criminal matters. It is a curious fact

8 And they troubled[b] the people, and the rulers of
the city, when they heard these things.
9 And when they had taken security of Jason, and
of the other, they let them go.
10 And the brethren immediately sent away[c] Paul
and Silas by night unto Berea: who coming *thither*,
went into the synagogue of the Jews.

11 These were more[d] noble than those in Thessalonica, in that they received the word with all readiness[e]
of mind, and searched the scriptures[f] daily, whether
those things were so.
12 Therefore many of them believed; also of honourable women which were Greeks, and of men, not a
few.

b Matt. 2 : 3; John 11 : 48....c verse 14; ch. 9 : 25....d Ps. 119 : 99, 100....e James 1 : 21; 1 Pet. 2 : 2....f Isa. 34 : 16; Luke 16 : 29; 24 : 44; John 5 : 39.

that the Greek word here used to designate this chief magistrate, *politarch* (πολιτάρχης), which is not employed in classic Greek as a designation of municipal rulers, is found on the ruins of an ancient arch at Thessalonica, in an inscription which informs us that the magistrates of Thessalonica were called *politarchs*, and that they were seven in number; and it is a curious coincidence that three of the name are identical with those of Paul's friends in this region, — Sopater of Berea (ch. 20 : 4), Gaius the Macedonian (ch. 19 : 29), and Secundus of Thessalonica (ch. 20 : 4).—**These that have turned the world upside down.** An unconsciously true characterization of the office of Christianity. Evidently the fame of the new religion had penetrated heathenism.—**These all,** *i. e.*, these Christians wherever found.—**Contrary to the decrees of Cæsar.** The Julian Laws gave a very vague and general definition of treason; "whoever violated the majesty of the state," was declared a traitor, and almost any offence could be easily brought by any magistrate within the terms of so general a definition. —**There is another king.** This charge here corresponds to that presented before Pilate against Jesus (Luke 23 : 2; John 19 : 12). Not improbably the report of that accusation had reached the Jews at Thessalonica, and was borrowed by them for this occasion. Some color was given to it by the peculiar character of Paul's preaching at Thessalonica, in which Christ's kingly character, second advent, and final kingdom upon the earth, appear to have been prominent (1 Thess. 1 : 10; 2 : 19; 3 : 13; 4 : 13–18; 5 : 1, 2; 2 Thess. 1 : 5, 7–10; 2 : 1–12; 3 : 5).

8, 9. Troubled the people. See on ver. 5. Mental perplexity and agitation are indicated. —**When they had taken security of Jason and of the other.** Possibly bail, that they would appear and answer when summoned for a future trial (so *Lewin*); but this seems to me improbable, since treason was not a bailable offence. More probably, security that the city should be no more troubled by them; and this view is confirmed by the next verse. This pledge could be carried out only by sending Paul and Silas out of the city, which was done immediately. Whether any further proceedings were taken against Jason is unknown, but Paul's expressions in his subsequent letters indicate that the persecution was in some form continued (2 Thess. 1 : 4). With this, too, agree the admonitions of his epistles (1 Thess. 4 : 11; 2 Thess. 3 : 11).

In studying this incident observe (1) the unscrupulousness of religious animosity. The Jews invite the co-operation of the heathen, and of the lowest class of the heathen; they throw the whole city into tumult; they present what they know to be a false charge; they apostatize from their own faith in repudiating a Messiah, and demanding the punishment of one of their own nation for preaching that kingdom of God which was, and still is, the stay and hope of the devout Jew in his exile. (2.) The incidental and striking confirmation of Luke's historical accuracy. "He takes notice in the most artless and incidental manner of minute details which a fraudulent composer would judiciously avoid, and which, in the mythical result of mere oral tradition, would surely be loose and inexact. Cyprus is a 'proconsular' province. Philippi is a 'colony.' The magistrates of Thessalonica have an unusual title, unmentioned in ancient literature; but it appears, from a monument of a different kind, that the title is perfectly correct. And the whole aspect of what happened at Thessalonica, as compared with the events at Philippi, is in perfect harmony with the ascertained difference in the political position of the two places. There is no mention of the rights and privileges of Roman citizenship (comp. ch. 16 : 21); but we are presented with the spectacle of a mixed mob of Greeks and Jews, who are anxious to show themselves to be 'Cæsar's friends.' Comp. ch. 17 : 7 with John 19 : 12. No lictors (ch. 16 : 35, 38), with rods and fasces, appear upon the scene; but we hear something distinctly of a demus (ch. 17 : 5), or free assembly of the people (but *quere*, see on ver. 5). Nothing is said of religious ceremonies (ch. 16 : 21) which the citizens, 'being Romans,' may not lawfully adopt; all the anxiety, both of people and magistrates, is turned to the one point of showing their loyalty to the emperor (ch. 17 : 7). And those magistrates by whom the question at issue is ultimately decided, are not Roman prætors (ch. 16 : 20, 22, 35, etc.), but Greek politarchs."—(*Conybeare and Howson.*)

10-12. By night. To avoid danger from the mob.—**Unto Berea.** A walled city on the eastern slope of the Olympian range, about 50 miles from Thessalonica, on the left bank of the river Haliacmon, about five miles from where that

13 But when the Jews of Thessalonica had knowledge that the word of God was preached of Paul at Berea, they came thither also, and stirred up[g] the people.
14 And then immediately the brethren sent away[h] Paul, to go as it were to the sea: but Silas and Timotheus abode there still.
15 And they that conducted Paul brought him unto Athens: and receiving a commandment unto Silas and Timotheus[i] for to come to him with all speed, they departed.

g Luke 12 : 51....h Matt. 10 : 23....i ch. 18 : 5

river breaks through an immense rocky ravine from the mountains to the plain. Though possessed of many natural advantages, that which has rendered it famous was its seclusion. It was a retreat, though not an idle one for Paul, after the Thessalonian trouble. According to Cicero it afforded, under widely different circumstances, a refuge from the complaints of an exasperated people, for Piso, who, while præfect of Macedonia, had shamefully outraged his office. Under Roman authority it was assigned to the third region of Macedonia. It is well shaded with plane trees, and so abundantly watered, that in almost every street there is a running stream. It is described as one of the most agreeable towns in Rumili. It boasts of a present population of 15,000 or 20,000, and is placed in the second rank of cities in European Turkey. There still remains some ruins of the Greek and Roman period. There seems to be a general opinion that the inhabitants were of a superior culture and disposition, but no other authority is given than the expression here.—**More noble than those in Thessalonica.** Literally of better birth. Not as in our English version *in that they received the word;* two statements are made by the historian, one that the Jews at Berea were a better class than those at Thessalonica, the other, a result and an evidence of this fact, that they received the word with *readiness of mind, i. e.,* a willingness to consider, and, if true, to receive it. Observe their readiness was not that of a superstitious credulity, as that of the Lycaonians (ch. 14 : 11), for they searched the Scriptures daily to see whether these things were so. They illustrate Paul's directions to the Thessalonians (1 Thess. 5 : 21).—**Honorable women.** Occupying an honorable position in the community. See ch. 13 : 50, note.—**Greeks.** Greek proselytes; heathen would not have searched the Jewish Scriptures for evidence of Paul's message.

13, 14. Observe that Anti-Christ, as well as Christ, has his missionaries. How long Paul remained at Berea we have no means of knowing; he twice attempted to go back to Thessalonica (1 Thess. 2 : 18), and as 1st Thessalonians was written from Corinth, we may assume that the endeavor therein mentioned was made while at Berea. By the phrase *as it were to the sea,* we are to understand, not that he made a pretence of going by sea, to deceive his enemies, and then went by land, which would have involved a journey of over two hundred miles, but that he started in the direction of the sea. The historian did not go with him, and writes only what he personally knew.

15. They that conducted Paul. The delegation from the church at Berea which accompanied him. They went with him to Athens, and returning brought the command from Paul to Silas, who had remained at Berea, and to Timothy, who had meanwhile gone back to Thessalonica, either from Berea or from Athens (1 Thess. 3 : 2); but Silas and Timothy do not seem to have rejoined Paul until he reached Corinth. We have no direct information what became of Luke in the meantime.

Ch. 17 : 16–34. PAUL AT ATHENS. PANTHEISM, MATERIALISM, POSITIVISM, REFUTED. See Note on Paul at Athens.

PRELIMINARY NOTE.—To understand aright, either the significance of Paul's course at Athens, the meaning of the incidental allusions to his surroundings, or the full force of his marvellous address, it is necessary that the reader should have a measurably correct apprehension of both the external aspects of the city and the character of its people. Athens, the pre-eminent ancient city in civilization, arts and arms,—distinguished for philosophy and learning,—famous for its architecture and statuary, and the mother of the most celebrated warriors, poets, statesmen and philosophers,—was situated in the plain of Attica, the city proper being about three miles from the sea, although as described by Lewin and Smith it consisted of two circular wall-enclosed cities, united by another long and narrow portion, also wall-enclosed. One of the circular portions included the sea-ports Pireus and Phalerum, the other the inland settlement; the connecting fortification, known as the "Long Walls," being a populous street, making a third city, whose inhabitants were shut out from all view of the country by the vast wall on either side. It needs no graphic words to picture the misery of a people thus imprisoned, when to their ordinary suffocating crowding was added the horror of the plague, or the terrors of a siege. The plain on which Athens was built was fertile only in architectural material, but the exquisite clearness of the air, the beautiful outlook over rocky eminences to the sea, with the dark green lines of olive groves winding through the valley, formed a landscape both picturesque and inspiring.

Athens is said to have been built by Cecrops and an Egyptian colony, about 1550 years before Christ, and hence was called Cecropia even in later times, but to have received the name Athens from the prominence given to the worship of the goddess Athenæ, or Minerva, whose olive-wood statue and temple erected by Erectheus I. were most sacred in the eyes of the people. After some centuries of growth under various rulers, heroes, or despots, during which time some magnificent temples and other public buildings were erected, Athens was captured by Xerxes, who reduced it almost to ashes, B. C. 480. But later an increased maritime power brought a greater prosperity, and her wealth, largely augmented by the tribute paid her by subject states, afforded ample means for the re-embellishment of the city. Under the administrations of Themistocles, Cimon and Pericles most of her public buildings were erected. Subsequently through various vicissitudes, being alternately ruinously ravaged and magnificently adorned, Athens came into the hands of the Romans, under whose rule the commerce of the city was annihilated, but philosophy, literature and art continued to thrive. During the middle ages it degenerated into an insignificant town, until the thirteenth century, when it became again the football of contest, and has since suffered greatly in the various sieges to which it has been subjected. In 1834 Athens was declared the capital of the new kingdom of Greece, but it has little to glory in, except its treasures of antiquity, which commend it to scholars. It has only a small university, and its trade is described as consisting of "walking-sticks and smoking-tubes made of the black thorn of Old Parnassus."

ANCIENT ATHENS RESTORED.

The city as Paul entered it is easily reproduced. Though he left no minute description, we have the records of a traveler, Pausanias, who visited it only 50 years after Paul, during which time there had probably been but little change. We may presume that he landed at the Port Phalerus, the nearest port to Macedonia, although Port Pireus, on the other side of the peninsula, was the more commonly used. Here at these two ports, was maritime Athens, once thriving, now, though retaining some outward features of its former prosperity, degenerated into a mere harbor for the upper city. Temples to Ceres, Minerva and Jupiter were the first objects to meet the eye of the apostle as he stepped upon the shore; and as he passed further on, altars erected to the deified heroes and to "unknown gods" (see ver. 23, note) met his view on every side. Paul's course would lead him between the ruins of the "Long Walls." The remnants of this fortress still remained scattered about, although some of its material had been used in the Roman siege for other military works. The foundations of these immense solid walls, probably sixty feet high, are still to be traced here and there on the plain. Still a third fortifying wall, called the Phaleric, had connected the main or upper city with the coast, but this had been allowed to fall into decay when the second or southern of the two Long Walls had been erected. Arrived at the city walls, a distance of forty stadia or four and one-half miles, and entering by the Piraic gate, the Pnyx lay on the left, the museum hill on the right, and opposite the gate ran a street directly to the Agora (the market of verse 17). The walls were some seven and a half miles in circumference, about the same length as those enclosing the Port cities. There are eleven gates mentioned by name, and others the names of which are unknown. At the very gate the eye must have been bewildered with the multitude of temples and statues. On either side of the street was a colonnade, under whose porticoes were shops displaying their costly wares, with rows of bronze statues in front. At the end of the street was the Agora, the forum or market-place, which had been the centre of a glorious

ATHENS—MODERN.

public life, but which could only impress the apostle as the meeting-place for lounging, conversation and business, of a people who spent their time in nothing else but either to tell or to hear some new thing. In one sense, the whole quarter known as the Agora was a market, for at the same time that it contained some of the finest temples, statues and public buildings of Athens, it was one grand bazaar, where could be found the flower piazza, the slave mart, men's clothing here and women's clothing there, fish-stalls, book-stalls, pottery, perfumes, fruit and vegetables. This strange medley of commodities was to be found among the finest works of art the world has ever seen. Here were statues of the celebrities of Athens—Solon, Conon, Demosthenes, the mythical Hercules and Theseus, and all the fabled divinities of Olympus. Every public building was the sanctuary of some deity and adorned with his statue. Here was the Temple of Apollo, called the Patroum; the Temple of the Mother of the Gods, or the Metroum; the Senate house, the altar of the Twelve Gods; the Tholus, with its circular stone dome, where the prytanes took their meals and offered their sacrifices. Here while the morning marketing and traffic called together a concourse, Socrates had come to find an audience, and here were the great informal gatherings of the people for general purposes. The Agora occupied a central position in the city. The Pnyx, where met the political assemblages, adjoined it on the west. In this semi-circular area, capable of holding 12,000 people, the assembled citizens stood or sat on the bare rock early in the morning, "at daybreak," to listen to their great orators. From the Bema of this Pnyx, of which there are still some remains, Demosthenes, Pericles, Themistocles, Aristides and Solon have addressed the Athenian people. On the east, wall-enclosed, was the Acropolis—the citadel—a square, craggy rock, rising abruptly about 150 feet, with a flat summit of about 1000 feet from east to west, by 500 feet from north to south. This, the original site of the ancient city—it had long before ceased to be inhabited—was appropriated to the worship of Athena and the other guardian deities of the city. Art having offered her sacrifices of mas-

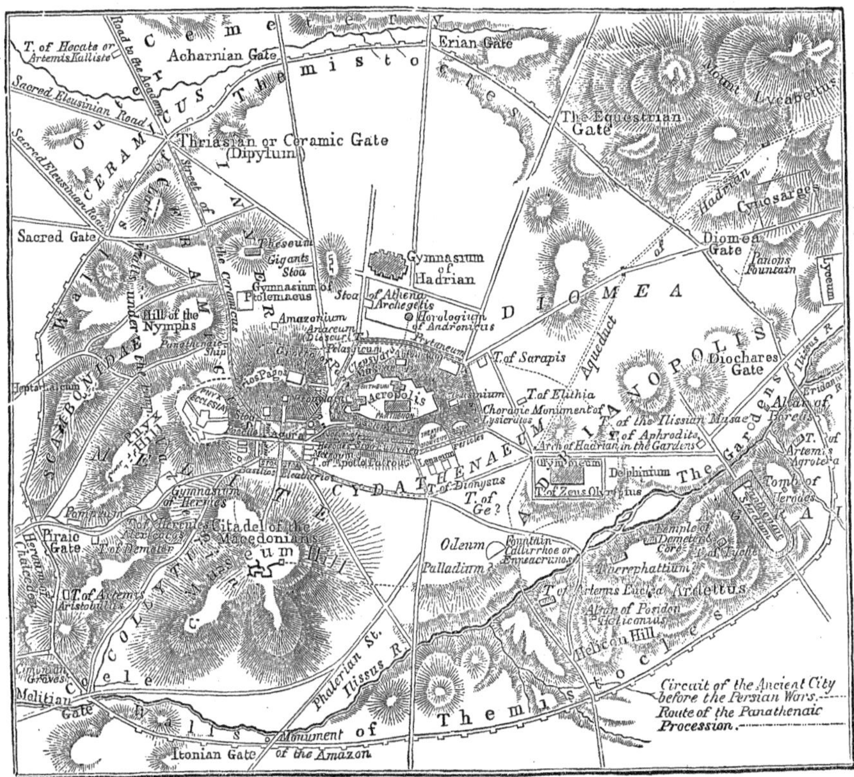

PLAN OF ATHENS.

ter-pieces here, it became a museum. It was a votive offering to the unconscious deities, of all that architecture, sculpture and painting could combine, and Nature crowned it with the unrivalled tinting which the sunlight in a wondrously clear atmosphere could produce. But to the Christian student the great attraction is the Areopagus. North of the Agora, between the Pnyx and the Acropolis, was a rocky height which was the meeting-place of the Upper Council, and the site of the legendary trial of Mars for the murder of the son of Poseidon. Here the greatest criminals had received sentence, and the most solemn questions of religion had been discussed and passed upon. The judges sat in the open air upon seats hewn out in the rock, on a platform which was reached by a flight of stone steps directly from the Agora, sixteen of which still remain. On the brow of the eminence was a temple of Mars, and in a broken cleft of the rock just below the judges' seat was the sanctuary of the Furies. This spot was regarded with superstitious reverence, and was a "place of awe in the midst of the gay and

16 Now while Paul waited for them at Athens,[j] his spirit was stirred in him, when he saw the city wholly given to idolatry.
17 Therefore disputed he in the synagogue with the Jews, and with the devout[k] persons, and in the market daily with them that met with him.
18 Then certain philosophers[l] of the Epicureans, and of the Stoics, encountered him. And some said, What will this babbler say? other some, He seemeth to be a setter forth of strange gods: because he preached unto them Jesus, and the resurrection.

j Ps. 119 : 136; 2 Pet. 2 : 8....k ch. 8 : 2....l Col. 2 : 8.

frivolous city." Between the Areopagus and Pnyx was the street Cerameicus, a sort of corso running from the Agora through the Ceramic gate to the outer Cerameicus, the place of burial of all who were honored with a public funeral, where were monuments to all the illustrious dead of Athens. These were the most important points of the city.

But while the public buildings were grand and beautiful, the streets adorned at every possible point with statuary of bronze or marble, and temples of every shape and material crowded every public place, the private dwellings were, as a rule, mean; the streets narrow and crooked, unpaved and dirty; with poor supply of water, and very meagre sewerage. A people taught by the sages, the philosophers and the statesmen, which were the pride of Greece, ought to have been noble men, but Paul found the Athenians frivolous and profligate—their very culture luring them to vice, and their religion an incentive to shameless debauchery. The philosophy which had been their especial glory, having no root in the Divinity, had ceased to flourish; while the uneducated were given up to vice and superstition, the thinkers were "given up to a scornful skepticism." That the schools of philosophy still had their adherents we know, but there was no great leader in Athens to meet the apostle Paul. Such was the city in which, such the people to which, Paul preached on Mars Hill.

16. His spirit was stirred in him. Literally *sharpened*, or *whetted*, like a sword. The presence of ignorance and superstition, so far from discouraging, aroused his courage; as the challenge of Goliath aroused the military ardor of David.—**The city full of idols.** Not, as in our English version, *wholly given to idolatry.* The actual presence of the idols and temples which crowded the streets, is indicated, rather than the spirit or character of the people, except as the former showed the latter. Petronius says, satirically, that it was easier to find a god than a man in Athens; Pausanias, that it had more images than all the rest of Greece put together; Xenophon, that the whole city was an altar, a votive offering to the gods. Similar testimony is borne by Socrates, Cicero, Livy, Strabo, Lucian and others.

17. Therefore disputed he. Rather, he reasoned or discussed. Paul's method in preaching the Gospel to those unacquainted with it was never controversial, and the idea of controversy is not involved in the original here.—**And with the devout persons,** *i. e.*, the Jewish proselytes from heathenism.—**And in the market.** Literally, *the Agora.* In all the larger Greek cities there was a place of public assembly so entitled, used both for traffic and for the transaction of public business. In the times of Homer enclosed with large stones sunk into the earth and provided with seats of stone for the chiefs, it grew in later times into a magnificent structure—an open space enclosed by porticoes or colonnades, and surrounded with statues, altars, temples, and other structures for public business, for the administration of justice, and for market purposes. It was the centre of political and commercial intercourse and of religious life, answering to the gateway of the Jewish city. Here were celebrated the first festive

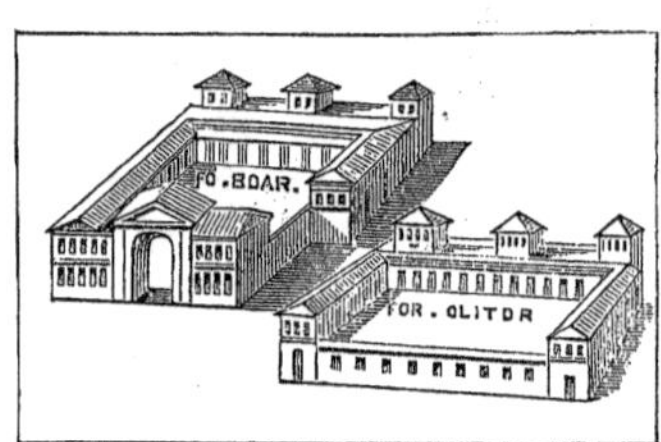

THE AGORA.
(From Rich's Companion to the Latin Dictionary.)

games, here centred the great highways of the city, from here started the great religious processions, here originally the great public assemblages of the citizens took place, here the different sorts of merchandise were gathered partly in permanent shops and partly in temporary booths, and here was the place of social and fashionable resort. This, at least, was the Agora in its original conception, though, in the larger cities, the commercial, the religious, and the political centres became more or less separated, and in Rome almost every class of provision dealers had a market of their own. During the market hours the Agora was a place of general resort; it was also frequented in the afternoon and evening, somewhat in the manner of our public parks to-day, except that, unlike the latter, the ancient Agora was resorted to by the wealthy and the cultured, and it was even deemed discreditable not to be seen therein. Socrates habitually frequented it for the purposes of conversation and instruction. The accompanying illustration, from an ancient painting, gives some idea of the simpler kind of Agora. As Christ's example sanctions field-preaching, so Paul's street-preaching. For further description of the Agora at Athens, see Prel. Note.—**Them that met with him.** His instruction was conversational, not oratorical; his first direct conflict with idolatry was a hand-to-hand combat.

18. Then certain of the philosophers, of the Stoics and the Epicureans. The two principal schools of Greek philosophy. The founder of Stoicism was Zeno (340–260 B. C.). He opened his school in a porch, called the *Stoa Pœcile* ("Painted Portico"), at Athens, whence the origin of the name of the sect. The Stoics in theory condemned the worship of images and the use of temples, but in practice justified the popular Polytheism, allowing any and all ways of conceiving and worshipping the Supreme Being. They were Pantheists; and much of their language is a curious anticipation of the phraseology of modern Pantheism. In their view, God was merely the spirit or reason of the universe; the world was itself a rational soul; matter was inseparable from the Deity; he did not create, he only organized; the soul was corporeal, and at death would be absorbed in God. Thus, a resurrection from the dead was to Stoicism an impossibility. Nor was their moral system less hostile to the teachings of Christ. According to Stoicism, all outward things were alike to the wise. Pleasure was no good; pain no evil. All actions conformable to reason were equally good; all actions contrary to reason were equally evil. Thus their philosophy, while it approached the truth in holding one Supreme Being, compromised it in allowing any and all ways of conceiving and worshipping him, and contravened it, in its Pantheistic belief that all souls are emanations of him. In *spirit* it was directly opposed to the Gospel—holding the dependence of man on no being but himself, together with the subjection of God and man alike to the stern laws of an inevitable fate. Christianity is the school of humility; Stoicism was the education of pride.

PHILOSOPHER STUDYING A ROLL OF PAPYRUS BEFORE A SUN-DIAL. (From an antique gem.)

Epicurus, the founder of the Epicureans, who are referred to in the N. T. only here, was born B. C. 341, in the island of Samos. In B. C. 306 he opened a school in a garden at Athens. His life was simple, chaste, and temperate. Of the three hundred works he is said to have written, nothing has come down to us except three letters, giving a summary of his views for the use of his friends, a number of detached sayings, preserved by Diogenes Laertius, and others, and some fragments of his work on nature, found at Herculaneum. The additional sources of our knowledge of Epicurus are the works of his opponents, Cicero, Seneca, Plutarch, and of his follower Lucretius. Theologically, the philosophy of the Epicureans was a system of materialism, in the strictest sense of the word. The world was formed by an accidental concourse of atoms; the gods were merely phantoms, which had no objective reality, or at least exercised no active influence on the physical world or the business of life; the universe was a great accident and sufficiently explained itself without any reference to a higher power; as there was no creator, so there was no moral governor; all notions of retribution and of a judgment to come were, of course, forbidden by such a creed; the soul was nothing without the body; both body and soul were dissolved together and dissipated into the elements; and when this occurred, all the life of man was ended. In morals the Epicureans were the utilitarians of the first century. They held that pleasure is the only good; pain is the only evil; virtue is no good to be sought for itself, vice no evil to be for itself avoided; the one is to be sought for the happiness it produces, the other avoided for the suffering it entails. As originally taught by Epicurus, this doctrine was not sensualistic. Epicurus declares: "When we say that pleasure is the end of life, we do not mean the pleasures of the debauchee or the sensualist, as some, from ignorance or from malignity represent, but freedom of the body from pain, and of the soul from anxiety." But in Paul's time the philosophy had degenerated into that debased form which its founder seems to have apprehended, and its current motive was, "Let us eat and drink for to-morrow we die" (1 Cor. 15 : 32).

A third school of philosophy at Athens, scarcely less important than the others, was that of the followers of Plato. He was accustomed to meet his disciples in a garden, a grove once belonging to Academicus; hence the name, Academicians. The variations of doctrine among the successors of Plato gave rise to successive schools of philosophy, known as the Old, the Middle, and the New Academy. The essential principle of the Academicians in Paul's time was that nothing was or could be known; thus they represented, religiously, that form of skepticism which neither asserts nor denies that there

19 And they took him, and brought him unto Areopagus, saying, May we know what this new[m] doctrine, whereof thou speakest, *is?*

20 For thou bringest certain[n] strange things to our ears: we would know therefore what these things mean.

m John 13:34; 1 John 2:7, 8....n Hosea 8:12.

is a Divine Being, but denies that anything can be known concerning Him. Though not distinctly mentioned in this account, we may safely assume, that the altar to the unknown God represented their philosophy, or, at least, that universal outreaching after God, which such skeptical philosophy can neither prevent nor appease. Such, without entering into details at once abstruse and unprofitable, were the three great schools of philosophy whose representatives encountered Paul at Athens, and who not unnaturally mocked when they heard of the resurrection. Let the reader observe how the apostle's address brings out in clear contrast with these philosophies the existence and the personality of a Divine Creator, and the resurrection of the soul and its accountability to God, as well as the further truth in which he would have beforehand the sympathies of the intellectual leaders, that the Deity could not be adequately represented by idols.

Some said, What will this babbler say? Other some, He seemeth to be a setter forth of strange gods. The first ridiculed him as a talker of nonsense, literally, a *seed-picker*, a retailer of small talk, of gossip; the others, regarding the matter more seriously, accused him of what was a serious offence under Roman law, and for which he had already been beaten and imprisoned in Philippi (ch. 16:21, note). It was for setting forth strange gods that Athens put Socrates to death, B. C. 399.—**Because he preached unto them Jesus and the resurrection.** The preaching of strange gods was charged upon him, not because he preached Jehovah, as the one only true God, for Jehovah was not a strange God in Athens, where was a synagogue of the Jews, and where, by public vote of the council, a statue of Hyrcanus, the high-priest of the Jews, had been erected in the temple of Demus and the Graces (see Jos. Ant. 14:8, 5); nor because he preached Jesus *and* the resurrection, in such a form that the people imagined that the resurrection was a god or goddess distinct from Jesus, an hypothesis which imputes equal obscurity to Paul and stupidity to his auditors. The plural, setter forth of strange *gods*, is employed, not because he preached a multiplicity of gods, or set forth the Trinity, in such a way as to give color to the belief that he was a polytheist, but because that was the technical characterization of an offence recognized under both Greek and Roman law (see above). He set forth Jesus as the manifestation of God in the flesh; they supposed that he desired to add another to the superabundant deities which they already possessed; and his address is devoted to correcting this error, and setting forth the *one* and *only God*, the God of all nations and times, and Jesus as the *man* by whom he will judge the world (ver. 31, note).

MARS HILL—THE AREOPAGUS.

19, 20. And they took him. Not with violence. Their spirit is not that of aroused hostility; the act is not that of a mob.—**And brought him unto Areopagus.** *Mars Hill;* the word is the same so rendered in ver. 22. For description, see Prel. Note. It was famous chiefly as the official site of a council which bore the same name, which existed from very early antiquity, which had general charge of order in the city, which had jurisdiction as a criminal court in cases of willful murder, and which exercised a general censorship over religious matters in Athens. Thus, if a formal com-

21 (For all the Athenians, and strangers which were
there, spent their time in nothing else, but either to
tell, or to hear some new thing.)
22 Then Paul stood in the midst of Mars' Hill, and
said, *Ye* men of Athens, I perceive that in all things ye
are too superstitious.[o]
23 For as I passed by, and beheld your devotions, I
found an altar with this inscription, TO THE UN-
KNOWN GOD. Whom therefore ye ignorantly worship, him declare I unto you.
24 God[p] that made the world, and all things therein,

o Jer. 50 : 38. . . . p ch. 14 : 15.

plaint had been lodged against Paul, it would have been naturally brought to trial before this court. This does not, however, seem to have been the case. Possibly there may have been an imperfectly formed purpose to present charges against him, but it was not executed. It is evident from the form of their request here, *May we know?* from the explanation of the next verse, which attributes their action to curiosity, and from the final result (ver. 32), that it is not a judicial proceeding which is here described, but a popular assembly.—**May we know?** The language is courteous; that of Greeks, famous for their politeness, to one whose teaching had thus far been, outside of the synagogue, of a purely personal and private character. See ver. 17, note.

21. A just characterization of the Athenian people at this period of their history. Dissatisfied alike with the religion and the philosophy of the past, and too well educated to remain contentedly in ignorance, they were famed throughout the land for intellectual restlessness. There is a certain subtle satire in the original, inadequately rendered in our English version. We may translate it, *have time for nothing else but either to hear or to tell the latest news* (καινότερον, in the comparative, signifies something newer than what has gone before).

22. Then Paul stood in the midst of Mars Hill. To appreciate the courage of the apostle in this address, and his unfaltering faith in God and truth, we must stand, in imagination, where he stood, the temple of the Eumenides immediately below him, behind him the temple of Theseus, on his left the colossus of Minerva, the champion of Athens, to the right the temple of Victory, and opposite, at the distance of 200 yards, the Acropolis, so entirely occupied with temples and statues as to be, in the language of Aristides, "one great offering to the gods." History has justified his faith; the Parthenon became a Christian temple; Athens ceased to be a city full of images; and the repugnance of the Greeks to images and image worship became so great, as to be a principal cause of the schism between the churches of the East and the West, in the eighth century.—**In every point of view.** One can readily imagine the apostle emphasizing these words with a sweep of the hand toward the statues and images spread out in the city below.—**I see you more than others reverential to the gods.** It is almost impossible to give accurately in the English the exact significance of the original. "Superstition," says Cicero, "is a senseless fear of God; religion, the pious worship of God." To render Paul's language here *too superstitious*, as in our English version, carries with it reprobation; to translate it, as Hackett, *more religious than others*, carries with it commendation. Paul neither reprobates nor condemns; he simply states as a fact, witnessed by all the monuments about him, the exceeding reverence for the gods, leaving it unsuggested whether that be the reverence of love which Socrates commended, or that of fear which Plutarch condemned. But his language is unquestionably sympathetic; and puts him *en rapport* with his audience from the beginning. From this general reference, he naturally passes to the altar to an Unknown God, and to show how, so far from being a setter forth of strange gods, he has come to disclose to them the true nature of this Unknown.

23. For passing through (the city), **and looking about, upon** (*reconnoitering, considering*, not merely beholding) **the objects of your worship** (not *your devotions*, the acts of worship, but your *altars, statues and temples*, the objects of your worship), **I found even an altar on which was inscribed, To an Unknown God.** Several such altars existed in Athens, according to Pausanias. See Prel. Note. He reports the inscription as, "To unknown *gods*," but this may be because he refers to several altars, each bearing an inscription such as Paul reports. That is not, as in our English version, To *the* Unknown God; the definite article is wanting in the Greek; nor to *God the Unknown*, for this rendering there is no grammatical authority; it has been apparently invented to harmonize the language of the inscription more closely with Paul's speech. The origin of these altars is accounted for in different ways. There is a legend that in the time of a plague, it being uncertain which god was offended, a number of sheep were let loose, and wherever one lay down, an altar was erected to the unknown offended deity. Some suppose that these altars were originally dedicated to some particular god, but the name having been lost, the place was thus sacredly kept. Others still imagine—for there seems to be no basis for the opinion—that Jehovah was really intended, and that it was an at-

seeing that he is[q] Lord of heaven and earth, dwelleth[r]
not in temples made with hands;
25 Neither is worshipped with men's hands, as
though[s] he needed any thing, seeing, he[t] giveth to all
life, and breath, and[u] all things;

26 And hath made of one[v] blood all nations of men,
for to dwell on all the face of the earth; and hath determined the times[w] before appointed, and the bounds[x]
of their habitation;
27 That they should seek the Lord, if haply they

q Matt. 11 : 25....r ch. 7 : 48....s Ps. 50 : 8....t Job 12 : 10; Zech. 12 : 1....u Rom. 11 : 36....v Mal. 2 : 10....w Ps. 31 : 15....x Isa. 45 : 21.

tempt on the part of the Athenians to conciliate the Jews. The real underlying reason appears to be a sense, in the more cultivated Greeks, that all the attempts to "find God" through statues, and altars, and temples, were, after all, in vain, and that he was still unknown; of this the writings of the best classic authors afford abundant illustration. The accompanying cut gives the reader an idea of the structure of the

ANCIENT ALTARS.

ancient altars. The altar to an Unknown God probably resembled these in structure. There was a cavity in the top in which the fire was kindled, and an orifice at the side or bottom, through which the libations of wine, or pieces of the burnt-offering, flowed.—**Whom, therefore, not knowingly, ye worship, him declare I unto you.** Not *ignorantly*, which involves reprobation, if not contempt. He borrows his word (ἀγνοοῦντες) from the inscription on their altar (ἀγνώστῳ). Observe that he speaks with respect of the worship, "an important lesson for all who have to deal with Paganism and Romanism."—(*Alford.*)

24. The God that made the world and all things therein. In a single sentence he sets forth the fundamental tenet of the Christian religion, in contrast with Epicureanism, which taught that there was no God, and that the world was only a happy accident; with Stoicism, which taught that the world was God and God the world; and with popular mythology, which believed in as many gods or goddesses as domains in nature or political divisions in the state.—**He that is Lord** (*master*) **of heaven and of earth, not in hand-made temples dwells.** Though this truth had been impressed on the mind of the Jewish nation by the O. T. prophets, and was recognized by some of the better thinkers even in heathendom, it was nevertheless a radical and startling doctrine to preach in the heart of Athens. Observe that Paul begins with the foundation; he does not preach Christ crucified as a Redeemer till he has preached the one only God as Creator, and this for the reason well stated by Stier: "Only on the firm foundation of the O. T. doctrine of creation can we rightly build the N. T. doctrine of Redemption; and only he who scripturally believes and apprehends by faith the earliest words of Revelation concerning the Creator of all things, can also apprehend, know, and Scripturally worship, THE MAN, in whom God's word, down to its latest canonical revelation, gathers all things." For a confirmation of this truth, see Paul's language in the synagogue at Antioch (ch. 13 : 26, note). Observe in his phraseology here, *hand-made temples*, what we may well believe is a reminiscence of Stephen's language in his last speech (ch. 7 : 48, note).

25. Neither by human hands is served. Not *worshipped;* the Greek will not bear this meaning, and the declaration, so rendered, is not true. On the contrary he calls for *worship* from men's hands (Psalm 29 : 2; 89 : 7; Isaiah 56 : 6, 7; Hab. 2 : 20; John 4 : 23; 1 Tim. 2 : 8; Heb. 12 : 28). But this worship is not *service;* in it God serves us, we do not serve him. The heathen brought costly offerings, and food and drink, supposing that the gods consumed them; this idea of the dependence of God on men, the reversal of the truth, and one common to all heathen and heathenish systems, Paul disclaims and disproves (comp. Psalm 50 : 9-15).—**As though he needeth any thing.** This clause limits and defines the term *served* (mistranslated *worshipped*) in the preceding clause.—**He that gives to all life and death and all things.** The fact that *all* comes from God, and is constantly preserved by God, is a sufficient evidence that we cannot *serve* him by giving anything to him. (Comp. 1 Chron. 29 : 14.)

26. Has made of one blood all the nations of the earth, that they may dwell together. Or, *Has caused all the nations of the earth* (*sprung*) *of one blood, to dwell together*. The latter meaning is preferred by Alford, De Wette, and Meyer; the former is the more general view, and seems to me the better one, both because simpler grammatically, and also because it better accords with the context. The point is not that God has caused the nations to dwell together, for in fact they had worshipped different and even rival gods, and lived in perpetual conflict;

might feel after him, and find him, though[y] he be not far from every one of us:
28 For[z] in him we live, and move, and have our being; as[a] certain also of your own poets have said, For we are also his offspring.

29 Forasmuch then as we are the offspring of God, we ought not[b] to think that the Godhead is like unto gold, or silver, or stone, graven by art and man's device.

y ch. 14 : 17. . . . z Col. 1 : 17. . . . a Titus 1 : 12. . . . b Isa. 40 : 18, etc.

but that he had made them of *one blood*, in order that they might dwell together in peace. Having asserted the unity of God, Paul proceeds to assert the unity of the race. There is some doubt whether the word *blood* is authentic or not. Alford retains, Tischendorf omits it. The question is only important in its bearing on the scientific question, whether the various races of men descended from a common parentage or not. The whole religious significance of Paul's address is preserved, by the reading which omits the word *blood*, and understands his reference to be to the divine origin of men, all races being offspring of one Father (see ver. 28). This truth corrects, not merely national pride, which was a strongly marked characteristic of the Athenians, who claimed to be aboriginal, sprung from the earth, but also controverts the fundamental idea of polytheism, which gives to every nation a different origin, a different religion, and a different god.—**Having fixed the appointed seasons and limits of their abode.** So Dr. Hackett, who gives the significance well: "The apostle, by adding this, admonishes the Athenians that they, like every other people, had not only received their peculiar advantages from the common Creator, but that they could hold them only during the continuance of his good will and favor. In assigning to the nations their respective abodes, he had fixed both the *seasons* of their prosperity and the limits of their territory, *i. e.*, it was he who decided *when*, and *how long* they should flourish, and *how far* their dominion should extend. We have the same idea exactly in Job 12 : 23." Let me add that the truths embodied in this verse are peculiarly applicable to our own age and nation, in which all races intermingle, and in which self-conceit is the predominant national vice.

27. That they should seek the Lord. Rather, *God*, which is the best reading. The whole object of the divine providence, *in his dealings with nations as well as with individuals*, is to bring them to a knowledge of the one true God. This is the declaration of the apostle; that it has important bearings on the Christian conception of national life, and one peculiarly applicable to our own times, is apparent.—**If haply they might feel after him.** As a blind man gropes for some object which he is unable to see. The same Greek word is used in the Septuagint in Gen. 27 : 12, 21, 22, which see for illustration. How the heathen became so blinded that they must thus *grope* after God, see Rom. 1 : 21. Observe that idols result from a groping after a mediator able to reveal an unknown God to the soul. *If haply*, indicates a contingency not likely to happen. In fact, so far as history indicates, the instances of such finding of the true God by the groping of the heathen, though not unknown, are rare.—**Though he be not far from us.** He is hard to find, not because *he* withdraws from us, but because *we* withdraw from him. Our iniquities separate us from him (Isaiah 59 : 2; Jer. 23 : 23, 24; Rom. 10 : 6, 8).

28. For in him we live and move and have our being. Comp. Ephes. 1 : 10; Col. 1 : 17; Heb. 1 : 3. The whole is to be taken literally, not of spiritual life and being merely. "A climax rising higher with each term; out of God we should have no life, nor even movement, which some things without life have (plants, water, etc.), nay, not any existence at all; we should not have been."—(*Meyer.*) This declaration gives no countenance to pantheism; *that* asserts that God is all, and all is God; *this*, that God is *in* all, and all is dependent upon God.—**As certain also of your own poets have said.** The reference is probably to Aratus. He lived about B. C. 270; was a native of Cilicia, Paul's native province, perhaps, though that is not quite certain, of Tarsus; lived, in his later years, in Macedonia; wrote several poems and some prose works. Only two astronomical poems have been preserved, one of which asserts in the introduction the dependence of all things upon Jupiter, and contains the words here quoted, "For we are also his offspring." Cleanthes, who lived about 300 B. C., and was born at Assos in Troas, uses very nearly the same language in a well-known hymn to Jupiter. Plato, in the same spirit, declares that God is the "father of noble children;" and Plutarch, that the soul is "not only made by him, but begot by him." (Comp. Matt. 6 : 9, note.) Observe that Paul does not quote the Bible, but a heathen poet; he quotes as an authority that which his audience will accept as such. Contrast his course in the synagogue at Antioch (ch. 13), where his whole address is based on Scripture.

29. We ought not to think. He classes himself with them, as though this error had formerly been his also. To those not under the law he becomes as not under the law, that he may win those not under the law (1 Cor. 9 : 20). Observe how, without directly declaring the

30 And the times of this ignorance God winked[c] at;
but now[d] commandeth all men every where to repent:
31 Because he hath appointed[e] a day, in the which
he will judge the world in righteousness, by *that* man whom he hath ordained; *whereof* he hath given assurance unto all *men*, in that he hath raised him from the dead.

32 And when they heard of the resurrection of the dead,[f] some mocked: and others said, We will hear thee again[g] of this *matter*.
33 So Paul departed from among them.
34 Howbeit certain men clave unto him, and believed: among the which *was* Dionysius the Areopagite, and a woman named Damaris, and others with them.

c Rom. 3 : 25....d Luke 24 : 47: Titus 2 : 10, 11....e Rom. 2 : 16....f ch. 26 : 8....g ch. 24 : 25; Luke 14 : 18.

N. T. doctrines of incarnation and atonement, he leads toward them. If we are God's offspring, then we ought not to think that he is like the work of our hands and device, for he is like us; then his highest manifestation will be looked for in a perfect Son, that man whom he hath ordained (ver. 31). The argument here against idolatry is exactly analogous in spirit to that of Ps. 115 : 3–8 and Isa. 46 : 5–7. Observe that it applies to all use of images for the purpose of bringing God near to the soul through the imagination. This is the reason given for their use in the Romish church to-day; the truth is, however, that the Godhead is not like to such images, and this is equally true of art representations of Christ, since what is adorable in him is not the fleshly form (2 Cor. 5 : 16), but the inward, impalpable spirit.

30, 31. The times of this ignorance God overlooked. Comp. ch. 14 : 16, where the thought is substantially the same. As in his infinite mercy God is said to forget the sins which he pardons, so full and complete is his forgiveness (Jer. 31 : 34), so here he is said to overlook, *i. e.*, not to see, the sins which are the fruits of ignorance. Eternal life has ever been given to even those in idolatrous nations and times, who, by patient continuance in well-doing, sought for glory and honor and immortality (Rom. 2 : 7, 10), and their idolatry, if it has not been accompanied by *works* of darkness, has been overlooked.—**But now commandeth all men everywhere to repent.** The command to repentance was not something new, for conscience, convicting the Gentiles of sin, carried with it a command to repent (Rom. 2 : 14, 15). What was characteristic of the *now* was the fact that this command, heretofore expressed directly by written or spoken word only to the Jews, was henceforth, through the Gospel of Jesus Christ, to be carried to all men, everywhere. Parallel is the declaration of ch. 11 : 18, "Then hath God also to the Gentiles granted repentance unto life."—**Because he hath appointed a day.** The reason, not why he commands, but why men should make haste to obey the command.—**In the which he will judge the world.** The language certainly implies a definite and fixed occasion of judgment in the future. It is hardly consistent with the idea of a continuous judgment, before which the souls of the dying appear immediately upon death, and certainly not with the idea of a gradual development in the future life, carried on in all alike, from the stage attained by the discipline of earth. See Matt. 25 : 31–46, Prel. Note.—**By that man whom he hath ordained.** Jesus Christ. See John 5 : 25–29. Observe that Paul here refers to Jesus as that *man*, saying nothing of his divine nature, his incarnation, his kingdom, because he would then be liable to misapprehension, and might be thought to be adding to the deities of Athens another deified Jewish hero. But in Thessalonica he speaks of Christ's kingdom and second coming (ver. 7, note), and in Corinth of his incarnation (1 Cor. 1 : 22–24). He adapts his preaching to the needs and the understanding of his auditors. The word *that* is not in the original; the definite article is wanting; but it is implied by the construction. See Alford's *Greek Test.*—**Giving assurance.** Literally *giving* or *offering faith*, *i. e.*, a ground for faith to rest upon.—**In that he hath raised him from the dead.** The resurrection of Jesus is, historically, the basis for faith in a supernatural Christianity. See Vol. I, p. 330, Note on the Resurrection of Jesus Christ.

32-34. But hearing of the resurrection of the dead. The resurrection of *all the dead* was necessarily implied by Paul's statements, viz., that the dead should all come into judgment, and that the assurance of this general rising was afforded by the resurrection of the One by whom the judgment should be conducted.—**Some mocked; and others said.** The latter were no more serious, but only more courteous, than the former. It was only curiosity that brought them together; when that was satisfied they departed. There is no reason for supposing that the one class were Epicureans or the others Stoics.—**But certain men clave unto him.** Following him personally and becoming associated with him. See ch. 5 : 13, note.—**Dionysius the Areopagite.** That is, a member of the court of Areopagus. According to Eusebius he became afterward bishop of the church at Athens, and died a martyr. The writings which have been attributed to him are undoubtedly spurious, probably the products of the fifth or sixth century.—**Damaris.** Nothing else is known of her; there is no adequate reason for the conjecture that she was the wife of Dionysius.

PAUL AT ATHENS.—In considering the practi-

CHAPTER XVIII.

AFTER these things, Paul departed from Athens, and came to Corinth;

2 And found a certain Jew named[h] Aquila, born in Pontus, lately come from Italy, with his wife Priscilla; (because that Claudius had commanded all Jews to depart from Rome;) and came unto them.

h Rom. 16 : 3.

cal lessons of this eventful day in Paul's life observe, (1.) His courage of faith. Alone, in the intellectual metropolis of idolatrous Greece, whose religion was interwoven with its national and social life, and sustained by pride, pecuniary interests, political ambition, and a habit of generations, he does not hesitate to set against it the simple theism of Christianity—One invisible God, Creator of the world and all that it contains—and to demand of his auditors that they repent of their idolatries, as of sin, basing his demand on no other authority than their own consciousness, sustained by the utterances of one of their own poets, and by the inscription on one of their idolatrous altars. (2.) His wisdom in (*a*) the adaptation of truth. He preaches redemption and justification to the Jews at Antioch in Pisidia (ch. 13), the kingdom of a coming Messiah to the few Jewish women in the proseuchæ at Philippi (ch. 16 : 13, note), Christ crucified, the glory and wisdom of God, to wealthy and aristocratic Corinth (1 Cor. 1 : 23, 24), the One only true God, the Creator of all things, to skeptical, atheistic, and idolatrous Athens. (*b*.) His courteous and conciliatory spirit. He speaks of their superstition in *terms* of respect rather than of reprobation, and recognizes their reverence as real, while he endeavors to lead them from the worship of the false to the worship of the true. (*c*.) His method. He finds a point of agreement with them in the inscription, To the Unknown God, and in the language of one of their own poets, We are his offspring, and from that point deduces the doctrine of the unity and spirituality of the Divine Being. (*d*.) He lays a foundation for Christianity in preaching theism. It is useless to preach the higher doctrines of the Gospel to those who deny the fundamental tenet—the existence, personality, and power of God. (3.) The seemingly small results. In Philippi, where Paul is beaten; in Thessalonica, from which he is driven; in Corinth, where opposition arouses a mob, large and prosperous churches are early formed. In Athens, where there is no opposition, where curiosity invites him to preach, and receives his message either with courteous skepticism or mocking disdain, he does not live to see any results; there is no indication of a Christian church in Athens in his time; in the time of the Antonines (2d century) paganism still flourished there. Indifference is more discouraging than open opposition. (4.) The parallelism to our own time. The forms of unbelief have changed; their essential spirit and character are unchanged. Stoicism answers to modern pantheism, the doctrine that God is all and all is God; Epicureanism answers to modern materialism, the doctrine that there is no spirit, nothing but a mode of motion; the inscription to the Unknown God represents the aspirations which, in a different form, still express themselves in the writings of those who declare the Deity to be the Unknown and the Unknowable. Paul's treatment of the skepticism of Athens is equally applicable to the parallel skepticism of our own times. We are to recognize it as a fact; to unhesitatingly attack it; to treat it as a genuine conviction, with respect, and yet as a spiritual blindness that is a sin to be repented of; and we are to meet it, not by arguments drawn from Scripture, whose authority it does not recognize, nor by preaching the higher doctrines of Christianity—the incarnation, atonement, and second coming of Christ—but by appealing to the inner consciousness of men, witnessed in and by themselves, and by laying the foundation, in demonstrating the truth of theism, for a demonstration of the truth of Christianity.

Ch. 18 : 1-22. PAUL AT CORINTH. IN SEASON AND OUT OF SEASON, PAUL THE TENT-MAKER IS STILL PAUL THE APOSTLE.—THE MINISTER MAY SOMETIMES LEAVE THE SINNER, AND YET KEEP HIS OWN CONSCIENCE CLEAN.—THE LORD IS WITH HIS CHILDREN IN THE HOUR OF THEIR TREMBLING AND WEAKNESS (comp. vers. 9, 10, with 1 Cor. 2 : 3).—OVERRULING PROVIDENCE ILLUSTRATED.—THE WRATH OF MAN PRAISES GOD.—THE CHRISTIAN'S RIGHT SOMETIMES TO STOP WORK FOR THE SAKE OF WORSHIP (ver. 21).

1. And came to Corinth. A city of Greece remarkable in every aspect. It was about forty-five miles from Athens; by sea, and with a fair wind, the voyage can be made in from three to five hours. Pre-eminently advantageous in situation, notable in commerce and manufactures, foremost, in time as well as proficiency, in the fine arts, mentally and manually active, it had an important place in the history of Greece and Rome. The Christian student is attracted to it from the fact of its having received so long a visit from the Apostle Paul and been the scene of the initial Christian correspondence, the most important of the epistles having all been written from or to Corinth. See Chron. Table, p. 20. From ancient Greece, or Hellas proper, the portion called Peloponnesus, or the island of Pelops, was almost severed by two seas—the Western, flowing in from the Adriatic and the Mediterranean, called the Corinthiacus Sinus, now Gulf of Patras and Lepanto; the Eastern, from the Ægean Sea, called the Sinus Saronicus, now the Gulf of Egina. That this separation was not complete was owing to a narrow, rocky, sterile plain, scarcely three and a half miles wide at its narrowest point. This was the Isthmus, Pindar's "Bridge of the Sea," Xenophon's "Gate of the Peloponnesus," the home of the Isthmian games. From this, *the* Isthmus, all such connecting strips of land have received their name. Entirely across the northern end of the Isthmus stretched the Geraneian mountains through which there were only three passes; on the southern end was the Oneian ridge not spanning the Isthmus entirely—for between the ridge and the Sinus Corinthiacus rose the Acrocorinthus, a sort of offshoot of the ridge separated from it by a ravine, leaving still a narrow level place between the Acrocorinthus and the sea. Thus there were three passes on the south, one on the shore of the Saronic Gulf, one through the ravine, and one at the foot of the Acrocorinthus. This path then, for all the traffic between northern Greece and Peloponnesus, this bridge, over which the richly freighted Levantine vessels were dragged from sea to sea to avoid the stormy passage around the peninsula, was a place of the utmost importance, and here Corinth, planting herself upon the slope of her citadel, the Acrocorinthus, reaching out her left hand, her port town Lachæum, to the Corinthian sea, her right, the port town Cenchræa, to the Saronic Gulf, supervised and controlled the communication between the East and the West. Although she looked out upon no fertile lands, excepting the narrow plain, which gave rise to the proverbial expression for great wealth, "To possess what lies between Corinth and Sicyon," the scene from the summit of the Acrocorinthus was not a dull one. On one side, over across the sea, forty-five miles away, could be seen the Acropolis of Athens, with the mountains of Attica and Bœotia, and the islands of the Archipelago; on the other hand were the mountains of northeastern Greece, "Parnassus towering above Delphi"; just below, the little plain resolutely keeping the waters of the East and the waters of the West from uniting, the busy life of the two harbors, and the city itself, spread out to view. Could a city thus distinguished endure? Satisfied, elated, intoxicated, would she not fall from her regality? Her history answers. Though concerned in many contests, with great expenditure of men and treasure, its early history had been one of general prosperity, but poisoned with jealousy it became inimical to both Athens and Sparta, in turn joining one against the other, then became subject to the Macedonian kings, and finally to Rome. Still, however, it enjoyed a measure of supremacy, being united to the Achæan league. In 146 B. C., after the Romans were angered by the maltreatment of certain ambassadors who were in Corinth for the purpose of conferring with deputies from the Achæan league, the city was entered by Mummius, and an uncalled-for and inexcusable destruction ordered. The works of art, many and valuable, were carried to Rome, the males slaughtered, the women and children sold as slaves, the city pillaged by the soldiery, and set on fire. All rebuilding on the site, which was accursed and dedicated to the gods, was prohibited, and "the eye of Hellas" was utterly extinguished. After a century, Julius Cæsar resolved to rebuild it, and 46 B. C. sent thither a colony of veterans and freedmen, among whom were probably many of the Jewish race. The city which Paul visited one hundred years after was not the Grecian Corinth, but Corinth of Rome, a colony (see ch. 16 : 12, note), still the capital of Achaia, and as such the residence of its proconsul Gallio. In the arts and literature Corinth had early established her superiority. It gave birth to painting, the most elaborate order of architecture received from her its name, the finest bronze was the Aes Corinthiacum, and here the most beautiful terra-cotta vases were sought. Although none of her sons are mentioned among the illustrious writers of Greece, poetry flourished in the early days of the city. It had been pre-eminent, too, in licentiousness; its patron goddess was Aphrodite, the Greek Venus, in one of whose temples a thousand courtezans were kept for the service of strangers; its most famous monument, that to the courtezan Lais, who took such sums from the merchants, who came to the city, as utterly to ruin them. Pausanias, who visited Corinth in the 2d century, describes the temples and monuments to the numerous gods and goddesses, and especially the famous fountain of Peirene, which is said to have received its waters, which were delicious and abundant, by some secret spring from a fountain on the summit of the Acrocorinthus. Nothing remains to us of ancient Corinth except a few Doric columns in ruins, and some possible remains of a bath of Hadrian, an amphitheatre of still later date. It is now a small unhealthy malarious town called Gortho. For further description of place and people, see Intro. to Epistles to Corinthians.

2. And found a certain Jew named Aquila. Of Aquila and Priscilla we have no knowledge outside the Scripture narrative. From the fact of their holding Christian meetings at their house both at Ephesus and Rome it has been supposed that they were persons of some wealth. The Roman form of their names may have come, as did Paul's, from some connection with a Roman family. They accompanied Paul to Ephesus, and there Aquila rendered him

3 And because he was of the same craft, he abode with them, and [i] wrought: for by their occupation they were tentmakers.

4 And he reasoned in the [j] synagogue every sabbath, and persuaded the Jews and the Greeks.
5 And when Silas [k] and Timotheus were come from

i ch. 20 : 34.... j ch. 17 : 2.... k ch. 17 : 14, 15.

most important services. It appears that Priscilla was a woman of marked ability, being not only mentioned as sharing in the hospitality of the family, but also in the theological instruction of Apollos. From the fact that her name is always mentioned first it has been inferred that she was the more energetic of the two, but it is a fact worthy of note that the two are always mentioned together, from which we may conclude that they furnish a happy example of harmony and sympathy in Christian life.—**Born in Pontus.** On Pontus, see ch. 2 : 9, note.—**Lately come from Italy.** None other than the ordinary geographical sense is meant by the N. T. reference to this country, which consisted of the peninsula between the Alps and the straits of Messina. There are three, or more properly four, references in the N. T. to it; they illustrate the military relations of the imperial peninsula and the provinces (Acts 10 : 1), the subsisting trade between the peninsula and the Mediterranean (Acts 27 : 1), the spread of the Gospel in the West (Heb. 13 : 24), and this verse alludes to the large Jewish population which from other sources we learn it contained.—**Because that Claudius.** Fourth Roman emperor; his full name was Tiberius Claudius Nero Durus Germanicus. He was called from a quiet and obscure life to succeed Caligula A. D. 41. He had been considered from childhood lacking in intellect, the natural irresoluteness of his character had been increased by contemptuous treatment from his relatives, and harshness and cruelty from servants. The evil wrought during his reign is ascribed to others rather than to him, and he is said to have been good and honest. Herod Agrippa the First, who was concerned in nominating him to power, received accessions of territory from the emperor in return. After a weak and foolish reign Claudius was poisoned by his fourth wife, Agrippina, the mother of the infamous Nero.—**Had commanded all Jews to depart from Rome.** To what decree reference is here made is uncertain. There is no question that the Jews were a general object of dislike among the Romans; they were persecuted by three successive Roman emperors; see ch. 6 : 9, note. Suetonius says that Claudius drove the Jews from Rome because they were incessantly raising tumults at the instigation of a certain Chrestus. Chrestus was a common name, Christus was not; the two were often used interchangeably; the pronunciation was the same, or nearly so; hence the surmise is not unreasonable that Christianity had already reached Rome at this time; that the Jews instigated riots against their Christian brethren, as in other places in the Roman empire—Corinth (ver. 12), Berea (ch. 17 : 13), Thessalonica (ch. 17 : 5), Iconium (ch. 14 : 19), Antioch in Pisidia (ch. 13 : 50); and that Suetonius, who wrote half a century after the event, which he dismisses in a sentence, formed the impression that this Christus or Chrestus was somehow responsible for the outbreaks, and therefore represented him as their instigator. The decree, whatever it was, did not remain long in force, for we find Aquila not long after in Rome (Rom. 16 : 3), and many Jews resident there (ch. 28 : 15).

3, 4. And because he (Paul) **was of the same craft.** I can see no reason for the surmise that Aquila and Priscilla were Christians before this time. The language of ver. 2, *A certain Jew*, seems to me inconsistent with that opinion; if previously converted, Aquila would have been designated as a certain *brother*. What brought Paul and Aquila together was their common industry, and the practical lesson drawn by Conybeare and Howson is legitimate: "The trade which St. Paul's father had taught him in his youth was thus the means of procuring him invaluable associates in the noblest work in which man was ever engaged. No higher example can be found of the possibility of combining diligent labor in the common things of life with the utmost spirituality of mind."—**And wrought, for by occupation they were tent-makers.** Every Jew was required by Rabbinical laws to teach his sons a trade, that he might be independent; this was rendered the more necessary since the religious teachers, prophets, scribes, rabbis, had no state pay, and nothing answering to the modern annuities often given by government to distinguished literary men. So Jesus himself was probably taught the carpenter's trade (Mark 6 : 3), and Paul the trade of a tent-maker. These tents were made of a cloth woven out of goat's-hair, supplied by the goats of Paul's native province, and hence known as *Cilicium*. The same tents of goat's-hair are still seen covering the plains of Cilicia in harvest. The use of tents was then and still is very great in the East, and the business of manufacture and repair was and is an important one. "Tent-making constitutes an important occupation in Western Asia at the present day. In all the larger cities, and particularly at Constantinople, there is a portion of the bazaar, or business part of the town, entirely devoted to this branch of industry. Here may

Macedonia, Paul was pressed in the spirit, and testified to the Jews *that* Jesus *was* Christ.
6 And when they opposed[l] themselves, and blasphemed, he shook[m] *his* raiment, and said unto them, Your[n] blood *be* upon your own heads: I *am* clean: from henceforth I will go unto the Gentiles.

l 2 Tim. 2 : 25.... m Neh. 5 : 13.... n Ezek. 33 : 4.

be seen men engaged in cutting and sewing canvas, in constructing or finishing off tents of various forms and sizes, in mending and repairing those long used, or packing them up for their customers. This is what we have described as the military tent, for the black tent of the nomads is made exclusively by themselves. But the military tent is not employed solely for the purpose of warfare. The civilian often carries it with him on his journey, and pitches it at night; it is frequently seen beside some hot spring, whose sanitary waters are sought to mitigate the sufferings of the sick; and one of the most refreshing sights of the advancing spring is the herds of horses feeding on the barley sown for the purpose in the neighborhood of every town, with the conical tents of their keepers scattered here and there over the valley or plain. The apostle Paul was a tent-maker (Acts 18 : 3), and the tents he constructed were doubtless employed by the Roman soldiers, since no military power existed in his day in the lands where he wrought. The Roman tent, like the Grecian, is probably identical with the tent still used in the same lands."—(*Van Lennep's Bible Lands*, p. 415.) Women, as well as men, engage

WOMEN WEAVING TENT-CLOTH.

in the manufacture both of the cloth and of the tents; the cloth is used also for garments. Mr. Rawson, whose sketch of modern tents and tent-makers accompanies this note, informs me that he has a cloak made from this cloth by an Arab woman. There is no reason for understanding by the language here that Paul was engaged in *weaving the cloth;* the natural meaning of the original is that conveyed by our English version, which represents him as a *tent-maker*, employing for that purpose probably the manufactured hair-cloth. It is, however, possible that the raw material was an article of commerce, and that he wove the cloth as well as made it into tents. There was in those days no such division of labor as exists in our day. The ancient tent was sometimes made, as generally with us, simply of canvas or skin, stretched upon ends, and sometimes in whole or in part of wood, and covered with canvas or skins.—**And persuaded the Jews and the Greeks.** *Was persuading;* some measure of success is indicated by this word. The *Greeks* are here the proselytes, who attended the synagogue. Prominent among them was Justus (ver. 7).

5. And when Silas and Timotheus were come from Macedonia. Silas from Berea, Timothy from Thessalonica. It is not necessarily implied that they came together. Comparing ch. 17 : 14–16 with 1 Thess. 1 : 1, 2, I believe the facts to be that Timothy was sent back to Thessalonica from Berea, not from Athens; that Paul, finding no opening for his work in Athens, proceeded to Corinth, and that Timothy probably rejoined Silas at Berea, whence they both came on to Corinth and rejoined Paul there. For other views, see Conybeare and Howson, I : 406, note.—**Paul was wholly given to the word.** The best reading is *to the word*, not *in the spirit.* The meaning is not perfectly clear. It may indicate (as Alford and Alexander) that Silas and Timothy found Paul "more than usually absorbed in the work of testifying to the Jews, a crisis in the work being imminent, which resulted in their rejection of the word of life;" or it may mean (as Hackett and Robinson) that after they came he gave himself wholly to the word, being relieved by the contribution which they brought him from the Macedonian churches (2 Cor. 11 : 9) from the necessity of devoting a considerable part of his time to manual labor, in order to earn his daily bread. Up to this time he had been "in fear and in much trembling" (1 Cor. 2 : 3), not from apprehension of personal injury, but from a sense of his own weakness and inability to cope with the corruption and wickedness which he saw about him. This experience, here and in Athens (ch. 17 : 16), indicates in Paul a strong sense of need of human sympathy and fellowship, such as is

7 And he departed thence, and entered into a certain *man's* house, named Justus, *one* that worshipped God, whose house joined hard to the synagogue.
8 And Crispus,[o] the chief ruler of the synagogue, believed on the Lord with all his house; and many of the Corinthians hearing, believed, and were baptized.
9 Then spake the Lord to Paul in the night by a vision, Be not afraid, but speak, and hold not thy peace:
10 For I[p] am with thee, and no man shall set on thee, to hurt thee: for I have much people in this city.
11 And he continued *there* a year and six months, teaching the word of God among them.
12 And when Gallio was the deputy of Achaia, the Jews made insurrection with one accord against Paul, and brought him to the judgment seat,

o 1 Cor. 1 : 14....p Matt. 28 : 20.

often found in strong, independent, self-reliant natures.—**Testifying to the Jews the Messiah Jesus.** Not merely, as in our English version, that Jesus was Christ, but the whole truth respecting the life of Jesus, and how his life fulfilled the prophecies of the O. T. concerning the Messiah (see ch. 13).

6. Shaking his garments. Shaking off the dust as a testimony against them; a common symbolical act among the Hebrews. See ch. 13 : 51, and Matt. 10 : 14, note.—**Your blood be upon your own heads.** Comp. Ezek. 33 : 4. Paul's act here illustrates the principle laid down there. Contrast also Matt. 27 : 24. Like Pilate, Paul declares himself innocent; like Pilate, Paul employs a symbol to emphasize his declaration. But Pilate, though he uses the symbol, yet is in fact guilty, in that he condemns the innocent to death; Paul is guiltless, in that he does not turn from the Jews till they refuse to hear his message of salvation.—**I shall henceforth, with a pure conscience, go to the Gentiles.** So Alford. It is literally, *I, clean, henceforth go*, etc. Observe in this sentence a hint of the motive which led Paul always first to preach to the Jews: because he could not, with a good conscience, go to the Gentiles without first offering the Gospel to his own people. Comp. Rom. 9 : 1-3; 10 : 1.

7, 8. And he departed thence. From the synagogue, where he was denied a hearing.—**And entered into a certain man's house named Justus.** Not to live, but to preach. The fact that it adjoined the synagogue made it convenient for this purpose. The implication is that, as he was preaching, he was vehemently interrupted in the service by the outcries of the Jews, and that he responded by shaking off the dust against them, referring to Ezekiel 33 : 4 in a citation which they would readily understand, and departing immediately to the adjoining house—many of the congregation, perhaps including the chief ruler, going out with him. The court-yard of any of the larger Greek houses would afford a convenient place for religious services. Of Justus nothing more is known than the statement here. The Syriac and Arabic versions have Titus, while the Vulgate combines the two names, Justus Titus. The description of him as *one that worshipped God*, indicates that he was a heathen proselyte, but not necessarily at this time a Christian, though sympathizing with Paul rather than with his heathen persecutors.—**And Crispus.** He was baptized by Paul (1 Cor. 1 : 14) and is said to have subsequently become bishop of Egina. His name, which is foreign, indicates some connection with heathen nationalities; his office that he was a Jew.—**The chief ruler of the synagogue.** On the constitution of the synagogue, its method of worship and form of government, etc., see Matt. 4 : 23, note. This ruler of the synagogue was the president of its board of elders.—**With all his house.** Comp. ch. 16 : 15, 34. Among the believers were Gaius and Stephanas (1 Cor. 1 : 14, 16), who, with Crispus, were baptized by Paul's own hand. The others were baptized probably by Silas or Timothy, not by Paul.

9-11. By a vision. That is, by some supernatural appearance to him, though, very possibly, in a dream. Comp. ch. 27 : 23.—**Be not afraid.** Possibly, after so determined and bold a renunciation of the Jews, the apostle suffered a reaction, and doubted whether he had not destroyed the hope of further work.—**Speak, and hold not thy peace.** The double form, affirmative and negative, adds emphasis. Comp. Isaiah 58 : 1; Job 2 : 3.—**For I am with thee.** Comp. Jer. 1 : 8; Matt. 28 : 20; John 14 : 18-23.—**Shall set on thee to hurt thee.** *So as to hurt thee;* a promise fulfilled in the experiences which followed.—**I have much people in this city.** Literally, *There is for me much people in this city.* Not many people already consecrated to God, but many whom God recognized as his; and this may imply either that there were many who were appointed to become his own, or many in whom he saw a preparedness to receive the Gospel.—**And he continued there a year and six months.** As the result of Paul's labors at Corinth, a Christian church was established, not only in Corinth, but also in its port town Cenchrea (Rom. 16 : 1), and apparently elsewhere in Achaia (2 Cor. 1 : 1). The year and six months probably includes the whole of his Corinthian ministry, during which time the incident narrated in vers. 12-17 occurred; some, however, regard it as extending only to that incident, the *yet a good while* of ver. 18 indicating a still further stay in the city.

13 Saying, This *fellow* persuadeth men to worship God contrary to the law.
14 And when Paul was now about to open *his* mouth, Gallio said unto the Jews, If it were a matter of wrong, or wicked lewdness, O *ye* Jews,[q] reason would that I should bear with you:
15 But if it be a question of words and names, and *of* your law,[r] look ye *to it;* for I will be no judge of such *matters*.
16 And he drave them from the judgment seat.
17 Then all the Greeks took[s] Sosthenes, the chief ruler of the synagogue, and beat *him* before the judgment seat. And Gallio cared for none of those things.
18 And Paul *after this* tarried *there* yet a good

q Rom. 13 : 3 .... r chaps. 23 : 29 ; 25 : 11, 19 ; John 18 : 31 .... s 1 Cor. 1 : 1.

12. Gallio being deputy of Achaia. *Proconsul.* On the difference between imperial and senatorial provinces, see ch. 13 : 7, 8, note. Achaia was originally a senatorial province, was made an imperial province by Tiberius, remained so under Caligula, but was restored to the senate by Claudius, and was at this time, therefore, governed by proconsuls. Originally a narrow strip of land in the north of the Peloponnesus, whose cities were confederated in an ancient League, in the N. T. *Achaia* signifies the Roman province, which, with Macedonia, included all of Greece. Hence the use of the terms together. *Gallio*, mentioned in the N. T. only here, was the elder brother of Annæus Seneca, the philosopher; his own name was Annæus Novatus, and he received the name by which he is known to us, because of his adoption into the family of Junius Gallio, the rhetorician. He died in A. D. 66, having, probably, but shortly before left Achaia for a sea-voyage for the benefit of his health. His brother's allusions to him, which are exceedingly affectionate, indicate that he was a man of integrity and honesty, and beloved on account of his amiability and suavity, and the account here is in harmony with such a character.—**Made insurrection.** Rather, made an assault.—**With one accord.** Indicating preconcerted action. The indications from ver. 17 are that Sosthenes had replaced Crispus as chief ruler of the synagogue, and was a leader in this movement.—**To the judgment-seat.** A movable, or sometimes a permanent, throne or chair of state, used by the emperors at Rome, and in the provinces by the proconsuls and other chief magistrates, in administering justice. For illustration and description, see John 19 : 13, note.

13-17. This fellow. Though the word *fellow* is not in the original, the language is that of contempt, and is rightly represented in our English version.—**Contrary to the law.** The same accusation had resulted in the scourging and imprisonment of Paul and Silas at Philippi. See ch. 16 : 21, note. But this judge was a very different type of Roman from the prætors of Philippi. He perceived that it was not attachment to the Roman law which had aroused the rage of the Jews, and he would have nothing to do with the settlement of their own religious controversies. Some take the accusation as meaning against the law of Moses, but without good reason; no such complaint would be preferred by Jews to a Roman magistrate.—**If it were a matter of injustice** (a plain violation of law, infringing on the rights of others), **or wicked mischief** (even a mischievous act of a malicious kind, not directly contravening any special statute), **reason would that I should bear with you.** The language is significant as indicating that he was, as a Roman, impatient of the contentions of the Jews, who already had the reputation of being a factious and disquiet people. See on ver. 2.—**Concerning words.** Rather *doctrines;* here Jewish theology.—**And names.** To a Roman, the question whether Jesus was the Christ would seem to be a mere question of names.—**And your laws.** Comp. Pilate's action (John 18 : 30) and that of Lysias (Acts 23 : 29) and Festus (Acts 25 . 20). But Gallio was a more courageous man than either Pilate or Festus. Moreover, the influence of the Jews at Corinth was insignificant; at Jerusalem and Cæsarea it was all-important for the Roman ruler to keep them at peace.—**I do not wish to be judge of these things.** Observe, as an indication of the simple truthfulness of the narrative, that the narrator does not hesitate to describe the contempt of a Roman official for the Jewish nation and the Christian cause.—**And he drave them from the judgment-seat.** Not necessarily, yet not impossibly, with force. — **Then all the Greeks.** The word *Greeks*, omitted by Tischendorf and Alford, and wanting in the best MSS., is doubtless an addition by a later hand, probably invented to prevent the possible impression that the friends of Paul beat Sosthenes. The interpolation probably correctly represents the facts. The Greeks took the occasion to beat the chief religious representative of the Jews; a very small occasion was sufficient to call into action their latent hatred and contempt of the Jewish people. The opinion advocated by some, that he was a Christian and beaten by the Jews, is highly improbable. A Sosthenes of Corinth is afterward mentioned by Paul as a Christian (1 Cor. 1 : 1), but whether it is this person, or another of the same name, we have no means of knowing. The name is not an uncommon one.—**And Gallio cared for none of these things.** An often misapplied text. It does not refer to religious indifference to Christian truth, for there is no indication that any Christian truth was

while, and then took his leave of the brethren, and
sailed thence into Syria, and with him Priscilla and
Aquila; having shorn[t] *his* head in Cenchrea:[u] for he
had a vow.
19 And he came to Ephesus, and left them there:
but he himself entered into the synagogue, and reasoned[v] with the Jews.
20 When they desired *him* to tarry longer time with
them, he consented not;
21 But bade them farewell, saying, I must by all
means keep this feast that cometh in Jerusalem:[w] but
I will return again unto you, if[x] God will. And he
sailed from Ephesus.
22 And when he had landed at Cæsarea, and gone
up, and saluted the church, he went down to Antioch.

t ch. 21 : 24; Numb. 6 : 18 . . . . u Rom. 16 : 1 . . . . v ch. 17 : 2 . . . . w chaps. 19 : 21; 20 . 16 . . . . x 1 Cor. 4 : 19; James 4 : 15.

brought before him; he did not even hear Paul speak; but to his indifference to the Jewish excitement, and to the mob violence against Sosthenes. With an easy indifference to anything that did not threaten to weaken Roman authority, or impair seriously the peace of the city, he left the Jews to settle their own religious questions among themselves, and Sosthenes to the mercies of the mob.

18. Tarried yet a good while. Probably this time is included in the eighteen months mentioned in ver. 11. See note there.—**Of the brethren.** Perhaps leaving Silas behind; he is not mentioned again in Acts; Timothy is next mentioned at Ephesus, in ch. 19 : 22.—**Unto Syria.** In that direction; stopping at Ephesus on the way.—**Having shorn his head.** Some think that it was Aquila, not Paul, of whom this was said. The great body of critics, however, apply it to Paul. The other view appears to be an afterthought, suggested by the supposed incongruity of an O. T. vow entered into by Paul, who so vigorously repudiated the obligations of the ceremonial law. But (1) there is no reason why the historian should mention Aquila's shaving his head, while this act by Paul was probably connected with his journey to Jerusalem, where the vow would require to be perfected by some sacrifices in the Temple (see ch. 21 : 29), and is thus stated to explain his refusal to remain at Ephesus, and his earnestness to proceed. (2.) The form of the sentence almost necessarily connects the statement with Paul, not with Aquila. "There are from verses 18 to 23 inclusive, no less than nine aorist participles, eight of which indisputably apply to Paul as the subject of the section, leaving it hardly open to question that the participle *having shorn* must be referred to him also."—(*Alford.*) The vow here is very generally thought to be that of the Nazarite. The restrictions of this vow were threefold. There must be entire abstinence from all strong drink, from the juice of the grape, and from everything belonging to the vine. The hair of the Nazarite was to be permitted to grow, no razor touching his head during all the days of his separation, and he should on no account defile himself for the dead. When the term of the vow expired, the Nazarite brought a sin-offering, a burnt-offering, and a peace-offering, with the usual appendages, his hair being shorn or shaven, and cast into the fire which was under the sacrifice of the peace-offerings, indicating the ordinary state of friendly communion with God. If the vow here mentioned was that of the Nazarite, Paul must have shorn, that is, *trimmed*, not *shaved* his head at Cenchrea, preparatory to the vow, purposing not to cut his hair again till he had fulfilled the vow by the offering at Jerusalem, or else the obligation of the Nazarite had been changed since O. T. times. The customary term of the Nazarite vow, when not for life, was, according to the rabbis, thirty days. The law concerning it is found in Numbers, ch. 6; Scripture instances are those of Samson (Judges 13 : 5), Samuel (1 Sam. 1 : 11), and John the Baptist (Luke 1 : 15).—**In Cenchrea.** The eastern and most important harbor of Corinth, distant from it about eight or nine miles. A double wall, extending from Corinth to its nearest harbor Lechæum, protected the Corinthian shore, and the fortifications at Cenchrea were of great moment to the safety of the pass along the Saronic shore. It was a natural harbor, while Lechæum was an artificial one, and possessed a life within itself which the nearness of Corinth prevented at Lechæum. Its idolatry partook of the same licentious character as that at Corinth, and the temples and monuments which Paul must have seen are described by Pausanias. There was an organized Christian church at Cenchrea (Rom. 16 : 1), and tradition gives the name Lucius as that of its first bishop, appointed by Paul himself. It is now deserted, but the spot retains a form of the name, and some ruins of its foundations remain.

19-22. And he came to Ephesus. A voyage of two or three days. On the place, see ch. 19 : 1, note, and Intro. to Epis. to the Ephesians.—**They desired him to tarry longer time with them.** The only occasion in which he was urged to remain and preach the Gospel in the synagogue and to the Jews. The vow that called him to Jerusalem must have been one of peculiar sacredness in his eyes, to have enabled him to resist such a call.—**Saying, I must by all means keep this feast that is coming in Jerusalem.** Tischendorf omits these words, and there is some uncertainty respecting them. They are, however, retained by Olshausen, De Wette, Meyer, Alford. The feast was either the Passover or the Pentecost; most probably the latter. This is indicated by the fact that

23 And after he had spent some time *there*, he
departed, and went over *all* the country of Galatia[y] and Phrygia in order, strengthening[z] all the disciples.
24 And a certain Jew named[a] Apollos, born at Alexandria, an eloquent man, *and* mighty in the scriptures,
came to Ephesus.
25 This man was instructed in the way of the Lord;
and being fervent[b] in the spirit, he spake and taught
diligently the things of the Lord, knowing[c] only the
baptism of John.

y Gal. 1 : 2 .... z chaps. 14 : 22 ; 15 : 32, 41 .... a 1 Cor. 1 : 12 ; 3 : 4-6 ; Titus 3 : 13 .... b Rom. 12 : 11 ; James 5 : 16 .... c ch. 19 : 3.

navigation was not ordinarily open early enough to make the voyage from Corinth possible in time to reach Jerusalem in March or early April. Observe that he here postpones Christian work, in order to get the benefit of personal communion with other Christians, and an opportunity for public worship.—**Landed at Cæsarea.** For description and illustration of Cæsarea, see ch. 8 : 40, note.—**And gone up and saluted the church.** At Jerusalem. This was still regarded as the mother church. Only here could he have kept the feast.—**He went down to Antioch.** In Syria, whence he had originally started (ch. 15 : 35, 36). This completes Paul's second missionary tour.

Ch. 18 : 23-28.—PAUL'S THIRD MISSIONARY TOUR. HIS EARLY MINISTRY AT EPHESUS.—GOD USES ALL INSTRUMENTS.

A. D. 54. With this verse begins the third missionary tour of the apostle Paul. For its general course, see map, p. 21. The first portion of this tour we are unable to trace with accuracy. Paul began (autumn, A. D. 54), as before, by revisiting the churches which he had previously founded in the provinces of Galatia and Phrygia; thence, by what route we have no means of determining, he came to Ephesus, which was to the province of Asia a centre, as Athens and Corinth were to Greece. There he remained for a period of two years and upward (A. D. 55, 56; see ver. 10); thence he went into Macedonia and Greece (ch. 20 : 2), probably revisiting the churches at Philippi, Berea, Thessalonica, Corinth, and Cenchrea, perhaps Athens also; thence he returned, by a route nearly every stage of which we can trace by the geographical references in chaps. 20 and 21, to Jerusalem. This was the end of his third missionary journey. His arrest there prevented his returning to the point of his departure, Antioch in Syria. The whole duration of this tour is believed to be about four years, viz., from the autumn of A. D. 54 to the summer or fall of A. D. 58. During this tour he is thought also to have written the following Epistles, viz.: From Ephesus, spring, 57, 1 Corinthians; from Macedonia, autumn, 57, 2 Corinthians; from Corinth, winter, 57, Galatians; from Corinth, spring, 58, Romans. See Chronol. Table, p. 20.

23. And after he had spent some time there. There is nothing to indicate the length of time; probably a few months. Conybeare and Howson, whose chronology is generally well considered, suppose that he reached Antioch in the summer and left in the fall of A. D. 54. On Galatia and Phrygia, see ch. 16 : 6, note. Comp. with this revisitation of the churches ch. 15 : 41, and observe how Paul is not less concerned to strengthen the saints than to convert sinners.

24, 25. And a certain Jew named Apollos. Of whom nothing is known besides the information here given, except the facts that his eloquence attracted many at Corinth who would fain have made him the leader of a Christian sect in the church (1 Cor. 3 : 6); that he would not permit it, and, probably for this reason, refused to return to Corinth, though earnestly urged to do so by Paul (1 Cor. 16 : 12), who testifies his regard for him in Titus 3 : 13. He is regarded by some critics as the author of the Epistle to the Hebrews.—**Born at Alexandria.** A celebrated city and seaport of Egypt, on the Mediterranean, twelve miles from the mouth of the river Nile, named in honor of Alexander the Great, who founded it, B. C. 332. He selected it for the Greek colony which he proposed to found, from the great natural advantages which it possessed, and from the admirable harbor formed by the deep water between Rhacotis and the isle of Pharos. It was built upon a strip of land between the sea and Lake Marcotis, and connected with the isle of Pharos by a long mole nearly a mile in length. Two main streets, 240 feet wide, crossing each other at right angles in the middle of the city, left a free passage for the sea-breezes. Though mentioned in the N. T. only incidentally in the Book of Acts (chaps. 6 : 9; 27 : 6), it exerted a powerful influence on the history of the development of Christianity. It was a great literary and philosophic centre, was the site of the largest library in the world, which under Cleopatra contained 700,000 volumes, was a mother of philosophy and arts, and was a cosmopolitan city, in which Greeks, Egyptians, and Jews had their respective quarters. At this time nearly one-third of its population were Jews; they had, however, materially modified their religious belief, to conform it to the dreamy philosophy of the Orient, which there found a home. On this philosophy, see John, ch. 1, Prel. Note. The Alexandrian Jews, though more learned in foreign philosophy than those of Palestine, or even of Asia Minor, were despised by their

26 And he began to speak boldly in the synagogue: whom when Aquila and Priscilla had heard, they took him unto *them*, and expounded unto him the way of God more[d] perfectly.
27 And when he was disposed to pass into Achaia, the brethren wrote, exhorting the disciples to receive him: who, when he was come, helped[e] them much which had believed[f] through grace:
28 For he mightily convinced the Jews, *and that* publicly, shewing by[g] the scriptures that Jesus was Christ.

d Heb. 6 : 1; 2 Pet. 3 : 18.... e 1 Cor. 3 : 6.... f Ephes. 2 : 8.... g John 5 : 39.

brethren, because of their departure from the orthodox faith of the fathers. Presumptively, Apollos was a pupil of the Alexandrian school, a rhetorician, who had learned, in a very imperfect way, the facts respecting the life of Jesus. See below.—**An eloquent man.** This is probably the meaning of the original here, though it may also be rendered, *a learned man.*—**Mighty in the Scriptures.** That is, in the O. T. Scriptures. Observe, not merely *learned* in them, but *powerful* in the use of them. Comp. 2 Tim. 3 : 17. One reason of his power is indicated in the next verse; he was *fervent in spirit*, and he taught out of them the *things of the Lord.* Comp. John 5 : 39. A fervent spirit, a good knowledge of the Bible, and a search in it always for the things concerning Christ, are the elements that give *power* in its use. Observe, too, that, ignorant as he was in almost the first principles of Christian theology, he was powerful, through the Scriptures.—**Was instructed in the way of the Lord.** The word rendered *instructed* (κατηχέω) literally indicates oral instruction; hence, learning by rumor, report, or hearsay. Comp. ch. 21 : 21, 24. That appears to be its meaning here. He had heard, in an imperfect way, the story of Christ's life, death, and resurrection; it exactly accorded with the O. T. prophecies of the Messiah (see ch. 3 : 18, note), and without further instruction he began to preach to the Jews from the O. T. that the Messiah had come. But of the nature of his kingdom, and especially of the baptism which he commanded, into the name of the Father, the Son, and the Holy Ghost (Matt. 28 : 19), he knew nothing. He baptized simply as John, unto repentance from sin (Matt. 3 : 6).—**Knowing only the baptism of John.** That is, knowing no other baptism. He knew, probably, that the Christians were baptized, but knew nothing of any difference between their baptism and that which John employed.

26-28. Aquila and Priscilla. Observe, a woman is here the instructor of the religious teacher, working equally with her husband for his enlightenment. Observe, too, that God, who uses the imperfectly instructed Apollos to preach his Gospel to the Jews, and to aid the Gentile Christians in replying to them, uses a layman and his wife, tent-makers, to instruct the learned and eloquent Apollos.—**More perfectly.** In what respect is not indicated; hardly on the point of baptism, since the Christians at Ephesus, where Priscilla and Aquila dwelt, seem to have been in ignorance on this point. See ch. 19 : 3, 4.—**Into Achaia.** See ch. 18 : 12, note. —**He mightily convinced.** Or *vehemently*, as in Luke 23 : 10; the adverb indicates the character of his speech, as fervid, vehement, impassioned. With this agrees the description of Apollos as an eloquent man, and fervent in the spirit.—**The Jews.** In the controversies which everywhere took place in the early church between the Jewish and Gentile converts, and between the Christians and the Jews, who were at first their bitterest opponents, Apollos was an effective ally, by reason of his knowledge of O. T. Scripture, of which the Gentile converts, and even the proselytes, were comparatively ignorant. His labors in Achaia appear to have been specially carried on in Corinth, where his learning and eloquence, in marked contrast with the simplicity of Paul's unoratorical preaching (1 Cor. 2 : 1-4), attracted many friends, who endeavored to organize a party or sect under his name (1 Cor. 1 : 12; 3 : 4-6). See on ver. 24.

This "historical episode," as Meyer calls it, appears to be introduced for the purpose of showing what agencies were employed by the Spirit of God in promoting the spread of the Gospel. Preaching was not confined to those that were ordained by the apostles, nor even to such as were directly instructed in the Gospel from the fountain head. The incident illustrates and is partially parallel to Luke 9 : 49, 50. Comp. Rev. 22 : 17, "Let him that heareth say Come." Analogous to this story of Apollos are some incidents in the experience of modern missionaries in foreign lands. Dr. Chamberlain, of the Reformed (Dutch) Mission, has narrated such an one to me. A Hindoo purchased a Bible from a native who had bought it from a mission station; the purchaser was converted, with his wife, by reading the Bible; they gathered the villagers together and read it aloud to them, organized a *quasi* Christian church, without, however, baptism or the Lord's Supper, the necessity and nature of which they did not understand; he became known far and near as "the man with the book." His church some seven or eight years thereafter, was found by some missionaries during a missionary journey through the country, and after being more perfectly instructed in Christian doctrine, was received by them into the visible "communion of saints."

CHAPTER XIX.

AND it came to pass, that, while Apollos[h] was at Corinth, Paul having passed through the upper coasts, came to Ephesus; and finding certain disciples,

2 He said unto them, Have ye received the Holy Ghost since ye believed? And they said unto him, We have not[i] so much as heard whether there be any Holy Ghost.

h 1 Cor. 3 : 4-6. . . . i ch. 8 : 16; 1 Sam. 3 : 7.

Ch. 19 : 1-41. PAUL AT EPHESUS. THE CONDITION AND THE CONSUMMATION OF CHRISTIAN EXPERIENCE: REPENTANCE AND FAITH IN CHRIST ARE THE CONDITIONS; THE RECEIVING OF THE SPIRIT OF GOD IS THE CONSUMMATION (vers. 1-7).—PECULIAR EXIGENCIES REQUIRE PECULIAR POWERS; GOD ADAPTS HIS GIFTS TO OUR NEEDS (vers. 11, 12).—THE WORK OF GOD AND THE WORKS OF DARKNESS IN CONFLICT: CHRISTIANITY CONTRASTED WITH WITCHCRAFT (vers. 13-17).—GENUINE REPENTANCE IS APT TO COST SOMETHING (ver. 19).—THE GREATER THE GOOD THE FIERCER THE ENMITY (vers. 10, 20, with 26).—GAIN IS NOT GODLINESS (vers. 25-27; 1 Tim. 6 : 5).—THE TWOFOLD ENEMY OF CHRISTIANITY: WORLDLINESS AND SUPERSTITION (ver. 27). — GOD RAISES UP FRIENDS AND DEFENDERS IN UNEXPECTED PLACES (vers. 31, 35).—THE SERVANT OF THE LORD MUST NOT STRIVE (ver. 37; 2 Tim. 2 : 24).

A. D. 54-57. Paul probably arrived at Ephesus in the winter of A. D. 54 or the spring of A. D. 55, and left in the summer of A. D. 57. See Chronol. Table, p. 20. The episode related in the preceding chapter probably occurred while Paul was making the tour of visitation described in ch. 18 : 23. Thence, by what route we do not know, he came to Ephesus, where he had preached for a single Sabbath in the synagogue about a year previous, on his way to Jerusalem (ch. 18 : 19). The incident narrated in verses 1-7 has given rise to much perplexity, and not inconsiderable controversy. It is foreign to my purpose to enter into these controversies, or to cumber my notes with statements in detail of interpretations which seem to me to be forced, and invented for theological or controversial reasons. I shall, therefore, simply indicate what appears to me to be clearly the meaning of this passage, and the lessons which are evidently taught by it. Much of the difficulty here, as elsewhere in Acts, has been increased, if not created, by forgetting the fact that in this early stage of church history, neither doctrine, church order, nor church ceremonials, had come into a definite system, such as that in which they now exist. Christianity, as a system, both of doctrine and order, was, as yet, growing; and it is not at all surprising that Christian converts should have got only fragments of it.

1. Having passed through the upper coasts. The eastern parts of Asia Minor, beyond the river Halys, or in that direction, are here intended. See map, p. 21. — **Came to Ephesus.** The capital and most important city of the province of Asia—one of the chief of the free cities which were the nucleus of the Ionian league—the emporium of the trade of the East. Situated on the projecting forehead of the peninsula since known as Asia Minor, it was called one of the eyes of Asia—Smyrna, forty miles distant, being the other. Partly on the ridge of Mt. Coressus, partly on Mt. Prion or Pion, and partly on the plain in the valley of the river Cayster, from which these eminences arose, the city was built. This plain, about five miles long from east to west, and three miles broad, was bounded on three sides by mountains, and on the fourth by the Icarian, one of the divisions of the Ægean sea. The outer port of the city was formed by the channel of the Cayster and the bay into which it flowed; the inner port was a sort of lake, connected with the river, a short distance above its mouth, by a canal. The land about was low, the waters abundant, and marshes and lagoons, and a continual change of form was the consequence. The wash of the sea and the accumulations of silt had already, at the time of Paul's visit, impaired the harbor; and its subsequent destruction, by the continuance of the same process, proved the death of the town. Ephesus has scanty material for history. Founded by Androchus, son of Codrus, Ephesus was the royal residence of the Ionian kings, was a kind of sacred city, holding peculiar religious festivals, was successively under the dominion of the Persian and Lydian kings, and came finally under the Roman rule—the province of Asia, with Ephesus for its capital, being formed 129 B. C. At the time of Paul's stay there it was a free city and assize town, with thriving commerce and a fair cultivation of the arts and literature, with a fervor of idolatry, and bewitched with sorcery. Although there are remains of some beautiful buildings, the only ones which interest us as students of the Bible are the stadium, the theatre, and the temple. From the ruins of the edifices and the descriptions of contemporaneous visitors, we have very minute information respecting these three buildings. The stadium, or circus, 685 feet long and 200 wide, was the arena of the beast fights, foot-racing, wrestling, and pugilistic combats. It lay at the end of a broad paved street, which led off to the north along the foot of Mt. Coressus. Out of the hill itself the seats on the south were excavated, while those on the north were supported on arches. The eastern end was of circular form, like a theatre; the other extremity was built straight across, with open spaces on the north and south for the two entrances to the stadium. The theatre, excavated from the sloping side of Mt. Coressus, looked toward the west, faced with a portico, but, like other ancient theatres, without a roof. It is said to have been the largest edifice of the kind ever erected by the Greeks. It would seat 50,000 people. From the agora just below, the crowd quite naturally rushed into the theatre, when matters came to so serious a pass with the Ephesians as to threaten an interference with the honor paid to the great Diana, and with the manufacture of her shrines. But the crowning glory of Ephesus was the great temple of Artemis or Diana, one of the seven great wonders of the world, and whose magnificence has been a marvel ever since. It glittered in brilliant beauty at the head of the harbor, and it was said that the sun saw nothing in his course more magnificent than Diana's temple. From the earliest settlement of the city this deity had been honored. A temple reported to have been a grand one had given place to one yet more grand, commenced in the Macedonian period, and reared amid the admiring Greeks and Asiatics, with all the beauty which the most noted architects, aided by the most skillful workmen, could produce. After the long years spent in its creation, it was left but a short time to adorn the city. An Ephesian, Herostratus by name, set it on fire, and on the birthnight of Alexander the Great it was destroyed. Tradition says that the divinity was absent from Ephesus superintending the advent of Alexander, and the temple, thus left without a protector, was lost. But the temple was immediately rebuilt, with still greater magnificence. The women contributed their jewels, and all Asia joined to restore to its idol a fitting home. Made of the purest marble, upon substantial foundations, which in that marshy ground were at once costly and essential, it confronted the mariner immediately at the landing-place. It was 425 feet long, and 220 broad; its columns, of Parian marble, were 60 feet high, and 36 of them were magnificently carved. The porticos in front and rear consisted each of 32 columns, 8 abreast and 4 deep, and around the sides were two rows, the entire number of columns, 127, being given each one by a king. Before entering the temple the worshippers must purify themselves at the lavatory in front. The great doors were of carved cypress, with jambs of marble, and an enormous transom of a single block, so immense that it is a marvel how it could have been put in its place. A legend says that the architect despaired of raising it, but while he slept the goddess herself lifted it, and the stone was found properly adjusted in the morning. The hall was adorned with the most wonderful statuary and paintings, the works of Polycletus, of Phidias, and other famous sculptors, the masterpiece of Calliphon, and the greatest of all, Alexander the Great, painted by Apelles. This last cost $35,000, equivalent, Chandler says, to $193,250 at the present day. In the centre of the court, under a roof of cedar supported by eight columns of green jasper—now in the mosque of St. Sophia at Constantinople—was the altar, rich with the carvings of Praxiteles. Around, hung the gifts of devotion from the rich and the poor, and beyond the altar hung the purple veil which concealed the deity worshipped by "all the world." The goddess herself, the object of all this magnificence, was a very unattractive image, made of wood, so timeworn that its kind, whether vine,

TEMPLE OF DIANA (from an ancient coin).

cedar, or ebony, cannot be told, with a staff or trident in each hand, the upper part of the body covered with paps, the emblem of fecundity, the lower part, a block or pyramid upside down, covered with rude carvings (see ver. 35). Behind the shrine was an apartment for the safe-keeping of the treasures of nations and rulers. So great was the veneration of the people, that no one would have dared to venture into this safe, much less disturb anything there. To go to the roof of the temple, a staircase ascended, which was made of the wood of a single vine from Cyprus. From the corner of the roof Mithridates shot the arrow to mark the boundary of the sanctuary or asylum of the temple, "and the shaft went to the length of more than a furlong." The attendants on the temple were many, including eunuchs under a high-priest, a host of virgins, and a great number of slaves (see ver. 31, note). The sacred emblem of Diana was a bee, and the priestesses were called Mellissæ (bees). The city was personified as a devotee of Diana, and boastfully exhibited on her coins "*Neocoros*," or "*temple-sweeper*" (see ver. 35, note). Ephesus was a hotbed of sorcery. The incantations used there had a wide reputation as Ephesian charms (see ver. 13, note). The remains of Ephesus are partly covered with rubbish, and overgrown with vegetation. They have been visited by many travelers, and the ruins are full of interest to antiquarians. The site is now an utter desolation. Lewin says that in 1862 he could not even

3 And he said unto them, Unto what then were ye baptized? And they said, Unto[j] John's baptism.
4 Then said Paul, John[k] verily baptized with the baptism of repentance,[l] saying unto the people, that they should believe on him which should come after him, that is, on Christ Jesus.
5 When they heard *this*, they were baptized in the name[m] of the Lord Jesus.

j ch. 18 : 25.... k Matt. 3 : 11.... l John 1 : 15, 27, 30.... m ch. 8 : 16; 1 Cor. 1 : 13.

find a hut on the site of the capital of Asia. The only inhabitants within her walls were the beasts of the field and the fowls of the air.

And finding certain disciples. Not *Jews* (as *Conybeare and Howson*), nor *disciples of John the Baptist* (as, apparently, *Baumgarten*), nor *men so called because they acknowledged the name of Christ as soon as it was made known to them* (*Hackett*); all these interpretations are results of an attempt to get rid of the implication that one could be a disciple and not know of the Holy Spirit; and they take from the incident one of its chief lessons, viz., that a genuine discipleship is not inconsistent with great spiritual ignorance. One may be a pupil, and yet at the beginning know little or nothing. That these were *Christian disciples* is evident from (1) the word here used (μαθητής), which is never employed in the N. T. except to designate Christian disciples; (2) from Paul's distinct recognition of them as *believers* (ver. 2), *i. e.*, evidently believers in Christ. Nor is there any reason to suppose that these disciples were strangers who had just arrived at Ephesus, a purely gratuitous surmise. The unquestioned facts in the case are these: Paul coming from Corinth, from six to nine months before, stopped at Ephesus, and preached one sermon in the synagogue, produced a favorable impression, but declined to remain (ch. 18 : 19-21). If we take his sermon at Antioch in Pisidia (ch. 13) as a type of his preaching to the Jews, and it is the only fully reported sermon to his own countrymen which we possess, he did not undertake to set the whole Christian system before them, but simply the truths, (1) that Jesus is the Messiah; (2) that through him, by repentance, is remission of sins; nothing was probably said about the Trinity, the gift of the Holy Ghost, the form or nature of Baptism, or church order or organization. Having planted this seed, the apostle departed. He was followed by Apollos; but Apollos knew the facts of Christianity only by rumor, and very imperfectly (ch. 18 : 24-28), and nothing concerning the gift of the Holy Ghost, or the nature of Christian baptism. Was this knowledge imparted to these Ephesian Christians by Aquila and Priscilla? There is no evidence that it was; in a city of so many thousand inhabitants they may have never met, or even heard of these strangers from Corinth. Moreover, there is nothing to indicate that the latter were Christian teachers, or had acquired anything more than the rudiments of Christianity. There is no distinct statement even of their conversion in ch. 18; or that they went to Ephesus as missionaries, rather than for the purposes of their trade, which originally brought them and Paul together (ch. 18 : 2, note). And it is evident from 1 Corinthians, chaps. 1, 2, 3, that Paul's preaching in Corinth was of the simplest description; he told the story of the cross, nothing else, and he baptized only three or four disciples (1 Cor. 1 : 14-16; 2 : 2; 3 : 1, 2, etc.). That there was at this time no Christian church in Ephesus is indicated by the fact that Paul preached in the synagogue (ver. 8). I believe, then, that, as a result of the preaching of Paul and Apollos, a few Jews had accepted the truth that Jesus is the Messiah, and had been baptized as a symbol of repentance, perhaps by Apollos, certainly with a baptism like that of John; that insomuch as they accepted Jesus as the Messiah, they are recognized as disciples, *i. e.*, pupils, though ignorant of some of the fundamental principles of Christian theology; that they received no further instruction from Apollos, who proceeded immediately to Greece, nor from Aquila and Priscilla, who were not rabbis, and had no opportunity to teach what they knew, publicly, in the synagogue, and who, for aught that appears in the narrative, had never met these disciples, and were, as yet, imperfectly instructed themselves.

2. Did ye receive the Holy Ghost when ye believed? This is a better rendering than our English version. So *Alford*, *Hackett*, *Alexander*.—**We did not hear whether there be any Holy Ghost.** That is, nothing was said about it at the time of our conversion and acceptance of Christianity. They believed that Jesus was the promised Messiah; but the further truth that another Comforter had come, who was given for light and life to all that would receive him (ch. 2 : 38, 39), they had heard nothing of. The church still contains many Ephesian Christians, who believe in God the Father, and Christ as the Redeemer, but not practically in a Holy Spirit, on whom they may daily and hourly rely, and in whose inspiration and guidance there is perfect liberty. They have accepted the doctrine of repentance, baptism, and the remission of sins; but they have not gone on to receive the gift of the Holy Ghost.

3, 4. Into what (εἰς) **were ye baptized?** Christ had commanded his disciples to baptize into the name (εἰς τὸ ὄνομα) of the Father, the Son, and the Holy Ghost (Matt. 28 : 19).—**Into John's baptism.** That is, into the baptism which he, and, after him, his disciples, adminis-

6 And when Paul had laid[n] *his* hands upon them, the
Holy Ghost came on them;[o] and they spake with
tongues, and[p] prophesied.
7 And all the men were about twelve.
8 And he went into the synagogue, and spake boldly for the space of three months, disputing,[q] and persuading[r] the things concerning the kingdom of God.

9 But when divers were hardened,[s] and believed
not, but spake evil[t] of that[u] way before the multitude,
he departed[v] from them, and separated the disciples,
disputing daily in the school of one Tyrannus.
10 And this continued by the space[w] of two years;
so that all they which dwelt in Asia[x] heard the word
of the Lord Jesus, both Jews and Greeks.

n ch. 8 : 17....o chaps. 2 : 4; 10 : 46 ...p 1 Cor. 14 : 1, etc....q ch. 18 : 19....r ch. 28 : 23....s Rom. 11 : 7; Heb. 3 : 13....t 2 Tim. 1 : 15; 2 Pet. 2 : 2; Jude 10....u verse 23....v 1 Tim. 6 : 5....w ch. 20 : 31....x ch. 20 : 18.

tered, the nature of which is here explained, as a baptism of repentance. See below. On John's baptism, see Matt., ch. 3, notes, and Luke 3 : 1–18, notes.

5-7. When they heard this, they were baptized into the name of the Lord Jesus. This has been interpreted for controversial reasons as a part of Paul's speech, as though he said, *They*, John's auditors, *when they heard this*, his prophecy of a coming Messiah, *were baptized into the name of Jesus.* This interpretation is manifestly false, since when John preached and baptized, he did not at first even know that Jesus was the Messiah, and never baptized in his name. It is pronounced by Hackett as now obsolete. Paul's re-baptism of these Ephesian converts affords no authority for re-baptizing those who have received Christian baptism. Whatever ground there may be for that practice, it is not sustained by Paul's example here, since the reason why he re-baptized was not an error or informality in the previous baptism, but the fact that that baptism was not into Jesus Christ, and therefore not into covenant relations with the Triune God.—**The Holy Ghost came upon them.** There is nothing in this language inconsistent with the opinion that they had been previously converted by the power of the Spirit of God. On the meaning of the phraseology, see ch. 8 : 17, note, where also is discussed *laying on of hands.*—**All the men were about twelve.** Apparently, they were all *men.* Of their previous and subsequent history nothing is known; and nothing of their character, except what can be deduced from the language of the historian here. From their ignorance concerning the Holy Ghost, whose presence and influence is a matter of O. T. teaching, it is surmised that they were of Gentile rather than of Jewish extraction; but this is far from certain.

While it is true that this episode suggests "many questions, the solution of which our imperfect knowledge of the first Christian age has put beyond our reach" (*Hackett*), it teaches very plainly some very important truths. (1.) The personality of the Holy Spirit. The language of the narrative, especially verse 2, is hardly consistent with the view that the Holy Spirit is only an impersonal, divine influence. (2.) The nature of Christian baptism. This is not a mere symbolic act by which the recipient publicly confesses his sins and his acceptance of Jesus as the Christ. It also symbolizes the mutual act of God and man, by which the latter is received into covenant with the Father, has his sins washed away through the Son, *and receives, as the principle and power of his future life, the gift of the Holy Ghost.* Comp. ch. 2 : 38. (3.) The nature of Christian experience. This is not merely repentance and acceptance of Christ. It is consummated only by the reception of a personal, present, and continuous gift of the Holy Ghost, as the power of a new life, to be maintained in, with, and by God, in which we have the liberty of the sons of God, being brought into his likeness by his indwelling. Comp. Rom. 7 : 6; 12 : 2; 1 Cor. 1 : 9; 2 : 12; 12 : 13; 2 Cor. 3 : 18; Ephes. 4 : 14. And observe the importance which Paul attaches to this aspect of Christian experience, in that he addresses to these disciples at once the question whether they have received this consummating gift of the Holy Ghost. It is not without significance that it is for the Ephesian church he subsequently lifts up the prayer of Ephes. 3 : 18–21.

8, 9. Concerning the kingdom of God. Thus his theme here, as at Thessalonica (ch. 17 : 7, note), was the same as that of John the Baptist and of Jesus (Matt. 3 : 2; 4 : 17). To the Jews he spoke of that kingdom of God which all the Jews throughout the world were expecting.—**Spake evil of that way before all the multitude.** Public debate with open enemies of the grace of God is rarely profitable. Paul eschewed it. Comp. ch. 18 : 6.—**School of one Tyrannus.** Of him nothing is known. He may have been the teacher of a Jewish school, such as was generally organized in every city, often in connection with the synagogue; or a Greek sophist converted to Christianity through the labors of Paul, and gladly allowing his school of philosophy or rhetoric, to be converted into a school of Christ; or the founder of a school, whose building, hired by Paul for a preaching-place, still bore his name; and this last hypothesis seems to me the most probable. The reason assigned by Baumgarten appears conclusive against the first hypothesis: "But what consistency was it to depart from the synagogue, on account of the general prevalence of unbelief in it, and to characterize it as an unclean place for the disciples to frequent, and thereupon to pass at once into a Rabbinical school?" The reference to *one* Ty-

11 And God wrought special[y] miracles by the hands of Paul:
12 So that from his body were brought unto the sick handkerchiefs[z] or aprons, and the diseases departed from them, and the evil spirits went out of them.
13 Then certain of the vagabond Jews, exorcists, took upon them[a] to call over them which had evil spirits the name of the Lord Jesus, saying, We adjure[b] you by Jesus, whom Paul preacheth.

y Mark 16 : 20.... z ch. 5 : 15.... a Mark 9 : 38; Luke 9 : 49.... b Josh. 6 : 26.

rannus appears inconsistent with the second opinion; if converted to Christianity, he would have been designated as a believer.

10-12. And this continued by the space of two years. During this time Paul wrote 1 Corinthians (1 Cor. 16 : 8, 9); it is probable also that at this time the church at Colossæ was formed, not directly by Paul, but by one of the disciples, named Epaphras (Col. 1 : 7). Churches appear also to have been organized, probably at this time, at Laodicea and Hierapolis (Col. 4 : 13, 15, 16). Out of this ministry may also have grown other of the seven churches in Asia, mentioned in Rev., chaps. 1-3. Paul's address to the elders of the Ephesian church (ch. 20 : 17-35) gives us a definite and graphic picture of his ministry during these two years.—**Special miracles.** Literally, *uncommon powers*, *i. e.*, uncommon signs of power. Ephesus (see above) was a centre of magic and witchcraft, as well as of idolatry; and as Moses wrought special miracles to break down the power of the magicians and sorcerers of Egypt, so here was given to Paul special power to break the bonds which enthralled this superstitious people. It is notable that Luke makes little account, generally, of the miracles wrought by the apostles, sometimes not even mentioning them. Thus, but for 2 Cor. 12 : 12, we should not know that Paul wrought any miracles in Corinth.—**Handkerchiefs or aprons.** The former are his handkerchiefs, with which he had wiped the sweat from his brow; the latter are the aprons which he had worn in his daily toil, by which, in Ephesus as in Corinth, he maintained himself (ch. 20 : 34). Thus, as Baumgarten, "the thought is both natural and obvious that in these working garments, in this pouring out of his sweat, the people saw and reverenced the plenitude of infinite love and power, which had shone forth in the apostle Paul." In respect to these miracles observe (1) that they were exceptional, and not numerous; this is implied by the phrase "special miracles," and by the consideration that Paul could hardly have possessed an unlimited supply of handkerchiefs and aprons; (2) that they required a special act of faith in the healed, or their friends, since the garments of the apostle were sent for and carried away, and that thus the case is different from that recorded in ch. 5 : 15, where, as I believe (see note there), no healing was wrought by the shadow of Peter; (3) that the only analogous N. T. miracle is that of the woman healed of an issue of blood by touching the hem of Christ's garment (Mark 5 : 24-34, notes); hence the skepticism respecting the account here is hardly fairly dealt with by the commentators, since it is founded, not on the impossibility of God's working by what instruments he will, but on the fact that he in no other authenticated instance wrought miracles in this way, while the method here described has certain at least external resemblances to the legendary accounts of cure by relics, etc.; (4) that the true answer to this objection is that the circumstances were special and called for special measures, that only special miracles could have had the effect, which by Paul's ministry was produced, to suppress magical arts and abate idolatrous worship (vers. 19, 26); (5) that the incident here gives no countenance to relic worship or the legendary miracles alleged to have been wrought by relics; rather the reverse; for the reason stated by Alford: "In no cases but these do we find the power, even in the apostolic days; and the general cessation of all extraordinary gifts of the Spirit would lead us to the inference that these, which were even then the rarest, have ceased also."

13. Certain of the vagabond Jews, exorcists. Though Ephesus was a Greek city, the manners of its inhabitants were half Oriental. The image of its tutelary goddess resembled an Indian idol, its religion was intermixed with Asiatic superstition; it was thus the centre both of an Oriental philosophy and the practice of witchcraft. Mysterious symbols, called Ephesian letters, were employed to charm away evil spirits, either by being pronounced by the charmer, or written upon parchment or engraved upon stone, and so employed as an amulet. The study of these symbols was an elaborate science, and books both numerous and costly were compiled by its professors. These magical arts were practised by not a few of the Jews; the very severity with which the O. T. forbids such practices (Exod. 22 : 18; Lev. 20 : 27; Deut. 18 : 10, 11; 1 Sam. 28 : 3, 9) indicates a national tendency toward them. The Talmud and Josephus give evidence of a continuance of these practices at a later period, as do references in Paul's epistles (Gal. 5 : 20; 2 Tim. 3 : 13). A knowledge of magic was a requisite qualification of a member of the Sanhedrim, that he might be able to try those who were accused of employing it, and the art was believed among the Jews to have been derived from King Solomon. The instruments employed

14 And there were seven sons of *one* Sceva, a Jew,
and chief of the priests, which did so.
15 And the evil spirit answered and said, Jesus I
know, and Paul I know; but who are ye?
16 And the man in whom the evil spirit was, leaped[c]
on them, and overcame them, and prevailed against
them, so that they fled out of that house naked and
wounded.
17 And this was known to all the Jews and Greeks
also dwelling at Ephesus; and fear[d] fell on them all,
and the name of the Lord Jesus was magnified.
18 And many that believed came, and confessed,[e]
and shewed their deeds.
19 Many of them also which used curious arts
brought their books together, and burned them before
all *men*: and they counted the price of them, and
found *it* fifty thousand *pieces* of silver.
20 So mightily grew[f] the word of God, and prevailed.
21 After[g] these things were ended, Paul purposed in
the spirit, when he had passed through Macedonia and
Achaia, to go to Jerusalem, saying, After I have been
there, I must also see Rome.[h]
22 So he sent into Macedonia two of them that ministered unto him, Timotheus and Erastus:[i] but he himself stayed in Asia for a season.

c Luke 8 : 29....d Luke 1 : 65; chaps. 2 : 43; 5 : 5, 11....e Matt. 3 : 6; Rom. 10 : 10....f ch. 12 : 24... g Gal. 2 : 1....h Rom. 15 : 23-28.... i Rom. 16 : 23; 2 Tim. 4 : 20.

in its practice were chiefly fumigations, incantations, use of certain herbs, and the employment of charms, written or spoken. The exorcists here mentioned treated the name of Jesus as such a charm, the mere pronunciation of which they thought would have power to expel evil spirits. Thus they classed Paul with themselves, and Christianity with magic. Their action indicates a certain degree of sincerity in their superstition; they were given over to believe a lie (2 Thess. 2 : 11); while the language of ver. 18 indicates that they were also consciously guilty of fraud, and, in the event which followed, publicly confessed it. On ancient magic, see further chaps. 8 : 9, note; 13 : 6, note.

14-20. Seven sons of one Sceva. Mentioned only here. Nothing more is known of him. It is not certain that he resided at Ephesus because his sons did so, nor whether he had been one of the chief priests, that is, chief of the twenty-four priestly courses at Jerusalem, or was an apostate Jew and was one of the priests of Diana. The Greek word rendered *chief-priest* was not only in general use among the heathen, but occurs repeatedly on coins and in other inscriptions relating to the worship of Diana at Ephesus.—**Jesus I know, and Paul I know.** Two different Greek verbs are rendered by the same English verb *know;* it may be rendered, *I know who Jesus is, and as for Paul I am well acquainted with him.*—**Naked and wounded.** Not literally nude, but partially stripped of their raiment; perhaps here, as elsewhere, of the cloak or outer garment. The best manuscripts indicate that only two of the sons were engaged in this unsuccessful attempt at exorcism.—**The name of the Lord Jesus was magnified.** See Matt. 5 : 16. There is no ground for Olshausen's remark, "This proceeding served, as one would expect, greatly to raise the reputation of St. Paul." It was the Master, not the servant, who was magnified.—**Many that believed.** The context would seem to indicate here that belief in these magical arts is intended; but the phrase, when used as here without qualification, always indicates in the N. T. belief in Jesus Christ. The implication of the narrative, then, is that many of the Ephesian Christians continued their belief in and practice of heathen magic, and that the sons of Sceva endeavored, like Simon Magus (ch. 8 : 18, 19), to employ the power of Christianity for their own benefit.—**And confessed.** Not their sins in general, but their participation in magical arts. —**Many also of them which used curious arts.** The *many* of ver. 18 are the dupes, those who had consulted the wizards; the *many* of ver. 19 are the wizards themselves.—**Fifty thousand pieces of silver.** That is, drachms, equivalent to between $8,000 and $10,000. This burning is very different from and gives no warrant for the burning of heretical books by the Roman Catholic church; in the one case, the books are burned voluntarily by the owners, in the other in spite of the owners.

21, 22. After he had passed through Macedonia and Achaia. For account of the execution of this purpose, see ch. 21.—**I must also see Rome.** This purpose was executed, but in a manner very different from that anticipated by the apostle; he went to Jerusalem, was there arrested, and sent as a prisoner to Rome. The object of his visit to Jerusalem was probably, as before (ch. 18 : 21), to attend one of the feasts and to report to the Christian church the result of his ministry; incidentally also to carry thither collections from the richer churches of Asia Minor and Greece (1 Cor. 16 : 1-4); the object of his visit to Rome was not to see the imperial city, but to have spiritual communion with the few converts there gathered (Rom. 1 : 9-12). —**So he sent into Macedonia two,** etc. One of the many incidental confirmations of the authenticity of the Book of Acts is afforded by a comparison of the language here with 1 Cor. 16 : 8-10 and with Rom. 1 : 13; 15 : 23-28.—**Erastus.** Probably a deacon or attendant of Paul's at Ephesus, mentioned again as at Corinth in 2 Tim. 4 : 20; not to be confounded with the treasurer of the city of Corinth mentioned in Rom. 16 : 23. That an attendant upon Paul at Ephesus could have gone forward into Greece to

23 And the same time there arose no small stir[j] about that way.
24 For a certain *man* named Demetrius, a silversmith, which made silver shrines for Diana, brought no small[k] gain unto the craftsmen;
25 Whom he called[l] together with the workmen of like occupation, and said, Sirs, ye know that by this craft we have our wealth.
26 Moreover, ye see and hear, that not alone at Ephesus, but almost throughout all Asia, this Paul hath persuaded and turned away much people, saying that[m] they be no gods, which are made with hands:
27 So that not only this our craft is in danger to be set at nought; but also that the temple of the great goddess Diana should be despised,[n] and her magnificence should be destroyed, whom all Asia and the world[o] worshippeth.
28 And when they heard *these sayings*, they were full of wrath,[p] and cried out, saying, Great *is* Diana of the Ephesians!
29 And the whole city was filled with confusion: and having caught Gaius[q] and Aristarchus,[r] men of Macedonia, Paul's companions in travel, they rushed with one accord into the theatre.

j 2 Cor. 1 : 8; 6 : 9....k ch. 16 : 16-19....l Rev. 18 : 11....m Ps. 115 : 4; Isa. 44 : 10-20....n Zeph. 2 : 11....o 1 John 5 : 19; Rev. 13 : 8.... p Jer. 50 : 38....q Rom. 16 : 23; 1 Cor. 1 : 14....r Col. 4 : 10.

prepare the way for Paul's ministry and have been straightway made chamberlain of the city of Corinth, is highly improbable.—**But he himself stayed in Asia.** Some critics (see *Conybeare and Howson*) suppose that Paul made a short visit to Corinth at this time, referred to in 2 Cor. 12 : 14; 13 : 1, where he speaks of coming to them a third time. On this doubtful question, see notes there.

23-27. About that way. The way of the Lord, the Gospel (ch. 9 : 2, note).—**Demetrius, a silversmith, which made silver shrines.** Small, portable images or models of the temple of the Ephesian Diana. Similar images are found on the coins of many cities. It was the custom to carry these shrines on journeys and military expeditions, and set them up as objects of worship in private dwellings; the material might be wood, gold or silver; the manufacturing of them furnished an extensive and profitable traffic, visitors to Ephesus taking them away as sacred memorials of their visit. Of Demetrius nothing more is known. It is evident from the account here that he was a wholesale dealer and gave employment to various workmen. The word rendered *gain* should rather be rendered *work* or *employment*.—**Whom he called together with the workmen of like occupation.** The *craftsmen* (ver. 24) are probably his own workmen; *the workmen of like occupation* are probably others engaged in the manufacture, either of other memorials, or amulets, connected with the worship of Diana, or those not in the employ of Demetrius, but engaged either in the same work, or in getting out the rough material for the shrines. All the men pecuniarily interested in maintaining the worship of Diana were brought together on this occasion.—**Almost throughout all Asia.** An indication of the extent of the effect of Paul's labors. Comp. ver. 10. —**That they be no gods which are made with hands.** An indication of the character of Paul's preaching. Comp. ch. 17 : 23-25, 29. But see below on ver. 37. While the higher heathen philosophy taught that the images were only intended to represent the gods to the imagination, the superstitious and ignorant then, as now, regarded the idols themselves as deities. —**Not only this our craft is in danger, but even that the temple of the great goddess Diana should be despised.** *Diana*, the Latin name for the Greek Artemis is here used for the tutelary deity of the Ephesians, an Artemis quite unlike the Greek divinity, and more nearly resembling Astarte. Her worship was said to have been established at Ephesus by the Amazons, and the Greeks on coming to Ionia, fancying some points of resemblance between this Asiatic divinity and their own Artemis, invested her with some of her peculiarities and gave it her name. She was the goddess of productiveness, and was represented with a mural crown, many breasts, a bar of metal or sort of trident in each hand, and the lower part of the body a mere "pyramid upside down," covered with figures of mystical animals. There was nothing attractive or impressive in this rude, mummy-like figure, but the very contrast to her magnificent temple (see on ver. 1), added to the superstitious devotion to this image.—**Whom all Asia and the world worshippeth.** An extravagant expression, yet with some ground of truth; the temple had been built at the common expense of all the Greek cities in Asia, and pilgrims repaired thither from all nations and countries.

28, 29. And cried out. *Were crying out;* the imperfect tense indicates continuous action. Probably at first a tumultuous procession marched through the streets of the city swelling their ranks by this war-cry, "Great is Diana of the Ephesians." The mob having been thus sufficiently aroused, Paul's traveling companions were seized and a rush was made for the theatre, which in the Greek cities was used for public gatherings as well as for sports.—**Gaius and Aristarchus.** Of *Gaius* nothing more is known. He is not the Gaius of ch. 20 : 4, who was of Derbe, nor the Gaius of Rom. 16 : 23 and 1 Cor. 1 : 14, who was evidently a Corinthian. *Aristarchus* was from Thessalonica (ch. 20 : 4), sailed with Paul to Rome (ch. 27 : 2) and in Paul's epistle to the Colossians (4 : 10) is mentioned as a fellow-prisoner, and in his epistle to Philemon (ver. 24) as a fellow-

30 And when Paul would have entered in unto the
people, the disciples suffered him not.
31 And certain of the chief of Asia, which were his
friends, sent unto him, desiring[s] *him* that he would not
adventure himself into the theatre.
32 Some[t] therefore cried one thing, and some another: for the assembly was confused: and the more
part knew not wherefore they were come together.

33 And they drew Alexander out of the multitude,
the Jews putting him forward. And Alexander[u] beckoned with the hand, and would have made his defence
unto the people.
34 But when they knew that he was a Jew, all with
one voice, about the space of two hours, cried out,
Great *is* Diana of the Ephesians!

s ch. 21 : 12.... t ch. 21 : 34.... u 1 Tim. 1 : 20; 2 Tim. 4 : 14.

laborer. — **With one accord into the theatre.** The theatre of the ancients was usually semi-circular in form and open to the air; the seats were ranged around in tiers one above another, and the performances took place on a stage level with the lowest seats on the straight side of the building. Thus it resembled the modern hippodrome rather than the modern theatre. The remains of the theatre here mentioned are still extant and attest its vast dimensions and convenient situation. See further on ver. 1. The temple of Diana could be seen from it across the market-place.

THEATRE AT EPHESUS.

30, 31. Paul would have entered in. To rescue his traveling companions, or to share their danger. This slight incident is very significant of his character.—**Certain of the chief of Asia.** Literally, *Asiarchs.* These were officers, elected by the cities of the province of Asia, to preside over their games and religious festivals. Each town chose one of its wealthiest citizens, and out of the number thus chosen ten were selected for this honored office. Such an Asiarch is mentioned by Eusebius as presiding at the martyrdom of Polycarp. The Ephesian games in honor of Diana took place in the month of May, which was consecrated to the glory of the goddess, and was named, in her honor, Artemision. "Receiving no emolument from their office, but being required rather to expend large sums for the amusement of the people and their own credit, they (the Asiarchs) were necessarily persons of wealth. Men of consular rank were often willing to receive the appointment, and it was held to enhance the honor of any other magistracies with which they might be invested. They held for the time a kind of sacerdotal position; and when, robed with mantles of purple and crowned with garlands, they assumed the duty of regulating the great gymnastic contests and controlling the tumultuary crowd in the theatre, they might literally be called the 'chief of Asia.'"—(*Conybeare and Howson.*) That Paul should have secured the friendship of one of these Asiarchs is a remarkable, but not an incredible circumstance. God raises up friends for his people where they are needed. To this incident of the presence of his traveling companions in the theatre Paul perhaps refers in 1 Cor. 4 : 9.

32-34. Most part knew not wherefore they were come together. They had rushed into the theatre by a common impulse, the mob swayed, as is common, by a few master minds, without knowing the object or occasion of the concourse.—**And they put forward Alexander out of the multitude, the Jews putting him forward.** Fearful lest the mob, which is always unreasonable, should direct its fury against them, the Jews put forward one of their number to defend them, probably to explain that they were not to be confounded with the Christians. It is not improbable that this Alexander is the coppersmith mentioned by Paul in 2 Tim. 4 : 14, and was one of the "workmen of like occupation" of ver. 25, and hence likely to have considerable influence with his guild. This, which is the view of Alexander, Hackett, Olshau-

35 And when the town-clerk had appeased the people, he said, *Ye* men[v] of Ephesus, what man is there
that knoweth not how that the city of the Ephesians is
a worshipper of the great goddess Diana, and of the
image which fell down from Jupiter?
36 Seeing then that these things cannot be spoken
against, ye ought to be quiet, and to do[w] nothing
rashly.
37 For ye have brought hither these men, which are
neither robbers[x] of churches, nor yet blasphemers of
your goddess.
38 Wherefore if Demetrius, and the craftsmen which
are with him, have a matter against any man, the law
is open, and there are deputies: let them implead one
another.
39 But if ye inquire any thing concerning other matters, it shall be determined in a lawful assembly.
40 For we are in danger to be called in question for
this day's uproar, there being no cause whereby we
may give an account of this concourse.
41 And when he had thus spoken, he dismissed the
assembly.[y]

v Ephes. 2 : 12.... w Prov. 14 : 29.... x ch. 25 : 8.... y 2 Cor. 1 : 8–10.

sen, and others, seems to me far more probable than that suggested by Meyer and Alford, that he was a Christian, put forward by the Jews maliciously, to bear the brunt of the mob's attack. The mob had already in their hands two of Paul's traveling companions (ver. 29), and it is not probable that a third would have ventured into the mob, where Alexander was.—**Would have made his defence.** Defence for himself and his nation.—**All with one voice for about the space of two hours cried out, saying, Great is Diana of the Ephesians.** This was itself, according to the Oriental ideas prevalent at Ephesus, an act of worship. See Matt. 6 : 7; 1 Kings 18 : 26. The Jews were recognized enemies of image worship, and the mob was in no mood to hear from them.

35-37. The town-clerk. Rather, *The secretary.* The original (γραμματεύς), like our word *secretary*, is a word of various meanings, used to characterize officers of very different rank. The title appears on coins of Ephesus, and in such connection with the title Asiarch as to suggest a *quasi* religious office. The secretary of the Greek cities kept the records of the public assemblages and read the laws in the public gatherings of the people; was present when money was deposited in the temple; and received and opened letters addressed to the city. That this man was one of no inconsiderable influence and authority is evident from the narrative here.—**Had appeased the people.** Rather *quelled them; i. e.*, by his appearance and the mere weight of his authority.—**He said.** "The speech is a pattern of candid argument and judicious tact. He first allays the fanatical passions of his listeners by a simple appeal. Then he bids them remember that Paul and his companions had not been guilty of profaning the temple or calumnious expressions against the goddess. Then he points out that the remedy for any injustice was amply provided by the assizes, or by an appeal to the proconsul. And finally he reminds them that such an uproar exposed them to the displeasure of the Roman government."—(*Conybeare and Howson.*)—**The city of the Ephesians is a worshipper of the great goddess Diana.** The term here rendered worshipper (νεωκόρος, *neocoros*) is literally, *temple-keeper* or *temple-sweeper*, but no exact equivalent can easily be found for it in any single English word or phrase. The title is found in the inscriptions

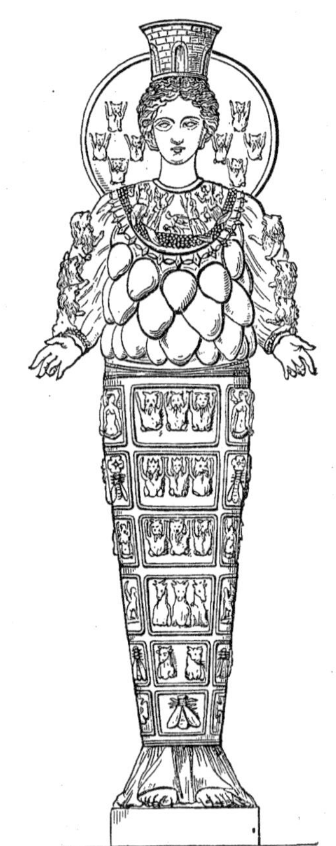

IMAGE OF DIANA.

on Ephesian coins. It was a title of honor given to any city noted for the worship of a particular deity in whose honor it had constructed a well-

CHAPTER XX.

AND after the uproar[z] was ceased, Paul called unto *him* the disciples, and embraced *them*, and departed for to go[a] into Macedonia.

2 And when he had gone over those parts, and had given them much[b] exhortation, he came into Greece,
3 And *there* abode three months. And when the Jews laid wait[c] for him, as he was about to sail into Syria, he purposed to return through Macedonia.

z ch. 19 : 40. . . . a 1 Cor. 16 : 5; 1 Tim. 1 : 3. . . . b 1 Thess. 2 : 3, 11. . . . c chaps. 23 : 12; 25 : 3; 2 Cor. 11 : 26.

known temple. Originally an expression of humility, signifying literally *temple-sweeper*, and applied to the verger or sexton of the temple, it became an honorable appellation, coveted by the greatest cities.—**Which fell down from Jupiter.** "Like the Palladium of Troy, like the more ancient Minerva of the Athenian Acropolis, like the Paphian Venus, or Cybele of Pessinus, like the Ceres in Sicily mentioned in Cicero, it was believed to have fallen down from the sky." —(*Conybeare and Howson.*) The origin of this legend may possibly be traced to the fall of some remarkable meteoric stones. — **Seeing these things are indisputable.** The real difficulty was that they were not indisputable; and a secret sentiment of doubt angered the people against the men who impugned their religion, and consequently endangered the fame and traffic of their city. Assurance of faith always produces calmness, and religious phrensy is generally a sign of unconscious skepticism.—**Neither sacrilegious.** So Wickliffe renders it. The apostle had not in any way profaned the temple.—**Nor yet blasphemers of your goddess,** *i. e., evil speakers against her.* An indication of the character of Paul's preaching. He had preached an affirmative Gospel—the unity and spirituality of the Godhead—as in Athens; he had not held up to derision or contempt even the superstitious worship of the Ephesians—a lesson to religious controversialists in our own day.

38-41. And the craftsmen that were with him. His workmen, or possibly the guild to which he belonged, and of which, in this matter, he was a leader.—**The law is open and there are deputies.** Rather, *The courts are in session* and *there are proconsuls.* On the office of proconsul, see ch. 13 : 7, note. At certain times of the year, fixed by the proconsul, the people of each Roman province assembled in the chief town of the district, in a *conventus.* The holding of such a convention was expressed by the phrase, *conventus agere* (equivalent to ἀγόραιοι ἄγονται here). At such a *conventus*, litigants applied to the proconsul, who selected a number of judges from the *conventus* to try the cause or causes, he himself presiding at the trials and pronouncing the sentence. The *deputies* (ἀνθύπατοι) here are either the proconsuls, or possibly the judges selected by him for the trial of causes, and the language implies that such a *conventus* was now actually in session at Ephesus.—**If ye enquire anything concerning other matters.** That is, if the public welfare, not private interests, are threatened, so that it cannot be left to a lawsuit. —**It shall be determined in a lawful assembly.** Which this was not. It was neither regularly called, nor legally organized; and was quite incompetent for the legal transaction of business. Such assemblies (ἐκκλησία), answering somewhat to an American town-meeting, were either regular or special, the former being held at stated times, the latter on special occasions of extreme importance, by special call. The former were entitled, as here, *lawful assemblies* (νόμιμος ἐκκλησία), and to these regular meetings of the people for the transaction of local business, the secretary here alludes. If Demetrius has a private grievance, he can lay it before the courts—the *conventus* even now in session; if the matter concerns the public, it should be brought before one of the stated assemblages of the people; in neither case is there any justification for a mob—this is the alternative put by the speaker to the people.—**To be called in question.** By the Roman government, which did not tolerate tumultuous assemblages of any kind, in the subjugated provinces, and punished participation in them with death. The hint was therefore significant.

Ch. 20 : 1-36. PAUL LEAVES EPHESUS : JOURNEY TOWARD JERUSALEM. A PRIMITIVE CHURCH SERVICE (vers. 7-12). — A PICTURE OF APOSTOLIC LIFE AND LABORS (vers. 17-35).—THE ESSENTIAL CHARACTERISTICS OF A SUCCESSFUL CHRISTIAN MINISTRY.

A. D. 57, 58. Paul leaves Ephesus in the spring of A. D. 57, spends the summer, fall and early winter in Macedonia and Greece, leaving Corinth toward spring, reaching Philippi in Passover week, March, A. D. 58, and thence going up to Jerusalem, reaching it in time for the feast of the Pentecost. For diary of this journey, see ver. 6, note.

1, 2. After the uproar was ceased. Not merely an indication of time; Paul waited until the disturbance was at an end, both that he might not seem to be a fugitive, and also that he might assure himself of the safety of the church.—**Embraced them.** Not literally; the verb simply signifies saluting, either in welcome or farewell.—**Into Macedonia.** Where were the churches of Philippi, Thessalonica, and Berea. For description of the province, see ch. 16 : 9, note.—**And when he had gone over these**

4 And there accompanied him into Asia, Sopater of Berea; and of the Thessalonians, Aristarchus[d] and Secundus; and Gaius of Derbe, and Timotheus;[e] and of Asia, Tychicus[f] and Trophimus.[g]
5 These going before, tarried for us at Troas.
6 And we sailed away from Philippi after the days[h] of unleavened bread, and came unto them to Troas[i] in five days: where we abode seven days.
7 And upon the first[j] *day* of the week, when the disciples came together to break bread,[k] Paul preached unto them, ready to depart on the morrow; and continued his speech until midnight.

d ch. 19 : 29....e ch. 16 : 1....f Ephes. 6 : 21; Col. 4 : 7; 2 Tim. 4 : 12; Titus 3 : 12....g ch. 21 : 29; 2 Tim. 4 : 20....h Exod. 23 : 15.... i 2 Tim. 4 : 13....j 1 Cor. 16 : 2; Rev. 1 : 10....k ch. 2 : 42. 46; 1 Cor. 10 : 16; 11 : 20-34.

parts * * * he came into Greece. This word occurs only here in the N. T. It is the name given by the Romans to the country called Hellas, whose boundaries it is somewhat difficult precisely to fix. It did not include Peloponnesus and extended only to the fortieth degree of latitude—not including Epirus. It is here used as opposed to Macedonia, and equivalent to Achaia. He delayed on the way some time at Troas waiting for Titus (2 Cor. 2 : 12, 13); full of anxiety because of the dissensions in the Corinthian church, proceeded on his way, meeting Titus in Macedonia with news from Corinth (2 Cor. 7 : 5-7); traveled as far westward as the confines of Illyricum, the western borders of Macedonia (Rom. 15 : 19), laying the foundation of future Christian churches in every principal town (Rom. 15 : 23); came at length to Corinth, where his burdens were increased by intelligence of the defection in the Galatian churches, and where he wrote his epistles to the Galatians and the Romans. To this period of his life belongs the peculiar experience of sorrow and spiritual conflict described in 2 Cor. 12 : 7-10.

3, 4. The Jews laid wait for him. Comp. for analogous plots ch. 9 : 23, 29; 23 : 12; 2 Cor. 11 : 32. Of this plot nothing more is known. Of most of the associates of Paul mentioned in this verse but little is known. *Sopater* is described in ancient MSS. as *of Pyrrhus, i. e.*, the son of Pyrrhus, but no such person is mentioned elsewhere in the N. T. Some identify this Sopater with Sosipater of Rom. 16 : 21. *Aristarchus* is probably the person of the same name mentioned in ch. 19 : 29. See note there. *Secundus* is not elsewhere mentioned in the N. T. *Gaius* is described as of Derbe, in Lycaonia, to distinguish him from the Gaius of Macedonia mentioned in ch. 19 : 29; John's third epistle is addressed to a person of the same name, but there is no special reason for regarding them as identical. On *Timothy*, see ch. 16 : 1, note. *Tychicus* is here first mentioned. He was one of Paul's most faithful companions and fellow-laborers. He was probably a native of Ephesus, and staid there or at Miletus, while Paul went to Jerusalem. He shared Paul's first imprisonment, and with Onesimus was the bearer of Paul's epistles to the Colossians (Col. 4 : 7), Ephesians (Eph. 6 : 21), and Philemon. Deserted by his other Asiatic friends, Paul still had Tychicus as a companion in his second imprisonment; at the time of the second epistle to Timothy, he had been dispatched on some mission to Ephesus (2 Tim. 4 : 12). It is thought he was one of the two brethren (2 Cor. 8 : 16-24) who managed the collection for the poor Christians in Judea. The other of the two is thought to have been the *Trophimus* here mentioned. He accompanied Paul to Jerusalem, and was there the innocent cause of the tumult which resulted in Paul's journey to Rome (ch. 21 : 29).

5, 6. These going before. Various hypotheses have been proposed to account for the separation, but they are arbitrary surmises.—**After the days of unleavened bread.** The Passover; Paul's aim was to reach Jerusalem in time for the Pentecost forty-nine days later (ver. 16). Conybeare and Howson indicate the probable course of the journey. "Paul stayed at least *seven* days at Philippi after the Passover (ver. 6), *five* days were spent on the journey to Troas, *six* days (for so we may reckon them) were spent at Troas, *four* were occupied on the voyage by Chios to Miletus (vers. 13-15), two were spent at Miletus, in *three* days Paul went by Cos and Rhodes to Patara (21 : 1), *two* days would suffice for the voyage to Tyre (ch. 21 : 2, 3), six days were spent at Tyre (ch. 21 : 4), *two* were taken up in proceeding by Ptolemais to Cæsarea (ch. 21 : 7, 8). This calculation gives us *thirty-seven* days in all; thus leaving thirteen before the festival of Pentecost, after the arrival at Cæsarea, which is more than the conditions require. We may add, if necessary, two or three days more during the voyage, in the cases where we have reckoned inclusively."—**In five days.** Paul had previously made the voyage from Troas to Philippi in two days (ch. 16 : 11, 12). A difference in the direction of the wind would be amply sufficient to account for the difference in the length of the voyage.

7, 8. On the first day of the week. It seems to have been the practice of the early Christians from a very early period to meet in commemoration of the resurrection. Gradually this Christian day supplanted the Sabbath, though, for a time, both days were observed. The Jews demanded that the Gentile Christians should observe the Jewish Sabbath, a demand to which Paul told them not to accede (Col. 2 : 16). The Christian weekly festival was called the Lord's Day (Rev. 1 : 10); Sunday is a later title of heathen origin, being equivalent to Day of the Sun. There is no direct authority in the N. T.

8 And there were many lights in the upper chamber,[l] where they were gathered together.
9 And there sat in a window a certain young man named Eutychus, being fallen into a deep sleep: and as Paul was long preaching, he sunk down with sleep, and fell down from the third loft, and was taken up dead.
10 And Paul went down, and fell[m] on him, and embracing *him*, said,[n] Trouble not yourselves; for his life is in him.
11 When he therefore was come up again, and had broken bread, and eaten, and talked a long while, even till break of day, so he departed.
12 And they brought the young man alive, and were not a little comforted.
13 And we went before to ship, and sailed unto Assos, there intending to take in Paul: for so had he appointed, minding himself to go afoot.
14 And when he met with us at Assos, we took him in, and came to Mitylene.

l ch. 1 : 13.... m 1 Kings 17 : 21; 2 Kings 4 : 34.... n Matt. 9 : 24.

for any change of the day from the seventh to the first, except such as may be deduced from the apostolic practice.—**To break bread.** In the East bread is never cut with a knife, but always broken with the hand; hence to "break bread" is, in Oriental language, the same as to eat. In N. T. usage, it generally indicates an observance of the Lord's Supper, usually in connection with the *agapæ*, or love-feasts, which were a prominent feature in the social services of the apostolic churches. See 1 Cor. 11 : 20, etc. The best manuscripts have here *we* came, instead of *the disciples* came.—**There were many lights.** The language of an eye-witness depicting vividly the scene.—**In the upper chamber.** A guest chamber used for company and feasts; in Greek houses, it usually occupied the upper story; it was sometimes devoted to the lodging of the slaves, and did not ordinarily extend over the whole of the lower story. For illustration and description, see Luke 22 : 12, note.

9-12. Sat in a window. Only the rooms in the upper story were lighted by windows; they were small, about three feet by two, closed by a wooden shutter, sometimes protected by a lattice-work, and occasionally, in the houses of the wealthiest, enclosed with a thin, transparent stone, or even with glass. Eutychus was sitting on the ledge of the window-sill, the shutter being open, and the window evidently being unprotected by lattice. He is called a youth (νεανίας) here, and a boy (παῖς) in ver. 12. Neither indicates his age at all definitely. He is not again mentioned in the N. T., and nothing more is known of him.—**Falling into a deep sleep * * * sunk down in sleep.** This is not a repetition; having fallen asleep, he became entirely relaxed, and sank down in such a way that the sill no longer protected him.—**From the third loft.** *The third story.*—**Was taken up dead * * * his life is in him.** By some critics (De Wette, Olshausen, Meyer) it is supposed that Eutychus was not dead, that he was merely taken up *for* dead, and that Paul, with clearer discernment, perceived that he was only stunned. The answer of Alford to this view seems to me conclusive: "The youth falls, and is taken up dead; so much is plainly asserted. Paul, not a physician, but an apostle, gifted, not with medical discernment, but with miraculous power, goes down to him, falls on him and embraces him, a strange proceeding for one bent on discovering suspended animation, but not so for one who bore in mind the action of Elijah (1 Kings 17 : 21) and Elisha (2 Kings 4 : 34), each time over a *dead body; and having done this, not before*, he bids them not to be troubled, for *his life was in him.* I would ask any unbiased reader, taking these details into consideration, which of the two is the natural interpretation—and whether there can be any reasonable doubt that *the intent of Luke* is to relate a miracle of raising the dead, and that he mentions falling on and embracing him as the outward significant means taken by the apostle to that end?" Add to this that there is no significance apparent in the incident, and no reason for the narrative, if it be not a miracle—the only one, I believe, in the N. T. performed within the church, or at night, or without the attestation of unbelievers to its reality.—**Talked a long while.** Rather, *Had much companionship*; the preaching was over; social converse, with a meal, followed. In this whole story is a graphic picture of the early services, held at night, in an upper room, the guest-chamber of some Christian or a friendly unbeliever; and of the zeal of Paul, preaching till midnight, continuing in social converse till daybreak, and then starting (ver. 13) on a foot journey of twenty miles.

13, 14. Sailed unto Assos. A seaport of the Roman province of Asia, in the ancient district of Mysia. It was a splendid and populous city, situated on the top of a rocky eminence by the shore of the gulf of Adramyttium, and, being about half way from Troas to Mitylene, was a convenient halting-place for vessels going from one place to the other. The harbor was protected by a large and excellent mole or pier, but the slope from the town to the beach was so steep that it gave rise to a proverb, "Go to Assos and break your neck." There was a curious kind of stone in the neighborhood, called sarcophagus (*flesh-eater*), because it consumed flesh, a body entombed in it disappearing, all but the teeth, in forty days! The inhabitants were mostly Greeks; Fellows found there no trace of the Romans, and Leake says that from the re-

15 And we sailed thence, and came the next *day*
over against Chios; and the next *day* we arrived at
Samos, and tarried at Trogyllium; and the next *day*
we came to Miletus.

16 For Paul had determined to sail for Ephesus, because he would not spend the time in Asia; for he hasted, if it were possible for him, to be at Jerusalem[o] the day of Pentecost.[p]

o chaps. 18 : 21; 24 : 17. . . . p ch. 2 : 1; 1 Cor. 16 : 8.

mains, which are numerous and well-preserved, may be had "perhaps the most perfect idea of a Greek city that anywhere exists." From its citadel it commanded a glorious view, and must have presented a splendid appearance from the sea. The name Asso still exists in the neighborhood, but the place of the remains is called Beahsahm.—**To go afoot.** It was only 19 or 20 miles distant from Troas, on an excellent Roman road, and the apostle could traverse this distance in a much shorter time than the ship required to double the promontory terminating in Cape Lectum. The narrative indicates that he was found at Assos on the arrival of the ship. Observe the indication of his vigor. Comp. vers. 31, 34; 2 Cor. 11 : 24–28.—**Came to Mitylene.** The chief town of the island of Lesbos—famous for having been the birthplace of Sappho and Alcæus, who originated the Sapphic and Alcaic metres, and of Pittæus, one of the seven wise men of Greece. It was a free city, under Roman rule, at the time when Paul's ship anchored for the night in its excellent harbor or roadstead, and was a fine sight, with its noble buildings and the background of mountains. It was probably the time of a dark moon, and daylight would be needed to accomplish safely the intricate navigation between the island and the mainland. It is one of the few cities of the Ægean which have continued to flourish to the present day, and the island and the town are called Mytilni.

15. And came the next day over against Chios. The island, well known under its modern name Scio, for the dreadful sufferings of its inhabitants in the Greek war of independence. It has no other connection with the Scripture narrative than thus to mark out the apostle's course in this journey. It is possible the ship was becalmed. Herod, in his voyage to join Marcus Agrippa, was here once detained, and gave liberally toward the restoration of some public works. His journey, as described by Josephus, affords an interesting comparison with Paul's. The island was only about five miles from the mainland, but it is not certain that it was ever a part of the Roman province. Its outline is mountainous and bold, and it has always been celebrated for its beauty and fruitfulness.—**We arrived at Samos.** An illustrious Greek island off the coast of Asia Minor, where Ionia joins Caria. It was once a powerful member of the Ionic confederacy, and has had part in many famous contests. The name denotes a height, especially by the sea-shore, and correctly describes this lofty and commanding island. At this time it was in the province of Asia, and was a convenient port where passengers or merchandise might have been landed from this ship; and this business dispatched, she sailed across the strait to—**Trogyllium.** This was an anchorage about a mile from Samos, the termination of the promontory of Mycale, well known in the annals of Greek victory over the Persians. A little to the east of this place there is still an anchorage, called *St. Paul's Port.* The apostle had passed in front of the bay into which the Cayster emptied, and was now but a short distance from Ephesus. See map, p. 21.—**And the next day came to Miletus.** This city, more ancient than Ephesus, had been at the height of its prosperity 500 years before this visit of the apostle. The Ionians coming to Asia Minor, found it a Carian town, situated on a peninsula formed in the south-west of the Latmus bay by Mt. Grion. Across the bay, 40 stadia distant, was the mouth of the river Meander, which has obtained over the town a more complete victory than the Persians or the Greeks. Before the Ionians made it their capital city it had borne many names; but then commenced its great prosperity. After founding more than 75 colonies, many of them important, pushing its commerce even to the Atlantic, it fell a victim to the Persians, and still later suffered at the hands of Alexander. From that time it sunk into ruin. Although still possessing its four harbors, at this time it was only a second-rate shipping town. Such has been the active deposit of the river Meander, that the group of islands lying opposite Miletus, which were at once a protection to its harbor and a hiding-place for smugglers and pirates, have come to be only gentle eminences rising out of a plain, the mouth of the Meander, many miles further toward Trogyllium, having made a lake of the Latmus bay, and covered the site of Miletus and the territory about it with a pestilential swamp. The ruins of Mysa, a town on the shore of the Meander, have been erroneously supposed to be those of Miletus. The inhabitants were, with the rest of the Ionians, notorious for their voluptuousness and effeminacy, having lost their brave and warlike character in the years of their prosperity. They were not wholly idle, for their couches and furniture were very famous, and their woollen cloths and carpets were highly esteemed. Ephesus was be-

17 And from Miletus he sent to Ephesus, and called
the elders of the church.
18 And when they were come to him, he said unto
them, Ye know, from the first day that I[q] came into
Asia, after what manner I have been with you at all
seasons,
19 Serving the Lord with all humility[r] of mind, and
with many tears,[s] and temptations,[t] which befell me by
the lying[u] in wait of the Jews:
20 *And* how I[v] kept back nothing that was profitable
unto you, but have shewed you, and have taught
you publicly, and from house[w] to house,
21 Testifying both to the Jews, and also to the
Greeks, repentance[x] toward God, and faith toward
our Lord Jesus Christ.
22 And now, behold, I go bound[y] in the spirit unto
Jerusalem, not knowing[z] the things that shall befall
me there:
23 Save that the Holy Ghost witnesseth in every
city, saying that bonds[a] and afflictions abide me.
24 But none[b] of these things move me, neither count
I my life dear unto myself, so that I might finish[c] my
course with joy, and the ministry,[d] which I have received[e]
of the Lord Jesus, to testify the gospel of the
grace of God.
25 And now, behold, I know that ye all, among

q ch. 19 : 1, 10....r 1 Cor. 15 : 9, 10....s Phil. 3 : 18....t 2 Cor. 4 : 8-11....u verse 3....v verse 27....w 2 Tim. 4 : 2....x Mark 1 : 15; Luke 24 : 47... y ch. 19 : 21....z James 4 : 14....a chaps. 9 : 16; 21 : 11....b ch. 21 : 13; Rom. 8 : 35, 37; 2 Cor. 4 : 16....c 2 Tim. 4 : 7.... d 2 Cor. 4 : 1....e Gal. 1 : 1.

tween 20 and 30 miles distant. From the statement that these Ephesian brethren accompanied Paul to the ship (ver. 38), it seems that the landing-place had already come to be some distance from the city.

16. Had determined to sail by Ephesus. That is, not to stop there. By going up from Miletus to Ephesus, a distance of twenty-eight miles, he might have missed his ship; Paul neither owned nor chartered one, and was dependent upon the movements, always uncertain, of those engaged in commerce. On the possibility of Paul's reaching Jerusalem in time for the feast of Pentecost, see ver. 6, note.

17-19. The elders of the church. The body who administered the government, perhaps including its teachers, the distinction in office between governing and teaching not being clearly defined. On eldership in the apostolic churches, see note on ch. 11 : 30.—**In all seasons.** Rather, *all the time.* This whole ministry in Asia was pursued in Ephesus, though its effects were felt throughout the province, and Christian churches were established at Hierapolis, Colosse, and elsewhere. See on ch. 19 : 10.—**Serving the Lord Jesus.** The minister is the servant, not of the church, but of Christ.—**With all humility.** Lowliness of mind, neither refusing minor and seemingly insignificant work, *e. g.*, in personal conversation as at Athens (ch. 17 : 17), nor hesitating to engage in manual labor for his own support and that of others (ver. 34), nor arrogating to himself to be a lord over God's heritage (1 Pet. 5 : 3). He here addresses them as *overseers* or bishops (ver. 28), not claiming that office himself, a significant fact. With his language of self-commendation here, comp. 1 Cor. 9 : 4-15; 2 Cor. 6 : 3, 4; 12 : 14, etc.; 1 Thess. 2 : 5-10; 2 Thess. 3 : 7-9; and observe that to know our own fidelity, and to call others to attest it, is not inconsistent with true humility. But also observe, that Paul never does this for self-praise, but only as a means of stimulating others to similar fidelity.—**And with many tears.** An evidence of Paul's warm and demonstrative character. Comp. 2 Cor. 2 : 4; Phil. 3 : 18; Ps. 126 : 6.—**And temptations.** Rather, *trials.* Perhaps including the temptation in his flesh alluded to in Gal. 4 : 14 and again in 2 Cor. 12 : 7, but also the opposition encountered from practitioners of magic and others (see ch. 19), among whom were some of his own nation, and the temporary defection of some of the Christian believers (ch. 19 : 18, note).—**By the lying in wait of the Jews.** No such Jewish company in Ephesus is mentioned directly by Luke; it may have been connected with the one referred to in ver. 3, though that originated at Corinth. See note there.

20, 21. Kept back nothing that was profitable. The word here rendered *kept back* is in ver. 27 rendered *shunned.* Neither fear of personal danger, nor impaired popularity, had restrained his teaching. Personal prudence may make us cautious *how* we present the truth, but it can never justify an absolute suppression of the truth. Observe the qualification, *profitable to you.* What, as yet, they were unprepared for, he may have kept back till the time for presenting it should arrive. All scripture is profitable, but not to all men at all times. See John 16 : 12; 1 Cor. 3 : 1, 2.—**Publicly and from house to house.** Observe, that personal work was a characteristic feature in Paul's ministry, as it has always been in the work of spiritually successful men.—**The repentance that is toward God, and the faith that is toward the Lord Jesus Christ.** The first is illustrated by Ps. 51 : 4 and Luke 15 : 18, the second by John 14 : 1; Acts 2 : 38; 16 : 31. Repentance may not lead to faith, but repentance *toward God* the sense of sin as against him, brings with it a conscious need of a mediator and an atonement, and so leads to faith towards the mediator between God and man (2 Cor. 5 : 20, 21; 1 Tim. 2 : 5).

22-24. And now, behold, I go bound in the Spirit. Not *Constrained by the Holy Spirit*, for the term Holy Spirit in the next verse is apparently used to distinguish it from the spirit, Paul's own spirit, referred to here; nor, *In imagination bound, i. e.*, foreseeing himself as literally bound, for the original will not bear this

whom I have gone preaching the kingdom of God, shall see my face no more.
26 Wherefore I take you to record this day, that I *am* pure[f] from the blood of all *men.*
27 For I have not shunned to declare unto you all the counsel[g] of God.
28 Take heed[h] therefore unto yourselves, and to all the flock, over the which the Holy Ghost hath made

f 2 Cor. 7 : 2. . . . g Ephes. 1 : 11. . . . h Col. 4 : 17; 1 Tim. 4 : 16.

significance, and in the very next clause he declares himself ignorant of what is to befall him; nor exactly, as Hackett, "*constrained by an invincible impulse or sense of duty;*" more than this is implied by the peculiar language here. The word (δέω) rendered *bound*, is used by Paul to indicate *obligation* (Rom. 7 : 2; 1 Cor. 7 : 27, 39. Comp. Matt. 16 : 19, note); Paul, who does not hold himself under obligation to obedience to the apostles as ecclesiastical superiors (Gal. 1 : 17-22; 2 : 8, 9, 11), nor to the law, as a system of external rules and regulations (Gal. 4 : 4, 5; 5 : 1-4), recognizes himself as *under obligation to God*, whose will is revealed *by* the Holy Spirit, *to* and *in* his own Spirit. Under this spiritual obligation, he is going up now to Jerusalem; the impulse being from above, and one not to be gainsaid or resisted (ch. 21 : 13, 14).—**Witnesses in every city.** By the mouth of inspired prophets (ch. 21 : 4, 11); also, perhaps, by his personal experiences of bonds and afflictions. See ch. 9 : 23, 29; 13 : 50; 14 : 5, 19; 16 : 23; 17 : 5, 10, 13; 18 : 12; 20 : 3, for such experience prior to this time.—**But on no account do I esteem my life of value to myself.** There is some uncertainty as to the reading; this is the one adopted by Tischendorf and Alford. Observe, that he does not say he esteemed his life of no value, but of no value *to himself;* he measures it wholly by its value to Christ by whom, and for whom, he lives. Comp. Gal. 2 : 20; Phil. 1 : 21.—**So that I might finish my course.** A suggested metaphor borrowed from the foot-race, a common Grecian sport. It is a favorite figure with Paul. See Phil. 2 : 16; 2 Tim. 4 : 7. *With joy* has been added by the copyists in analogy to Phil. 1 : 4; Col. 1 : 11, etc.; but really weakens the force of Paul's language. It is the *work*, not the *reward*, which is here uppermost. Beware of considering *so that* (ὡς) an adverb of comparison. He does not say, I esteem my life of no value, in comparison with the completion of my course; but absolutely, I esteem my life of no value, so long as I am enabled to complete my course. As the object of the race is the goal, so the object of this earthly life is the completion of the work assigned us by God, and it is of no value except for that purpose. Comp. 2 Tim. 4 : 8; Heb. 12 : 1, 2. If his afflictions can redound to the larger success of his work, in the glory of the Gospel, he welcomes them (Phil. 1 : 12, 13).

25-27. Behold, I know that ye all * * * shall see my face no more. The knowledge may have been disclosed to him by the Spirit of God, or through some prophet; or the language may indicate simply one of those premonitions, not uncommon in experience today, or simply a firm conviction derived from his purpose of going to Rome and thence still further west. The language does not necessarily imply inspired knowledge. Alford refers to ch. 26 : 27, in which Paul expresses his conviction that Agrippa was a believer in the prophets, but does not imply an infallible knowledge of his heart. There is, however, no evidence that Paul was at Ephesus again, though it is probable that he subsequently traversed this region, after his first Roman imprisonment. The *all* here signifies not merely the elders, but those whom they represented, the members of the Christian church at Ephesus, and perhaps those of other Christian churches in Asia, and even in Macedonia and Achaia. The language, *among whom I have gone, heralding the kingdom*, indicates a wide circuit of labor, not confined within a single city.—**I take you to record.** I invoke your testimony. He appeals to their own knowledge of his ministry. Comp. the analogous appeal of Samuel in 1 Sam. 12 : 1-5.—**Pure from the blood of all.** See ch. 18 : 6, note.—**All the will of God.** Not merely the plan of God respecting the salvation of men, but his whole will, as revealed by the O. T., and by the teachings of the Holy Spirit.

28. Unto yourselves and to all the flock. Observe, the first duty of the watchman is to watch over himself (Luke 12 : 41-44). The metaphor of the flock, borrowed from Christ, and by him from the O. T. (John 10 : 1-16), and used by Peter (1 Peter 2 : 25), is not elsewhere used by Paul, unless Heb. 13 : 20 be an exception.—**Hath made you overseers.** The word *overseer* is a literal translation of the original (ἐπίσκοπος, *episkopos*), from which comes our English word *episcopal;* it is, however, everywhere else in the N. T. rendered *bishop.* It is agreed by nearly, if not quite all scholars, that the words *bishop* and *elder* (ἐπίσκοπος and πρεσβύτερος), in the language of the N. T., signify the same office. Thus Conybeare and Howson: "These terms are used in the N. T. as equivalent. The former (*bishop*) denoting, as its meaning of *overseer* implies, the duties; the latter (*elder*) denoting the rank of the office." So Alford: "The English version has hardly dealt fairly in this case with the sacred text, in the rendering 'overseers,' where-

you[i] overseers, to feed the church[j] of God, which he
hath purchased[k] with his own blood.
29 For I know this, that after my departing shall
grievous wolves[l] enter in among you, not sparing[m]
the flock.
30 Also of your[n] own selves shall men arise, speaking perverse things, to draw away disciples after
them.
31 Therefore watch,[o] and remember, that by the
space of three years I ceased not to warn[p] every one
night and day with tears.
32 And now, brethren, I commend you to God, and
to the word of his grace, which is able[q] to build you
up, and to give you an inheritance[r] among all them
which are sanctified.
33 I[s] have coveted no man's silver, or gold, or apparel.
34 Yea, ye yourselves[t] know, that these hands have
ministered unto my necessities, and to them that were
with me.
35 I have shewed you all things, how that so labour-
ing ye ought to support[u] the weak, and to remember
the words of the Lord Jesus, how he said, It[v] is more
blessed to give than to receive.
36 And when he had thus spoken, he kneeled[w]
down, and prayed with them all.
37 And they all wept sore, and fell[x] on Paul's neck,
and kissed him,
38 Sorrowing most of all for the words[y] which he
spake, that they should see his face no more. And
they accompanied him unto the ship.

---

i Heb. 13 : 17....j Prov. 10 : 21; Jer. 3 : 15; John 21 : 15-17; 1 Pet. 5 : 2, 3....k Ephes. 1 : 14; Col. 1 : 14; Heb. 9 : 12, 14; 1 Pet. 1 : 18, 19; Rev. 5 : 9....l Matt. 7 : 15; 2 Pet. 2 : 1....m Jer. 13 : 20; 23 : 1; Ezek. 34 : 2, 3; Zech. 11 : 17....n 1 John 2 : 19; Jude 4, etc....o 2 Tim. 4 : 5....p Col. 1 : 28....q John 17 : 17....r ch. 26 : 18; Col. 1 : 12; Heb. 9 : 15; 1 Pet. 1 : 4....s 1 Sam. 12 : 3; 1 Cor. 9 : 12; 2 Cor. 7 : 2....t ch. 18 : 3; 1 Cor. 4 : 12; 1 Thess. 2 : 9; 2 Thess. 3 : 8....u Rom. 15 : 1; Ephes. 4 : 28; 1 Thess. 5 : 14....v Luke 14 : 12-14....w ch. 21 : 5....x Gen. 46 : 29....y verse 25.

---

as it ought there, as in all other places, to have been 'bishops.'" Rather, in all other places it should be rendered "overseers."—**To shepherd the church of God.** Not merely to *feed*, but to act as shepherd of the church, including feeding with doctrine, leading by example, and perhaps administering government (1 Peter 5 : 2, 3). The question whether this verse should read the church of *God*, or the church of *the Lord* is one of the most uncertain in textual criticism. For arguments *pro* and *con*, see Alford's Greek Testament; he thus states his conclusion: "On the whole, then, weighing the evidence on both sides, seeing that it is more likely that the alteration should have been made to *of the Lord* (κυρίου) than to *of God* (θεοῦ), more likely that the speaker should have used *of God* than *of the Lord*, and more consonant to the evidently emphatic position of the word. I have, on a final revision of this volume, decided for the received reading, which, in the first writing of it, I had rejected." The difference is important, because of the closing clause of the verse, *Which he hath purchased with his own blood.* If this declaration is made respecting God, the verse becomes a conclusive evidence of the divinity of Jesus Christ. The representation of salvation as a purchased redemption is again employed by Paul in Ephes. 1 : 13.

29, 30. Shall grievous wolves enter in * * * Also of your own selves shall men arise. Grievous wolves are not persecutors from without the church, but false teachers within (Matt. 7 : 15). The distinction is between false teachers coming to Ephesus from other places and false teachers springing up within the church. On the fulfillment of this prophecy, see 2 Tim. 2 : 17, 18, written to Timothy from Rome, while the latter was in the vicinity of Ephesus; see also Rev. 2 : 2. The wolves ravaged the flock; the Christian temple of Ephesus rivaled in magnificence and superstition that of the heathen Diana; these gave place to the mosque of Mohammed; which has, in turn, given place to utter desolation. — **Perverse things.** Perverted things; the truth distorted and made an instrument of error. Comp. ch. 13 : 10, note.

31, 32. The *three years* consists of three months' preaching in the synagogue (ch. 19 : 8), two years' ministry in the school of Tyrannus (ch. 19 : 10), and three months or thereabouts in Paul's subsequent ministry. Observe how every word in this sentence here has its significance: *every one* indicates personal work; *night and day*, ceaseless industry; *with tears*, warmth of feeling. *I commend you to God*, is, I place you in God's hands, as for safe-keeping; *the word of his grace* is in contrast with the law, and indicates the possession by the church at Ephesus of one or more gospels; the metaphor of an *inheritance* is a favorite one with the apostle.

33-35. Contrast with Paul's spirit that of Demetrius (ch. 19 : 25, 26), and comp. his admonitions to Timothy respecting the danger of covetousness (1 Tim. 6 : 1-11). With his reference here to his manual labor agrees 1 Cor. 4 : 11, 12; comp. 1 Thess. 3 : 8. These references indicate that the tent-making referred to only by Luke in ch. 18 : 3, was Paul's dependence for support; observe that he supports his traveling companions also, an indication that he was a successful artisan. *The weak* are not the weak in faith, nor the poor, but those who, from any infirmity, were dependent on charity for support. The words of the Lord Jesus here quoted are not in the gospels; they are referred to by Paul as though familiar to his auditors and are quoted either from tradition or from a lost gospel. Analogous in spirit is Luke 14 : 12–14.

36-38. The scene here is a touching one; the simplicity of Luke's description heightens the effect. "We feel instinctively that the eye must have seen what the pen has portrayed in so natural a manner."—(*Hackett.*)

The student will do well to compare this ad-

CHAPTER XXI.

AND it came to pass, that after we were gotten from them, and had launched, we came with a straight course unto Coos, and the *day* following unto Rhodes, and from thence unto Patara:

2 And finding a ship sailing over unto Phenicia, we went aboard, and set forth.
3 Now when we had discovered Cyprus, we left it on the left hand, and sailed into Syria, and landed at Tyre: for there the ship was to unlade her burden.
4 And finding disciples, we tarried there seven days:

---

dress of Paul with the analogous expressions of experience in the epistles, particularly his metaphors in vers. 24, 28, 32. The parallelisms noticeable to the English reader are still more noticeable to the Greek student. No other passage in the N. T. of the same length presents so clear and vivid a picture of the characteristic features of Paul's ministry: his *theme*, repentance and faith (ver. 21), enforced by a heralding of the kingdom of God (ver. 25), a kingdom and inheritance of grace (ver. 32); his *spirit*, humility (ver. 19), courage (vers. 20, 27), unswerving purpose (ver. 24), ceaseless industry, ardent feeling (ver. 31), unselfishness (vers. 33-35); his *method*, both a public preaching and personal and private conversation (ver. 20). This address thus affords a suggestion of what are the essential elements of a successful Christian ministry.

Chaps. 21, 22, 23. PAUL GOES TO JERUSALEM. HIS EXPERIENCE THERE. THE CHRISTIAN IN EXPERIENCES OF TRIAL.—THE PROVIDENCE OF GOD ILLUSTRATED.

A. D. 58. Paul, bound in the Spirit, goes up to Jerusalem, in spite of the remonstrances of prophets and of personal friends (ch. 21: 4, 11, 12); he yields to the solicitations of James and the elders at Jerusalem, and participates in a Jewish ceremonial in order to remove the prejudices of the Jews and the Jewish Christians against him; the plan fails; this act is made an occasion of a mob, from which he is rescued by the Roman soldiery; and, after a second mob, and a plan for his assassination, he is sent, under an escort, to Cæsarea for trial before Felix, the Roman procurator. Except the story of the shipwreck (ch. 27), there is no part of Paul's life more dramatic than that recorded in this chapter. His own courage, calmness, and dignity, and the contrast between his character and that of the Jews on the one hand and of Claudius Lysias on the other, carry their own lesson; he will best learn that lesson who acquaints himself with the external aspects of the history, and then reads the story, and takes in the inspiration of Paul's lordly bearing, in his bonds, and before his enemies. Like the story of Joseph, this history of Paul affords, also, a remarkable illustration of the strange way in which God works out his plans. The hate of Joseph's brethren sends Joseph into Egypt to prepare for their succor; the hate of the Jews provides for Paul the opportunity to make, without expense to himself or the infant church the journey he had so long desired to make to Rome. See at close of ch. 27.

Ch. 21 : 1-3. When now it came to pass that we put to sea, having departed from them, having run straight (*i. e.*, before the wind), **we came to Coos.** More properly *Cos*, an island, "the garden of the Ægean," famous for its wines, ointments and textile fabrics, about twenty-three miles south of Miletus, opposite Cnidus and Halicarnassus. Reference is here made probably to its principal town, which lay at the eastern extremity of the island, and possessed a fine harbor, which has since become a malarious lagoon. It must have been of special interest to Luke, the physician, since it was the birth-place of Hippocrates, and boasted of a school of medicine traditionally connected with Esculapius, whose temple was so filled with votive models, as to be in reality a museum of pathology and anatomy. The city is still in existence under the name Stanchio, a corruption of "*es tan Co*" (toward Cos); and in the walls of a Turkish castle there, which, however, Christian travelers are not allowed to enter, are said to be some sculptures from the ancient temple to the god of healing.—**And the day following** (having probably lain at anchor over night) **unto Rhodes.** One of the most illustrious of the Ægean islands, famous for its historical record, its fertile, though broken and rocky soil, and its climate, there being a proverb that the sun shines every day in Rhodes. In this city were the famous temple of the sun, an idolatrous temple erected by a Jew, and the chief of the seven great wonders of the world, the Colossus. The city, founded and raised to a capital by the three ancient towns of the island, and built by the architect Hippodamus, "rose," it is said, "in the midst of its perfumed gardens, and its amphitheatre of hills, with unity so symmetrical, that it appeared like one house." The wonderful Colossus, which had been thrown from its height of more than 100 feet by an earthquake, lay for over 900 years along the margin of the port. — **And from thence unto Patara.** The port of the city of Xanthus, the capital of Lycia. It had a convenient haven, and was, therefore, a resort for the coasting vessels, one of which Paul found ready to take him on. Patara was a city of some pretensions, and especially noted for its temple and oracle of Apollo, some remains of which, among other ruins, are supposed to be still seen, although the harbor, which was the occasion of its mention in the

who said[z] to Paul through the Spirit, that he should
not go up to Jerusalem.
5 And when we had accomplished those days, we
departed and went our way: and they all brought us
on our way, with wives and children, till *we were* out
of the city: and we kneeled[a] down on the shore, and
prayed.
6 And when we had taken our leave one of another,
we took ship; and they returned home again.
7 And when we had finished *our* course from Tyre,
we came to Ptolemais, and saluted the brethren, and
abode with them one day.
8 And the next *day*, we that were of Paul's company
departed, and came unto Cæsarea: and we entered
into the house of Philip[b] the evangelist,[c] which was
one of the seven;[d] and abode with him.
9 And the same man had four daughters, virgins,
which[e] did prophesy.
10 And as we tarried *there* many days, there came
down from Judæa a certain prophet, named Agabus.[f]

z verse 12....a ch. 20 : 36....b ch. 8 : 26-40....c Ephes. 4 : 11; 2 Tim. 4 : 5....d ch. 6 : 5....e ch. 2 : 17; Joel 2 : 28....f ch. 11 : 28.

Christian narrative, is now only a pestilential swamp.—**Unto Phenicia.** On the northwestern coast of Syria (see map, p. 21); also known in the N. T. by its principal cities as "the coasts of Tyre and Sidon." For description, see Matt. 11 : 21, note.—**Having discovered Cyprus.** Literally, *having been shown Cyprus*. For description of the island, see ch. 11 : 19, note. Without a mariner's compass, the Greeks seldom ventured out into the open sea, the headlands of the coasts or the islands serving them as guides. The direct course from Rhodes to Tyre would leave Cyprus on the left.—**Into Syria.** Here used in a general sense for the whole of the Holy Land. See 15 : 41, note.—**Landed at Tyre.** See ch. 12 : 20, note. There the ship was to unload, an indication that Paul traveled by an ordinary merchant vessel.

4-6. And finding disciples. The Gospel had been preached at Tyre in the early persecution instigated by Paul (ch. 11 : 19).—**Through the spirit.** By the mouth of some prophet.—**That he should not go up to Jerusalem.** This must be interpreted by the prophecy in ver. 11; the prophet foretold what would befall Paul, the disciples drew thence the conclusion that he should not go up. But he went "bound in the spirit" (ch. 20 : 22), the disclosure of the divine will to his own soul being to him a higher authority than the words of the prophet.—**We kneeled down on the beach and prayed.** A level, sandy beach extends for a considerable distance on both sides of the ancient Tyre. Observe, the parting meeting is a prayer-meeting; observe, too, that there is none of that false reserve so common in modern Protestantism, to forbid the gathering for prayer where they are liable to observation; the implication of the narrative is, that the spot was between the city and the point of embarkation.

7-9. And having finished the voyage, we came from Tyre unto Ptolemais. Mentioned in Judges (1 : 3) by its ancient name Accho, by Greek and Roman writers as Acē, and more recently as Acre. It had at this time passed out of the hands of the Ptolemies, from one of whom it received its name here, and was a Roman colony, recently established by the Emperor Claudius. Situated about midway between Tyre and Cæsarea, older than either and outliving them both, it has had a continuous history, from a very early period to the present time. It was largely populated by Jews, for, at the outbreak of the Jewish war, besides those who were imprisoned, 2,000 were slain. It is evident there was already a Christian church here, and possibly its members were known to Paul. Here the apostle's voyage terminated and the forty-two miles, or two days' journey to Cæsarea, were traversed by land. The town has now a population of about 10,000, and is at the terminus of the great road from Damascus to the sea. The present anchorage, the best on the Syrian coast, is at some distance from the former one, the mole which protected that being now in ruins.—**That were of Paul's company.** These words are wanting in the best MSS.; there is nothing in the original to indicate any separation from Paul.—**Philip the evangelist.** One of the seven deacons (ch. 6 : 5). The last preceding mention of him in the N. T. is at Cæsarea (ch. 8 : 40).—**Four daughters.** Observe, that in the apostolic church women are not only teachers (ch. 18 : 26), as in the Jewish church (ch. 22 : 14), but also inspired teachers. On the nature of prophecy, see ch. 13 : 1.

10-14. Agabus. That this is the same person referred to in ch. 11 : 28 is every way probable; his name, office, and residence, are the same.—**Paul's girdle.** The girdle was an essential article of dress in the East, worn by both men and women. It was sometimes made of leather (2 Kings 1 : 8; Matt. 3 : 4), sometimes of linen embroidered with silk, or gold or silver thread Jer. 13 : 1; Ezek. 16 : 10; Dan. 10 : 5; Rev. 1 : 3; 15 : 6); it was sometimes fastened by a clasp, sometimes tied in a knot. The symbolic act of Agabus is analogous to the methods of the O. T. prophets (1 Kings 22 : 11; Isa. 20 : 2; Jer. 13 : 1; Ezek. 14 : 1; 5 : 1). Observe that the prophetic language of the O. T. is, *Thus saith the Lord;* in the N. T., *Thus saith the Holy Ghost*. For fulfillment of this prophecy, see ver. 33. Observe that it is fulfilled in the spirit, not in the letter: Paul is bound by the Gentiles, not by the Jews, and he is forcibly taken by the Gentiles from the Jews, who would otherwise have slain him. Observe, too, that the fulfillment of this prophecy afforded an answer, though in an unex-

11 And when he was come unto us, he took Paul's
girdle, and bound his own hands and feet, and said,
Thus saith the Holy Ghost, So shall[g] the Jews at Jerusalem bind the man that owneth this girdle, and shall
deliver *him* unto the hands of the Gentiles.
12 And when we heard these things, both we, and
they of that place, besought[h] him not to go up to Jerusalem.
13 Then Paul answered, What mean ye to weep and
to break mine heart? for I am ready[i] not to be bound
only, but also to die at Jerusalem for the name of the
Lord Jesus.
14 And when he would not be persuaded, we ceased,
saying, The will[j] of the Lord be done.
15 And after those days we took up our carriages,
and went up to Jerusalem.
16 There went with us also *certain* of the disciples
of Cæsarea, and brought with them one Mnason of
Cyprus, an old disciple,[k] with whom we should lodge.
17 And when we were come to Jerusalem, the brethren received us[l] gladly.
18 And the *day* following Paul went in with us unto
James;[m] and all the elders were present.
19 And when he had saluted them, he declared particularly what things[n] God had wrought among the
Gentiles by his[o] ministry.
20 And when they heard *it*, they glorified the Lord;
and said unto him, Thou seest, brother, how many
thousands of Jews there are which believe; and they
are all zealous[p] of the law:
21 And they are informed of thee, that thou teachest
all the Jews which are among the Gentiles to forsake
Moses, saying that they ought not to circumcise[q] *their*
children, neither to walk after the customs.

g verse 33; ch. 20:23....h Matt. 16:22, 23....i 2 Tim. 4:6....j Matt. 6:10; 26:42....k Prov. 16:31....l ch. 15:4....m ch. 15:13, etc.; Gal. 1:19....n Rom. 15:18, 19... o ch. 20:24; 2 Cor. 12:12 ...p ch. 22:3; Rom. 10:2....q Gal. 5:3.

THE GIRDLE.

pected manner, to Paul's prayers for an opportunity to visit Rome (Rom. 1:10).—**And to break mine heart.** An indication of the strength of Paul's sympathies; though not to be shaken in his purpose, he is deeply affected by the tears and entreaties of his friends.—**The will of the Lord be done.** There is small ground for Alford's deduction from this sentence that the Lord's Prayer was used in the apostolic church, though it is every way probable that such was the fact. The disciples recognized in Paul's determination an indication of the divine will. Their course illustrates the nature of true submission; they exercise their own judgment, exert all their influence for the course which seems to them wise, but cheerfully acquiesce when convinced that the Lord's will is otherwise.

15, 16. We packed up our baggage. Carriages in the modern sense of the term were unknown to the ancients. Chariots and rude carts were sometimes employed, but travel was, for the most part, then, as now, on horseback, or on camels; the term *carriage* in the Bible is generally used in the old English sense of baggage. There is some uncertainty as to the reading here, some MSS. give (ἀποσκευάζω) *having packed away*, *i. e.* stored, in Cæsarea the luggage required on the sea-voyage; others give (ἐπισκευάζω) *having packed up*, *i. e.*, in bundles upon mules or horses for the journey to Jerusalem.—**And brought us to one Mnason of Cyprus.** This is the most probable rendering. So Hackett and Alford. The words *with them* are not in the original. Nothing more is known of Mnason; he was probably a resident at Jerusalem, and a disciple from the days of Pentecost; or possibly, as Alford surmises, he may have been a personal disciple of Christ.

17-19. The *brethren* are the lay members of the church at Jerusalem; *James* is the brother of the Lord, who occupied, perhaps by reason of his relationship to the Lord, a position of special prominence in the church (see ch. 15:13, note); the *elders* are the officers of the local church; the apostles are not mentioned, probably because absent from the city in the work of the ministry. Some may already have been dead. Paul, after the personal and informal interviews with the lay brethren, probably at the house of Mnason, mentioned in ver. 17, meets with the officers of the church, to give them a *quasi* official report of his work, which he does *particularly*, *i. e.*, in detail.

20, 21. And when they (the elders) **heard it, they glorified God.** The best MSS. have *God*, not *the Lord*. A service of prayer or praise is indicated.—**Thou seest.** They appeal to Paul's own experience and observation.—**How many myriads of Jews there are.** A general phrase, signifying simply a large number. Not only the dwellers at Jerusalem, but also those who had come up to the feast, would be included in this number. On the early growth of the church at Jerusalem, see chaps. 2:41-47; 4:4, 31-33; 5:12-16. While these converted Jews believed that Jesus was the Messiah, and perhaps looked for his second coming, they still

22 What is it therefore? the multitude must needs
come together: [r] for they will hear that thou art come.
23 Do therefore this that we say to thee: We have
four men which have a vow on them;
24 Them take, and purify thyself with them, and be
at charges with them, that they may shave [s] *their*
heads: and all may know, that those things, whereof
they were informed concerning thee, are nothing; but
that thou thyself also walkest orderly, and keepest the
law.
25 As touching the Gentiles which believe, we [t] have
written, *and* concluded that they observe no such
thing, save only that they keep themselves from *things*
offered to idols, and from blood, and from strangled,
and from fornication.
26 Then Paul took the men,[u] and the next day puri-

r ch. 19 : 32. . . . s ch. 18 : 18; Numb. 6 : 2, 13, 18. . . . t ch. 15 : 20, 29. . . . u 1 Cor. 9 : 20.

held to the obligations of the ceremonial law, and that Gentiles could become Christians only through circumcision, that is, by first becoming Jews (ch. 15 : 1).—**They are informed of thee.** Rather, *they are possessed of the idea concerning thee.* The strength of the original is inadequately rendered by our English version.—**That thou teachest,** etc. What Paul did teach was that neither circumcision nor uncircumcision was of any consequence (Gal. 5 : 6; 6 : 15); that the uncircumcised need not be circumcised, and that the circumcised should not become uncircumcised (1 Cor. 7 : 18, 19); that Jew and Gentile are alike guilty before God, and are saved only by the grace of God through Jesus Christ (Rom. chaps. 1-3). He is accused of teaching the Jews to apostatize (αποστασία) from the law of Moses and to discontinue circumcision, and this, not as their liberty, but as an obligation imposed on them by the Gospel.

22-25. What is it, therefore? That the occasion requires.—**It must needs be that a multitude will come together.** Not *the* multitude, *i. e.*, of Christians in an orderly assemblage for consultation, but *a* multitude, *i. e.*, of Jews and Jewish Christians, hostile to Paul and excited by his presence.—**We have four men.** The language implies that they were Christian believers.—**Which have a vow on them.** Probably the Nazarite vow; for description of which, see ch. 18 : 18, note. Baumgarten remarks that this is a vow of the most extreme abstinence and purification; Paul's public approbation of it, therefore, would be a complete refutation of the charge that he forbade Jews from obeying the ceremonial law.—**Become a Nazarite with them.** This appears to be the significance of the original. The Greek verb rendered purify thyself (ἁγνίζω) is used in the Septuagint (Numb. 6 : 3) in describing the Nazarite's duties. Paul was to enter upon the same course of abstinence and religious consecration as the four men.—**And be at charges for them.** The offerings required (Numb. 6 : 13-18) involved considerable expense; others than the Nazarites sometimes shared in it, and thus indirectly participated in the supposed advantages of the vow. Thus Agrippa I, on arriving from Rome to take possession of his throne, as a means of purchasing popularity, paid the expense of numerous indigent Nazarites.—**That**

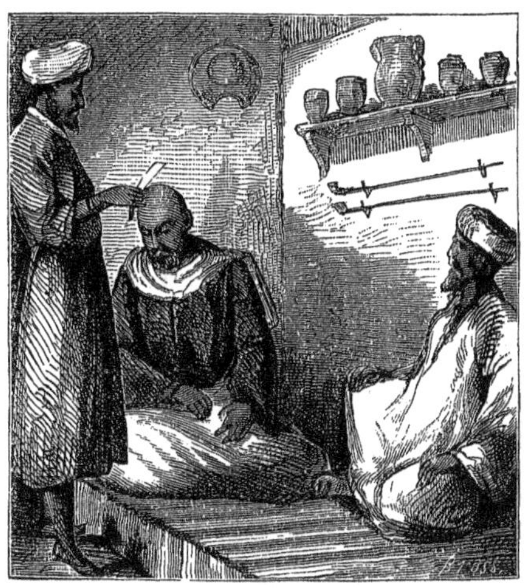

they may shave their heads. Not until the appointed offerings had been made, could the vow be fulfilled and the hair cut. The shaving of heads in connection with religious vows is customary among the Mohammedans to the present day. The modern barber's shop is probably the same in essential characteristics as that of the days of Ezekiel (Ezek. 5 : 1). The customer sits on the divan, or on a low chair, and often leans against the side of the room. The barber is the newsvender of the East; while he shaves he chats and exchanges the latest news with his customers. Pipes and coffee are brought from the nearest shop for those who may wish for them while waiting to be served. The hand-basin used for washing the beard has a crescent-shaped piece cut from the side, as shown on the wall, the better to fit close under the chin. This basin and the razor are the signs of a barber in the East.—**Walkest orderly.** Literally, according to rule, *i. e.*, the Jewish ceremonial. But there is small evidence that Paul did so. Partly owing to natural temperament, partly to a more teachable disposition, partly to the very thoroughness of the change wrought in his intellectual convictions at the time of his conversion, and partly from the broadening effect of travel, Paul was emancipated from the law more thoroughly than James and the elders who had re-

fying himself with them, entered[v] into the temple, to
signify the accomplishment[w] of the days of purification, until that an offering should be offered for every
one of them.
27 And when the seven days were almost ended, the
Jews[x] which were of Asia, when they saw him in the
temple, stirred up all the people, and laid hands[y] on
him,
28 Crying out, Men of Israel, help: this is the man,
that teacheth[z] all *men* every where against the people, and the law, and this place: and further, brought
Greeks also into the temple, and hath polluted this
holy place.
29 (For they had seen before with him, in the city,
Trophimus[a] an Ephesian, whom they supposed that
Paul had brought into the temple.)
30 And all the city was moved, and the people ran
together: and they took Paul, and drew him out of
the temple: and forthwith the doors were shut.
31 And as they went about[b] to kill him, tidings came
unto the chief captain of the band, that all Jerusalem
was in an uproar:

v ch. 24 : 18....w Numb. 6 : 13....x ch. 24 : 18....y ch. 26 : 21....z chaps. 6 : 13, 14; 24 : 5, 6....a ch. 20 : 4....b 2 Cor. 11 : 23, etc.

mained at Jeausalem. The commentators generally appear solicitous to show that Paul, in following this advice, did nothing inconsistent with his teaching. Perhaps not. Yet it appears to me very clear that he did from *policy* what he would not have done from preference, nor felt called on to do by religious principle, and that the lesson which this incident is intended to teach is this, that embittered prejudices are seldom overcome, and the cause of truth is seldom advanced by *any* policy, however adroit, which involves any veiling or concealment of the truth. — **We have written.** In the resolutions passed by the so-called council of Jerusalem (ch. 15 : 23–29).

26-30. In the temple. For plan and full description, see John 2 : 13–17, notes; for illustration, vol. I, p. 257. It must suffice here to say that the Temple consisted of a series of courts; the court of the priests, the court of Israel, the court of the women, and the court of the Gentiles, and that no Gentile was permitted to pass this outer court into the interior of the Temple under pain of death. The tower of Antonia, built upon the same broad platform of solid rock with the Temple, and adjoining it, overlooked the Temple courts; it was at once the palace of the Roman governor and the barracks of his legions. "The inward parts had the largeness and form of a palace, it being parted into all kinds of rooms and other conveniences, such as courts, and places for bathing, and broad spaces for camps, insomuch that, by having all conveniences that cities wanted, it might seem to be composed of several cities, but by its magnificence, it seemed a palace; and, as the entire structure resembled a tower, it contained also four other distinct towers at its four corners, whereof the others were but 50 cubits high; whereas that which lays upon the southeast corner was 70 cubits high, that from thence the whole Temple might be viewed; but on the corner where it joined to the cloisters of the Temple, it had passages down to them both, through which the guard (for there lay in this tower a Roman legion) went several ways among these cloisters with their arms, on the Jewish festivals, in order to watch the people, that they might not there attempt to make any innovations."—(*Josephus' Wars*, 5 : 5, 8). Paul entered into the inner Temple, the court of Israel, with his four companions; the mob caught him and drew him out into the court of the Gentiles; the gates leading from the court of the Gentiles into the Temple proper were then closed; news of the mob being carried to the chief-captain, he came at once with a guard from the adjoining tower of Antonia and rescued the apostle. — **Making known** (to the ministers of the Temple) **the accomplishment of the days of the purification,** *i. e.*, that he had come to accomplish them. This appears to be the significance of the original.—**And when the seven days were almost ended.** What seven days are intended is uncertain; apparently the vow of these Nazarites extended for seven days further, at the expiration of which time, they would be released from it. According to the Rabbis, the shortest term of the vow was thirty days.—**The Jews which were of Asia.** The province where Paul had been teaching, and where he encountered, as everywhere, opposition from the Jews (ch. 19 : 8).—**Laid hands on him.** This was not a legal arrest by the Temple police, but an act of mob violence.—**Crying out * * * hath polluted this holy place.** By bringing Gentiles into this inner court, which was forbidden them. Observe how malice puts an uncharitable construction upon a doubtful act and judges without investigation. Seeing strangers with Paul in the Temple, the Jews assume that they are Gentiles brought in for the purpose of polluting the sacred place; they do not even inquire whether they may be Jews engaged in an act of orderly worship. Observe, too, how Paul here is subjected to the same charge brought with his approbation against Stephen (ch. 6 : 13). — **The doors were shut.** By the Levites who had charge of the Temple. This was done possibly to prevent Paul's escaping from the mob to the altar for refuge (Exod. 21 : 13, 14; 1 Kings 2 : 28); more probably to shut out the mob, whose incursion would pollute the Holy Place. The Levites were careful to protect the court, but not the life of a worshipper. See Luke 10 : 31, 32.

31-36. Unto the chief-captain of the band. The chiliarch or tribune, Claudius Lysias (ch. 23 : 26). Nothing is known of him, except

32 Who[c] immediately took soldiers and centurions,
and ran down unto them: and when they saw the
chief captain and the soldiers, they left beating of Paul.
33 Then the chief captain came near, and took him,
and commanded *him* to be bound[d] with two chains;
and demanded who he was, and what he had done.
34 And some cried one thing, some another, among
the multitude: and when he could not know the certainty for the tumult, he commanded him to be carried
into the castle.[e]
35 And when he came upon the stairs, so it was, that
he was borne of the soldiers, for the violence[f] of the
people.
36 For the multitude of the people followed after,
crying, Away[g] with him!
37 And as Paul was to be led into the castle, he said
unto the chief captain, May I speak unto thee? Who
said, Canst thou speak Greek?
38 Art not thou that Egyptian, which before these
days madest an uproar, and leddest out into the wilderness four thousand men that were murderers?
39 But Paul said, I[h] am a man *which am* a Jew of
Tarsus, *a city* in Cilicia, a[i] citizen of no mean city:
and, I beseech thee, suffer me to speak unto the people.
40 And when he had given him licence, Paul stood
on the stairs, and beckoned[j] with the hand unto the
people. And when there was made a great silence, he
spake unto *them* in the Hebrew tongue, saying,

CHAPTER XXII.

MEN,[k] brethren, and fathers, hear ye my defence,[l] *which I make* now unto you.
2 (And when they heard that he spake in the Hebrew
tongue to them, they kept the more silence: and he
saith,)
3 I am[m] verily a man *which am* a Jew, born in Tarsus, *a city* in Cilicia, yet brought up in this city, at the
feet of[n] Gamaliel, *and* taught according[o] to the perfect manner of the law of the fathers, and was[p] zealous toward God, as ye[q] all are this day.

c chaps. 23 : 27; 24 : 7....d verse 11; ch. 20 : 23; Ephes. 6 : 20....e ch. 23 : 10, 16....f Ps. 55 : 9; Hab. 1 : 3....g ch. 22 : 22; Luke 23 : 18; John 19 : 15; 1 Cor. 4 : 13.... h chaps. 9 : 11; 22 : 3....i ch. 22 : 25....j ch. 12 : 17....k ch. 7 : 2....l 1 Pet. 3 : 15....m ch. 21 : 39; 2 Cor. 11 : 22; Phil. 3 : 5....n ch. 5 : 34....o ch. 26 : 5....p Gal. 1 : 14....q ch. 21 : 20; Rom. 10 : 2.

such information as is afforded by the account of him, in this and the succeeding chapter. The Roman army was divided into legions of from three thousand to six thousand soldiers, each legion being under six tribunes, who commanded in turn. This *chief-captain* was such a tribune, answering somewhat to a colonel, or perhaps a brigade commander in the U. S. army.—**Soldiers and centurions.** The centurion was the commander of a century, equivalent to the modern company, and varying in strength from fifty to one hundred men.—**Ran down.** From the adjoining tower of Antonia. See above.—**When they saw.** The sight of the Roman soldiery was enough to intimidate the mob; they did not wait for actual interference.—**Bound with two chains.** To two soldiers, one on each side of him. See chaps. 12 : 6, note; 28 : 16.—**Into the castle.** Literally, the *garrison* or *barracks; i. e.*, that portion of the tower occupied by the troops; it furnished quarters for five hundred soldiers.—**Upon the stairs.** Leading up into the tower.—**He was borne of the soldiers.** That is, lifted up from the ground and carried bodily into the tower.—**Away with him.** The same cry which echoed before this same tower of Antonia against Paul's Lord (John 19 : 15).

37-40. As Paul was about to be led into the barracks. Either for imprisonment or for scourging (ch. 23 : 23, 24). —**Canst thou speak Greek?** In which language Paul had addressed him. His speech surprises the chief-captain, who had confounded Paul with the Egyptian impostor mentioned in the next verse. —**Art not thou that Egyptian?** Rather, *Thou art not, then.* The allusion is here evidently to something well known and comparatively recent in occurrence. Josephus speaks of an Egyptian impostor, giving two different and somewhat discrepant accounts of him. It seems, however, from both, that an Egyptian, with a band of robbers called Sicarii, probably the *Assassins*, whose organized depredations are a matter of history, gathered a rabble from the neighborhood of Jerusalem, and took them out of the city, promising to show them that the walls of Jerusalem would fall at his command. Felix scattered them, killing, wounding and taking prisoners a part, the rest dispersing or following the false prophet into the wilderness. For a fuller account, see his *Wars of the Jews* 2 : 13, 5, and *Ant.* 20 : 7, 6.—**Of Tarsus.** See ch. 9 : 30, note, for description and illustration.—**I beseech thee suffer me to speak,** etc. Observe the indications of Paul's self-possession, confidence in his cause, native dignity, and personal power. Unawed by the mob, he desires to address them; by his personal weight secures permission from the chief-captain; and there, chained to the two soldiers, his hair and garments still disordered by the rough handling he has received, with a gesture he silences the crowd, and secures an audience. We no longer wonder that this man wished to go into the theatre at Ephesus and face the mob there (ch. 19 : 30).

Ch. 22 : 1, 2. In the Hebrew tongue. The Syro-Chaldaic, the mother-tongue of the Jews in Judea at this time, and the one, therefore, most likely to secure the attention of the mob. Observe that Paul speaks with equal fluency the Greek and the Hebrew. Comp. ch. 21 : 37. Luke's version of this speech is, of course, Greek; the peculiarities in the phraseology indicate that it was translated from the Hebrew by Luke, who was present in Jerusalem (ch. 21 : 17), and not improbably himself heard the speech.

3. I am a man a Jew. That is, by parentage. Both parents were Hebrews (Phil. 3 : 5).—**In**

4 And I persecuted[r] this way unto the death, binding and delivering into prisons both men and women.
5 As also the high priest doth bear me witness, and
all the estate of the elders: from whom also I received
letters unto the brethren, and went to Damascus,[s] to
bring them which were there bound unto Jerusalem,
for to be punished.
6 And it came to pass, that, as I made my journey,
and was come nigh unto Damascus about noon, suddenly there shone from heaven a great light round
about me.
7 And I fell unto the ground, and heard a voice saying unto me, Saul, Saul, why persecutest thou me?
8 And I answered, Who art thou, Lord? And he
said unto me, I am Jesus of Nazareth, whom thou persecutest.
9 And they that were with me saw[t] indeed the light,
and were afraid: but they heard not the voice of him
that spake to me.
10 And I said, What shall I do, Lord? And the Lord
said unto me, Arise, and go into Damascus; and there
it shall be told thee of all things which are appointed
for thee to do.
11 And when I could not see for the glory of that
light, being led by the hand of them that were with
me, I came into Damascus.
12 And one Ananias,[u] a devout man according to the
law, having a good[v] report of all the Jews which
dwelt *there*,

r chaps. 8 : 3; 26 : 9-13; Phil. 3 : 6; 1 Tim. 1 : 13....s ch. 9 : 2, etc....t Dan. 10 : 7....u ch. 9 : 17....v ch. 10 : 22; 1 Tim. 3 : 7; Heb. 11 : 2.

Tarsus of Cilicia. For description and illustration, see ch. 9 : 30, note.—**Brought up in this city.** The original implies, as in ch. 7 : 21, from early youth. See ch. 26 : 4.—**At the feet of Gamaliel.** On his history and character, see ch. 5 : 34, note. Schools were established in connection with every Jewish community; the proper number of pupils to the single teacher was fixed by Rabbinical regulations at twenty-five, the proper age to go to school at six. Besides these primary schools, there were higher institutions at Jerusalem, where young men were trained who proposed to become teachers of Israel. The principal themes of study were the law and the commentaries of the Scribes thereon, but all subjects were discussed—theology, philosophy, jurisprudence, astronomy, astrology, medicine, botany, geography, arithmetic, architecture. The mode of teaching was chiefly catechetical. The master delivered his lecture and the disciples in turn asked questions; or he interrogated them and based his teaching on the various replies given. Stories, anecdotes, riddles, and parables, were all woven into the discussions. The pupils generally sat on the floor cross-legged, and the teacher on a platform or dais a little raised above them; this, at least, is the modern Oriental fashion, and it probably has descended unchanged from the first century.—**Taught according to the strict interpretation** (ἀκρίβεια) **of the law of the fathers.**—That is, according to the stricter school of the Pharisees, who were divided into two parties, the conservative or stricter sect, and the progressive or liberal sect. Paul was educated according to the former. So in ch. 26 : 5, "After the most straitest sect of our religion, I lived a Pharisee."—**And was zealous toward God.** But not full of the Spirit of God; on the contrary, full of self-confidence. This is implied in Phil. 3 : 4. Zeal, without humility and love, may only lead to sin and death.—**As ye all are this day.** Observe how Paul seeks to find a foundation of sympathy between himself and his auditors. Comp. ch. 17 : 22, note.

4, 5. I persecuted this way. That is, those that were in the way of the Lord (Matt. 3 : 3); in other words, followers of Christ. So in ch. 9 : 2; 18 : 25; 19 : 9, etc.—**Unto the death.** Paul gives fuller details of this persecution in his speech before Agrippa (ch. 26 : 10, 11).—**The high-priest.** Theophilus, the brother and successor to Jonathan, who succeeded Caiaphas. He was still living, and to his witness Paul appeals.—**And all the estate of the elders.** Here the lay members of the Sanhedrim which issued the letters of authority, at his request (ch. 9 : 2).—**Unto the brethren.** That is, his Jewish brethren at Damascus. In ch. 9 : 2 the language is "to the synagogues." Here Paul is emphasizing his Jewish character; to the mob of Jews he speaks as himself a Jew.—**Them which were there.** In the previous persecution Christians may have fled as far as Damascus (ch. 8 : 1), or after the Pentecost Damascus converts may have returned thither.

6-11. Of Saul's conversion there are three accounts, viz., here and in chaps. 9 and 26. For a comparison of the three, showing real or apparent discrepancies, and a consideration of their true harmony, see notes on ch. 9 : 1-9. The words in ver. 9, *And were afraid*, are omitted by Tischendorf, but retained by Alford and Meyer. The words "They heard not the voice of him that spake to me," signifies, not that they heard nothing, but that they did not distinguish articulate words. The account here expressly states, what the other accounts only imply, that the cause of Paul's temporary blindness was "the glory of that light."

12-16. A devout man, according to the law, having a good report, etc. Facts not mentioned in Luke's account of Paul's conversion, where Ananias is only described as a disciple (ch. 9 : 10); referred to by Paul here, the better to give acceptance with his Jewish auditors, to his account of the divine commission entrusted to him.—**Came unto me,** etc. The account is more full in ch. 9 : 17, 18.—**The God of our fathers.** Paul again classes himself with the Jews.—**Hath destined thee.** Literally, *Hath*

13 Came unto me, and stood, and said unto me,
Brother Saul, receive thy sight. And the same hour I
looked up upon him.
14 And he said, The[w] God of our fathers hath chosen[x] thee, that thou shouldest know his will, and see[y]
that Just[z] One, and shouldest hear the voice[a] of his
mouth.
15 For thou[b] shalt be his witness unto all men, of
what thou hast seen and heard.
16 And now, why tarriest thou? arise, and be baptized, and wash[c] away thy sins, calling[d] on the name
of the Lord.
17 And it came to pass, that when I was come again
to Jerusalem, even while I prayed in the temple, I was
in a trance;[e]
18 And saw[f] him saying unto me, Make haste, and
get thee quickly out of Jerusalem: for they will not
receive thy testimony concerning me.
19 And I said, Lord, they[g] know that I imprisoned
and beat in every synagogue them that believed on
thee:
20 And when the blood of thy martyr Stephen was
shed, I[h] also was standing by, and consenting[i] unto
his death, and kept the raiment of them that slew him.
21 And he said unto me, Depart: for[j] I will send
thee far hence unto the Gentiles.
22 And they gave him audience unto this word, and
then lifted up their voices, and said, Away with such
a *fellow* from the earth: for[k] it is not fit that he should
live.
23 And as they cried out, and cast off *their* clothes,
and threw dust into the air,

w chaps. 3 : 13; 5 : 30....x ch. 9 : 15; Gal. 1 : 15....y verse 18; 1 Cor. 9 : 1; 15 : 8....z chaps. 3 : 14; 7 : 52....a 1 Cor. 11 : 23: Gal. 1 : 12....
b chaps. 23 : 11; 26 : 16, etc....c Heb. 10 : 22; 1 Pet. 3 : 21....d Rom. 10 : 13; 1 Cor. 1 : 2....e 2 Cor. 12 : 2....f verse 14....g verse 4....
h ch. 7 : 58....i ch. 8 : 1....j ch. 13 : 2, 47; Rom. 1 : 5; 11 : 13; 15 : 16; Gal. 2 : 7, 8; Ephes. 3 : 7, 8; 1 Tim. 2 : 7....k ch. 25 : 24.

taken thee in hand. The language here interprets that of ch. 9 : 15, *He is a chosen vessel unto me.*—**That thou shouldest know his will.** Being guided by his Spirit (Rom. 12 : 2; Ephes. 5 : 17; Col. 1 : 9).—**And see that Just One,** etc. The reference is to the revelation made to Paul just previously (ch. 9 : 17, 27; 1 Cor. 9 : 1; 15 : 8).—**Why tarriest thou?** If one might ever tarry till his sins are partly purged away, before coming to Christ for a free pardon, Paul might (1 Tim. 1 : 12-16). The words of Ananias to Paul are the Gospel's response to the spirit of procrastination. Observe that redemption does not merely relieve from punishment, but *washes away sin* (Isa. 1 : 18), and that sin is washed away, not by baptism, but by the gift of God which is accepted in baptism. See Ezek. 36 : 25-27.

17. When I was come again to Jerusalem. A space of three years (Gal. 1 : 18) is passed over by Paul without a word. His object is not to furnish an autobiography, but to give the Jews his divine authority for preaching to the Gentiles. This he does by narrating (1) the Lord's direction to him to go into Damascus and receive his commission there (ver. 10); (2) his commission, as given by Ananias (vers. 14, 15); (3) the further command given directly by the Lord to him in the Temple, and accepted by him, apparently with reluctance.—**While I prayed in the Temple.** Still maintaining, therefore, his respect for the holy place. Special sacredness attached, in the Jewish estimate, to prayers there offered.—**In a trance.** See ch. 10 : 10, note.

18-21. The connection appears to be this. Paul is accused of preaching against the law, and profaning the Temple (ch. 21 : 21, 28); in his defence he asserts that, after his conversion, he came up to Jerusalem to preach the Gospel to his own countrymen; the Lord commanded him to leave the city; he remonstrated, urging that he was peculiarly fitted to preach the Gospel to the Jews, because known to them as one who had before persecuted the Christians. The providence of God enforced the Word of God, and drove him out of Jerusalem (ch. 9 : 29, 30). On the use of synagogues as a place of trial and punishment, see Matt. 4 : 23, note. On Paul's participation in the martyrdom of Stephen, see ch. 7 : 58, note; 8 : 1, note. The word *martyr* (μάρτυρ) signifies literally *witness*, and might be so rendered here. In early ecclesiastical literature, the word is used in its modern sense, and this appears to be the meaning here and in Rev. 17 : 6; everywhere else in the N. T. the word is rendered *witness*. By his sufferings the martyr is a witness to the strength of that grace which sustains him in them.

22, 23. The doctrine that the Messiah was not exclusively for the Jews, but inaugurated a kingdom of God for all humanity, invariably roused the ire of the Jewish people, especially of those in Jerusalem, who hoped to see their city the mistress of the world. For this teaching

ORIENTALS CASTING OFF THEIR CLOTHES.

Christ was mobbed in Nazareth (Luke 4 : 28, 29); the same teaching in the Passover week was the immediate occasion of his crucifixion; and for reit-

24 The chief captain commanded him to be brought
into the castle, and bade that he should be examined
by scourging; that he might know wherefore they
cried so against him.
25 And as they bound him with thongs, Paul said
unto the centurion that stood by, Is it lawful for you
to scourge a man that is a Roman,[l] and uncondemned?
26 When the centurion heard *that*, he went and told
the chief captain, saying, Take heed what thou doest:
for this man is a Roman.
27 Then the chief captain came, and said unto him,
Tell me, art thou a Roman? He said, Yea.
28 And the chief captain answered, With a great
sum obtained I this freedom. And Paul said, But I
was *free* born.
29 Then straightway they departed from him which
should have examined him: and the chief captain also
was afraid, after he knew that he was a Roman, and
because he had bound him.
30 On the morrow, because[m] he would have known
the certainty wherefore he was accused of the Jews,
he loosed him from *his* bands, and commanded the
chief priests and all their council to appear, and
brought Paul down, and set him before them.

---

l chaps. 16 : 37; 25 : 16.... m ch. 23 : 28.

---

erating it, Stephen was put to death by a mob. The men did not lay off their clothes, as in the case of Stephen, to stone Paul, for he was in the custody of the soldiers, and the force was too great to be despised; nor was this a formal religious act, the mere shaking off the dust as a testimony against Paul, according to the religious usages of the East (see ch. 18 : 6, note), but an act of vehement and uncontrollable rage, increased by their very sense of impotence. It is still not uncommon in the East to throw off the outer garment and trample it in the dust, as an expression of anger and scorn. The accompanying illustration by Mr. Rawson, represents this act as he has seen it in the East.

24, 25. Paul's speech has been unintelligible to the Roman chief-captain; he judges its character only by its results, and without further inquiry proceeds to examine into the matter by ordering his prisoner to be scourged, till he reports what he has done and said to excite the ire of the mob. For illustration of the Roman scourge, see Matt. 27 : 26, note. For this purpose Paul is brought into the soldiers' barracks; while, with the thongs, a sort of leathern gear, they are binding him to the post for the scourge, he addresses to the centurion, who is charged with the execution of the sentence, the inquiry in form, the remonstrance in fact, of ver. 25.

26-28. A false claim of Roman citizenship was punishable with death, and, being easily detected, was seldom made. The centurion, therefore, unhesitatingly credits Paul's implied claim of citizenship, enforced with the quiet dignity with which it was preferred; the chief-captain comes at once and asks Paul, not because he doubts the statement, but in consequence of his own surprise, and perhaps to elicit an explanation of the fact. This is implied by his own statement in ver. 28. The inhabitants of the Roman empire were divided into three classes, Cives or citizens, Latini or Latins, and Peregrini or foreigners. The foreigners were without political rights; the citizens had full political rights, including, under the republic, suffrage and eligibility to office; the Latins possessed part, but not all, the rights of citizenship. The privileges of citizenship might be acquired in several ways, chiefly by purchase or by parentage. In what way Paul acquired them is a matter of surmise. They would not, as assumed by some writers, belong to him merely as a native of Tarsus, though a free city; this is evident, because the chief-captain knew him to be a native of Tarsus (ch. 21 : 39) before ordering him to be scourged. Captives taken in war were often reduced to slavery, and there were many such Jewish slaves in the Roman empire. For special services these were sometimes set free, and the slave, manumitted with due formalities, became a citizen, his children inheriting citizenship from him. Paul's frequent references in his epistles to himself as a bondman or slave of Jesus Christ, coupled with the fact that he customarily drew his illustrations so largely from his own experience, gives some color to the hypothesis that he was the son of a slave thus manumitted. To scourge a Roman citizen, to subject him to any personal violence, to deprive him of a fair hearing on any charge preferred against him, to deny him the right of appeal, under the republic to the Senate, under the empire to the emperor, was an unpardonable offence, punishable, as treason, with death. See ch. 16 : 38, note.

29, 30. Paul having been bound, the chief-captain cannot undo what he has done; it is, therefore, his interest to secure an accusation which will serve as a justification for his course. The subordinate officers charged with the examination by scourging, withdraw at once, without waiting for orders, as soon as they learn the facts; Paul is left bound, not to the pillar, but with chains, as a prisoner, until the morrow; and Lysias then summons the Sanhedrim, to learn what charges are preferred against him. The result is nothing tangible (ch. 23 : 9, 10), and he consequently seeks to avoid the danger of being called to account, by the form of his report to Felix, in which he represents himself as rescuing Paul, because he was a Roman, from the mob (ch. 23 : 26-30). The meeting of the Sanhedrim here described could not have taken place in the Temple, which no Gentile was allowed to enter. It probably was convened in a room on Mount Zion, across the valley of the Tyropœan from the Temple site; according to tradition, the San-

CHAPTER XXIII.

AND Paul, earnestly beholding the council, said,
Men *and* brethren, I[n] have lived in all good conscience before God until this day.
2 And the high priest Ananias commanded them that
stood by him to smite him[o] on the mouth.
3 Then said Paul unto him, God shall smite thee,
thou whited wall: for sittest thou to judge me after the
law, and commandest me to be smitten[p] contrary to
the law?
4 And they that stood by said, Revilest thou God's
high priest?
5 Then said Paul, I wist not, brethren, that he was
the high priest: for it is written,[q] Thou shalt not speak
evil of the ruler of thy people.

---

n ch. 24 : 16 ; 2 Cor. 1 : 12 ; Heb. 13 : 18....o John 18 : 22....p Lev. 19 : 35 ; Deut. 25 : 1, 2 ; John 7 : 51....q Exod. 22 : 28 ; Eccles. 10 : 20 ; 2 Pet. 2 : 10 ; Jude 8.

---

hedrin transferred its sessions to such a room a little prior to this time. See Lewin 2 : 149.

Ch. 23 : 1-3. And Paul, earnestly beholding the council. Among them were probably some of those with whom he had been associated in the martyrdom of Stephen twenty years before, and from whom he had received letters of authority for pursuing the Christians unto Damascus (ch. 22 : 4, 5). Alford regards the language here, *earnestly* beholding, as an indication of that infirmity of sight with which the apostle seems to have been afflicted (Gal. 4 : 13-15, note); I should rather regard it as an indication of that power of the eye which is often a characteristic of the most effective orators. See ch. 13 : 9, note.—**Men and brethren, I have lived in all good conscience before God.** Observe Paul addresses them as an equal, having been himself probably a member of the Sanhedrin (ch. 7 : 58, note). It is difficult to express in English the full significance of the original Greek verb here inadequately rendered *lived* (πολιτεύω). It may be paraphrased, *I have ordered my life and conduct as a good citizen* unto God. He is accused (ch. 21 : 21) of teaching the Jews to apostatize from the laws of Moses; he replies that he has lived according to those laws. Comp. with his language here ch. 24 : 16; 2 Tim. 1 : 3; Heb. 13 : 18. For the characteristics and accompaniment of a good conscience, see 1 Tim. 1 : 5, 19; 3 : 9; 2 Tim. 1 : 3; 1 Pet. 3 : 15, 16. See also 1 Cor. 8 : 7, 12; 1 Tim. 4 : 2; Tit. 1 : 15; Heb. 10 : 22.—**And the high-priest Ananias.** The son of Nehedacus, appointed high-priest by Herod, king of Chalcis, A. D. 48, and succeeding Joseph, son of Camithus. He was sent to Rome A. D. 52 by the Procurator Cumanus, on a charge of oppression brought against him by the Samaritans, but was acquitted, and probably resumed his office. He was deposed shortly before Felix quitted his government, and was assassinated by the sicarii at the beginning of the last Jewish war.—**To smite him on the mouth.** This mode of enjoining silence is practised at the present day in the Oriental courts.—**God shall smite thee, thou whited wall.** A reference to the annual whitewashing of the sepulchres by the Jews, that all might know that the place was unclean, and to be avoided. See Matt. 23 : 27, note. As a prophecy these words were fulfilled by the death of Ananias, by assassins.—**Sittest thou to judge me after the law,** etc. The meaning appears to be this, Do you judge me, for a disregard of the ceremonial law, and yourself disregard that judgment which is one of the weightier matters of the law? (Matt. 23 : 23.) The act of Ananias violated the Mosaic precepts (Lev. 19 : 35; Deut. 19 : 17, 18; 25 : 1), which required careful investigation before punishment, and gave the accused a right always to be heard in his own defence. Paul's indignant outburst was natural, and accords with his impulsive character, but not with the example of Christ under similar circumstances (John 18 : 22, 23), and we lose the significance of the lesson if we fail to note the contrast between the course of the Master, who never for an instant lost his self-control, and that of the servant, who recovered it, and apologized for his undue heat. "That Paul thus answered might go far to *excuse* a like fervid reply in a Christian or a minister of the Gospel, but must never be used to *justify* it. It may serve for an *apology*, but never for an *example*."—(*Alford*.)

4, 5. I had not perceived, brethren, that he is the high-priest. It is best to take Paul's language here in this, which is the most natural meaning. It is no objection to this interpretation that the high-priest would have been distinguished by his dress, for the meeting of the Sanhedrim was a special one, irregularly summoned by the Roman chief-captain on short notice, and there is no evidence that the high-priest had on his pontifical robes, or that the council was regularly organized, as it would have been for the conduct of a formal trial, or that the command from Ananias came in such form that he was recognized by Paul; the voice came from the throng, the speaker may not have been seen. Nor is Paul's language in ver. 3 any objection, for it would have been equally applicable to any member of the Sanhedrim who undertook to prevent a prisoner from being heard in his own defence. The principal other interpretations are (1) *I did not consider that he was high-priest* (*Bengel*, *Olshausen*, *Neander*), thus interpreting it as an apology; but the Greek verb (οἶδα) will not bear this meaning; (2) *I could not be supposed to know that one who conducted himself so cruelly and illegally could be the high-priest*

6 But when Paul perceived that the one part were
Sadducees, and the other Pharisees, he cried out in the
council, Men *and* brethren, I[r] am a Pharisee, the son
of a Pharisee: of[s] the hope and resurrection of the
dead I am called in question.
7 And when he had so said, there arose a dissension
between the Pharisees and the Sadducees: and the
multitude was divided.
8 For the Sadducees[t] say that there is no resurrection, neither angel, nor spirit: but the Pharisees confess both.
9 And there arose a great cry: and the scribes *that*
were of the Pharisees' part arose, and strove, saying,
We find[u] no evil in this man: but if a spirit[v] or an
angel hath spoken to him, let us not[w] fight against
God.
10 And when there arose a great dissension, the
chief captain, fearing lest Paul should have been pulled
in pieces of them, commanded the soldiers to go down,
and to take him by force from among them, and to
bring *him* into the castle.
11 And the night following, the Lord stood[x] by him,
and said, Be of good cheer, Paul: for as thou hast testified of me in Jerusalem, so must thou bear witness
also at Rome.[y]
12 And when it was day, certain[z] of the Jews band-

r ch. 26:5; Phil. 3:5....s chaps. 24:15, 21; 26:6; 28:20....t Matt. 22:23; Mark 12:18; Luke 20:27....u chaps. 25:25; 26:31....
v ch. 22:17, 18....w ch. 5:39....x chaps. 18:9; 27:23, 24; Ps. 46:1, 7....y ch. 28:30, 31; Rom. 1:15....z vers. 21, 30; ch. 25:3.

(*Calvin*); thus interpreting it as a bitter irony, a meaning imputed to, not drawn from, the language; (3) *I do not know that he is high-priest*, thus interpreting it as denial by Paul of the official character claimed by, and imputed to, Ananias, and in support of this interpretation is the fact that there is some question whether he was, at this time, regularly in the office, from which he had been at one time deposed (see above). But if this had been Paul's meaning, he would have used the present, not the pluperfect tense, *I do not recognize*, not *I did not know*, and the language of the historian (ver. 2) appears to leave no question that Ananias was, in fact, at this time high-priest.—**It is written.** In Exod. 22:28.

6-8. For a full description of the Pharisees and the Sadducees, see Matt. 3:7, note. The former were the orthodox Jews, the latter the infidels among the Jews. The controversy between them was a bitter one and had existed for years. The first persecutors of the apostolic church were the Sadducees, and this because the apostles taught the resurrection of the dead (ch. 14:1-3, note), and in that first persecution they were defended by Gamaliel, one of the principal Pharisaic rabbis (ch. 5:34, note). Paul, who was familiar not only with the history of these sects, but also with the division of sentiment which existed respecting the early persecutions, avails himself of his knowledge to divide the court, before whom there is no hope of a fair trial. His statement, *Of the hope and resurrection of the dead I am called in question*, is the truth, though not the whole truth; the fundamental fact of Christianity being the resurrection of Jesus Christ from the dead in attestation of his Messiahship (chaps. 2:32, 33; 3:15; 4:10). With Paul's description of himself as a Pharisee and the son of Pharisees (not *of a Pharisee* as in our English version), comp. Phil. 3:5. Charged with being a violator of the law, he asserts his Pharisaic origin and faith.

9, 10. Paul's purpose is accomplished; the Pharisees take sides against the Sadducees, and the court breaks up in confusion. The words, *let us not fight against God*, are wanting in the best MSS.; the sentence in the original is broken off, as if by the violence of the tumult; it may be rendered, *What if a spirit hath spoken to him or an angel!* The reference is to his account, on the preceding day, of his conversion and the vision in the Temple. The diversion in Paul's favor appears to have been more than transient in its effects, for the Sadducees abandoned the hope of securing a legal conviction and execution, and resorted to plans for assassination (vers. 12-14). *Lest Paul should have been pulled in pieces*, is probably to be taken literally; in the *melee*, the Pharisees endeavoring to protect and the Sadducees to destroy Paul, there was danger that he would be literally torn asunder. The language, *go down*, is exact; the barracks being in a tower from which the soldiers must descend to the street and thence to the council-room. See ch. 21:26, note.

11. Three such experiences of divine encouragement afforded to the apostle, under circumstances of peculiar peril or anxiety, are recorded in the Acts; one when he was "in weakness and in fear and in much trembling" in Corinth (ch. 18:9, 10), once during the long storm at sea (ch. 27:24). Comp. analogous experiences in the life of Christ (Mark 1:13; Luke 22:43). Paul had come to Jerusalem despite the counsel of prophets and the entreaties of friends (ch. 21:4, 10-14); no longer in the presence of immediate danger, suffering the reaction consequent in a man of his temperament from the excitement of the preceding days, unsupported by sympathizing friends, doubts respecting the past, and forebodings respecting the future, may well have combined to produce in him extreme depression. Observe both the form and the significance of the Lord's words. Paul has declared that he counts his life nothing, so that he may finish his course and his testimony (ch. 20:24). The Lord declares that he shall finish his course and his testimony, bearing witness in Rome, as he has already borne witness in Jerusalem. The Lord's answer thus indicates the nature of Paul's depression to which it was responsive, a fear, not for his life, but lest his prayers to visit Rome (Rom. 1:10) are not to be answered. Alford well notes the power of comfort which these words of the Lord possessed, in his subsequent experi-

ed together, and bound themselves under a curse, saying that they would neither eat nor drink[a] till they
had killed Paul.
13 And they were more than forty which had made
this conspiracy.
14 And they came to the chief[b] priests and elders,
and said, We have bound ourselves under a great
curse, that we will eat nothing until we have slain
Paul.
15 Now therefore ye, with the council, signify to the
chief captain that he bring him down unto you to-morrow, as though ye would inquire something more perfectly concerning him: and we, or ever he come near,
are ready[c] to kill him.
16 And when Paul's sister's son heard of their lying
in wait, he[d] went and entered into the castle, and told
Paul.
17 Then[e] Paul called one of the centurions unto *him*,
and said, Bring this young man unto the chief captain;
for he hath a certain thing to tell him.
18 So he took him, and brought *him* to the chief captain, and said, Paul the prisoner[f] called me unto *him*,
and prayed me to bring this young man unto thee, who
hath something to say unto thee.
19 Then the chief captain took him by the hand, and
went *with him* aside privately, and asked *him*, What
is that thou hast to tell me?
20 And he said, The Jews have[g] agreed to desire
thee that thou wouldest bring down Paul to-morrow
into the council, as though they would inquire somewhat of him more perfectly.
21 But[h] do not thou yield unto them: for there lie
in wait for him of them more than forty men, which
have bound themselves with an oath, that they will
neither eat nor drink till they have killed him: and
now are they ready, looking for a promise from thee.
22 So the chief captain *then* let the young man depart, and charged *him*, *See thou* tell no man that thou
hast shewed these things to me.
23 And he called unto *him* two centurions, saying,
Make ready two hundred soldiers to go to Cæsarea,
and horsemen threescore and ten, and spearmen two
hundred, at the third hour of the night;
24 And provide *them* beasts, that they may set Paul
on, and bring *him* safe unto Felix the governor.

a Ps. 31 : 13....b Hosea 4 : 9....c Ps. 21 : 11; 37 : 32, 33....d 2 Sam. 17 : 17....e Prov. 22 : 3; Matt. 10 : 16....f ch. 28 : 17; Ephes. 3 : 1; 4 : 1; Philemon 9....g verse 12....h Exod. 23 : 2.

ences, "(1) in the *uncertainty of his life from the Jews*; (2) in the *uncertainty of his liberation from prison at Cæsarea*; (3) in the *uncertainty of his surviving the storm in the Mediterranean*; (4) in the *uncertainty of his fate on arriving at Rome.* So may one crumb of divine grace and help be multiplied to feed five thousand wants and anxieties."

12-15. Such oaths by which men bound themselves to the performance of some act, were not uncommon among the Jews. See 1 Sam. 14 : 24. Josephus narrates a similar conspiracy to assassinate Herod (Ant. 15 : 8 : 1-4). Several similar conspiracies had been previously formed against Paul (chaps. 9 : 24, 29; 20 : 3, 19). Analogous attempts were made at Jerusalem on the life of Christ (John 7 : 19; 8 : 40; 10 : 39). That more than forty persons should unite in such a conspiracy and should, without scruple, propose it to the supreme court of the land, seems to a modern almost incredible, but accords with the Jewish opinions and practices of that age. Thus Philo, who is one of the purest religious teachers outside the N. T., directly justifies the assassination of apostates from Judaism. "It is highly proper that all who have a zeal for virtue should have a right to punish with their own hands, without delay, those who are guilty of this crime; not carrying them before a court of judicature, or the council, or, in short, before any magistrate, but they should indulge the abhorrence of evil, the love of God, which they entertain, by inflicting immediate punishment on such impious apostates, regarding themselves for the time as all things, senators, judges, prætors, sergeants, accusers, witnesses, the laws, the people; so that, hindered by nothing, they may without fear, and with all promptitude, espouse the cause of piety."—(*Philo.*) From such an oath as that here taken, *not to eat*, etc., it was easy to secure absolution, under Rabbinical regulations.

16-19. Nothing is known of Paul's sister, nor of her son, beyond the information here given; neither are elsewhere referred to in the N. T. Alford surmises that the son may have been at school in Jerusalem, as Paul had been, and thus heard the proposed assassination or Paul discussed. It is evident that Paul had the liberty of the prison, as subsequently at Cæsarea (ch. 24 : 23), and as John the Baptist at Machærus (Matt. 11 : 2, note). He may have been bound to a soldier, and this is indicated by the words, "Paul the *prisoner*" (δέσμιος), and still enjoyed some degree of privacy and liberty, as in Rome (ch. 28 : 16). The readiness of the centurion to comply with Paul's request, and of the chief-captain to give audience to the young man, and the special heed given to his message, in taking him aside privately, indicate the influence which Paul, though a prisoner, had already secured by his personal character. Similar indications are afforded in the account of the shipwreck (ch. 27 : 30-37). Observe the promptness, vigor, and wisdom of Paul's course.

20-22. Comp. the account here given by the young man of the conspiracy with Luke's account above. The implication of the language, *there lie in wait for him*, is that the ambuscade, as well as the conspiracy, had already been formed. The chief-captain enjoins secrecy, because he will avoid all hazard of an assault; for the same reason he starts Paul and his escort out by night.

23, 24. The *two hundred soldiers* are the common foot-soldiers of the Roman army. See ch. 10 : 7 for illustration. The *horsemen* are the ordinary Roman cavalry. The *spearmen* cannot be definitely identified. The Greek word (δεξιολάβος) signifying literally, *taking the right*, is not found in classic Greek. It probably describes

25 And he wrote a letter after this manner:
26 Claudius Lysias unto the most excellent governor
Felix *sendeth* greeting.
27 This man[i] was taken of the Jews, and should
have been killed of them: then came I with an army,
and rescued him, having understood that he was a
Roman.
28 And[j] when I would have known the cause wherefore they accused him, I brought him forth into their
council:
29 Whom I perceived to be accused of questions[k]
of their law, but to have nothing[l] laid to his charge
worthy of death or of bonds.
30 And when[m] it was told me, how that the Jews
laid wait for the man, I sent straightway to thee, and
gave[n] commandment to his accusers also, to say before thee what *they had* against him. Farewell.
31 Then the soldiers, as it was commanded them,
took Paul, and brought *him* by night to Antipatris.
32 On the morrow they left the horsemen to go with
him, and returned to the castle:
33 Who, when they came to Cæsarea, and delivered
the epistle[o] to the governor, presented Paul also before him.
34 And when the governor had read *the letter*, he
asked of what province he was. And when he understood that *he was* of Cilicia;[p]
35 I will hear thee, said he, when thine accusers[q] are
also come. And he commanded him to be kept in[r]
Herod's judgment hall.

i chaps. 21 : 33; 24 : 7....j ch. 22 : 30....k chaps. 18 : 15; 25 : 19....l ch. 26 : 31....m vers. 20, 21....n chaps. 24 : 8; 25 : 6....o vers. 25-30....p ch. 21 : 39....q chaps. 24 : 1, etc.; 25 : 16....r Matt. 27 : 27.

some light-armed troops furnished with spears and javelins, used by the right hand alone. The *third hour of the night* is nine o'clock. The distance from Jerusalem to Cæsarea is about sixty-eight miles, and would have occupied nearly two days; to prevent delay a relay of horses is provided for Paul (*beasts* not *beast*). For a detailed description of the route, see Conybeare and Howson, ch. 21. The size of the escort, 470 in all, seems disproportionate to the danger, but note that, in addition to the ordinary peril from the robbers and assassins which then infested Judea, Jerusalem had been in a state of tumult. The soldiery had been already twice required to rescue Paul. The extent of the present conspiracy could only be surmised, and Lysias, having endangered himself by binding and threatening to scourge a Roman citizen, would naturally be ready to afford abundant and conspicuous protection to him.

25-30. This letter has evident marks of being a verbatim copy of the original. It is probable that the original might have been shown to Paul, and a copy procured through him, or it may have been obtained from the records of the Roman procurator's court. The Roman law required that the subordinate officer, in sending a prisoner to the proper magistrate for trial, should send with him a written statement embodying the facts in the case. The governor, on receiving such a communication, was required to give the prisoner an independent hearing. On Claudius Lysias, see ch. 21 : 31, note. Lysias was probably his original Greek name, Claudius, a Latin name, assumed when he purchased the rights of citizenship. On the character of Felix, see 24 : 3, note. He was procurator of Judea, the office filled by Pilate at the time of Christ's crucifixion; as such, he was directly responsible to the emperor for the administration of the province, which was imperial, not senatorial. See ch. 13 : 7, note. Comp. the account in this letter of the rescue of Paul with the actual facts (ch. 22 : 22-28). Claudius seized Paul, believing him to be the Egyptian leader of the assassins, intended to examine him by scourging, and abandoned his purpose after learning, to his surprise, that he is a Roman. Observe the parallelism between Paul's experience and Christ's. Claudius, like Pilate, perceives that the accused has done nothing guilty of death (John 19 : 4), and that the accusation against him is one respecting Jewish laws; and, as Pilate sought to rid himself of responsibility by sending Jesus to Herod (Luke 23 : 7), so Claudius Lysias is glad to rid himself of responsibility by sending Paul to the procurator. This spirit of indifference to Jewish questions is analogous to that of Gallio in Corinth (ch. 18 : 12-16).

31-35. And brought him by night to Antipatris. The precise site is unknown; the old itinerants indicate the general locality, viz., about forty-two miles from Jerusalem, and twenty-six from Cæsarea. Two good military roads connected the two cities, the remains of which are still distinguishable. By a forced march the troops could have reached Antipatris in ten hours, arriving there, therefore, about seven A. M.—**On the morrow.** Not necessarily on the day after leaving Jerusalem; more probably, as Alford surmises, the day after arriving at Antipatris, where they, perhaps, remained for a day's rest.—**Cæsarea;** *i. e.*, of course, Cæsarea Palestina, the military headquarters of the Roman governor. For description and illustration, see ch. 8 : 40.—**Of Cilicia.** Of which province Tarsus was the principal city. For description, see ch. 15 : 23.—**I will hear thee.** As, in such a case, he was required by Roman law to do. See above.—**Herod's judgment-hall.** Literally, *Prætorium of Herod;* the palace built by him at Cæsarea, and now occupied as the residence of the Roman procurators. The ancient palace often had in connection with it rooms for the incarceration of prisoners of state.

Ch. 24 : 1-27. PAUL BEFORE FELIX. A HEATHEN LAWYER AND A CHRISTIAN PROPHET IN CONTRAST.—THE CHRISTIAN UNDER FALSE ACCUSATION.—THE DARING OF INNOCENCE.—THE HOPE AND THE LIFE OF THE

CHAPTER XXIV.

AND after five days, Ananias[s] the high priest descended with the elders, and *with* a certain orator
named Tertullus, who informed[t] the governor against
Paul.
2 And when he was called forth, Tertullus began to
accuse *him*, saying, Seeing that by thee we enjoy
great quietness, and that very worthy deeds[u] are done
unto this nation by thy providence,
3 We accept *it* always, and in all places, most noble
Felix, with all thankfulness.
4 Notwithstanding, that I be not further tedious unto
thee, I pray thee that thou wouldest hear us of thy
clemency a few words.
5 For we have found this man *a* pestilent *fellow*,[v]
and a mover of sedition among all the Jews throughout the world, and a ringleader of the sect of the Nazarenes:
6 Who also hath gone about to profane[w] the temple: whom we took, and would have judged[x] according to our law.
7 But the chief[y] captain Lysias came *upon us*, and
with great violence took *him* away out of our hands,
8 Commanding his accusers[z] to come unto thee: by
examining of whom, thyself mayest take knowledge
of all these things, whereof we accuse him.
9 And the Jews also assented, saying that these
things were so.
10 Then Paul, after that the governor had beckoned

s chaps. 23 : 2; 25 : 2....t Ps. 11 : 2....u Ps. 12 : 2....v chaps. 6 : 13; 16 : 20; 17 : 6; 21 : 28; Luke 23 : 2; 1 Pet. 2 : 12, 19....w chaps. 19 : 37; 21 : 28....x John 18 : 31....y ch. 21 : 33....z ch. 23 : 30.

CHRISTIAN.—A TRUE COURT PREACHER.—A LAWFUL END DOES NOT JUSTIFY UNLAWFUL MEANS: THE APOSTLE WILL NOT BRIBE A JUDGE TO RENDER EVEN A JUST JUDGMENT.

A. D. 58-60. Paul is tried before Felix; no ground for condemnation is found in him; he is reserved for further trial by the governor, who hopes to receive a bribe for his release, and who, by retaining him in custody, seeks to please the Jews. The account of this trial accords with what we know concerning proceedings in the Roman provincial courts. See notes below.

1. After five days, *i. e.*, the fifth day from Paul's departure from Cæsarea.—**With the elders,** *i. e.*, with a deputation from the Sanhedrim.—**And with a certain orator, Tertullus.** Nothing is known of him except the mention here. His name indicates that he was a Roman. The proceedings may have been either in the Greek or the Latin language. "Under the emperors trials were permitted in Greek in Rome itself, as well in the senate as in the forum; and it is unlikely that greater strictness should have been observed in a distant province."—(*Lewin.*) Paid advocates were employed both in the Greek and the Roman courts, and in criminal actions both for the prosecution and the defence. The time of the speaker was limited by the court. Both parties were usually allowed to make two speeches, the complainant beginning, the defendant following, the complainant replying, and the defendant closing the case. As a general rule the accused, even when his case was conducted by a paid advocate, was expected to address the court himself, for the judges liked to form an opinion of him from his voice, look, and demeanor. The description of Tertullus here as an *orator* (ῥήτωρ) indicates that he was a paid advocate. It was common for young Roman lawyers to qualify themselves for practice in the Roman courts by provincial practice.—**Who informed the governor,** *i. e.*, who formally presented the accusation against Paul.

2-4. Antoninus Felix, a freedman of the emperor Claudius, and therefore sometimes called Claudius Felix, was the governor of Judea at this time. The circumstances and date (probably about A. D. 52) of his appointment are involved in doubt, Josephus and Tacitus differing somewhat in their accounts. There is no difference, however, in their estimate of his character and their statements respecting his ill-conduct. He was ferocious in his cruelty, pursuing his enemies without regard to law, and gave his lustful passions the same unbridled license. Some instances of his quelling seditions, and subduing bands of robbers, are given, but it cannot be that his administration was eminently successful even in that regard, since, when he was recalled, and gave up his office to Festus (A. D. 60) his province was, it is said, "wasted and harassed by bands of robbers and sicarii, and the old plague of false prophets." Tertullus appeals with great subtlety of flattery to this man, whose feelings were easily wrought upon, though not permanently moved. In this he complies with a well-recognized precept among the ancient rhetoricians, which counselled the advocate always to begin his plea by praising the judge.

5-9. The accusation against Paul is threefold; he is charged (1) with causing factious disturbances among the Jews throughout the whole Roman empire, an offence distinctively recognized and punished with death by the Roman law; (2) with being a ringleader of the heretical sect of Nazarenes, a name applied to the Christians by the Jews in derision, but occurring in the N. T. only here; this was charged, not as against Roman law, but as against the law of Moses; (3) with an attempt to profane the Temple at Jerusalem, an offence against both Roman and Jewish law, since the former protected the Jews in the exercise of their worship. The object of Tertullus, however, appears to be, not the condemnation and punishment of Paul by Felix, but his surrender to the Jewish authorities for trial. He therefore proceeds to misstate the facts respecting Paul's rescue. Paul was

unto him to speak, answered, Forasmuch as I know that thou hast been of many years a judge unto this nation, I do the more cheerfully answer[a] for myself:
11 Because that thou mayest understand that there are yet but twelve days since I went up to[b] Jerusalem for to worship.
12 And they neither[c] found me in the temple disputing with any man, neither raising up the people, neither in the synagogues, nor in the city:
13 Neither can they prove[d] the things whereof they now accuse me.
14 But this I confess unto thee, that after the way which they call heresy, so[e] worship I the God of[f] my fathers, believing all things which are[g] written in the law and[h] in the prophets;
15 And have hope[i] toward God, which they themselves also allow, that there shall be a resurrection[j] of the dead, both of the just and unjust.
16 And herein do I exercise myself, to have[k] always a conscience void of offence toward God, and *toward* men.

a 1 Pet. 3 : 15....b ch. 21 : 15....c chaps. 25 : 8; 28 : 17....d 1 Pet. 3 : 16....e Micah 4 : 5....f 2 Tim. 1 : 3....g chaps. 26 : 22; 28 : 23; Luke 24 : 27....h ch. 13 : 15; Matt. 22 : 40; Luke 16 : 16; John 1 : 45; Rom. 3 : 21....i chaps. 23 : 6, etc.; 26 : 6, 7; 28 : 20, etc.. .j Dan. 12 : 2; John 5 : 28, 29; 1 Cor. 15 : 12-27; Rev. 20 : 6, 13....k ch. 23 : 1.

assailed by a mob, and would have been slain without trial but for the intervention of Lysias; Tertullus represents him as arrested legally, and taken from the hands of the Jewish authorities by the despotic act of the chief-captain. It should, however, be added, that the whole of ver. 7 and part of ver. 8 are of doubtful authority; they are omitted by Tischendorf, Griesbach, and Bengel, and doubted by Alford. But while external evidence is conflicting, internal evidence is in favor of their retention. Tertullus refers to no witnesses; the accusers to whom he refers in ver. 8 are the deputation from the Sanhedrim, who have no direct personal knowledge of the matter; the Asiatic Jews who first accused Paul of profaning the Temple (ch. 21 : 27) have not been brought up to Cæsarea, perhaps because their testimony would tend rather for Paul than against him. Of this fatal omission on the part of the prosecution Paul wisely avails himself in his defence (vers. 17-21).

10-16. Paul in his defence follows the course of Tertullus, and answers in detail his charges: (1) The charge of sedition he simply and emphatically denies, and he demands the proof (vers 11-13); (2) he admits and avoids the charge of heresy, *i. e.*, admits that he belongs to the sect of the Nazarenes, but declares that its doctrines accord with the law and the prophets, and in nothing sanction an immoral life (vers. 14-16); (3) to the charge of profaning the Temple he replies with an account of the reasons which led him to the Temple, and with demanding the production of the Asiatic Jews who falsely accused him in Jerusalem (vers. 17-19); finally (vers. 20, 21), with the boldness of innocence, he appeals to the Jews who are present to testify to the result of the informal trial before the Sanhedrim (ch. 23 : 1-9), and in which the Pharisees declared him without evil.—**Thou hast been of many years a judge.** Felix was now in the seventh year of his procuratorship. The contrast between the exordium of Paul's speech and that of Tertullus is noteworthy; Paul, without using flattery, wisely expresses a good ground of his confidence in Felix, as one who is well skilled in the manners and the spirit of the Jewish nation. Analogous in its purport is Christ's response to Pilate (John 18 : 34, note).—**It is in thy power to learn.** By independent testimony, and, as a conclusive evidence that he, Paul, had not been stirring up sedition in the province in which Felix was governor. As to the charge of sedition in other parts of the world, it would be characteristic of Roman administration to refer them to the governors of the disturbed provinces (Luke 23 : 6, 7).—**There are yet but twelve days.** There is some disagreement among the critics in their reckoning of these twelve days. It seems to me clear that the time from Paul's going up to Jerusalem to the time of his plea before Felix is all embraced in these twelve days, and probable, from the language of ch. 21 : 26, 27, that seven of these days elapsed before the mob and the arrest in the Temple. This would allow the rest of the time to be thus accounted for: eighth day, appearance before the Sanhedrim; ninth day, departure from Jerusalem; three or four days subsequent, between that departure and the arrival of Ananias and Tertullus at Cæsarea for the trial before Felix. — **Neither can they prove the things.** A direct challenge to his accusers; and note, in this case, an illustration of the justice of the apothegm that no man is to be condemned without a hearing; for the circumstances were adverse to Paul.—**But.** From a denial of the false charge Paul passes to a statement of the truth respecting himself and his religious opinions.—**After that way which they called heresy.** The same word translated *sect* in ver. 5 is here translated *heresy*. Paul admits himself to be a Nazarene.—**So worship I the God of my fathers.** Conybeare and Howson give the argument well. "Our nation is divided into religious parties which are called *sects;* thus there is the sect of the Pharisees and the sect of the Sadducees, and so now we are called the sect of the Nazarenes. I do not deny that I belong to the latter sect; but I claim for it the same toleration which is extended by the Roman law to the others. I claim the right which you allow to all the nations under your government, of worshipping their national gods."—**And herein,** *i. e.*, in this hope; his religious faith led to no violation of the law, neither that of Moses nor that of Rome, but to carefulness and conscien-

17 Now after many years, I came[l] to bring alms to
my nation, and offerings.
18 Whereupon certain Jews from Asia found me
purified in the temple, neither with multitude, nor
with tumult:
19 Who ought to have been here[m] before thee, and
object, if they had aught against me.
20 Or else let these same *here* say, if they have found
any evil doing in me, while I stood before the council,
21 Except it be for this one voice, that I cried standing among them, Touching the resurrection of the
dead, I am called in question by you this day.
22 And when Felix heard these things, having more
perfect knowledge of *that* way, he deferred them, and
said, When Lysias[n] the chief captain shall come down,
I will know the uttermost of your matter.
23 And he commanded a centurion to keep Paul,
and to let *him* have liberty,[o] and that he should forbid
none of his acquaintance to minister or come unto him.
24 And after certain days, when Felix came with his
wife Drusilla, which was a Jewess, he sent for Paul,
and heard him concerning the faith in Christ.
25 And as he reasoned of[p] righteousness, temperance,[q] and judgment[r] to come, Felix trembled,[s] and
answered, Go[t] thy way for this time; when I have a
convenient season, I will call for thee.
26 He hoped also that money[u] should have been
given him of Paul, that he might loose him: wherefore
he sent for him the oftener, and communed with him.
27 But after two years, Porcius Festus came into
Felix' room: and Felix, willing to shew[v] the Jews a
pleasure, left Paul bound.

l chaps. 11 : 29, 30; 20 : 16; Rom. 15 : 25....m ch. 25 : 16....n verse 7....o chaps. 27 : 3; 28 : 16....p Prov. 16 : 12; Jer. 22 : 15-17; Dan. 4 : 27; John 16 : 8....q Prov. 31 : 4, 5; Dan. 5 : 1-4; Hosea 7 : 5; 1 Pet. 4 : 4....r Ps. 50 : 3, 4; Dan. 12 : 2; Matt. 25 : 31-46; 2 Cor. 5 : 10; Rev. 20 : 12....s Ps. 99 : 1; Isa. 32 : 11; Hab. 3 : 16; Heb. 4 : 1, 12....t Prov. 1 : 24-32; Matt. 22 : 5; 25 : 1-10....u Exod. 23 : 8....v ch. 25 : 9; Mark 15 : 15.

tiousness, both toward God and man. Observe the force of the phrase, *I exercise myself*, implying training one's self, as in an art that requires practice for its perfection. Comp. 1 Cor. 9 : 27; 1 John 3 : 3. See also ch. 23 : 1, note and refs.

17-19. After many years. It was five years since Paul's previous visit to Jerusalem.—**Alms to my nation, and offerings.** Two objects of this visit are specified; one, charity to the poor; the other, offerings to God in the Temple service.—**Whereupon certain Jews from Asia,** etc. Observe the points implied in this and the next verse. The accusation came not from the officer of the Temple, but from Asiatic Jews; the apostle, so far from profaning the Temple, was there to complete a process of ceremonial purification; he was not responsible for the disturbance, since the tumult was raised and the multitude called together by others; and the original accusers should have been present to substantiate the accusation, not leaving it to hearsay evidence. This demand was in accordance with the Roman custom, which was, not to judge a prisoner, without allowing him to meet face to face with his accusers.

20, 21. Or let these persons themselves say what offence they found in me, when I stood before the Sanhedrim; except it be for this one saying, which I cried out, as I stood in their midst. Paul refers to the inquiry before the Jewish court, reported in ch. 23 : 1–9, in which no other ground of condemnation was found, than that afforded by his emphatic declaration of faith in the doctrine of the resurrection made before the court.

22, 23. Having more perfect knowledge of that way, *i. e.*, of the Christian religion. In this sense, the phrase *this way* or *the way* is used in the Acts (ch. 9 : 2, 17; 19 : 9, 23). Félix, as governor, would have known something of it, but chiefly through the misstatements of the Jews, who habitually represented the Christians as seditious in spirit (John 19 : 12; Acts 16 : 20, 21; 17 : 6. Comp. ch. 21 : 38). Paul's speech corrected this misapprehension, and Felix, perceiving that no offence had been committed against the Roman government, and yet desirous not to offend the Jews, made an excuse for deferring the case. There is no reason to suppose that he ever sent for Lysias, or even intended to do so. The Roman procurator was not bound to fix any definite time for the trial of an accused, but might hold him in custody indefinitely.—**To keep Paul, and to let him have liberty.** Three kinds of custody were recognized by Roman law: (1) Confinement in the common jail, for description of which, see ch. 16 : 24, note; (2) free custody, according to which the accused party was committed to the charge of a magistrate, who became responsible for his appearance on the day of trial, this answered to the modern bail; (3) military custody, according to which the accused was given into the charge of soldiers, who were responsible for his safe-keeping. He was then often chained to a soldier. It was to the military custody Paul was here committed, but the language, *let him have liberty* (ἔχειν τε ἄνεσιν), implies that he was not bound. A form of military custody, entitled *observatio*, in which the soldier kept watch of his prisoner, but was not chained to him, was recognized by the law. Because Felix left Paul bound (ver. 27) when he resigned the administration of the province into the hands of Festus, it does not follow that he kept him bound during his own administration.

24-27. With his wife Drusilla. She was not really his wife, having been seduced from her husband Azizus, prince of Emesa, by Felix, through the intervention of the Cyprian sorcerer Simon (ch. 8 : 9). She was the daughter of Herod Agrippa I, and sister of Agrippa II. She had been at the age of six years betrothed to Antiochus Epiphanes, prince of Comagene, but his refusal to submit to circumcision and become a Jew, prevented the marriage. While living thus in adultery with Felix, she bore him a son, Agrip-

CHAPTER XXV.

NOW when Festus was come into the province, after three days he ascended from Cæsarea to Jerusalem.
2 Then the high priest and the chief of the Jews informed him against Paul, and besought him,
3 And desired favour against him, that he would send for him to Jerusalem, laying[w] wait in the way to kill him.
4 But Festus answered, that Paul should be kept at Cæsarea, and that he himself would depart shortly *thither*.
5 Let them therefore, said he, which among you are able, go down with *me*, and accuse this man, if there be any wickedness in him.

w ch. 23 : 14, 15.

pa; both mother and son perished in the eruption of Vesuvius in the reign of Titus.—**Heard him concerning the faith in Christ.** So Herod was accustomed to hear John the Baptist, while keeping him a prisoner (Mark 6 : 20).—**As he reasoned of righteousness,** etc. The apostle availed himself of this opportunity, not to plead further in his own defence, but to preach the truth of God to one unaccustomed to hear it. Comp. ch. 28 : 30, 31; Phil. 1 : 13. *Righteousness* is rectitude of conduct and character according to the law of God; *temperance* is not abstinence from strong drink, but self-control and moderation as to all the animal appetites and passions. Instruction in and exhortation to both, were specially applicable to Felix, of whom Tacitus says that "he exercised the authority of a king with the disposition of a slave, in all manner of cruelty and lust."—**Felix becoming alarmed, answered.** Fear sent away, not the sin, but the preacher.—**When I have an opportunity.** Not a convenient time for repentance, for there is no indication of any penitent feeling in Felix, but an opportunity for further hearing. —**He hoped also that money should have been given him.** Such bribery was exceedingly common in the Roman provinces. Albinus, who succeeded Festus, encouraged this kind of bribery to such an extent, that none were held in prison who were able and willing to buy their way out. Doubtless the money for this purpose could easily have been raised among Paul's friends, but he would not employ corrupt measures to escape even a palpable injustice.—**Wherefore he sent for him,** etc. Not because of any interest in Paul's person or doctrine, but from a hope of obtaining money through him or his friends, Felix had these conferences with the apostle.—**Porcius Festus.** See ch. 25 : 1, note.—**Left Paul bound.** Still in military custody, and perhaps, on transferring him to Festus, actually in chains.

Chaps. 25 : 1 to 26 : 32. PAUL BEFORE FESTUS AND AGRIPPA. THE CHRISTIAN PUT UPON HIS SELF-DEFENCE: HIS DIGNITY; HIS COURAGE; HIS SELF-RESTRAINT; HIS SELF-DEFENCE IS A DEFENCE OF THE GOSPEL.—THE COMMISSION OF THE CHRISTIAN MINISTRY.—THE SKEPTIC, THE SCORNER, THE CHRISTIAN, IN CONTRAST.

A. D. 60. For the fourth time Paul presents his defence; the first being before the mob at Jerusalem (ch. 22), the second before the Sanhedrim (ch. 23), the third before Felix (ch. 24). The contrast between the conduct of Felix and Festus agrees with what we know of their respective characters. The latter does not do full justice to Paul, but, making due allowances for the times and the ordinary course of Roman governors, his course is relatively commendable, though I cannot agree with Lewin in thinking it worthy of all admiration. The general lesson of these chapters, scarcely noticed by the commentators, is the apostolic example of the spirit with which the Christian should meet false accusation, resisting palpable injustice by meekness without weakness, and dignity without pride or wrath, and making even the wrong-doing of his enemies and those of his Lord an occasion of preaching the Gospel. No words can add to the moral power of the simple contrast between Paul, the Christian prisoner, Festus, the cold and skeptical Roman, and Agrippa, the ambitious, lustful and scornful man of the world.

1-5. Now when Festus. Porcius Festus was sent by Nero to succeed Felix, probably in the late summer or autumn of A. D. 60, and remained in office till the summer of A. D. 62, a little less than two years, during which time Judea was disturbed with the same difficulties with sicarii, robbers, and sorcerers, as during the administration of Felix. Festus is represented as being more efficient in their subjection than his predecessor, and a much more just and honorable man. He had a difference with the Jews concerning a high wall which they had built to prevent Agrippa from overlooking the court of the Temple from his palace. This wall also prevented the Roman guard appointed to watch the Temple during the festival, from a view of it. The procurator took sides with Agrippa against the Jews. But he permitted them to send to Rome for a decision, and Nero's wife influenced it in their favor. Festus was succeeded by Albinus.—**Into the province.** This term is used popularly not accurately; Judea being a procuratorship attached to the province of Syria.—**From Cæsarea.** The military headquarters of the Roman governor.—**To Jerusalem.** For conference with the Jewish authorities on taking possession of the office.—**The high-priest.** Ismael, the son of Phali, the successor of Ana-

6 And when he had tarried among them more than ten days, he went down unto Cæsarea; and the next day sitting on the judgment seat, commanded Paul to be brought.

7 And when he was come, the Jews which came down from Jerusalem stood round about, and laid many and grievous complaints against Paul, which[x] they could not prove.

8 While he answered for himself, Neither against the law of the Jews, neither against the temple, nor yet against Cæsar, have I offended any thing at all.

9 But Festus, willing to do the Jews a pleasure, answered Paul, and said, Wilt thou go up to Jerusalem, and there be judged of these things before me?

10 Then said Paul, I stand at Cæsar's judgment seat, where I ought to be judged: to the Jews have I done no wrong, as thou very well knowest.

11 For if I be an offender, or have committed any thing worthy of death, I refuse not to die: but if there be none of these things whereof these accuse me, no man may deliver me unto them. I appeal[y] unto Cæsar.

12 Then Festus, when he had conferred with the council, answered, Hast thou appealed unto Cæsar? unto Cæsar shalt thou go.

13 And after certain days, king Agrippa and Bernice came unto Cæsarea, to salute Festus.

14 And when they had been there many days, Fes-

x ch. 24 : 5, 13; Ps. 35 : 11; Matt. 5 : 11, 12.... y ch. 26 : 32.

nias. Time had not cooled the hatred of the Jews. — **And desired favor.** It is little consonant with our ideas of justice that condemnation should be asked of a judge as a political favor, but it was no strange thing for a Roman governor both to release and to condemn prisoners, as a means of ingratiating himself with the people. — **Laying wait in the way to kill him.** The implication is that arrangements were already perfected for an ambuscade, perhaps by those who had two years before prepared one (ch. 23 : 12-15). We know from Josephus that the land was full of assassins who were hired by various parties to kill their adversaries. — **But Festus answered,** etc. The reason for this answer is given in ver. 16. See note there. He would, however, have subsequently complied with their request (ver. 9) but for Paul's protest and appeal.—**Let them, therefore, said he, which among you are in authority.** Not which are able to go, for the Roman magistrate would not make the trial of Paul dependent upon the convenience of the accusers. He calls for those who are officially able to represent the Sanhedrim.

6-9. More than ten days. The best readings have *Not more than eight or ten days.*—**Sitting on the judgment-seat.** The official throne, or chair of state, used in administering justice. For illustration and description, see John 19 : 13, note.—**Many and grievous complaints.** Their nature is indicated by the speech of Tertullus in the preceding chapter, and by the summary of Paul's defence here. They included charges of violating Jewish law, profaning the Temple, and inciting sedition against Cæsar.—**Which they could not prove.** The good fruit of Paul's caution is noteworthy; not even malice could find plausible ground for his condemnation. Paul exemplifies his own precepts (Rom., ch. 13; 14 : 16. Comp. 1 Pet. 4 : 14-16).—**Wilt thou go up to Jerusalem?** The ostensible reason for this request of Festus is given in ver. 20, viz., because he desires more light on the religious questions involved; the real reason is given here, viz., his desire to curry favor with the Jews. That this was not the real reason is evident, (1) from the language of the historian here; (2) from Paul's dignified and emphatic language in ver. 10; (3) from the confessed perplexity of Festus when it becomes necessary to formulate the charges against his prisoner, to be sent with him to Rome. The proposition to transfer the trial to Jerusalem was also, in effect, a proposition to transfer the proceedings to the Jewish Sanhedrim which had accused Paul. *Before me* indicates, not that Festus would conduct the trial personally, but that he would be present and supervise it. Alford supposes that Festus anticipated Paul's refusal, but desired to make it appear to the Jews that the obstacle to compliance with their request came from Paul, not from himself. Paul, having declared himself a Roman citizen, and no good ground of condemnation having been made to appear, he could not be transferred from the Roman to the Jewish tribunal, without his consent.

10-12. But said Paul, At the judgment-seat of Cæsar I am standing; there it is right for me to be judged. The Jews in nothing have I wronged, as also thou knowest better (than to prefer this request). **If indeed I have wronged** (any) **and done aught worthy of death, I do not entreat not to die; but if there is nothing in these things of which they accuse me, no one shall sacrifice me to them. To Cæsar I appeal.** This translation will aid in giving the spirit of Paul's response. It was his right, as a Roman citizen, to be judged before the Roman tribunal; he had not transgressed the Jewish law; there was, therefore, no reason for going before a Jewish tribunal. *I do not entreat not to die* presents Paul in contrast with his accusers. They ask Paul's condemnation as a favor: he demands acquittal as a matter of justice. *Deliver me unto them,* is literally, Grant me to them as a matter of favor. Paul, as a Roman citizen, refuses to be used by Festus for his own political advantage. *Cæsar* is here Nero; it was a general title of the Roman emperors, as Pharaoh of the Egyptian kings. The courage and dignity of

tus declared Paul's cause unto the king, saying, There is a certain man left in bonds by Felix:
15 About whom, when[z] I was at Jerusalem, the chief priests and the elders of the Jews informed *me*, desiring *to have* judgment against him.
16 To whom I answered, It is not the manner of the Romans to deliver any man to die, before that he which is accused have the accusers face to face, and have licence to answer for himself concerning the crime laid against him.
17 Therefore, when[a] they were come hither, without any delay on the morrow I sat on the judgment seat, and commanded the man to be brought forth.
18 Against whom, when the accusers stood up, they brought none accusation of such things as I supposed:
19 But[b] had certain questions against him of their own superstition, and of one Jesus, which was dead, whom Paul affirmed to be alive.
20 And because I doubted of such manner of questions, I asked *him* whether he would go to Jerusalem, and there be judged of these matters.
21 But when Paul had appealed to be reserved unto the hearing of Augustus, I commanded him to be kept till I might send him to Cæsar.
22 Then Agrippa said unto Festus, I would also hear the man myself. To-morrow, said he, thou shalt hear him.
23 And on the morrow, when Agrippa was come, and Bernice, with great[c] pomp, and was entered into the place of hearing, with the chief captains, and principal men of the city, at Festus' commandment Paul[d] was brought forth.

z verses 2, 3.... a verse 6.... b ch. 18 : 15.... c Ezek. 7 : 24.... d ch. 9 : 15.

Paul in this response indicate some secret ground of courage. This was twofold, (1) such promises of God in the O. T., a copy of which Paul doubtless possessed, as Ps. 37 : 5–9; Isa. 41 : 10–14; (2) his rights as a Roman citizen. Among these rights was that of appeal from the decision of a provincial magistrate, under the republic to the people, under the empire to the emperor. No written appeal was required; the pronunciation of the single word *appello, I appeal*, suspended all further proceedings. There were, however, certain cases of great crime, where there was no doubt as to the facts, in which the appeal might be disallowed, *e. g.*, in the case of bandits or pirates taken in the act. Hence, here Festus confers with his council before allowing the appeal. This council consisted of a certain number of citizens selected for the trial of accused persons, in conference with the proconsul. —**And to Cæsar shalt thou go.** Thus Festus unconsciously aided to fulfill the promise of God to Paul in ch. 23 : 11.

13. Agrippa and Bernice. Herod Agrippa II, who was educated at the court of Claudius. Being only seventeen years old at the time of the death of his father, Agrippa the Great, he was not allowed to succeed to his kingdom, which included all that of Herod the Great. Instead, Claudius gave him the principality of Chalcis, the presidency of the Temple at Jerusalem and of its treasures, and the appointment of the high-priest, adding afterward the former tetrarchy of Philip, with the title of *king*. This jurisdiction was still further increased by Nero. But he made himself obnoxious to the Jews by his capricious changes of the high-priesthood, and especially offended them by constructing a magnificent room in his palace to overlook the Temple, and by the partiality and lavish favors which he bestowed upon the city of Berytus. At the outbreak of the war with the Romans, he sided with them, after vainly attempting to dissuade the people from rebellion. At the siege of Gamala he was wounded, but was afterward invested with the dignity of prætor at Rome, whither he went with his sister Bernice, after the capture of Jerusalem. He died in the third year of Trajan, at about seventy years of age, and was the last prince of the house of the Herods. Bernice, his sister, who had been the wife of her uncle Herod, is charged with having lived in criminal intimacy with him. To escape the scandal, she married Polemon, king of Cilicia, but she remained with him only a little time, returning to Agrippa to live under the same scandalous appearances. About A. D. 65 she was at Jerusalem performing a vow, when she interceded with Gessius Florus against his cruel massacre of the Jews, the sole redeeming act of an otherwise utterly infamous life. She is reported to have won to her homage both Vespasian and Titus, the former by her magnificent presents, the latter by her beauty.

14-21. There is nothing to indicate whence the sacred writer obtained his report of this interview—apparently a private one—between Festus and Agrippa. The substance of it may have been communicated by Festus to Paul or some of his friends; but in its phraseology it may reasonably be regarded as a dramatic representation, by the historian, of the substantial facts, after the manner customary in both ancient and modern history. See Intro., p. 15. Agrippa, one of the Herodian family, was familiar with the Jewish religion, had the right of appointment of the high-priest, and was president of the Temple; it was therefore natural for Festus to communicate the facts respecting Paul to Agrippa, whose life and character made him familiar with Jewish laws and usages. Chaps. 23 : 30; 24 : 19; 25 : 5 illustrate the declaration of ver. 16, which is abundantly sustained by classical authorities. It is more reasonable to presume that Festus correctly reports his answer to the request of the Jews, the result of which only is recorded by Luke in ver. 4, than to suppose that he added this declaration respecting Roman law to gain credit with Agrippa. The language of ver. 19 indicates a real perplexity in the mind of the Roman governor, to whom the question whether Jesus was alive or dead

24 And Festus said, King Agrippa, and all men which are here present with us, ye see this man, about whom all[e] the multitude of the Jews have dealt with me, both at Jerusalem, and *also* here, crying that[f] he ought not to live any longer.

25 But when I found that he had committed nothing[g] worthy of death, and that he himself hath appealed[h] to Augustus, I have determined to send him.

26 Of whom I have no certain thing to write unto my lord. Wherefore I have brought him forth before you, and specially before thee, O king Agrippa, that, after examination had, I might have somewhat to write.

27 For[i] it seemeth to me unreasonable, to send a prisoner, and not withal to signify the crimes *laid* against him.

CHAPTER XXVI.

THEN Agrippa said unto Paul, Thou art permitted to speak for thyself. Then Paul stretched forth the hand, and answered for himself:

2 I think myself happy, king Agrippa, because I shall answer for myself this day before thee, touching all the things whereof I am accused of the Jews:

3 Especially, *because I know* thee to be expert[j] in all customs and questions which are among the Jews: wherefore I beseech thee to hear[k] me patiently.

4 My manner[l] of life from my youth, which was at the first among mine own nation at Jerusalem, know all the Jews;

5 Which knew me from the beginning, if they would testify, that after the most straitest sect of our religion, I lived a Pharisee.[m]

e vers. 3, 7....f ch. 22 : 22....g chaps. 23 : 9, 29; 26 : 31....h vers. 11, 12....i Prov. 18 : 13; John 7 : 51....j Deut. 17 : 18....k ch. 24 : 4....l 2 Tim. 3 : 10....m ch. 22 : 3; Phil. 3 : 5.

appeared to be a matter of no importance. Comp. the indifference of Gallio, ch. 18 : 12–17. Ver. 20 assigns a reason for the proposition of Festus to transfer the case to Jerusalem, which would be agreeable to Agrippa, to whose judgment on matters of Jewish law and custom Festus deferred. The real reason is given in ver. 9. See note there. *Augustus* is not here the name of that Cæsar so known in history. The title, an adjective denoting *venerable* or *august*, is strictly religious in its character, and was first given to Octavius, the first emperor, from whom it was inherited by his successors. The Cæsar now on the throne was the infamous Nero, whose reign lasted from A. D. 54 to A. D. 68.

22-27. The plea of Paul before Agrippa is in direct fulfillment of our Lord's prophecy in Matt. 10 : 18; Mark 13 : 9. He was summoned before the king for exhibition rather than for trial, for the appeal already allowed took the case out of the hands of the procurator, who could no longer render judgment either for or against the prisoner (ch. 26 : 32). Analogous to the course of Festus here is that of Pilate in sending Christ before Herod (Luke 23 : 6–12). *The place of hearing* was the *auditorium*, a hall or room in the palaces of the Roman emperors, and in the residences of the provincial governors, for the purposes of public receptions, the trial of causes, and other state business. *The chief-captains* are the tribunes or chief military officers (see ch. 21 : 31, note); *the principal men of the city* are prominent civilians. The pomp of the royal auditors is described in contrast with the lowliness of the prisoner in chains. It is necessary that Festus should afford some excuse for this public exhibition of his prisoner; hence the explanation of vers. 26, 27. The perplexity was, however, a real one, for the governor was required to send, in writing, with the prisoner, a statement of the accusation (see ch. 23 : 25, note); to send Paul without such written statement, or with one of a trivial character, would subject Festus to criticism, if not to censure. It should, however, have occurred to him that, if Paul had been kept in prison for two years, without even a definite accusation, it was quite time that he were set at liberty.

Ch. 26 : 1-3. In the speech which follows Paul begins by expressing his gratification in being permitted to speak before one familiar with Jewish laws and life, and then enters at once into what is a response to the question of Festus—a statement of the real offence which has aroused the enmity of the Jews. He accordingly narrates his early experience as a Pharisee, his conversion, his commission from Christ, and his course in obedience to that commission, for which causes the Jews sought to slay him. Festus, regarding him as a religious enthusiast, breaks in upon his discourse with the interruption of ver. 24; from Festus the apostle appeals to king Agrippa to attest the truth of his representation of the prophetic teachings; Agrippa replies with the sarcastic response of ver. 28, eliciting from Paul, whose ardor neither skepticism nor sarcasm can quench, the rejoinder of ver. 29, with which the audience closes.

Thou art permitted to speak for thyself. But he does not; he speaks for Christ, and for those whom he addresses, preaching the Gospel in season and out of season.—**Stretched forth the hand;** that was chained; a significant and eloquent reminder that he, against whom Festus can find no definite accusation, is a prisoner.—**Answered for himself.** The Greek word (ἀπολογέομαι) is not the same so rendered in Agrippa's permission. It simply means to plead or answer before a tribunal.—**Especially because thou art expert in all Jewish customs,** whether established by law or usage, **and questions,** including the religious disputes between the different Jewish sects.

4-8. Know all the Jews. Not to be taken literally; yet an indication that Paul was before his conversion a man of considerable reputation, and this is confirmed by the few known facts of

6 And now[n] I stand and am judged for the hope of the promise[o] made of God unto our fathers:
7 Unto which *promise* our twelve tribes, instantly serving[p] *God* day and night, hope to come. For which hope's sake, king Agrippa, I am accused of the Jews.
8 Why[q] should it be thought a thing incredible with you, that God should raise the dead?
9 I[r] verily thought with myself, that I ought to do many things contrary to the name of Jesus of Nazareth.
10 Which thing I also did in[s] Jerusalem: and many of the saints did I shut up in prison, having received authority[t] from the chief priests; and when they were put to death, I gave my voice against *them*.
11 And I punished them oft in[u] every synagogue, and compelled *them* to blaspheme; and being exceedingly mad against them, I persecuted *them* even unto strange cities.
12 Whereupon as I went[v] to Damascus, with authority and commission from the chief priests,

n ch. 23:6....o ch. 13:32; Gen. 3:15; 22:18; 49:10; Deut. 18:15; 2 Sam. 7:12; Ps. 132:11; Isa. 4:2; 7:14; 9:6, 7; Jer. 23:5; 33:14-16; Ezek. 34:23; Dan. 9:24; Micah 7:20; Zech. 13:1, 7; Mal. 13:1; Gal. 4:4....p Luke 2:37; 1 Thess. 3:10....q 1 Cor. 15:12, 20....r 1 Tim. 1:13....s ch. 8:3; Gal. 1:13....t ch. 9:14....u ch. 22:19....v ch. 9:3.

his early history.—**If they would testify.** To their testimony Paul appealed in his address before the mob on the tower stairs (ch. 22:5).—**After the most straitest sect.** The Pharisees were divided into two classes, the followers of Hillel and the followers of Shammai, the former liberal and catholic, the latter rigid and narrow in their spirit. See Matt. 3:7. Paul belonged to the straiter or more rigorous faction, not to that which embraced such men as Nicodemus, Joseph of Arimathea, and Gamaliel. Comp. his description of his character and experience in Phil. 3:4–6.—**For the hope of the promise made by God.** This promise was of a Messiah, who should deliver Israel, and should prove himself King of kings and Lord of lords. For Agrippa no further reference or description of this promise was necessary; Paul wisely does not describe it, because any attempt to do so would be liable to be misunderstood by the Roman procurator, who doubtless knew that the Jews expected a political Messiah, and who could not have been made to understand the spiritual nature of the kingdom that fulfilled the hope to which Paul referred.—**Unto which our twelve tribes, in zealous worship day and night, hope to come.** That is, it is the hope of the fulfillment of this prophecy which inspires the Jews in their zeal for the ceremonialism of the law; *serving* (λατρεύω) indicates ritualistic or ceremonial worship.—**Why is it judged by you incredible if God raises the dead?** That is, If God sees fit to raise the dead, what is there in that past your belief? The appeal is to Agrippa, who professed to believe the O. T. Scriptures (ver. 27), which contain unquestionable cases of resurrection from the dead (1 Kings 17:22, 23; 2 Kings 4:32–35; 13:21).

9-11. I thought within myself. Or, *in myself*. The language implies a spirit of self-reliance, in contrast with the prayer which accompanied his conversion, "What shall I do, Lord?" (ch. 22:10). See also ch. 9:11, which certainly implies that he had not before really sought counsel and guidance of God. This is the secret, in part, of his sin; he thought he ought to persecute the Christians because he had confidence in self, not that spirit of humility which makes its possessor seek direction from God.—**Ought to do many things against the name of Jesus of Nazareth.** That is, against the cause which centred about and was represented by that name. But observe, he does not say that he thought he ought to persecute to death. His conscience justified his opposition to Christianity; his pride and self-will embittered him against its adherents.—**Received authority from the chief-priests.** This commission was prior to that asked and obtained to pursue the converts to Damascus.—**I gave my voice against them.** Literally, *I cast my pebble, i. e.*, my vote. In voting in ancient times, small round pebbles were used, the white for acquittal, the black for condemnation. The language here clearly implies that Paul had, at that time, a position which entitled him to vote in the tribunal before which the Christians were brought for trial; and as the Jewish law allowed the infliction of the death-sentence only by the Sanhedrim, the conclusion has been very generally drawn that he was a member of that court. In that case, according to Rabbinical rules, he must have been at least 30 years of age.—**And I punished them oft in every synagogue.** The synagogue was a court as well as a house of worship, and was used as a place of punishment by scourging (Matt. 10:17).—**Compelled them to blaspheme.** Literally, *To speak evil of;* here of the name of Christ, *i. e.*, to recant from their faith, and renounce Christ. The original indicates rather Paul's purpose than his success; that they actually did blaspheme is not necessarily implied, but is very probable. Such apostasies have occurred in all times of persecution, and did occur in the primitive church (2 Tim. 1:15; 4:10; Heb. 6:6).—**And being exceeding mad against them.** This language effectually disposes of the position of those who suppose that in all this persecution Paul was acting under the impulse of conscience alone, and in a devout though mistaken service of God. He may have thought he did God service in slaying Christ's disciples (John 16:2), but it is clear that he was acting under the influence of pride and passion, which unfits the mind for moral judgment. What one who is "exceeding mad" thinks he ought to do is no

13 At midday, O king, I saw in the way a light from
heaven, above the brightness of the sun, shining round
about me and them which journeyed with me.
14 And when we were all fallen to the earth, I heard
a voice speaking unto me, and saying in the Hebrew
tongue, Saul, Saul, why persecutest thou me? *it is*
hard for thee to kick against the pricks.
15 And I said, Who art thou, Lord? And he said, I
am Jesus whom thou persecutest.
16 But rise, and stand upon thy feet: for I have appeared unto thee for this purpose, to make thee a minister[w] and a witness[x] both of these things which thou
hast seen, and of those things in the which I will appear unto thee;
17 Delivering thee from the people, and *from* the
Gentiles, unto[y] whom now I send thee,
18 To open[z] their eyes, *and* to turn[a] *them* from darkness to light, and *from* the power[b] of Satan unto God,
that they may receive forgiveness[c] of sins, and inheritance[d] among them which are[e] sanctified by faith[f]
that is in me.
19 Whereupon, O king Agrippa, I was not disobedient unto the heavenly vision:
20 But shewed[g] first unto them of Damascus, and at
Jerusalem, and throughout all the coasts of Judæa,
and *then* to the Gentiles, that they should repent and
turn to God, and do works[h] meet for repentance.
21 For these causes the Jews[i] caught me in the temple, and went about to kill *me*.
22 Having therefore obtained help of God, I continue
unto this day, witnessing both to small and great, saying none other things than those which[j] the prophets
and Moses did say should come:
23 That Christ should suffer, *and* that he should be
the first[k] that should rise from the dead, and should
shew light unto the people, and to the Gentiles.

w Ephes. 3 : 7; Col. 1 : 23, 25....x ch. 22 : 15....y ch. 22 : 21; Rom. 11 : 13....z Isa. 35 : 5; 42 : 7; Ephes. 1 : 18....a Luke 1 : 79; John 8 : 12; 2 Cor. 4 : 6; 1 Pet. 2 : 9....b Col. 1 : 13....c Luke 1 : 77; Ephes. 1 : 7; Col. 1 : 14....d Ephes. 1 : 11; Col. 1 : 12; 1 Pet. 1 : 4.... e ch. 20 : 32; John 17 : 17; 1 Cor. 1 : 30; Rev. 21 : 27....f Ephes. 2 : 8; Heb. 11 : 6....g ch. 9 : 19, etc....h Matt. 3 : 8....i ch. 21 : 30.... j Luke 24 : 27, 46....k 1 Cor. 15 : 23.

trustworthy guide.—**Strange cities.** Literally, *Cities without*, *i. e.*, without the bounds of Judea. He was not content to drive heresy from his own land; he determined to extirpate it. To understand Paul's conversion it is necessary to form a clear idea of his previous state of mind; and this certainly was not that of a humble, devout, but mistaken child of God. Coupling the account here with other references in Acts and the Epistles, we may ascertain its essential character. He was proud and self-confident (Phil. 3 : 4), scrupulous concerning the letter rather than the spirit (Phil. 3 . 5), angered by the determined endurance of the Christians (ver. 11), full of and breathing out threatenings and slaughter (ch. 9 : 1), relentless, sparing neither men nor women (ch. 9 : 2), pursuing the disciples into private houses, ravaging the church like a wild beast (ch. 8 : 3, note), and adding his own taunts and revilings to punishment (1 Tim. 1 : 13, note), being all the time uneasy in his own conscience, and by its reproaches only goaded to more bitter anger (ch. 9 : 5, note).

12-15. For a consideration of the discrepancies, real and apparent, between the three accounts of Saul's conversion here and in chaps. 9 and 22, see 9 : 1-9, notes. Paul's account here is the fullest of the three, and contains several features peculiar to it, viz., the description of the light as *above the brightness of the sun*, the language of the heavenly voice, *in the Hebrew tongue*, the revelation of Paul's own interior struggles, *It is hard for thee to kick against the pricks*. The latter occurs in our English version in ch. 9 : 5, but was inserted there by the copyists from this place. On the meaning of the metaphor and its spiritual significance, see note there.

16-18. I believe, with Alford, that Paul here embodies in one account the revelation of the divine will made to him by Ananias (ch. 9 : 15), and subsequently in the Temple at Jerusalem (ch. 22 : 18-21). See note on the Conversion of Saul, p. 111, 1, *d*. These verses, constituting Paul's commission, indicate also the commission of all Christian ministers. They are appointed to be witnesses to those things made known or to be made known to them by the Spirit of God; their protector is the Lord, who is with them alway even to the end of the world (Matt. 28 . 20); the result of their testimony is the opening of the eyes of the blind, that they may be turned from darkness to light, from Satan to God; therein receiving the remission, *i. e.*, the putting away, of their sins, and an inheritance among the holy, all of which is accomplished by faith in Christ. *By faith that is in me* qualifies *receive;* the meaning is, *That they may receive, by the faith that is in me, forgiveness of sin and inheritance*, etc. *The people* are the people of Israel, in contrast with the Gentiles.

19-21. I was not disobedient. It does not necessarily follow that Paul devoted himself forthwith exclusively to preaching; and since, in his description of the regions in which he preached, Arabia is not mentioned, the language here tends to confirm the hypothesis that his sojourn in Arabia (Gal. 1 : 17) was rather for study and meditation than for public ministry. His preaching in Damascus followed immediately his conversion (Acts 9 : 20-22); then, after his visit to Arabia, followed a brief ministry in Jerusalem (ch. 9 : 28); but there is no distinct account of any public ministry by him throughout the province of Judea. Observe the threefold elements in Christian experience: repentance, *i. e.*, abandonment of sin; return to God, *i. e.*, faith; and works meet for repentance, *i. e.*, the fruits of repentance and faith in practical godliness. See Isa. 55 : 6, 7; Luke 3 : 8-14; Ephes. 2 : 10.—**For these causes.** Paul has been requested by Felix, impliedly, to give an account himself of the crimes laid against him. This he has done in what is, in fact, a gospel sermon, though in form partially a self-defence.

22, 23. I continue unto this day. Rather, *Even unto this day I have stood; i. e.*, against

24 And as he thus spake for himself, Festus said with a loud voice, Paul, thou art beside thyself; much learning doth make thee mad.[l]

25 But he said, I am not mad, most noble Festus; but speak forth the words of truth and soberness.

26 For the king knoweth of these things, before whom I speak freely: for I am persuaded that none of these things are hidden from him; for this thing was not done in a corner.

27 King Agrippa, believest thou the prophets? I know that thou believest.

28 Then Agrippa said unto Paul, Almost thou [m] persuadest me to be a Christian.

29 And Paul said, I would [n] to God, that not only thou, but also all that hear me this day, were both almost, and altogether such as I am, except these bonds.

30 And when he had thus spoken, the king rose up, and the governor, and Bernice, and they that sat with them:

31 And when they were gone aside, they talked between themselves, saying, This man doeth nothing worthy of death or of bonds.

32 Then said Agrippa unto Festus, This man might have been set at liberty, if he had not appealed unto Cæsar.

l 2 Kings 9 : 11.... m James 1 : 23, 24.... n 1 Cor. 7 : 7.

foes without and fears within (2 Cor. 4 : 8, 9; 11 : 24–27), thus exemplifying his exhortation in Ephes. 6 : 13.—**Both to small and great.** To the few women without the walls of Philippi (Acts 16 : 13); to the procurator Felix and king Agrippa.—**Saying none other things.** So far from impugning the law and the prophets, he has proclaimed their fulfillment in a Messiah suffering, crucified, and risen from the dead, and so bringing light, not only to the people of Israel, but also to the Gentiles. For prophecies of which this was a fulfillment, see Isa. 42 : 6; 49 : 9; 60 : 1–3.

24-27. Festus, the cold and skeptical Roman, could not comprehend Paul's enthusiasm respecting the resurrection of "one Jesus" (ch. 25 : 20), whom the Jews asserted to be dead, and Paul affirmed to be alive; to him the apostle seemed a religious fanatic, as did Jesus to Pilate. Paul responds that his words are those *of truth and soberness*, *i. e.*, rooted in the truth, and coming from a sane and self-restrained mind; and he appeals to king Agrippa, as one that knows both the facts respecting the life and death of Jesus, and the testimony in the O. T. prophets which those facts fulfilled.

28, 29. In a little thou persuadest me to become a Christian. There are two difficult questions respecting the proper interpretation of this verse, (1) The rendition of the idiom; (2) the spirit of the speaker. Some scholars supply after the words *in a little*, the word *time*, thus making the declaration, *In a little time thou wilt persuade*, etc.; this necessitates rendering Paul's reply, *Whether in a little time or in much time;* a substitution of *or* (ἤ) for *and* (καὶ), for which there seems to be no warrant in the Greek, though this substitution is made, without explanation, by Hackett, Alford, and Conybeare and Howson. Others supply the word *labor* or *endeavor*, *i. e.*, *with a little endeavor*, *easily*, *thou persuadest;* but this is open to the same objection. I would supply, as Alexander, the word *degree*, thus rendering the passage as in our English version. In respect to the spirit of the speaker there are three views: The first regards Agrippa as expressing a serious conviction; the second as expressing a courtly and complimentary appreciation of Paul's eloquence, implying a recognition of the truth of what he had said respecting Jesus Christ and the prophets; the third as ironical. I incline to adopt the latter view, from the considerations, that the term Christian was one of ill-repute, never, apparently, used by the disciples among themselves (see ch. 11 : 26, note), and that this interpretation accords better than either of the others with what we know of the character of Agrippa, and also with Paul's answer, and the abrupt conclusion of the hearing. I would render, then, the passage thus, *Then Agrippa said unto Paul, In a little measure thou persuadest me to become a Christian; and Paul said, I could wish to God, that both in a measure and in full, not only thou, but also all those who hear me to-day, were even such as I am, excepting only these bonds.* The last words refer to Paul's captivity, but may have been enforced by holding up to view the chains upon his wrists.

30-32. Paul's response brings the hearing to an end. Festus had already decided that Paul has not done anything worthy of condemnation under the Roman law (ch. 25 : 17–20). Agrippa adjudges that he is guilty of no offence against Jewish law. But the appeal made by Paul and accepted by Festus, has taken the case out of the governor's hands, and he has no longer power either to acquit or to condemn.

Ch. 27. PAUL'S VOYAGE AND SHIPWRECK. DIVINE PROVIDENCE AND CHRISTIAN TRUST ILLUSTRATED. See note at end of chapter.

PRELIMINARY NOTE.—A. D. 60. The date of the events in this chapter is fixed by ver. 9 (see note there), as extending from the early fall into and through the winter, the mid-winter months (ch. 28 : 11) being spent in the island of Malta, and Rome being reached in the early spring of A. D. 61. For the correct understanding of the chapter, some knowledge of ancient ships and navigation is necessary. I have not only in this note, but throughout this chapter, borrowed largely from, and followed closely, Mr. James Smith's monograph on the Voyage and Shipwreck of St. Paul, which is the recognized standard work on the subject, not only in England, but also upon the Continent. Conybeare and Howson draw largely from it; Lewin furnishes some suggestive details; the other commentators add but very little information to these original authorities. For an elaborate description of ancient ships, the student is referred, in addition, to *William Smith's Dict. of Antiq.*, art. Navis.

OF ANCIENT NAVIGATION. — The Mediterranean was called by the ancients the Great Sea; it was the theatre of an extensive commerce, but one necessarily rude and imperfect. The Greeks and Romans were ignorant of the use of the compass; they were without exact chronometers; the instruments with which they took observations were very imperfect compared with those of modern times; charts were almost, if not quite, unknown; it was therefore generally considered necessary to remain in sight of the coast or of some island by day, steering by the stars by night; in winter, navigation generally ceased altogether. The ancient ship was comparatively rude, both in build and rig—the stern built exactly like the prow; the sails generally square, though triangular top-sails seem to have been known to the Romans. Merchant ships were constructed of large size, quite equal to those of a large modern merchant vessel. The ship of Lucian described below, is estimated at from 1,200 to 1,500 tons. Paul's ship carried 276 crew and passengers (ver. 37), that in which Josephus was wrecked, 600. The prow of the ancient ship was generally ornamented on both sides with figures; very commonly an eye was represented on each side. Hence, probably, the expression, *to eye* or *face the wind* (ver. 15, note). The stern was like the prow, variously adorned, especially with an image of the tutelary deity of the vessel (ch. 28 : 11, note). Banks of oars were used in the naval vessels; the great vessel of Ptolemæus Philopator had 4,000 rowers; but it is not necessary to enter here into a discussion concerning the arrangement of these oarsmen, since they were not a feature of merchant vessels. The rudder was not like our own; it was an oar, or more generally two oars, with

BOAT WITH TACKLING, ETC.

broad blades, projecting one from each side of the stern, and in larger ships joined by a pole which kept the rudders parallel, and brought them under the control of one steersman. Ropes or rudder-bands were provided by which these rudders could be drawn out of the water and fastened to the side of the vessel when not in use (ver. 40). Ships were constructed with one, two or three masts, made usually of fir. In three-masted vessels the largest mast was nearest the stern; the main-yard was attached to the mainmast by a wooden hoop made to slide up and down by means of ropes and pulleys. The anchors did not differ materially in form from those of modern times, except that they were often constructed with one fluke and sometimes with none. A peculiarity of the ship furniture were the under-girders used for frapping or undergirding the ship in time of danger (ver. 17, note). The ancient vessel could not at all compete with the modern in sailing against the wind, but when running before the wind, made fair progress. The voyage from Rhegium to Puteoli, 182 miles, made in one day, 24 hours (ch. 28 : 13), though a quick, was not an unprecedented passage. These general features of an ancient ship will be made clearer to the reader by the accompanying illustration from an ancient picture, representing the casting of Jonah to the whale. In the centre is the main-mast with the sail reefed up to the yard; in the stern are the two rudders; in the prow is the foresail, miscalled mainsail in ver. 40. A vivid picture of an Alexandrian corn-ship just such as that in which the apostle Paul was wrecked is described by Lucian, who lived next after the apostolic age. The vessel, the Isis, like that in which Paul sailed, had gone around by Syria, and along the coast of Asia Minor, and then, encountering adverse winds, had been driven into the Piræus. It was an unusual sight in the port of Athens, and soon attracted a crowd of idlers from the city. Lucian introduces a dialogue amongst a party who had just examined the Isis; and one of them is made to

CHAPTER XXVII.

AND when it was determined that we should sail
into Italy, they delivered Paul[o] and certain other
prisoners unto *one* named Julius, a centurion of Augustus' band.
2 And entering into a ship of Adramyttium, we
launched, meaning to sail by the coasts of Asia; *one*
Aristarchus,[p] a Macedonian of Thessalonica, being
with us.
3 And the next *day* we touched at Sidon. And Julius courteously entreated[q] Paul, and gave *him* liberty to go unto his friends to refresh himself.
4 And when we had launched from thence, we sailed
under Cyprus, because the winds were contrary.
5 And when we had sailed over the sea of Cilicia and
Pamphylia, we came to Myra, *a city* of Lycia.

o ch. 25 : 12, 25.... p ch. 19 : 29.... q chaps. 24 : 23; 28 : 16.

say, "But what a ship it was! the carpenter said it was 180 feet long and 45 wide, and from the deck down to the pump at the bottom of the hold 45¼ feet, and for the rest, what a mast it was! and what a yard it carried! and with what a cable it was sustained! and how gracefully the stern was rounded off! and was surmounted with a golden goose, the sign of a corn-ship. And at the other end how gallantly the prow sprang forward, carrying on either side the goddess after whom the ship was named! and all the rest of the ornament, the painting, and the flaming pennants, and above all the anchors, and the capstans, and windlasses, and the cabin next to the stern, all appear to be perfectly marvellous. All the multitude of sailors one might compare to a little army, and it was said to suffice for a year's consumption for all Attica, and this unwieldy bulk was all managed by that little, shriveled old gentleman, with a bald pate, who sat at the helm, twisting about with a bit of handle those two monstrous paddles, one on each side, which serve as rudders."

1, 2. And when it was determined that we should sail. Literally, *sail from;* a nautical term used in the N. T. only by Luke. It is evident from the use of the first person throughout this and the next chapter, that Luke accompanied Paul on this voyage to Rome. See Col. 4 : 14; Philem. 24.—**Certain other prisoners.** A motley crowd, probably such as no modern convict-ship could present. Like his Lord, Paul was numbered among the transgressors.—**Julius a centurion.** A commander of a hundred, answering to our captain. See ch. 10 : 1, note. He comes down to history as one who treated Paul courteously; was perhaps one of the guard which had accompanied Festus to Cæsarea, and was now returning to Rome. It is possible that he is the Julius Priscus of whom Tacitus writes, who was a centurion, and afterward prefect of the Prætorians. Observe, in the influence of Paul, a prisoner, obtained in this journey over Julius, as previously over Festus (ch. 25), the chief-captain (ch. 23), and the Asiarchs of Ephesus (ch. 19 : 31), indications of the apostle's dignity of character and personal power over men.—**Of Augustus' band.** Probably a part of the great Imperial or Prætorian guard, amounting at this time to 10,000 men; possibly identical with the Italian band mentioned in Acts 10 : 1 (see note there), sometimes spoken of as Italian, because levied in Italy, and sometimes as Augustan, because attached to the emperor. It is not indicated that the band was in Cæsarea, but only that Julius belonged to it. —**A ship of Adramyttium.** A seaport in the province of Asia, situated in the district called Æolis, and also Mysia (Acts 16 : 7). It was a place of considerable traffic, for it lay on the great Roman road between Assos, Troas, and the Hellespont, on the north; and Pergamos, Ephesus, and Miletus, on the south; and was also the terminus of similar roads into the interior. That it was the centurion's plan to take the vessel to Adramyttium, thence journeying to Rome by land, is indicated, (1) by the language here, *meaning to sail by the coasts of Asia;* (2) by that of ver. 6, which implies that the centurion found unexpectedly the Alexandrian ship; (3) by the fact that the time of the closing of navigation was near at hand. The overland road which conjecture thus assumes to have been their proposed route, is the same by which some years after the martyr Ignatius, under a guard of ten soldiers, was conveyed from Antioch to Rome, under similar circumstances. Tradition says Adramyttium was a settlement of the Lydians in the time of Crœsus. It afterwards became a Roman colony, and became under the kingdom of Pergamos a seaport of consequence. Pliny speaks of it as at this time a Roman assize town. The modern *Adramytti* is a poor village, but has some trade and shipbuilding.—**Aristarchus * * * being with us.** See ch. 19 : 29, note. He was possibly one of the other prisoners mentioned in the preceding verse. See Col. 4 : 10. That he left Paul at Myra, and afterward went to Rome, seems to me very improbable; while it is not at all improbable that he was arrested with Paul at Jerusalem, or was allowed of his own choice to share the apostle's imprisoment and subsequent voyage.

3-5. The next day we touched at Sidon. Or Zidon, the modern Saida, not quite twenty miles north of Tyre, and often mentioned in connection with it. It was within the tribal territory of Asher (Josh. 19 : 28), but was never conquered by the Israelites (Judges 1 : 31; 3 : 3), was destroyed under Artaxerxes Ochus, was rebuilt, passed under the control of Alexander, keeping its own

6 And there the centurion found a ship of Alexandria sailing into Italy; and he put us therein.
7 And when we had sailed slowly many days, and
scarce were come over against Cnidus, the wind not
suffering us, we sailed under Crete, over against Salmone;
8 And, hardly passing it, came unto a place which is
called The fair havens; nigh whereunto was the city
of Lasea.

---

vassal kings, was alternately ruled by Egyptian and Syrian until conquered by the Romans. It was famous in early history for the manufacture of glass, linen, silversmiths' work, workers in timber, and other manufacturing arts. It was also a famous commercial city, and Sidonian ships were celebrated. It is described as having had two harbors, one of which was large, with a narrow entrance, where merchant ships could winter in safety. The harbor was filled up dur-

SIDON.

ing the wars of the middle ages, and it is now a scene of utter desolation. It is sixty-seven miles from Cæsarea; as only one day was occupied in the voyage, they must have had a leading wind, probably a westerly; and this is the prevailing wind in this part of the Mediterranean.—**And when we had launched from thence.** Another nautical term characteristic of Luke (ἀνάγω). We have no English term which exactly corresponds; it is nearly equivalent to our phrase, *get under way.*—**We sailed under Cyprus.** That is, under the lee, so as to be sheltered by it; whether to the north or the south would therefore depend on the direction of the wind. The question, though unimportant, has been hotly debated. But the facts that the wind was *contrary*, which would not be true of a northerly or northeasterly wind, and that the prevailing winds in this part of the Mediterranean in the summer are the westward, which would be contrary, justify the opinion embodied in the map (p. 22) that the ship sailed directly for the Cilician coasts, and then beat up against the wind along the coast. This is confirmed by the language of the next verse, *When we had sailed on the sea of Cilicia and Pamphylia, i. e.*, that part of the Mediterranean lying immediately contiguous to these provinces. For description of Cyprus, see ch. 11 : 19, note.—**We came to Myra.** One of the most important cities of Lycia, afterward its capital, situated on the river Andracus, partly on a hill and partly on the slope of it, a distance of twenty stadia from the sea. It lay at the opening of a long and wonderful gorge which was the passage from the interior of Lycia to the sea. Its port, Indriace, was one of the many excellent harbors in the southwestern part of Asia Minor, and was a common resort of ships when winds were contrary. Myra still exists bearing its ancient name, though called by the Turks *Dembre.* It is remarkable for its fine ruins which are among the most beautiful of Lycia.

6-8. Found a ship of Alexandria. Not

merely an Alexandrian vessel, but one from that port; this at least is probably, though not certainly, the meaning. Egypt was one of the granaries of Rome; ships of great size conveyed the grain thence to Italy. These were sometimes as large as our largest class of merchant ships. The cargo was wheat. The implication of the language is that this finding of a ship sailing direct for Rome was unexpected. Myra appears far out of the course of a ship sailing from Alexandria to Italy; but with the westerly winds which prevailed in these seas, ships unprovided with a compass, and ill calculated to work to windward, would naturally stand to the north till they made the land of Asia Minor, and thence sail eastward along its coast, which is very bold, and, from the elevation of the mountains, visible at a great distance.—**And when we had sailed slowly many days, and with difficulty were come over against Cnidus.** This was a city of great consequence, situated at the extreme southwest of the peninsula of Asia Minor, on a promontory now called *Cape Crio*, which projects between the islands of Cos and Rhodes. The distance from Myra is 130 miles, easily accomplished in one day with a fair wind. The language here implies, not calms, but contrary winds. The word rendered *scarce* implies, not that they did not quite reach Cnidus, but that it was reached with difficulty. It is the same word (*μόλις*) rendered *hardly* in the next verse.—**The wind not suffering,** *i. e.*, not suffering them to get on in a direct course.—**We sailed under Crete, by Salmone.** Crete, the modern Candia, is a large, bold, and mountainous, but fruitful island, situated in the Ægean basin of the Mediterranean sea, and closing in the Greek Archipelago on the south. It has a conspicuous place in the mythology and early history of Greece, boasting especially of having given birth to Minos. It was noted in early history for its hundred cities. Tacitus has a story that the Jews were of Cretan origin, which may have come from some confusion respecting their early history, but it is quite certain that there had long been an acquaintance between the Cretans and Jews, and that many Jews settled on the island before the destruction of Jerusalem. At a subsequent period there appear to have been numerous churches in Crete, the foundations of which were probably laid by Cretans present on the day of Pentecost (ch. 2:11); and Paul, with Titus, visited the island, probably subsequent to his first imprisonment in Rome (Titus 1:5). Salmone is a promontory on the eastern extremity of the island. The wind was probably in a northwesterly direction; the ship beat up against the wind under the shore till it reached Cnidus; here the land suddenly trends to the north, at the opening of the Ægean sea; the ship therefore changed her course, and ran, as a northwesterly wind would have enabled her to do, under the lee of Crete. Along this shore they could work up against the wind in a similar manner till they reached Fair Havens, the last harbor before reaching Cape Matala, where the land trends suddenly to the north, so that beyond it an ancient ship could not go with northwesterly winds.—**And with difficulty passing it, came unto a place called Fair Havens.** A city of Crete, not mentioned in any other ancient writings, but its position is undoubtedly established as on the south of the island, four or five miles to the east of Cape Matala, the most conspicuous headland on its southern coast. It was probably the port of Lasea. As a winter harbor, Fair Havens would not be so safe as Phenice, though recent explorations indicate that it was somewhat protected, and Paul's advice was to adhere to a tolerable shelter rather than run a great risk for a better one.

VIEW OF CRETE—MT. IDA IN THE DISTANCE. (From Searing's Virgil's Æneid.)

9 Now when much time was spent, and when sailing was now dangerous, because the fast was already
past, Paul admonished *them*,
10 And said unto them, Sirs, I perceive[r] that this
voyage will be with hurt and much damage, not only
of the lading and ship, but also of our lives.
11 Nevertheless, the centurion[s] believed the master
and the owner of the ship, more than those things
which were spoken by Paul.
12 And because the haven was not commodious to
winter in, the more part advised to depart thence also,
if by any means they might attain to Phenice, *and*
there to winter; *which is* an haven of Crete,[t] and lieth
toward the south-west and north-west.
13 And when the south wind blew softly, supposing
that they had obtained *their* purpose, loosing[u] *thence*,
they sailed close by Crete.
14 But not long after there arose against it a tempestuous[v] wind, called Euroclydon.
15 And when the ship was caught, and could not
bear up into the wind, we let *her* drive.
16 And running under a certain island which is
called Clauda, we had much work to come by the
boat;

r 2 Kings 6 : 9, 10; Dan. 2 : 20; Amos 3 : 7 . . . . s Prov. 27 : 12 . . . . t verse 7 . . . . u verse 21 . . . . v Ps. 107 : 25.

The ruins of Lasea were discovered by a yachting party in 1856.

9-13. During the winter months navigation was in so far dangerous in the Mediterranean that the sailing season was considered closed from November to March. The fast here mentioned is the fast of expiation (Lev. 16 : 29, etc.; 23 : 26, etc.), which came on the 10th of Tisri, answering to our October—about the time of the autumnal equinox. The question presented for their consideration was whether they should winter at Fair Havens, an imperfectly protected winter harbor, or endeavor to proceed to Phenice, which was much safer. The centurion naturally accepted the counsels of the ship's master, rather than those of his prisoner. In this he acted not unwisely, certainly not wrongly. Calvin suggests the reason why Paul was led to give this counsel, viz., that it might subsequently serve to commend him and his advice to the centurion. *Hurt and damage* are rather *violence and damage.* There is not much doubt that the Phenice here mentioned is the modern Lutro; it is the only good harbor on the south side of the island of Crete, and was a customary winter resort of Alexandrian ships. Considerable difference of opinion exists, however, respecting the proper interpretation of the peculiar phrase in ver. 12, the proper rendering of which is, *which looks toward the south-west and north-west.* The harbor of Lutro lies open to the east, and is perfectly land-locked from westerly and north-westerly winds, against which the ship desired protection. The most natural explanation is that of Dr. Howson, that "sailors speak of everything from their own point of view, and that such a harbor does look, from the water toward the land which encloses it, in the direction of south-west and north-west."

14-17. But not long after there came down from it (*i. e.*, from the high lands of Crete) **a tempestuous wind**—literally a *typhonic wind* (τυφωνικός), *i. e.*, a wind accompanied by those phenomena which ordinarily accompany a sudden change in the direction of the wind, whirling eddies and currents, violent blasts, a tossed and angry appearance of the clouds, and a violent sea—**called euro-equilo.** There is small doubt that this is the correct reading. An eastern wind was *eurus*, a northeast wind *equilus;* this was *euro-equilo*, east-northeast. This is the most probable interpretation of a disputed and doubtful word. Of the direction of the wind there is no reasonable doubt.—**And not being able to look the wind in the face** (ἀντοφθαλμέω). This is the literal meaning of the original, the nautical term being probably derived from the custom of painting eyes on either side of the prow of a vessel, as in the annexed illustration, from a wall painting at Herculaneum.—**We let her drive.** Unable to face the wind, they were compelled to scud before it. The Greek is, literally, *given over to* (the wind), *we were borne along* (by it). Sudden changes from a southerly to a northerly or north-easterly wind are common in this region, partly owing to the mountainous character of the island. The fact appears in this case to be that the ship, under the influence of a southern wind, weighed anchor, sailed close along the shore to Cape Matala, doubled the cape, was proceeding prosperously on its course with a fair prospect of reaching Phenice (Lutro), only 34 miles distant, in a few hours, when this sudden change drove her from her course. At the time the ship was caught in the gale, she must have been near a small group of islands called the Paximader, in the gulf of Messara. The island of Clauda lay about twenty-three miles to leeward, and is a little south of west of Cape Matala.—**We had much difficulty to come by the boat.** The skiff, which had been towing behind. It had been left there at first because the weather was fair and the anticipated journey short; during the first fury of the storm it could not be taken on board; the difficulty experienced now in raising it was probably from its being nearly filled with water, yet, in case of shipwreck, it might have been of the utmost importance. In the result, this boat, secured with so much difficulty, threatened to become an instrument of destruction (vers. 30, 31).—**They used helps un-**

BOAT WITH EYES.

17 Which when they had taken up, they used helps, undergirding the ship; and fearing lest they should fall[w] into the quicksands, strake sail, and so were driven.

18 And we being exceedingly tossed[x] with a tempest, the next *day* they lightened the ship;
19 And the third *day* we cast out[y] with our own hands the tackling of the ship.

w verse 41. . . . x Ps. 107 : 27. . . . y Job 2 : 4; Jonah 1 : 5.

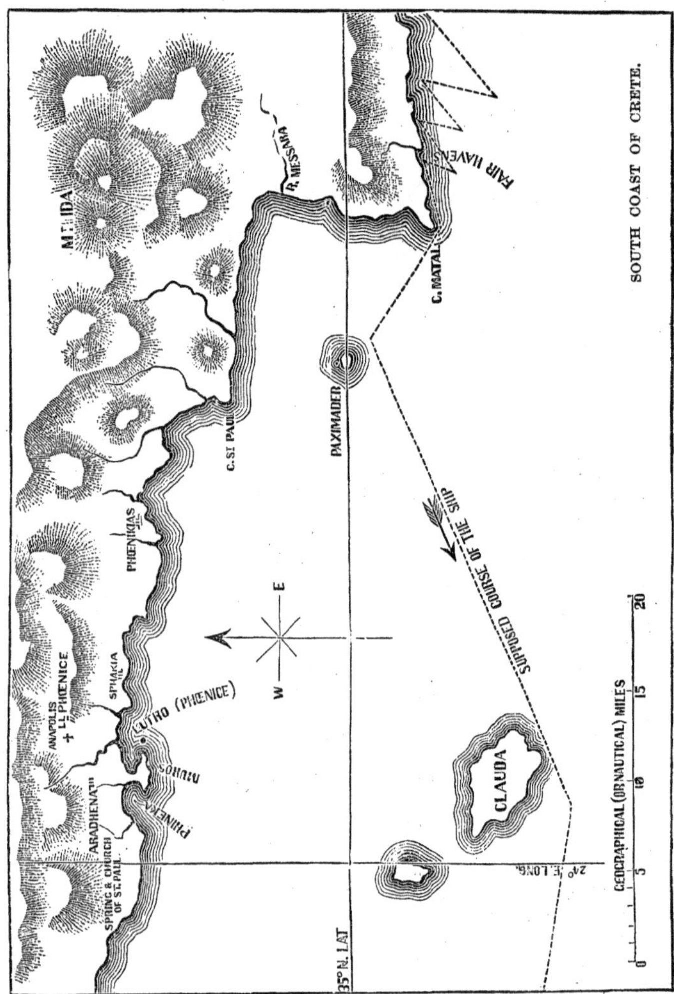

dergirding the ship. This was done by passing ropes under the ship, not from stem to stern, as, by a curious mistake, it has been represented by some authorities, but around the middle of the ship, at right angles to its length, and near the mizzen-mast. This was a common practice among the ancients, the object being to prevent the working of the planks and timbers. Special cables for this purpose were a part of the ordinary furniture of an ancient vessel. The extensive application of iron in modern shipbuilding has rendered this contrivance less common, but Mr. James Smith and Conybeare and Howson give several illustrations from modern times. It is now called *frapping.*—**Fall into the quicksands.** The Syrtis on the African coast, directly to the southwest of the vessel and in the direction in which they were being driven by the wind. These quicksands were regarded by the sailors as peculiarly dangerous. The object of the undergirding may have been in part to enable the vessel to stand the shock, for a longer time, if it was driven upon this dangerous shoal.—**Lowered the gear and so were driven.** Not *strake sail.* On the contrary, a stern-sail must have been set. Exactly what was lowered is not clear; probably that which was connected with the fair weather sails. The language is nautical and accords with modern nautical phraseology. A ship similarly situated is said now to "send down" her top-gallant-masts, etc. If this ship had strake-sail and scud before the wind, she would have been driven directly on the quick-

20 And when neither[z] sun nor stars in many days
appeared, and no small tempest lay on *us*, all hope[a]
that we should be saved was then taken away.
21 But after long abstinence, Paul stood forth in the
midst of them, and said, Sirs, ye should have heark-
ened[b] unto me, and not have loosed[c] from Crete, and
to have gained this harm and loss.
22 And now I[d] exhort you to be of good cheer: for
there shall be no loss of *any man's* life among you, but
of the ship.
23 For there stood by me this night[e] the angel[f] of
God, whose[g] I am, and whom[h] I serve,
24 Saying, Fear not, Paul; thou must be brought
before Cæsar: and, lo, God hath given thee[i] all them
that sail with thee.
25 Wherefore, sirs, be of good cheer; for I[j] believe
God, that it shall be even as it was told me.
26 Howbeit, we must be cast upon a certain island.[k]
27 But when the fourteenth night was come, as we
were driven up and down in Adria, about midnight

z Ps. 105 : 28....a Ezek. 37 : 11....b verse 10....c verse 13....d Job 22 : 29; Ps. 112 : 7; 2 Cor. 4 : 8, 9....e ch. 23 : 11....f Heb. 1 : 14....g Deut. 32 : 9; Ps. 135 : 4; Isa. 44 : 5; Mal. 3 : 17; John 17 : 9, 10; 1 Cor. 6 : 20; 1 Pet. 2 : 9, 10....h Ps. 116 : 16; Isa. 44 : 21; Dan. 3 : 17; 6 : 16; John 12 : 26; Rom. 1 : 9; 2 Tim. 1 : 3....i Gen. 19 : 21, 29....j Luke 1 : 45; Rom. 4 : 20, 21; 2 Tim. 1 : 12....k ch. 28 : 1.

sands, which were so much dreaded. What was undoubtedly done was this: Under the lee of the island she was brought round with her head to the gale, facing the north or a little east of north, so as to take the storm on her starboard or right quarter. The fair weather sails and spars were taken down, a storm sail was set, and she was then suffered to drift before the storm. In this position navigators calculate that she would drift in a direction west by north, at the rate of thirty-six miles in twenty-four hours. Thirteen days and a fraction of drifting in this direction, and at this rate, would bring her to the island of Malta, and to that part of the island which tradition identifies with the scene of the shipwreck. In this respect, therefore, modern calculations exactly confirm the Scripture narrative. For calculations in detail, see Mr. Smith's treatise, pp. 123–126.

18-20. And we being exceedingly tempest-tossed, they made a casting out. The language here is, as elsewhere throughout this chapter, nautical. What was thrown overboard was a part of the cargo (comp. Jonah 1 : 5), but probably not the wheat, which constituted an important part of it (ver. 38). Matthew Henry quaintly remarks, that "any man will rather make shipwreck of his goods than of his life; but many will rather make shipwreck of faith and of a good conscience than of their goods."—**We cast out with our own hands the tackling of the ship.** Alford supposes the ship's furniture, including the beds, cooking utensils, spare rigging, and other movables. Mr. Smith suggests the main-yard, an immense spar, probably as long as the ship, which would require the united effort of passengers and of crew to launch overboard; he adds that the relief which a ship would experience by this would be of the same kind as in a modern ship when the guns are thrown overboard. There is some uncertainty as to the reading of ver. 19; Alford reads, *with their own hands they cast out;* internal evidence, however, seems to me to confirm the accepted reading, which indicates such degree of danger, that the passengers took part with the sailors in relieving the ship. The course of the sailors thus far has exactly corresponded with that pursued by modern navigators in similar circumstances, (1) undergirding or frapping; (2) lowering the top gear; (3) laying the ship to; (4) lightening the ship, first of its cargo, then of its tackling.—**At last all hope that we should be saved was taken away.** Why? The situation, without compass and without means of observation, was one of great danger, but not necessarily one of despair. The hopelessness of their condition was probably due to the ship leaking; they could not tell which way to make for the nearest land in order to run ashore; and unless they did make the land, they must inevitably founder at sea. This conjecture is confirmed by the repeated lightenings of the ship.

21-26. But after long abstinence. This abstinence was not only by Paul, but by all on board (ver. 33), and was due, not to a religious fast (*Blunt*), nor to the absence of any eatables (see ver. 35), but to the impossibility of cooking, the injury to provisions from water, and the general anxiety and distress.—**Thus would you have been spared this harm and loss.** Either *harm* to their persons and *loss* to their property, or *violence and loss.* See on ver. 10. Paul's object in thus recalling the correctness of his former advice is to induce those on board to credit his present assertions.—**The angel of God.** "Paul knows not where he is himself; yet God's angel knows where to find him out."—(*Matthew Henry.*)—**Whose I am, and whom I serve.** In time of danger the Christian's security is this, that he belongs to God. His opportunity is this, that by his courage he may serve God. Observe the implication that his previous conduct had made him known and respected as an avowed servant of God.—**God hath bestowed on thee all them that sail with thee.** The language implies giving as matter of favor, and here in answer to prayer. Here is a true intercession of saints. Observe how one godly man saves many ungodly men (Gen. 18 : 23-33). "This is a singular pledge of God's love toward us, that he maketh certain drops of his goodness distil from us unto others."—(*Calvin.*)—**Wherefore, men, be of good cheer, for I believe in God that it shall be,** etc. In time of disaster good cheer is in the proportion of a living faith in God.

the shipmen deemed that they drew near to some country;
28 And sounded, and found *it* twenty fathoms: and when they had gone a little further, they sounded again, and found *it* fifteen fathoms.

29 Then fearing lest they should have fallen upon rocks, they cast four anchors out of the stern, and wished[1] for the day.
30 And as the shipmen were about to flee out of the ship, when they had let down the boat into the sea,

1 Ps. 130 : 6.

We must be cast upon a certain island. This fact had probably been disclosed to Paul in the vision.

27-29. When the fourteenth night was come. From the time when the ship left Fair Havens. The storm had therefore lasted a little over thirteen days. "A gale of such duration, though not very frequent, is by no means unprecedented in that part of the Mediterranean, especially toward winter."—(*Conybeare and Howson.*) —**As we were driven about in Adria,** *i. e.*, the Adriatic Sea. This phrase included not only the Venetian Gulf, but was used also in a more extended sense, so as to include that portion of the Mediterranean south of Greece.—**About midnight the sailors conjectured that some land was nearing them.** The graphic language of seamen, to whom the ship is the principal object, while the land rises and sinks, nears and recedes. What was the cause of this conjecture? Certainly not the smell of land, for the wind blew toward shore; hardly the sight of breakers, for it was midnight and raining (ch. 28 : 2); probably the *sound* of breakers. "If we assume that St. Paul's Bay in Malta is the actual scene of the shipwreck, we can have no difficulty in explaining what these indications must have been. No ship can enter it from the east without passing within a quarter of a mile of the point of Koura; but, before reaching it, the land is too low, and too far from the track of a ship driven from the eastward to be seen in a dark night. When she does come within this distance, it is impossible to avoid observing the breakers; for, with northeasterly gales, the sea breaks upon it with such violence, that Admiral Smyth, in his view of the headland, has made the breakers its distinctive character."—(*James Smith.*)—**And casting the lead, they found twenty fathoms * * * fifteen fathoms.** These soundings exactly correspond with those of St. Paul's Bay, supposing the ship to have drifted in a westerly direction as indicated on the annexed map. The ancient fathom (ὀργυιά), etymologically, the space which one can measure by extending the arms laterally, corresponds almost exactly to the modern one, six feet. —**They cast four anchors out of the stern.** Ordinarily, anchoring, in ancient as in modern navigation, was from the bow; but the ancient ships possessed hawser-holes aft; there was, therefore, nothing to prevent anchoring from the stern; and there were two reasons for so doing: (1) the fear of swinging round and falling on the rocks to the leeward; (2) the purpose of running the ship ashore as soon as daylight enabled them to select a spot for this purpose. In the naval battle of Copenhagen, the English ships anchored thus from the stern, and it is stated by Conybeare and Howson that Nelson stated after the battle that he had been reading the twenty-seventh chapter of Acts that morning.—**And wished for day.** The occasion was still one of great danger; for the shore is full of rocky precipices, upon which the sea must have been breaking with great violence. Happily, the anchorage here is good. It is thus described in the *English Sailing Directions*, "The harbor of St. Paul is open to easterly and north-

ROMAN SHIPS.

under colour as though they would have cast anchors
out of the foreship,
31 Paul said to the centurion and to the soldiers, Except these abide in the ship, ye cannot be saved.
32 Then the soldiers cut off the ropes of the boat,
and let her fall off.
33 And while the day was coming on, Paul besought
them all to take meat, saying, This day is the fourteenth day that ye have tarried, and continued fasting,
having taken nothing.
34 Wherefore I pray you to take *some* meat; for
this[m] is for your health: for there[n] shall not an hair
fall from the head of any of you.
35 And when he had thus spoken, he took bread, and
gave thanks[o] to God in presence of them all: and
when he had broken *it*, he began to eat.
36 Then were they all of good cheer, and they also
took *some* meat.
37 And we were in all in the ship, two hundred
threescore and sixteen souls.

m Matt. 15 : 32; 1 Tim. 5 : 23....n 1 Kings 1 : 52; Matt. 10 : 30; Luke 12 : 7; 21 : 18....o 1 Sam. 9 : 13; Matt. 15 : 36; Mark 8 : 6; John 6 : 11, 23; 1 Tim. 4 : 3, 4.

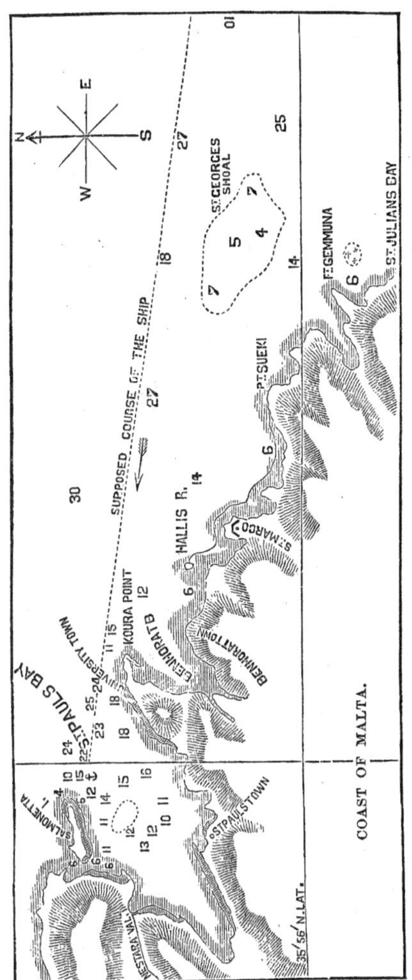

east winds. It is, notwithstanding, safe for small ships, the ground generally very good, and while the cables hold there is no danger, *as the anchors will never start*."

30-32. Had let down the boat into the sea, under pretence as though they would have cast anchors out of the fore ship. As if to carry out the anchors to the extent of the cable which was loosened. Their design to make good their own escape in apparently the only boat is penetrated by Paul; it is not necessary to suppose that it was supernaturally communicated to him.—**Except these abide in the ship, ye cannot be saved.** Paul, with his usual tact, says nothing to the sailors, but addresses the soldiers and centurion; and without words, they cut the rope, and the boat is instantly borne off by the sea. Humanly speaking, the presence of the sailors was necessary to the safety of the rest, for everything depended on their subsequent management of the ship. The language here is not inconsistent with that of ver. 22; for, in fact, it was God's will that the sailors should abide in the ship, and they did so.

33-37. And until it began to be day, *i. e.*, in the interval between the attempted escape of the sailors and daybreak. Paul did not make a speech to the multitude, which the howling of the tempest would doubtless have rendered inaudible, but went from group to group personally cheering and exhorting them.—**And continued fasting.** Not an absolute abstinence is intended; they had eaten so little that it is legitimately regarded as nothing. See on ver. 21.—**For this is for your safety.** Because weakened by previous abstinence, they might otherwise be unable to endure the hardship and peril which followed. —**He gave thanks to God.** Even in this hour of dire peril, Paul does not forget this simple ceremonial; this instance affords a strong argument for the habitual use of grace before meat. His own courage is imparted to the others, and commends him to the consideration and respect of the centurion.—**And we were in all in the ship two hundred three-score and sixteen souls.** "By this time the dawn of day was approaching. A faint light showed more of the terrors of the storm, and the objects on board the ship began to be more distinctly visible. Still, toward the land all was darkness, and their eyes followed the spray in vain as it drifted off toward the leeward. A

38 And when they had eaten enough, they lightened
the ship, and cast out the wheat into the sea.
39 And when it was day, they knew not the land:
but they discovered a certain creek with a shore, into
the which they were minded, if it were possible, to
thrust in the ship.
40 And when they had taken up the anchors, they
committed *themselves* unto the sea, and loosed the rudder bands, and hoisted up the mainsail to the wind, and
made toward shore.
41 And falling into a place where two seas met, they
ran the ship aground; and the forepart stuck fast, and
remained unmoveable, but the hinder part was broken
with the violence of the waves.
42 And the soldiers' counsel[p] was to kill the prisoners, lest any of them should swim out, and escape.
43 But the centurion, willing to save Paul,[q] kept
them from *their* purpose; and commanded that they
which could swim should cast *themselves* first *into the
sea*, and get to land:
44 And the rest, some on boards, and some on *broken
pieces* of the ship. And so[r] it came to pass, that they
escaped all safe to land.

p Ps. 74 : 20 .... q 2 Cor. 11 : 25 .... r verse 22; Ps. 107 : 28-30.

slight effort of the imagination suffices to bring before us an impressive spectacle, as we think of the dim light just showing the haggard faces of the 276 persons clustered on the deck and holding on by the bulwarks of the sinking vessel."—(*James Smith.*)

38, 39. They lightened the ship, casting the wheat into the sea. Not the ship's provisions (*Alford*), an hypothesis neither in accordance with the original Greek nor with the circumstances of the case, but the cargo. Grain was the principal commodity exported from Egypt to Italy. The object of throwing it out was not merely to lighten the ship, so that she might more readily approach the shore; it is probable, from the ship having been so long thrown partially on one side, that the cargo had shifted; this rendered it necessary to cast out part of the wheat so as to right the ship again, and enable her to be more accurately steered toward the land.—**They knew not the land.** The tense is the imperfect and indicates an endeavor to recognize it. It has been thought strange, that if Malta was the island it should not have been known to some of the crew; but St. Paul's Bay is remote from the great harbor, and possesses no marked features by which in the early dawn, and through the driving rain (ch. 28 : 2), it could be recognized. —**But they discovered a certain inlet having a sandy beach, upon which they determined, if it were possible, to strand the ship.** This beach no longer exists on the island of Malta; "but every geologist must know that it must have had one, and that at a period, geologically speaking, from the dip of the beds, by no means remote."—(*James Smith.*) See below. The implication of the narrative that the rest of the coast was rocky and full of danger accords exactly with its present character.

40, 41. And cutting round the anchors, they left them to the sea; at the same time loosing the rudder-bands and raising the foresail, they held fast for the shore, and falling into a place where two seas met, they beached the ship; and the bows, having stuck fast, remained immovable, but the stern was broken off by the violence of the waves. This translation, which follows closely the original, embodies the material points in which it differs from our English version. The operations of cutting the anchors, preparing the rudders, and raising the foresail, were simultaneous. (1.) They did not take up the anchors, which could have been of no possible further use, and would have added weight to the ship; but cut them round, that is, cut round the stern the four anchor-cables, leaving the anchors in the sea. (2.) The rudders, which were oars (see Prel. Note), and of which there were always two, had been drawn out of the water and lashed to the ship's side when the anchors were cast out of the stern; these lashings were now loosened, and the rudders let down into the water, in order to steer the vessel. (3.) There is some doubt as to the nature of the sail which was raised; the original Greek term (ἀρτέμων) has been rendered mainsail, mizzensail, topsail, mast, yard, rudder, vane, etc. Mr. Smith, however, has shown pretty clearly that it was the foresail. This was the best possible sail that could be set in order to run the ship ashore, bow on. (4.) They *held fast for the shore* is a nautical phrase, indicating holding the ship firm toward the land by the rudders. (5.) *A place where two seas met* describes exactly the appearance presented to the sailors as they neared the land; the island of Salmonetta (see map) is a long rocky ridge separated from the main land by a channel of not more than a hundred yards in breadth, and two currents, one flowing from east and the other from the north, meet at the point where the ship was beached. (6.) *The stern was broken off*, not merely broken; the vessel parted amidships. The rocks of Malta disintegrate into exceedingly minute particles of sand and clay, which, when acted upon by the currents or surface agitation, form a deposit of tenacious clay; but in still water, where these causes do not act, mud is formed; but it is only in the creeks, where there are no currents, and at such a depth as to be undisturbed by the waves, that the mud occurs. In Admiral Smyth's chart of the bay, the nearest soundings to the mud indicate a depth of about three fathoms, which is about what a large ship would draw. A ship, therefore, impelled

CHAPTER XXVIII.

AND when they were escaped, then they knew that the island[s] was called Melita.

2 And the barbarous[t] people shewed us no little kindness: for they kindled a fire, and received us[u] every one, because of the present rain, and because of the cold.

s ch. 27 : 26.... t Rom. 1 : 14 ; Col. 3 : 11.... v Matt. 10 : 42 ; Heb. 13 : 2.

by the force of a gale into a creek with a bottom such as that laid down on the chart, would strike a bottom of mud, graduating into tenacious clay, into which the fore part would force itself and be held fast, whilst the stern was exposed to the force of the waves.

42-46. The proposition to kill the prisoners is not unaccordant with the character of the Roman soldiery. Observe, that for the third time Paul is the means of saving the lives of those with him, first, by the promise of God in answer to his prayers (ver. 24); then by his interference to prevent the escape of the sailors from the ship; now, by the consideration paid to the other prisoners for his sake.

The commentators generally have given more attention to the historic and dramatic details of Paul's remarkable experiences of danger and deliverance, than to the religious lessons which this chapter in his life is intended to inculcate. What the story of Joseph is in the O. T., that is the story of Paul's voyage to Rome in the N. T. —a striking illustration of the truth and the method of divine providence. It had been Paul's earnest prayer that he might be permitted to visit the Christian brethren at Rome (Rom. 1 : 9-13). Many obstacles prevented; among others, the length and expense of the journey. God provides carriage without cost; an escort which ensures protection from assault by the inimical Jews; brings him into dangers which call forth the exhibition of his noblest qualities of patience, endurance, courage, and cheerfulness—qualities appreciated readily by those who did not comprehend the faith which was their source; thus introduces him into Rome without an accuser or an accusation, and with the friendly countenance of the Roman centurion, who, if Julius Priscus (see ver. 1, note), was a person of some influence and consequence in Rome; as a result, Paul had larger liberty of preaching the Gospel to both Jew and Gentile as a prisoner in Rome than as a freeman in Jerusalem, his very bonds aiding to the more effective preaching of the Gospel in the Roman camp, and to the servants of Cæsar (Phil. 1 : 12-18), whom, as a Jew not officially sent to Rome, he could not have hoped to reach. Thus all things—the mob at Jerusalem, the unjust Felix, the irresolute Festus, the infamous Agrippa, the tempest, the bonds—work together for his good, and for the promotion of that work to which he has consecrated his whole life. The fullness of his trust, the restfulness of his soul in God, in the irksome period of enforced inaction during the long imprisonment in Cæsarea, under the dangers involved before the judgment-seat, first of Felix, then of Festus, and throughout the voyage and shipwreck, in which he, the prisoner, becomes the leader, and, as it were, the captain of all there are with him, exemplify the power and value of the Christian's trust in times of darkness and danger.

Ch. 28. PAUL AT ROME. THE PRAYER OF THE APOSTLE ANSWERED (Rom. 1 : 13).—THE PROPHECY OF OUR LORD FULFILLED (ch. 1 : 8).—THE POWER OF FAITH EXEMPLIFIED.

1, 2. Melita. Some few writers have identified this island with Meleda, an island of Austria in the Adriatic Sea, nineteen miles W.N.W. of Ragusa; but this opinion is rejected by all the best modern scholars, is inconsistent with the general course of the narrative, places Fair Havens on the north side of Crete, makes the Euroclydon (ch. 27 : 14), the hot sirocco blowing from the coasts of Africa, and, therefore, certainly not on to the quicksands which lie on that coast, and as certainly not a wind to have brought rain and cold. It is shown in the notes above that St. Paul's Bay in Malta answers exactly to the description given in the preceding chapter, and lies exactly where a ship thrown by an E.N.E. wind would be brought by a tempest of thirteen days. The following objections are urged to Malta: (1.) That the inhabitants of Malta were not barbarians; but this term was customarily used by Jewish writers to distinguish Gentiles from Jews, or other races from Greeks and Romans (Rom. 1 : 14; 1 Cor. 14 : 11); it implies very much what our word *natives* does. (2.) That there are no vipers in Malta; but Malta, though now denuded of wood, and so without vipers, was anciently well wooded; it is not strange that they have now disappeared. (3.) That the disorder of the father of Publius does not belong to a locality so dry and rocky as that of Malta; but, in fact, the disease is not uncommon there. (4.) That Malta is not in the Adriatic Sea; but (see ver. 27, note) this term had a much wider geographical import formerly than now. (5.) That the sailors should have known the land; but their ignorance of an unfamiliar part of it, in the darkness of the night and in the driving storm, is not strange (ch. 27 : 39, note), and they did know it as soon as they had landed.—**Because of the rain which had come upon us.** Not necessarily suddenly, yet

3 And when Paul had gathered a bundle of sticks,
and laid *them* on the fire, there came a viper out of the
heat, and fastened on his hand.
4 And when the barbarians saw the *venomous* beast
hang on his hand, they said among themselves, No
doubt[v] this man is a murderer, whom, though he hath
escaped the sea, yet vengeance suffereth not to live.
5 And he shook off the beast into the fire, and felt[w]
no harm.
6 Howbeit, they looked when he should have swol-
len, or fallen down dead suddenly: but after they had
looked a great while, and saw no harm come to him,
they changed their minds, and said[x] that he was a god.
7 In the same quarters were possessions of the chief
man of the island, whose name was Publius; who received us, and lodged us three days courteously.
8 And it came to pass, that the father of Publius lay
sick of a fever, and of a bloody flux: to whom[y] Paul
entered in, and prayed, and laid[z] his hands on him, and
healed him.
9 So when this was done, others also, which had diseases in the island, came, and were healed;
10 Who also honoured[a] us with many honours; and
when we departed, they laded *us* with such things[b] as
were necessary.
11 And after three months we departed in a ship of
Alexandria, which had wintered in the isle, whose sign
was Castor and Pollux.
12 And landing at Syracuse, we tarried *there* three
days.
13 And from thence we fetched a compass, and came
to Rhegium: and after one day the south wind blew,
and we came the next day to Puteoli;

v John 7 : 24....w Mark 16 : 18; Luke 10 : 19....x ch. 14 : 11... y James 5 : 14, 15....z ch. 19 : 11; Matt. 9 : 18; Mark 6 : 5; 7 : 32; 16 : 18; Luke 4 : 40; 1 Cor. 12 : 9, 28....a 1 Thess. 2 : 6; 1 Tim. 5 : 17....b Matt. 6 : 31-34; 10 : 8-10; 2 Cor. 9 : 5-11; Phil. 4 : 11, 12.

the implication is that the rain had not fallen throughout all the tempestuous time.

3, 4. When Paul had gathered a bundle of sticks. Probably dead wood from the forest. Observe that Paul does not leave this work to the sailors and soldiers. — **There came a viper out of the heat.** "The viper was probably in a torpid state, and was suddenly restored to activity by the heat. It was now cold, in consequence both of the storm and lateness of the season (ver. 2), and such reptiles become torpid as soon as the temperature falls sensibly below the mean temperature of the place which they inhabit. Vipers, too, lurk in rocky places, and that is the character of the region where the incident occurred. They are accustomed, also, to dart at their enemies, sometimes several feet at a bound; and hence the one mentioned here could have reached the hand of Paul, as he stood in the vicinity of the fire."—(*Hackett.*) The Greek word, like the English, implies a venomous serpent; but the word *venomous* in ver. 4 is added by the translators.—**A murderer whom * * * justice suffereth not to live.** A striking illustration of the injustice of forming sudden judgments, based upon appearances.

5, 6. In this incident Paul experiences a fulfillment of the promise of Christ in Mark 16 : 18. It is true that Luke does not expressly say that the serpent was poisonous, nor that he bit Paul, nor that Paul was saved from injury by divine intervention; but the whole course of the narrative implies a miracle. The view of the rationalistic commentators is well answered by Alford: "According to these rationalists, a fortunate concurrence of accidents must have happened to the apostles, unprecedented in history or probability. Besides, did not the natives themselves in this case testify to the fact? None were so well qualified to judge of the virulence of the serpent, none so capable of knowing that the hanging on Paul's hand implied the communication of the venom; yet they change him from a murderer into a god on seeing what took place. Need we further evidence that the divine power which they mistakenly attributed to Paul himself, was really exerted on his behalf by him who had said, 'They shall take up serpents?'"

7-10. Were estates of the chief man of the island. The Greek word rendered here *chief man* (πρῶτος) probably does not signify the principal person in the island, but is an official title. Malta belonged to the province of Sicily, and Alford supposes that Publius was the legate of the prætor of the province, and therefore his representative upon the island. Of Publius here mentioned nothing more is known; the name indicates that he was a Roman. The capital of Malta, now Civita Vecchia, about 5 miles from St. Paul's Bay, and commanding a view of it, was probably the residence of Publius, and here probably the cure of his father took place. —**Three days.** Probably till they could find suitable lodging.—**Sick of a fever and dysentery.** This language, like that of Luke elsewhere, is medically accurate.—**Honored us with many honors.** Not, as some commentators, *with many gifts*, an interpretation which does not accord with the original, and scarcely with the spirit of Christ's directions in Matt. 10 : 8.

11-13. After three months. These were the winter months, when navigation on the Mediterranean was impracticable. Alford places the date of their probable departure as early in March.—**With the sign of Castor and Pollux.** The ancient ship commonly carried a picture or image on the prow, which gave to it its name, and a *tutela*, or figure of the tutelary god of the ship, upon the stern; in this case the two seem to have been the same. Castor and Pollux, the twin sons of Jupiter, were the patrons of the sailors; in this vessel Castor was probably upon one side of the prow, and Pollux on the other.—**Syracuse.** A celebrated city on the eastern coast of Sicily, and a Roman colony. It was important both as a strategical and a com-

14 Where we found brethren, and were desired to tarry with them seven days: and so we went toward Rome.
15 And from thence, when the brethren heard of us, they came[c] to meet us as far as Appii forum, and The three taverns; whom when Paul saw, he thanked God, and took courage.[d]
16 And when we came to Rome, the centurion de-

c ch. 21 : 5; 3 John 6-8.... d Josh. 1 : 6, 7, 9; 1 Sam. 30 : 6; Ps. 27 : 14.

mercial point. It is about 80 miles a little east of north of Malta, a day's sail with a fair wind. The tarrying at Syracuse was either for purposes of trade (*Lewin*) or for a favorable change in the wind (*Alford*).—**From thence we fetched a compass** (rather *sailed circuitously*), **and arrived at Rhegium.** A town at the southern entrance of the straits of Messina, and now existing under the name of Reggio, with a population of 10,000; it is about the same distance from Syracuse as Syracuse from Malta. The prevailing wind in this part of the Mediterranean is W.N.W.; either the ship was obliged to beat up against this wind, or, more probably, being under the shelter of the high mountain range of Ætna, was obliged to stand out to sea in order to fill the sails, and so come to Rhegium by a circuitous sweep; either hypothesis explains sufficiently the language here descriptive of their course.—**The south wind blew.** This (see map, p. 21) would be favorable for passing through the dangerous straits of Messina, and for the rest of the voyage, for Puteoli lies nearly due north from Rhegium, about 182 miles. In this sail they would pass through the famous passage between Scylla and Charybdis, even at the present time considered dangerous.—**To Puteoli.** A maritime city of Campania, on the bay of Naples. Just across the inner bay of Puteoli was Baiæ, the fashionable watering-place of Rome. Adjoining it was Baulos, the emperor's marine villa. Puteoli was the Liverpool of Rome, and, though distant from the capital 150 miles, was the customary harbor for ships from the East, whence not only passengers, but merchandise of all kinds, were transported to the imperial city. The harbor, besides its natural advantages, was protected by an extensive mole, thrown out into the bay, and supported on stone piers with arches between them. The remains of this mole are still to be seen, as in the accompanying illustration. Lewin says that in 1851 he counted the ruins of 13 of these piers. The modern Pozzuoli, while

PUTEOLI.

CUMÆ.

retaining interesting relics of its former greatness, is a poor place of about 8,000 inhabitants.

14, 15. Where we found brethren. Who had probably been long hoping and praying for Paul's coming. Four years before he had written his letter to them, expressive of his purpose to visit Rome.—**Were desired to tarry with them.** This request was apparently complied with; this is both indicated by the language following, *So* (*i. e.*, after tarrying) *we went toward Rome*, and also by the fact that intelligence of their coming was forwarded to the brethren at Rome. Their journey took them over the great Appian Way. Puteoli lay some miles to the westward of this celebrated road, but communicated with it by well-traveled cross-roads. Paul's course probably lay through Cumæ, a city on the coast, about six miles north of Puteoli, thence along the coast to Sinuessa, where he would strike the Via Appia. This was certainly the ordinary way of travel 20 years later, and a branch of the Via Appia, the Via Domitiana, was constructed by the emperor Domitian for its accommodation. The track of the Appian road still remains. "It was from thirteen to fifteen feet broad, the foundation was of concrete or cemented rubblework, and the surface was laid with large polygonal blocks of the hardest stone, usually basaltic lava, irregular in form, but fitted together with the greatest nicety. The distances were marked by milestones, and at intervals of about 20 miles were 'mansions,' or post-sta-

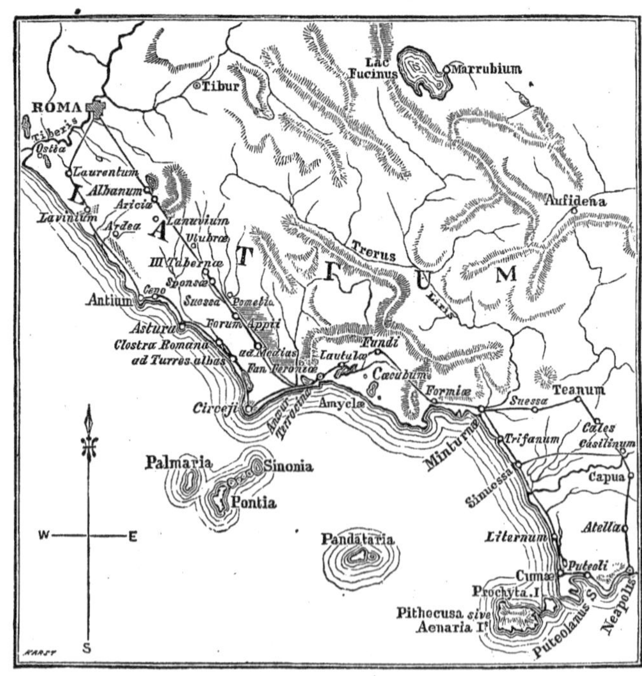

MAP OF PAUL'S ROUTE TO ROME.

livered the prisoners to the captain of the guard: but
Paul was suffered to dwell by himself[e] with a soldier
that kept him.
17 And it came to pass, that after three days Paul
called the chief of the Jews together: and when they
were come together, he said unto them, Men *and*
brethren, though[f] I have committed nothing against
the people, or customs of our fathers, yet was I delivered[g] prisoner from Jerusalem into the hands of the
Romans:
18 Who, when[h] they had examined me, would have
let *me* go, because there was no cause of death in me.
19 But when the Jews spake against *it*, I was constrained to appeal[i] unto Cæsar; not that I had aught
to accuse my nation of.
20 For this cause therefore have I called for you, to
see *you*, and to speak with *you*: because that for the
hope[j] of Israel I am bound with this chain.[k]
21 And they said unto him, We neither received letters out of Judæa concerning thee, neither any of the
brethren that came shewed or spake any harm of thee.
22 But we desire to hear of thee what thou thinkest:
for as concerning this sect, we know that every where[l]
it is spoken against.

e chaps. 24 : 23; 27 : 3....f chaps. 24 : 12, 13; 25 : 8....g ch. 21 : 33, etc....h chaps. 24 : 10; 26 : 31....i ch. 25 : 11....j ch. 26 : 6, 7.... k ch. 26 : 29; Ephes. 3 : 1; 4 : 1; 6 : 20; 2 Tim. 1 : 16; 2 : 9; Phile. 10, 13....l ch. 24 : 5, 14; Luke 2 : 34; 1 Pet. 2 : 12; 4 : 14.

tions, where vehicles and horses and mules were provided for the convenience of travelers and the transmission of government despatches."—(*Lewin.*) From Terracina, 47 miles from Sinuessa, there were two routes, one by land around the Pontine marshes, another by canal directly across the morass. These two routes met at Appii Forum, a small town 18 miles from Terracina and 43 from Rome. The terminus of the canal, it was the ordinary lodging-place for travelers at the end of the first day's journey from Rome, and is described by Horace as full of insolent bargemen and exorbitant tavern-keepers. There are now no inhabitants on the spot, but the site is clearly marked by considerable ruins, as well as by the 43d milestone.—**Three taverns** (*Tres Tabernæ*). A well-known station 10 miles from Appii Forum. A branch road from Antium here joined the Appian Way, making it a place of some importance. The exact site is now unknown, although a spot is fixed upon about three miles from modern Cisterna. Here more of the brethren met Paul, and from this point his progress was more like a triumphal procession than like the march of a criminal.—**Took courage.** Paul was by no means indifferent to human sympathy, and the presence of these brethren gave him new hope, not for himself only, but for the fulfillment of his earnest prayers (Rom. 1 : 10-12). Their very presence was a partial answer to these prayers.

16. We came to Rome. For description of the ancient city of Rome, see Intro. to the Epistle to the Romans.—**To the captain of the guard.** The *prefectus prætoris*, the commander of the troops, who guarded the emperor's person. At this time a purely military office, it subsequently became, like that of the Vizier of the East, one including the superintendence of all departments of the State. This officer was the one put in charge of all prisoners from the provinces.—**With a soldier that kept him.** To this soldier it would appear, from ver. 20, Paul was bound with a chain, after the custom of the Romans. Comp. Phil. 1 : 13. It does not follow from the language there, *My bonds are manifested in all the palace*, that he dwelt either in the prætorian camp established outside the walls of the city, or in any portion of the palace of Cæsar, or even in its vicinity. Wherever he resided, a soldier was his constant companion, and as the guard was continually changed, and Paul was engaged in preaching the Gospel, the report of

A PRISONER BETWEEN TWO ROMAN SOLDIERS.

his preaching was carried throughout the household of Cæsar. From the fact that he was permitted at this time to receive and hold conference with the leading men of the Jews, it is presumable that he was from the first permitted to dwell in his own hired house, which had, perhaps, been obtained for him by the Christian brethren at Rome. There is nothing extraordinary in this permission, since no prosecutor presented charges against him. Festus, if he sent letters, probably expressed a favorable opinion, and the influence of Julius, the centurion, would also have been in his favor.

17-20. It is not strange that Paul's conference with the Jews is the only Christian work described, for Luke rarely mentions any work of the apostle among churches already formed; he here, therefore, follows his usual custom in describing Paul as a missionary, first to the Jews and then to the Gentiles. The object of Paul's address is less to set himself right before them than to open the way for the preaching of the Gospel. He therefore explains that he is not an offender against Jewish law, that he appealed to Cæsar only as a necessary act of self-protection, and not for the purpose of presenting any charge against the Jews, and that, as a herald of the

23 And when they had appointed him a day, there
came many to him into *his* lodging;[m] to whom he expounded[n] and testified the kingdom of God, persuading them concerning Jesus, both[o] out of the law of
Moses, and *out of* the prophets, from morning till
evening.
24 And some[p] believed the things which were spoken, and some believed not.
25 And when they agreed not among themselves,
they departed, after that Paul had spoken one word,
Well spake the Holy Ghost by Esaias[q] the prophet
unto our fathers,
26 Saying, Go unto this people, and say, Hearing ye
shall hear, and shall not understand; and seeing ye
shall see, and not perceive:
27 For the heart of this people is waxed gross, and
their ears are dull of hearing, and their eyes have they
closed; lest they should see with *their* eyes, and hear
with *their* ears, and understand with *their* heart, and
should be converted, and I should heal them.
28 Be it known therefore unto you, that the salvation of God is sent unto the Gentiles,[r] and *that* they
will hear it.
29 And when he had said these words, the Jews departed, and had great reasoning among themselves.
30 And Paul dwelt two whole years in his own hired
house, and received all that came in unto him,
31 Preaching[s] the kingdom of God, and teaching
those things which concern the Lord Jesus Christ, with
all confidence, no man forbidding him.

m Philemon 22....n chaps. 17:3; 19:8; Luke 24:27....o ch. 26:6, 22....p chaps. 14:1; 17:4; 19:9; Rom. 3:3....q Ps. 81:11, 12; Isa. 6:9; Jer. 5:21; Ezek. 3:6, 7; 12:2; Matt. 13:14, 15; Rom. 11:8....r chaps. 13:46, 47; 18:6; 22:21; 26:17, 18; Matt. 21:41; Rom. 11:11....s ch. 4:31; Ephes. 6:19.

hope of Israel, *i. e.*, of the Messiah, he is in bonds.

21, 22. We neither received letters, etc. There is nothing remarkable, certainly nothing incredible, in this statement; for (1) before his appeal, the Jews had no reason to send forward any complaints against Paul, having no expectation that he would be forwarded to Rome; and (2) since his appeal there had probably been no opportunity to do so. Had any deputation from the Jews followed Paul to Jerusalem, they would probably have been impeded by the same storm which impeded him; but it is not at all probable that they would have undertaken to present their trivial complaints to the emperor in person.—**Every where it is spoken against.** This was emphatically true; the Christians being denounced, not only by the Jews, but by the Romans, as guilty of various and enormous crimes. The very fact of their combination in religious organizations, subjected them to distrust; and a little subsequent to this time they were subjected to the most ferocious persecutions by Nero, with apparently the hearty approbation of the Roman people.

23-28. To whom he set forth, bearing witness, the kingdom of God * * * both out of the law of Moses, etc. Both the subject and the method of Paul's ministry are indicated. He set forth the true nature of the kingdom of God for which the Jews were hoping; he bore personal witness out of his own experience, to its spiritual power and worth; and he maintained the truth by an exposition of the O. T. Scriptures; thus his preaching was both expository and experimental.—**From morning till evening.** When the preacher and hearers are both greatly in earnest no sermon seems long.—**Well spake the Holy Ghost by Isaiah.** Isa. 6:9. On its meaning, see Matt. 13:14, 15, note. The solemnity of this admonition from the O. T. is strengthened by Paul's prophetic addition in ver. 28.

29-31. Ver. 29 is omitted as spurious by most of the critics; Alford queries it.—**And Paul dwelt two whole years in his own hired house.** The implication is, without a trial and still in custody, for nothing is said of his preaching in the synagogues or elsewhere, and the statement that he preached with all confidence, no man forbidding him, indicates that there were reasons why interference might have been expected; moreover, in the epistles written from Rome, he refers to himself as a prisoner (Eph. 6:19, 20; Col. 4:3, 4). This delay of his trial is not strange. The personal presence of the prosecutor was required by Roman law, and there is no indication that any deputation came to prosecute the apostle from Jerusalem. Not until later did the law provide that a failure for a year of the prosecutor was tantamount to an abandonment of the prosecution. Josephus gives the account of some Jewish prisoners sent by Felix to Rome, there detained for three years, and then released only by Josephus' special interference. Among those who were Paul's companions at this time were Luke (Col. 4:14; Philemon 24), Timothy (Philemon 1; Col. 1:1; Phil. 1:1), Tychicus (Col. 4:7; Ephes. 6:21), Mark (2 Tim. 4:11), Demas (Philemon 24; Col. 4:14), who, however, subsequently abandoned the apostle (2 Tim. 4:10), Aristarchus (Col. 4:10; Philemon 24), and Epaphras (Col. 1:7; Philemon 23). During this captivity Paul is believed to have written the epistles to Philemon, the Colossians, and the Philippians. The latter especially gives an account of his experience at this time. For the traditional account of the subsequent life of Paul, see Intro., pp. 18, 19.—**With all confidence, unforbidden.** Yet not without a hungering desire for human sympathy (Ephes. 6:19; Col. 4:18), so characteristic of Paul's royally endowed nature. The secret source of this confidence he has imparted in his Epistle to the Philippians, "I can do all things through Christ which strengtheneth me." Thus the Book of Acts, exemplifying Christian truth in action, fittingly closes with an account of the fulfillment of that promise of our Lord, which constitutes the close of the first Gospel, "So I am with you alway, even unto the end of the world."